RitualSong

A HYMNAL AND SERVICE BOOK FOR ROMAN CATHOLICS

GIA PUBLICATIONS, INC.

CHICAGO

PREFACE

If seriousness can be measured by the resources and amount of time expended on an effort, this publisher could be regarded as having produced its first serious hymnal in 1975. That book, *Worship II,* was the product of extensive preparation by a committee of competent editors. But that was just the beginning.

GIA has always firmly believed in a bound hymnal as the ideal printed resource for the worshiping community. In a time when the Church is marked by a diversity of approaches to worship, it has become increasingly clear that no single hymnal/service book can satisfy all. *RitualSong* is the seventh hymnal for parish worship published by GIA in these twenty-one years. Two of those have been replaced by revisions, which are among the five choices currently available to Roman Catholic parishes from this publisher.

Worship II was eventually replaced in 1986 by *Worship—Third Edition,* GIA's premier classical hymnal. And *Gather,* a collection of contemporary "folk-style" music published in 1988 as a companion book to *Worship,* was replaced in 1995 by *Gather—Second Edition. Worship* and *Gather* used together offer parishes the most extensive repertoire available today in a published program. A spinoff of these hymnals, *Gather Comprehensive,* is the entire *Gather— Second Edition* with a significant amount of organ-based music added.

Since the first publication of *Worship* and *Gather,* GIA has heard some parish musicians and liturgists speak of using the combination of these two books as perhaps the ideal, but nonetheless one that was not suitable for their particular parish circumstances. These pastoral practitioners have ultimately influenced GIA's decision to combine the substance of *Worship* and *Gather* into one book, *RitualSong.*

The editors of *RitualSong* set out to create a truly comprehensive hymnal, reflective of the growing trend in the Church today toward an eclectic approach to selecting music for liturgy.

While *RitualSong* may be thought of as the best of *Worship* and *Gather* somewhat equally combined into one book, it is actually much more. *RitualSong* is a fairly even mix of those two earlier hymnals in terms of style, quality, and much of the content, but it actually contains many things never before included in a single hymnal or combination program.

RitualSong contains more psalms and canticles than any other published hymnal, including up to five different settings of some of the psalms that are used most frequently. It has more service music than any other hymnal GIA has ever published, and it offers a collection of 500 hymns and songs—many appearing for the first time in a GIA hymnal.

Special recognition for this project is given to Jeffry Mickus (project coordinator), Marc Southard (typesetting, music engraving, and book layout), Alec Harris (technical coordinator), Clarence Reiels and Edwina Schaufler (proofreaders), Victoria Krystansky (copyright permissions and editorial services), and last but far from least, one who is clearly the world's most experienced and competent hymnal indexer, Robert H. Oldershaw.

Michael A. Cymbala
    Project Director
Robert J. Batastini
    Senior Editor
David Anderson
Marty Haugen
Jean McLaughlin
    Editors
Edward J. Harris
    Publisher

Contents

Hymns

Appendix

Indexes

The Liturgy of the Hours

When darkness gives way before the sun's light and a new day begins, people of all religions have had their rites of morning: words and songs and gestures with which to pray. It has been the same at the end of the day's light, and again in the last moments before sleep.

Christians, following the example of their Jewish ancestors, continued to pray at morning and evening and night. These moments are the hinges of daily life. As they came round each day they have been occasions to repeat what every child has learned by heart: words to praise God for a new morning, to thank the Father for Christ who is our light as evening comes, to invoke God's strong protection through the hours of night.

The daily prayers of Christians were fashioned at first from very simple things: the sign of the cross, the Lord's Prayer, a few verses and songs and short psalms, inter- cessions. And for most Christians morning and night remain times for such simple prayers always said by heart.

The pages of this present section offer a form of daily prayer that grew from this same tradition. When Christians have gathered in the early morning, at day's end, just before retiring, the simple prayers for the individual have grown more elabo- rate. The daily assemblies of Christians gave shape to what became known as the divine office or "liturgy of the hours." In recent times, these prayers have been restored to some of their original simplicity and are again being prayed in parish churches and Christian households.

In using and in adapting the forms of morning, evening and night prayer given below, two things are especially important. First, these are not to be prayers which could be prayed any time. Rather, they are prayers (in word, song, gesture, silence) which are prompted by the morning itself, by the evening, by the night. Their con- tent and pace should reflect what is unique to each of these moments. Second, these prayers are not meant to be followed in and read from books. The assembly's parts are to be gradually learned by heart. Simplicity, repetition, care for times of silence, the use of refrains: all make it possible for these prayers to belong fully to those who assemble.

INVITATORY

All make the sign of the cross on their lips.

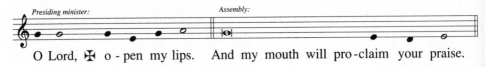

O Lord, ✠ o-pen my lips.   And my mouth will pro-claim your praise.

2 PSALM 95

The psalm may begin with an appropriate antiphon.

A. ADVENT

Come,   let us   wor-ship   the   Lord,   the
King   who   is   to   come.

B. CHRISTMAS

Christ   is   born   for   us;   come,   let us a - dore him.

C. LENT

To - day   if   you   hear   the   voice   of   the
Lord,   hard-en   not   your   hearts.

D. EASTER

The   Lord   is   ris-en,   al - le - lu - ia.

E. GENERAL

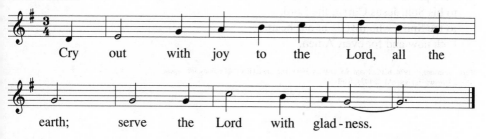

Cry out with joy to the Lord, all the earth; serve the Lord with glad-ness.

Psalm Tone

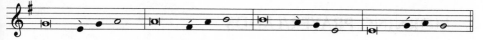

Verses

1. Come, ring out our joy tò the Lord;
   hail the róck who saves us.
   Let us come before God, gìving thanks,
   with songs let us háil the Lord.

2. A mighty God is the Lord,
   a great king abòve all gods,
   in whose hands are the depths of the earth;
   the heights of the mountáins as well.
   The sea belongs to Gòd, who made it
   and the dry land shaped bý his hands.

3. Come in; let us bow ànd bend low;
   let us kneel before the Gód who made us
   for this is our God and we
   the people who belong tò his pasture,
   the flock that is led bý his hand.

4. O that today you would listen tò God's voice!
   "Harden not your hearts ás at Meribah,
   as on that day at Massah in the desert
   when your ancestors put me tò the test;
   when they tried me, though they sáw my work.

5. For forty years I was wearied of these people
   and I said: 'Their hearts àre astray,
   these people do not knów my ways.'
   Then I took an oath ìn my anger:
   'Never shall they entér my rest.'"

6. Give praise to the Fathèr almighty,
   to his Son, Jesus Chríst, the Lord,
   to the Spirit who dwells ìn our hearts,
   both now and for evér. Amen.

Text: Antiphons, © 1974, ICEL; Psalm 95, © 1963, 1993, The Grail, GIA Publications, Inc., agent
Music: Howard Hughes, SM, © 1974, ICEL

3 MORNING PRAYER/LAUDS

The church's sense for how to pray in the morning comes from our Jewish heritage. Whatever the day, whatever the difficulties, the tradition has been to begin the day with praise for the creator. Thus the whole of morning prayer is in the verse: "O Lord, open my lips. And my mouth will proclaim your praise." The sign of the cross, first traced on the Christian at baptism, is again made to begin the new day and its prayer. In the hymn and the psalms, in the scripture and intercessions, each one who prays and the community together finds what it is to stand at the beginning of a new day as a Christian. The morning's prayer gives the day its meaning when, through the years, these prayers become one's own.

The following verse and response are omitted when the hour begins with the invitatory.

All make the sign of the cross.

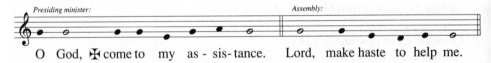

Presiding minister: / *Assembly:*

O God, ✠ come to my as - sis - tance. Lord, make haste to help me.

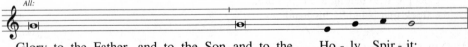

All:

Glory to the Father, and to the Son, and to the Ho - ly Spir - it:

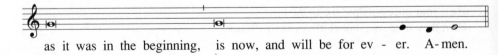

as it was in the beginning, is now, and will be for ev - er. A - men.

Added outside Lent:

Al - le - lu - ia.

HYMN

4

1. This day God gives me Strength of high heav - en,
2. This day God sends me Strength as my guar - dian,
3. God's way is my way, God's shield is 'round me,
4. Ris - ing I thank you, Might - y and strong One,

Sun and moon shin - ing, Flame in my hearth,
Might to up - hold me, Wis - dom as guide.
God's host de - fends me, Sav - ing from ill.
King of cre - a - tion, Giv - er of rest,

Flash - ing of light - ning, Wind in its swift - ness,
Your eyes are watch - ful, Your ears are lis - t'ning,
An - gels of heav - en, Drive from me al - ways
Firm - ly con - fess - ing God in three Per - sons,

Depths of the o - cean, Firm - ness of earth.
Your lips are speak - ing, Friend at my side.
All that would harm me, Stand by me still.
One - ness of God - head, Trin - i - ty blest.

Text: Ascribed to St. Patrick; James Quinn, S.J., b.1919, © 1969. Used by permission of Selah Publishing Co., Inc., Kingston, N.Y.
Tune: BUNESSAN, 5 5 5 4 D; Gaelic; acc. by Marty Haugen, b.1950, © 1987, GIA Publications, Inc.

PSALMODY

5

The singing of one or more psalms is a central part of Morning Prayer. Psalm 63/Ant. II (no. 89) is one of the premier morning psalms. Psalm 51/Ant. V (no. 82) is commonly substituted for Psalm 63 on Wednesday and Friday, as well as during Lent. Other appropriate psalms for morning are Psalms 5, 8, 33, 42, 66, 72, 80, 85, 93, 95, 98, 100, 118, 148, 149 and 150.

READING

6 RESPONSE TO THE WORD OF GOD

A. ADVENT

Cantor, then all:

Christ, Son of the liv-ing God, have mer - cy on us.

Cantor: All:

You are the one who is to come; have mer - cy on us.

Cantor:

Glo-ry to the Fa-ther, and to the Son, and to the Ho-ly Spir-it:

All:

Christ, Son of the liv-ing God, have mer - cy on us.

B. CHRISTMAS

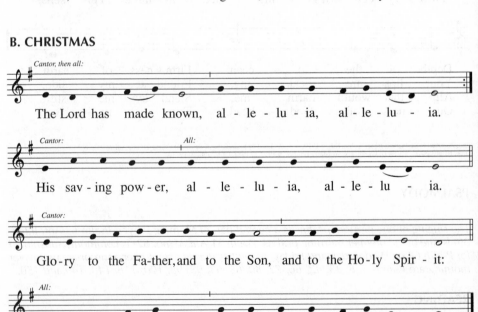

Cantor, then all:

The Lord has made known, al - le - lu - ia, al - le - lu - ia.

Cantor: All:

His sav - ing pow - er, al - le - lu - ia, al - le - lu - ia.

Cantor:

Glo-ry to the Fa-ther, and to the Son, and to the Ho-ly Spir - it:

All:

The Lord has made known, al - le - lu - ia, al - le - lu - ia.

C. LENT

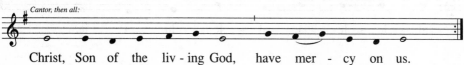

Cantor, then all:

Christ, Son of the liv-ing God, have mer - cy on us.

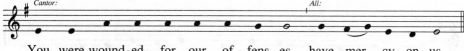

Cantor: *All:*

You were wound-ed for our of - fens - es, have mer - cy on us.

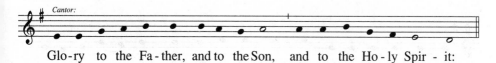

Cantor:

Glo-ry to the Fa - ther, and to the Son, and to the Ho - ly Spir - it:

All:

Christ, Son of the liv - ing God, have mer - cy on us.

D. EASTER

Cantor, then all:

Christ, Son of the liv - ing God, have mer - cy on us,

al - le - lu - ia, al - le - lu - ia.

Cantor: *All:*

You have ris - en from the dead, al - le - lu - ia, al - le - lu - ia.

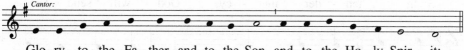

Cantor:

Glo-ry to the Fa - ther, and to the Son, and to the Ho - ly Spir - it:

All:

Christ, Son of the liv - ing God, have mer - cy on us,

al - le - lu - ia, al - le - lu - ia.

E. GENERAL

Cantor, then all:

Christ, Son of the liv - ing God, have mer - cy on us.

Cantor: All:

You are seat-ed at the right hand of the Fa-ther, have mer - cy on us.

Cantor:

Glo - ry to the Fa - ther, and to the Son, and to the Ho - ly Spir - it:

All:

Christ, Son of the liv - ing God, have mer - cy on us.

Text: *Liturgy of the Hours,* © 1974, ICEL
Tune: Robert Le Blanc, © 1986, GIA Publications, Inc.

7   GOSPEL CANTICLE

All make the sign of the cross.

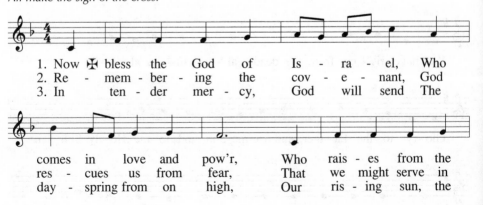

1. Now ✠ bless the God of Is - ra - el, Who
2. Re - mem - ber - ing the cov - e - nant, God
3. In ten - der mer - cy, God will send The

comes in love and pow'r, Who rais - es from the
res - cues us from fear, That we might serve in
day - spring from on high, Our ris - ing sun, the

roy - al house De - liv - 'rance in this hour.　Through
ho - li - ness And peace from year to year;　And
light of life For those who sit and sigh.　God

ho - ly proph - ets　God has sworn To
you, my child, shall　go be - fore To
comes to guide our　way to peace, That

free us from a - larm,　To save us from the
preach, to proph - e - sy,　That all may know the
death shall reign no more.　Sing prais - es to the

heav - y hand Of all who wish us harm.
ten - der love, The grace of God most high.
Ho - ly One! O wor - ship and a - dore!

Text: *Benedictus*, Luke 1:68-79; Ruth Duck, b.1947, © 1992, GIA Publications, Inc.
Tune: FOREST GREEN, CMD; English; harm. by Ralph Vaughan Williams, 1872-1958

INTERCESSIONS 8

In place of the following, a more familiar form may be used.

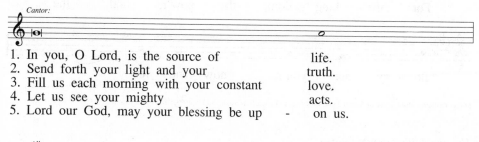

Cantor:

1. In you, O Lord, is the source of　life.
2. Send forth your light and your　truth.
3. Fill us each morning with your constant　love.
4. Let us see your mighty　acts.
5. Lord our God, may your blessing be up - on us.

All:

In your light we　shall see light.
Let these　be our guide.
That we may sing and be glad　all our life.
May your children see your glo - ri - ous might.
And give us success in　all we do.

Praise God in Song, © 1979, GIA Publications, Inc.

9 LORD'S PRAYER

Our Fa - ther, who art in heav - en, hal-lowed be thy name;

thy king - dom come; thy will be done on earth as it

is in heav - en. Give us this day our dai - ly bread;

and for - give us our tres - pass - es as we for - give

those who tres - pass a - gainst us; and lead us not

in - to temp - ta - tion, but de - liv - er us from e - vil.

All:

For the king - dom, the pow'r, and the

glo - ry are yours, now and for ev - er.

Music: Traditional chant, adapt. by Robert Snow, 1964; acc. by Robert J. Batastini, © 1975, 1993, GIA Publications, Inc.

The concluding prayer follows.

DISMISSAL

Music: David Clark Isele, © 1979, GIA Publications, Inc.

Dismissal, if the leader is not a priest or deacon:

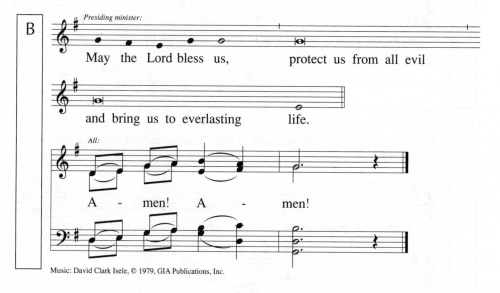

Music: David Clark Isele, © 1979, GIA Publications, Inc.

11 EVENING PRAYER/VESPERS

The church gathers in the evening to give thanks for the day that is ending. In the earliest tradition, this began with the lighting of the lamps as darkness fell and the hymn of praise of Christ who is "radiant Light. . .of God the Father's deathless face." The evening psalms and the Magnificat bring the day just past to focus for the Christian: "God has cast down the mighty from their thrones, and has lifted up the lowly"; "God has remembered the promise of mercy, the promise made to our ancestors." Prayers of intercession are almost always part of the church's liturgy, but those which conclude evening prayer are especially important. As day ends, the church again and again lifts up to God the needs and sorrows and failures of all the world. Such intercession is the daily task and joy of the baptized.

All make the sign of the cross.

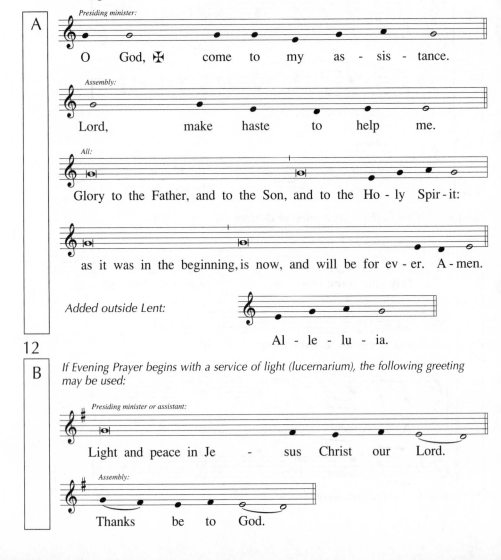

A

Presiding minister:

O God, ✠ come to my as - sis - tance.

Assembly:

Lord, make haste to help me.

All:

Glory to the Father, and to the Son, and to the Ho - ly Spir - it:

as it was in the beginning, is now, and will be for ev - er. A - men.

Added outside Lent:

Al - le - lu - ia.

12

B

If Evening Prayer begins with a service of light (lucernarium), the following greeting may be used:

Presiding minister or assistant:

Light and peace in Je - sus Christ our Lord.

Assembly:

Thanks be to God.

HYMN

13

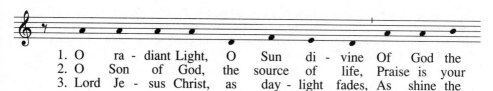

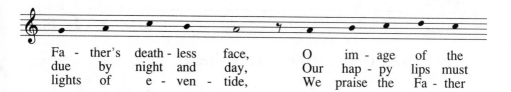

1. O ra - diant Light, O Sun di - vine Of God the
2. O Son of God, the source of life, Praise is your
3. Lord Je - sus Christ, as day - light fades, As shine the

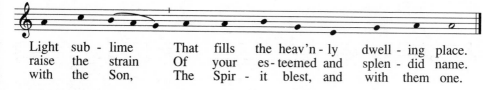

Fa - ther's death - less face, O im - age of the
due by night and day, Our hap - py lips must
lights of e - ven - tide, We praise the Fa - ther

Light sub - lime That fills the heav'n - ly dwell - ing place.
raise the strain Of your es - teemed and splen - did name.
with the Son, The Spir - it blest, and with them one.

Text: *Phos Hilaron* Greek, c.200; tr. by William G. Storey, ©
Music: JESU DULCIS MEMORIA, LM; Mode I; acc. by Richard Proulx, © 1975, GIA Publications, Inc.

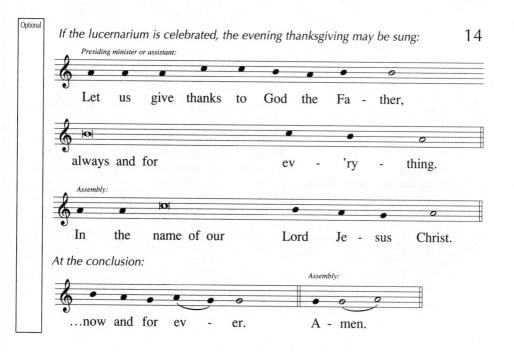

Optional

If the lucernarium is celebrated, the evening thanksgiving may be sung: 14

Presiding minister or assistant:

Let us give thanks to God the Fa - ther,

always and for ev - 'ry - thing.

Assembly:

In the name of our Lord Je - sus Christ.

At the conclusion:

Assembly:

...now and for ev - er. A - men.

PSALMODY

The singing of one or more psalms is a central part of Evening Prayer. Psalm 141, given below, is one of the premier evening psalms (see also no. 188 and 189). It is customary to use incense as it is sung. Other appropriate psalms for evening are Psalms 19, 23, 27, 84, 91, 104, 117, 118, 121, 122, 130 and 145.

15   PSALM 141/INCENSE PSALM

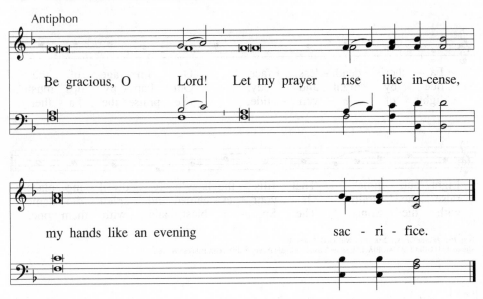

Antiphon

Be gracious, O   Lord!   Let my prayer   rise   like in-cense,

my hands like an evening   sac - ri - fice.

Verses

1. I have called to you,   Lord,   has - ten   to help me!
3. Set, O   Lord,   a guard o - ver my mouth;
5. Never al   -   low me   to share   in their feasting.
7. Their leaders were thrown down   by the side   of the rock;
9. To you, Lord   God,   my   eyes are turned;
11. Let the wicked   fall   into the traps they have set

1. Hear my voice when I cry to you.
3. keep watch, O Lord, at the door of my lips!
5. If the upright strike or reprove me it is kind - ness;
7. then they understood that my words were kind.
9. in you I take refuge; spare my soul!
11. whilst I pursue my way un - harmed.

2. Let my prayer arise before you like incense,
4. Do not turn my heart to things that are wrong,
6. but let the oil of the wick - ed not a - noint my head.
8. As a mill - stone is shattered to pieces on the ground,
10. From the trap they have laid for me keep me safe;
12. Give praise to the Fa - ther, the Son and Ho - ly Spirit,

2. the raising of my hands like an evening ob - la - tion.
4. to evil deeds with those who are sin - ners.
6. Let my prayer be ever against their mal - ice.
8. so their bones were strewn at the mouth of the grave.
10. keep me from the snares of those who do e - vil.
12. both now and for ages unending. A - men.

Text: Psalm 141; © 1963, 1993, The Grail, GIA Publications, Inc., agent
Music: KONTAKION; Russian Orthodox Liturgy, adapt. by Richard Proulx, © 1985, GIA Publications, Inc.

READING

16 RESPONSE TO THE WORD OF GOD

A. ADVENT

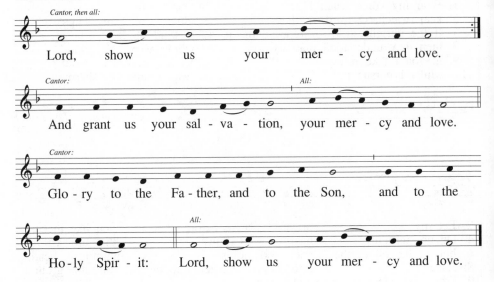

Cantor, then all:

Lord, show us your mer - cy and love.

Cantor: *All:*

And grant us your sal - va - tion, your mer - cy and love.

Cantor:

Glo - ry to the Fa - ther, and to the Son, and to the

All:

Ho - ly Spir - it: Lord, show us your mer - cy and love.

B. CHRISTMAS

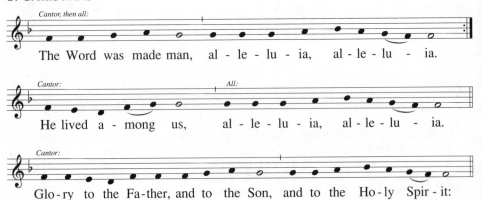

Cantor, then all:

The Word was made man, al - le - lu - ia, al - le - lu - ia.

Cantor: *All:*

He lived a - mong us, al - le - lu - ia, al - le - lu - ia.

Cantor:

Glo - ry to the Fa - ther, and to the Son, and to the Ho - ly Spir - it:

All:

The Word was made man, al - le - lu - ia, al - le - lu - ia.

C. LENT

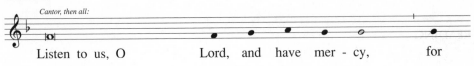

Cantor, then all:

Listen to us, O Lord, and have mer - cy, for

D. EASTER

E. GENERAL

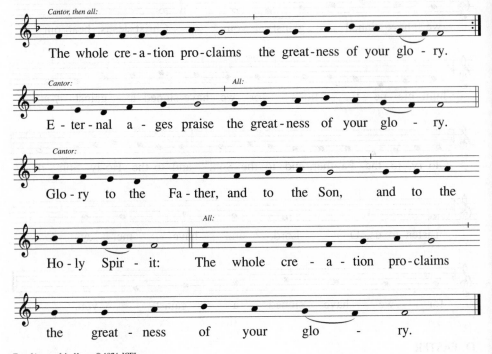

Cantor, then all:

The whole cre-a-tion pro-claims the great-ness of your glo-ry.

Cantor: ... *All:*

E-ter-nal a-ges praise the great-ness of your glo-ry.

Cantor:

Glo-ry to the Fa-ther, and to the Son, and to the

All:

Ho-ly Spir-it: The whole cre-a-tion pro-claims

the great-ness of your glo-ry.

Text: *Liturgy of the Hours,* © 1974, ICEL
Music: Robert Le Blanc, © 1986, GIA Publications, Inc.

17 GOSPEL CANTICLE

1. My  heart sings out with joy-ful praise To
2. The arm of God is strong and just To
3. The prom-ise made in a-ges past At

God who rais-es me, Who came to me when
scat-ter all the proud. The ty-rants tum-ble
last has come to be, For God has come in

I was low And changed my des-ti-ny.
from their thrones And van-ish like a cloud.
pow'r to save, To set all peo-ple free.

The Ho - ly One, the Liv - ing God,
The hun - gry all are sat - is - fied;
Re - mem - b'ring those who wait to see

Is al - ways full of grace To
The rich are sent a - way. The
Sal - va - tion's dawn - ing day, Our

those who seek their Mak - er's will
poor of earth who suf - fer long
Sav - ior comes to all who weep

In ev - 'ry time and place.
Will wel - come God's new day.
To wipe their tears a - way.

Text: *Magnificat,* Luke 1:46-55; Ruth Duck, b.1947, © 1992, GIA Publications, Inc.
Tune: KINGSFOLD, CMD; English traditional; harm. by Ralph Vaughan Williams, 1872-1958

INTERCESSIONS   18

The response will be indicated by the leader.

LORD'S PRAYER

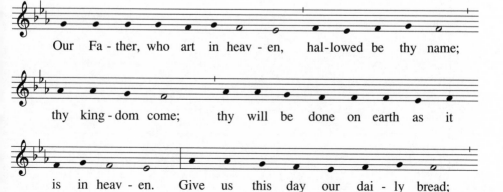

Our Fa - ther, who art in heav - en, hal-lowed be thy name;

thy king - dom come; thy will be done on earth as it

is in heav - en. Give us this day our dai - ly bread;

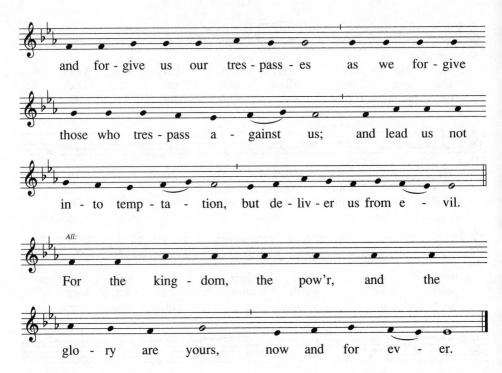

and for-give us our tres-pass-es as we for-give

those who tres-pass a - gainst us; and lead us not

in - to temp-ta - tion, but de-liv-er us from e - vil.

All:

For the king - dom, the pow'r, and the

glo - ry are yours, now and for ev - er.

Music: Traditional chant, adapt. by Robert Snow, 1964; acc. by Robert J. Batastini, © 1975, 1993, GIA Publications, Inc.

The concluding prayer follows.

DISMISSAL

Music: David Clark Isele, © 1979, GIA Publications, Inc.

Dismissal, if the leader is not a priest or deacon:

20

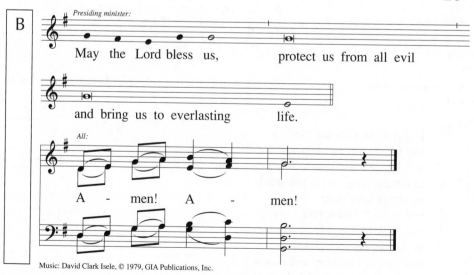

Music: David Clark Isele, © 1979, GIA Publications, Inc.

All may conclude the celebration by exchanging a sign of peace.

21 NIGHT PRAYER/COMPLINE

The church's prayers at night are direct and simple. The Christian remembers with sorrow the day's evil and failure, and places this before the mercy of God. Before surrendering to sleep, there is prayer for God's protection through the night and an expression of acceptance: "Now, Lord, you may dismiss your servant." The night prayer concludes by binding together the sleep of this night with the final falling asleep in the Lord: "May the all-powerful Lord grant us a restful night and a peaceful death." Night's last words are often a gentle invocation of our mother, "When this exile is ended, show us your womb's blessed fruit, Jesus."

All make the sign of the cross.

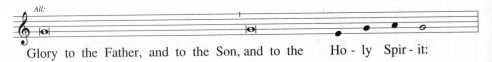

Presiding minister: O God, ✠ come to my as-sis-tance. *Assembly:* Lord, make haste to help me.

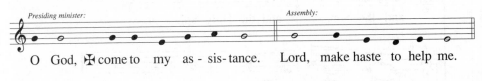

All: Glory to the Father, and to the Son, and to the Ho-ly Spir-it:

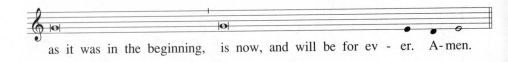

as it was in the beginning, is now, and will be for ev-er. A-men.

Added outside Lent:

Al - le - lu - ia.

A brief examination of conscience may be made. At its conclusion, the following may be said:

> Optional
>
> I confess to almighty God,
> and to you, my brothers and sisters,
> that I have sinned through my own fault
> in my thoughts and in my words,
> in what I have done,
> and in what I have failed to do;
> and I ask blessed Mary, ever virgin,
> all the angels and saints,
> and you, my brothers and sisters,
> to pray for me to the Lord our God.

HYMN 22

1. We praise you, Fa - ther, for your gift of dusk and
2. With - in your hands we rest se - cure; in qui - et
3. Your glo - ry may we ev - er seek in rest, as

night - fall o - ver earth, fore - shad - ow - ing the
sleep our strength re - new, yet give your peo - ple
in ac - tiv - i - ty, un - til its full - ness

mys - ter - y of death that leads to end - less day.
hearts that wake in love to you, un - sleep-ing Lord.
is re - vealed, O Source of Life, O Trin - i - ty.

Text: Benedictine Nuns of St. Mary's Abbey, West Malling, Kent, © 1967
Music: TE LUCIS ANTE TERMINUM, LM; adapt. by Howard Hughes, SM, © 1982, GIA Publications, Inc.

PSALMODY 23

The proper psalms for Night Prayer are: Sunday, Psalm 91/Ant. III (no. 122); Monday, Psalm 86/Ant. II (no. 115); Tuesday, Psalm 143:1-11 (no. 190); Wednesday, Psalm 31:1-6/Ant. III (no. 63) and Psalm 130/Ant. III (no. 175); Thursday, Psalm 16/Ant. I (no. 34); Friday, Psalm 88 (no. 116); and Saturday, Psalm 4/Ant. I (no. 29) and Psalm 134 (no. 181).

READING 24

RESPONSORY 25

Cantor:

In - to your hands, O Lord, I com - mend my spir - it.

All:

In - to your hands, O Lord, I com - mend my spir - it.

Cantor:

You have re - deemed us, Lord God of truth.

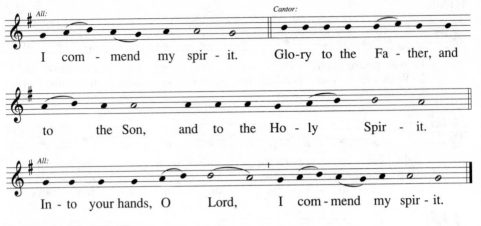

All: I com - mend my spir - it. *Cantor:* Glo-ry to the Fa - ther, and

to the Son, and to the Ho - ly Spir - it.

All: In - to your hands, O Lord, I com - mend my spir - it.

Text: *Liturgy of the Hours,* © 1974, ICEL
Music: IN MANUS TUAS; Sarum Tone, adapt. by Richard Proulx, © 1986, GIA Publications, Inc.

26 GOSPEL CANTICLE

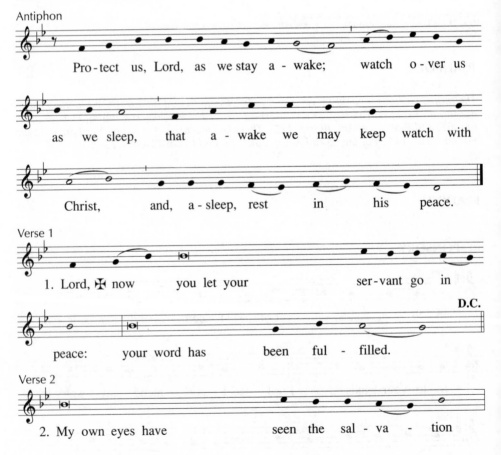

Antiphon

Pro-tect us, Lord, as we stay a - wake; watch o - ver us

as we sleep, that a - wake we may keep watch with

Christ, and, a - sleep, rest in his peace.

Verse 1

1. Lord, ✠ now you let your ser - vant go in

D.C.

peace: your word has been ful - filled.

Verse 2

2. My own eyes have seen the sal - va - tion

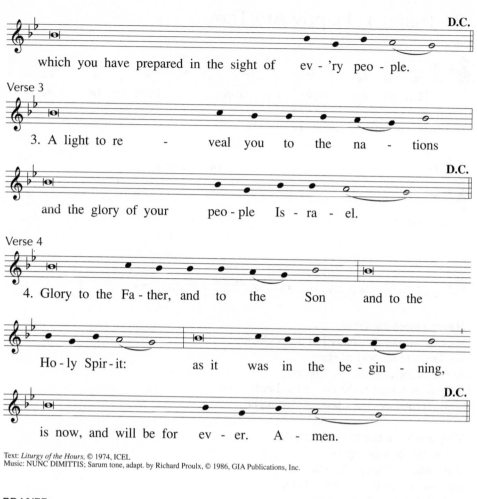

which you have prepared in the sight of ev - 'ry peo - ple.

Verse 3

3. A light to re - veal you to the na - tions

and the glory of your peo - ple Is - ra - el.

Verse 4

4. Glory to the Fa - ther, and to the Son and to the

Ho - ly Spir - it: as it was in the be - gin - ning,

is now, and will be for ev - er. A - men.

Text: *Liturgy of the Hours*, © 1974, ICEL
Music: NUNC DIMITTIS; Sarum tone, adapt. by Richard Proulx, © 1986, GIA Publications, Inc.

PRAYER

27

CONCLUSION

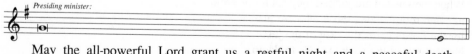

Presiding minister:

May the all-powerful Lord grant us a restful night and a peaceful death.

All:

A - men! A - men!

Music: David Clark Isele, © 1979, GIA Publications, Inc.

The Marian antiphon, "Salve Regina," no. 894, or during Easter season, "Regina Caeli," no. 584, may follow.

28 Psalm 1: Happy Are They

Antiphon

Hap-py are they who hope, who hope in the Lord.

Text: *Lectionary for Mass*, © 1969, 1981, ICEL
Music: Robert J. Thompson, © 1975, GIA Publications, Inc.

Psalm Tone ⌐Repeat for 6-line stanza⌐

Music: Robert Kennedy Knox, © 1979

Gelineau Tone ⌐Omit for 4-line stanza⌐

¹ **Happy** indeed are thòse
who **fol**low not the **coun**sel of the **wíck**ed,
nor **lin**ger in the **way** of sìnners
nor **sit** in the **com**pany of scórners,
² but whose de**light** is the **law** of the Lòrd
and who **pon**der God's **law** day and níght.

³ **They** are like a **tree** that is plànted
be**side** the flowing wáters,
that **yields** its **fruit** in due sèason
and whose **leaves** shall **never** fáde;
and **all** that they **do** shall pròsper.
⁴ Not **so** are the **wick**ed, not só!

For **they** like **win**nowed chàff
shall be **driven** away by the wínd.
⁵ When the **wicked** are **judg**ed they shall not stànd,
nor find **room** among **those** who are júst
⁶ for the **Lord** guards the **way** of the jùst
but the **way** of the **wicked** leads to dóom.

Give **praise** to the **Father** Almìghty,
to his **Son**, Jesus **Christ**, the Lórd,
to the **Spirit** who **dwells** in our hèarts,
both **now** and for **ever**. Amén.

Text: Psalm 1; The Grail
Music: Joseph Gelineau, SJ
© 1963, 1993, The Grail, GIA Publications, Inc., agent

Psalm 4: Have Mercy, Lord 29

Antiphon I

Have mer - cy, Lord, and hear my prayer.

Text: *Liturgy of the Hours,* © 1974, ICEL
Music: Eugene Englert, © 1986, GIA Publications, Inc.

Antiphon II (Vs. 2.4.7.8.9)

Lord, let your face shine on us.

Text: *Lectionary for Mass,* © 1969, ICEL
Music: Robert LeBlanc, © 1986, GIA Publications, Inc.

Psalm Tone

Music: A. Gregory Murray, OSB, © L. J. Carey and Co., Ltd.

Gelineau Tone

² When I **call**, **an**swer me, O **Gòd** of **jus**tice;
  from **an**guish you re**leased** me, have **mer**cý and **hear** me!

³ You **reb**els, how **long** will your **heàrts** be **closed**,
  will you **love** what is **fu**tile and **seek** whát is **false**?

⁴ It is the **Lord** who grants **fav**ors to **those** whò are **mer**ciful;
  the **Lord hears** me whenevér I **call**.

⁵ **Trem**ble; do not **sin**: **pon**der on your **bed** ànd be **still**.
⁶ Make **jus**tice your **sac**rifice and **trust** ín the **Lord**.

⁷ "**What** can bring us **hap**piness?" **màn**y say.
  Lift up the **light** of your **face** on **ús**, O **Lord**.

⁸ You have **put** into my **heart** a **greàt**er **joy**
  than **they** have from a**bun**dance of **corn** ánd new **wine**.

⁹ I will **lie** down in **peace** and **sleep** còmes at **once**
  for **you** alone, **Lord**, make me **dwéll** in **safe**ty.

Give **praise** to the **Fath**er, the **Son** and **Hòl**y **Spir**it,
both **now** and for **ag**es unend**ing**. **Amen**.

Text: Psalm 4; The Grail
Music: Joseph Gelineau, SJ
© 1963, 1993, The Grail, GIA Publications, Inc., agent

30 Psalm 4: Let Your Face Shine upon Us

Refrain

Lord, let your face shine up - on us, shine up - on us, shine up - on us.

Verses

1. Listen to my song, hear me when I call, Oh Lord, my God, be gracious,
   hear my prayer.

2. You have called my name, set your seal upon my heart,
   you hear me when I call.

3. Fill me with your joy, grant to me your peaceful rest,
   to dwell in safety with my Lord.

Text: Psalm 4:2, 4, 9; Marty Haugen
Music: Marty Haugen
© 1980, GIA Publications, Inc.

31 Psalm 8: How Great Is Your Name

Antiphon I

How great is your name, O Lord our God, through all the earth!

Text: Psalm 8:2, The Grail
Music: A. Gregory Murray, OSB
© 1963, The Grail, GIA Publications, Inc., agent

Antiphon II (St. 3-5)

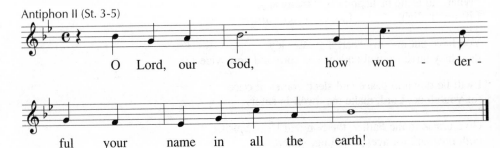

O Lord, our God, how won - der - ful your name in all the earth!

Text: *Lectionary for Mass*, © 1969, 1981, ICEL
Music: J. Robert Carroll, © 1975, GIA Publications, Inc.

Psalm Tone

Music: Chant tone 5; acc. by Robert J. Batastini, © 1975, GIA Publications, Inc.

Gelineau Tone

Omit for 2-line stanza

*²How **great** is your **name**, O Lòrd our **God**,
  thróugh all the **earth**!

  Your **majesty** is **praised** above the **hèa**vens;
³ on the **lips** of **chíl**dren and of **babes**
  you have found **praise** to **foil** your **è**nemy,
  to **si**lence the **fóe** and the **reb**el.

⁴When I see the **heav**ens, the **work** of yòur **hands**,
  the **moon** and the **stárs** which you ar**ranged**,
⁵ what are **we** that you should **keep** us in **mìnd**,
  mere **mor**tals thát you **care** for **us**?

⁶ Yet you have **made** us little **less** than **gòds**;
  and **crowned** us with **gló**ry and **hon**or,
⁷ you gave us **power** over the **work** of yòur **hands**,
  put **all** things **únd**er our **feet**.

⁸ **All** of them, **sheep** and **càt**tle,
  yes, **e**ven thé **sav**age **beasts**,
⁹ **birds** of the **air**, and **fish**
  that **make** their **way** thróugh the **waters**.

*¹⁰ How **great** is your **name**, O Lòrd our **God**,
  thróugh all the **earth**!

  Give **glo**ry to the **Fa**ther Al**mìght**y,
  to his **Son**, Jésus **Christ**, the **Lord**,
  to the **Spir**it who **dwells** in òur **hearts**,
  both **now** and for **év**er. **Amen**.

Omitted when Antiphon I is used.

Text: Psalm 8; The Grail
Music: Joseph Gelineau, SJ
© 1963, 1993, The Grail, GIA Publications, Inc., agent

32 Psalm 8: How Glorious Is Your Name

Refrain

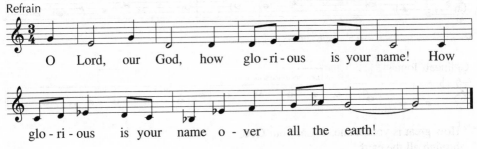

O Lord, our God, how glo-ri-ous is your name! How glo-ri-ous is your name o-ver all the earth!

Verses

1. When I see the heavens, the work of your hands,
   the moon and the stars which you arranged,
   What are we that you keep us in mind?
   Your children that you remember them at all?

2. Yet you have made us little less than gods, with glory and honor you crowned us,
   Gave us pow'r over the work of your hands, dominion over all that you have made.

3. All sheep and oxen, birds of the air, all things that swim in the sea.
   Beasts without number, life without names, you have placed under our feet.

Text: Psalm 8:4-5, 6-7, 8-9; Rory Cooney
Music: Rory Cooney
© 1990, GIA Publications, Inc.

33 Psalm 15: The Just Will Live

Antiphon

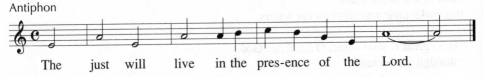

The just will live in the pres-ence of the Lord.

Text: *Lectionary for Mass*, © 1981, ICEL
Music: Robert J. Batastini, © 1995, GIA Publications, Inc.

Psalm Tone — Omit for 2-line stanza

Music: Chrysogonus Waddell, OCSO, © Gethsemani Abbey

Gelineau Tone — Omit for 2-line stanza

[1] Lord, **who** shall be admitted tò your **tent**
and **dwell** on your **holý mountain**?

[2] **Those** who **walk** wìthout **fault**,
those who **act** wíth **justice**
and **speak** the **truth** from thèir **hearts**,
[3] **those** who do not **slan**der with théir **tongue**,

those who **do no wrong** tò their **kin**dred,
who **cast** no **slur** on théir **neigh**bors,
[4] who **hold** the **god**less in dìs**dain**,
but **hon**or those who **fear** thé **Lord**;

those who **keep** their **word**, cóme what **may**,
[5] who **take** no **in**terest on á **loan**
and ac**cept** no **bribes** against thè **in**nocent.
Such people will **stand** firm fór **ever**.

Give **praise** to the **Fathèr** Al**might**y,
to his **Son**, Jesus **Christ**, thé **Lord**,
to the **Spir**it who **dwells** in oùr **hearts**,
both **now** and for **ever**. Á**men**.

Text: Psalm 15; The Grail
Music: Joseph Gelineau, SJ
© 1963, 1993, The Grail, GIA Publications, Inc., agent

34   Psalm 16: In You, My God

Antiphon I

In you, my God, my bod - y will rest in hope.

Text: *Liturgy of the Hours,* © 1974, ICEL
Music: Eugene Englert, © 1986, GIA Publications, Inc.

Antiphon II (Vs. 5.8.9-10.11)

Keep me safe, O God; you are my hope.

Text: *Lectionary for Mass,* © 1969, 1981, ICEL
Music: Richard Proulx, © 1986, GIA Publications, Inc.

Antiphon III (Vs. 1-2.5.7-8.9-10.11)

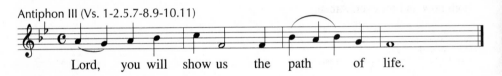

Lord, you will show us the path of life.

Text: *Lectionary for Mass,* © 1969, 1981, ICEL
Music: Michael Joncas, © 1986, GIA Publications, Inc.

Antiphon IV (Vs. 1-2.5.7-8.9-10.11)

You are my in - her - i - tance, you, O Lord.

Text: *Lectionary for Mass,* © 1969, 1981, ICEL
Music: Michael Joncas, © 1986, GIA Publications, Inc.

Psalm Tone

Omit for 3-line stanza   Repeat for 5-line stanza

Music: Laurence Bevenot, OSB, © 1969, Ampleforth Abbey Trustees

Gelineau Tone

Omit for 4-line stanza   Omit for 3-line stanza

St. 1-5

St. 6-7

Omit for 3-line stanza

¹ Preserve me, God, I take refùge in you.
² I say to you Lord: "You áre my God.
  My happiness lies in yóu alone."

³ You have put into my heart a marvèlous love
  for the faithful ones who dwell ín your land.
⁴ Those who choose other gods incrèase their sorrows.
  Never will I offer their offerings of blood.
  Never will I take their name upón my lips.

⁵ O Lord, it is you who are my portìon and cup,
  it is you yourself who áre my prize.
⁶ The lot marked out for me is mỳ delight,
  welcome indeed the heritage that fálls to me!

⁷ I will bless you, Lord, you gìve me counsel,
  and even at night diréct my heart.
⁸ I keep you, Lord, ever ìn my sight;
  since you are at my right hand, I sháll stand firm.

⁹ And so my heart rejoices, my sòul is glad;
  even my body shall rést in safety.
¹⁰ For you will not leave my soul amòng the dead,
  nor let your beloved knów decay.

¹¹ You will show me the pàth of life,
  the fullness of joy ín your presence,
  at your right hand happinéss for ever.

Give praise to the Fathèr Almighty,
to his Son, Jesus Chríst, the Lord,
to the Spirit who dwells ìn our hearts,
both now and forevér. Amen.

Text: Psalm 16; The Grail
Music: Joseph Gelineau, SJ
© 1963, 1993, The Grail, GIA Publications, Inc., agent

35 Psalm 16: Keep Me Safe, O God

Refrain

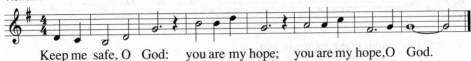

Keep me safe, O God: you are my hope; you are my hope, O God.

Verses

1. I say to God, "you are my only God, I have no good except in you."

2. I find in God always my cup of joy; and God will keep my life secure.

3. I bless my God: God who has counseled me. At night my heart gives counsel too.

4. I keep my God always before my eyes; with God beside me I'm secure.

5. And so my heart always is glad in God; my body too shall dwell secure.

6. For you will not ever abandon me, or let your servant lose the path.

7. The path of life you have revealed to me, and in your presence is my joy.

Text: Psalm 16; John Foley, SJ, © 1993, GIA Publications, Inc.; refrain trans., © 1969, ICEL.
Music: John Foley, SJ, © 1993, GIA Publications, Inc.

36 Psalm 16: You Will Show Me the Path of Life

Refrain I

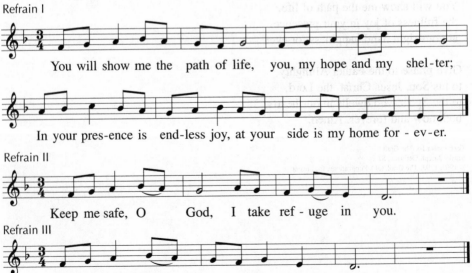

You will show me the path of life, you, my hope and my shel-ter;

In your pres-ence is end-less joy, at your side is my home for - ev-er.

Refrain II

Keep me safe, O God, I take ref-uge in you.

Refrain III

You are my in - her - i - tance, O Lord.

Verses

1. Faithful God, I look to you, you alone my life and fortune,
   never shall I look to other gods, you shall be my one hope.

2. From of old you are my heritage, you my wisdom and my safety,
   through the night you speak within my heart, silently you teach me.

3. So my heart shall sing for joy, in your arms I rest securely,
   you will not abandon me to death, you shall not desert me.

Text: Psalm 16:1-2, 6-8, 9-10; Marty Haugen, © 1988, GIA Publications, Inc.; refrain III trans., © 1969, ICEL
Music: Marty Haugen; refrain II and III adapt. by Diana Kodner, © 1988, 1994, GIA Publications, Inc.

Psalm 17: Lord, When Your Glory Appears   37

Refrain

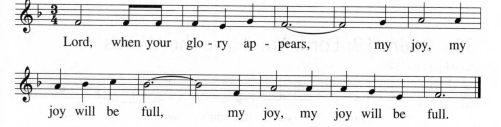

Lord, when your glo-ry ap-pears, my joy, my joy will be full, my joy, my joy will be full.

Verses

1. Hear, O Lord, a just suit, attend to my outcry.
   Hear the prayer of my lips; lips without deceit.

2. My steps are fast in your path, my feet have faltered not.
   I call and you answer me; incline your ear to me.

3. Keep me in your gentle care. Hide me under your wings.
   In justice shall I see your face, on waking shall I be content.

Text: Psalm 17:1, 5-6, 8-9, 15; Roy James Stewart, © 1993, GIA Publications, Inc.; refrain trans. © 1969, ICEL
Music: Roy James Stewart, © 1993, GIA Publications, Inc.

38 Psalm 18: I Love You, Lord, My Strength

Refrain

I love you, Lord, my strength, my strength.

Verses

1. I love you, Lord, my strength, my rock, my fortress, my savior.
   God, you are the rock where I take refuge;
   my shield, my mighty help, my stronghold.
   Lord, you are worthy of all praise, when I call I am saved from my foes.

2. Long life to you, Lord, my rock! Praise to you, God, who saves me,
   You have given great victories to your king and shown your love for your anointed.

Text: Psalm 18:2-3, 3-4, 47, 51; © 1963, 1993, The Grail, GIA Publications, Inc., agent; refrain trans. © 1969, ICEL
Music: Michel Guimont, © 1994, GIA Publications, Inc.

39 Psalm 19: Lord, You Have the Words

Antiphon I (St. 5-8)

Lord, you have the words of

ev - er - last - ing life.

Text: *Lectionary for Mass,* © 1969, ICEL
Music: Richard Proulx, © 1975, GIA Publications, Inc.

Antiphon II (St. 5.7.9.10)

The pre-cepts of the Lord give joy to the heart.

Text: *Lectionary for Mass,* © 1969, ICEL
Music: Randolph Currie, © 1986, GIA Publications, Inc.

Antiphon III (St. 1-2)

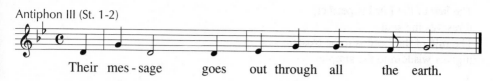

Their mes - sage goes out through all the earth.

Text: *Lectionary for Mass,* © 1969, ICEL
Music: James J. Chepponis, © 1986, GIA Publications, Inc.

Antiphon IV (St. 5.6.7.11)

Your words, Lord, are spir - it and life.

Text: *Lectionary for Mass,* © 1969, ICEL
Music: Chrysogonus Waddell, OCSO, © 1986, GIA Publications, Inc.

Psalm Tone

Repeat for 3-line stanza

Music: A. Gregory Murray, OSB, © L. J. Carey and Co., Ltd.

Gelineau Tone

St. 1-4   Omit for 3-line stanza

St. 5-12

[2] The **heav**ens pro**claim** the **glor**ỳ of **God**,
    and the **firm**ament shows **forth** the **work** óf God's **hands**.
[3] **Day** unto **day takes** ùp the **story**
    and **night** unto **night** makes kn**ówn** the **mes**sage.

[4] No **speech**, no **word**, no **vòice** is **heard**
[5] yet their **span** ex**tends** through **áll** the **earth**,
    their **words** to the **utmost bounds** óf the **world**.

    There God has **placed** a **tent** fòr the **sun**;
[6] it comes **forth** like a **bride**groom **com**ing fróm his **tent**,
    re**joic**es like a **champ**ion to **rún** its **course**.

[7] At the **end** of the **sky** is the **rising** òf the **sun**;
    to the **furth**est **end** of the **sky** ís its **course**.
    There is **noth**ing con**cealed** from its **búrn**ing **heat**.

⁸ The **law** of the **Lòrd** is **per**fect,
  it revíves the **soul**.
The **rule** of the **Lord** is tò be **trust**ed,
  it gives **wis**dom tó the **simple**.

⁹ The **pre**cepts of the **Lòrd** are **right**,
  they **glad**dén the **heart**.
The com**mand** of the **Lòrd** is **clear**,
  it gives **light** tó the **eyes**.

¹⁰ The **fear** of the **Lòrd** is **ho**ly,
  abidíng for **ever**.
The de**crees** of the **Lòrd** are **truth**
  and **all** óf them **just**.

¹¹ They are **more** to be desìred than **gold**,
  than the **pur**ést of **gold**
  and **sweet**er are **thèy** than **hon**ey,
  than **hon**ey fróm the **comb**.

¹² So in **them** your **ser**vant finds in**struc**tion;
  great re**ward** is ín their **keep**ing.
¹³ But **can** we dis**cern** àll our **er**rors?
  From **hid**den fáults ac**quit** us.

¹⁴ From pre**sump**tion re**stràin** your **ser**vant
  and **let** ít not **rule** me.
Then shall **Ì** be **blame**less,
  clean fróm grave **sin**.

¹⁵ May the **spok**en **words** òf my **mouth**,
  the **thoughts** óf my **heart**,
  win **fa**vor in your **sìght**, O **Lord**,
  my **res**cuér, my **rock**!

Praise the **Father**, the **Son**, and Hòly **Spir**it,
  both **now** ánd for **ever**,
the **God** who **is**, who **was**, ànd who **will** be,
  world wíthout **end**.

Text: Psalm 19; The Grail
Music: Joseph Gelineau, SJ
© 1963, 1993, The Grail, GIA Publications, Inc., agent

Psalm 19: Lord, You Have the Words   40

Refrain

Lord, you have the words of ev-er-last-ing life.

Verses

1. The law of the Lord is perfect, refreshing the soul;
   the Lord's rule is to be trusted, the simple find wisdom.

2. The fear of the Lord is holy, abiding for ever;
   the decrees of the Lord are true, all of them just.

3. The precepts of the Lord are right, they gladden the heart,
   the command of the Lord is clear, giving light to the eye.

4. They are worth more than gold, than the finest gold,
   sweeter than honey, than honey from the comb.

Text: Psalm 19:8, 9, 10, 11; David Haas, © 1983, GIA Publications, Inc.; refrain trans. © 1969, ICEL
Music: David Haas, © 1983, GIA Publications, Inc.

Psalm 22: I Will Praise You, Lord   41

Refrain

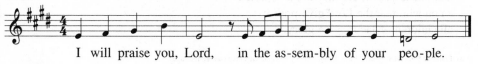

I will praise you, Lord, in the as-sem-bly of your peo-ple.

Verses

1. My vows I will pay before those who fear God.
   The poor shall eat and shall have their fill.
   Those who seek the Lord shall praise the Lord.
   May their hearts live for ever and ever!

2. All the earth shall remember and return to the Lord,
   all families of the nations shall bow down in awe.
   They shall bow down in awe, all the mighty of the earth,
   all who must die and go down to the dust.

3. My soul shall live for God and my children too shall serve.
   They shall tell of the Lord to generations yet to come;
   declare to those unborn, the faithfulness of God.
   These things the Lord has done.

Text: Psalm 22:26-27, 28, 30, 31-32; © 1963, 1993, The Grail, GIA Publications, Inc., agent; refrain trans. © 1969, ICEL
Music: Michel Guimont, © 1994, GIA Publications, Inc.

42 Psalm 22: My God, My God

Antiphon

My God, my God, why have you for - sak-en me?

Verses

1. All who see me deride me.
   They curl their lips, they toss their heads.
   "He trusted in the Lord, let him save him,
   and release him if this is his friend."

2. Many dogs have surrounded me,
   a band of the wicked beset me.
   They tear holes in my hands and my feet.
   I can count every one of my bones.

3. They divide my clothing among them.
   They cast lots for my robe.
   O Lord, do not leave me alone,
   my strength, make haste to help me!

4. I will tell of your name to my people
   and praise you where they are assembled.
   "You who fear the Lord give praise;
   all children of Jacob, give glory."

43 Psalm 22: My God, My God

Refrain

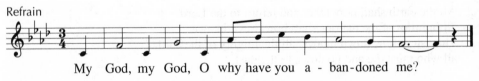

My God, my God, O why have you a - ban-doned me?

Verses

1. All who see me laugh at me, they mock me and they shake their heads:
   "He relied on the Lord, let the Lord be his refuge."

2. As dogs around me, they circle me about.
   Wounded me and pierced me, I can number all my bones.

3. My clothing they divided, for my garments casting lots,
   O Lord, do not desert me, but hasten to my aid.

4. I will praise you to my people, and proclaim you in their midst,
   O fear the Lord, my people, give glory to God's name.

Psalm 23: The Lord Is My Shepherd   44

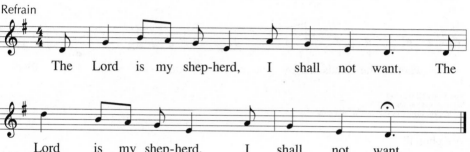

Verses

1. The pastures are fresh where you give me rest;
   Calm waters lift up my soul.
   You lead me on paths that are righteous and good;
   Your name is hallowed by all.

2. Though I am brought down to the valley deep,
   No evil great will I fear;
   The strength of your rod and the pow'r of your staff
   Will give me comfort and cheer.

3. A feast you have held in the sight of foes;
   Oil has anointed my head;
   My cup overflows with your mercy and love:
   With blessings great am I fed.

4. Today and for all of my days to come
   Goodness and love follow me,
   And now I will dwell in the house of the Lord
   As long as life there shall be.

45 Psalm 23: My Shepherd Is the Lord

Antiphon I

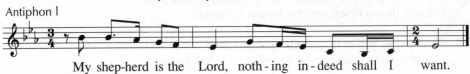

My shep-herd is the Lord, noth-ing in-deed shall I want.

Text: Psalm 23; The Grail
Music: Joseph Gelineau, SJ
© 1963, The Grail, GIA Publications, Inc., agent

Antiphon II

The Lord is my shep - herd, noth-ing shall I

want: he leads me by safe paths, noth-ing shall I fear.

Text: Psalm 23; The Grail
Music: A. Gregory Murray, OSB
© 1963, The Grail, GIA Publications, Inc., agent

Antiphon III

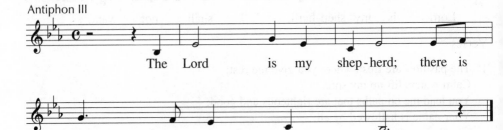

The Lord is my shep-herd; there is

noth - ing I shall want.

Text: *Lectionary for Mass*, © 1969, ICEL
Music: Richard Proulx, © 1975, GIA Publications, Inc.

Antiphon IV

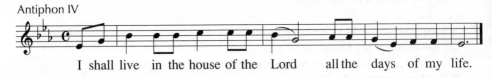

I shall live in the house of the Lord all the days of my life.

Text: *Lectionary for Mass*, © 1969, ICEL
Music: Robert J. Batastini, © 1975, GIA Publications, Inc.

Psalm Tone

Omit for 4-line stanza

Music: Richard Proulx, © 1975, GIA Publications, Inc.

Gelineau Tone

Omit for 4-line stanza

¹ **Lord, you** are mỳ **shep**herd;
  there is **noth**ing Í shall **want.**
² **Fresh** and **green** are thè **pas**tures
  where you **give** me ré**pose.**
  Near **rest**ful **wat**ers yòu **lead** me,
³ to re**vive** my droopíng **spirit.**

  You **guide** me alòng the rìght **path;**
  You are **true** tó your **name.**
⁴ If I should **walk** in the **val**ley òf **dark**ness
  no evil would Í **fear.**
  You are **there** with your **crook** and yòur **staff;**
  with **these** you give mé **comfort.**

⁵ You have pre**pared** a **ban**quet fòr **me**
  in the **sight** óf my **foes.**
  My **head** you have a**noin**ted wìth **oil;**
  my **cup** is ové**rflowing.**

⁶ Surely **good**ness and **kind**ness shàll **fol**low me
  all the **days** óf my **life.**
  In the **Lord's** own **house** shall Ì **dwell**
  for **ever** ánd **ever.**

  To the **Fa**ther and **Son** gìve **glory,**
  give **glo**ry tó the **Spir**it.
  To God who **is,** who **was,** and whò **will** be
  for **ever** ánd **ever.**

Text: Psalm 23; The Grail
Music: Joseph Gelineau, SJ
© 1963, 1993, The Grail, GIA Publications, Inc., agent

46 Psalm 23: Nada Me Falta

Refrain

El Se - ñor es mi pas - tor, na - da me fal - ta. El Se -
ñor es mi pas - tor, na-da me fal - ta - rá.

Verses

1. El Señor es mi pastor, nada me falta: En verdes praderas me hace recostar;
   Me conduce hacia fuentes tranquilas y repara mis fuerzas.

2. Me guía por el sendero justo en gracia de su nombre.
   Aunque camine por cañadas oscuras, nada temo porque tú vas conmigo:
   tu vara y tu cayado me sosiegan.

3. Preparas una mesa ante mí, enfrente de mis enemigos;
   me unges la cabeza con perfume, y mi copa rebosa.

4. Tu bondad y tu engencia me acompañan. Todos los días de mi vida,
   y habitaré en la casa del Señor por siempre.

Text: Psalm 23, *Leccionario Edición Hispanoamericana;* Donna Peña
Music: Donna Peña; acc. by Diana Kodner
© 1988, 1993, GIA Publications, Inc.

47 Psalm 24: We Long to See Your Face

Refrain I

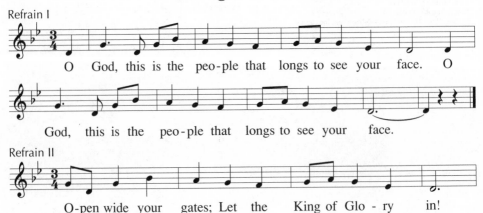

O God, this is the peo-ple that longs to see your face. O
God, this is the peo-ple that longs to see your face.

Refrain II

O-pen wide your gates; Let the King of Glo - ry in!

O-pen wide your gates; Let the King of Glo - ry in!

Verses

1. All the earth is yours, O God, the world and those who dwell on it.
   You have founded it upon the seas and established it upon the rivers.

2. Who can ascend your mountain, God? Or who may stand in this holy place?
   Those whose hands are sinless, hearts are clean, and desire not the vanity of earth.

3. They shall receive your blessing, God, their Savior shall reward them.
   Such is the face that seeks for you, that seeks your face, O God of Jacob.

Text: Psalm 24; Kevin Keil, © 1993, GIA Publications, Inc.; refrain 1 trans. © 1969, ICEL
Music: Kevin Keil, © 1993, GIA Publications, Inc.

Psalm 24: Let the Lord Enter 48

Antiphon

Let the Lord en-ter; he is king of glo-ry.

Text: *Lectionary for Mass*, © 1969, ICEL
Music: Richard Proulx, © 1975, GIA Publications, Inc.

Verses

1. The Lord's is the earth and its fullness,
   the world and all its peoples.
   It is God who set it on the seas;
   who made it firm on the waters.

2. Who shall climb the mountain of the Lord?
   Who shall stand in God's holy place?
   Those with clean hands and pure heart,
   who desire not worthless things.

3. They shall receive blessings from the Lord
   and reward from the God who saves them.
   These are the ones who seek,
   seek the face of the God of Jacob.

Text: Psalm 24:1-2, 3-4, 5-6; © 1963, 1993, The Grail, GIA Publications, Inc., agent

49 Psalm 24: Who Is This King

Refrain

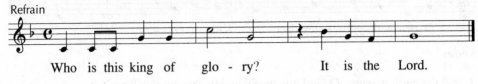

Who is this king of glo - ry? It is the Lord.

Verses

1. O gates, lift high your heads;
   grow higher, ancient doors.
   Let the king of glory enter!

2. Who is the king of glory?
   The Lord, the mighty, the valiant,
   the Lord, the valiant in war.

3. O gates, lift high your heads;
   grow higher, ancient doors.
   Let the king of glory enter!

4. Who is the king of glory?
   The Lord of heavenly armies.
   This is the king of glory.

50 Psalm 25: To You, O Lord

Refrain

To you, O Lord, I lift up my soul.

Verses

1. Lord, make me know your ways.
   Lord, teach me your paths.
   Make me walk in your truth, and teach me,
   for you are God my savior.
   In you I hope all the day long.

2. The Lord is good and upright,
   showing the path to those who stray,
   guiding the humble in the right path,
   and teaching the way to the poor.

3. God's ways are steadfastness and truth
   for those faithful to the covenant decrees.
   The Lord's friendship is for the God-fearing;
   and the covenant is revealed to them.

Text: Psalm 25:4-5, 8-9, 10, 14; © 1963, 1993, The Grail, GIA Publications, Inc., agent

Psalm 25: To You, O Lord 51

Refrain

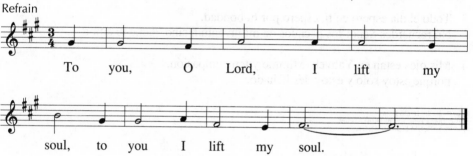

To you, O Lord, I lift my soul, to you I lift my soul.

Verses

1. Lord, make me know your ways.
   Lord, teach me your paths.
   Make me walk in your truth, and teach me,
   for you are God my savior.
   In you I hope all the day long.

2. The Lord is good and upright,
   showing the path to those who stray,
   guiding the humble in the right path,
   and teaching the way to the poor.

3. God's ways are steadfastness and truth
   for those faithful to the covenant decrees.
   The Lord's friendship is for the God-fearing;
   and the covenant is revealed to them.

Text: Psalm 25:4-5, 8-9, 10, 14; © 1963, 1993, The Grail, GIA Publications, Inc., agent; refrain trans. © 1969, ICEL
Music: Michel Guimont, © 1995, GIA Publications, Inc.

52 Psalm 25: Levanto Mi Alma

Refrain

Oh Dios mí-o, le-van-to mi al - ma,

le - van-to a ti Se-ñor, mi sal - va - ción.

Verses

1. Sólo en ti confio, estaré sin vergüenza. Y no triunfaran mis enemigos.
   No hay dudas.

2. Muestrame tus caminos. Enséñame tus sendas.
   Guíame Señor en tu verdad y a mi salvación.

3. Todo el día espero en ti, espero por tu bondad.
   No recuerdes Señor los pecados de mi juventud, sino, dame tu amor.

4. Mis ojos estan en Yahveh. Mirame y ten compasión,
   porque estoy solo y estoy desdichado.

Text: Psalm 25; Donna Peña
Music: Donna Peña; acc. by Diana Kodner
© 1988, 1993, GIA Publications, Inc.

53 Psalm 25: To You, O Lord

Refrain I

To you, O Lord, I lift my soul, to

you, I lift my soul.

Refrain II

Your ways, O Lord, are love and truth, to

those   who   keep   your   cov - e - nant.

Verses

1. Lord, make me know your ways, teach me your paths
   and keep me in the way of your truth, for you are God, my Savior.

2. For the Lord is good and righteous, revealing the way to those who wander,
   gently leading the poor and the humble.

3. To the ones who seek the Lord, who look to God's word, who live God's love,
   God will always be near, and will show them mercy.

Text: Psalm 25:4-5, 8-9, 12-14; Marty Haugen, © 1982, GIA Publications, Inc.; refrain trans. © 1969, ICEL
Music: Marty Haugen, © 1982, GIA Publications, Inc.

Psalm 25: Remember Your Mercies   54

Refrain I

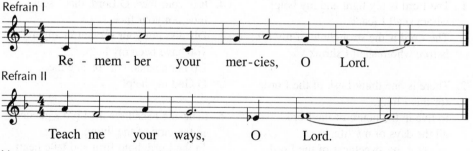

Re - mem - ber   your   mer-cies,   O   Lord.

Refrain II

Teach me   your   ways,   O   Lord.

Verses

1. Your ways, O Lord, make known to me, teach me your paths.
   Guide me, teach me, for you are my Savior.

2. Remember your compassion, Lord, and your kindness of old.
   Remember this, and not my sins, in your goodness, O Lord.

3. Good and just is the Lord, the sinners know the way.
   God guides the meek to justice, and teaches the humble.

Text: Psalm 25:4-5, 6-7, 8-9; David Haas, © 1985, GIA Publications, Inc.; refrain trans. © 1969, ICEL
Music: David Haas, © 1985, GIA Publications, Inc.

55   Psalm 27: I Believe That I Shall See

Antiphon I (St. 1.2.3)

I be - lieve that I shall see   the good things of the

Lord   in   the   land   of the   liv - ing.

Text: *Lectionary for Mass*, © 1969, ICEL
Music: Columba Kelly, OSB, harm. by Richard Proulx, © 1975, GIA Publications, Inc.

Antiphon II (St. 1.3.4.5 or 1.2.5)

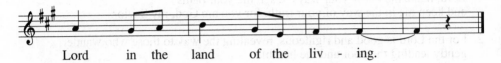

The Lord is my light and my sal - va - tion.

Text: *Lectionary for Mass*, © 1969, ICEL
Music: Richard Proulx, © 1975, GIA Publications, Inc.

Verses

1. The Lord is my light and my help;
   whom shall I fear?
   The Lord is the stronghold of my life;
   before whom shall I shrink?

2. There is one thing I ask of the Lord,
   for this I long,
   to live in the house of the Lord,
   all the days of my life,
   to savor the sweetness of the Lord,
   to behold his temple.

3. O Lord, hear my voice when I call;
   have mercy and answer.
   Of you my heart has spoken:
   "Seek God's face."

4. It is your face, O Lord, that I seek;
   hide not your face.
   Dismiss not your servant in anger;
   you have been my help.
   Do not abandon or forsake me,
   O God my help!

5. I am sure I shall see the Lord's goodness
   in the land of the living.
   In the Lord, hold firm and take heart.
   Hope in the Lord!

Text: Psalm 27:1, 4, 7-8, 8-9, 13-14; © 1963, 1993, The Grail, GIA Publications, Inc., agent

Psalm 27: In the Land of the Living 56

Refrain

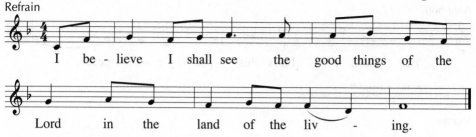

I be - lieve I shall see the good things of the
Lord in the land of the liv - ing.

Verses

1. The Lord is my light, the Lord is my help, of whom should I be afraid?
   The Lord is the stronghold of my life, before whom should I shrink?

2. When I cry out, O Lord, hear my voice! Have mercy on me and answer.
   My heart has told me, "seek his face!" It is your face, Lord, I seek.

3. There is only one thing I ask of the Lord: to live in God's house forever,
   to savor the sweetness of the Lord, to behold his temple.

Text: Psalm 27; *The Jerusalem Bible,* © 1966, Darton, Longman and Todd, Ltd. and Doubleday, a division of Bantam Doubleday Dell
    Publishing Group, Inc.
Music: Carl Johengen, © 1993, GIA Publications, Inc.

Psalm 27: The Lord Is My Light 57

Refrain

The Lord is my light and my sal - va - tion, of
whom should I be a - fraid, of whom should I be a - fraid?

Verses

1. The Lord is my light and my help; whom should I fear?
   The Lord is the stronghold of my life; before whom should I shrink?

2. There is one thing I ask of the Lord; for this I long:
   to live in the house of the Lord all the days of my life.

3. I believe I shall see the goodness of the Lord in the land of the living;
   hope in God, and take heart. Hope in the Lord!

Text: Psalm 27:1-2, 4, 13-14; David Haas
Music: David Haas
© 1983, GIA Publications, Inc.

58 Psalm 29: The Lord Will Bless His People

Antiphon

The Lord will bless his peo - ple with peace.

Text: *Lectionary for Mass,* © 1981, ICEL
Music: Robert J. Batastini, © 1995, GIA Publications, Inc.

Verses

1. O give the Lord, you children of God,
   give the Lord glory and power;
   give the Lord the glory of his name.
   Adore the Lord, resplendent and holy.

2. The Lord's voice resounding on the waters,
   the Lord on the immensity of waters;
   the voice of the Lord, full of power,
   the voice of the Lord, full of splendor.

3. The God of glory thunders.
   In his temple they all cry: "Glory!"
   The Lord sat enthroned over the flood;
   the Lord sits as king for ever.

Text: Psalm 29:1-2, 3-4, 3, 9-10; © 1963, 1993, The Grail, GIA Publications, Inc., agent

59 Psalm 30: I Will Praise You, Lord

Refrain

I will praise you, Lord, for you have res - cued me.

Verses

1. I will praise you, Lord, you have rescued me
   and have not let my enemies rejoice over me.
   O Lord, you have raised my soul from the dead,
   restored me to life from those who sink into the grave.

2. Sing psalms to the Lord, you faithful ones,
   give thanks to his holy name.
   God's anger lasts a moment; God's favor all through life.
   At night there are tears, but joy comes with dawn.

3. The Lord listened and had pity.
   The Lord came to my help.
   For me you have changed my mourning into dancing,
   O Lord my God, I will thank you for ever.

Text: Psalm 30:2, 4, 5-6, 11-13; © 1963, 1993, The Grail, GIA Publications, Inc., agent; refrain trans. © 1969, ICEL.
Music: Michel Guimont, © 1995, GIA Publications, Inc.

Psalm 30: I Will Praise You, Lord 60

Refrain

I will praise you, Lord, you have res-cued me, I will praise you, Lord, for your mer-cy. I will praise you, Lord, you have res-cued me: I will praise you, Lord.

Verses

1. I will praise you, Lord, you have rescued me
   and have not let my enemies rejoice over me.
   O Lord, you have raised my soul from the dead,
   restored me to life from those who sink into the grave.

2. Sing psalms to the Lord, all you faithful, give thanks to his holy name.
   God's anger lasts but a moment; God's favor through life.
   At night there are tears, but joy comes with dawn.

3. The Lord listened and had pity. The Lord came to my help.
   For me you have changed my mourning into dancing;
   O Lord my God, I will thank you for ever.

Text: Psalm 30:2, 4, 5-6, 11-13; © 1963, 1993, The Grail, GIA Publications, Inc., agent; refrain, Paul Inwood, © 1985, alt.
Music: Paul Inwood, © 1985
Published by OCP Publications

61 Psalm 31: I Put My Life in Your Hands / Pongo Mi Vida

Refrain

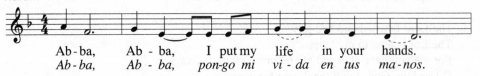

Ab - ba, Ab - ba, I put my life in your hands.
Ab - ba, Ab - ba, pon-go mi vi - da en tus ma - nos.

Ab-ba, Ab-ba, I put my life in your hands.
Ab-ba, Ab-ba, pon-go mi vi-da en tus ma - nos.

Verses

1. In you, O Lord I take refuge; let me never be put to shame.
   In your justice rescue me, in your hands I commend my spirit.

2. For all my foes reproach me; all my friends are now put to flight.
   I am forgotten, like the dead, like a dish that now is broken.

3. I place my trust in you; in your hands is my destiny.
   Let your face shine upon your servant, in your hands I will place my life.

1. *En ti busco protección. No me defraudes nunca jamás.*
   Ponme a salvo pues tú eres justo. En tus manos encomiendo mi espíritu.

2. *En ti pongo toda mi fe hablaré de tu bondad,*
   por favor está siempre conmigo. Tú haces la luz del caos.

3. *Tú eres mi esperanza; sólo tú mi salvación.*
   Con tu misericordia, ven. Escucha mi oración.

Text: Psalm 31; David Haas; Spanish trans. by Jeffrey Judge
Music: David Haas
© 1993, GIA Publications, Inc.

Psalm 31: Father, I Put My Life in Your Hands 62

Refrain

Fa - ther, I put my life in your hands.

Verses

1. In you, O Lord, I take refuge;
   let me never be put to shame.
   In your justice rescue me.
   Into your hands I commend my spirit;
   you will redeem me, O Lord, O faithful God.

2. For all my foes I am an object of reproach,
   a laughingstock to my neighbors,
   and a dread to my friends;
   they who see me abroad flee from me.
   I am forgotten like the unremembered dead;
   I am like a dish that is broken.

3. But my trust is in you, O Lord;
   I say, "You are my God."
   In your hands is my destiny;
   rescue me from the clutches of my enemies and my persecutors.

4. Let your face shine upon your servant;
   save me in your kindness.
   Take courage and be stouthearted,
   all you who hope in the Lord.

Text: Psalm 31:2, 6, 12-13, 15-16, 17-25; *New American Bible*, © 1970, Confraternity of Christian Doctrine; refrain trans. © 1969, ICEL
Music: Howard Hughes, SM, © 1980, GIA Publications, Inc.

63 Psalm 31: Father, I Put My Life in Your Hands

Antiphon I (Vs. 2.6.12-13.15-16.17.25)

Fa - ther, I put my life in your hands.

Text: *Lectionary for Mass,* © 1969, 1981, ICEL
Music: S. DeLaSalle McKeon, CSJ, © 1975, GIA Publications, Inc.

Antiphon II (Vs. 2-3.3-4.17.25)

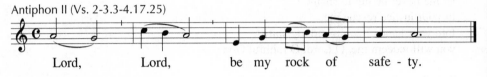

Lord, Lord, be my rock of safe - ty.

Text: *Lectionary for Mass,* © 1969, 1981, ICEL
Music: Marie Kremer, © 1986, GIA Publications, Inc.

Antiphon III

Lord God, be my ref - uge and my strength.

Text: *Liturgy of the Hours,* © 1974, ICEL
Music: Randolph Currie, © 1986, GIA Publications, Inc.

Psalm Tone

Omit for 3-line stanza

Music: A. Gregory Murray, OSB, © L. J. Carey and Co., Ltd.

Gelineau Tone

St. 1-5

St. 6-13

St. 14-19

Omit for 3-line stanza

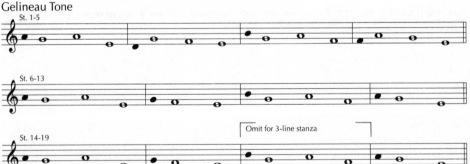

² In **you**, O **Lord**, Ì take **ref**uge.
Let me **nev**er be **pút** to **shame**.
In your **jus**tice, **sèt** me **free**,
³ **hear** me and **speed**ily **rés**cue me.

Be a **rock** of **ref**ùge for **me**,
a **mighty** **strong**hóld to **save** me,
⁴ for **you** are my **ròck**, my **strong**hold.
For your **name's** sake, **lead** mé and **guide** me.

⁵ Re**lease** me from the **snares** thèy have **hid**den
for **you** are my **réf**uge, **Lord**.
⁶ Into your **hands** I com**mènd** my **spir**it.
It is **you** who will re**deém** me, **Lord**.

O **God** of **truth**, yòu de**test**
those who **wor**ship **false** and **émp**ty **gods**.
⁸ As for **me**, I **trust** ìn the **Lord**;
let me be **glad** and re**joice** ín your **love**.

You who have **seen** mỳ af**flic**tion
and taken **heed** of my **sóul's** dis**tress**,
⁹ have not **hand**ed me over tò the **en**emy,
but **set** my **féet** at **large**.

¹⁰ Have **mer**cy on **mè**, O **Lord**,
for I am ín dis**tress**.
Tears have **wast**èd my **eyes**,
my **throat** ánd my **heart**.

¹¹ For my **life** is **spènt** with **sor**row
and my **yéars** with **sighs**.
Af**flic**tion has **brok**en dòwn my **strength**
and my **bones** **wáste** a**way**.

¹² In the **face** of **àll** my **foes**
I am á re**proach**,
an **ob**ject of **scorn** tò my **neigh**bòrs
and of **fear** tó my **friends**.

Those who **see** me ìn the **street**
run **far** awáy from **me**.
¹³ I am like the **dead**, for**gott**èn by **all**,
like a **thing** thrówn a**way**.

¹⁴ I have **heard** the **slan**der òf the **crowd**,
fear is **áll** a**round** me,
as they **plot** togethèr a**gainst** me,
as they **plan** to táke my **life**.

¹⁵ But as for **me**, I **trùst** in **you**, Lord;
I **say**: "**You** áre my **God**.
¹⁶ My **life** is in your **hands**, de**lìv**er me
from the **hands** of thóse who **hate** me.

¹⁷ Let your **face** **shine** òn your **ser**vant.
Save me ín your **love**.
¹⁸ Let me **not** be put to **shame** fòr I **call** you,
let the **wick**éd be **shamed**!

Let them be **si**lenced ìn the **grave**,
¹⁹ let **ly**ing **líps** be **mute**,
that speak **haugh**tily a**gàinst** the **just**
with **pride** ánd con**tempt**."

²⁰ How **great** is the **gòod**ness, **Lord**,
that you **keep** for thóse who **fear** you,
that you **show** to **thòse** who **trust** you
in the **síght** of **all**.

²¹ You **hide** them in the **shel**ter òf your **pres**ence
from **hú**man **plots**;
you **keep** them **safe** withìn your **tent**
from dis**pút**ing **tongues**.

²² **Bless**ed be the **Lord** whò has **shown** me
such a **stéad**fast **love**
in a **for**tí**fied** **city**.

²³ "I am **far** re**moved** fròm your **sight**"
I **said** in **mý** a**larm**.
Yet you **heard** the **voice** òf my **plea**
when I **crí**ed for **help**.

²⁴ **Love** the **Lord**, àll you **saints**.
The **Lord** guárds the **faith**ful
but in **turn** will re**pay** tò the **full**
those who **áct** with **pride**.

²⁵ Be **strong**, let your **hèart** take **cour**age,
all who **hope** ín the **Lord**.
Praise the **Fa**ther, the **Son**, and **Hòly** **Spir**it,
for **ev**ér and **ever**.

Text: Psalm 31; The Grail
Music: Joseph Gelineau, SJ
© 1963, 1993, The Grail, GIA Publications, Inc., agent

64 Psalm 32: I Turn to You, Lord

Refrain

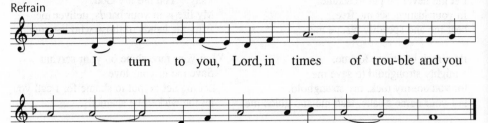

I turn to you, Lord, in times of trou-ble and you
fill me with the joy of sal - va - tion.

Verses

1. Happy the one whose sin is forgiven,
   whose sin is remitted by the Lord.
   Happy the one whom the Lord imputes no guilt,
   whose spirit has no guile.

2. But now I acknowledge all my sin,
   my guilt I hide not from the Lord.
   I will confess my sin to the Lord, my God,
   Lord forgive the guilt of my sin.

3. Rejoice, rejoice in the Lord our God,
   exult, you who are just.
   O come, come ring out your joy
   all you upright of heart.

Psalm 32: Lord, Forgive the Wrong 65

Refrain

Lord, for - give the wrong I have done.

Verses

1. Happy those whose offense is forgiven,
   whose sin is remitted.
   O happy those to whom the Lord
   imputes no guilt,
   in whose spirit is no guile.

2. But now I have acknowledged my sins;
   my guilt I did not hide.
   I said: "I will confess
   my offense to the Lord."
   And you, Lord, have forgiven
   the guilt of my sin.

3. You are my hiding place, O Lord;
   you save me from distress.
   (You surround me with cries of deliverance.)

4. Rejoice, rejoice in the Lord,
   exult, you just!
   O come, ring out your joy,
   all you upright of heart.

Text: Psalm 32:1-2, 5, 7, 11; © 1963, 1993, The Grail, GIA Publications, Inc., agent; refrain trans. © 1969, ICEL
Music: Michel Guimont, © 1995, GIA Publications, Inc.

66 Psalm 33: Let Your Mercy Be on Us

Refrain I

Let your mer-cy be on us, O God, as we place our trust in you.

Refrain II

The earth is full of the good-ness of God, the good-ness of our God.

Refrain III

Hap-py are the peo-ple the Lord has cho-sen, cho-sen to be his own.

Verses

1. Your words, O God, are truth indeed, and all your works are ever faithful;
   you love justice and right, your compassion fills all creation.

2. See how the eye of God is watching, ever guarding all who wait in hope,
   to deliver them from death and sustain them in time of famine.

3. Exult, you just, in the Lord, for praise is the song of the righteous!
   How happy the people of God, the ones whom God has chosen!

4. Our soul is waiting for God, for God is our help and our shield.
   May your kindness, O God, be upon us who place our hope in you.

Text: Psalm 33:1, 4-5, 12, 18-19, 20, 22; Marty Haugen; refrain I trans. © 1969, ICEL; refrains II, III, and verses © 1987, 1994, GIA Publications, Inc.
Music: Marty Haugen; refrain III adapt. by Diana Kodner, © 1987, 1994, GIA Publications, Inc.

Psalm 33: Happy the People 67

Antiphon I (St. 2.4.6.7 or 1.6.7)

Hap - py the peo - ple the Lord has

cho - sen to be his own.

Text: *Lectionary for Mass,* © 1969, 1981, ICEL
Music: Columba Kelly, OSB, © 1975, GIA Publications, Inc.

Antiphon II (St. 2.3.5.7)

The earth is full of the

good-ness the good-ness of the Lord.

Text: *Lectionary for Mass,* © 1969, 1981, ICEL
Music: J. Robert Carroll, © 1975, GIA Publications, Inc.

Verses

1. Ring out your joy to the Lord, O you just;
   for praise is fitting for loyal hearts.
   They are happy, whose God is the Lord,
   the people who are chosen as his own.

2. For the word of the Lord is faithful
   and all his works done in truth.
   The Lord loves justice and right
   and fills the earth with love.

3. By God's word the heavens were made,
   by the breath of his mouth all the stars.
   God collects the waves of the ocean;
   and stores up the depths of the sea.

4. By God's word the heavens were made,
   by the breath of his mouth all the stars.
   For God spoke; it came to be.
   God commanded; it sprang into being.

5. They are happy, whose God is the Lord,
   the people who are chosen as his own.
   From the heavens the Lord looks forth
   and sees all the peoples of the earth.

6. The Lord looks on those who fear him,
   on those who hope in his love,
   to rescue their souls from death,
   to keep them alive in famine.

7. Our soul is waiting for the Lord.
   The Lord is our help and our shield.
   May your love be upon us, O Lord,
   as we place all our hope in you.

Text: Psalm 33:1&12, 4-5, 6-7, 6&9, 12-13, 18-19, 20&22; © 1963, 1993, The Grail, GIA Publications, Inc., agent

68 Psalm 33: Lord, Let Your Mercy

Refrain

Lord, let your mer-cy be on us, as we place our trust in you.

Verses

1. For the word of the Lord is faithful
   and all his works done in truth.
   The Lord loves justice and right
   and fills the earth with love.

2. The Lord looks on those who fear him,
   on those who hope in his love,
   to rescue their souls from death,
   to keep them alive in famine.

3. Our soul is waiting for the Lord.
   The Lord is our help and our shield.
   May your love be upon us, O Lord,
   as we place all our hope in you.

Text: Psalm 33:4-5, 18-19, 20, 22; © 1963, 1993, The Grail, GIA Publications, Inc., agent; refrain trans. © 1969, ICEL
Music: Michel Guimont, © 1995, GIA Publications, Inc.

69 Psalm 34: The Cry of the Poor

Refrain

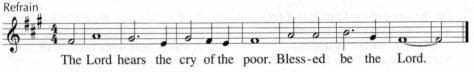

The Lord hears the cry of the poor. Bless-ed be the Lord.

Verses

1. I will bless the Lord at all times, with praise ever in my mouth.
   Let my soul glory in the Lord, who will hear the cry of the poor.

2. Let the lowly hear and be glad: the Lord listens to their pleas;
   and to hearts broken, God is near, who will hear the cry of the poor.

3. Every spirit crushed, God will save; will be ransom for their lives;
   will be safe shelter for their fears, and will hear the cry of the poor.

4. We proclaim your greatness, O God, your praise ever in our mouth;
   every face brightened in your light, for you hear the cry of the poor.

Text: Psalm 34:2-3, 6-7, 18-19, 23; John Foley, SJ
Music: John Foley, SJ
© 1978, 1991, John B. Foley, SJ, and OCP Publications

Psalm 34: Taste and See   70

Refrain

Taste   and   see   the   good-ness   of   the   Lord,   the   good - ness   of   the   Lord.

Verses

1. I will bless the Lord at all times, God's praise ever in my mouth.
   Glory in the Lord for ever, and the lowly will hear and be glad.

2. Glory in the Lord with me, let us together extol God's name.
   I sought the Lord, who answered me and delivered me from all my fears.

3. Look to God that you might be radiant with joy,
   and your faces free from all shame.
   The Lord hears the suffering souls, and saves them from all distress.

Text: Psalm 34:2-3, 4-5, 6-7; Marty Haugen, © 1980, GIA Publications, Inc.; refrain trans. © 1969, ICEL
Music: Marty Haugen, © 1980, GIA Publications, Inc.

71 Psalm 34: Taste and See

Refrain I (St. 1.2.3.4 or 1.5.6.7 or 1.8.9.10.11)

Taste and see the good - ness of the Lord.

Refrain II (Vs. 2-3.17-18.19.23)

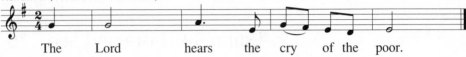

The Lord hears the cry of the poor.

Verses

1. I will bless the Lord at all times,
   God's praise always on my lips;
   in the Lord my soul shall make its boast.
   The humble shall hear and be glad.

2. Glorify the Lord with me.
   Together let us praise God's name.
   I sought the Lord and was heard;
   from all my terrors set free.

3. Look towards God and be radiant;
   let your faces not be abashed.
   When the poor cry out the Lord hears them
   and rescues them from all their distress.

4. The angel of the Lord is encamped
   around those who fear God, to rescue them.
   Taste and see that the Lord is good.
   They are happy who seek refuge in God.

5. Revere the Lord, you saints.
   They lack nothing, who revere the Lord.
   Strong lions suffer want and go hungry
   but those who seek the Lord lack no blessing.

6. Come, children, and hear me
   that I may teach you the fear of the Lord.
   Who are those who long for life
   and many days, to enjoy their prosperity?

7. Then keep your tongue from evil
   and your lips from speaking deceit.
   Turn aside from evil and do good;
   seek and strive after peace.

8. The eyes of the Lord are toward the just
   and his ears toward their appeal.
   The face of the Lord rebuffs the wicked
   to destroy their remembrance from the earth.

9. They call and the Lord hears
   and rescues them in all their distress.
   The Lord is close to the brokenhearted;
   those whose spirit is crushed God will save.

10. Many are the trials of the upright
    but the Lord will come to rescue them,
    keeping guard over all their bones,
    not one of their bones shall be broken.

11. Evil brings death to the wicked;
    those who hate the good are doomed.
    The Lord ransoms the souls of the faithful.
    None who trust in God shall be condemned.

Psalm 34: Taste and See   72

Refrain

Taste and see, taste and see that the Lord is good, the Lord is good.

Verses

1. I will bless the Lord at all times,
   his praise always on my lips.
   The Lord shall be the glory of my soul;
   the humble shall hear and be glad.

2. Glorify the Lord with me,
   together let us praise his name.
   I sought the Lord: he answered me;
   he set me free from all my fear.

3. Look upon the Lord and be radiant;
   hide not your face from the Lord.
   He heard the cry of the poor;
   he rescued them from all their woes.

4. The angel of the Lord is with his people
   to rescue those who trust in him.
   Taste and see the goodness of the Lord;
   seek refuge in him and be glad.

5. Saints of the Lord, revere him;
   those who fear him lack nothing.
   Lions suffer want and go hungry,
   but those who seek him lack no blessing.

6. Children of the Lord, come and hear,
   and learn the fear of the Lord.
   Who is he who longs for life,
   whose only love is for his wealth?

7. Keep evil words from your tongue,
   your lips from speaking deceit.
   Turn aside from evil and do good;
   seek and strive after peace.

Text: Psalm 34; Stephen Dean
Music: Stephen Dean
© 1981, published by OCP Publications

73 Psalm 34: Taste and See

Antiphon I (St. 1.2.3.4. or 1.5.6.7. or 1.8.9.10.11)

Taste and see the good - ness of the Lord.

Text: *Lectionary for Mass,* © 1969, 1981, ICEL
Music: Richard Proulx, © 1975, GIA Publications, Inc.

Antiphon II (St. 1-4)

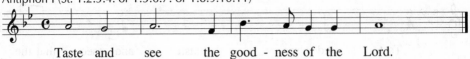

The an-gel of the Lord will res - cue those who fear him.

Text: *Lectionary for Mass,* © 1969, 1981, ICEL
Music: Howard Hughes, SM, © 1975, GIA Publications, Inc.

Psalm Tone

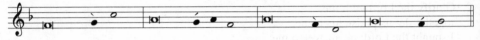

Music: Richard Proulx, © 1986, GIA Publications, Inc.

Gelineau Tone

² I will **bless the Lord** at àll **times,**
  God's **praise al**ways ón my **lips;**
³ in the **Lord** my **soul** shall make ìts **boast.**
  The **hum**ble shall **hear** and bé **glad.**

⁴ **Glorify** the **Lord** wìth **me.**
  To**geth**er let us **práise** God's **name.**
⁵ I **sought** the **Lord** and wàs **heard;**
  from all my **terrors sét free.**

⁶ **Look** towards **God** and bè **radiant;**
  let your **faces not** bé **abashed.**
⁷ When the **poor** cry **out** the **Lòrd hears** them
  and **rescues** them from **all** their **dístress.**

⁸ The **angel** of the **Lord** is èn**camped**
  around **those** who fear **Gód,** to **rescue** them.
⁹ **Taste** and **see** that the **Lord** ìs **good.**
  They are **happy** who seek **refuge** ín **God.**

¹⁰ Revere the **Lord**, yòu **saints**.
   They lack **noth**ing, who revére the **Lord**.
¹¹ Strong **lions** suffer **want** and gò **hun**gry
   but **those** who seek the **Lord** lack nó **bless**ing.

¹² **Come**, **chil**dren, ànd **hear** me
   that I may **teach** you the **fear** óf the **Lord**.
¹³ Who are **those** who **long** fòr **life**
   and many **days**, to en**joy** their prós**per**ity?

¹⁴ Then **keep** your **tongue** fròm **evil**
   and your **lips** from **speak**íng de**ceit**.
¹⁵ Turn a**side** from evil and dò **good**;
   seek and **strive** aftér **peace**.

¹⁶ The **eyes** of the **Lord** are toward thè **just**
   and his **ears** toward **theír** ap**peal**.
¹⁷ The **face** of the **Lord** rebuffs thè **wick**ed
   to de**stroy** their remem**brance** from thé **earth**.

¹⁸ They **call** and the **Lòrd hears**
   and **res**cues them in **all** théir dis**tress**.
¹⁹ The **Lord** is **close** to the **brokèn**heart**ed**;
   those whose **spirit** is **crushed** God wíll **save**.

²⁰ **Man**y are the **trials** of thè **up**right
   but the **Lord** will cóme to **res**cue them,
²¹ keeping **guard** over **all** thèir **bones**,
   not **one** of their **bones** shall bé **broken**.

²² **Evil** brings **death** to thè **wick**ed;
   those who **hate** the **góod** are **doomed**.
²³ The **Lord ran**soms the **souls** of thè **faith**ful.
   None who **trust** in **God** shall be cón**demned**.

Give **praise** to the **Father** Àl**mighty**,
to his **Son**, Jesus **Chríst**, the **Lord**,
to the **Spir**it who **dwells** in òur **hearts**,
both **now** and for **ever**. Ámen.

Text: Psalm 34; The Grail
Music: Joseph Gelineau, SJ
© 1963, 1993, The Grail, GIA Publications, Inc., agent

74 Psalm 40: Here I Am

Refrain

Here I am, Lord, here I am. I come to do your will.

Verses

1. Long was I waiting for God, and then he heard my cry.
   It was he who taught this song to me, a song of praise to God.

2. You asked me not for sacrifice, for slaughtered goats or lambs.
   No, my heart, you gave me ears to hear you, then I said, "Here I am."

3. You wrote it in the scrolls of law what you would have me do.
   Doing that is what has made me happy, your law is in my heart.

4. I spoke before your holy people, the good news that you save.
   Now you know that I will not be silent, I'll always sing your praise.

Text: Psalm 40; Rory Cooney, © 1971, 1991, North American Liturgy Resources.; refrain trans. © 1969, ICEL
Music: Rory Cooney, © 1971, 1991, North American Liturgy Resources.
Published by OCP Publications.

75 Psalm 40: Here Am I

Antiphon I (Vs. 2.4.7-8.8-9.10 or st. 4.5.6.7)

Here am I, Lord; I come to do your will.

Text: *Lectionary for Mass,* © 1969, 1981, ICEL
Music: Richard Proulx, © 1986, GIA Publications, Inc.

Antiphon II (St. 1.2.3.8)

Lord, come to my aid!

Text: *Lectionary for Mass,* © 1969, 1981, ICEL
Music: Robert J. Batastini, © 1975, GIA Publications, Inc.

Verses

1. ²I waited, I waited for the Lord
   who stooped down to me,
   and heard my cry.

2. [3]God drew me from the deadly pit,
   from the miry clay,
   and set my feet upon a rock
   and made my footsteps firm.

3. [4]God put a new song into my mouth,
   praise of our God.
   Many shall see and fear
   and shall trust in the Lord.

4. [7]You do not ask for sacrifice and offerings,
   but an open ear.
   You do not ask for holocaust and victim.
   [8]Instead, here am I.

5. In the scroll of the book it stands written
   [9]that I should do your will.
   My God, I delight in your law
   in the depth of my heart.

6. [10]Your justice I have proclaimed
   in the great assembly.
   My lips I have not sealed;
   you know it, O Lord.

7. [11]I have not hidden your justice in my heart
   but declared your faithful help.
   I have not hidden your love and your truth
   from the great assembly.

8. [18]As for me, wretched and poor,
   the Lord thinks of me.
   You are my rescuer, my help,
   O God, do not delay.

76 Psalm 41: Lord, Heal My Soul

Antiphon

Lord, heal my soul, for I have sinned a - gainst you.

Text: *Lectionary for Mass*, © 1969, 1981, ICEL
Music: J. Robert Carroll, © 1975, GIA Publications, Inc.

Verses

1. Happy those who consider the poor and the weak.
   The Lord will save them in the evil day,
   will guard them, give them life, make them happy in the land
   and will not give them up to the will of their foes.

2. The Lord will give them strength in their pain,
   will bring them back from sickness to health.
   As for me, I said: "Lord, have mercy on me,
   heal my soul for I have sinned against you."

3. If you uphold me I shall be unharmed
   and set in your presence for evermore.
   Blessed be the Lord, the God of Israel
   from age to age. Amen. Amen.

Text: Psalm 41:2-3, 4-5, 13-14; © 1963, 1993, The Grail, GIA Publications, Inc., agent

77 Psalm 42-43: Like a Deer That Longs

Antiphon

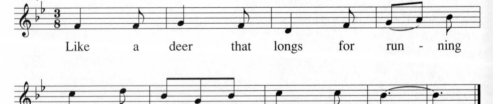

Like a deer that longs for run - ning

streams, my soul longs for you, my God.

Text: *Lectionary for Mass*, © 1969, 1981, ICEL
Music: William A. Bauman, © 1975, GIA Publications, Inc.

Verses

1. My soul is thirsting for God,
   the God of my life;
   when can I enter and see
   the face of God?

2. How I would lead the rejoicing crowd
   into the house of God,
   amid cries of gladness and thanksgiving,
   the throng wild with joy.

3. O send forth your light and your truth;
   let these be my guide.
   Let them bring me to your holy mountain,
   to the place where you dwell.

4. And I will come to your altar, O God,
   the God of my joy.
   My redeemer, I will thank you on the harp,
   O God, my God.

Text: Psalm 42:3, 5; 43:3, 4; © 1963, 1993, The Grail, GIA Publications, Inc., agent

Psalm 45: The Queen Stands at Your Right Hand   78

Refrain

The queen stands at your right hand, ar-rayed in gold.

Verses

1. Listen, O daughter, give ear to my words:
   forget your own people and your father's house.

2. So will the king desire your beauty;
   he is your lord, pay homage to him.

3. They are escorted amid gladness and joy;
   they pass within the palace of the king.

Text: Psalm 45:11, 12, 16; © 1963, 1993, The Grail, GIA Publications, Inc., agent; refrain trans. © 1969, ICEL
Music: Michel Guimont, © 1995, GIA Publications, Inc.

79   Psalm 47: God Mounts His Throne

Antiphon

God mounts   his throne   to

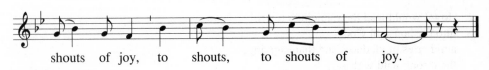

shouts   of joy,   to   shouts,   to   shouts   of   joy.

Text: *Lectionary for Mass,* © 1969, 1981, ICEL
Music: Richard Proulx, © 1975, GIA Publications, Inc.

Verses

1. All peoples, clap your hands,
   cry to God with shouts of joy!
   For the Lord, the Most High, we must fear,
   great king over all the earth.

2. God goes up with shouts of joy;
   the Lord goes up with trumpet blast.
   Sing praise for God, sing praise,
   sing praise to our king, sing praise.

3. God is king of all the earth,
   sing praise with all your skill.
   God is king over the nations;
   God reigns enthroned in holiness.

Text: Psalm 47:2-3, 6-7, 8-9; © 1963, 1993, The Grail, GIA Publications, Inc., agent

80   Psalm 47: God Mounts His Throne

Ostinato Refrain*

God   mounts his   throne   to   shouts   of   joy,   O

sing   your   prais-es   to   the   Lord!

May be sung in canon.

Verses

1. All you peoples, clap your hands, shout to God in gladness,
   the Lord we must fear, king of all the earth.

2. God goes up to shouts of joy, sound the trumpet blast.
   Sing praise to our God, praise unto our king!

3. God is king of all the earth, sing with all your skill
   to the king of all nations, God enthroned on high!

Text: Psalm 47:2-3, 6-7, 8-9; Marty Haugen
Music: Marty Haugen
© 1983, GIA Publications, Inc.

Psalm 50: To the Upright 81

Refrain

To the up-right I will show   the sav-ing power of God.

Verses

1. The God of gods, the Lord, has spoken and summoned the earth,
   from the rising of the sun to its setting,
   "I find no fault with your sacrifices, your offerings are always before me.

2. Were I hungry, I would not tell you, for I own the world and all it holds.
   Do you think I eat the flesh of bulls, or drink the blood of goats?

3. Offer to God your sacrifice; to the Most High pay your vows.
   Call on me in the day of distress. I will free you and you shall honor me."

Text: Psalm 50:1, 8, 12-13, 14-15; © 1963, 1993, The Grail, GIA Publications, Inc., agent; refrain trans. © 1969, ICEL
Music: Michel Guimont, © 1994, GIA Publications, Inc.

82 Psalm 51: Have Mercy, Lord

Antiphon I

Have mer - cy, Lord, cleanse me from all my sins.

Text: Psalm 51; The Grail
Music: Joseph Gelineau, SJ
© 1963, 1993, The Grail, GIA Publications, Inc., agent

Antiphon II (St. 1.2.6.7ab & 8cd)

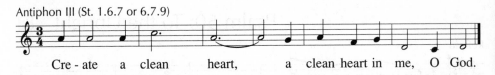

Be mer - ci - ful, O Lord, for we have sinned.

Text: *Lectionary for Mass*, © 1969, 1981, ICEL
Music: Patricia Craig, © 1975, GIA Publications, Inc.

Antiphon III (St. 1.6.7 or 6.7.9)

Cre - ate a clean heart, a clean heart in me, O God.

Text: *Lectionary for Mass*, © 1969, ICEL
Music: Frank Schoen, alt., © 1975, GIA Publications, Inc.

Antiphon IV (Vs. 3-4.12-13.17.19)

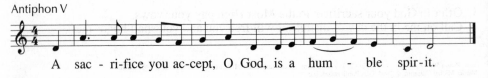

I will rise and go to my fa - ther.

Text: *Lectionary for Mass*, © 1969, 1981, ICEL
Music: James J. Chepponis, © 1986, GIA Publications, Inc.

Antiphon V

A sac - ri-fice you ac-cept, O God, is a hum - ble spir-it.

Text: *Praise God in Song*, 1979
Music: Michael Joncas, acc. by Robert J. Batastini
© 1979, 1995, GIA Publications, Inc.

Psalm Tone

Music: Chrysogonus Waddell, OCSO, © Gethsemani Abbey

Gelineau Tone

3 Have mercy on me, **God**, ìn your **kind**ness.
  In your compassion blot **out** my óffense.
4 O **wash** me more and **more** from mỳ **guilt**
  and **cleanse** me **from** mý **sin**.

5 My offenses trulỳ I **know** them;
  my **sin** is **al**ways bé**fore** me.
6 Against **you**, you al**one**, have Ì **sinned**;
  what is **evil** in your **sight** I háve **done**.

  That you may be **justified when** yòu
      give **sen**tence
  and be with**out** re**proach** when yóu **judge**,
7 O **see**, in **guilt** I wàs **born**,
  a **sin**ner was I cón**ceived**.

8 **Indeed** you love **truth** ìn the **heart**;
  then in the **secret** of my **heart** teach mé **wisdom**.
9 O **purify** me, **then** I shall bè **clean**;
  O **wash** me, I shall be **whiter** thán **snow**.

10 Make me **hear** rejoicìng and **gladness**
   that the **bones** you have **crushed** máy re**vive**.
11 From my **sins** turn a**way** yòur **face**
   and **blot** out **all** mý **guilt**.

12 A **pure** heart cre**ate** for mè, O **God**,
   put a **steadfast spirit** wíthin me.
13 Do not **cast** me a**way** from yòur **presence**,
   nor de**prive** me of your **holý spirit**.

14 Give me a**gain** the **joy** òf your **help**;
   with a **spirit** of **fervor** sús**tain** me,
15 that I may **teach** trans**gressors** yòur **ways**
   and **sinners** may re**turn** tó **you**.

16 O **rescue** me, **Gòd**, my **help**er,
   and my **tongue** shall **ring** out yóur **good**ness.
17 O **Lord**, open mỳ **lips**
   and my **mouth** shall de**clare** yóur **praise**.

18 For in **sacrifice** you **take** nò de**light**,
   burnt **offering** from **me** you would ré**fuse**;
19 my **sacrifice**, a **contrìte spirit**,
   a **humbled**, contrite **heart** you will nót **spurn**.

20 In your **goodness**, show **favòr** to **Zion**;
   re**build** the **walls** of Jéru**salem**.
21 **Then** you will be **pleased** with lawfùl
       sacrifice,
   (burnt **offerings wholly** cònsumed),
   then you will be **offered** young **bulls**
       on yóur **altar**.

   Give **glory** to the **Fathèr Almighty**,
   to his **Son**, Jesus **Christ**, thé **Lord**,
   to the **Spirit** who **dwells** in oùr **hearts**,
   both **now** and for **ever**. **Ámen**.

Text: Psalm 51; The Grail
Music: Joseph Gelineau, SJ
© 1963, 1993, The Grail, GIA Publications, Inc., agent

83 Psalm 51: Be Merciful, O Lord

Refrain

Be mer-ci-ful, O Lord, for we have sinned; be

mer-ci-ful, O Lord, for we have sinned.

Verses

1. Have mercy on me, God, in your kindness,
   in your compassion, blot out my offense.
   O wash me more and more from my guilt and my sorrow,
   and cleanse me from all of my sin.

2. My offenses, truly I know them, and my sins are always before me;
   against you alone have I sinned, O Lord, what is evil in your sight I have done.

3. Create in me a clean heart, O God, put your steadfast spirit in my soul.
   Cast me not away from your presence, O Lord, and take not your spirit from me.

4. Give back to me the joy of your salvation, let your willing spirit bear me up
   and I shall teach your way to the ones who have wandered,
   and bring them all home to your side.

Text: Psalm 51:3-4, 5-6, 12-13, 14-15; Marty Haugen, © 1983, GIA Publications, Inc.; refrain trans. © 1969, ICEL
Music: Marty Haugen, © 1983, GIA Publications, Inc.

84 Psalm 51: Create in Me

Refrain

Cre - ate in me, cre - ate in me a clean heart, O God.

Verses

1. A pure heart create for me, O God,
   put a steadfast spirit within me.
   Do not cast me away from your presence,
   nor deprive me of your holy spirit.

2. Give me again the joy of your help;
   with a spirit of fervor sustain me,
   that I may teach transgressors your ways
   and sinners may return to you.

3. For in sacrifice you take no delight,
   burnt offering from me you would refuse;
   my sacrifice, a contrite spirit,
   a humbled, contrite heart you will not spurn.

Text: Psalm 51:12-13, 14-15, 18-19; © 1963, 1993, The Grail, GIA Publications, Inc., agent; refrain trans. ©1969, ICEL
Music: Michel Guimont, © 1995, GIA Publications, Inc.

Psalm 51: Create in Me   85

Refrains

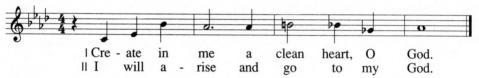

I Cre - ate in me a clean heart, O God.
II I will a - rise and go to my God.

Verses

1. Have mercy on me, O God. In the greatness of your love,
   cleanse me from my sin. Wash me.

2. Stay close to me, O God. In your presence keep me safe.
   Fill me with your spirit. Renew me.

3. Your salvation is joy to me. In your wisdom show the way.
   Lead me back to you. Teach me.

Text: Psalm 51:3-4, 12-13, 14-15; David Haas, © 1987, GIA Publications, Inc.; refrain I trans. © 1969, ICEL
Music: David Haas, © 1987, GIA Publications, Inc.

86 Psalm 54: The Lord Upholds My Life

Refrain

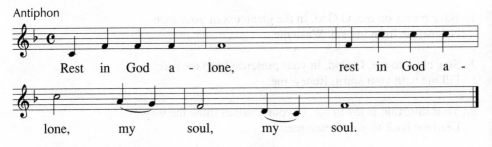

The Lord up - holds my life.

Verses

1. O God, save me by your name; by your power, uphold my cause.
   O God, hear my prayer; listen to the words of my mouth.

2. For the proud have risen against me, ruthless foes seek my life.
   They have no regard for God. (They have no regard for God).

3. But I have God for my help. The Lord upholds my life.
   I will sacrifice to you with willing heart and praise your name,
   O Lord, for it is good.

Text: Psalm 54:3-4, 6-8; © 1963, 1986, The Grail, GIA Publications, Inc., agent; refrain trans. © 1969, ICEL
Music: Michel Guimont, © 1994, GIA Publications, Inc.

87 Psalm 62: Rest in God

Antiphon

Rest in God a - lone, rest in God a -

lone, my soul, my soul.

Text: *Lectionary for Mass,* © 1969, 1981, ICEL
Music: Robert J. Batastini, © 1975, GIA Publications, Inc.

Verses

1. In God alone is my soul at rest;
   from God comes my help.
   God alone is my rock, my stronghold,
   my fortress; I stand firm.

2. In God alone be at rest, my soul;
   from God comes my hope.
   God alone is my rock, my stronghold,
   my fortress; I stand firm.

3. In God is my safety and glory,
   the rock of my strength.
   Take refuge in God, all you people,
   trusting always.
   Pour out your hearts to the Lord.

Psalm 62: In God Alone   88

Refrain

In God a - lone is my soul at rest, the God who is my help. The Lord is my rock, my strength and my hope; my for - tress, my God.

Verses

1. Only in God is my soul at rest, from my God comes my salvation.
   God is my rock, the salvation of my life.
   I shall not be shaken, for the Lord is my strength!

2. Only in God is my soul at rest, from my God comes my hope.
   God is my rock, my salvation and my hope.
   I will rest in the Lord. I will not be afraid!

3. Glory and safety, God is my joy, God is my rock and my strength.
   God is my refuge, I trust with all my strength.
   Pour out your hearts before the Lord!

89 Psalm 63: My Soul Is Thirsting

Antiphon I

My soul is thirst-ing for you, O Lord, thirst-ing for you my God.

Text: *Lectionary for Mass,* © 1969, 1981, ICEL
Music: Richard Proulx, © 1975, GIA Publications, Inc.

Antiphon II

In the morn-ing I will sing, will sing glad songs of praise to you.

Text: *Praise God in Song*
Music: David Clark Isele
© 1979, GIA Publications, Inc.

Psalm Tone

Music: Richard Proulx, © 1986, GIA Publications, Inc.

Gelineau Tone

Omit for 4-line stanza

2 O **God**, you are my **God**, for yòu I **long**;
for yóu my **soul** is **thirst**ing.
My **body pìnes** for **you**
like a **dry**, weary **lánd** with<u>out</u> **wa**ter.
3 So I **gaze** on **you** in the **sànc**tuary
to **see** your **stréngth** and <u>your</u> **glory**.

4 For your **love** is **bèt**ter than **life**,
my **líps** will **speak** your **praise**.
5 So I will **bless** you **àll** my **life**,
in your **name** I will **líft** up <u>my</u> **hands**.
6 My **soul** shall be **filled** as wìth a **ban**quet,
my **mouth** shall **práise** you <u>with</u> **joy**.

7 On my **bed** I re**mèm**ber **you**.
On **you** I **múse** through <u>the</u> **night**
8 for **you** have **bèen** my **help**;
in the **shad**ow of your **wíngs** I re**joice**.
9 My **soul clìngs** to **you**;
your **ríght** hand **holds** me **fast**.

Give **praise** to the **Fà**ther Al**mighty**,
to his **Son**, **Jé**sus **Christ** the **Lord**,
to the **Spirit** who **dwèlls** in our **hearts**,
both **now** and for **éver**. <u>A</u>men.

Text: Psalm 63:2-9; The Grail
Music: Joseph Gelineau, SJ
© 1963, The Grail, GIA Publications, Inc., agent

Psalm 63: My Soul Is Thirsting 90

Refrain

My soul is thirst - ing, my soul is thirst - ing,

my soul is thirst - ing for you, O Lord my God.

Verses

1. O God, you are my God whom I seek;
   O God, you are my God whom I seek;
   for you my flesh pines, my soul thirsts like the earth,
   parched, lifeless, without water.

2. Thus have I gazed toward you in your holy place
   to see your power and your glory.
   Your kindness is a greater good than life itself;
   my lips will glorify you.

3. Thus will I bless you while I live;
   Lifting up my hands I will call upon your name.
   As with a banquet shall my soul be satisfied;
   with exultant lips my mouth shall praise you.

4. For you have been my help, you have been my help;
   in the shadow of your wings I shout for joy.
   My soul clings fast to you; your right hand holds me firm;
   in the shadow of your wings I sing for joy.

Text: Psalm 63:2, 3-4, 5-6, 8-9; verses adapt. © 1970, Confraternity of Christian Doctrine, Washington, D.C.; refrain by Michael Joncas, © 1987, GIA Publications, Inc.
Music: Michael Joncas, © 1987, GIA Publications, Inc.

91 Psalm 63: My Soul Is Thirsting

Refrain

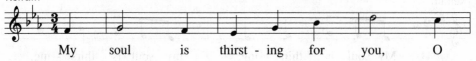

My soul is thirst-ing for you, O

Lord, my God, O Lord, my God.

Verses

1. O Lord, you are my God whom I seek.
   For you my soul pines.
   Like the earth, parched and lifeless
   without water.

2. I seek you in this holy place,
   to see your power and glory.
   For your mercy is greater than life,
   my lips glorify you.

3. My God you are my help;
   my soul clings fast to you.
   In the shadow of your wings,
   I shout for joy.

Text: Psalm 63:2-4, 8-9; Roy James Stewart, © 1993, GIA Publications, Inc.; refrain trans. © 1969, ICEL
Music: Roy James Stewart, © 1993, GIA Publications, Inc.

92 Psalm 65: The Seed That Falls on Good Ground

Refrain

The seed that falls on good ground will yield a fruit-ful har-vest.

Verses

1. You care for the earth, give it water; you fill it with riches.
   Your river in heaven brims over to provide its grain.

2. And thus you provide for the earth; you drench its furrows;
   you level it, soften it with showers; you bless its growth.

3. You crown the year with your goodness. Abundance flows in your steps;
   in the pastures of the wilderness it flows.

4. The hills are girded with joy, the meadows covered with flocks,
   the valleys are decked with wheat. They shout for joy, yes they sing.

Text: Psalm 65:10-11, 12-13, 14; © 1963, 1993, The Grail, GIA Publications, Inc., agent; refrain trans. © 1969, ICEL
Music: Michel Guimont, © 1994, GIA Publications, Inc.

Psalm 66: Let All the Earth   93

Refrain

Let all the earth cry out in joy to the Lord;

Let all the earth cry out in joy to the

| 1.-3. | To verses | Last time |

Lord!   Lord!   to the Lord!

Verses

1. Cry out in joy to the Lord, all peoples on earth,
   sing to the praise of God's name, proclaiming for ever,
   "tremendous your deeds for us."

2. Leading your people safe through fire and water,
   bringing their souls to life, we sing of your glory, your love is eternal.

3. Hearken to me as I sing my love of the Lord,
   who answers the prayer of my heart. God leads me in safety, from death unto life.

Text: Psalm 66:1-3, 12, 16; Marty Haugen
Music: Marty Haugen
© 1982, GIA Publications, Inc.

94   Psalm 67: May God Bless Us in His Mercy

Refrain I

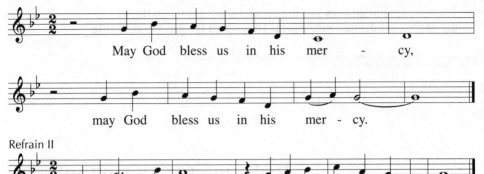

May God bless us in his mer - cy,

may God bless us in his mer - cy.

Refrain II

O God, O God, let all the na-tions praise you.

Verses

1. O God, be gracious and bless us and let your face shed its light upon us.
   So will your ways be known upon earth and all nations learn your saving help.

2. Let the nations be glad and exult for you rule the world with justice.
   With fairness you rule the peoples, you guide the nations on earth.

3. Let the peoples praise you, O God; let all the peoples praise you.
   May God still give us blessing till the ends of the earth stand in awe.

Text: Psalm 67:2-3, 5, 6, 6-8; © 1963, 1993, The Grail, GIA Publications, Inc., agent; refrain trans. © 1969, ICEL
Music: Michel Guimont, © 1994, GIA Publications, Inc.

95   Psalm 67: May God Bless Us in His Mercy

Antiphon I (St. 1.3.6ab & 5cd)

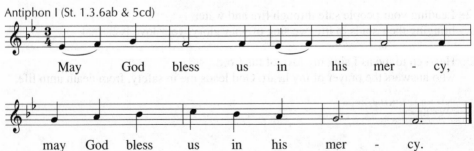

May God bless us in his mer - cy,

may God bless us in his mer - cy.

Text: *Lectionary for Mass,* © 1969, 1981, ICEL
Music: Robert J. Batastini, © 1975, GIA Publications, Inc.

Antiphon II (St. 1.3.6ab & 5cd)

O God, O God, let all the na-tions praise you!

Antiphon III (St. 1.3.5)

The earth has yield - ed its fruits;

God, our God has blessed us.

Psalm Tone

Gelineau Tone Omit for 2-line stanza

2 O **God**, be **gracìous** and **bless** us
  and let your **face** shed its **líght** upon us.
3 So will your **ways** be **known** ùpon **earth**
  and all **na**tions learn your **sáving help**.

4 Let the **peoples praise** yòu, O **God;**
  let **all** the **péo**ples **praise** you.

5 Let the **nations** be **glad** ànd **exult**
  for you **rule** the **wórld** with **justice**.
  With **fairness** you **rùle** the **peoples**,
  you **guide** the **na**tions on **earth**.

6 Let the **peoples praise** yòu, O **God;**
  let **all** the **péo**ples **praise** you.

7 The **earth** has **yieldèd** its **fruit**
  for **God**, our **Gód**, has **blessed** us.
8 May **God** still **gìve** us **blessing**
  till the **ends** of the **earth** stánd in **awe**.

  Let the **peoples praise** yòu, O **God;**
  let **all** the **péo**ples **praise** you.
  To the **Father**, the **Son** and **Hòly Spirit**,
  give **praise** for evér. **Amen**.

96 Psalm 68: You Have Made a Home for the Poor

Refrain

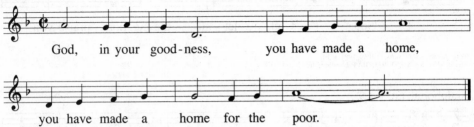

God, in your good-ness, you have made a home,

you have made a home for the poor.

Text: *Lectionary for Mass*, © 1969, 1981, ICEL
Music: Rory Cooney, © 1991, GIA Publications, Inc.

Verses

1. But the just shall rejoice at the presence of God,
   they shall exult and dance for joy.
   O sing to the Lord, make music to God's name;
   Rejoice in the Lord, exult before God.

2. Father of the orphan, defender of the widow,
   such is God in the holy place.
   God gives the lonely a home to live in;
   and leads the prisoners forth into freedom.

3. You poured down, O God, a generous rain;
   when your people were starved you gave them new life.
   It was there that your people found a home,
   prepared in your goodness, O God, for the poor.

Text: Psalm 68:4-5, 6-7, 10-11; The Grail, © 1963, 1993, GIA Publications, Inc. agent

97 Psalm 69: Turn to the Lord in Your Need

Refrain

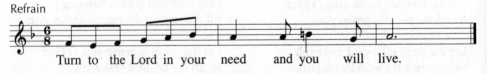

Turn to the Lord in your need and you will live.

Verses

1. This is my prayer to you, my prayer for your favor.
   In your great love, answer me, O God, with your help that never fails;
   Lord, answer, for your love is kind; in your compassion turn towards me.

2. As for me in my poverty and pain, let your help, O God, lift me up.
   I will praise God's name with a song; I will glorify God with thanksgiving.

3. The poor when they see it will be glad and God-seeking hearts will revive;
   for the Lord listens to the needy and does not spurn captives in their chains.

4. For God will bring help to Zion and rebuild the cities of Judah.
   The children of God's servants shall inherit it;
   those who love God's name shall dwell there.

Text: Psalm 69:14, 17, 30-31, 33-34, 36, 37; © 1963, 1993, The Grail, GIA Publications, Inc., agent; refrain trans. © 1969, ICEL
Music: Michel Guimont, © 1994, GIA Publications, Inc.

Psalm 69: Lord, in Your Great Love   98

Antiphon

Lord,   in   your great love,   an-swer me.

Text: *Lectionary for Mass*, © 1969, 1981, ICEL
Music: Alexander Peloquin, © 1975, GIA Publications, Inc.

Verses

1. It is for you that I suffer taunts,
   that shame covers my face,
   that I have become a stranger to my family,
   an alien to my brothers and sisters.
   I burn with zeal for your house
   and taunts against you fall on me.

2. This is my prayer to you,
   my prayer for your favor.
   In your great love, answer me, O God,
   with your help that never fails;
   Lord, answer, for your love is kind;
   in your compassion, turn towards me.

3. The poor when they see it will be glad
   and God-seeking hearts will revive;
   for the Lord listens to the needy
   and does not spurn captives in their chains.
   Let the heavens and the earth give God praise,
   the sea and all its living creatures.

Text: Psalm 69:8-10, 14, 17, 33-35; © 1963, 1993, The Grail, GIA Publications, Inc., agent

99 Psalm 71: I Will Sing

Refrain

I will sing of your sal - va - tion, I will sing, I will sing.

Verses

1. In you, O Lord, I take refuge;
    let me never be put to shame.
    In your justice rescue me, and deliver me;
    incline your ear to me and save me.

2. Be my rock of refuge,
    a stronghold to give me safety,
    for you are my rock and my fortress.
    O my God, rescue me from the hand of the wicked.

3. For you are my hope, O Lord;
    my trust, O God, from my youth.
    On you I depend from birth;
    from my mother's womb you are my strength.

4. My mouth shall declare your justice,
    day by day, your salvation.
    O God, you have taught me from my youth,
    and till the present I proclaim your wondrous deeds.

Text: Psalm 71:1-2, 3-4, 5-6, 15, 17; © 1963, 1993, The Grail, GIA Publications, Inc., agent; refrain trans. © 1969, ICEL
Music: Randolph Currie, © 1995, World Library Publications, Inc.

100 Psalm 71: Since My Mother's Womb

Refrain

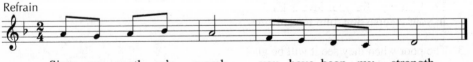

Since my moth - er's womb, you have been my strength.

Verses

1. In you, O Lord, I take refuge;
    let me never be put to shame.
    In your justice rescue me, free me;
    pay heed to me and save me.

2. Be a rock where I can take refuge,
   a mighty stronghold to save me;
   for you are my rock, my stronghold.
   Free me from the hand of the wicked.

3. It is you, O Lord, who are my hope,
   my trust, O Lord, since my youth.
   On you I have leaned from my birth;
   from my mother's womb you have been my help.

4. My lips will tell of your justice
   and day by day of your help.
   O God, you have taught me from my youth
   and I proclaim your wonder still.

Text: Psalm 71:1-2, 3-4, 5-6, 15, 17; © 1963, 1993, The Grail, GIA Publications, Inc., agent; refrain trans. © 1969, ICEL
Music: Michel Guimont, © 1995, GIA Publications, Inc.

Psalm 72: Justice Shall Flourish 101

Refrain

Jus - tice shall flour - ish in his time, and full - ness of peace for ev - er.

Verses

1. O God, give your judgment to the king,
   to a king's son your justice,
   that he may judge your people in justice
   and your poor in right judgment.

2. In his days justice shall flourish
   and peace till the moon fails.
   He shall rule from sea to sea,
   from the Great River to earth's bounds.

3. For he shall save the poor when they cry
   and the needy who are helpless.
   He will have pity on the weak
   and save the lives of the poor.

4. May his name be blessed for ever
   and endure like the sun.
   Every tribe shall be blessed in him,
   all nations bless his name.

Text: Psalm 72:1-2, 7-8, 12-13, 17; © 1963, 1993, The Grail, GIA Publications, Inc., agent; refrain trans. © 1969, ICEL
Music: Michel Guimont, © 1995, GIA Publications, Inc.

102 Psalm 72: Every Nation on Earth

Refrain I

Ev-'ry na-tion on earth will a-dore you, Lord;

ev-'ry na-tion on earth will a-dore you, Lord.

Refrain II

In his days jus-tice will flou-rish;

in his days full-ness of peace for-ev-er-more.

Verses

1. O God, with your judgment endow the king;
   with your justice endow the king's son.
   With justice he will govern your people,
   your afflicted ones with right judgment.

2. Justice shall flow'r in his days,
   lasting peace 'til the moon be no more.
   May he rule from sea to sea,
   from the river to the ends of the earth.

3. The kings of Tarshish and the Isles offer gifts,
   those from Seba and Arabia bring tribute.
   All kings shall pay him their homage,
   all nations shall serve him.

4. He rescues the poor when they cry out,
   the afflicted with no one to help.
   The lowly and poor he shall pity,
   the lives of the poor he will save.

Text: Psalm 72:1-2, 7-8, 10-11, 12-13; Michael Joncas
Music: Michael Joncas
© 1987, 1994, GIA Publications, Inc.

Psalm 72: Lord, Every Nation on Earth   103

Antiphon

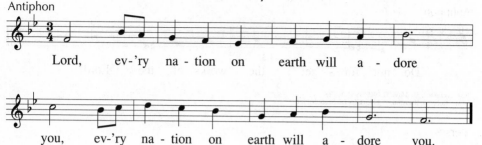

Lord, ev-'ry na - tion on earth will a - dore you, ev-'ry na - tion on earth will a - dore you.

Text: *Lectionary for Mass,* © 1969, ICEL
Music: Marty Haugen, © 1995, GIA Publications, Inc.

Verses

1. O God, give your judgment to the king,
   to a king's son your justice,
   that he may judge your people in justice
   and your poor in right judgment.

2. In his days justice shall flourish
   and peace till the moon fails.
   He shall rule from sea to sea,
   from the Great River to earth's bounds.

3. The kings of Tarshish and the seacoasts shall pay him tribute.
   The kings of Sheba and Seba shall bring him gifts.
   Before him all rulers shall fall prostrate,
   all nations shall serve him.

4. For he shall save the poor when they cry
   and the needy who are helpless.
   He will have pity on the weak
   and save the lives of the poor.

Text: Psalm 72:1-2, 7-8, 10-11, 12-13; © 1963, 1993, The Grail, GIA Publications, Inc., agent

104 Psalm 78: Do Not Forget

Antiphon

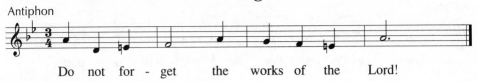

Do not for - get the works of the Lord!

Text: *Lectionary for Mass,* © 1969, 1981, ICEL
Music: Robert J. Batastini, © 1975, GIA Publications, Inc.

Verses

1. Give heed, my people, to my teaching;
   turn your ear to the words of my mouth.
   I will open my mouth in a parable
   and reveal hidden lessons of the past.

2. When God slew them they would seek him,
   return and seek him in earnest.
   They remembered that God was their rock,
   God, the Most High their redeemer.

3. But the words they spoke were mere flattery;
   they lied to God with their lips.
   For their hearts were not truly sincere;
   they were not faithful to the covenant.

4. Yet the one who is full of compassion
   forgave them their sin and spared them.
   So often God held back the anger
   that might have been stirred up in rage.

Text: Psalm 78:1-2, 34-35, 36-37, 38; © 1963, 1993, The Grail, GIA Publications, Inc., agent

105 Psalm 78: The Lord Gave Them Bread

Antiphon

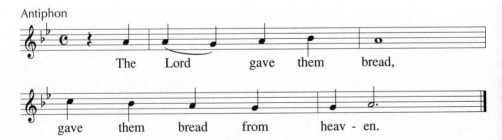

The Lord gave them bread,

gave them bread from heav - en.

Text: *Lectionary for Mass,* © 1969, 1981, ICEL
Music: Randolph Currie, © 1975, GIA Publications, Inc.

Verses

1. The things we have heard and understood,
   the things our ancestors have told us,
   these we will not hide from their children
   but will tell them to the next generation.

2. The glories and might of the Lord
   and the marvelous deeds God has done.

3. Yet God commanded the clouds above
   and opened the gates of heaven;
   rained down manna for their food,
   and gave them bread from heaven.

4. Mere mortals ate the bread of angels.
   The Lord sent them meat in abundance.
   So God brought them to that holy land,
   to the mountain that was won by his hand.

Text: Psalm 78:3-4, 23-34, 25, 54; © 1963, 1993, The Grail, GIA Publications, Inc., agent

Psalm 80: The Vineyard of the Lord   106

Refrain

The vine-yard of the Lord   is the house of Is - ra - el.

Verses

1. You brought a vine out of Egypt, to plant it you drove out the nations.
   It stretched out its branches to the sea,
   to the Great River it stretched out its shoots.

2. Then why have you broken down its walls?
   It is plucked by all who pass by.
   It is ravaged by the boar of the forest; devoured by the beasts of the field.

3. God of hosts, turn again, we implore, look down from heaven and see.
   Visit this vine and protect it, the vine your right hand has planted.

4. And we shall never forsake you again;
   give us life that we may call upon your name.
   God of hosts, bring us back;
   let your face shine on us and we shall be saved.

Text: Psalm 80:9, 12-14, 15-16, 19-20; © 1963, 1993, The Grail, GIA Publications, Inc., agent; refrain trans © 1969, ICEL
Music: Michel Guimont, © 1994, GIA Publications, Inc.

107 Psalm 80/85/Luke 1: Lord, Make Us Turn to You

Refrain

Lord, make us turn to you, show us your face, and

we shall be saved.

Verses

1. Shepherd of Israel, hearken from your throne and shine forth,
   O rouse your power, and come to save us.

2. We are your chosen vine, only by your care do we live,
   reach out your hand, O Lord, unto your people.

3. If you will dwell with us, we shall live anew in your love,
   O shine upon us, great Lord of life.

4. Lord, we are present here, show us your kindness and love,
   O speak your word of peace unto your people.

5. Lord, let salvation rain, shower down your justice and peace,
   the earth shall bring forth truth, the skies your love.

6. See, Lord, we look to you, you alone can bring us to life,
   O walk before us to light our pathways.

7. You have done wondrous things, holy is your name for all time,
   your mercy and your love are with your people.

8. You are my joy and song, I would have my life speak your praise,
   on me your love has shown, your blessings given.

9. You fill all hungry hearts, sending the rich empty forth,
   and holding up in love the meek and lowly.

Text: Psalm 80:2-3, 15-16, 18-20; Psalm 85:9-14; Luke 1:46-55; Marty Haugen
Music: Marty Haugen
© 1982, GIA Publications, Inc.

Psalm 80: Lord, Make Us Turn to You   108

Refrain

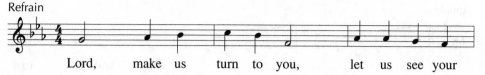

Lord, make us turn to you, let us see your

face and we shall be saved.

Verses

1. O shepherd of Israel, hear us,
   shine forth from your cherubim throne.
   O Lord, rouse up your might,
   O Lord, come to our help.

2. God of hosts, turn again, we implore,
   look down from heaven and see.
   Visit this vine and protect it,
   the vine your right hand has planted.

3. May your hand be on the one you have chosen,
   the one you have given your strength.
   And we shall never forsake you again;
   give us life that we may call upon your name.

109 Psalm 81: Sing with Joy to God

Antiphon

Sing with joy to God! Sing to God, our help!

Text: *Lectionary for Mass,* © 1969, 1981, ICEL
Music: Randolph Currie, © 1986, GIA Publications, Inc.

Verses

1. Raise a song and sound the timbrel,
   the sweet-sounding harp and the lute;
   blow the trumpet at the new moon,
   when the moon is full, on our feast.

2. For this is Israel's law,
   a command of the God of Jacob,
   imposed as a law on Joseph's people,
   when they went out against the land of Egypt.

3. A voice I did not know said to me:
   "I freed your shoulder from the burden;
   your hands were freed from the load.
   You called in distress and I saved you.

4. Let there be no foreign god among you,
   no worship of an alien god.
   I am the Lord your God,
   who brought you from the land of Egypt."

Text: Psalm 81:3-4, 5-6, 6-8, 10-11; © 1963, 1993, The Grail, GIA Publications, Inc., agent

Psalm 84: How Lovely Is Your Dwelling Place   110

Antiphon

How love-ly is your dwell-ing place, O Lord of hosts.

Text: Psalm 84:2, The Grail
Music: A. Gregory Murray, OSB
© 1963, The Grail, GIA Publications, Inc., agent

Psalm Tone

Repeat for 5-line stanza
Omit for 2-line stanza

Music: Chrysogonus Waddell, © Gethsemani Abbey

Gelineau Tone

Repeat for 5-line stanza
Omit for 2-line stanza

² How **lovely is** your **dwèll**ing place,
Lord, God óf hosts.

³ My **soul** is **longìng** and **yearn**ing,
is **yearn**ing for the **courts** of thé **Lord.**
My **heart** and my **soul** ring out thèir **joy**
to **God,** the **livíng God.**

⁴ The **sparrow herself** finds a **home**
and the **swallow** a **nest** for hér **brood;**
she **lays** her **young** by yòur **altars,**
Lord of **hosts,** my **king** and mý **God.**

⁵ They are **happy,** who **dwell** ìn your **house,**
for **ever singing** yóur **praise.**

⁶ They are **happy,** whose **strength** is ìn **you,**
in whose **hearts** are the **roads** tó **Zion.**

⁷ As they **go** through the **Bìtter Valley**
they **make** it a **place** óf **springs,**
(the **autumn** rain **covers** it wíth **blessings**).

⁸ They **walk** with **ever** growing **strength,**
they will **see** the God of **gods** ín **Zion.**

⁹ O **Lord** God of **hosts,** hèar my **prayer,**
give **ear,** O **God** óf **Jacob.**

¹⁰ **Turn** your **eyes,** O **God,** òur **shield,**
look on the **face** of your **ánoin**ted.

¹¹ **One** day withìn your **courts**
is **better** than a **thou**sánd **else**where.
The **threshold** of the **house** òf **God**
I **prefer** to the **dwell**ings of thé **wicked.**

¹² For the Lord **God** is a **rampàrt,** a **shield.**
The **Lord** will **give** us **favor** ánd **glory.**
The **Lord** will not re**fuse** anỳ **good**
to **those** who **walk** withóut **blame.**

¹³ **Lord,** Gòd of **hosts,**
happy are **those** who **trust** ín **you!**

Give **praise** to **Fathèr Almighty,**
to his **Son,** Jesus **Christ** thé **Lord,**
to the **Spirit** who **dwells** in òur **hearts,**
both **now** and for **ever. Ámen.**

Text: Psalm 84:2-10; The Grail
Music: Joseph Gelineau, SJ
© 1963, 1993, The Grail, GIA Publications, Inc., agent

111 Psalm 84: Happy Are They

Refrain

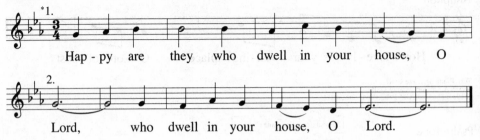

Hap - py are they who dwell in your house, O Lord, who dwell in your house, O Lord.

Verses

1. My soul yearns and pines for the courts of the Lord.
   My heart and my flesh cry to the living God.

2. The sparrow finds a home and the swallow a nest;
   Your altars, O Lord, my King and my God.

3. Happy are they who abide in your house.
   You are their strength, your praises they will sing.

May be sung in canon.

Text: Psalm 84:2, 3, 4, 5-6; Thomas J. Porter
Music: Thomas J. Porter
© 1987, GIA Publications, Inc.

112 Psalm 85: Lord, Let Us See Your Kindness

Refrain

Lord, let us see your kind-ness; Lord, let us see your kind-ness.

Verses

1. Let us hear what our God proclaims: Peace to the people of God,
   salvation is near to the ones who fear God.

2. Kindness and truth, justice and peace;
   truth shall spring up as the water from the earth,
   justice shall rain from the heavens.

3. The Lord will come and you shall know his love,
   justice shall walk in his pathways, salvation the gift that he brings.

Text: Psalm 85:9-10, 11-12, 13-14; Marty Haugen, © 1983, GIA Publications, Inc.; refrain trans. © 1969, ICEL
Music: Marty Haugen, © 1983, GIA Publications, Inc.

Psalm 85: Lord, Let Us See Your Kindness 113

Antiphon I

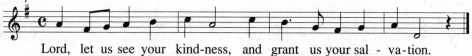

Lord, let us see your kind-ness, and grant us your sal - va-tion.

Text: *Lectionary for Mass,* © 1969, 1981, ICEL
Music: J. Robert Carroll, © 1975, GIA Publications, Inc.

Antiphon II

The Lord speaks of peace to his peo - ple.

Text: *Lectionary for Mass,* © 1969, 1981, ICEL
Music: Richard Proulx, © 1986, GIA Publications, Inc.

Verses

1. I will hear what the Lord has to say,
   a voice that speaks of peace,
   peace for his people and friends
   and those who turn to God in their hearts.
   Salvation is near for the God-fearing,
   and his glory will dwell in our land.

2. Mercy and faithfulness have met;
   justice and peace have embraced.
   Faithfulness shall spring from the earth
   and justice look down from heaven.

3. The Lord will make us prosper
   and our earth shall yield its fruit.
   Justice shall march in the forefront,
   and peace shall follow the way.

Text: Psalm 85:9-10, 11-12, 13-14; © 1963, 1993, The Grail, GIA Publications, Inc., agent

114 Psalm 85: Come, O Lord, and Set Us Free

Refrain I

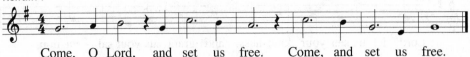

Come, O Lord, and set us free. Come, and set us free.

Refrain II

Lord, let us see your kind - ness; Lord, grant us your sal-va - tion.

Verses

1. Now I will hear what God proclaims, the Lord who speaks of peace.
   Near to us now, God's saving love for those who believe.

2. Mercy and faithfulness shall meet, in justice and peace, embrace.
   Truth shall blossom from the earth as the heavens rejoice.

3. Our God shall grant abundant gifts, the earth shall yield its fruit.
   Justice shall march before our God and guide us to peace.

Text: Psalm 85; refrains I and II, © 1969, ICEL; verses by Mike Balhoff, Gary Daigle, Darryl Ducote, © 1978, 1993, Damean Music.
Distributed by GIA Publications, Inc.
Music: Mike Balhoff, Gary Daigle, Darryl Ducote, © 1978, 1993, Damean Music. Distributed by GIA Publications, Inc.

115 Psalm 86: O Lord, Our God

Antiphon I

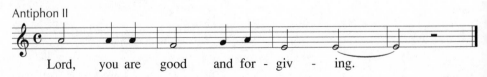

O Lord, our God, un - wea-ried is your love for us.

Text: Liturgy of the Hours, © 1974, ICEL
Music: John Schiavone, © 1986, GIA Publications, Inc.

Antiphon II

Lord, you are good and for - giv - ing.

Text: Lectionary for Mass, © 1969, 1981, ICEL
Music: Chrysogonus Waddell, OCSO, © 1986, GIA Publications, Inc.

Psalm Tone

Omit for 3-line stanza | Repeat for 5-line stanza

Gelineau Tone

Omit for 3-line stanza | Repeat for 5-line stanza

¹ Turn your **ear**, O **Lord**, ànd give **an**swer
  for **I** am pó**or** and nee**dy**.
² Pre**serve** my **life**, for Ì am **faith**ful;
  save the **ser**vant who **trústs** in **you**.

³ You are my **God**, have **mer**cy òn me, **Lord**,
  for I **cry** to you **all** thé **day** long.
⁴ Give **joy** to your **ser**vànt, O **Lord**,
  for to **you** I **lift** úp my **soul**.

⁵ O **Lord**, you are **good** ànd for**giv**ing,
  full of **love** to **áll** who **call**.
⁶ Give **heed**, O **Lord**, tò my **prayer**
  and at**tend** to the **sound** óf my **voice**.

⁷ In the **day** of dis**tress** Ì will **call**
  and **sure**ly **you** wíll re**ply**.
⁸ Among the **gods** there is **none** like yòu, O
    Lord,
  nor **work** to com**páre** with **yours**.

⁹ All the **na**tions shall **come** tò a**dore** you
  and **glo**rify your **náme**, O **Lord**,
¹⁰ for you are **great** and do **mar**vèlous **deeds**,
  you who a**lóne** are **God**.

¹¹ **Show** me, **Lòrd**, your **way**
  so that **I** may **walk** ín your **truth**.
  Guide my **heart** to **féar** your **name**.

¹² I will **praise** you, Lord my **God**, with àll
  my **heart**
  and **glo**rify your **náme** for **ever**;
¹³ for your **love** to **me** hàs been **great**,
  you have **saved** me from the **depths** óf
  the **grave**.

¹⁴ The **proud** have ri**sèn** a**gainst** me;
  ruthless **en**emies **séek** my **life**;
  to **you** they **páy** no **heed**.

¹⁵ But **you**, God of **mer**cy ànd com**pas**sion,
  slow to an**gér**, O **Lord**,
  a**bound**ing in **lòve** and **truth**,
¹⁶ **turn** and take pi**tý** on **me**.

O **give** your **strength** tò your **ser**vant
and **save** your **hánd**maid's **child**.
¹⁷ **Show** me a **sign** òf your **fa**vor
  that my **foes** may **see** tó their **shame**
  that you con**sole** me and **give** mé your
    help.

Give **praise** to the **Fathèr** Al**might**y,
to his **Son**, Jesus **Chríst**, the **Lord**,
to the **Spi**rit who **dwells** ìn our **hearts**,
both **now** and for **evér**. **Amen**.

116 Psalm 88: Day and Night

Antiphon

Day and night I cry to you, my God.

Text: *Liturgy of the Hours*, © 1974, ICEL
Music: Suzanne Toolan, SM, © 1986, GIA Publications, Inc.

Psalm Tone

Music: Chrysogonus Waddell, OCSO, © Gethsemani Abbey

Gelineau Tone

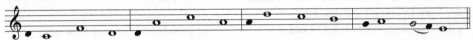

² Lord my **God**, I call for **hèlp** by **day**;
 I **cry** at **night** béfore you.
³ Let my **prayer** come **into** yòur **presence**.
 O **turn** your **ear** to mý **cry**.

⁴ For my **soul** is **filled** with **evils**;
 my **life** is on the **brink** of thé **grave**.
⁵ I am **reck**oned as **one** in thè **tomb**;
 I have **reached** the **end** of mý **strength**,

⁶ like one **alone** amòng the **dead**,
 like the **slain lying** in théir **graves**,
 like **those** you re**mem**ber nò **more**,
 cut **off**, as they **are**, from yóur **hand**.

⁷ You have **laid** me in the **depths** òf the **tomb**,
 in **places** that are **dark**, in thé **depths**.
⁸ Your **anger weighs** down ùpon me;
 I am **drowned** be**neath** yóur **waves**.

⁹ You have **taken** awày my **friends**
 and **made** me **hateful** in théir **sight**.
 Im**prisoned**, I **cannot** èscape;
¹⁰ my **eyes** are **sunk**en wíth **grief**.

I **call** to you, **Lord**, all thè day **long**;
 to **you** I **stretch** out mý **hands**.
¹¹ Will you **work** your **won**ders for thè **dead**?
 Will the **shades** stand ánd **praise** you?

¹² Will your **love** be **told** ìn the **grave**
 or your **faithfulness** among thé **dead**?
¹³ Will your **won**ders be **known** in thè **dark**
 or your **justice** in the **land** of óblivion?

¹⁴ As for **me**, Lord, I **call** to yòu for **help**;
 in the **morning** my **prayer** comes béfore you.
¹⁵ **Lord**, **why** do you rèject me?
 Why do you **hide** yóur **face**?

¹⁶ **Wretch**ed, close to **death** fròm my **youth**,
 I have **borne** your **trials**; I ám **numb**.
¹⁷ Your **fury** has **swept** down ùpon me;
 your **terrors** have **utterly** déstroyed me.

¹⁸ They sur**round** me all the **day** lìke a **flood**,
 they as**sail** me **all** tógether.
¹⁹ **Friend** and **neighbor** you have **taken** àway;
 my **one** com**panion** ís **darkness**.

Give **praise** to the **Fathèr** Al**might**y,
to his **Son**, Jesus **Christ**, thé **Lord**,
to the **Spir**it who **dwells** in òur **hearts**,
both **now** and for **ever**. Ámen.

Text: Psalm 88; The Grail
Music: Joseph Gelineau, SJ
© 1963, 1993, The Grail, GIA Publications, Inc., agent

Psalm 89: For Ever I Will Sing 117

Refrain (St. 1.2.5 or 2.3.5 or 1.3.4)

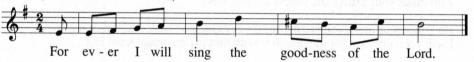

For ev - er I will sing the good-ness of the Lord.

Verses

1. I will sing for ever of your love, O Lord;
   through all ages my mouth will proclaim your truth.
   Of this I am sure, that your love lasts for ever,
   that your truth is firmly established as the heavens.

2. "With my chosen one I have made a covenant;
   I have sworn to David my servant:
   I will establish your dynasty for ever
   and set up your throne through all ages."

3. Happy the people who acclaim such a God,
   who walk, O Lord, in the light of your face,
   who find their joy every day in your name,
   who make your justice the source of their bliss.

4. For you, O Lord, are the glory of their strength;
   by your favor it is that our might is exalted;
   for our ruler is in the keeping of the Lord;
   our king in the keeping of the Holy One of Israel.

5. He will say to me: 'You are my father,
   my God, the rock who saves me!'
   I will keep my love for him always;
   with him my covenant shall last.

Text: Psalm 89:2-3, 4-5, 16-17, 18-19, 27, 29; © 1963, 1993, The Grail, GIA Publications, Inc., agent; refrain trans. © 1969, ICEL
Music: Michel Guimont, © 1995, GIA Publications, Inc.

118 Psalm 89: For Ever I Will Sing

Refrain

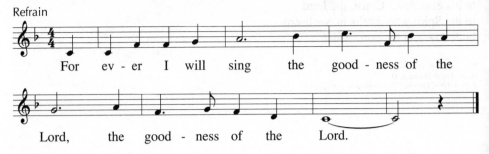

For ev - er I will sing the good - ness of the

Lord, the good - ness of the Lord.

Verses

1. "With my chosen one I have made a covenant; I have sworn to David my servant:
   I will establish your dynasty forever and set up your throne through all ages."

2. Happy the people who acclaim such a God,
   who walk, O Lord, in the light of your face,
   who find their joy ev'ry day in your name,
   who make your justice the source of their bliss.

3. He will say to me: "You are my father, my God, the rock who saves me!"
   I will keep my love for him always; with him my covenant shall last.

Alternate Verses

1. I have found David my servant,
   with my holy oil I have anointed him,
   that my hand may ever be with him
   and my arm make him strong.

2. My faithfulness and love shall be with you,
   in my Name your name will be exalted.

3. He shall cry to me, "My God, my rock of salvation, my salvation."

Text: Psalm 89: 4-5, 16-17, 27-29, © 1963, 1993, The Grail, GIA Publications, Inc., agent; alt. verses 21-22, 25, 27, Marty Haugen, © 1988, 1994,
    GIA Publications, Inc.; refrain trans. © 1969, ICEL
Music: Marty Haugen, © 1988, 1994, GIA Publications, Inc.

Psalm 89: For Ever I Will Sing   119

Antiphon I (St. 1.2.5 or 2.3.5 or 1.3.4)

For ev - er I will sing the good - ness of the Lord.

Text: *Lectionary for Mass,* © 1969, 1981, ICEL
Music: J. Robert Carroll, © 1975, GIA Publications, Inc.

Antiphon II (St. 1.2.5)

The Son of Da - vid will live for ev - er.

Text: *Lectionary for Mass,* © 1969, 1981, ICEL
Music: Randolph Currie, © 1986, GIA Publications, Inc.

Verses

1. I will sing for ever of your love, O Lord;
   through all ages my mouth will proclaim your truth.
   Of this I am sure, that your love lasts for ever,
   that your truth is firmly established as the heavens.

2. "With my chosen one I have made a covenant;
   I have sworn to David my servant:
   I will establish your dynasty for ever
   and set up your throne through all ages."

3. Happy the people who acclaim such a God,
   who walk, O Lord, in the light of your face,
   who find their joy every day in your name,
   who make your justice the source of their bliss.

4. For you, O Lord, are the glory of their strength;
   by your favor it is that our might is exalted;
   for our ruler is in the keeping of the Lord;
   our king in the keeping of the Holy One of Israel.

5. He will say to me: 'You are my father,
   my God, the rock who saves me!'
   I will keep my love for him always;
   with him my covenant shall last.

Text: Psalm 89:2-3, 4-5, 16-17, 18-19, 27, 29; © 1963, 1993, The Grail, GIA Publications, Inc., agent

120 Psalm 90: In Every Age

Antiphon I (St. 2.3.7.8ab & 9cde)

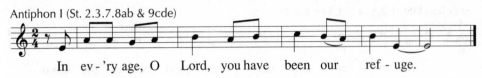

In ev - 'ry age, O Lord, you have been our ref - uge.

Text: *Lectionary for Mass,* © 1969, 1981, ICEL
Music: Eugene Englert, © 1986, GIA Publications, Inc.

Antiphon II (St. 7.8.9)

Fill us with your love, O Lord, and we will sing for joy!

Text: *Lectionary for Mass,* © 1969, 1981, ICEL
Music: Robert J. Batastini, © 1975, 1995, GIA Publications, Inc.

Antiphon III (Vs. 2.3-4.12-13.14.16)

Lord, give suc - cess to the work of our hands.

Text: *Lectionary for Mass,* © 1969, 1981, ICEL
Music: Richard Proulx, © 1986, GIA Publications, Inc.

Psalm Tone
Repeat for 5-line stanza

Music: A. Gregory Murray, OSB, © L. J. Carey and Co., Ltd.

Gelineau Tone
Omit for 4-line stanza

¹ O **Lord, you** have bèen our **refuge**
 from **one** generation tó the **next.**
² Before the **mountàins** were **born**
 or the **earth** or the **wòrld** brought **forth,**
 you are **God,** without begínníng or **end.**

³ You **turn** us **back** ìnto **dust**
 and say: "Go **back, children** óf the **earth.**"
⁴ To your **eyes** a **thòu**sand **years**
 are like **yesterday, còme** and **gone,**
 no **more** than a **watch** ín the **night.**

⁵ You **sweep** us a**way** lìke a **dream,**
 like **grass** which springs **up** ín the **morning.**
⁶ In the **morning** it **springs** ùp and **flowers;**
 by **evening** it **withérs** and **fades.**

⁷ So **we** are de**stroyed** ìn your **anger,**
 struck with **terror** ín your **fury.**
⁸ Our **guilt** lies o**pèn** be**fore** you,
 our **secrets** in the **light** óf your **face.**

⁹ All our **days** pass a**way** ìn your **anger.**
 Our **life** is **over** líke a **sigh.**
¹⁰ Our **span** is se**vènty years,**
 or **eighty** for **those** whó are **strong.**

And **most** of these are **emptinèss** and **pain**.
They pass **swiftly** and **wé** are **gone**.
[11] Who **understands** the **pow**er òf your **an**ger
and **fears** the **strength** óf your **fury**?

[12] Make us **know** the **short**ness òf our **life**
that **we** may gain **wisd**óm of **heart**.
[13] Lord, re**lent**! Is your **an**gèr for **ever**?
Show **pity** tó your **servants**.

[14] In the **morn**ing, **fill** us wìth your **love**;
we shall ex**ult** and re**joice** áll our **days**.
[15] Give us **joy** to **bal**ance òur af**fliction**
for the **years** when we **knéw** mis**fortune**.

[16] Show **forth** your **work** tò your **servants**;
let your **glory shine** ón their **chil**dren.
[17] Let the **fa**vor of the **Lord** bè up**on** us:
give suc**cess** to the **work** òf our **hands**
(give suc**cess** to the **work** óf our **hands**).

Give **praise** to the **Fa**thèr **Almighty**,
to his **Son**, Jesus **Chríst**, the **Lord**,
to the **Spi**rit who **dwells** ìn our **hearts**,
both **now** and for **evér**. **Amen**.

Text: Psalm 90; The Grail
Music: Joseph Gelineau, SJ
© 1963, 1993, The Grail, GIA Publications, Inc., agent

Psalm 90: Fill Us with Your Love, O Lord   121

Refrain

Fill us with your love, O Lord, and we will sing for joy!

Verses

1. Teach us to number our days, that we may gain wisdom of heart.
   Return, O Lord our God, have pity on your servants.

2. Fill us at dawn with your kindness,
   that we may shout for joy and gladness.
   Make us glad for the days when you afflicted us,
   for the years when we saw evil.

3. Let your work be seen by your servants, and your glory by their children.
   May your gracious care be ours. Prosper the work of our hands.

Text: Psalm 90; Roy James Stewart, © 1993, GIA Publications, Inc.; refrain trans. © 1969, ICEL
Music: Roy James Stewart, © 1993, GIA Publications, Inc.

122 Psalm 91: My Refuge, My Stronghold

Antiphon I

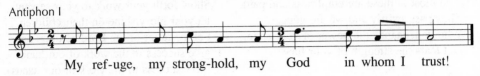

My ref-uge, my strong-hold, my God in whom I trust!

Text: The Grail
Music: A. Gregory Murray, OSB
© 1963, The Grail, GIA Publications, Inc., agent

Antiphon II

Call up - on the Lord and he will hear you.

Text: The Grail
Music: Joseph Gelineau, SJ
© 1963, The Grail, GIA Publications, Inc., agent

Antiphon III

Night holds no ter-rors for me sleep - ing un - der God's wings.

Text: *Liturgy of the Hours,* © 1974, ICEL
Music: Peter Hallock, acc. by Michael Connolly, © 1986, GIA Publications, Inc.

Psalm Tone

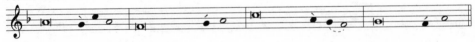

Music: Richard Proulx, © 1986, GIA Publications, Inc.

Gelineau Tone

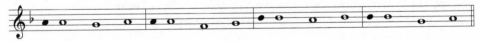

¹ Those who **dwell** in the **shel**ter of thè Most **High**
   and abide in the **shade** of the Álmighty
² **say** to the **Lord**: "Mỳ refuge,
   my **strong**hold, my **God** in whom Í **trust!**"

³ It is **God** who will **free** you fròm the **snare**
   of the **fowl**er who **seeks** to déstroy you;
⁴ **God** will conceal you with hìs **pinions,**
   and **un**der his **wings** you will fínd **refuge.**

⁵ You will not **fear** the **ter**ror òf the **night**
  nor the **ar**row that **flies** bý **day**,
⁶ nor the **plague** that **prowls** in thè **dark**ness
  nor the **scourge** that lays **waste** át **noon**.

⁷ A **thou**sand may **fall** àt your **side**,
  ten thousand **fall** at yóur **right**,
  you, it will **never** àp**proach**;
⁴ᶜ God's **faith**fulness is **buck**ler ánd **shield**.

⁸ Your **eyes** have onlỳ to **look**
  to **see** how the **wick**ed are ré**paid**,
⁹ **you** who have **said**: "**Lord**, mỳ **refuge**!"
  and have **made** the Most **High** yóur **dwell**ing.

¹⁰ Upon **you** no evìl shall **fall**,
  no **plague** approach where yóu **dwell**.
¹¹ For **you** God has com**mand**ed thè **angels**,
  to **keep** you in **all** yóur **ways**.

¹² They shall **bear** you upòn their **hands**
  lest you **strike** your **foot** against á **stone**.
¹³ On the **lion** and the **vi**per you wìll **tread**
  and **tram**ple the young **lion** and thé **dragon**.

¹⁴ You **set** your love on **me** so Ì will **save** you,
  pro**tect** you for you **know** mý **name**.
¹⁵ When you **call** I shall **answer**: "I àm **with** you,"
  I will **save** you in dis**tress** and give yóu **glory**.

¹⁶ With **length** of **days** I wìll content **you**;
  I shall **let** you see my sav**íng** **power**.
  To the **Father**, the **Son** and Holỳ **Spirit**
  give **praise** for **ever**. Ámen.

Text: Psalm 91; The Grail
Music: Joseph Gelineau, SJ
© 1963, 1993, The Grail, GIA Publications, Inc., agent

123 Psalm 91: Be with Me

Refrain

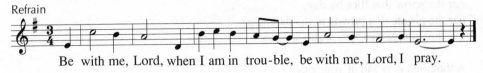

Be with me, Lord, when I am in trou-ble, be with me, Lord, I pray.

Verses

1. You who dwell in the shelter of the Lord, Most High,
   who abide in the shadow of our God,
   say to the Lord: "My refuge and fortress, the God in whom I trust."

2. No evil shall befall you, no pain come near,
   for the angels stand close by your side,
   guarding you always and bearing you gently, watching over your life.

3. Those who cling to the Lord live secure in God's love,
   lifted high, those who trust in God's name,
   call on the Lord, who will never forsake you.
   God will bring you salvation and joy.

Text: Psalm 91:1-2, 10-11, 14-15; Marty Haugen
Music: Marty Haugen
© 1980, GIA Publications, Inc.

124 Psalm 92: Lord, It Is Good

Refrain

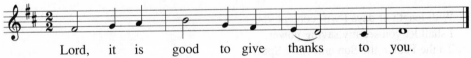

Lord, it is good to give thanks to you.

Verses

1. It is good to give thanks to the Lord,
   to make music to your name, O Most High,
   to proclaim your love in the morning
   and your truth in the watches of the night.

2. The just will flourish like the palm tree and grow like a Lebanon cedar.
   Planted in the house of the Lord they will flourish in the courts of our God.

3. Still bearing fruit when they are old, still full of sap, still green,
   to proclaim that the Lord is just. My rock, in whom there is no wrong.

Text: Psalm 92:2-3, 13-14, 15-16; © 1963, 1993, The Grail, GIA Publications, Inc., agent; refrain trans. © 1969, ICEL
Music: Michel Guimont, © 1994, GIA Publications, Inc.

Psalm 92: Lord, It Is Good   125

Antiphon

Lord,   it   is   good   to give thanks   to   you.

Text: *Lectionary for Mass,* © 1969, 1981, ICEL
Music: Richard Proulx, © 1975, GIA Publications, Inc.

Verses

1. It is good to give thanks to the Lord,
   to make music to your name, O Most High,
   to proclaim your love in the morning
   and your truth in the watches of the night.

2. The just will flourish like the palm tree
   and grow like a Lebanon cedar.
   Planted in the house of the Lord
   they will flourish in the courts of our God.

3. Still bearing fruit when they are old,
   still full of sap, still green,
   to proclaim that the Lord is just.
   My rock, in whom there is no wrong.

Text: Psalm 92:2-3, 13-14, 15-16; © 1963, 1993, The Grail, GIA Publications, Inc.,agent

126 Psalm 93: The Lord Is King for Evermore

Antiphon I

The Lord is King for ev - er - more.

Text: Psalm 93; The Grail
Music: A. Gregory Murray, OSB
© 1963, The Grail, GIA Publications, Inc., agent

Antiphon II

Al - le - lu - ia, al - le - lu - ia, al - le - lu - ia.

Music: A. Gregory Murray, OSB, © 1963, The Grail, GIA Publications, Inc., agent

Psalm Tone

Music: Psalm tone 8-g; acc. by Richard Proulx, © 1975, GIA Publications, Inc.

Gelineau Tone

¹ The Lord is **king**, with **maj**esty en**rōbed**;
the **Lord** is **robed** with **mìght**,
and **gird**ed **róund** with **pow**er.

The **world** you made **firm**, not to be **mōved**;
² your **throne** has stood **firm** from of **òld**.
From all e**ter**nitý, O **Lord**, you **are**.

³ The **wa**ters have **lift**ed up, O **Lōrd**,
the **wa**ters have **lift**ed up their **vòice**,
the **wa**ters have **lift**ed **úp** their **thun**der.

⁴ **Great**er than the **roar** of mighty **watērs**,
more **glor**ious than the **surg**ings of the **sèa**,
the **Lord** is **glór**ious on **high**.

⁵ **Tru**ly your de**crees** are to be **trustēd**.
Holiness is **fit**ting to your **hòuse**,
O **Lord**, un**tíl** the **end** of **time**.

Give **glo**ry to the **Fath**er Al**mightý**,
to his **Son**, Jesus **Christ**, the **Lòrd**,
to the **Spir**it who **dwélls** in our **hearts**.

Text: Psalm 93; The Grail
Music: Joseph Gelineau, SJ
© 1963, 1993, The Grail, GIA Publications, Inc., agent

Psalm 95: If Today You Hear His Voice   127

Refrain

If to - day you hear his voice,

hard - en not your hearts.

Verses

1. Come, ring out our joy to the Lord;
   hail the rock who saves us.
   Let us come before God, giving thanks,
   with songs let us hail the Lord.

2. Come in; let us bow and bend low;
   let us kneel before the God who made us
   for this is our God and we
   the people who belong to his pasture,
   the flock that is led by his hand.

3. O that today you would listen to God's voice!
   "Harden not your hearts as at Meribah,
   as on that day at Massah in the desert
   when your ancestors put me to the test;
   when they tried me, though they saw my work."

Text: Psalm 95:1-2, 6-7, 8-9; © 1963, 1993, The Grail, GIA Publications, Inc., agent; refrain trans. © 1969, ICEL
Music: Michel Guimont, © 1995, GIA Publications, Inc.

128 Psalm 95: If Today You Hear His Voice

Refrain

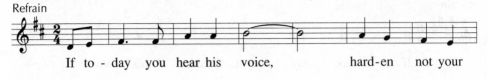

If to-day you hear his voice, hard-en not your hearts, hard-en not your hearts.

Verses

1. Come, let us sing joyfully to the Lord;
   let us acclaim the rock of our salvation.
   Let us greet him with thanksgiving,
   sing joyful psalms to him.

2. Come, let us bow down in worship;
   let us kneel before the Lord who made us,
   for he is our God and we the flock he guides.

3. O, that today you would hear his voice!
   Harden not your hearts as in the days in the desert
   where your fathers tested me.

Text: Psalm 95:1-2, 6-7, 8-9; Roy James Stewart, © 1993, GIA Publications, Inc.; refran trans. © 1969, ICEL
Music: Roy James Stewart, © 1993, GIA Publications, Inc.

129 Psalm 95: If Today You Hear God's Voice

Refrain

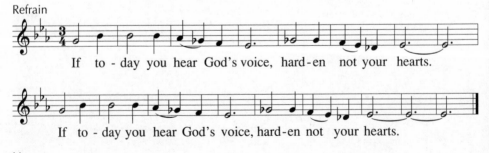

If to-day you hear God's voice, hard-en not your hearts.

If to-day you hear God's voice, hard-en not your hearts.

Verses

1. Come, ring out our joy to the Lord, hail the rock who saves us,
   let us come now before our God, with songs let us hail the Lord.

2. Come, let us bow and bend low, let us kneel before God who made us,
   for here is our God; we the people, the flock that is led by God's hand.

3. O that today you would hear God's voice, "Harden not your hearts,
   as on that day in the desert, when your parents put me to the test."

Text: Psalm 95:1-2, 6-7, 8-9; David Haas
Music: David Haas
© 1983, 1994, GIA Publications, Inc.

Psalm 96: Today Is Born Our Savior   130

Refrain

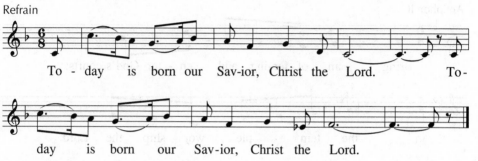

To - day   is   born our   Sav-ior, Christ the   Lord.   To-

day   is   born   our   Sav-ior, Christ the   Lord.

Verses

1. Sing to the Lord a new song;
   sing to the Lord, all you lands.
   Sing to the Lord; bless his name.

2. Announce his salvation, day after day.
   Tell his glory among the nations;
   Among all peoples, his wondrous deeds.

3. Let the heavens be glad and the earth rejoice;
   let the sea and what fills it resound;
   let the plains be joyful and all that is in them!
   Then shall all the trees of the forest exult.

4. They shall exult before the Lord, for he comes;
   for he comes to rule the earth.
   He shall rule the world with justice
   and the peoples with his constancy.

Text: Psalm 96; verses trans. © 1970, Confraternity of Christian Doctrine, Washington, D.C.; refrain trans. © 1969, ICEL
Music: Howard Hughes, SM, © 1976, GIA Publications, Inc.

131 Psalm 96: Great Is the Lord

Antiphon I

Great is the Lord, wor - thy of praise; tell all the na - tions "God is King"; spread the news of his love.

Text: Psalm 96:3-4; The Grail
Music: Joseph Gelineau, SJ
© 1963, The Grail, GIA Publications, Inc., agent

Antiphon II

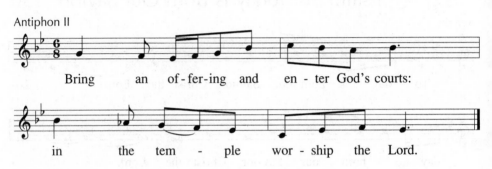

Bring an of - fer-ing and en - ter God's courts: in the tem - ple wor - ship the Lord.

Text: Psalm 96:6; The Grail
Music: Clifford Howell, SJ
© 1963, 1993, The Grail, GIA Publications, Inc., agent

Antiphon III (St. 1.2.8.9)

To - day is born our Sav-ior, Christ the Lord.

Text: *Lectionary for Mass,* © 1969, 1981, ICEL
Music: Howard Hughes, SM, © 1975, GIA Publications, Inc.

Antiphon IV (Vs. 1.3.4-5.7-8.9-10)

Give the Lord glo-ry, glo-ry and hon - or.

Text: *Lectionary for Mass,* © 1969, 1981, ICEL
Music: Richard Proulx, © 1986, GIA Publications, Inc.

Psalm Tone

Music: Chant tone 5; acc. by Robert J. Batastini, © 1975, GIA Publications, Inc.

Gelineau Tone

For 3-line stanza   For 4-line stanza

¹ O **sing** a new **song** to the **Lōrd**,
  sing to the **Lord** all the **èarth**.
² O **sing** to the **Lórd**, bless his **name**.

  Proclaim God's **help** day by **dãy**,
³ **tell** among the **nations** his **glòry**
  and his **wonders** amóng all the **peoples**.

⁴ The Lord is **great** and **worthy** of **prāise**,
  to be **feared** above all **gòds**;
⁵ the **gods** of the **héathens** are **naught**.

  It was the **Lord** who **made** the **heavēns**.
⁶ his are **majesty** and **honor** and **pòwer**
  and **splendor** ín the **holy** place.

⁷ Give the **Lord**, you **families** of **peoplēs**,
  give the **Lord** glory and **pòwer**;
⁸ give the **Lord** the **glóry** of his **name**.

  Bring an **offering** and **enter** God's **cōurts**,
⁹ **wor**ship the **Lord** in the **tèmple**.
  O **earth**, stand in **féar** of the **Lord**.

¹⁰ **Proclaim** to the **nations**: "God is **kĭng**."
  The **world** was made **firm** in its **plàce**;
  God will **judge** the **péo**ples in **fairness**.

¹¹ Let the **heavens** re**joice** and earth be
    glàd,
  let the **sea** and all with**ín** it thunder **praise**,
¹² let the **land** and all it **bears** re**jòice**,
  all the **trees** of the **wóod** shout for **joy**

¹³ at the **presence** of the **Lord** who **còmes**,
  who **cómes** to **rule** the **earth**.
  Comes with **justice** to **rule** the **wòrld**,
  and to **judge** the **péo**ples with **truth**.

  Give **praise** to the **Father** Al**mìght**y,
  to his **Son**, **Jésus** **Christ**, the **Lord**,
  to the **Spirit** who **dwells** in **òur** **hearts**,
  both **now** and for **éver**. **Amen**.

Text: Psalm 96; The Grail
Music: Joseph Gelineau, SJ
© 1963, 1993, The Grail, GIA Publications, Inc., agent

132　Psalm 96: Proclaim to All the Nations

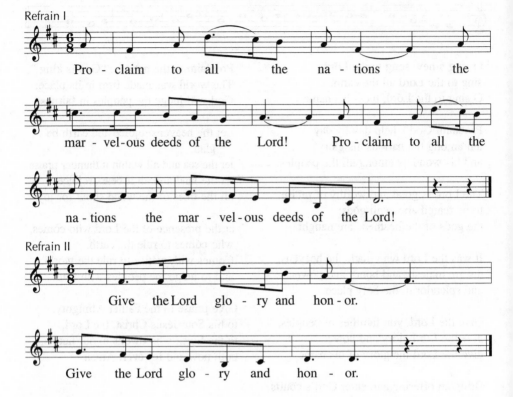

Refrain I

Pro - claim to all the na - tions the mar - vel-ous deeds of the Lord! Pro - claim to all the na - tions the mar - vel-ous deeds of the Lord!

Refrain II

Give the Lord glo - ry and hon - or.

Give the Lord glo - ry and hon - or.

Verses

1. Sing to the Lord a new song. Sing to the Lord all you lands!
   Sing to the Lord with all your heart, and bless God's name!

2. Announce salvation day by day, God's glory throughout the earth!
   Among all the people in every land, God's wondrous deeds!

3. Give to the Lord, you nations, praise to the Lord of all!
   Sing glory and praise and sing to the name, above all names!

4. Worship the Lord, and tremble, proclaim the one who reigns!
   Say to the nations: "The Lord is King;" who rules with justice!

Psalm 97: The Lord Is King 133

Antiphon (St. 1.3.4 or 1.2.4)

The Lord is king, the most high o - ver all the earth.

Text: *Lectionary for Mass,* © 1969, 1981, ICEL
Music: Richard Proulx, © 1975, GIA Publications, Inc.

Verses

1. The Lord is king, let earth rejoice,
   let all the coastlands be glad.
   Surrounded by cloud and darkness;
   justice and right, God's throne.

2. The mountains melt like wax
   before the Lord of all the earth.
   The skies proclaim God's justice;
   all peoples see God's glory.

3. The skies proclaim God's justice;
   all peoples see God's glory.
   All you spirits, worship the Lord.

4. For you indeed are the Lord
   most high above all the earth,
   exalted far above all spirits.

Text: Psalm 97:1-2, 5-6, 6-7, 9; © 1963, 1993, The Grail, GIA Publications, Inc., agent

Psalm 97: A Light Will Shine 134

Antiphon

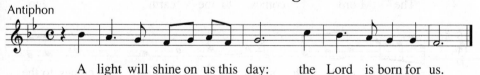

A light will shine on us this day: the Lord is born for us.

Text: *Lectionary for Mass,* © 1969, 1981, ICEL
Music: J. Robert Carroll, © 1975, GIA Publications, Inc.

Verses

1. The Lord is king, let earth rejoice,
   let all the coastlands be glad.
   The skies proclaim God's justice;
   all peoples see God's glory.

2. Light shines forth for the just
   and joy for the upright of heart.
   Rejoice, you just, in the Lord;
   give glory to God's holy name.

Text: Psalm 97:1, 6, 11-12; © 1963, 1993, The Grail, GIA Publications, Inc., agent

135 Psalm 98: All the Ends of the Earth

Refrain I

All the ends of the earth have seen the pow-er of God; all the ends of the earth have seen the pow - er of God.

Refrain II

Sing to the Lord a new song, for God has done won - der - ful deeds. Sing to the Lord a new song, for God has done won - der - ful deeds.

Refrain III

The Lord comes to the earth to rule the earth with jus - tice. The Lord comes to the earth to rule the earth with jus - tice.

Verses

1. Sing to the Lord a new song, for God has done wondrous deeds;
   whose right hand has won the vict'ry for us, God's holy arm.

2. The Lord has made salvation known, and justice revealed to all,
   remembering kindness and faithfulness to Israel.

3. All of the ends of earth have seen salvation by our God.
   Joyfully sing out all you lands, break forth in song.

4. Sing to the Lord with harp and song, with trumpet and with horn.
   Sing in your joy before the king, the king, our Lord.

Psalm 98: All the Ends of the Earth   136

Refrain I (St. 1-4)

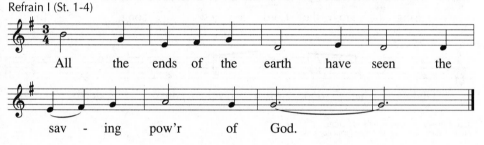

Refrain II (St. 1-3)

Verses

1. Sing a new song to the Lord
   who has worked wonders;
   whose right hand and holy arm
   have brought salvation.

2. The Lord has made known salvation;
   has shown justice to the nations;
   has remembered truth and love
   for the house of Israel.

3. All the ends of the earth have seen
   the salvation of our God.
   Shout to the Lord, all the earth,
   ring out your joy.

4. Sing psalms to the Lord with the harp
   with the sound of music.
   With trumpets and the sound of the horn
   acclaim the King, the Lord.

137 Psalm 98: All the Ends of the Earth

Antiphon I (St. 1-4)

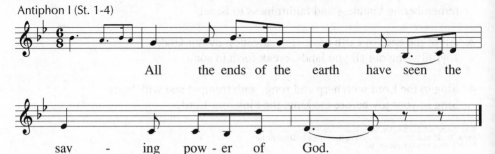

All the ends of the earth have seen the sav - ing pow-er of God.

Text: *Lectionary for Mass,* © 1969, 1981, ICEL
Music: Richard Proulx, © 1975, GIA Publications, Inc.

Antiphon II (St. 1-3)

Sing to the Lord a new song, for God has done mar - vel - ous deeds.

Text: *Lectionary for Mass,* © 1969, 1981, ICEL
Music: J. Robert Carroll, © 1975, GIA Publications, Inc.

Antiphon III (St. 1-3)

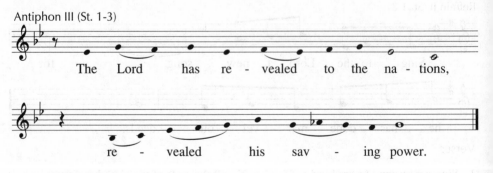

The Lord has re - vealed to the na - tions, re - vealed his sav - ing power.

Text: *Lectionary for Mass,* © 1969, 1981, ICEL
Music: Michael Joncas, © 1986, GIA Publications, Inc.

Verses

1. Sing a new song to the Lord
who has worked wonders;
whose right hand and holy arm
have brought salvation.

2. The Lord has made known salvation;
has shown justice to the nations;
has remembered truth and love
for the house of Israel.

3. All the ends of the earth have seen
   the salvation of our God.
   Shout to the Lord, all the earth,
   ring out your joy.

4. Sing psalms to the Lord with the harp
   with the sound of music.
   With trumpets and the sound of the horn
   acclaim the King, the Lord.

Text: Psalm 98:1, 2-3, 3-4, 5-6; © 1963, 1993, The Grail, GIA Publications, Inc., agent

Psalm 100: We Are God's People 138

Ostinato Refrain

We are God's peo - ple, the flock of the Lord.

Verses

1. Cry out with joy to the Lord, all you lands, all you lands.
   Serve the Lord now with gladness, come before God singing for joy!

2. Know that the Lord is God! Know that the Lord is God,
   who made us, to God we belong, God's people, the sheep of the flock!

3. Go, now within the gates giving thanks, giving thanks.
   Enter the courts singing praise, give thanks and bless God's name!

4. Indeed, how good is the Lord, whose mercy endures for ever,
   for the Lord is faithful, is faithful from age to age!

Text: Psalm 100:1-2, 3, 4, 5; David Haas
Music: David Haas
© 1983, GIA Publications, Inc.

139 Psalm 100: Arise, Come to Your God

Antiphon I

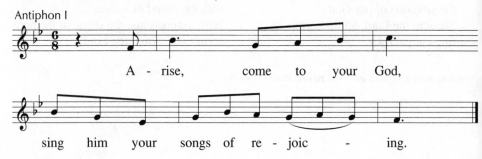

A - rise, come to your God,

sing him your songs of re - joic - ing.

Text: Joseph Gelineau, SJ
Music: Joseph Gelineau, SJ
© 1963, The Grail, GIA Publications, Inc., agent

Antiphon II

Al - le - lu - ia, al - le - lu - ia, al - le - lu - ia.

Music: A. Gregory Murray, OSB, © 1963, The Grail, GIA Publications, Inc., agent

Psalm Tone

Music: Chant tone 8-g; acc. by Richard Proulx, © 1975, GIA Publications, Inc.

Gelineau Tone

¹ Cry out with **joy** to the **Lord,** all the **ēarth.**
² **Serve** the **Lord** with **glàd**ness.
Come be**fore** God, **síng**ing for **joy.**

³ **Know** that the **Lord** is **Gōd,**
our **Mak**er, to **whom** we be**lòng.**
We are God's **people, shéep** of the **flock.**

⁴ **Enter** the **gates** with thanks**givīng,**
God's **courts** with **sòngs** of **praise.**
Give **thanks** to **Gód** and **bless** his **name.**

⁵ **Indeed,** how **good** is the **Lōrd,**
whose **mer**ciful **love** is et**èrnal;**
whose **faith**fulness **lásts** for **ever.**

Give **glory** to the **Father** Al**mightȳ,**
to his **Son,** Jesus **Chrìst,** the **Lord,**
to the **Spir**it who **dwélls** in our **hearts.**

Text: Psalm 100; The Grail
Music: Joseph Gelineau, SJ
© 1963, 1993, The Grail, GIA Publications, Inc., agent

Psalm 103: The Lord Is Kind and Merciful   140

Refrain

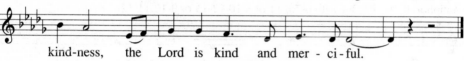

The Lord is kind and mer-ci-ful; the Lord is kind and mer-ci-ful. Slow to an-ger, rich in kind-ness, the Lord is kind and mer-ci-ful.

Verses

1. Bless the Lord, O my soul; all my being bless God's name.
   Bless the Lord, O my soul; forget not all God's blessings.

2. The Lord is gracious and merciful, slow to anger, full of kindness.
   God is good to all creation, full of compassion.

3. The goodness of God is from age to age,
   blessing those who choose to love.
   And justice toward God's children; on all who keep the covenant.

Text: Psalm 103; Jeanne Cotter
Music: Jeanne Cotter
© 1993, GIA Publications, Inc.

141 Psalm 103: The Lord Has Set His Throne

Antiphon I (St. 1.5.9)

The Lord has set his throne in heav-en.

Text: *Lectionary for Mass,* © 1969, 1981, ICEL
Music: Marty Haugen, © 1986, GIA Publications, Inc.

Antiphon II (Vs. 1-2.3-4 with 6-7.8.11 or 8.10.12-13 or 9-10.11-12)

The Lord is kind and mer - ci - ful.

Text: *Lectionary for Mass,* © 1969, 1981, ICEL
Music: David Haas, © 1986, GIA Publications, Inc.

Antiphon III (St. 1-4)

The Lord's kind - ness is ev - er -

last - ing to those who fear him.

Text: *Lectionary for Mass,* © 1969, 1981, ICEL
Music: Howard Hughes, SM, © 1975, GIA Publications, Inc.

Psalm Tone

Music: Richard Proulx, © 1975, GIA Publications, Inc.

Gelineau Tone

St. 1-7

Omit for 4-line stanza

St. 8-11

Omit for 4-line stanza

1 My soul, give thanks tò the Lord,
 all my being, bléss God's holy name.
2 My soul, give thanks to the Lòrd
 and never forget áll God's blessings.

3 It is God who forgives àll your guilt,
 who heals every óne of your ills,
4 who redeems your life from the gràve,
 who crowns you with love ánd
   compassion,
5 who fills your life wìth good things,
 renewing your youth líke an eagle's.

6 The Lord does deeds of jùstice,
 gives judgment for áll who are oppressed.
7 The Lord's ways were made known to
   Mòses;
 the Lord's deeds to Isráel's children.

8 The Lord is compassion ànd love,
 slow to anger and rích in mercy.
9 The Lord will not always chìde,
 will not be ángry for ever.
10 God does not treat us according tò our sins
 nor repay us accórding to our faults.

11 For as the heavens are high abòve the
   earth
 so strong is God's love fór the God-fearing.
12 As far as the east is fròm the west
 so far does hé remove our sins.

13 As parents have compassion on their chìldren,
 the Lord has pity on those whó are God-fearing
14 for he knows of what wè are made,
 and remembers thát we are dust.

15 As for us, our days are like gràss;
 we flower like the flówer of the field;
16 the wind blows and wè are gone
 and our place never sées us again.

17 But the love of the Lord is everlàsting
 upon those whó fear the Lord.
 God's justice reaches out to children's children
18 when they keep his covenant ìn truth,
 when they keep his wíll in their mind.

19 The Lord has set his throne in hèaven
 and his kingdom rúles over all.
20 Give thanks to the Lord, all you angels,
 mighty in power, fulfilling Gòd's word,
 who heed the vóice of that word.

21 Give thanks to the Lord, all you hòsts,
 you servants whó do God's will.
22 Give thanks to the Lord, all his works,
 in every place where Gòd rules.
 My soul, give thánks to the Lord!

Give praise to the Father Almìghty,
 to his Son, Jésus Christ, the Lord,
 to the Spirit who dwells in òur hearts,
 both now and for éver. Amen.

Text: Psalm 103; The Grail
Music: Joseph Gelineau, SJ
© 1963, 1993, The Grail, GIA Publications, Inc., agent

142 Psalm 103: The Lord Has Set His Throne

Refrain

The Lord has set his throne in heav - en.

Verses

1. My soul, give thanks to the Lord,
   all my being, bless God's holy name.
   My soul, give thanks to the Lord
   and never forget all God's blessings.

2. For as the heavens are high above the earth
   so strong is God's love for the God-fearing;
   As far as the east is from the west
   so far does he remove our sins.

3. The Lord has set his throne in heaven
   and his kingdom rules over all.
   Give thanks to the Lord, all you angels,
   mighty in power, fulfilling God's word.

143 Psalm 103: The Lord Is Kind and Merciful

Refrain

The Lord is kind and mer-ci - ful, the

Lord is kind and mer - ci - ful.

Verses

1. Bless the Lord, O my soul, and all my being bless God's name;
   bless the Lord, and forget not God's benefits.

2. God pardons all your iniquities, and comforts your sorrows,
   redeems your life from destruction and crowns you with kindness.

3. Merciful, merciful, and gracious is our God;
   slow to anger, abounding in kindness.

Text: Psalm 103:1-2, 3-4, 8; para. by Marty Haugen, © 1983, GIA Publications, Inc.; refrain trans. © 1969, ICEL
Music: Marty Haugen, © 1983, GIA Publications, Inc.

Psalm 104: Lord, Send Out Your Spirit   144

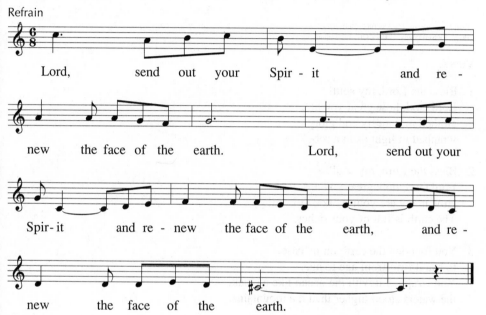

Refrain

Lord,   send   out   your   Spir - it   and   re -
new   the face of the   earth.   Lord,   send out your
Spir- it   and re - new   the face of the   earth,   and re -
new   the   face   of   the   earth.

Text: *Lectionary for Mass,* © 1969, 1981, ICEL
Music: Alexander Peloquin, © 1971, GIA Publications, Inc.

Verses

1. Bless the Lord, my soul!
   Lord God, how great you are,
   How many are your works, O Lord!
   The earth is full of your riches.

2. You take back your spirit, they die,
   returning to the dust from which they came.
   You send forth your spirit, they are created;
   and you renew the face of the earth.

3. May the glory of the Lord last for ever!
   May the Lord rejoice in creation!
   May my thoughts be pleasing to God.
   I find my joy in the Lord.

Text: Psalm 104:1, 24, 29-30, 31, 34; © 1963, 1993, The Grail, GIA Publications, Inc., agent

145 Psalm 104: Lord, Send Out Your Spirit

Antiphon (St. 1.3.4.5.6 or 1.6.7.8 or 2.8.9)

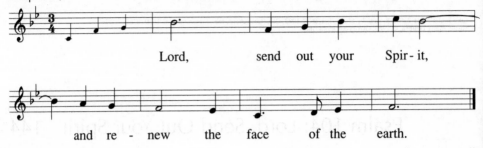

Lord, send out your Spir-it,

and re - new the face of the earth.

Text: *Lectionary for Mass,* © 1969, 1981, ICEL
Music: Richard Proulx, © 1975, GIA Publications, Inc.

Verses

1. Bless the Lord, my soul!
   Lord God, how great you are,
   clothed in majesty and glory,
   wrapped in light as in a robe!

2. Bless the Lord, my soul!
   Lord God, how great you are.
   How many are your works, O Lord!
   The earth is full of your riches.

3. You founded the earth on its base,
   to stand firm from age to age.
   You wrapped it with the ocean like a cloak:
   the waters stood higher than the mountains.

4. You make springs gush forth in the valleys;
   they flow in between the hills.
   On their banks dwell the birds of heaven;
   from the branches they sing their song.

5. From your dwelling you water the hills;
   earth drinks its fill of your gift.
   You make the grass grow for the cattle
   and the plants to serve our needs,
   that we may bring forth bread from the earth.

6. How many are your works, O Lord!
   In wisdom you have made them all.
   The earth is full of your riches.
   Bless the Lord, my soul.

7. All of these look to you
to give them their food in due season.
You give it, they gather it up;
you open your hand, they have their fill.

8. You take back your spirit, they die,
returning to the dust from which they came.
You send forth your spirit, they are created;
and you renew the face of the earth.

9. May the glory of the Lord last for ever!
May the Lord rejoice in creation!
May my thoughts be pleasing to God.
I find my joy in the Lord.

Text: Psalm 104:1-2, 1, 24, 5-6, 10, 12, 13-14, 24, 35, 27-28, 29-30, 31, 34; © 1963, 1993, The Grail, GIA Publications, Inc., agent

Psalm 104: Lord, Send Out Your Spirit 146

Refrain

Lord, send out your Spir-it, and re - new the face of the earth!

Verses

1. Bless the Lord, O my soul; O Lord, my God, you are great indeed!
How manifold are your works, O Lord! The earth is full of your creatures!

2. If you take away their breath, they die and they return to their dust.
When you send forth your Spirit of life, they are created in your sight!

3. May his glory last for all time; may the Lord be glad in his works.
Pleasing to him will be my theme; I will be glad in the Lord!

May be sung in canon.

Text: Psalm 104:1, 24, 29-30, 31, 34; Paul Lisicky, © 1985, GIA Publications, Inc.; refrain trans. © 1969, ICEL
Music: Paul Lisicky, © 1985, GIA Publications, Inc.

147 Psalm 107: Give Thanks to the Lord

Antiphon

Give thanks to the Lord, his love is ev - er - last-ing.

Text: *Lectionary for Mass,* © 1969, 1981, ICEL
Music: J. Robert Carroll, © 1975, GIA Publications, Inc.

Verses

1. Some sailed to the sea in ships
   to trade on the mighty waters.
   They saw the deeds of the Lord,
   the wonders he does in the deep.

2. For God spoke and summoned the gale,
   tossing the waves of the sea
   up to heaven and back into the deep;
   their souls melted away in distress.

3. Then they cried to the Lord in their need
   and he rescued them from their distress.
   God stilled the storm to a whisper;
   all the waves of the sea were hushed.

4. They rejoiced because of the calm
   and God led them to the haven they desired.
   Let them confess the love of the Lord,
   the wonders God does for the people.

Text: Psalm 107:23-24, 25-26, 28-29, 30-31; © 1963,1993, The Grail, GIA Publications, Inc., agent

148 Psalm 110: You Are a Priest for Ever

Antiphon

You are a priest for ev - er, in the

line of Mel - chi - ze - dek.

Text: *Lectionary for Mass,* © 1969, 1981, ICEL
Music: Robert J. Batastini, © 1975, GIA Publications, Inc.

Verses

1. The Lord's revelation to my Master:
   "Sit on my right;
   your foes I will put beneath your feet."

2. The Lord will wield from Zion
   your scepter of power;
   rule in the midst of all your foes.

3. A prince from the day of your birth
   on the holy mountains;
   from the womb before the dawn I begot you.

4. The Lord has sworn an oath and will not change.
   "You are a priest for ever,
   a priest like Melchizedek of old."

Text: Psalm 110:1, 2, 3, 4; © 1963,1993, The Grail, GIA Publications, Inc., agent

Psalm 112: A Light Rises in the Darkness   149

Refrain

A light ris-es in the dark-ness; a light for the up-right.

Verses

1. They are lights in the darkness for the upright;
   they are generous, merciful and just.
   Good people take pity and lend, they conduct their affairs with honor.

2. The just will never waver, they will be remembered for ever.
   They have no fear of evil news; with firm hearts they trust in the Lord.

3. With steadfast hearts they will not fear. Openhanded, they give to the poor;
   their justice stands firm for ever. Their heads will be raised in glory.

Text: Psalm 112:4-5, 6-7, 8-9; © 1963, 1993, The Grail, GIA Publications, Inc., agent; refrain trans. © 1969, ICEL
Music: Michel Guimont, © 1994, GIA Publications, Inc.

150 Psalm 113: Praise God's Name

Refrain

Al - le - lu - ia! Al-le-lu-ia! Al - le - lu - ia!

Verses

1. You servants of the Lord, bless the Lord: Blessed be the name for ever!
   From east to west, praised be the name of the Lord our God!

2. High above the nations the Lord is God;
   high above the heavens God's glory!
   Who is like God, enthroned on the stars above earth and sky?

3. Raising up the lowly and the poor from the dust,
   God gives them a home among rulers:
   blessing the barren, giving them children singing for joy!

4. Glory to the Father and glory to the Son; glory to the Holy Spirit:
   glory and honor, wisdom and power for evermore!

Text: Psalm 113; Michael Joncas, alt.
Music: Michael Joncas
© 1979, OCP Publications

151 Psalm 113: Praise the Lord

Refrain

Praise the Lord, praise the Lord who lifts up the poor.

Verses

1. Praise, O servants of the Lord; praise the name of the Lord!
   May the name of the Lord be blessed both now and for evermore!

2. High above all nations is the Lord, above the heavens God's glory.
   Who is like the Lord, our God, the one enthroned on high,
   who stoops from the heights to look down,
   to look down upon heaven and earth?

3. From the dust God lifts up the lowly,
   from the dungheap God raises the poor
   to set them in the company of rulers, yes, with the rulers of the people.

Text: Psalm 113:1-2, 4-6, 7-8; © 1963, 1993, The Grail, GIA Publications, Inc. agent; refrain trans. © 1969, ICEL
Music: Michel Guimont, © 1994, GIA Publications, Inc.

Psalm 116: The Name of God   152

Refrain I

I will take the cup of life, I will call God's name all my days.

Refrain II

Our bless-ing-cup is a com-mun-ion with the Blood of Christ.

Refrain III

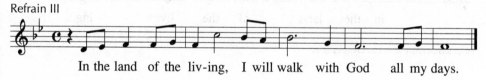

In the land of the liv-ing, I will walk with God all my days.

Verses

1. How can I make a return for the goodness of God?
   This saving cup I will bless and sing, and call the name of God!

2. The dying of those who keep faith is precious to our God.
   I am your servant called from your hands, you have set me free!

3. To you I will offer my thanks and call upon your name.
   You are my promise for all to see. I love your name, O God!

Text: Psalm 116; David Haas, © 1987, GIA Publications, Inc.; refrain II trans. © 1969, ICEL
Music: David Haas, © 1987, GIA Publications, Inc.

153   Psalm 116: I Will Take the Cup of Salvation

Antiphon I (Vs. 12-13.15-16.17-18)

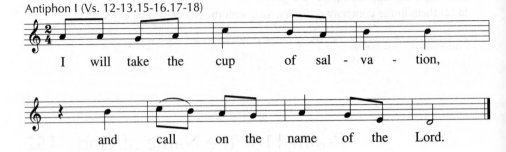

I will take the cup of sal - va - tion,

and call on the name of the Lord.

Text: *Lectionary for Mass,* © 1969, 1981, ICEL
Music: A. Gregory Murray, OSB, © 1975, GIA Publications, Inc.

Antiphon II (St. 6ab & 8cd.9.10 or vs. 1-2.3-4.5-6.8-9)

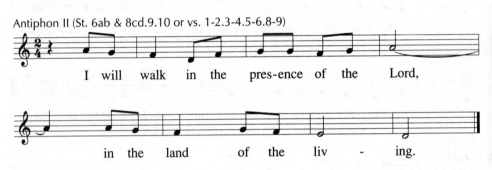

I will walk in the pres-ence of the Lord,

in the land of the liv - ing.

Text: *Lectionary for Mass,* © 1969, 1981, ICEL
Music: Richard Proulx, © 1975, GIA Publications, Inc.

Antiphon III (Vs. 12-13.15-16.17-18)

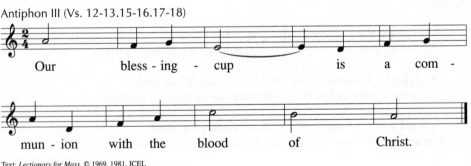

Our bless - ing - cup is a com -

mun - ion with the blood of Christ.

Text: *Lectionary for Mass,* © 1969, 1981, ICEL
Music: Alexander Peloquin, © 1975, GIA Publications, Inc.

Psalm Tone   Omit for 2-line stanza

Music: Richard Proulx, © 1986, GIA Publications, Inc.

Gelineau Tone

Omit for 2-line stanza

Repeat for stanza 4

Repeat for stanza 2

I love the **Lord**, for the **Lòrd** has **heard**
the **cry** of my **áppeal.**
[2] The **Lord** was attentive tò **me**
in the **day** when **Í called.**

[3] They surr**ound**ed me, the **snàres** of **death,**
with the **anguish** of thé **tomb;**
they **caught** me, **sorrow** and dì**stress.**
[4] I **called** on the **Lord's name.**
O **Lord,** my **God,** dé**liver** me!

[5] How **gracious** is the **Lòrd,** and **just;**
our **God** has **cómpassion.**
[6] The **Lord** protects the simplè **hearts;**
I was **helpless** so **Gód saved me.**

[7] Turn **back,** my **soul,** tò your **rest**
for the **Lord** has béen **good,**
[8] and has **kept** my **soul** from **death,**
(my **eyes** fròm **tears,**)
my **feet** fróm **stumbling.**

[9] I will **walk** in the **presence** òf the **Lord**
in the **land** of thé **living.**

[10] I **trusted, even** whèn I **said:**
"I am **sorely áfflicted,**"
[11] and **when** I **said** in my à**larm:**
"**There** is no one I **cán trust.**"

[12] How **can** I repày the **Lord**
for his **goodness** tó **me**?
[13] The **cup** of salvation I wìll **raise;**
I will **call** on thé **Lord's name.**

[14] My **vows** to the **Lord** I wìll ful**fill**
before all thé **people.**
[15] O **precious** in the **eyes** of thè **Lord**
is the **death** of thé **faithful.**

[16] Your **servant,** Lord, your **servànt** am I;
you have **loosened mý bonds.**
[17] A **thanks**giving **sacrifice** Ì **make;**
I will **call** on thé **Lord's name.**

[18] My **vows** to the **Lord** I wìll ful**fill**
before all thé **people,**
[19] in the **courts** of the **house** of thè **Lord,**
in your **midst,** O Jé**rusalem.**

Praise the **Father,** the **Son** and **Hòly Spirit,**
both **now** and fór **ever,**
the God who **is,** who **was,** and is tò **come,**
at the **end** of thé **ages.**

Text: Psalm 116; The Grail
Music: Joseph Gelineau, SJ
© 1963, 1993, The Grail, GIA Publications, Inc., agent

154 Psalm 116: I Will Walk in the Presence of God

Refrain

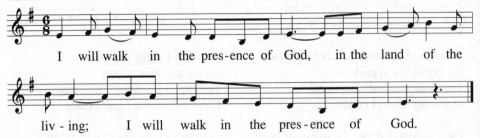

I will walk in the pres-ence of God, in the land of the liv-ing; I will walk in the pres-ence of God.

Verses

1. In my hour of despair, bereft and betrayed,
   I prayed, "Save me! Be my breath!"
   The death of a servant cuts close to your heart,
   For God of the living you are.

2. Your servant am I like my mother before me.
   You restore me, loosing my bonds.
   My hands in thanksgiving to God I will raise.
   O join me in glorious praise!

3. My vows I will make, and may ev'ryone hear me!
   Draw near me, O servants of God.
   I stand here in the midst of them:
   Your house, your heart, Jerusalem.

155 Psalm 116: Our Blessing-Cup

Refrain

Our bless-ing-cup is a com-mun-ion with the Blood of the Lord.

Verses

1. How can I make a return to the Lord for all God has done for me?
   The cup of salvation I will take up, I will call on the name of the Lord.

2. Precious, indeed, in the sight of the Lord is the death of his faithful ones;
   and I am your servant, your chosen one, for you have set me free.

3. Unto your name I will offer my thanks for the debt that I owe to you.
   In the presence of all who have called on your name,
   in the courts of the house of the Lord.

Text: Psalm 116:12-13, 15-16, 17-19; Marty Haugen
Music: Marty Haugen
© 1983. GIA Publications. Inc.

Psalm 117: Holy Is God, Holy and Strong 156

Refrain

Ho - ly is God!   Ho - ly and strong!

Ho-ly is God!   Ho-ly and strong!   Ho-ly and liv-ing for ev-er!

Verses

1. O praise the Lord, all you nations, acclaim God, all you peoples!
   Strong is God's love for us; the Lord is faithful for ever!

2. Give glory to the Father Almighty, to his Son Jesus Christ the Lord,
   to the Spirit who dwells in our hearts, both now and for ever. Amen!

Text: Psalm 117; © 1963, 1993, The Grail, GIA Publications, Inc., agent; refrain trans. © 1969, ICEL
Music: Michael Joncas, © 1979, GIA Publications, Inc.

157 Psalm 117: Go Out to All the World

Antiphon

Go out to all the world, and tell the Good News.

Text: *Lectionary for Mass,* © 1969, 1981, ICEL
Music: Alexander Peloquin, © 1975, GIA Publications, Inc.

Verses

1. O praise the Lord, all you nations,
   acclaim God all you peoples!

2. Strong is God's love for us;
   the Lord is faithful for ever.

Text: Psalm 117; © 1963, 1993, The Grail, GIA Publications, Inc., agent

158 Psalm 118: Let Us Rejoice

Refrain

This is the day the Lord has made, let us re-
Or: Al - le - lu - ia, al - le - lu - ia! Al - le -

joice and be glad; this is the day the Lord has
lu - ia! Al-le-lu - ia, al - le - lu -

made, let us re - joice and be glad!
ia! Al - le - lu - ia!

Verses

1. Give thanks to the Lord, for God is good; God's mercy endures for ever;
   Let the house of Israel say: "God's mercy endures for ever."

2. The hand of the Lord has struck with power, God's right hand is exalted,
   I shall not die, but live anew, declaring the works of the Lord.

3. The stone which the builders rejected has become the cornerstone,
   the Lord of love and mercy has brought wonder to our eyes!

Text: Psalm 118:1-2, 16-17, 22-23; Marty Haugen, © 1983, GIA Publications, Inc.; refrain trans. © 1969, ICEL
Music: Marty Haugen, © 1983, GIA Publications, Inc.

Psalm 118: Give Thanks to the Lord   159

Antiphon

Give thanks to the Lord for he is good, his love is ev - er - last - ing.

Text: *Lectionary for Mass*, © 1969, 1981, ICEL
Music: Chrysogonus Waddell, OCSO, © 1986, GIA Publications, Inc.

Verses

1. Let the family of Israel say:
   "God's love endures for ever."
   Let the family of Aaron say:
   "God's love endures for ever."
   Let those who fear the Lord say:
   "God's love endures for ever."

2. I was thrust down, thrust down and falling,
   but the Lord was my helper.
   The Lord is my strength and my song;
   and has been my savior.
   There are shouts of joy and victory
   in the tents of the just.

3. The stone which the builders rejected
   has become the cornerstone.
   This is the work of the Lord,
   a marvel in our eyes.
   This day was made by the Lord;
   we rejoice and are glad.

Text: Psalm 118:2-4, 13-15, 22-24; © 1963, 1993, The Grail, GIA Publications, Inc., agent

160 Psalm 118: This Is the Day

Antiphon

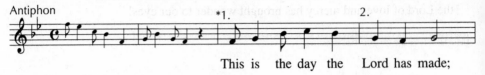

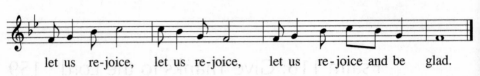

This is the day the Lord has made;

let us re-joice, let us re-joice, let us re-joice and be glad.

May be sung as a canon.

Text: *Lectionary for Mass,* © 1969, 1981, ICEL
Music: Richard Proulx, © 1975, GIA Publications, Inc.

Verses

1. Give thanks to the Lord who is good,
   for God's love endures for ever.
   Let the family of Israel say:
   "God's love endures for ever."

2. The Lord's right hand has triumphed;
   God's right hand raised me.
   The Lord's right hand has triumphed;
   I shall not die, I shall live
   and recount God's deeds,
   [and recount God's deeds.]

3. The stone which the builders rejected
   has become the cornerstone.
   This is the work of the Lord,
   a marvel in our eyes.

Text: Psalm 118:1-2, 16-17, 22-23, © 1963, 1993, The Grail, GIA Publications, Inc., agent

Psalm 118: The Stone Rejected   161

Refrain

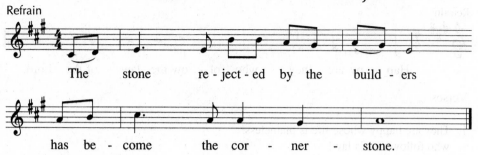

The stone re-ject-ed by the build-ers

has be-come the cor - ner - stone.

Verses

1. Give thanks to the Lord who is good,
   for God's love endures for ever.
   It is better to take refuge in the Lord
   than to trust in mortals;
   it is better to take refuge in the Lord
   than to trust in rulers.

2. I will thank you for you have answered
   and you are my savior.
   The stone which the builders rejected
   has become the cornerstone.
   This is the work of the Lord,
   a marvel in our eyes.

3. Blessed in the name of the Lord
   is he who comes.
   We bless you from the house of the Lord;
   the Lord God is our light.

4. I will thank you for you have answered
   and you are my savior.
   Give thanks to the Lord who is good;
   for God's love endures for ever.

Text: Psalm 118:1, 8-9, 21-23, 26, 21, 29; © 1963, 1993, The Grail, GIA Publications, Inc., agent; refrain trans. © 1969, ICEL
Music: Michel Guimont, © 1995, GIA Publications, Inc.

162 Psalm 119: Happy Are They

Refrain

Hap - py are they who fol - low the law of the Lord.

Verses

1. They are happy whose life is blameless,
   who follow God's law!
   They are happy who do God's will,
   seeking God with all their hearts.

2. You have laid down your precepts
   to be obeyed with care.
   May my footsteps be firm
   to obey your statutes.

3. Bless your servant and I shall live
   and obey your word.
   Open my eyes that I may see
   the wonders of your law.

4. Teach me the demands of your statutes
   and I will keep them to the end.
   Train me to observe your law,
   to keep it with my heart.

Text: Psalm 119:1-2, 4-5, 17-18, 33-34; © 1963, 1993, The Grail, GIA Publications, Inc., agent; refrain trans. © 1969, ICEL
Music: Michel Guimont, © 1995, GIA Publications, Inc.

163 Psalm 119: Lord, I Love Your Commands

Refrain

Lord, I love your com - mands.

Text: *Lectionary for Mass*, © 1969, 1981, ICEL
Music: Robert J. Batastini, © 1986, GIA Publications, Inc.

Verses

1. My part, I have resolved, O Lord, is to obey your word.
   The law from your mouth means more to me than silver and gold.

2. Let your love be ready to console me by your promise to your servant.
   Let your love come and I shall live for your law is my delight.

3. That is why I love your commands more than finest gold,
   why I rule my life by your precepts, and hate false ways.

4. Your will is wonderful indeed; therefore I obey it.
   The unfolding of your word gives light and teaches the simple.

Text: Psalm 119:57, 72, 76-77, 127-128, 129-130; © 1963, 1993, The Grail, GIA Publications, Inc., agent; refrain trans. © 1969, ICEL

Psalm 121: Our Help Comes from the Lord   164

Refrain

Our   help   comes   from   the   Lord,   the

mak - er   of   heav - en   and   earth.

Verses

1. I lift up my eyes to the mountains: from where shall come my help?
   My help shall come from the Lord who made heaven and earth.

2. May God never allow you to stumble! Let God sleep not, your guard.
   Neither sleeping nor slumbering, God, Israel's guard.

3. The Lord is your guard and your shade: and at your right side stands,
   By day the sun shall not smite you nor the moon in the night.

4. The Lord will guard you from evil: God will guard your soul.
   The Lord will guard your going and coming both now and for ever.

5. Glory to the Father, and to the Son, and to the Holy Spirit:
   as it was in the beginning, is now, and will be for ever. Amen.

Text: Psalm 121; © 1963, 1993, The Grail, GIA Publications, Inc., agent; refrain by Michael Joncas, © 1979, GIA Publications, Inc.
Music: Michael Joncas, © 1979, GIA Publications, Inc.

165 Psalm 122: I Rejoiced When I Heard

Antiphon

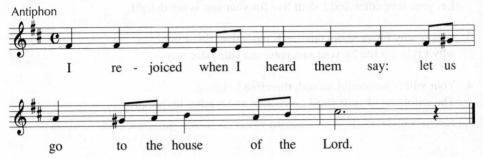

I re - joiced when I heard them say: let us go to the house of the Lord.

Text: *Lectionary for Mass*, © 1969, 1981, ICEL
Music: Robert J. Batastini, © 1975, GIA Publications, Inc.

Verses

1. I rejoiced when I heard them say:
   "Let us go to God's house."
   And now our feet are standing
   within your gates, O Jerusalem.

2. Jerusalem is built as a city
   strongly compact.
   It is there that the tribes go up,
   the tribes of the Lord.

3. For Israel's law it is,
   there to praise the Lord's name.
   There were set the thrones of judgment
   of the house of David.

4. For the peace of Jerusalem pray:
   "Peace be to your homes!
   May peace reign in your walls,
   in your palaces, peace!"

5. For love of my family and friends
   I say: "Peace upon you."
   For love of the house of the Lord
   I will ask for your good.

Text: Psalm 122; © 1963, 1993, The Grail, GIA Publications, Inc., agent

166 Psalm 122: I Was Glad

Refrain

I was glad when they said to me,
"Come with us to the house of the Lord!"

Verses

1. I was glad when they said to me: "Come with us to the house of the Lord."
   Now our feet are standing firm, within your gates, O Jerusalem!

2. Jerusalem— strongly built, walled around with unity.
   It is there that the tribes of God are lifted high, to the mountain of God!

3. Israel, this is your law: to praise the name of the Lord.
   Here are placed the judgment seats, for the just, here the house of David!

4. For the love of my fam'ly and friends, "may the peace of God be with you!"
   For the love of the house of God I will pray, I will pray for your good!

Text: Psalm 122; David Haas
Music: David Haas
© 1994, GIA Publications, Inc.

Psalm 122: Let Us Go Rejoicing   167

Refrain

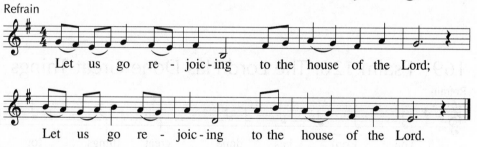

Let us go re-joic-ing to the house of the Lord;

Let us go re-joic-ing to the house of the Lord.

Verses

1. I rejoiced when I heard them say: "Let us go to the house of the Lord,"
   and now our feet are standing within your gates, O Jerusalem.

2. Jerusalem is a city built with unity and strength.
   It is there, it is there that the tribes go up, the tribes of the Lord.

3. For Israel's law is to praise God's name and there to give God thanks.
   There are set the judgment thrones for all of David's house.

4. Pray for the peace of Jerusalem! "May those who love you prosper;
   May peace ever reign within your walls, and wealth within your buildings!"

5. For love of my family and love of my friends, I pray that peace be yours.
   For love of the house of the Lord our God I pray for your good.

Text: Psalm 122; Michael Joncas, © 1987, GIA Publications, Inc.; refrain trans. © 1969, ICEL
Music: Michael Joncas, © 1987, GIA Publications, Inc.

168 Psalm 123: Our Eyes Are Fixed on the Lord

Refrain

Our eyes are fixed on the Lord, plead-ing for his mer - cy.

Verses

1. To you I have lifted up my eyes, you who dwell in the heavens;
   my eyes, like the eyes of slaves on the hand of their lords.

2. Like the eyes of a servant on the hand of her mistress,
   so our eyes are on the Lord our God till we are shown mercy.

3. Have mercy on us Lord, have mercy. We are filled with contempt.
   Indeed all too full is our soul with the scorn of the rich,
   (the disdain of the proud).

Text: Psalm 123:1-2, 3-4; © 1963, 1993, The Grail, GIA Publications, Inc., agent; refrain trans. © 1969, ICEL
Music: Michel Guimont, © 1994, GIA Publications, Inc.

169 Psalm 126: The Lord Has Done Great Things

Refrain

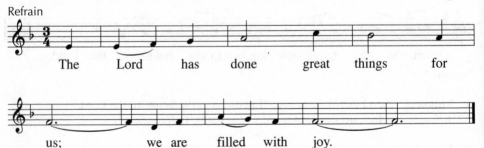

The Lord has done great things for

us; we are filled with joy.

Verses

1. When the Lord delivered Zion from bondage,
   it seemed like a dream.
   Then was our mouth filled with laughter,
   on our lips there were songs.

2. The heathens themselves said: "What marvels
   the Lord worked for them!"
   What marvels the Lord worked for us!
   Indeed we were glad.

3. Deliver us, O Lord, from our bondage
   as streams in dry land.
   Those who are sowing in tears
   will sing when they reap.

4. They go out, they go out, full of tears,
   carrying seed for the sowing;
   they come back, they come back, full of song,
   carrying their sheaves.

Text: Psalm 126; © 1963, 1993, The Grail, GIA Publications, Inc., agent; refrain trans. © 1969, ICEL
Music: Michel Guimont, © 1995, GIA Publications, Inc.

Psalm 126: The Lord Has Done Great Things   170

Refrain

The Lord has done great things for us and we are filled with joy.

Verses

1. When the Lord delivered Zion,
   we were like people dreaming.
   Then our mouth was filled with laughter,
   and our lips were filled with song.

2. The heathen marvelled at God,
   and the wonders he worked for them.
   What marvelous works the Lord has done,
   and we are glad indeed.

3. They go out full of tears,
   carrying seed for the sowing.
   They come back, they come back full of song,
   carrying their sheaves.

Text: Psalm 126:1-3, 6; Roy James Stewart, © 1993, GIA Publications, Inc.; refran trans. © 1969, ICEL
Music: Roy James Stewart, © 1993, GIA Publications, Inc.

171 Psalm 126: The Lord Has Done Great Things

Antiphon

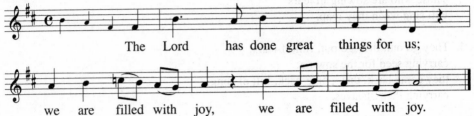

The Lord has done great things for us;

we are filled with joy, we are filled with joy.

Text: *Lectionary for Mass*, © 1969, 1981, ICEL
Music: Richard Proulx, © 1975, GIA Publications, Inc.

Psalm Tone

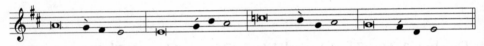

Music: Joseph B. Smith, © 1986, GIA Publications, Inc.

Gelineau Tone

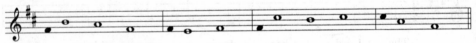

1 When the **Lord** delivered **Zìon** from **bond**age,
  it **seemed** líke a **dream.**
2 **Then** was our **mouth** fîlled with **laugh**ter,
  on our **lips** thére were **songs.**

  The **heath**ens them**selves** sàid: "What **mar**vels
  the **Lord** wórked for **them!**"
3 What **marvels** the **Lord** wòrked for **us!**
  Indeed wé were **glad.**

4 **Deliver** us, O **Lord**, fròm our **bond**age
  as **streams** ín dry **land.**
5 **Those** who are **sow**ìng in **tears**
  will **sing** whén they **reap.**

6 They go **out**, they go **out**, fùll of **tears**,
  carrying **seed** fór the **sowing;**
  they come **back**, they come **back**, fùll of **song**,
  carry**íng** their **sheaves.**

  Praise the **Father**, the **Son** and **Hòly Spir**it,
  both **now** ánd for **ever**,
  the God who **is**, who **was** ànd who **will** be,
  world wíthout **end.**

Text: Psalm 126; The Grail
Music: Joseph Gelineau, SJ
© 1963, 1993, The Grail, GIA Publications, Inc., agent

Psalm 128: May the Lord Bless and Protect 172

Antiphon I

May the Lord bless and pro-tect us all the days of our life.

Text: *Lectionary for Mass,* © 1969, 1981, ICEL
Music: A. Gregory Murray, OSB, © 1963, The Grail, GIA Publications, Inc., agent

Antiphon II

O hap - py are those who fear the

Lord and walk in his ways.

Text: *Lectionary for Mass,* © 1969, 1981, ICEL
Music: Joseph Gelineau, SJ, © 1963, The Grail, GIA Publications, Inc., agent

Verses

1. O blessed are you who fear the Lord
   and walk in God's ways!
   By the labor of your hands you shall eat.
   You will be happy and prosper.

2. Your wife like a fruitful vine
   in the heart of your house;
   your children like shoots of the olive,
   around your table.

3. Indeed thus shall be blessed
   those who fear the Lord.
   May the Lord bless you from Zion
   all the days of your life!

4. May you see your children's children
   in a happy Jerusalem!
   On Israel, peace!

Text: Psalm 128; © 1963, 1993, The Grail, GIA Publications, Inc., agent

173 Psalm 128: Blest Are Those Who Love You

Refrain I

Blest are those who love you, hap-py those who
fol-low you, blest are those who seek you, O God.

Refrain II

May the Lord bless us, May the Lord pro-
tect us, all the days, all the days of our life.

Verses

1. Happy all those who fear the Lord, and walk in God's pathway;
   you will find what you long for: the riches of our God.

2. Your spouse shall be like a fruitful vine in the midst of your home,
   your children flourish like olive plants rejoicing at your table.

3. May the blessings of God be yours all the days of your life,
   may the peace and the love of God live always in your heart.

Text: Psalm 128:1-2, 3, 5; Marty Haugen
Music: Marty Haugen; refrain II adapt. by Diana Kodner
© 1987, 1993, GIA Publications, Inc.

Psalm 130: With the Lord There Is Mercy   174

Refrain

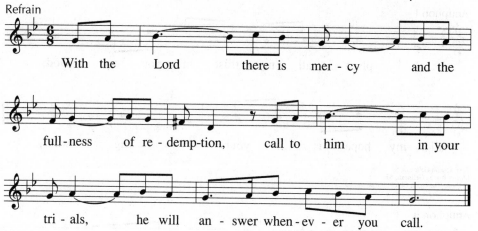

With the Lord there is mer - cy and the full-ness of re - demp-tion, call to him in your tri - als, he will an - swer when - ev - er you call.

Verses

1. Out of the depths I cry to you,
   I cry to you, O Lord.
   Lord, open your ears and hear my voice,
   attend to the sound of my plea.

2. If you, O Lord, should mark our guilt,
   then, Lord, who could hope to survive?
   But with you is found forgiveness of sin,
   and mercy that we might revere you.

3. Trust in the Lord, count on his word,
   wait for the Lord, my soul.
   I will wait for the Lord all the days of my life
   as sentinels wait for the dawn.

4. More than the sentinels wait for the dawn,
   let Israel wait for the Lord.
   For kindness is his, redemption for all,
   forgiveness of sins for his people.

Text: Psalm 130; Michael Joncas
Music: Michael Joncas
© 1983, OCP Publications

175 Psalm 130: I Place All My Trust

Antiphon I

I place all my trust in you, my God;

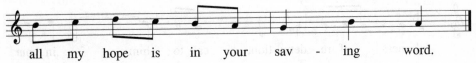

all my hope is in your sav - ing word.

Text: Joseph Gelineau, SJ
Music: Joseph Gelineau, SJ
© 1963, The Grail, GIA Publications, Inc., agent

Antiphon II

If you, O Lord, should mark our sins,

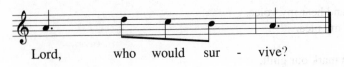

Lord, who would sur - vive?

Text: Psalm 130:3; The Grail
Music: Clifford W. Howell, SJ
© 1963, The Grail, GIA Publications, Inc., agent

Antiphon III

Out of the depths I cry to you, O Lord.

Text: *Liturgy of the Hours*, © 1974, ICEL
Music: Randolph Currie, © 1986, GIA Publications, Inc.

Antiphon IV

With the Lord there is mer-cy, and full-ness of re-demp-tion.

Text: *Lectionary for Mass*, © 1969, 1981, ICEL
Music: J. Robert Carroll, harm. by Richard Proulx, © 1975, GIA Publications, Inc.

Psalm Tone

Repeat for 6-line stanza

Music: A. Gregory Murray, OSB, © L. J. Carey and Co., Ltd.

Gelineau Tone

Repeat for 6-line stanza

¹ Out of the **depths** I **cry** to yòu, O **Lord**,
² **Lord**, héar my **voice**!
  O **let** your **ears** bè **att**entive
  to the **voice** óf my **pleading**.

³ If you, O **Lord**, should màrk our **guilt**,
  Lord, who wóuld survìve?
⁴ But with **you** is fòund for**give**ness:
  for **this** wé re**vere** you.

⁵ My **soul** is **wait**ing fòr the **Lord**.
  I **count** ón God's **word**.
⁶ My **soul** is **long**ing fòr the **Lord**
  more than **those** who wátch for **daybreak**.
  (Let the **watch**ers còunt on **day**break
⁷ and **Is**rael **ón** the **Lord**.)

Because with the **Lord** thère is **mercy**
and **full**ness óf re**demp**tion,
⁸ **Is**rael in**deed** God wìll re**deem**
from **all** íts in**iq**uity.

To the **Father** Al**mighty** give **glory**,
give **glory** tó his **Son**,
to the **Spir**it most **Holy** give **praise**,
whose **reign** ís for **ever**.

Text: Psalm 130; The Grail
Music: Joseph Gelineau, SJ
© 1963, 1993, The Grail, GIA Publications, Inc., agent

Psalm 130: With the Lord There Is Mercy   176

Refrain

With the Lord   there is   mer - cy,   and full-ness of   re - demp-tion.

Verses

1. From out of the depths, I cry unto you,
     Lord, hear my voice, come hear my prayer;
     O let your ear be open to my pleading.

2. If you, O Lord, should mark our guilt,
     then who could stand within your sight?
     But in you is found forgiveness for our failings.

3. Just as those who wait for the morning light,
     even more I long for the Lord, my God,
     whose word to me shall ever be my comfort.

Text: Psalm 130:1-2, 3-4, 5-6; Marty Haugen, © 1983, GIA Publications, Inc.; refrain trans. © 1969, ICEL
Music: Marty Haugen, © 1983, GIA Publications, Inc.

177 Psalm 130: If You, O God, Laid Bare Our Guilt

Refrain

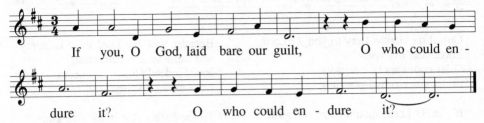

If you, O God, laid bare our guilt, O who could en -
dure it? O who could en - dure it?

Verses

1. Out of the depths I cry to you. Lord, hear my plea.
   Let your ear be attentive to the sound of my call.

2. If you, O God, lay bare our sin, Lord, who can stand?
   But with you is forgiveness, so your name is revered.

3. Waiting for you, our souls await, hoping in God.
   Like the sent'nel for daybreak, so our souls wait for you.

4. For with the Lord is steadfast love: pow'r to redeem.
   God will save us from sorrows, bring us back from our sin.

Text: Psalm 130; John Foley, SJ
Music: John Foley, SJ
© 1994, GIA Publications, Inc.

178 Psalm 131: My Soul Is Still

Refrain

In you, O Lord, I have found my
peace, I have found my peace.

Verses

1. My heart is not proud, my eyes not above you;
   You fill my soul. I am not filled with great things,
   nor with thoughts beyond me.

2. My soul is still, my soul stays quiet,
   longing for you like a weaned child
   in its mother's arms; so is my soul a child with you.

Text: Psalm 131; verses, David Haas, © 1985, GIA Publications, Inc.; refrain trans. © 1969, ICEL
Music: David Haas, © 1985, GIA Publications, Inc.

Psalm 131: In You, Lord   179

Antiphon

In you, Lord, in you, Lord, in

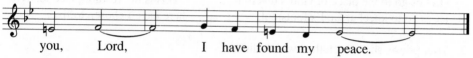

you, Lord, I have found my peace.

Text: *Lectionary for Mass,* © 1969, 1981, ICEL
Music: Robert J. Batastini, © 1975, GIA Publications, Inc.

Verses

1. O Lord, my heart is not proud
   nor haughty my eyes.
   I have not gone after things too great
   nor marvels beyond me.

2. Truly I have set my soul
   in silence and peace.
   A weaned child on its mother's breast,
   even so is my soul.

3. O Israel, hope in the Lord
   both now and for ever.

Text: Psalm 131; © 1963, 1993, The Grail, GIA Publications, Inc., agent

180 Psalm 132: Lord, Go Up

Antiphon

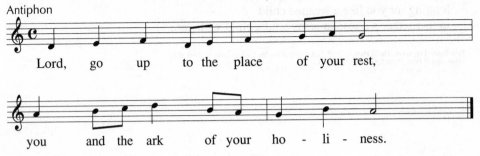

Lord, go up to the place of your rest, you and the ark of your ho - li - ness.

Text: *Lectionary for Mass*, © 1969, 1981, ICEL
Music: John Schiavone, © 1986, GIA Publications, Inc.

Verses

1. At Ephrata we heard of the ark;
   we found it in the plains of Yearim.
   "Let us go to the place of God's dwelling;
   let us go to kneel at God's footstool."

2. Your priests shall be clothed with holiness;
   your faithful shall ring out their joy.
   For the sake of David your servant
   do not reject your anointed.

3. For the Lord has chosen Zion;
   has desired it for a dwelling:
   "This is my resting-place for ever,
   here have I chosen to live."

Text: Psalm 132:6-7, 9-10, 13-14; © 1963, 1993, The Grail, GIA Publications, Inc., agent

181 Psalm 134: In the Silent Hours of Night

Antiphon

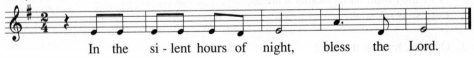

In the si - lent hours of night, bless the Lord.

Verses

1. O come, bless the Lord,
   all you who serve the Lord,
   who stand in the house of the Lord,
   in the courts of the house of our God.

2. Lift up your hands to the holy place
   and bless the Lord through the night.

3. May the Lord bless you from Zion,
   God who made both heaven and earth.

4. Glory to the Father, and the Son,
   and to the Holy Spirit:
   as it was in the beginning, is now,
   and will be for ever. Amen.

Text: Psalm 134; The Grail, © 1963, 1993, GIA Publications, Inc., agent; refrain text, from *Praise God in Song,* © 1979, GIA Publications, Inc.
Music: Howard Hughes, SM, © 1979, GIA Publications, Inc.

Psalm 137: Let My Tongue Be Silent   182

Antiphon

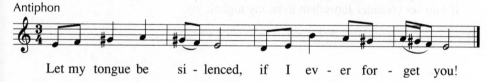

Let my tongue be   si - lenced, if   I   ev - er for - get you!

Text: *Lectionary for Mass,* © 1969, 1981, ICEL
Music: Frank Schoen, © 1975, GIA Publications, Inc.

Verses

1. By the rivers of Babylon
   there we sat and wept,
   remembering Zion;
   on the poplars that grew there
   we hung up our harps.

2. For it was there that they asked us,
   our captors, for songs,
   our oppressors, for joy.
   "Sing to us," they said,
   "one of Zion's songs."

3. O how could we sing
   the song of the Lord
   on alien soil?
   If I forget you, Jerusalem,
   let my right hand wither!

4. O let my tongue
   cleave to my mouth
   if I remember you not,
   if I prize not Jerusalem
   above all my joys!

Text: Psalm 137:1-2, 3, 4-5, 6; © 1963, 1993, The Grail, GIA Publications, Inc., agent

183 Psalm 137: Let My Tongue Be Silent

Refrain

Let my tongue be si - lent, if ev - er I for - get you!

Verses

1. By Babylonian rivers, we sat and wept, rememb'ring Zion.
   There on the poplars we retired our harps.

2. For there our captors demanded songs of joy:
   "Sing to us one of the songs of Zion!"

3. How can we sing the songs of the Lord while in a foreign land?
   How can we sing the songs of the Lord while in a foreign land?

4. If I should fail to remember you, O Zion, Let my tongue be silenced,
   let my right hand be forgotten,
   If I do not consider Jerusalem to be my highest joy.

Text: Psalm 137:1-6; Carl Johengen, © 1992, GIA Publications, Inc.; refrain trans. © 1969, ICEL
Music: Carl Johengen, © 1992, GIA Publications, Inc.

184 Psalm 138: In the Sight of the Angels

Antiphon I (St. 1.2.3.5)

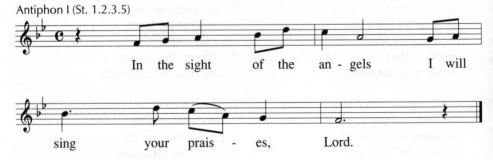

In the sight of the an - gels I will

sing your prais - es, Lord.

Text: *Lectionary for Mass*, © 1969, 1981, ICEL
Music: J. Robert Carroll, © 1975, GIA Publications, Inc.

Antiphon II (St. 1.2.4.5)

Lord, on the day I called for

help, you an - swered me.

Antiphon III (St. 1.2.4ab & 5cd)

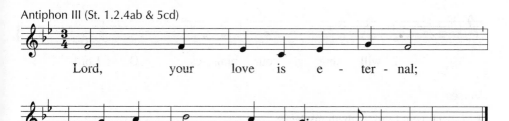

Lord, your love is e - ter - nal;

do not for - sake the work of your hands.

Psalm Tone

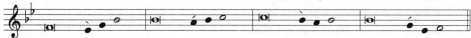

Gelineau Tone

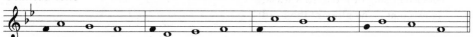

¹ I **thank** you, **Lord**, with àll my **heart**,
   you have **heard** the **words** óf my **mouth**.
   In the **pres**ence of the **an**gels Ì will **bless** you.
² I will a**dore** before your **hó**ly **tem**ple.

   I **thank** you for your **faith**fulnèss and **love**
   which ex**cel** all we **ev**er knéw of **you**.
³ On the **day** I càlled, you **an**swered;
   you in**creased** the **strength** óf my **soul**.

⁴ All the **rul**ers on **èarth** shall **thank** you
   when they **hear** the **words** óf your **mouth**.
⁵ They shall **sing** òf the **Lord's ways**:
   "How **great** is the **glo**ry óf the **Lord**!"

⁶ The Lord is **high** yet **looks** òn the **low**ly
   and the **haugh**ty God **knows** fróm a**far**.
⁷ Though I **walk** in the **midst** òf af**flic**tion
   you give me **life** and frus**trá**te my **foes**.

   You **stretch** out your **hànd** and **save** me,
   your **hand** ⁸will do **áll** things **for** me.
   Your **love**, O Lord, ìs e**ter**nal,
   dis**card** not the **work** óf your **hands**.

   Give **praise** to the **Fa**thèr Al**might**y,
   to his **Son**, Jesus **Chríst**, the **Lord**,
   to the **Spir**it who **dwells** ìn our **hearts**,
   both **now** and for **ev**ér. **Amen**.

185 Psalm 138: In the Sight of the Angels

Refrain

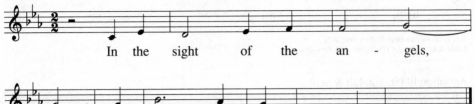

In the sight of the an - gels,
I will sing your prais - es, O Lord.

Verses

1. I thank you, Lord, with all my heart,
   you have heard the words of my mouth.
   In the presence of the angels I will bless you.
   I will adore before your holy temple.

2. I thank you for your faithfulness and love
   which excel all we ever knew of you.
   On the day I called, you answered;
   you increased the strength of my soul.

3. All the rulers on earth shall thank you
   when they hear the words of your mouth.
   They shall sing of the Lord's ways:
   "How great is the glory of the Lord!"

4. You stretch out your hand and save me,
   your hand will do all things for me.
   Your love, O Lord, is eternal,
   discard not the work of your hands.

Text: Psalm 138:1-2, 2-3, 4-5, 7-8; © 1963, 1993, The Grail, GIA Publications, Inc., agent; refrain trans. © 1969, ICEL
Music: Michel Guimont, © 1995, GIA Publications, Inc.

186 Psalm 139: Guide Me, Lord

Refrain

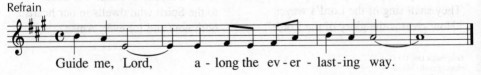

Guide me, Lord, a - long the ev - er - last-ing way.

Verses

1. O Lord, you have probed me and you know me;
   you know when I sit and when I stand;
   you understand my thoughts from afar.
   My journeys and my rest you scrutinize,
   with all my ways you are familiar.

2. Even before a word is on my tongue,
   behold, O Lord, you know the whole of it.
   Behind me and before, you hem me in
   and rest your hand upon me.
   Such knowledge is too wonderful for me;
   too lofty for me to attain.

3. Where can I go from your spirit?
   From your presence where can I flee?
   If I go up to the heavens, you are there;
   if I sink to the nether world, you are present there.

4. If I take the wings of the dawn,
   if I settle at the farthest limits of the sea,
   even there your hand shall guide me,
   and your right hand hold me fast.

5. If I say, "Surely the darkness shall hide me,
   and night shall be my light," for you
   darkness itself is not dark,
   and night shines as the day.

6. Truly you have formed my inmost being;
   you knit me in my mother's womb.
   I give you thanks that I am fearfully,
   wonderf'ly made; wonderful are your works.

7. My soul also you knew full well;
   nor was my frame unknown to you
   when I was made in secret,
   when I was fashioned in the depths of the earth.

8. Probe me, O God, and know my heart;
   try me, and know my thoughts;
   see if my way is crooked,
   and lead me in the way of old.

Text: Psalm 139:1-15, 23-24; *New American Bible,* © 1970, Confraternity of Christian Doctrine
Music: Howard Hughes, SM, © 1979, GIA Publications, Inc.

187 Psalm 139: I Praise You

Refrain

I praise you, O Lord, for I am won-der-ful-ly made.

Verses

1. O Lord, you search me and you know me,
   you know my resting and my rising,
   you discern my purpose from afar.
   You mark when I walk or lie down,
   all my ways lie open to you.

2. For it was you who created my being,
   knit me together in my mother's womb.
   I thank you for the wonder of my being,
   for the wonders of all your creation.

3. Already you knew my soul,
   my body held no secret from you
   when I was being fashioned in secret
   and molded in the depths of the earth.

Text: Psalm 139:1-3, 13-14, 14-15; © 1963, 1993, The Grail, GIA Publications, Inc., agent; refrain trans. © 1969, ICEL
Music: Michel Guimont, © 1995, GIA Publications, Inc.

188 Psalm 141: Let My Prayer Rise Like Incense

Refrain

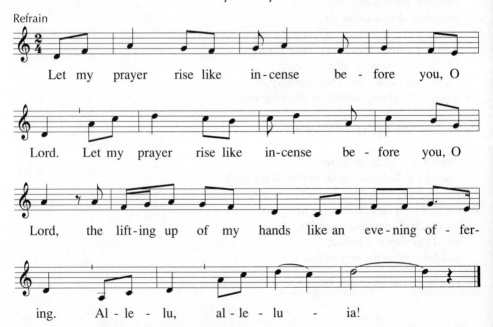

Let my prayer rise like in-cense be - fore you, O

Lord. Let my prayer rise like in-cense be - fore you, O

Lord, the lift-ing up of my hands like an eve-ning of - fer-

ing. Al - le - lu, al - le - lu - ia!

Verses

1. I have called to you, Lord; hasten to help me!
   Hear my voice when I cry to you.
   Let my prayer arise before you like incense,
   the raising of my hands like an evening oblation.

2. Set, O Lord, a guard over my mouth;
   keep watch, O Lord, at the door of my lips!
   Do not turn my heart to things that are wrong,
   to evil deeds with those who are sinners.

3. Never allow me to share in their feasting.
   If the upright strike or reprove me it is kindness;
   but let the oil of the wicked not anoint my head.
   Let my prayer be ever against their malice.

4. Their leaders were thrown down by the side of the rock;
   then they understood that my words were kind.
   As a millstone is shattered to pieces on the ground,
   so their bones were strewn at the mouth of the grave.

5. To you, Lord God, my eyes are turned;
   in you I take refuge; spare my soul!
   From the trap they have laid for me keep me safe;
   keep me from the snares of those who do evil.

6. Glory to the Father, and to the Son,
   and to the Holy Spirit:
   as it was in the beginning,
   is now, and will be for ever. Amen.

Text: Psalm 141; © 1963, 1993, The Grail, GIA Publications, Inc., agent
Music: Howard Hughes, SM, © 1978, GIA Publications, Inc.

189 Psalm 141: Evening Offering

Refrain

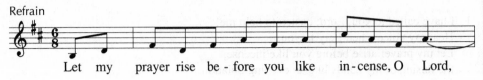

Let my prayer rise be-fore you like in-cense, O Lord,

and my hands like an eve - ning of - f'ring.

Verses

1. To you, O Lord, I call out for help.
   O hear my voice when I cry out to you.
   Let my prayer rise up before you like incense,
   my hands lifted at the end of the day.

2. May my words, O Lord, speak only your truth;
   my heart be filled with a longing for you.
   Keep my hands, O Lord, from all wicked deeds;
   let me not rejoice with those set against you.

3. Let your holy ones confront me in kindness;
   their words I hear as your wisdom for me.
   But the wicked ones shall never mislead me;
   I will pray for strength to conquer their evil.

4. I look to you, O Lord, for my hope.
   For you, my God, are the strength of my soul.
   Keep me safe from those who tempt me to sin,
   and free my heart to rest in your peace.

Tune: Psalm 141; Darryl Ducote
Music: Darryl Ducote; arr. by Gary Daigle
© 1985, 1993, Damean Music, Distributed by GIA Publications, Inc.

190 Psalm 143: Do Not Hide Your Face

Antiphon

Do not hide your face from me: In you I put my trust.

Text: *Liturgy of the Hours,* © 1974, ICEL
Music: Randolph Currie, © 1986, GIA Publications, Inc.

Psalm Tone

Music: Chrysogonus Waddell, OCSO, © Gethsemani Abbey

Gelineau Tone

Omit for 4-line stanza

Omit for 5-line stanza

¹ **Lord, listen** tò my **prayer,**
turn your **ear** to my **áppeal.**
You are **faithful,** you are **just;** gìve **answer.**
² Do not **call** your **ser**vant to **judg**ment
for **no** one is **just** in yóur **sight.**

³ The **enemy** pursùes my **soul;**
has **crushed** my **life** to thé **ground;**
has **made** me **dwell** ìn **dark**ness
like the **dead, long** fórgotten.*
⁴ **There**fore my **spir**ìt **fails;**
my **heart** is **numb** wíthin me.

⁵ I **remember** the **days** thàt are **past;**
I **pon**der **all** yóur **works.**
I **muse** on what your **hand** hàs **wrought**
⁶ and to **you** I **stretch** out mý **hands.****
Like a **parched** land my **soul** thirsts fór **you.**

⁷ **Lord,** make **hàste** and **answer;**
for my **spirit fails** wíthin me.
Do not **hide** yòur **face**
lest I be**come** like **those** in thé **grave.**

⁸ In the **morning** let me **knòw** your **love**
for I **put** my **trust** ín **you.**
Make me **know** the **way** I shòuld **walk;**
to **you** I **lift** up mý **soul.**

⁹ **Rescue** me, **Lord,** fròm my **enemies;**
I have **fled** to **you** fór **refuge.**
¹⁰ **Teach** me to **do** yòur **will**
for **you,** O **Lord,** are mý **God.***
Let your good **spir**ìt **guide** me
in **ways** that are **level** ánd **smooth.**

¹¹ For your **name's** sake, **Lord,** sàve my **life;*****
in your **justice** save my **soul** from **dís**tress.
Give **praise** to the **Fathèr Almighty,**
to his **Son,** Jesus **Christ,** thé **Lord,**
to the **Spir**it who **dwells** in òur **hearts,**
both **now** and for **ever. Ámen.**

*Repeat C + D
** Repeat D
***Omit B + C

Text; Psalm 143:1-11; The Grail
Music: Joseph Gelineau, SJ
© 1963, 1993, The Grail, GIA Publications, Inc., agent

191 Psalm 145: The Lord Is Near

Antiphon I (St. 1.2.5)

The Lord is near to all who call on him.

Text: *Lectionary for Mass,* © 1969, 1981, ICEL
Music: Robert J. Batastini, © 1995, GIA Publications, Inc.

Antiphon II (St. 3.4.5 or 2.4.5)

The hand of the Lord feeds us: he an-swers all our needs.

Text: *Lectionary for Mass,* © 1969, 1981, ICEL
Music: Columba Kelly, OSB, © 1975, GIA Publications, Inc.

Verses

1. I will bless you day after day
   and praise your name for ever.
   You are great, Lord, highly to be praised,
   your greatness cannot be measured.

2. You are kind and full of compassion,
   slow to anger, abounding in love.
   How good you are, Lord, to all,
   compassionate to all your creatures.

3. All your creatures shall thank you, O Lord,
   and your friends shall repeat their blessing.
   They shall speak of the glory of your reign
   and declare your might, O God.

4. The eyes of all creatures look to you
   and you give them their food in due season.
   You open wide your hand,
   grant the desires of all who live.

5. You are just in all your ways
   and loving in all your deeds.
   You are close to all who call you,
   who call on you from their hearts.

Text: Psalm 145:2-3, 8-9, 10-11, 15-16, 17-18; © 1963, 1993, The Grail, GIA Publications, Inc., agent

192 Psalm 145: I Will Praise Your Name for Ever

Refrain

I will praise your name for ev - er, my King and my God.

Text: *Lectionary for Mass,* © 1969, 1981, ICEL
Music: Leon Roberts, © 1987, GIA Publications, Inc.

Verses

1. I will give you glory, O God my king,
   I will bless your name for ever.
   I will bless you day after day
   and praise your name for ever.

3. All your creatures shall thank you, O Lord,
   and your friends shall repeat their blessing.
   They shall speak of the glory of your reign
   and declare your might, O God.

2. You are kind and full of compassion,
   slow to anger, abounding in love.
   How good you are, Lord, to all,
   compassionate to all your creatures.

4. You are faithful in all your words
   and loving in all your deeds.
   You support all those who are falling
   and raise up all who are bowed down.

Text: Psalm 145:1-2, 8-9, 10-11, 13-14; © 1963, 1993, The Grail, GIA Publications, Inc., agent

Psalm 145: I Will Praise Your Name   193

Refrain

I will praise your name, my King and my God.
I will praise your name, my King and my God.

Verses

1. I will give you glory, my God above, and I will bless your name for ever.
   Ev'ry day I will bless and praise your name for ever.

2. The Lord is full of grace and mercy, who is kind and slow to anger.
   God is good in ev'ry way, and full of compassion.

3. Let all your works give you thanks, O Lord,
   and let all the faithful bless you.
   Let them speak of your might, O Lord, the glory of your kingdom.

4. The Lord is faithful in word and deed,
   and always near, his name is holy.
   Lifting up all those who fall, God raises up the lowly.

Text: Psalm 145:1-2, 8-9, 10-11, 13b-14; David Haas
Music: David Haas
© 1983, GIA Publications, Inc.

194 Psalm 145: I Will Praise Your Name

Antiphon (St. 2.3.4 or 1.2.3.5)

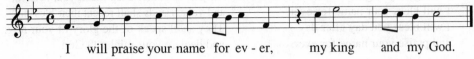

I will praise your name for ev - er, my king and my God.

Text: *Lectionary for Mass*, © 1969, 1981, ICEL
Music: J. Robert Carroll, © 1975, GIA Publications, Inc.

Verses

1. I will give you glory, O God my king,
   I will bless your name for ever.
   I will bless you day after day
   and praise your name for ever.

2. You are kind and full of compassion,
   slow to anger, abounding in love.
   How good you are, Lord, to all,
   compassionate to all your creatures.

3. All your creatures shall thank you, O Lord,
   and your friends shall repeat their blessing.
   They shall speak of the glory of your reign
   and declare your might, O God.

4. To make known to all your mighty deeds
   and the glorious splendor of your reign.
   Yours is an everlasting kingdom;
   your rule lasts from age to age.

5. You are faithful in all your words
   and loving in all your deeds.
   You support all those who are falling
   and raise up all who are bowed down.

Text: Psalm 145:1-2, 8-9, 10-11, 12-13, 13-14; © 1963, 1993, The Grail, GIA Publications, Inc., agent

195 Psalm 146: O Lord, Come and Save Us

Antiphon I

O Lord, come and save us.

Text: *Lectionary for Mass*, © 1969, 1981, ICEL
Music: Robert LeBlanc, © 1975, GIA Publications, Inc.

Antiphon II

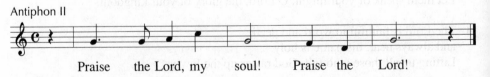

Praise the Lord, my soul! Praise the Lord!

Text: *Lectionary for Mass*, © 1969, 1981, ICEL
Music: Richard Proulx, © 1975, GIA Publications, Inc.

Verses

1. It is the Lord who keeps faith for ever,
   who is just to those who are oppressed.
   It is God who gives bread to the hungry,
   the Lord, who sets prisoners free.

2. The Lord who gives sight to the blind,
   who raises up those who are bowed down,
   the Lord, who protects the stranger
   and upholds the widow and orphan.

3. It is the Lord who loves the just
   but thwarts the path of the wicked.
   The Lord will reign for ever,
   Zion's God, from age to age.

Text: Psalm 146:6-7, 8-9, 9-10; © 1963, 1993, The Grail, GIA Publications, Inc., agent

Psalm 146: Happy the Poor 196

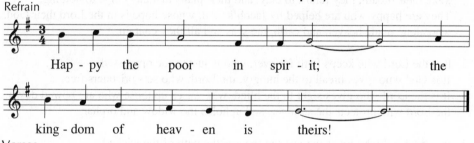

Refrain

Hap - py the poor in spir - it; the
king - dom of heav - en is theirs!

Verses

1. It is the Lord who keeps faith for ever,
   who is just to those who are oppressed.
   It is God who gives bread to the hungry,
   the Lord, who sets prisoners free.

2. The Lord who gives sight to the blind,
   who raises up those who are bowed down,
   It is the Lord who loves the just,
   the Lord, who protects the stranger.

3. The Lord upholds the widow and orphan,
   but thwarts the path of the wicked.
   The Lord will reign for ever,
   Zion's God, from age to age.

Text: Psalm 146:6-7, 8-9, 9-10; © 1963, 1993, The Grail, GIA Publications, Inc., agent; refrain trans. © 1969, ICEL
Music: Michel Guimont, © 1994, GIA Publications, Inc.

197   Psalm 146: I Will Praise the Lord

Refrain

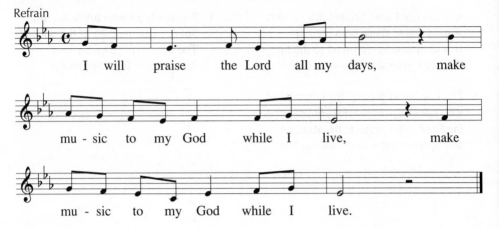

I will praise the Lord all my days, make mu-sic to my God while I live, make mu-sic to my God while I live.

Verses

1. Put no trust in the powerful, mere mortals in whom there is no help.
   Take their breath, they return to clay, and their plans that day come to nothing.
   They are happy who are helped by Jacob's God, whose hope is in the Lord their God,
   who alone made heaven and earth, the seas and all they contain.

2. It is the Lord who keeps faith for ever, who is just to the oppressed.
   It is God who gives bread to the hungry, the Lord, who sets prisoners free.
   It is the Lord who gives sight to the blind, who raises up those who are bowed down,
   the Lord who protects the stranger, and upholds the widow and orphan.

3. It is the Lord who loves the just but thwarts the path of the wicked.
   The Lord will reign for ever, Zion's God from age to age.

Text: Psalm 146; © 1963, 1993, The Grail, GIA Publications, Inc., agent
Tune: Michael Joncas, © 1990, GIA Publications, Inc.

198   Psalm 147: Praise the Lord

Refrain

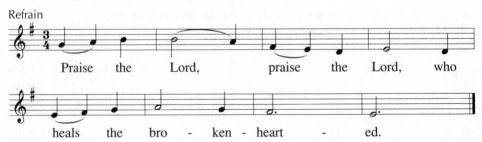

Praise the Lord, praise the Lord, who heals the bro - ken - heart - ed.

Verses

1. Sing praise to the Lord who is good;
   sing to our God who is loving:
   to God our praise is due.
   The Lord builds up Jerusalem
   and brings back Israel's exiles.

2. God heals the broken-hearted,
   and binds up all their wounds.
   God fixes the number of the stars;
   and calls each one by its name.

3. Our Lord is great and almighty;
   God's wisdom can never be measured.
   The Lord raises the lowly;
   and humbles the wicked to the dust.

Text: Psalm 147:1-2, 3-4, 5-6; © 1963, 1993, The Grail, GIA Publications, Inc., agent; refrain trans. © 1969, ICEL
Music: Michel Guimont, © 1995, GIA Publications, Inc.

Psalm 147: Praise the Lord   199

Antiphon

Praise the Lord, Je - ru - sa - lem.

Text: *Lectionary for Mass,* © 1969, 1981, ICEL
Music: Chrysogonus Waddell, OCSO, © 1986, GIA Publications, Inc.

Verses

1. O praise the Lord, Jerusalem!
   Zion, praise your God!
   God has strengthened the bars of your gates,
   and has blessed the children within you.

2. Has established peace on your borders,
   and feeds you with finest wheat.
   God sends out word to the earth
   and swiftly runs the command.

3. God makes his word known to Jacob,
   to Israel his laws and decrees.
   God has not dealt thus with other
     nations;
   has not taught them divine decrees.

Text: Psalm 147:12-13, 14-15, 19-20; © 1963, 1993, The Grail, GIA Publications, Inc., agent

200 Psalm 150: Praise God in This Holy Dwelling

Al-le - lu - ia, al - le-lu - ia, al-le-lu - ia.

1. Praise God in this ho - ly dwell - ing; Praise God on the
2. Praise God with the blast of trum - pet; Bring praise now with
3. Praise God with re - sound-ing cym - bals; With cym - bals that
4. Praise God, the al - might - y Fa - ther; Praise Christ, his be -

might - y throne; Prais - ing for all won - der - ful
lyre and harp; Prais - ing with the tim - brel and
crash, give praise; O let ev - 'ry - thing that has
lov - ed Son; Give praise to the Spir - it of

deeds; Sing praise to our sov - 'reign maj - es - ty.
dance; With the gen-tle sound of string and reed.
breath, Let all liv-ing crea - tures praise the Lord.
love; For ev - er the Tri - une God be praised.

Al - le - lu - ia, al - le - lu - ia,

1.-3.
al - le - lu - ia.

4.
lu - ia.

Text: Psalm 150:1-2, 3-4, 5-6; adapt. by Omer Westendorf
Music: Jan M. Vermulst; arr. by Charles G. Frischmann
© 1964, World Library Publications, Inc.

Exodus 15: Let Us Sing to the Lord 201

Refrain
with vigor

Let us sing to the Lord; Let us sing to the Lord; he has cov-ered him-self in glo-ry; he has cov-ered him-self in glo-ry!

Verses

1. I will sing to the Lord, for he is gloriously triumphant;
   horse and chariot he has cast into the sea.
   My strength and my courage is the Lord,
   and he has been my savior.
   He is my God, I praise him;
   the God of my father, I extol him.

2. The Lord is a warrior, Lord is his name!
   Pharaoh's chariots and army he hurled into the sea.
   At a breath of your anger the waters piled up,
   the flowing waters stood like a mound,
   the flood waters congealed in the midst of the sea.

3. The enemy boasted, "I will pursue and overtake them;
   I will divide the spoils and have my fill of them;
   I will draw my sword; my hand shall despoil them!
   When your wind blew, the sea covered them;
   like lead they sank in the mighty waters.

4. Who is like to you among the gods, O Lord?
   Who is like to you, magnificent in holiness?
   O terrible in renown, worker of wonders,
   when you stretched out your right hand,
   the earth swallowed them!

5. In your mercy you led the people you redeemed;
   in your strength you guided them to your holy dwelling.
   And you brought them in and planted them
   on the mountain of your inheritance—
   the place where you made your seat, O Lord,
   the sanctuary, O Lord, which your hands established.
   The Lord shall reign for ever and ever.

6. Glory to the Father, and to the Son,
   and to the Holy Spirit.
   As it was in the beginning,
   is now and will be for ever. Amen.

Text: Exodus 15, *New American Bible*, © 1970, Confraternity of Christian Doctrine
Music: Howard Hughes, SM, ©1979, 1988, GIA Publications, Inc.

202 Exodus 15: Song at the Sea

Refrain

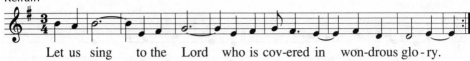

Let us sing to the Lord who is cov-ered in won-drous glo-ry.

Verses

1. I will sing to the Lord, in glory triumphant;
   horse and rider are thrown to the sea.
   God of strength, of song, of salvation, God of mine, hear these praises.

2. My God is a warrior whose name is "The Lord."
   Pharoah's army is thrown to the sea.
   Your right hand is magnificent in pow'r,
   your right hand has crushed the enemy.

3. In your mercy you led the people you redeemed.
   You brought them to your sacred home.
   There you will plant them on the mountain that is yours.
   The Lord shall reign for ever!

Text: Exodus 15; Niamh O'Kelly-Fischer
Music: Niamh O'Kelly-Fischer
© 1992, GIA Publications, Inc.

203 1Chronicles 29: We Praise Your Glorious Name

Refrain

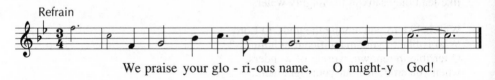

We praise your glo - ri-ous name, O might-y God!

Text: *Lectionary for Mass,* © 1969, ICEL
Music: Richard Proulx, © 1975, GIA Publications, Inc.

Verses

1. Blessed are you, O Lord,
   the God of Israel our father,
   for ever, for ages unending.

2. Yours, Lord, are greatness and power,
   and splendor, triumph and glory.
   All is yours, in heaven and on earth.

3. Yours, O Lord, is the kingdom,
   you are supreme over all.
   Both honor and riches come from you.

4. You are the ruler of all,
   from your hand come strength and power,
   from your hand come greatness and might.

Text: 1 Chronicles 29:10, 11, 11-12, 12; © 1963, The Grail, GIA Publications, Inc., agent

Isaiah 12: You Will Draw Water 204

Refrain

You will draw wa - ter joy - ful - ly

from the springs of sal - va - tion.

Verses

1. Truly, God is my salvation, I trust, I shall not fear.
   For the Lord is my strength, my song, he became my savior.
   With joy you will draw water from the wells of salvation.

2. Give thanks to the Lord, give praise to his name!
   Make his mighty deeds known to the peoples!
   Declare the greatness of his name.
   Sing a psalm to the Lord!

3. For he has done glorious deeds,
   make them known to all the earth!
   People of Zion, sing and shout for joy,
   for great in your midst is the Holy One of Israel.

Text: Isaiah 12:2-3, 4, 5-6; © 1963, The Grail, GIA Publications, Inc., agent; refrain trans. © 1969, ICEL
Music: Michel Guimont, © 1995, GIA Publications, Inc.

205 Isaiah 12: Cry Out with Joy and Gladness

Antiphon

Cry out with joy and glad - ness: for a-mong you is the great and Ho-ly One of Is - ra - el.

Text: *Lectionary for Mass*, © 1969, ICEL
Music: Robert J. Batastini, © 1975, GIA Publications, Inc.

Verses

1. Truly, God is my salvation,
   I trust, I shall not fear.

2. For the Lord is my strength, my song,
   he became my savior.

3. With joy you will draw water
   from the wells of salvation.

4. Give thanks to the Lord, give praise to his name!
   Make his mighty deeds known to the peoples!

5. Declare the greatness of his name,
   sing a psalm to the Lord!

6. For he has done glorious deeds,
   make them known to all the earth!

7. People of Zion, sing and shout for joy
   for great in your midst is the Holy One of Israel.

Text: Isaiah 12:2-3, 4-5, 5-6; © 1963, The Grail, GIA Publications, Inc., agent

Daniel 3:52-57 / Song of the Three Children 206

Cantor:

1. You are blest, Lord God of our fa - thers.
2. Blest be your glo - ri - ous ho - ly name.
3. You are blest in the tem - ple of your glo - ry.
4. You are blest on the throne of your king - dom.
5. You are blest who gaze in - to the depths.
6. You are blest who sit a - bove the cher - u - bim.
7. You are blest in the firm - a - ment of heav - en.
8. You are blest, Lord God, in all your works.

All:

To you glo - ry and praise for ev - er - more.

Text: Daniel 2:52-57; The Grail
Music: Joseph Gelineau, SJ
© 1963, The Grail, GIA Publications, Inc., agent

207 Daniel 3:57-88 / Song of the Three Children

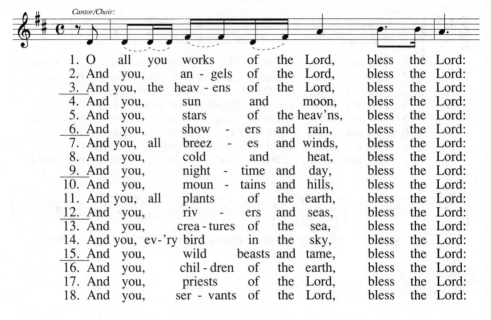

Cantor/Choir:

1. O all you works of the Lord, bless the Lord:
2. And you, an - gels of the Lord, bless the Lord:
3. And you, the heav - ens of the Lord, bless the Lord:
4. And you, sun and moon, bless the Lord:
5. And you, stars of the heav'ns, bless the Lord:
6. And you, show - ers and rain, bless the Lord:
7. And you, all breez - es and winds, bless the Lord:
8. And you, cold and heat, bless the Lord:
9. And you, night - time and day, bless the Lord:
10. And you, moun - tains and hills, bless the Lord:
11. And you, all plants of the earth, bless the Lord:
12. And you, riv - ers and seas, bless the Lord:
13. And you, crea - tures of the sea, bless the Lord:
14. And you, ev-'ry bird in the sky, bless the Lord:
15. And you, wild beasts and tame, bless the Lord:
16. And you, chil - dren of the earth, bless the Lord:
17. And you, priests of the Lord, bless the Lord:
18. And you, ser - vants of the Lord, bless the Lord:

All:

To God be high-est glo - ry and praise for ev - er.

Text: Daniel 3:57-88; The Grail
Music: A. Gregory Murray, OSB
© 1963, The Grail, GIA Publications, Inc., agent

208 Daniel 3:57-87 / Benedicite

Praise and ex - alt him for ev - er, O

praise and ex - alt him for ev - er.

Verses

1. Bless the Lord, all you works of the Lord,
   angels of the Lord, bless the Lord.

2. Heavens above, bless the Lord,
   waters o'er the heavens, bless the Lord.

3. All you hosts of the Lord, bless the Lord,
   sun and moon, bless the Lord.

4. Stars of heaven, bless the Lord,
   showers and dews, bless the Lord.

5. All you winds, bless the Lord,
   fire and heat, bless the Lord.

6. Cold and chill, bless the Lord,
   dew and rain, bless the Lord.

7. Ice and snow, bless the Lord,
   frost and chill, bless the Lord.

8. Nights and days, bless the Lord,
   light and darkness, bless the Lord.

9. Lightning and clouds, bless the Lord,
   let all the earth, bless the Lord.

10. Mountains and hills, bless the Lord,
    all growing things, bless the Lord.

11. Flowing springs, bless the Lord,
    seas and rivers, bless the Lord.

12. Dolphins and sea creatures, bless the Lord,
    birds of the skies, bless the Lord.

13. All you beasts, wild and tame,
    children of the Lord, bless the Lord.

14. Israel, bless the Lord,
    servants of the Lord, bless the Lord.

15. Souls of the just, bless the Lord,
    humble hearts, bless the Lord.

Text: Daniel 3:57-87, *New American Bible,* © 1970, Confraternity of Christian Doctrine
Music: Robert M. Hutmacher, OFM, © 1984, GIA Publications, Inc.

209 Luke 1:46-55 / Magnificat

Antiphon

My soul re-joic-es, my soul re-joic-es in my God.

Text: Luke 1:46; Robert J. Batastini
Music: Robert J. Batastini
© 1972, GIA Publications, Inc.

Psalm Tone

Music: *Lutheran Worship,* © 1982, Concordia Publishing House

Gelineau Tone

Stanzas 1, 2, 9, 10   Stanzas 3-8

1. My **soul glor**ifies the **Lord**,
   my **spir**it re**joic**es in **Gód**, my **Sav**ior.

2. He **looks** on his **ser**vant
   ìn her **noth**ingness;
   hence**forth** all **ag**es will
   cáll me **bless**ed.

3. The Al**mighty** works **mar**vèls for **me**.
   Holý his **name**!

4. His **mer**cy is from **àge** to **age**,
   on **thóse** who **fear** him.

5. He **puts** forth his **àrm** in **strength**
   and **scat**ters **thé** proud**heart**ed.

6. He **casts** the **might**y fròm their **thrones**
   and **raisés** the **low**ly.

7. He **fills** the **starv**ing wìth good **things**,
   sends the **rich** áway **empty**.

8. He pr**otects** Israèl his **ser**vant,
   remem**bering** his **mer**cy,

9. the **mer**cy **prom**ised tò our **fathers**,
   for **Abra**ham and his **sóns** for **ever**.

10. Praise the **Father**, the **Son**
    and **Hòly Spir**it,
    both **now** and for **ages** un**endíng**. **A**men.

Text: Luke 1:46-55; The Grail
Music: Joseph Gelineau, SJ
© 1963, The Grail, GIA Publications, Inc., agent

Luke 1:46-55 / Magnificat / Holy Is Your Name   210

Refrain

And ho - ly is your name through all gen - er - a-tions! Ev - er - last - ing is your mer-cy to the peo - ple you have cho-sen, and ho - ly is your name.

Verses

1. My soul is filled with joy as I sing to God my savior:
   you have looked upon your servant, you have visited your people.

2. I am lowly as a child, but I know from this day forward
   that my name will be remembered, for all will call me blessed.

3. I proclaim the pow'r of God, you do marvels for your servants;
   though you scatter the proud hearted, and destroy the might of princes.

4. To the hungry you give food, send the rich away empty.
   In your mercy you are mindful of the people you have chosen.

5. In your love you now fulfill what you promised to your people.
   I will praise you Lord, my savior, everlasting is your mercy.

Text: Luke 1:46-55, David Haas
Music: WILD MOUNTAIN THYME, Irregular; Irish traditional; arr. by David Haas
© 1989, GIA Publications, Inc.

211 Luke 1:46-55 / Magnificat

Refrain

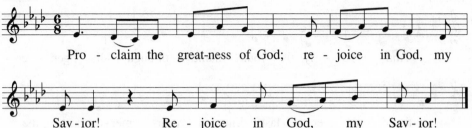

Pro - claim the great-ness of God; re - joice in God, my

Sav - ior! Re - joice in God, my Sav - ior!

Verses

1. For he has favored his lowly one, and all shall call me blessed.
   The almighty has done great things for me, and holy is his name.

2. He favors those who fear his name, in ev'ry generation.
   He has shown the might and strength of his arm,
   and scattered the proud of heart.

3. He has cast the mighty from their thrones, and lifted up the lowly.
   He has filled the hungry with all good gifts, and sent the rich away.

4. He has helped his servant Israel, remembering his mercy.
   He promised his mercy to Abraham and his children for evermore.

Text: Luke 1:46-55; James J. Chepponis
Music: James J. Chepponis
© 1980, GIA Publications, Inc.

Luke 2:29-32 / Canticle of Simeon   212

Antiphon

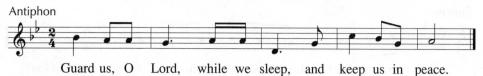

Guard us, O Lord, while we sleep, and keep us in peace.

Text: The Grail
Music: Guy Weitz and A. Gregory Murray, OSB
© 1963, The Grail, GIA Publications, Inc., agent

Psalm Tone

Music: Psalm tone 3-b; acc. by Richard Proulx, © 1975, GIA Publications, Inc.

Gelineau Tone

Omit for 3-line stanza

1. At **last** all-**pow**erful **Mas**ter,
   you give **leave** to your **sèr**vant to go
   in **peace**, ac**cord**ing to yóur **prom**ise.

2. For my **eyes** have **sèen** your sal**va**tion
   which **you** have pre**pared** for áll **na**tions,
   the **light** to en**lìght**en the **Gen**tiles
   and give **glo**ry to **Is**rael, yóur **peo**ple.

3. Give **praise** to the **Fà**ther Al**might**y,
   to his **Son**, Jesus **Chríst**, the **Lord**,
   to the **Spir**it who **dwèlls** in our **hearts**,
   both **now** and for **evér**. **Amen**.

Text: Luke 2:29-32; The Grail
Music: Joseph Gelineau
© 1963, The Grail, GIA Publications, Inc., agent

213 Revelation 19:1-7

Antiphon

All pow'r is yours, Lord God, our might-y King, al - le - lu - ia!

Refrain I

Al - le - lu - ia, al - le - lu - ia!

Verse   Refrain II

Al - le - lu - ia!

Verse   Refrain I

Al - le - lu - ia, al - le - lu - ia!

1. Salvation, glory and pòwer to our Gód: (Alleluia!)
   his judgements are hònest and trúe. (Alleluia, alleluia!)

2. Sing praise to our God, àll you his sérvants, (Alleluia!)
   all who worship him reverently, greàt and smáll. (Alleluia, alleluia!)

3. The Lord our all-powerful Gòd is Kíng; (Alleluia!)
   let us rejoice, sing pràise, and give him glóry. (Alleluia, alleluia!)

4. The wedding feast of the Làmb has begún, (Alleluia!)
   and his bride is prepàred to wélcome him. (Alleluia, alleluia!)

5. Glory to the Father, and to the Sòn, and to the Holy Spírit, (Alleluia!)
   as it was in the beginning, is now, and will be for èver. Amén. (Alleluia, alleluia!)

Text: Revelation 19:1-7; Howard Hughes, SM
Music: Howard Hughes, SM
© 1979, GIA Publications, Inc.

Christian Initiation of Adults

The passage of an adult into the Christian community takes place over an extended period of time. The members of the local church, the catechists and sponsors, the clergy and the diocesan bishop take part in the journey from inquiry through the catechumenate to baptism, confirmation and eucharist. The candidates are invited by example to pray, reflect on the scriptures, to fast and to join in the community's practice of charity. They are to learn the way of Jesus from the members of the church.

This journey of the candidates and community is marked by liturgical rites; thus the community publicly acknowledges, encourages and strengthens the candidates. The first of these is the rite of becoming catechumens. It concludes the sometimes lengthy period during which those who have come to ask about the way of the church and the life of a Christian have heard the gospel proclaimed and seen it practiced. Those who then feel called to walk in this way of Christ's church ask to begin the journey toward baptism. If the church judges the inquirers ready, they are accepted into the order of catechumens.

Those who have entered the catechumenate are already part of the household of Christ. During this time the catechumens are to hear and reflect on God's word, to learn the teachings and practices of the church, to become gradually accustomed to the ways of prayer and discipline in the church, to observe and to join in the good works of Christians. Ordinarily the catechumens are present on Sunday for the liturgy of the word and may be dismissed after the homily—to continue prayer and study with their catechists—since they cannot join in the eucharist.

Rites of exorcism and blessing may be celebrated during the catechumenate. Through such rites the church prays that the catechumens will be purified, strengthened against all evil and thus eagerly grow in faith and good works. The very presence of the catechumens—at the Sunday liturgy, in these special rites and in everyday life—is itself a source of strength and blessing to the faithful.

Each year as Lent begins, the bishop, with the help of the local pastor and others involved with the catechumens, is to call those catechumens who are judged ready to prepare themselves for baptism at the Easter Vigil. Thus the catechumens become the "elect", the chosen, and for the forty days of Lent they make preparations: praying, fasting, doing good works. All the faithful join them in this. On several Sundays in Lent the rites of scrutiny take place when the assembled church prays over the elect. During Lent also the catechumens may publicly receive the words of the church's profession of faith (creed) and the Lord's Prayer.

Good Friday and Holy Saturday are days of prayer, fasting and preparation for the rites of the Easter Vigil. On the night between Saturday and Easter Sunday, the church assembles to keep vigil and listen to many readings from scripture. Then the catechumens are called forward for baptism and confirmation. These rites are found in the Easter Vigil.

The newly baptized, now called neophytes, take a special place in the Sunday eucharist throughout the fifty days of Eastertime. This is a time for their full incorporation into the local community.

All of these stages of initiation take place in the midst of the community. In various rites, the faithful affirm their support for the catechumens. The daily lives of the faithful show the Christian life to the inquirers and catechumens. In turn, the faithful are strengthened and challenged in their faith by the presence of the catechumens.

Those who seek to belong to the Roman Catholic church and who are already baptized may take some part in the catechumenate but they are not baptized again. Rather, they are received into the full communion of the Roman Catholic Church by a profession of faith.

215 ACCEPTANCE INTO THE ORDER OF CATECHUMENS

INTRODUCTORY RITES
The priest greets the assembly: candidates, sponsors, members of the parish. The candidates are asked what it is that they seek and each replies. After each candidate has responded, one of the following acclamations may be sung by the assembly:
216

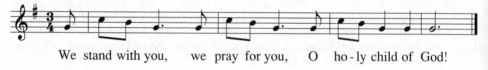

We stand with you,   we pray for you,   O   ho-ly child of God!

Text: David Haas, b.1957
Tune: David Haas, b.1957
© 1988, GIA Publications, Inc.

217

We   praise you,   Lord,   we   praise you, Lord,

we   praise you,   Lord,   and we   bless   you.

Music: Marty Haugen, © 1995, GIA Publications, Inc.

CANDIDATES' FIRST ACCEPTANCE OF THE GOSPEL 218

The priest solemnly asks if the candidates are ready to begin walking this way of the gospel.
The sponsors and all present are asked if they stand ready to assist the candidates as they
strive to know and follow Christ. All respond: **We are.**

SIGNING OF THE CANDIDATES WITH THE CROSS 219

The sign of the cross marks the candidates for their new way of life. The priest signs each on
the forehead saying:

N., receive the cross on your forehead.
It is Christ himself who now strengthens you
with this sign of his love.
Learn now to know him and follow him.

Sponsors and others also sign the candidates. Ears and eyes and other senses may also be
signed. The priest prays that the catechumens may share in the saving power of the cross.

One of the following musical settings with assembly acclamations may be used:

220

Priest: Receive the sign of the cross....

Christ will be your strength! Learn to know and fol-low him.

Music: David Haas, © 1988, GIA Publications, Inc.

221

Refrain I

In the cross of Christ, our glo - ry,

Christ, our sto - ry, Christ, our song.

Refrain II

Glo - ry and praise to you, Lord Je - sus Christ!

Text: Adapt. by Marty Haugen
Music: Marty Haugen
© 1995, GIA Publications, Inc.

222 INVITATION TO THE CELEBRATION OF THE WORD OF GOD

The assembly may go into the church for the liturgy of the word singing the following psalm:

Come, my chil - dren, come to me, and

you will know the fear of the Lord.

I will bless the Lord at all times,
God's song is always on my lips.
In the Lord my soul shall make its boast,
the humble will hear and be glad.

Look to God and shine with joy!
May God free your faces from all shame!
God hears the cry of all the poor,
and saves all who live in their fear.

Glory in the Lord with me,
May God's name always be our joy.
God answered me when I cried,
and freed me from my fear.

Text: Psalm 34; adapted by David Haas
Music: David Haas
© 1988, GIA Publications, Inc.

223 LITURGY OF THE WORD

There may be one or more readings from scripture, together with a responsorial psalm. After the homily, a book containing the scriptures may be given to the new catechumens for their study and prayer throughout the time of the catechumenate.

INTERCESSIONS

All join in prayer for the new catechumens.

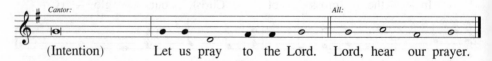

Cantor: *All:*

(Intention)   Let us pray to the Lord.   Lord, hear our prayer.

Music: Byzantine chant

If the eucharist is to be celebrated, the catechumens may be dismissed.

RITES OF THE CATECHUMENATE   224

DISMISSAL OF THE CATECHUMENS

When the catechumens are present at Mass, they are usually dismissed after the homily. Only when they have been baptized are they able to join the faithful in the reception of the eucharist. After their dismissal, the catechumens remain together and are joined by their catechists or others to pray and reflect on the scripture.

One of the following settings may be sung to accompany the dismissal:

225

Text: *Rite of Christian Initiation of Adults*, © 1985, ICEL
Music: Lynn Trapp, © 1991, Morning Star Music Publishers

226

Text: Natalie Sleeth, *Sunday Songbook*
Tune: Natalie Sleeth, *Sunday Songbook*
© 1976, Hinshaw Music, Inc.

227 CELEBRATIONS OF THE WORD OF GOD

On Sundays, after the catechetical sessions, before the liturgical seasons and at other times the catechumens and others may join for liturgy: song, reading of scripture, psalmody, prayer and silence are normally part of such a service.

228 MINOR EXORCISMS

At appropriate times during the catechumenate, the catechists or other ministers may lead the community in prayers of exorcism over the catechumens. These prayers acknowledge the struggle against evil and ask that God strengthen the catechumens.

229 BLESSINGS OF THE CATECHUMENS

Prayers of blessing and the laying on of hands may take place whenever the catechumens gather for instruction of other purposes. Catechists or other ministers ask these blessings over the catechumens.

230 ANOINTINGS AND PRESENTATIONS

During the catechumenate or during Lent, the candidates may be anointed with the oil of catechumens as a sign of strength given for their struggle to live the gospel. At some point in this time they are publicly presented with the church's treasury of prayer and faith, the Our Father and the Creed.

231 RITE OF ELECTION OR ENROLLMENT OF NAMES

On the first Sunday of Lent, the following acclamation, with or without verses, may be sung while or immediately after the candidates sign their names in the book:

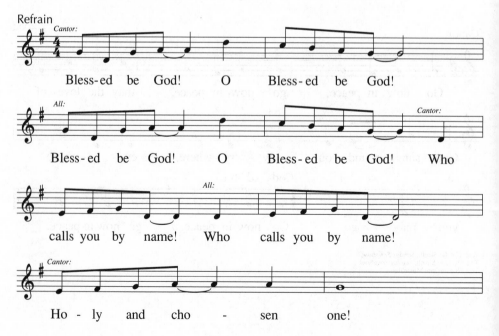

Ho - ly and cho - sen one!

Verses

1. Come, and re - turn to the Lord!
2. Seek to be chil - dren of light!
3. Sing now with all your heart!

Live by the Word of God,
Live in the love of God,
Praise and glo - ry be to our God,

who calls you by name! Who
who calls you by name! Who
who calls you by name! Who

D.C.

calls you by name!
calls you by name!
calls you by name!

Text: David Haas
Music: David Haas
© 1988, GIA Publications, Inc.

232   SCRUTINIES

The scrutinies occur on the third, fourth and fifth Sundays of Lent. The elect are called before the community for exorcism and prayer. This rite may conclude with the following song, sung prior to dismissal of the elect:

Refrain

First Scrutiny: God of all pow-er, foun-tain of grace: O liv-ing
Second Scrutiny: God of all mer-cy, re-store our sight: Lead us from
Third Scrutiny: God of the liv-ing, not of the dead: Raise us to

wa - ter, show your face! God of all pow-er, foun-tain of
dark-ness in - to light! God of all mer-cy, re - store our
life be-yond our death! God of the liv - ing, not of the

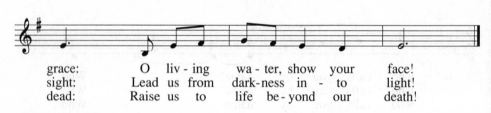

grace: O liv - ing wa - ter, show your face!
sight: Lead us from dark-ness in - to light!
dead: Raise us to life be-yond our death!

Text: David Haas, b.1957
Tune: David Haas, b.1957
© 1988, GIA Publications, Inc.

233   PREPARATORY RITES

Various preparation rites take place during the day on Holy Saturday. These include prayer, recitation of the Creed, and the rite of Ephpheta (opening of ears and mouth).

234   SACRAMENTS OF INITIATION

The sacraments of initiation take place at the Easter Vigil.

235   PERIOD OF MYSTAGOGIA

"Mystagogia" refers to the fifty-day period of postbaptismal celebration when the newly baptized are gradually drawn by the community into the fullness of Christian life and prayer. The newly baptized retain a special place in the assembly and are mentioned in the prayers of intercession. A special celebration, on Pentecost or just before, may mark the conclusion of the whole period of initiation.

The Baptism of Children

Children are baptized in the faith of the church: of parents, godparents, the local parish, the church throughout the world, the saints. Bringing their children for baptism, the parents profess their commitment to make a home where the gospel is lived. And the godparents and all members of the community promise to support the parents in this. Thus the children enter the waters of baptism and so are joined to this people, all baptized into the death and resurrection of Christ.

Baptism is celebrated above all at the Easter Vigil, but also on other Sundays, for Sunday is the Lord's day, the day when the church gathers to proclaim the paschal mystery. Although baptism may take place at the Sunday Mass, it is always to be celebrated in an assembly of members of the church.

RECEPTION OF THE CHILDREN   237

The parents and godparents are welcomed by all. The priest/deacon asks the names of the children and questions the parents about their own expectations and willingness to take on the responsibilities this baptism brings. The godparents are asked if they are ready to assist the parents to become Christian mothers and fathers.

With joy, then, the priest/deacon, the parents and godparents make the sign of the cross on the child's forehead: "I claim you for Christ our Savior by the sign of his cross."

All then go in procession to the place where the scriptures will be read. The following antiphon, or a hymn, may be sung during this procession:

Assembly repeats each phrase after the cantor.

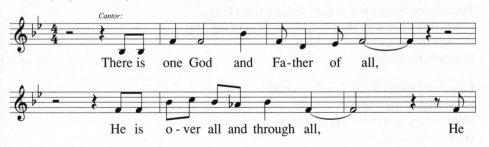

lives in all of us; All of us are one,

u - nit - ed in Christ Je - sus.

Text: ICEL, © 1969
Music: Marty Haugen, © 1995, GIA Publications, Inc.

238   LITURGY OF THE WORD

FIRST READINGS

One or more passages from scripture are read. At the conclusion of each:

   Reader: The word of the Lord.

Assembly: **Thanks be to God.**

RESPONSORIAL PSALM

The following psalm may follow the first reading:

The Lord is my light and my sal - va - tion.

Text: *Lectionary for Mass,* © 1969, ICEL
Music: Anthony E. Jackson, © 1984

The Lord is my light and my help;
whom shall I fear?
The Lord is the stronghold of my life:
before whom shall I shrink?

There is one thing I ask of the Lord, for this I long,
to live in the house of the Lord, all the days of my life,
to savor the sweetness of the Lord,
to behold his temple.

I am sure I shall see the Lord's goodness
in the land of the living.
Hope in him, hold firm and take heart.
Hope in the Lord!

Text: Psalm 27:1, 4, 13-14, © 1963, The Grail, GIA Publications, Inc., agent
Music: Cyril Baker, © The Antilles Episcopal Conference

GOSPEL

239

Before the gospel reading, this acclamation is sung:

Al - le - lu - ia,   al - le - lu - ia,   al - le - lu - ia.

Music: Chant Mode VI; acc. by Richard Proulx, © 1985, GIA Publications, Inc.

During Lent:

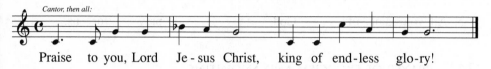

Praise to you, Lord Je - sus Christ, king of end - less glo-ry!

Text: ICEL, © 1969
Music: Frank Schoen, © 1970, GIA Publications, Inc.

Deacon (or priest): The Lord be with you.

> *Assembly:* **And also with you.**

> *Deacon:* A reading from the holy gospel according to **N.**

> *Assembly:* **Glory to you, Lord.**

After the reading:

> *Deacon:* The gospel of the Lord.

> *Assembly:* **Praise to you, Lord Jesus Christ.**

GENERAL INTERCESSIONS

240

All join in prayer for the church, the needs of the world, the poor, the children to be baptized and their parents.

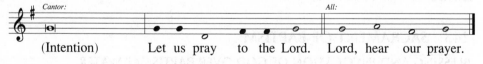

(Intention)   Let us pray   to the Lord. Lord, hear our prayer.

Music: Byzantine chant

241

This prayer concludes with the litany of the saints which may include the patron saints of the children and of the local church.

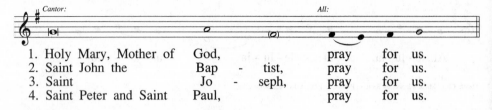

1. Holy Mary, Mother of God,   pray   for   us.
2. Saint John the   Bap - tist,   pray   for   us.
3. Saint   Jo - seph,   pray   for   us.
4. Saint Peter and Saint   Paul,   pray   for   us.

The names of other saints may be added here. The litany concludes:

5. All you saints of   God,   pray   for   us.

242   PRAYER OF EXORCISM AND ANOINTING

The priest/deacon stands before the parents with their infants and prays that God deliver these children from the power of evil. The children may be anointed with the oil of cate-chumens, an anointing which makes them strong for their struggle against evil in their lives or the priest/deacon may lay hands on each child. The priest/deacon lays hands on each child to show the love and concern the Church has for them. If there is a procession to the baptistry, the following may be sung:

We come to you, Lord Je - sus, fill us with your life.

Make us chil-dren of the Fa - ther and one in you.

Music: Ronald Arnatt, © 1984, GIA Publications, Inc.

243   SACRAMENT OF BAPTISM

BLESSING AND INVOCATION OF GOD OVER BAPTISMAL WATER

When all are gathered at the font, the priest/deacon leads a blessing of the water, unless the baptismal water has already been blessed.

RENUNCIATION OF SIN AND PROFESSION OF FAITH

The priest/deacon then questions the parents and godparents, and they make a renunciation of sin and evil and profess their faith. The assembly listens to their responses. The priest/deacon then invites all to give their assent to this profession of faith:

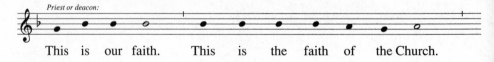

This is our faith. This is the faith of the Church.

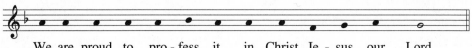

We are proud to pro - fess it, in Christ Je - sus our Lord.

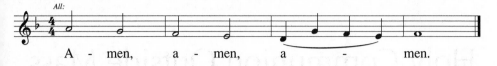

All:

A - men, a - men, a - men.

Music: Danish Amen

BAPTISM 244

One by one, the infants are brought to the font by their parents. There the parents express their desire to have their child baptized in the faith of the church which they have professed. The infant is then immersed in the water three times (or water is poured over the infant's head three times) as the priest/deacon says: "N., I baptize you in the name of the Father, and of the Son, and of the Holy Spirit." All may respond to each baptism with an acclamation.

Cantor, then All:

You have put on Christ, in him you have been bap - tized.

Al - le - lu - ia, al - le - lu - ia.

*May be sung in canon.

Text: ICEL, © 1969
Music: Howard Hughes, SM, © 1977, ICEL

ANOINTING WITH CHRISM 245

The priest/deacon anoints each child on the crown of the head with holy chrism, a mixture of oil and perfume. The word "Christ" means "anointed." The baptized child has been "Christ-ed" and the sweet smell of the anointing reminds all of this.

CLOTHING WITH THE BAPTISMAL GARMENT AND GIVING OF THE CANDLE

The infants are then clothed in baptismal garments and a candle for each of the newly baptized is lighted from the paschal candle.

> Optional | *The priest/deacon may touch the ears and mouth of each child: "May Jesus soon touch your ears to receive his word, and your mouth to proclaim his faith."*

CONCLUSION AND BLESSING

If baptism is celebrated at Mass, the liturgy continues with the eucharist. Otherwise, all process to the altar, carrying lighted candles. The above acclamation may be sung again during this procession. All then pray the Lord's Prayer, the parents are blessed and the liturgy concludes with a hymn of praise and thanksgiving.

Holy Communion Outside Mass

246
When for good reason communion cannot be received at Mass, the faithful may share in the paschal mystery through the liturgy of the word and the reception of holy communion.

INTRODUCTORY RITES
An appropriate hymn or psalm may be sung.

247   GREETING
If the minister is a priest or deacon, the usual form of greeting is used:
Assembly: **And also with you.**

If the minister is not a priest or deacon, another form of greeting may be used:
Assembly: **Blessed be God forever.**

PENITENTIAL RITE
The minister invites silent reflection and repentance. After some silence:
Assembly: **I confess to almighty God,**
and to you, my brothers and sisters,
that I have sinned through my own fault
in my thoughts and in my words,
in what I have done,
and in what I have failed to do;
and I ask blessed Mary, ever virgin,
all the angels and saints,
and you, my brothers and sisters,
to pray for me to the Lord our God.

The forms found at no. 289 may also be used.

CELEBRATION OF THE WORD OF GOD 248

FIRST READINGS

One or more passages from scripture are read. At the conclusion of each:

Reader: The word of the Lord.
Assembly: **Thanks be to God.**

RESPONSORIAL PSALM

The following psalm (or another appropriate psalm) may follow the first reading.

Taste and see the good - ness of the Lord.

Text: *Lectionary for Mass,* © 1969, 1981, ICEL
Music: Richard Proulx, © 1975, GIA Publications, Inc.

I will bless the Lord at all times,
God's praise always on my lips;
in the Lord my soul shall make its boast.
The humble shall hear and be glad.

Glorify the Lord with me.
Together let us praise God's name.
I sought the Lord and was heard;
from all my terrors set free.

Look towards God and be radiant;
let your faces not be abashed.
When the poor cry out the Lord hears them
and rescues them from all their distress.

The angel of the Lord is encamped
around those who fear God, to rescue them.
Taste and see that the Lord is good.
They are happy who seek refuge in God.

Text: Psalm 34:2-3, 4-5, 6-7, 8-9; The Grail
Music: Joseph Gelineau, SJ
© 1963, 1993, The Grail, GIA Publications, Inc., agent

THE GOSPEL 249

Before the gospel reading, this acclamation is sung:

Al - le - lu - ia, al - le - lu - ia, al - le - lu - ia.

Music: Chant Mode VI; acc. by Richard Proulx, © 1985, GIA Publications, Inc.

During Lent:

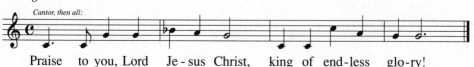

Praise to you, Lord Je - sus Christ, king of end-less glo-ry!

Text: ICEL, © 1969
Music: Frank Schoen, © 1970, GIA Publications, Inc.

Priest or deacon: The Lord be with you.

Assembly: **And also with you.**

Reader: A reading from the holy gospel according to N.

Assembly: **Glory to you, Lord.**

After the reading:

Reader: The gospel of the Lord.

Assembly: **Praise to you, Lord Jesus Christ.**

250 GENERAL INTERCESSIONS

The assembly joins in prayer for the needs of the world, of the poor and of the church.

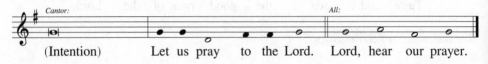

(Intention)   Let us pray   to the Lord.   Lord, hear   our prayer.

Music: Byzantine chant

251 HOLY COMMUNION

The minister invites all to join in the Lord's Prayer, then to exchange a sign of peace. The minister then raises the eucharistic bread and all respond to the invitation.

Assembly: **Lord, I am not worthy to receive you, but only say the word and I shall be healed.**

A psalm or hymn may be sung during communion. Afterwards, there may be a period of silence or the singing of a psalm or hymn. The minister then recites a concluding prayer.

CONCLUDING RITE

All are blessed and dismissed.

Presiding minister: Go in the peace of Christ.

Assembly: **Thanks be to God.**

Reconciliation of Several Penitents

252

The sacrament of penance, also called the sacrament of reconciliation, may be celebrated with one penitent or with many. The latter form, the communal penance service, is a gathering of a few or a large number of Christians. Together they listen to the scriptures, sing psalms and hymns, pray, individually confess their sins and receive absolution, then praise God whose mercy and love are greater than our evil. In the rite of penance, the members of the church confront the struggle that was entered at baptism. There has been failure, evil done and good undone, but the penitent church comes again and again to name and renounce its sins and to return to the way of the Lord.

INTRODUCTORY RITES

253

An appropriate hymn or psalm may be sung.

GREETING

The priest and people greet each other in these or other words:

> *Priest:* Grace, mercy, and peace be with you from God the Father and
> Christ Jesus our Savior.
>
> *Assembly:* **And also with you.**

OPENING PRAYER

After silent prayer, the priest concludes the gathering rite with a solemn prayer.

CELEBRATION OF THE WORD OF GOD

254

FIRST READINGS

One or more passages from scripture are read. At the conclusion of each:

> *Reader:* The word of the Lord.
>
> *Assembly:* **Thanks be to God.**

RESPONSORIAL PSALM

The following psalm may follow the first reading:

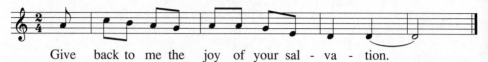

Give back to me the joy of your sal - va - tion.

Text: ICEL, © 1974
Music: Howard Hughes, SM, © 1986, GIA Publications, Inc.

Have mercy on me, God, in your kindness.
In your compassion blot out my offense.
O wash me more and more from my guilt
and cleanse me from my sin.

My offenses truly I know them;
my sin is always before me.
Against you, you alone, have I sinned;
what is evil in your sight I have done.

A pure heart create for me, O God,
Put a steadfast spirit within me.
Do not cast me away from your presence,
nor deprive me of your holy spirit.

Give me again the joy of your help;
with a spirit of fervor sustain me,
that I may teach transgressors your ways
and sinners may return to you.

Text: Psalm 51:3-4, 5-6, 12-13, 14-15
Music: Joseph Gelineau, SJ
© 1963, The Grail, GIA Publications, Inc., agent

255 GOSPEL

Before the gospel reading, this acclamation is sung:

Cantor, then all:

Al - le - lu - ia, al - le - lu - ia, al - le - lu - ia.

Music: Chant Mode VI; acc. by Richard Proulx, © 1985, GIA Publications, Inc.

During Lent:

Cantor, then all:

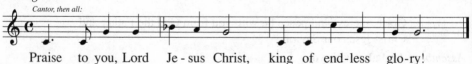

Praise to you, Lord Je - sus Christ, king of end - less glo - ry!

Text: ICEL, © 1969
Music: Frank Schoen, © 1970, GIA Publications, Inc.

Deacon (or priest): The Lord be with you.

Assembly: **And also with you.**

Deacon: A reading from the holy gospel according to N.

Assembly: **Glory to you, Lord.**

After the reading:

Deacon: The gospel of the Lord.

Assembly: **Praise to you, Lord Jesus Christ.**

HOMILY

EXAMINATION OF CONSCIENCE
In silence or through some other manner all reflect on their lives with sorrow for their sins.

SACRAMENT OF PENANCE   256

GENERAL CONFESSION OF SINS
Kneeling (or with another posture that expresses sorrow,) all join in confession. This form may be used:

**I confess to almighty God,
and to you, my brothers and sisters,
that I have sinned through my own fault
in my thoughts and in my words,
in what I have done,
and in what I have failed to do;
and I ask blessed Mary, ever virgin,
all the angels and saints,
and you, my brothers and sisters,
to pray for me to the Lord our God.**

257

Standing, all join in a litany using one of the following responses, or a song asking God's mercy. The Lord's Prayer is then recited or sung (see nos. 303, 464, and 465).

| A | **We pray you, hear us.** |

| B | **Lord, be merciful to me, a sinner.** |

| C | **Lord, have mercy.** |

INDIVIDUAL CONFESSION AND ABSOLUTION   258
One by one the penitents approach the priest confessors. All confess their sins, accept some fitting act of satisfaction and the counsel of the confessor. Then the priest extends his hands over the penitent's head and speaks the prayer of absolution, concluding: "Through the ministry of the church may God give you pardon and peace, and I absolve you from your sins in the name of the Father, and of the Son, and of the Holy Spirit." The penitent responds, "Amen." (Note: On those occasions when general absolution is permitted, the rest of the rite remains the same.)

259 PROCLAMATION OF PRAISE FOR GOD'S MERCY

The priest invites all to give thanks and to show by their lives—and in the life of the whole community—the grace of repentance. A psalm, canticle or hymn may be sung to proclaim God's mercy.

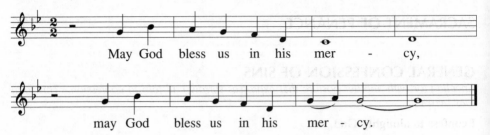

May God bless us in his mer - cy,

may God bless us in his mer - cy.

O God, be gracious and bless us
and let your face shed its light upon us.
So will your ways be known upon earth
and all nations learn your saving help.

Let the nations be glad and exult
for you rule the world with justice.
With fairness you rule the peoples,
you guide the nations on earth.

Let the peoples praise you, O God;
let all the peoples praise you.
May God still give us blessing
till the ends of the earth stand in awe.

Text: Psalm 67:2-3, 5, 6, 6-8; © 1963, 1993, The Grail, GIA Publications, Inc., agent; refrain trans. © 1969, ICEL
Music: Michel Guimont, © 1994, GIA Publications, Inc.

260 CONCLUDING PRAYER OF THANKSGIVING

This prayer is spoken by the priest.

BLESSING AND DISMISSAL

The priest blesses all present and the deacon or other minister dismisses the assembly. All respond:

Thanks be to God.

Marriage

Many rituals of various kinds and origins surround a wedding. These rites of preparation and of celebration are ways for the couple, the families and friends to share
in and to strengthen the making of a marriage. The marriage rite itself is a covenant
made by bride and groom, the consent each gives to and accepts from each other.
The church assembles to witness and bless this union.

LITURGY OF THE WORD

*The Sacrament of Marriage may be celebrated at Mass, or outside of Mass. In either case, the
rite begins with the reading of one or more passages from scripture. The form is similar to that
found in the Order of Mass (nos. 293 to 294).*

SACRAMENT OF MARRIAGE 262

*After the homily, the presiding minister invites the couple to give their consent to each other
freely in the presence of the church. When they have done so, the presiding minister receives
their consent in the name of the church. The wedding rings, a sign of love and fidelity, are
then blessed and exchanged.*

*Mass then continues with the Liturgy of the Eucharist and Communion (nos. 298 to 303).
If Mass is not celebrated, the rite concludes with the General Intercessions, Nuptial Blessing,
Lord's Prayer and Final Blessing.*

Anointing of the Sick

263
The sacrament of anointing is celebrated when a Christian's health is seriously impaired by sickness or old age. If possible, it is celebrated when the sick person is able to take part in the rite. When the sick person is able to receive holy communion, the rite of anointing may be celebrated within the liturgy of the Mass.

Through the anointing with the blessed oil of the sick, the church supports those who struggle against illness or injury and continues the healing work of Christ. The anointing is intended to bring hope and comfort to the one anointed and, to the gathered family and friends, a spirit of support and sharing in the sufferings of our brothers and sisters.

The Mass begins in the usual way; after the greeting the priest welcomes the sick.

264 LITURGY OF THE WORD

FIRST READINGS
One or more passages from scripture are read. At the conclusion of each:

Reader: The word of the Lord.

Assembly: **Thanks be to God.**

RESPONSORIAL PSALM
The following psalm may follow the first reading:

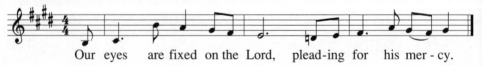

Our eyes are fixed on the Lord, plead-ing for his mer - cy.

To you I have lifted up my eyes,
you who dwell in the heavens;
my eyes, like the eyes of slaves
on the hand of their lords.

Like the eyes of a servant
on the hand of her mistress,
so our eyes are on the Lord our God
till we are shown mercy.

Have mercy on us Lord, have mercy.
We are filled with contempt.
Indeed all too full is our soul
with the scorn of the rich,
(the disdain of the proud.)

Text: Psalm 123:1-2, 3-4; ©1963, 1993, The Grail, GIA Publications, Inc., agent; refrain trans. © 1969, ICEL
Music: Michel Guimont, © 1994, GIA Publication, Inc.

GOSPEL 265

Before the gospel reading, this acclamation is sung:

Al - le - lu - ia, al - le - lu - ia, al - le - lu - ia.

Music: Chant Mode VI; acc. by Richard Proulx, © 1985, GIA Publications, Inc.

During Lent:

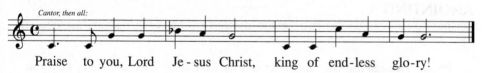

Praise to you, Lord Je - sus Christ, king of end-less glo-ry!

Text: ICEL, © 1969
Music: Frank Schoen, © 1970, GIA Publications, Inc.

Deacon (or priest): The Lord be with you .

 Assembly: **And also with you.**

  Deacon: A reading from the holy gospel according to N.

 Assembly: **Glory to you, Lord.**

After the reading:

  Deacon: The gospel of the Lord.

 Assembly: **Praise to you, Lord Jesus Christ.**

HOMILY

266 LITURGY OF ANOINTING

LITANY

The assembly joins in prayers for the sick and for those who care for them.

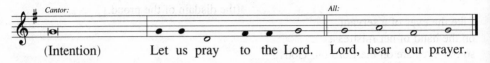

Music: Byzantine chant

LAYING ON OF HANDS

The priest silently lays hands on the head of each sick person in a gesture of prayer, healing and solidarity.

PRAYER OVER THE OIL

If the oil is already blessed, the priest leads a prayer of thanksgiving over it.
After each prayer:

Assembly: **Blessed be God who heals us in Christ.**

If the oil is not blessed, the priest leads the prayer of blessing.

ANOINTING

The priest anoints each sick person on the forehead in a sign of strength and soothing comfort.

> *Priest:* Through this holy anointing may the Lord in his love and mercy help you with the grace of the Holy Spirit.

Assembly: **Amen.**

The priest anoints the hands of each sick person.

> *Priest:* May the Lord who frees you from sin save you and raise you up.

Assembly: **Amen.**

The priest may anoint other parts of the body.

267 PRAYER AFTER ANOINTING

The priest prays for those who have been anointed. Then the liturgy of the eucharist is celebrated with special prayers for the sick.

[If the rite of anointing is celebrated outside of Mass, the liturgy begins with the greeting, rite of sprinkling and penitential rite. After the scripture readings and homily, the liturgy of anointing is celebrated as above. Then the Lord's Prayer is recited or sung and the rite may conclude with holy communion.]

Funeral Mass

268

The rites which surround the death of a Christian extend from the Viaticum (last communion) and final prayers before death through the wake service and funeral Mass to the burial of the body or ashes. In all of this the community affirms its faith in the communion of saints and the resurrection of the dead. The family and friends are helped in their time of sorrow with prayer and song. Thus they express present grief even as they hold to the church's lasting hope. Following is the rite of the funeral Mass.

INTRODUCTORY RITES

GREETING
269

The priest greets the assembly at the door, using these or similar words.

> *Priest:* The grace and peace of God our Father and the Lord Jesus Christ be with you.
>
> *All:* **And also with you.**

The body is sprinkled with holy water.

SONG

As the procession enters the church, an appropriate song is sung.

OPENING PRAYER
270

At the conclusion of the prayer all respond: **Amen.**

LITURGY OF THE WORD

READINGS
271

One or two passages from scripture are read before the gospel reading. At the conclusion of each:

> *Reader:* The word of the Lord.
>
> *All:* **Thanks be to God.**

272 RESPONSORIAL PSALM

One of the following, or another psalm may follow the first reading.

The Lord is my shep-herd; there is noth-ing I shall want.

Text: *Lectionary for Mass*, © 1969, ICEL
Music: Richard Proulx, © 1975, GIA Publications, Inc.

Lord, you are my shepherd;
there is nothing I shall want.
Fresh and green are the pastures
where you give me repose.
Near restful waters you lead me,
to revive my drooping spirit.

You guide me along the right path;
You are true to your name.
If I should walk in the valley of darkness
no evil would I fear.
You are there with your crook and your staff;
with these you give me comfort.

You have prepared a banquet for me
in the sight of my foes.
My head you have anointed with oil;
my cup is overflowing.

Surely goodness and kindness shall follow me
all the days of my life.
In the Lord's own house shall I dwell
for ever and ever.

Text: Psalm 23; The Grail
Music: Joseph Gelineau, SJ
© 1963, 1993, The Grail, GIA Publications, Inc.

B

Refrain

The Lord is my light and my sal - va - tion, of
whom should I be a - fraid, of whom should I be a - fraid?

The Lord is my light and my help;
whom should I fear?
The Lord is the stronghold of my life;
before whom should I shrink?

There is one thing I ask of the Lord;
for this I long;
to live in the house of the Lord
all the days of my life.

I believe I shall see the goodness of the Lord
in the land of the living;
hope in God, and take heart.
Hope in the Lord!

Text: Psalm 27:1-2, 4, 13-14; David Haas
Music: David Haas
© 1983, GIA Publications, Inc.

GOSPEL   273
Before the gospel one of the following, or another gospel acclamation is sung.

Cantor, then all:

Al - le - lu - ia, al - le - lu - ia, al - le - lu - ia.

Music: Chant Mode VI; acc. by Richard Proulx, © 1985, GIA Publications, Inc.

During Lent:

Cantor, then all:

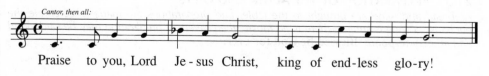

Praise to you, Lord Je - sus Christ, king of end - less glo - ry!

Text: ICEL, © 1969
Music: Frank Schoen, © 1970, GIA Publications, Inc.

The gospel is proclaimed by a deacon or a priest.

Deacon (or priest): The Lord be with you.

   All: **And also with you.**

Deacon (or priest): A reading from the holy gospel according to N.

   All: **Glory to you, Lord.**

After the gospel is proclaimed:

Deacon (or priest): The gospel of the Lord.

   All: **Praise to you, Lord Jesus Christ.**

HOMILY

274 GENERAL INTERCESSIONS

All pray for the Church, the local community, the deceased and those who mourn, using one of the forms below.

Reader: We pray to the Lord. (Let us pray to the Lord.)

   All: **Lord, hear our prayer.**

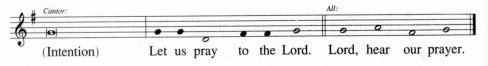

Music: Byzantine chant

Or:

Reader: Lord, in your mercy:

   All: **Hear our prayer.**

The priest concludes the petitions with a prayer and all respond: **Amen.**

LITURGY OF THE EUCHARIST

275 PREPARATION OF THE ALTAR AND GIFTS

As bread and wine are brought to the table, and preparations are made to celebrate the eucharist, a song is sung. If there is no music, the prayers of preparation may be said aloud and all may respond: **Blessed be God for ever.**

The priest then invites everyone to pray.

All: **May the Lord accept the sacrifice at your hands for the praise and glory of his name, for our good, and the good of all his Church.**

PRAYER OVER THE GIFTS
At the conclusion of the prayer over the gifts, all respond: **Amen.**

EUCHARISTIC PRAYER   276
This central prayer of the liturgy begins with the following dialogue:

Priest: The Lord be with you. *Assembly:* And al - so with you.

Priest: Lift up your hearts. *Assembly:* We lift them up to the Lord.

Priest: Let us give thanks to the Lord our God.

Assembly: It is right to give him thanks and praise.

Music: Sacramentary, 1974

The priest continues with the preface, which concludes with the Sanctus.

277 SANCTUS

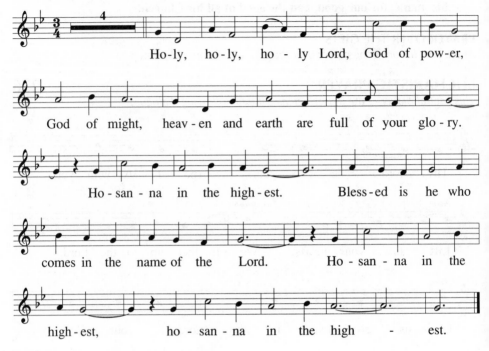

Ho-ly, ho-ly, ho - ly Lord, God of pow-er,
God of might, heav - en and earth are full of your glo - ry.
Ho - san - na in the high - est. Bless-ed is he who
comes in the name of the Lord. Ho - san - na in the
high - est, ho - san - na in the high - est.

Music: *Mass of Creation,* Marty Haugen, © 1984, GIA Publications, Inc.

After the words of institution the priest sings or says: "Let us proclaim the mystery of faith" and all respond with one of the following acclamations:

278 MEMORIAL ACCLAMATIONS

A

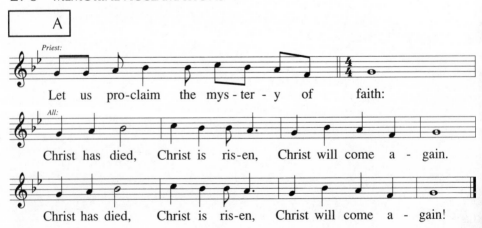

Priest:
Let us pro-claim the mys-ter - y of faith:

All:
Christ has died, Christ is ris-en, Christ will come a - gain.

Christ has died, Christ is ris-en, Christ will come a - gain!

Text: ICEL, © 1973
Music: *Mass of Creation,* Marty Haugen, © 1984, GIA Publications, Inc.

B

Priest:
Let us pro-claim the mys-ter-y of faith:

Cantor:
Dy - ing you de -

Cantor:
stroyed our death, ris - ing you re -

All:
Dy - ing you de - stroyed our death,

stored our life. Lord Je - sus, come in

ris - ing you re - stored our life. Lord

glo - ry.

Je - sus, come in glo - ry.

Text: ICEL, © 1973
Music: *Mass of Creation,* Marty Haugen, ©1990, GIA Publications, Inc.

C

Priest:
Let us pro-claim the mys-ter-y of faith:

All:
When we eat this bread, when we drink this cup, we pro - claim your

death, Lord Je - sus, un - til you come in glo - ry.

Text: ICEL, © 1973
Music: *Mass of Creation,* Marty Haugen, © 1993, GIA Publications, Inc.

D

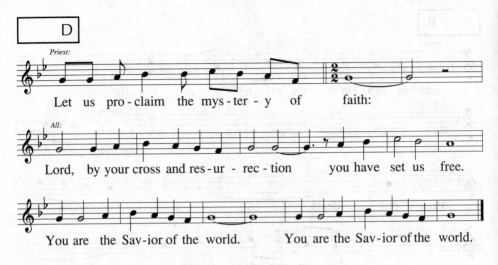

Priest:

Let us pro-claim the mys-ter-y of faith:

All:

Lord, by your cross and res-ur-rec-tion you have set us free.

You are the Sav-ior of the world. You are the Sav-ior of the world.

Text: ICEL, © 1973
Music: *Mass of Creation*, Marty Haugen, © 1993, GIA Publications, Inc.

279   *At the conclusion of the eucharistic prayer the priest sings or says:*

Priest: Through him, with him, in him, in the unity of the Holy Spirit, all glory and
honor is yours, almighty Father, for ever and ever.

All respond:

A - men, a - men, a - men!

A - men, a - men, a - men!

Music: *Mass of Creation*, Marty Haugen, © 1984, GIA Publications, Inc.

280 COMMUNION RITE
The priest invites everyone to sing or say the Lord's Prayer.

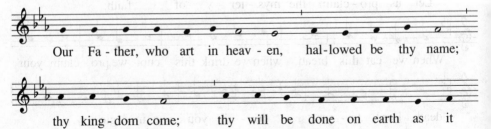

Our Fa-ther, who art in heav-en, hal-lowed be thy name;

thy king-dom come; thy will be done on earth as it

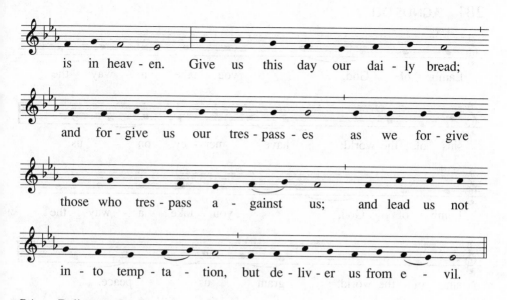

is in heav - en. Give us this day our dai - ly bread;

and for - give us our tres - pass - es as we for - give

those who tres - pass a - gainst us; and lead us not

in - to temp - ta - tion, but de - liv - er us from e - vil.

Priest: Deliver us, Lord...
for the coming of our Savior, Jesus Christ.

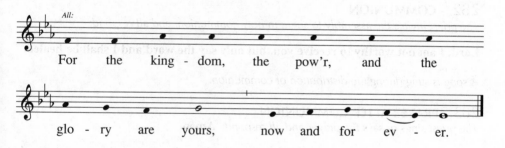

For the king - dom, the pow'r, and the

glo - ry are yours, now and for ev - er.

Music: Traditional chant, adapt. by Robert Snow, 1964; acc. by Robert J. Batastini, © 1975, 1993, GIA Publications, Inc.

SIGN OF PEACE

Following the prayer "Lord Jesus Christ," the priest invites all to exchange a sign of peace.

The peace of the Lord be with you al - ways. And al - so with you.

All exchange a sign of the peace of Christ.

281 AGNUS DEI

Cantor: *All:*

Lamb of God, you take a - way the

sins of the world: have mer - cy on us.

Cantor: *All:*

Lamb of God, you take a - way the

sins of the world: grant us peace.

Music: Agnus Dei XVIII, Vatican Edition; acc. by Robert J. Batastini, © 1993, GIA Publications, Inc.

282 COMMUNION

The priest invites the assembly to share in holy communion, and all respond:

Lord, I am not worthy to receive you, but only say the word and I shall be healed.

A song is sung during the distribution of communion.

283 PRAYER AFTER COMMUNION

The priest sings or says the prayer and all respond: **Amen.**

If the final commendation is to be celebrated at the place of committal, the procession to the place of committal immediately follows the prayer after communion.

FINAL COMMENDATION
The final commendation begins with an invitation to silent prayer.

SONG OF FAREWELL
The following or another appropriate responsory or song may be sung.

SAINTS OF GOD

Refrain

Re - ceive his/her soul, re - ceive his/her soul,

and pre - sent him/her to God the Most High,

and pre - sent him/her to God the Most High.

Verses

1. Saints of God, come to his/her aid!
   Hasten to meet him/her, angels of the Lord!

2. May Christ, who called you, take you to himself;
   may angels lead you to the bosom of Abraham.

3. Eternal rest grant unto him/her, O Lord, and let
   perpetual light shine upon him/her.

Text: *Order of Christian Funerals,* © 1985, ICEL
Music: Steven R. Janco, © 1990, GIA Publications, Inc.

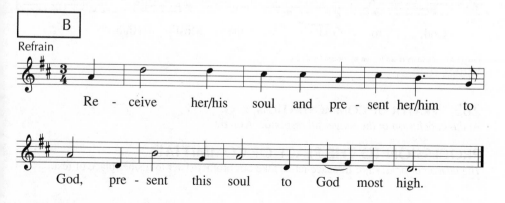

B

Refrain

Re - ceive her/his soul and pre - sent her/him to

God, pre - sent this soul to God most high.

Text: *Order of Christian Funerals;* para. by David Haas
Music: David Haas
© 1990, GIA Publications, Inc.

C

Cantor:

1. Saints of God, come to his/her aid!
2. May Christ who called you, take you to him - self;
3. Give him/her e - ter - nal rest, O Lord,

Come to meet him,/her, an - gels of the
may an - gels lead you to A - bra - ham's
and may your light shine on him/her for

Lord!
side. Re - ceive his/her soul and pre -
ev - er.

sent him/her to God, to God the Most High.

All:

Re - ceive his/her soul and pre - sent him/her to

God, to God the Most High.

Text: *Order of Christian Funerals;* para. by Richard Proulx
Music: Richard Proulx
© 1975, GIA Publications, Inc.

285 PRAYER OF COMMENDATION
At the conclusion of the prayer all respond: **Amen.**

PROCESSION TO THE PLACE OF COMMITTAL
The deacon or priest says: In peace let us take our brother/sister to his/her place of rest.

SONG

286

As the assembly leaves the church, the following or another appropriate responsory or song may be sung.

May the an - gels lead you in - to par - a-dise; may the mar-tyrs come to wel-come you and take you to the ho-ly cit - y, the new and e - ter - nal Je - ru - sa - lem.

Text: *Order of Christian Funerals,* © 1985, ICEL
Music: Steven R. Janco, © 1990, GIA Publications, Inc.

The Order of Mass

287

Each church gathers on the Lord's Day to listen to the Scriptures, to offer prayers, to give thanks and praise to God while recalling God's gifts in creation and saving deeds in Jesus, and to share in holy communion.

In these rites of word and eucharist, the Church keeps Sunday as the Lord's Day, the day of creation and resurrection, the "eighth day" when the fullness of God's kingdom is anticipated. The Mass or eucharistic celebration of the Christian community has rites of gathering, of word, of eucharist, of dismissal. All those who gather constitute the assembly. One member of this assembly who has been ordained to the presbyterate or episcopate—the priesthood—leads the opening and closing prayers and the eucharistic prayer, and presides over the whole assembly. A member ordained to the diaconate may assist, read the gospel, and preach. Other members of the assembly are chosen and trained for various ministries: These are the readers, servers, ushers, musicians, communion ministers. All of these assist the assembly. It is the assembly itself, all those present, that does the liturgy.

The Order of Mass which follows is familiar to all who regularly join in this assembly. It is learned through repetition. This Order of Mass leaves many decisions to the local community and others are determined by the various seasons of the liturgical year.

INTRODUCTORY RITES

The rites which precede the liturgy of the word assist the assembly to gather as a community. They prepare that community to listen to the Scriptures and to celebrate the eucharist together. The procession and entrance song are ways of expressing the unity and spirit of the assembly.

GREETING

All make the sign of the cross.

    Priest: In the name of the Father, and of the Son, and of the Holy Spirit.

    Assembly: **Amen.**

After the sign of the cross one of the greetings is given.

A

Priest: The grace of our Lord Jesus Christ and the love of God and the fellowship of the Holy Spirit be with you all.

Assembly: **And also with you.**

B

Priest: The grace and peace of God our Father and the Lord Jesus Christ be with you.

Assembly: **Blessed be God, the Father of our Lord Jesus Christ.**
or: **And also with you.**

C

Priest: The Lord be with you. (*Bishop:* Peace be with you.)

Assembly: **And also with you.**

BLESSING AND SPRINKLING OF HOLY WATER   288

On Sundays, especially during the season of Easter, instead of the penitential rite below, the blessing and sprinkling of holy water may be done. The following or another appropriate song is sung as the water is sprinkled.

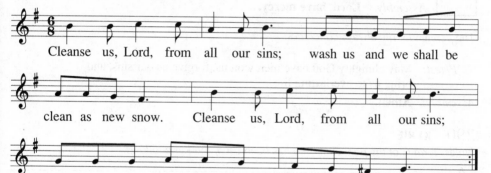

Cleanse us, Lord, from all our sins; wash us and we shall be clean as new snow. Cleanse us, Lord, from all our sins; wash us and we shall be clean as new snow.

Text: Psalm 51:9; Michael Joncas
Music: Michael Joncas
© 1988, GIA Publications, Inc.

PENITENTIAL RITE   289

The priest invites all to be mindful of their sins and of the great mercy of God. After a time of silence, one of the following forms is used.

A

Assembly: **I confess to almighty God,
and to you, my brothers and sisters,
that I have sinned through my own fault
in my thoughts and in my words,
in what I have done,
and in what I have failed to do;
and I ask blessed Mary, ever virgin,
all the angels and saints,
and you, my brothers and sisters,
to pray for me to the Lord our God.**

B

Priest: Lord, we have sinned against you:
Lord, have mercy.

Assembly: **Lord, have mercy.**

Priest: Lord, show us your mercy and love.

Assembly: **And grant us your salvation.**

C

The priest or another minister makes a series of invocations according
to the following pattern.

Priest: (Invocation)
Lord, have mercy.

Assembly: **Lord, have mercy.**

Priest: (Invocation)
Christ, have mercy.

Assembly: **Christ, have mercy.**

Priest: (Invocation)
Lord, have mercy.

Assembly: **Lord, have mercy.**

The penitential rite always concludes:

Priest: May almighty God have mercy on us, forgive us our sins, and
bring us to everlasting life.

Assembly: **Amen.**

290 KYRIE

Unless form C of the penitential rite has been used, the Kyrie follows.

Lord, have mer - cy.   Lord, have mer - cy.

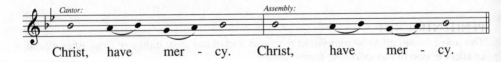

Christ, have mer - cy.   Christ, have mer - cy.

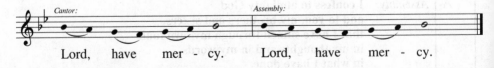

Lord, have mer - cy.   Lord, have mer - cy.

Music: *A Community Mass*, Richard Proulx, © 1971, 1977, GIA Publications, Inc.

GLORIA

The Gloria is omitted during Advent, Lent, and most weekdays.

Glo - ry to God in the high - est, and peace to his peo - ple on earth. Lord God, heav - en - ly King, al - might - y God and Fa - ther, we wor - ship you, we give you thanks, we praise you for your glo - ry.

Choir (Congr. ad lib):

Lord Je - sus Christ, on - ly Son of the Fa - ther, Lord God, Lamb of God, you take a - way the sin of the world: have mer - cy on us; you are seat - ed at the right hand of the Fa - ther: re - ceive our prayer.

All:

For you a - lone are the Ho - ly One, you a - lone are the

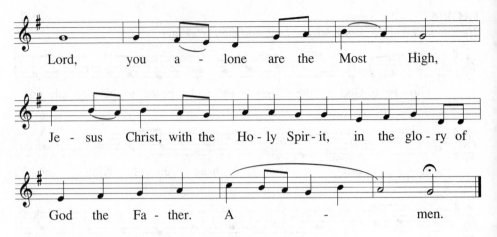

Lord, you a - lone are the Most High,

Je - sus Christ, with the Ho - ly Spir- it, in the glo - ry of

God the Fa - ther. A - men.

Music: *A New Mass for Congregations*, Carroll T. Andrews, © 1970, GIA Publications, Inc.

292 OPENING PRAYER

After the invitation from the priest, all pray for a while. The introductory rites conclude
with the proper opening prayer and the Amen of the assembly.

293 LITURGY OF THE WORD

When the Church assembles, the book containing the Scriptures (Lectionary) is
opened and all listen as the readers and deacon (or priest) read from the places
assigned. The first reading is normally from the Hebrew Scriptures (Old Testament),
the second from the letters of the New Testament, and the third from the Book of
Gospels. Over a three-year cycle, the Church reads through the letters and gospels
and a portion of the Hebrew Scriptures. During the Sundays of Ordinary Time, the
letters and gospels are read in order, each Sunday continuing near the place where
the previous Sunday's readings ended. During Advent/Christmas and Lent/Easter,
the readings are those which are traditional and appropriate to these seasons.

The Church listens to and—through the weeks and years—is shaped by the
Scriptures. Those who have gathered for the Sunday liturgy are to give their full
attention to the words of the reader. A time of silence and reflection follows each of
the two readings. After the first reading, this reflection continues in the singing of
the psalm. A homily, bringing together the Scriptures and the life of the community, follows the gospel. The liturgy of the word concludes with the creed, the dismissal of the catechumens and the prayers of intercession. In the latter, the assembly continues its constant work of recalling and praying for the universal Church
and all those in need.

This reading and hearing of the word—simple things that they are—are the foundation of the liturgical celebration. The public reading of the Scriptures and the rituals which surround this—silence and psalm and acclamation, posture and gesture,
preaching and litany of intercession—gather the Church generation after generation.
They gather and sustain and gradually make of us the image of Christ.

READING I

In conclusion:

> *Reader:* The word of the Lord.
> *Assembly:* **Thanks be to God.**

After a period of silence, the responsorial psalm is sung.

READING II

In conclusion:

> *Reader:* The word of the Lord.
> *Assembly:* **Thanks be to God.**

A time of silence follows the reading.

GOSPEL   294

Before the gospel, an acclamation is sung.

Al - le - lu - ia,   al - le - lu - ia,   al - le - lu - ia.

Music: Chant Mode VI; acc. by Richard Proulx, © 1985, GIA Publications, Inc.

During Lent one of the following acclamations replaces the alleluia.

A

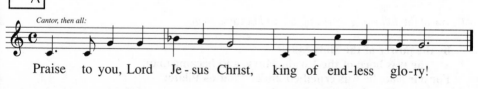

Praise to you, Lord Je - sus Christ, king of end - less glo - ry!

Text: ICEL, © 1969
Music: Frank Schoen, © 1970, GIA Publications, Inc.

Or:

B   **Praise and honor to you, Lord Jesus Christ!**

C   **Glory and praise to you, Lord Jesus Christ!**

D   **Glory to you, Word of God, Lord Jesus Christ!**

Deacon (or priest): The Lord be with you.

    Assembly: **And also with you.**

      Deacon: A reading from the holy gospel according to N.

    Assembly: **Glory to you, Lord.**

After the reading:

      Deacon: The gospel of the Lord.

    Assembly: **Praise to you, Lord Jesus Christ.**

HOMILY

295   PROFESSION OF FAITH

We believe in one God,
   the Father, the Almighty,
   maker of heaven and earth,
   of all that is seen and unseen.

We believe in one Lord, Jesus Christ,
   the only Son of God,
   eternally begotten of the Father,
   God from God, Light from Light,
   true God from true God,
   begotten, not made, one in Being with the Father.
   Through him all things were made.
   For us men and for our salvation he came down from heaven:

All bow at the following words up to: and became man.

   by the power of the Holy Spirit
      he was born of the Virgin Mary, and became man.
   For our sake he was crucified under Pontius Pilate;
      he suffered, died, and was buried.
      On the third day he rose again
      in fulfillment of the Scriptures;
      he ascended into heaven
      and is seated at the right hand of the Father.
   He will come again in glory to judge the living and the dead,
      and his kingdom will have no end.

We believe in the Holy Spirit, the Lord, the giver of life,
   who proceeds from the Father and the Son.
   With the Father and the Son he is worshiped and glorified.
   He has spoken through the Prophets.
   We believe in one holy catholic and apostolic Church.
   We acknowledge one baptism for the forgiveness of sins.
   We look for the resurrection of the dead,
      and the life of the world to come. Amen.

At Masses with children, the Apostles' Creed may be used:

We believe in God, the Father almighty,
   creator of heaven and earth.

We believe in Jesus Christ, his only Son, our Lord.
   He was conceived by the power of the Holy Spirit
       and born of the Virgin Mary.
   He suffered under Pontius Pilate,
       was crucified, died, and was buried.
   He descended to the dead.
   On the third day he arose again.
   He ascended into heaven,
       and is seated at the right hand of the Father.
   He will come again to judge the living and the dead.

We believe in the Holy Spirit,
   the holy catholic Church,
   the communion of saints,
   the forgiveness of sins,
   the resurrection of the body,
   and the life everlasting. Amen.

GENERAL INTERCESSIONS

The people respond to each petition as follows, or according to local practice.

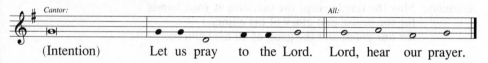

Cantor: (Intention) Let us pray to the Lord. All: Lord, hear our prayer.

Music: Byzantine chant

298 LITURGY OF THE EUCHARIST

To celebrate the eucharist means to give God thanks and praise. When the table has been prepared with the bread and wine, the assembly joins the priest in remembering the gracious gifts of God in creation and God's saving deeds. The center of this is the paschal mystery, the death of our Lord Jesus Christ which destroyed the power of death and his rising which brings us life. That mystery into which we were baptized we proclaim each Sunday at the eucharist. It is the very shape of Christian life. We find this in the simple bread and wine which stir our remembering and draw forth our prayer of thanksgiving. "Fruit of the earth and work of human hands," the bread and wine become our holy communion in the body and blood of the Lord. We eat and drink and so proclaim that we belong to one another and to the Lord.

The members of the assembly quietly prepare themselves even as the table is prepared. The priest then invites all to lift up their hearts and join in the eucharistic prayer. All do this by giving their full attention and by singing the acclamations from the "Holy, holy" to the great "Amen." Then the assembly joins in the Lord's Prayer, the sign of peace and the "Lamb of God" litany which accompanies the breaking of bread. Ministers of communion assist the assembly to share the body and blood of Christ. A time of silence and prayer concludes the liturgy of the eucharist.

PREPARATION OF THE ALTAR AND THE GIFTS

Bread and wine are brought to the table and the deacon or priest prepares these gifts. If there is no music, the prayers may be said aloud, and all may respond: **"Blessed be God for ever."** *The priest then invites all to pray.*

Assembly: **May the Lord accept the sacrifice at your hands**
for the praise and glory of his name,
for our good, and the good of all his Church.

The priest says the prayer over the gifts and all respond: **Amen.**

299 EUCHARISTIC PRAYER

The central prayer of the Mass begins with this greeting and invitation between priest and assembly.

Priest:

Let us give thanks to the Lord our God.

Assembly:

It is right to give him thanks and praise.

Music: Sacramentary, 1974

300

The Sanctus acclamation is sung to conclude the introduction to the eucharistic prayer.

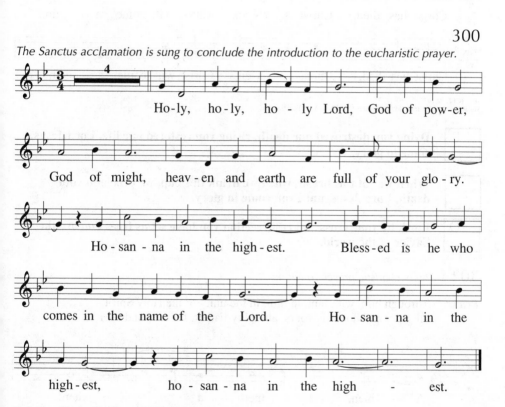

Ho-ly, ho-ly, ho - ly Lord, God of pow-er, God of might, heav - en and earth are full of your glo - ry. Ho - san - na in the high - est. Bless - ed is he who comes in the name of the Lord. Ho - san - na in the high - est, ho - san - na in the high - est.

Music: *Mass of Creation,* Marty Haugen, © 1984, GIA Publications, Inc.

301 *One of the following acclamations follows the priest's invitation: "Let us proclaim the mystery of faith."*

Priest:
Let us pro-claim the mys - ter - y of faith:

All:
Christ has died, Christ is ris-en, Christ will come a - gain.

Christ has died, Christ is ris-en, Christ will come a - gain!

Text: ICEL, © 1973
Music: *Mass of Creation*, Marty Haugen, © 1984, GIA Publications, Inc.

B **Dying you destroyed our death, rising you restored our life. Lord Jesus, come in glory.**

C **When we eat this bread, when we drink this cup, we proclaim your death, Lord Jesus, until you come in glory.**

D **Lord, by your cross and resurrection you have set us free. You are the Savior of the world.**

302 *The eucharistic prayer concludes:*

Priest: Through him, with him, in him, in the unity of the Holy Spirit,
all glory and honor is yours, almighty Father, for ever and ever.

A - men, a - men, a - men!

A - men, a - men, a - men!

Music: *Mass of Creation*, Marty Haugen, © 1984, GIA Publications, Inc.

COMMUNION RITE

303

The priest invites all to join in the Lord's Prayer.

Our Fa - ther, who art in heav - en, hal-lowed be thy name;

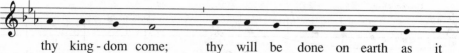

thy king - dom come; thy will be done on earth as it

is in heav - en. Give us this day our dai - ly bread;

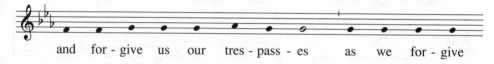

and for - give us our tres - pass - es as we for - give

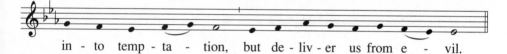

those who tres - pass a - gainst us; and lead us not

in - to temp - ta - tion, but de - liv - er us from e - vil.

Priest: Deliver us, Lord...for the coming of our Savior, Jesus Christ.

All:

For the king - dom, the pow'r, and the

glo - ry are yours, now and for ev - er.

Music: Traditional chant, adapt. by Robert Snow, 1964; acc. by Robert J. Batastini, © 1975, 1993, GIA Publications, Inc.

304

Following the prayer "Lord, Jesus Christ," the priest invites all to exchange the sign of peace.

Priest: The peace of the Lord be with you always.

Assembly: **And also with you.**

All exchange a sign of peace.

305 *Then the eucharistic bread is solemnly broken and the consecrated bread and wine
are prepared for holy communion. The litany "Lamb of God" is sung during the
breaking of the bread.*

Cantor or Choir: *All:*

*Lamb of God, you take a - way the

sins of the world, have mer-cy on us.

Last time

grant us peace.

**Alternates: 1. Emmanuel, 2. Prince of peace, 3. Son of God, 4. Word made flesh,
5. Paschal Lamb, 6. Bread of Life, 7. Lord Jesus Christ, 8. Lord of Love,
9. Christ the Lord, 10. King of kings.*

Music: *Holy Cross Mass;* David Clark Isele, © 1979, GIA Publications, Inc.

306 *The priest then invites all to share in holy communion.*

> *Priest:* This is the Lamb of God...his supper.
>
> *Assembly:* **Lord, I am not worthy to receive you,
> but only say the word and I shall be healed.**

Minister of communion: The body (blood) of Christ.

> *Communicant:* **Amen.**

*A song or psalm is ordinarily sung during communion. After communion, a time of silence
is observed or a song of thanksgiving is sung. The rite concludes with the prayer after communion to which all respond:* **Amen.**

CONCLUDING RITE

The liturgy of word and eucharist ends very simply. There may be announcements of events and concerns for the community, then the priest gives a blessing and the assembly is dismissed.

GREETING AND BLESSING

> *Priest:* The Lord be with you.
> *Assembly:* **And also with you.**

Optional | *When the bishop blesses the people he adds the following:*

> *Bishop:* Blessed be the name of the Lord.
> *Assembly:* **Now and for ever.**

> *Bishop:* Our help is in the name of the Lord.
> *Assembly:* **Who made heaven and earth.**

The blessing may be in a simple or solemn form. All respond to the blessing or to each part of the blessing: **Amen.**

DISMISSAL

The deacon or priest then dismisses the assembly:

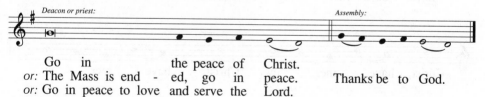

Go in the peace of Christ.
or: The Mass is end - ed, go in peace.
or: Go in peace to love and serve the Lord.

Thanks be to God.

EASTER DISMISSAL

The deacon or priest then dismisses the assembly:

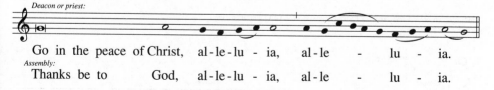

Go in the peace of Christ, al-le-lu - ia, al-le - lu - ia.
Thanks be to God, al-le-lu - ia, al-le - lu - ia.

Setting One

A COMMUNITY MASS

308 KYRIE

Cantor: Lord, have mer - cy. Assembly: Lord, have mer - cy.

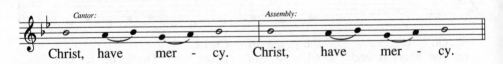

Cantor: Christ, have mer - cy. Assembly: Christ, have mer - cy.

Cantor: Lord, have mer - cy. Assembly: Lord, have mer - cy.

Music: *Litany of the Saints;* adapt. by Richard Proulx, © 1971, GIA Publications, Inc.

Or:

Cantor: Ky - ri - e e - le - i - son. Assembly: Ky - ri - e e - le - i - son.

Cantor: Chri - ste e - le - i - son. Assembly: Chri - ste e - le - i - son.

Ky - ri - e e - le - i - son. Ky - ri - e e - le - i - son.

Music: *Litany of the Saints;* adapt. by Richard Proulx, © 1971, GIA Publications, Inc.

GLORIA
309

Glo - ry to God in the high - est, and peace to his peo - ple on

earth. Lord God, heav-en - ly King, al -

might - y God and Fa - ther, We wor - ship you, we

give you thanks, we praise you for your glo - ry.

Lord Je - sus Christ, on - ly

Son of the Fa - ther, Lord, God,

Lamb of God, you take a - way the sin of the

world: have mer - cy on us;

You are seat - ed at the right hand of the

Fa - ther: re - ceive our pray'r, re -

ceive, re - ceive our pray'r.

For you a- lone are the Ho- ly One, you a-

lone are the Lord, you a - lone are the Most

High, Je - sus Christ with the Ho - ly Spir - it in the

glo - ry of God the Fa - ther. A -

men. A - men.

Music: *A Community Mass,* Richard Proulx, © 1971, 1977, GIA Publications, Inc.

SANCTUS 310

Ho - ly, ho - ly, ho - ly Lord, God of pow-er and might, heav'n and earth are full of your glo - ry. Ho - san - na in the high - est, ho - san-na in the high - est. Blest is he who comes in the name of the Lord. Ho - san - na in the high - est, ho - san-na in the high - est.

Music: *A Community Mass,* by Richard Proulx, © 1971, 1977, GIA Publications, Inc.

MEMORIAL ACCLAMATION 311

Christ has died; Christ is ris - en; Christ will come a - gain.

Text: ICEL, ©1973
Music: *A Community Mass,* Richard Proulx, © 1971, 1977, GIA Publications, Inc.

312 MEMORIAL ACCLAMATION

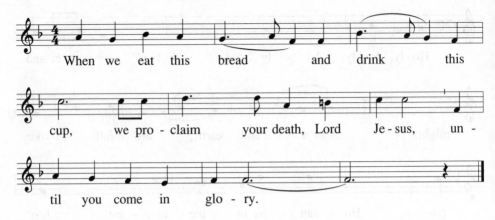

When we eat this bread and drink this cup, we pro - claim your death, Lord Je - sus, un - til you come in glo - ry.

Text: ICEL, © 1973
Music: *A Community Mass,* Richard Proulx, © 1988, GIA Publications, Inc.

313 AMEN

A - men, a - men, a - men.

Music: *A Community Mass,* Richard Proulx, © 1971, 1977, GIA Publications, Inc.

314 AGNUS DEI

Lamb of God, you take a - way the sins of the world: have mer - cy on us.

Lamb of God, you take a - way the sins of the world: grant us peace.

Music: *A Community Mass,* Richard Proulx, © 1971, 1977, GIA Publications, Inc.

Setting Two

MASS OF CREATION

Refrain

If we have died to our-selves in Je-sus, then we shall a - rise to

new life in him. Al - le - lu - ia, al - le - lu - ia!

Verses

1. We are fire and wa - ter, we are sym - bol and
2. In the wa - ter we seek him, in the well-spring of
3. In the fire we seek him, in the hun - gers and
4. In our dy - ing and ris - ing, we shall fol - low where
5. Flow-ing out of the des - ert, roll - ing down from the
6. Rain - ing down from the heav-ens, spring-ing up from the
7. Gift of love and of mer - cy, giv - en free - ly to

sign of grace, we are the mys - t'ry,
all that lives, all who are thirst - y,
pains we bear, hope for the hope - less,
he has gone, pil - grims and lov - ers,
moun - tain side, up from with - in you,
dri - est earth, sim - ple and ho - ly,
all who thirst, gen - tle and yield - ing,

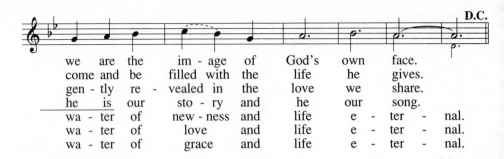

D.C.

we	are	the	im - age	of	God's	own	face.
come	and	be	filled with	the	life	he	gives.
gen - tly	re -	vealed in	the	love	we	share.
he	is	our	sto - ry	and	he	our	song.
wa - ter	of	new - ness	and	life	e - ter - nal.
wa - ter	of	love	and	life	e - ter - nal.
wa - ter	of	grace	and	life	e - ter - nal.

Text: *Mass of Creation*, Marty Haugen
Music: *Mass of Creation*, Marty Haugen
© 1984, GIA Publications, Inc.

316 KYRIE

Refrain

Lord, have mer - cy.   Christ, have mer - cy.

Lord, have mer - cy.

Music: *Mass of Creation*, Marty Haugen, © 1984, GIA Publications, Inc.

317 GLORIA

Refrain

Glo-ry to God in the high - est, and

peace to his peo - ple on earth.

Verses

1. Lord God, heavenly King, almighty God and Father,
   we worship you, we give you thanks,
   we praise you for your glory.

2. Lord Jesus Christ, only Son of the Father,
   Lord God, Lamb of God,
   you take away the sin of the world: have mercy on us;
   you are seated at the right hand of the Father:
   receive our prayer.

3. For you alone are the Holy One,
   you alone are the Lord,
   you alone are the Most High, Jesus Christ,
   with the Holy Spirit,
   in the glory of God, the Father. Amen! Amen!

Music: *Mass of Creation,* Marty Haugen, © 1984, GIA Publications, Inc.

GOSPEL ACCLAMATION   318

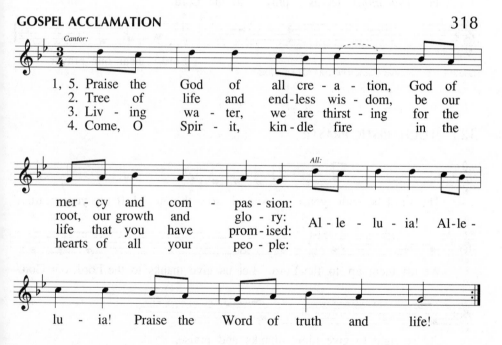

1, 5. Praise the God of all cre - a - tion, God of
2. Tree of life and end-less wis - dom, be our
3. Liv - ing wa - ter, we are thirst - ing for the
4. Come, O Spir - it, kin-dle fire in the

mer - cy and com - pas - sion:
root, our growth and glo - ry: Al - le - lu - ia! Al-le -
life that you have prom-ised:
hearts of all your peo - ple:

lu - ia!   Praise the Word of truth and life!

Text: *Mass of Creation,* Marty Haugen
Music: *Mass of Creation,* Marty Haugen
© 1984, GIA Publications, Inc.

319 LENTEN ACCLAMATION

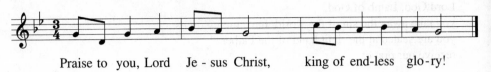

Praise to you, Lord Je - sus Christ, king of end-less glo-ry!

Text: ICEL, © 1969
Music: *Mass of Creation,* Marty Haugen, © 1984, GIA Publications, Inc.

320 GENERAL INTERCESSIONS

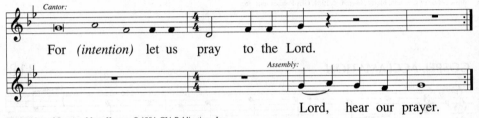

Cantor:
For *(intention)* let us pray to the Lord.

Assembly:
Lord, hear our prayer.

Music: *Mass of Creation,* Marty Haugen, © 1984, GIA Publications, Inc.

321 EUCHARISTIC PRAYER

Priest: The Lord be with you. *Assembly:* And al - so with you. *Priest:* Lift up your hearts.

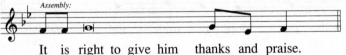

Assembly: We lift them up to the Lord. *Priest:* Let us give thanks to the Lord, our God.

Assembly: It is right to give him thanks and praise.

Music: *Mass of Creation,* Marty Haugen, © 1984, GIA Publications, Inc.

SANCTUS

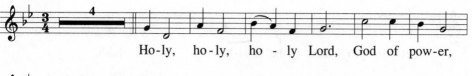

Ho-ly, ho-ly, ho-ly Lord, God of pow-er,

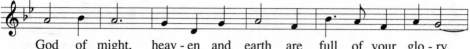

God of might, heav-en and earth are full of your glo-ry.

Ho-san-na in the high-est. Bless-ed is he who

comes in the name of the Lord. Ho-san-na in the

high-est, ho-san-na in the high - est.

Music: *Mass of Creation*, Marty Haugen, © 1984, GIA Publications, Inc.

MEMORIAL ACCLAMATION

323

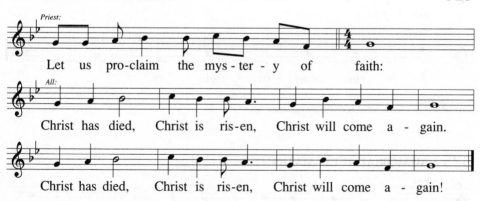

Priest:

Let us pro-claim the mys-ter-y of faith:

All:

Christ has died, Christ is ris-en, Christ will come a - gain.

Christ has died, Christ is ris-en, Christ will come a - gain!

Text: ICEL, © 1973
Music: *Mass of Creation*, Marty Haugen, © 1984, GIA Publications, Inc.

324 MEMORIAL ACCLAMATION

Priest: Let us pro-claim the mys-ter-y of faith:

Cantor: Dy-ing you de-stroyed our death,

Cantor: ris-ing you re-stored our life.

All: Dy-ing you de-stroyed our death, Lord Je-sus, come in glo-ry.

ris-ing you re-stored our life. Lord Je-sus, come in glo-ry.

Text: ICEL, © 1973
Music: *Mass of Creation*, Marty Haugen, © 1990, GIA Publications, Inc.

325 MEMORIAL ACCLAMATION

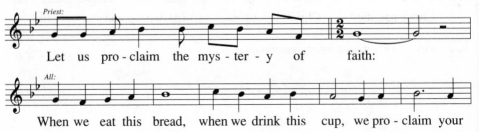

Priest: Let us pro-claim the mys-ter-y of faith:

All: When we eat this bread, when we drink this cup, we pro-claim your

death, Lord Je - sus, un - til you come in glo - ry.

Text: ICEL, © 1973
Music: *Mass of Creation*, Marty Haugen, © 1993, GIA Publications, Inc.

MEMORIAL ACCLAMATION 326

Priest:
Let us pro - claim the mys - ter - y of faith:

All:
Lord, by your cross and res - ur - rec - tion you have set us free.

You are the Sav-ior of the world. You are the Sav-ior of the world.

Text: ICEL, © 1973
Music: *Mass of Creation*, Marty Haugen, © 1993, GIA Publications, Inc.

AMEN 327

A - men, a - men, a - men!

A - men, a - men, a - men!

Music: *Mass of Creation*, Marty Haugen, © 1984, GIA Publications, Inc.

328 LORD'S PRAYER

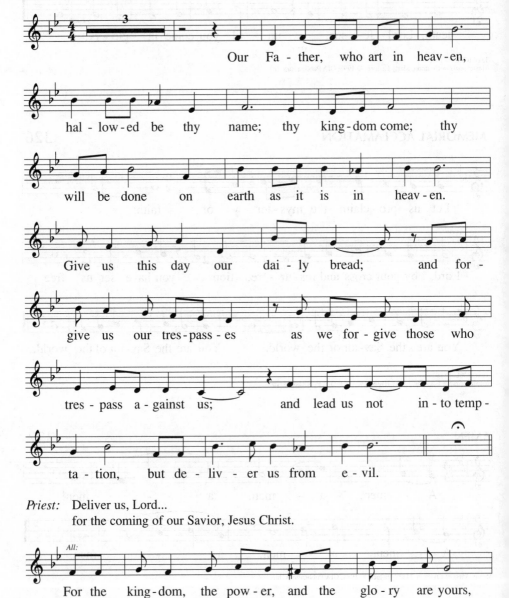

Our Fa - ther, who art in heav - en,
hal - low - ed be thy name; thy king - dom come; thy
will be done on earth as it is in heav - en.
Give us this day our dai - ly bread; and for -
give us our tres - pass - es as we for - give those who
tres - pass a - gainst us; and lead us not in - to temp -
ta - tion, but de - liv - er us from e - vil.

Priest: Deliver us, Lord...
for the coming of our Savior, Jesus Christ.

All:
For the king - dom, the pow - er, and the glo - ry are yours,
now and for ev - er - more. A - men.

Music: *Mass of Creation,* Marty Haugen, © 1984, GIA Publications, Inc.

AGNUS DEI

Cantor:

1. Je-sus, Lamb of
2. Je-sus, Bread of
3. Je-sus, Prince of

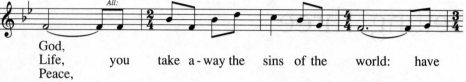

All:

God,
Life, you take a-way the sins of the world: have
Peace,

Last time
Cantor: *All:*

mer-cy on us. Je-sus, Lamb of God; you

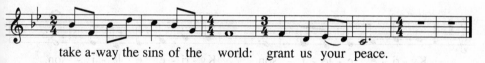

take a-way the sins of the world: grant us your peace.

Music: *Mass of Creation,* Marty Haugen, © 1984, GIA Publications, Inc.

Setting Three

MASS OF LIGHT

330 KYRIE

Ky - ri - e e - le - i - son. Ky - ri - e e - le - i - son.

Chri - ste e - le - i - son. Chri - ste e - le - i - son.

Ky - ri - e e - le - i - son. Ky - ri - e e - le - i - son.

Music: *Mass of Light*, David Haas, © 1988, GIA Publications, Inc.

GLORIA

331

Refrain

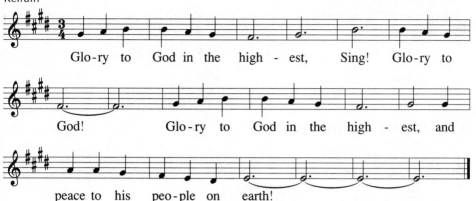

Glo-ry to God in the high - est, Sing! Glo-ry to

God! Glo-ry to God in the high - est, and

peace to his peo-ple on earth!

Verses

1. Lord God, heavenly King,
   almighty God and Father,
   we worship you, we give you thanks,
   we praise you for your glory.

2. Lord Jesus Christ, only Son of the Father,
   Lord God, Lamb of God,
   you take away the sin of the world:
   have mercy on us;
   you are seated at the right hand of the Father:
   receive our prayer.

3. For you alone are the Holy One,
   you alone are the Lord,
   the Most High, Jesus Christ,
   with the Holy Spirit,
   in the glory of God the Father.

332 ALLELUIA

Cantor or choir, then all:

Al - le - lu - ia! Al - le - lu - ia! Al - le - lu - ia!

Music: *Mass of Light,* David Haas, © 1988, GIA Publications, Inc.

333 GOSPEL ACCLAMATION

Cantor or choir, then all:

Glo-ry to you, O Word of God, Lord Je - sus Christ!

Text: ICEL, © 1969
Music: *Mass of Light,* David Haas, © 1988, GIA Publications, Inc.

334 PREFACE DIALOG

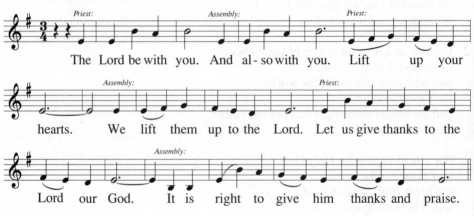

Priest: *Assembly:* *Priest:*

The Lord be with you. And al - so with you. Lift up your

Assembly: *Priest:*

hearts. We lift them up to the Lord. Let us give thanks to the

Assembly:

Lord our God. It is right to give him thanks and praise.

Music: *Mass of Light,* David Haas, © 1988, GIA Publications, Inc.

335 SANCTUS

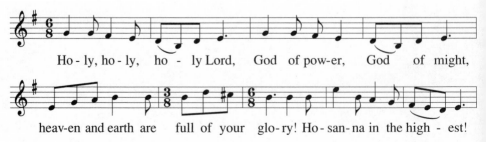

Ho - ly, ho - ly, ho - ly Lord, God of pow-er, God of might,

heav-en and earth are full of your glo-ry! Ho - san-na in the high - est!

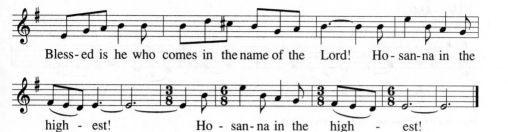

Bless-ed is he who comes in the name of the Lord! Ho-san-na in the

high - est! Ho - san-na in the high - est!

Music: *Mass of Light,* David Haas, © 1988, GIA Publications, Inc.

EUCHARISTIC ACCLAMATION I (OPTIONAL) *   336

Ho - san - na in the high - est!

*As in the Eucharistic Prayers for Masses with Children.

Music: *Mass of Light,* David Haas, © 1988, GIA Publications, Inc.

MEMORIAL ACCLAMATION   337

Dy-ing you de - stroyed our death, ris - ing you re - stored our life.

Lord Je - sus come! Lord Je - sus come in glo - ry!

Text: ICEL, © 1973
Music: *Mass of Light,* David Haas, © 1988, GIA Publications, Inc.

EUCHARISTIC ACCLAMATION II (OPTIONAL)   338

Hear us, hear us. Hear us, hear us.

Music: *Mass of Light,* David Haas, © 1988, GIA Publications, Inc.

339 AMEN

A - men, a - men! A - men, a - men!

Music: *Mass of Light*, David Haas, © 1988, GIA Publications, Inc.

340 AGNUS DEI

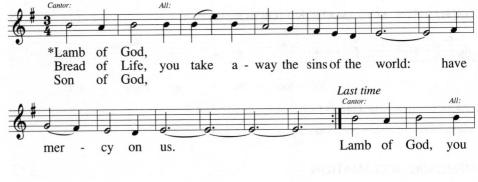

*Lamb of God,
Bread of Life, you take a - way the sins of the world: have
Son of God,

mer - cy on us.   Lamb of God, you

take a - way the sins of the world   grant us your peace.

*"Lamb of God" is sung the first and last times. Alternate intervening invocations include:
Saving Cup, Hope for all, Prince of Peace, Wine of Peace, etc.

Music: *Mass of Light*, David Haas, © 1988, GIA Publications, Inc.

Setting Four

MASS OF REMEMBRANCE

KYRIE
341

Ky - ri - e   e - le - i - son,   Chri - ste   e - le - i - son,

Ky - ri - e   e - le - i - son.

Music: *Mass of Remembrance*, Marty Haugen, © 1987, GIA Publications, Inc.

GLORIA
342

Refrain

Priest or cantor:

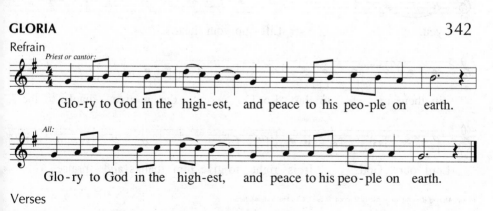

Glo-ry to God in the high-est,   and peace to his peo-ple on   earth.

All:

Glo-ry to God in the high-est,   and peace to his peo-ple on   earth.

Verses

Choir: Lord God, heavenly King, almighty God and Father,
   we worship you, we give you thanks,
   we praise you for your glory.
               All sing entire refrain

Lord Jesus Christ, only Son of the Father,
Lord God, Lamb of God, you take away the sin of the world:
have mercy on us;
you are seated at the right hand of the Father:
receive our prayer.
All sing entire refrain

For you alone are the Holy One, you alone are the Lord,
you alone are the Most High, Jesus Christ,
with the Holy Spirit, in the glory of God the Father. Amen.
All sing entire refrain

Music: *Mass of Remembrance*, Marty Haugen, © 1987, © GIA Publications, Inc.

343   ALLELUIA

Al - le - lu - ia,   al - le - lu - ia,   al - le - lu - ia!

Music: *Mass of Remembrance*, Marty Haugen, © 1987, GIA Publications, Inc.

344   PREFACE DIALOG

The   Lord be with   you.   And   al - so with

you.   Lift   up your   hearts.   We

lift them up   to the   Lord.   Let us give   thanks to the

Lord our   God.   It is right   to give him thanks and   praise.

Music: *Mass of Remembrance*, Marty Haugen, © 1987, GIA Publications, Inc.

EUCHARISTIC ACCLAMATION IA (OPTIONAL)*   345

Praise, thanks and glo-ry be to you, O God!

As in the Eucharistic Prayers for Masses with Children.

Music: *Mass of Remembrance*, Marty Haugen, © 1987, GIA Publications, Inc.

SANCTUS   346

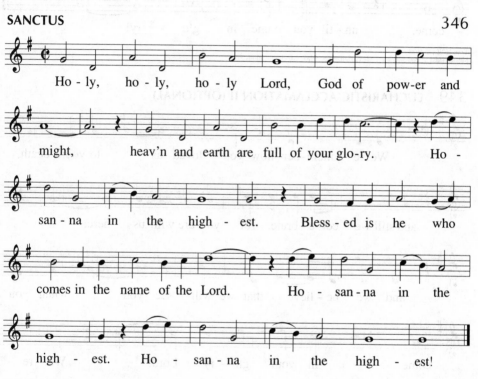

Ho - ly, ho - ly, ho - ly Lord, God of pow-er and

might, heav'n and earth are full of your glo-ry. Ho -

san - na in the high - est. Bless - ed is he who

comes in the name of the Lord. Ho - san - na in the

high - est. Ho - san - na in the high - est!

Music: *Mass of Remembrance*, Marty Haugen, © 1987, GIA Publications, Inc.

EUCHARISTIC ACCLAMATION IB (OPTIONAL)   347

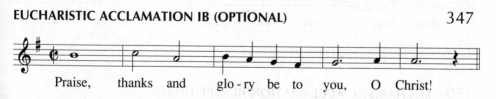

Praise, thanks and glo-ry be to you, O Christ!

Music: *Mass of Remembrance*, Marty Haugen, © 1987, GIA Publications, Inc.

348 MEMORIAL ACCLAMATION

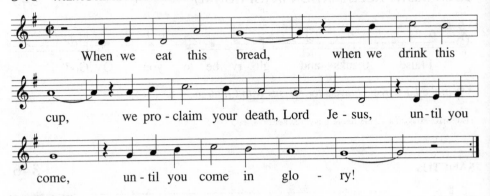

When we eat this bread, when we drink this cup, we pro - claim your death, Lord Je - sus, un - til you come, un - til you come in glo - ry!

Text: ICEL, © 1973
Music: *Mass of Remembrance*, Marty Haugen, © 1987, GIA Publications, Inc.

349 EUCHARISTIC ACCLAMATION II (OPTIONAL)

We re - mem-ber how you loved us to your death, and still we cel - e - brate, for you are with us here; and we be - lieve that we will see you when you come in your glo - ry, Lord. We re - mem - ber, we cel - e - brate, we be - lieve.

Music: *Mass of Remembrance*, Marty Haugen, © 1987, GIA Publications, Inc.

350 EUCHARISTIC ACCLAMATION III (OPTIONAL)

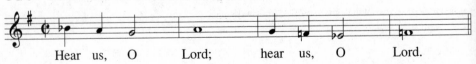

Hear us, O Lord; hear us, O Lord.

Music: *Mass of Remembrance*, Marty Haugen, © 1987, GIA Publications, Inc.

AMEN

Al - le - lu - ia,   a -   men!
Lent: Praise to   you,   Lord,   a -   men!

Al - le - lu - ia,   a -   men!
Praise to   you,   Lord,   a -   men!

Music: *Mass of Remembrance*, Marty Haugen, © 1987, GIA Publications, Inc.

AGNUS DEI

Cantors: *All:*   To repeat

1. *Lamb   of   God,
2. Prince of   Peace, you take a - way the sins of the world: have mer-cy on
3. Bread   of   Life,

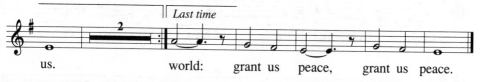

Last time

us.   world: grant us   peace,   grant us   peace.

*"Lamb of God" is sung the first and last times. Alternate intervening invocations
include: Ancient Cup, Bread of Peace, Wine of Hope, Lord of lords.

Music: *Mass of Remembrance*, Marty Haugen, © 1987, GIA Publications, Inc.

Setting Five

MISSA EMMANUEL

353   KYRIE

Lord,   have mer - cy.   Lord,   have mer - cy.

Christ,   have mer - cy.   Christ,   have mer - cy.

Lord,   have mer - cy.   Lord,   have mer - cy.

Music: *Missa Emmanuel*; Richard Proulx, © 1991, GIA Publications, Inc.

354   SANCTUS

Ho-ly, ho-ly, ho - ly Lord, God of pow'r and God   of might.

Heav - en and earth   are full of your glo -

ry. Ho - san - na in the high - est,

ho - san - na in the high - est.

All:
Ho - san - na in the high - est,

ho - san - na in the high - est.

Cantor:
Bless - ed is he who comes in the name

of the Lord. Ho - san - na in the

high - est, ho - san - na in the

All:
high - est. Ho - san - na in the high -

est, ho - san - na in the high - est.

Music: *Missa Emmanuel,* Richard Proulx, © 1991, GIA Publications, Inc.

355 MEMORIAL ACCLAMATION

Cantor, then all:

Christ has died, Christ is ris - en, Christ will come a - gain.

Text: ICEL, © 1973
Music: *Missa Emmanuel*, Richard Proulx, © 1991, 2002, GIA Publications, Inc.

356 AMEN

Cantor, then all:

A - men, a - men, a - men, a - men.

Music: *Missa Emmanuel*, Richard Proulx, © 1991, 2002, GIA Publications, Inc.

357 AGNUS DEI

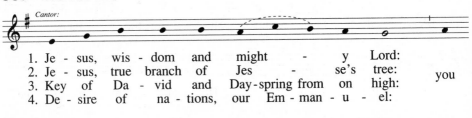

Cantor:

1. Je - sus, wis - dom and might - y Lord:
2. Je - sus, true branch of Jes - se's tree: you
3. Key of Da - vid and Day-spring from on high:
4. De - sire of na - tions, our Em - man - u - el:

1., 2., 3.

take a - way the sins of the world, have mer - cy on us, have

Assembly:

4.

mer - cy on us. grant us peace, grant us peace.

Assembly:

Music: *Missa Emmanuel*, Richard Proulx, © 1991, GIA Publications, Inc.

Setting Six

CORPUS CHRISTI MASS

KYRIE

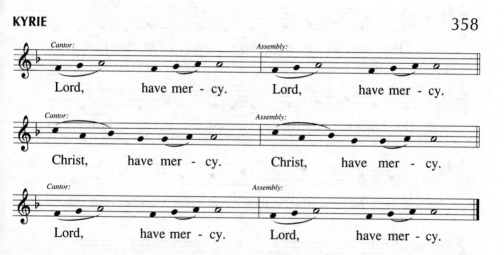

Cantor: Lord, have mer - cy. Assembly: Lord, have mer - cy.

Cantor: Christ, have mer - cy. Assembly: Christ, have mer - cy.

Cantor: Lord, have mer - cy. Assembly: Lord, have mer - cy.

Music: *Corpus Christi Mass*, Kyrie XVI, adapt. by Richard Proulx, © 1992, GIA Publications, Inc.

359 SANCTUS

Ho - ly, ho - ly, ho - ly Lord, God of pow'r and might.

Ho - ly, ho - ly, ho - ly Lord, God of pow'r and might.

Heav'n and earth are full of your glo - ry.

Ho - san - na in the high - est, in the high - est.

Ho - san - na in the high-est, in the high - est.

Blessed is he who comes in the name of the Lord.

Ho - san - na in the high - est, in the high - est.

Ho - san - na in the high - est, in the high - est.

Music: *Corpus Christi Mass, Adoro te devote,* setting by Richard Proulx, © 1992, GIA Publications, Inc.

MEMORIAL ACCLAMATION 360

Cantor, then all:

Christ has died, Christ is ris - en, Christ will come a - gain.

Text: ICEL, © 1973
Music: *Corpus Christi Mass, Adoro te devote,* setting by Richard Proulx, © 1992, GIA Publications, Inc.

AMEN 361

Cantor, then all:

A - men, a - men, a - men.

Music: *Corpus Christi Mass, Adoro te devote,* setting by Richard Proulx, © 1992, GIA Publications, Inc.

AGNUS DEI 362

Cantor:

1. Je - sus, Lamb of God, Bear - er of our sins,
2. Je - sus, Lamb of God, Sav - ior of the world, have
3. Je - sus, Lamb of God, Bread come down from heav'n,
4. Je - sus, Lamb of God, Shep - herd of our souls,

Assembly: *repeat as needed*

mer - cy on us, have mer - cy on us.

Cantor:

5. Je - sus, Lamb of God, gen - tle Prince of peace,

grant us peace, grant us peace.

Assembly:

Grant us peace, grant us peace.

Music: *Corpus Christi Mass, Adoro te devote,* setting by Richard Proulx, © 1992, GIA Publications, Inc.

Setting Seven

CANTUS MISSAE

363 **KYRIE**

Music: Vatican Edition VIII; acc. by Richard Proulx, © 1995, GIA Publications, Inc.

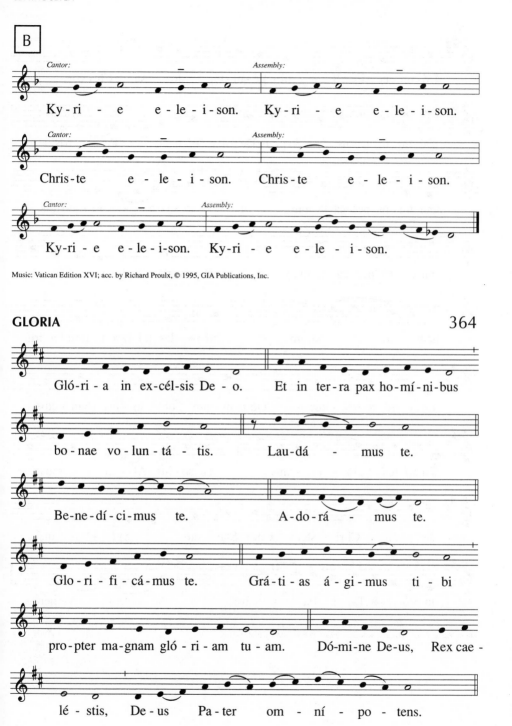

B

Cantor: Assembly:

Ky - ri - e e - le - i - son. Ky - ri - e e - le - i - son.

Cantor: Assembly:

Chris - te e - le - i - son. Chris - te e - le - i - son.

Cantor: Assembly:

Ky - ri - e e - le - i - son. Ky - ri - e e - le - i - son.

Music: Vatican Edition XVI; acc. by Richard Proulx, © 1995, GIA Publications, Inc.

GLORIA 364

Gló - ri - a in ex - cél - sis De - o. Et in ter - ra pax ho - mí - ni - bus

bo - nae vo - lun - tá - tis. Lau - dá - mus te.

Be - ne - dí - ci - mus te. A - do - rá - mus te.

Glo - ri - fi - cá - mus te. Grá - ti - as á - gi - mus ti - bi

pro - pter ma - gnam gló - ri - am tu - am. Dó - mi - ne De - us, Rex cae -

lé - stis, De - us Pa - ter om - ní - po - tens.

LITURGY OF THE WORD

THE FIRST READINGS 365

After the first reading:

Reader: Ver - bum Dó - mi - ni.
Assembly: De - o grá - ti - as.

After the second reading or if there is only one reading before the gospel:

Reader: Ver - bum Dó - mi - ni.
Assembly: De - o grá - ti - as.

GOSPEL 366

Before the gospel:

Deacon or priest: Dó - mi - nus vo - bís-cum.
Assembly: Et cum spí - ri - tu tu - o.

Deacon: Lé - cti - o sanc - ti E - van - gé - li - i se - cún - dum

N... Assembly: Gló - ri - a ti - bi, Dó - mi - ne.

After the gospel:

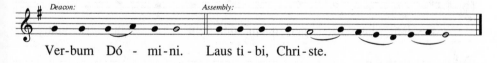

Deacon: Ver-bum Dó - mi-ni.
Assembly: Laus ti - bi, Chri - ste.

367 CREDO

Cre-do in u-num De - um, Pa - trem om - ni - po - tén-tem fa-

ctó-rem cae - li et ter-rae, vi - si - bí - li-um óm - ni-um

et in - vi - si - bí - li-um. Et in u - num Dó - mi - num

Je - sum Chri-stum, Fí - li - um De - i u - ni - gé - ni-tum.

Et ex Pa-tre na - tum an - te óm - ni - a sáe - cu - la.

De - um de De - o, lu - men de lú - mi - ne, De - um ve - rum

de De - o ve-ro. Gé - ni-tum, non fa - ctum, con-sub-stan - ti -

á - lem Pa - tri: per quem óm - ni - a fa - cta sunt.

Qui pro - pter nos hó - mi - nes et pro - pter no-stram sa - lú - tem de-

scén-dit de cae-lis. Et in-car-ná-tus est de Spí - ri - tu

San - cto ex Ma - rí - a Vír - gi - ne, et ho - mo fa-ctus est.

Cru - ci - fí - xus é - ti - am pro no - bis sub

Pón - ti - o Pi - lá - to, pas - sus et se - púl - tus est.

Et re - sur - ré - xit tér - ti - a di - e, se - cún - dum Scri - ptú - ras,

et a - scén - dit in cae - lum, se - det ad déx - te - ram Pa - tris.

Et í - te - rum ven - tú - rus est cum gló - ri -

a, ju - di - cá - re vi - vos et mór - tu - os, cu - jus re - gni non e - rit fi - nis.

Et in Spí - ri - tum San - ctum, Dó - mi - num et vi - vi - fi - cán - tem:

qui ex Pa - tre Fi - li - ó - que pro - cé - dit.

Qui cum Pa - tre et Fi - li - o si - mul a - do - rá - tur, en con - glo -

ri - fi - cá - tur: qui lo - cú - tus est per Pro - phé - tas. Et u -

nam, san - ctam, ca - thó - li - cam et a - po - stó - li - cam Ec - clé - si - am.

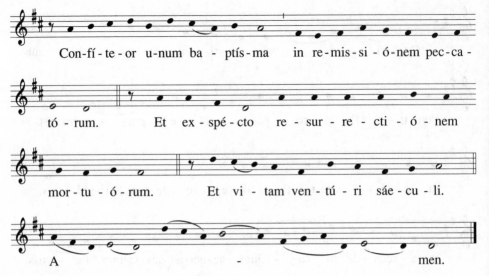

Con-fí - te - or u-num ba - ptís-ma in re-mis-si - ó-nem pec-ca -

tó - rum. Et ex - spé - cto re - sur - re - cti - ó - nem

mor-tu - ó - rum. Et vi - tam ven-tú - ri sáe-cu - li.

A - men.

Music: Vatican Edition III; acc. by Richard Proulx, © 1995, GIA Publications, Inc.

368 GENERAL INTERCESSIONS

After each intention:

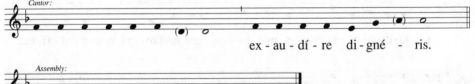

Cantor:

ex - au - dí - re di - gné - ris.

Assembly:

Te ro - gá - mus, aú - di - nos.

LITURGY OF THE EUCHARIST

369 PREFACE DIALOG

Priest:

Dó - mi - nus vo - bí - scum.

Assembly:

Et cum Spír - i - tu tu - o.

Priest:

Sur - sum cor - da.

Assembly:

Ha - bé - mus ad Dó - mi - num.

Priest:
Grá - ti - as a - gá - mus Dó - mi - no

De - o no - stro.

Assembly:
Di - gnum et iu - stum est.

SANCTUS 370

A

San - ctus, * San - ctus, San -

ctus Dó - mi - nus De - us Sá -

ba - oth. Ple - ni sunt cae - li et

ter - ra gló - ri - a tu - a. Ho - sán -

na in ex - cél - sis. Be - ne - dí - ctus qui

ve - nit in nó - mi - ne Dó - mi - ni. Ho - sán -

na in ex - cél - sis.

Music: Vatican Edition VIII; acc. by Richard Proulx, © 1995, GIA Publications, Inc.

B

San - ctus, San - ctus, San-ctus Dó - mi - nus De - us Sá - ba-oth.

Ple - ni sunt cae - li et ter - ra gló - ri - a tu - a. Ho-sán - na

in ex - cél - sis. Be - ne - dí - ctus qui ve - nit in nó - mi - ne

Dó - mi - ni. Ho - sán - na in ex - cél - sis.

Music: Vatican Edition XVIII; acc. by Richard Proulx, © 1995, GIA Publications, Inc.

371 MEMORIAL ACCLAMATION

A

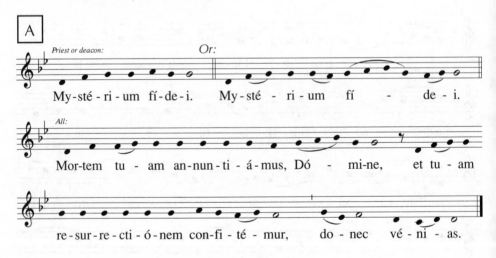

Priest or deacon: *Or:*

My - sté - ri - um fí - de - i.   My - sté - ri - um fí - de - i.

All:

Mor-tem tu - am an-nun-ti - á-mus, Dó - mi-ne, et tu - am

re - sur - re - cti - ó - nem con-fi - té - mur, do - nec vé - ni - as.

Music: Vatican Edition; acc. by Richard Proulx, © 1995, GIA Publications, Inc.

B

Priest or deacon:

My - sté - ri - um fí - de - i.

Mor-tem tu - am an - nun - ti - á - mus, Dó - mi - ne, et re - sur -

re - cti - ó - nem con - fi - té - mur, do - nec vé - ni - as.

Music: Vatican Edition; acc. by Richard Proulx, © 1995, GIA Publications, Inc.

AMEN 372
After the doxology:

After the doxology: *Assembly:*

per o - mni - a sae - cu - la sae - cu - lo - rum. A - men.

COMMUNION RITE

LORD'S PRAYER 373

Priest:

Prae - cé - ptis sa - lu - tá - ri - bus mó - ni - ti, et de - ví - na

in - sti - tu - ti - ó - ne for - má - ti, au - dé - mus dí - ce - re:

All:

Pa - ter no - ster, qui es in cae - lis: san - cti - fi - cé - tur no - men

tu - um; ad - vé - ni - at re - gnum tu - um; fi - at vo - lún - tas

tu - a, si - cut in cae - lo, et in ter - ra.

Pa - nem no - strum co - ti - di - á - num da no - bis hó - di - e;

et di - mít - te no - bis dé - bi - ta no - stra,

si - cut et nos di - mít - ti - mus de - bi -

tó - ri - bus no - stris; et ne nos in - dú - cas in ten -

ta - ti - ó - nem; sed lí - be - ra nos a ma - lo.

Priest: Libera nos...Iesu Christi.

Qui - a tu - um est re - gnum, et po - té - stas,

et gló - ri - a in sáe - cu - la.

374 SIGN OF PEACE

Priest:

Qui vivis et regnas in saecula sae - cu - lo - rum.

Assembly:

A - men.

Priest:

Pax Dó - mi - ni sit sem - per

Assembly:

vo - bís - cum. Et cum spí - ri - tu tu - o.

AGNUS DEI

Music: Vatican Edition VIII; acc. by Richard Proulx, © 1995, GIA Publications, Inc.

tol - lis pec - cá - ta mun - di: do - na no - bis pa - cem.

Music: Vatican Edition XVIII; acc. by Richard Proulx, © 1995, GIA Publications, Inc.

CONCLUDING RITE

376 DISMISSAL

I - te,   mis-sa est.
De - o   grá - ti - as.

Music: Vatican Edition VIII; acc. by Richard Proulx, © 1995, GIA Publications, Inc.

Service Music

Refrain

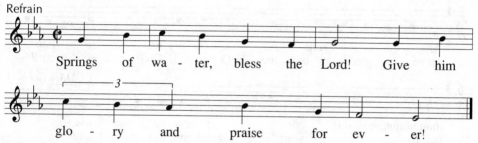

Springs of wa - ter, bless the Lord! Give him
glo - ry and praise for ev - er!

Each verse concludes:

Bless - ed be God for ev - er! Bless - ed be God for ev - er!

Text: Refrain trans. © 1973, ICEL; additional text by Marty Haugen, © 1994, GIA Publications, Inc.
Music: Marty Haugen, © 1994, GIA Publications, Inc.

This refrain may be used with the Asperges Me, which follows.

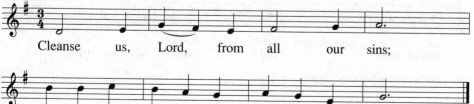

Cleanse us, Lord, from all our sins;
wash us and we shall be clean as new snow.

Text: *Roman Missal*
Music: Howard Hughes, SM, © 1986, GIA Publications, Inc.

379 RITE OF SPRINKLING

A - spér - ges me, Dó - mi - ne hys -
Cleanse me from sin, O Lord God, wash

só - po, et mun-dá - bor: la - vá - bis me,
me with hys - sop branch - es: cleanse me from guilt,

et su - per ni-vem de - al - bá - bor.
and I shall be clean as the new snow.

Mis - se - rére me - i, De - us, se - cún -
Have mer - cy on me, O my God, ac - cord -

D.C. *(ad lib.)*

dum magnam miseri - cór - di - am tu - am.
ing to your great com-pas - sion.

Gló - ri - a Patri, et Filio, et Spi - rí - tu - i San - cto:
Glo - ry be to the Father
and to the Son, and to the Ho - ly Spir - it:

Si - cut erat in princípio, et nunc, et sem - per,
As it was in the beginning, is now and ev - er shall be,

D.C.

et in saécula saé - cu - ló-rum. A - men.
world with - out end. A - men.

Text: *Roman Missal*; trans. by Richard Proulx, © 1975, GIA Publications, Inc.
Music: Vatican Edition, adapt. by Richard Proulx, © 1975, GIA Publications, Inc.

RITE OF SPRINKLING

380

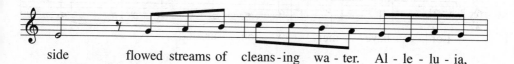

Lord Je-sus, from your wound-ed

side   flowed streams of   cleans-ing   wa - ter.   Al - le - lu - ia,

al - le - lu - ia,   al - le - lu   -   ia.   The   world   was

washed of   all   its   sin,   all   life made   new a-gain. Al - le - lu - ia,   al -

le - lu - ia,   al - le - lu   -   ia.

Music: *Festival Liturgy*, Richard Hillert, © 1983, GIA Publications, Inc.

KYRIE

381

Cantor, then all

(Invocation)   *Lord have mer-cy,   Lord have mer-cy.
Christ have mer-cy,   Christ have mer-cy.
Lord have mer-cy,   Lord have mer-cy.

*Alternate text, "Show us your mercy, be with us now!"

Music: Gary Daigle, © 1993, GIA Publications, Inc.

382 KYRIE

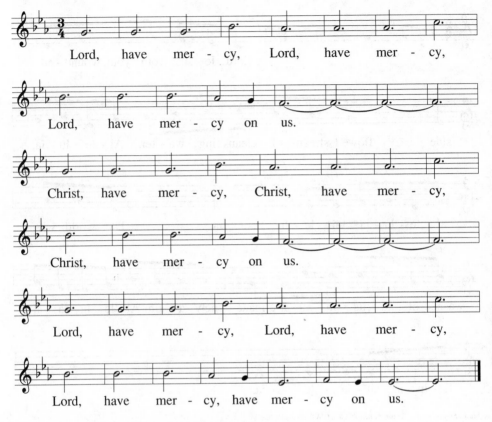

Lord, have mer - cy, Lord, have mer - cy,
Lord, have mer - cy on us.
Christ, have mer - cy, Christ, have mer - cy,
Christ, have mer - cy on us.
Lord, have mer - cy, Lord, have mer - cy,
Lord, have mer - cy, have mer - cy on us.

Music: *Mass of St. Augustine,* Leon C. Roberts, © 1981, GIA Publications, Inc.

383 KYRIE

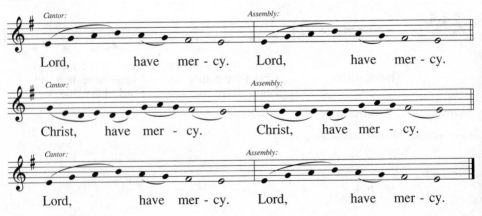

Cantor: Lord, have mer - cy. *Assembly:* Lord, have mer - cy.
Cantor: Christ, have mer - cy. *Assembly:* Christ, have mer - cy.
Cantor: Lord, have mer - cy. *Assembly:* Lord, have mer - cy.

Music: *Kyrie cum jubilo,* Vatican edition; acc. by Gerard Farrell, OSB, © 1986, GIA Publications, Inc.

KYRIE

Cantor or choir, then all:

Ky-ri - e e - le - i-son,

Ky-ri - e e - le - i-son, Ky-ri - e e - le - i - son.

Cantor or choir:

Chris - te e - le - i - son,

Chris - te e - le - i-son,

Chris - te e - le - i - son,

e - le - i - son.

All:

Ky-ri - e e - le - i-son, Ky-ri - e e - le - i-son,

Ky-ri - e e - le - i - son, e -

le - i - son.

Music: *Music for Celebration*, David Hurd, © 1979, GIA Publications, Inc.

385 KYRIE

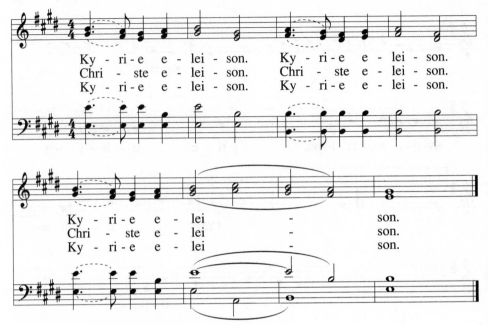

Ky - ri - e e - lei - son. Ky - ri - e e - lei - son.
Chri - ste e - lei - son. Chri - ste e - lei - son.
Ky - ri - e e - lei - son. Ky - ri - e e - lei - son.

Ky - ri - e e - lei - son.
Chri - ste e - lei - son.
Ky - ri - e e - lei - son.

Music: Russian Orthodox; arr. by John L. Bell, © 1990, Iona Community, GIA Publications, Inc., agent

386 KYRIE

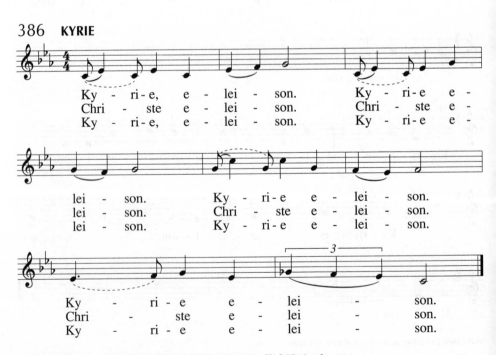

Ky - ri - e, e - lei - son. Ky - ri - e e -
Chri - ste e - lei - son. Chri - ste e -
Ky - ri - e, e - lei - son. Ky - ri - e e -

lei - son. Ky - ri - e e - lei - son.
lei - son. Chri - ste e - lei - son.
lei - son. Ky - ri - e e - lei - son.

Ky - ri - e e - lei - son.
Chri - ste e - lei - son.
Ky - ri - e e - lei - son.

Music: Dinah Reindorf, © 1987; arr. by John L. Bell, © 1990, Iona Community, GIA Publications, Inc., agent

GLORIA

Glo - ry to God in the high - est, and peace to his

peo-ple on earth. Lord God, heav-en - ly, King, Al-might-y,

God and Fa - ther, we wor-ship you, we give you thanks,

we praise you for your glo - ry. Lord Je - sus Christ,

on - ly Son of the Fa - ther, Lord God, Lamb of God,

you take a - way the sin of the world: have mer - cy on us;

you are seat - ed at the right hand of the Fa - ther:

re - ceive our prayer. For you a - lone are the Ho - ly One,

you a - lone are the Lord, you a - lone are the

Most High, Je - sus Christ, with the Ho - ly Spir - it,

in the glo - ry of God the Fa - ther. A - men.

Music: *New Plainsong,* David Hurd, © 1981, GIA Publications, Inc.

388 GLORIA

Music: Peter Jones, © 1981, 1982
Published by OCP Publications

389 GLORIA

Glo - ry to God in the high - est, and peace to his peo - ple on earth.

Verses

1. Lord God, heavenly King,
   almighty God and Father,
   we worship you, we give you thanks,
   we praise you for your glory.

2. Lord Jesus Christ, only Son of the Father,
   Lord God, Lamb of God,
   you take away sin of the world,
   have mercy on us;
   you are seated at the right hand of the Father,
   receive our prayer.

3. You alone are the holy one,
   you alone are the Lord,
   you alone are the Most High, Jesus Christ,
   with the Holy Spirit, in the glory of God the Father.

Music: *Assembly Mass,* Thomas Porter, © 1987, GIA Publications, Inc.

390 GLORIA

Glo - ry to God in the high - est, and peace to his peo - ple on earth.

Verses

1. Lord God, heavenly King, almighty God and Father.

2. We worship you, we give you thanks,
   we praise you, we praise you for your glory.

3. Lord Jesus Christ, only Son of the Father,
   Lord God, Lamb of God, you take away the sin of the world:
   have mercy on us; you are seated at the right hand of the Father:
   receive, receive our prayer.

4. For you alone are the Holy One, you alone are the Lord,
   you alone are the Most High, Jesus Christ,
   with the Holy Spirit in the glory of God the Father.

Music: *Melodic Gloria*, James J. Chepponis, © 1986, GIA Publications, Inc.

GLORIA

391

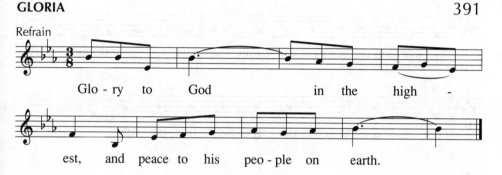

Refrain

Glo - ry to God in the high - est, and peace to his peo - ple on earth.

Verses

1. Lord God, heavenly King, almighty God and Father,
   we worship you, we give you thanks,
   we praise you for your glory.

2. Lord Jesus Christ, only Son of the Father,
   Lord God, Lamb of God, you take away the sin of the world:
   have mercy on us; you are seated at the right hand of the Father:
   receive our prayer.

3. For you alone are the Holy One, you alone are the Lord,
   you alone are the Most High, Jesus Christ,
   with the Holy Spirit, in the glory of God the Father. Amen.

Music: *Mass of Hope;* Becket Senchur, OSB, © 1992, GIA Publications, Inc.

392 GLORIA

I (Cantor/choir)
Glo-ry to God in the high - est, and peace to his peo-ple on earth.

II (Assembly)
Lord God, heav'n-ly King, al-might-y God and Fa - ther.

I
We wor-ship you, we give you thanks, we praise you for your glo - ry.

II
Lord Je - sus Christ, on - ly Son of the Fa - ther,

I
Lord God, Lamb of God, you take a - way the sin of the world:

II
have mer-cy on us; you are seat-ed at the right hand of the

Fa - ther: re - ceive our prayer.

I
For you a - lone are the Ho - ly One,

you a - lone are the Lord, you a -

II

lone are the Most High, Je - sus Christ, with the Ho - ly Spir - it,

Slower

in the glo - ry of God the Fa - ther. A - men.

Music: *Congregational Mass;* John Lee, © 1970, GIA Publications, Inc.

GLORIA

393

All:

Glo-ry to God in the high-est, and peace to his peo-ple on

earth. Glo - ry to God in the high-est, and

Cantor or T. B.:

peace to his peo - ple on earth. Lord God,

heav - en - ly King, al-might-y God and Fa - ther.

All:

Glo-ry to God in the high-est, and peace to his peo-ple on

Cantor or S. A.:

earth. We wor-ship you, we give you thanks,

All:

we praise you for your glo - ry. Glo-ry to God in the

Cantor or T. B.:
high-est, and peace to his peo-ple on earth. Lord Je - sus

Christ, on - ly Son of the Fa - ther.

All:
Glo-ry to God in the high-est, and peace to his peo-ple on earth.

T. B.:
Lord God, Lamb of God, you take a - way the

S. A.:
sin of the world; have mer - cy on us; you are

seat - ed at the right hand of the Fa-ther:

T. B.: re - ceive our pray-er. *All:* Glo-ry to God in the

high-est, and peace to his peo-ple on earth.

Glo-ry to God in the high-est, and peace to his peo-ple on

Cantor or T. B.:
earth. For you a - lone are the Ho - ly One,

Music: *Mass of the Bells;* Alexander Peloquin, © 1972, 1973, GIA Publications, Inc.

394 ALLELUIA

Al - le - lu - ia, al - le - lu - ia,

al - le - lu - ia, al-le-lu-ia, al-le-lu - ia.

Music: Joe Wise; acc. by Kelly Dobbs Mickus, © 1966, 1973, 1986, GIA Publications, Inc.

395 ALLELUIA

Al - le - lu - ia, al - le - lu - ia!

Al - le - lu - ia, al - le - lu - ia!

Text: *Celtic Alleluia;* Christopher Walker
Music: Fintan O'Carroll and Christopher Walker
© 1985, Fintan O'Carroll and Christopher Walker, published by OCP Publications

396 ALLELUIA

Hal-le, hal-le, hal-le - lu - jah! Hal-le, hal-le, hal-

le - lu - ia! Hal-le, hal-le, hal-le -

lu - jah! Hal-le-lu-jah! Hal-le-lu - jah!

Music: Traditional Caribbean, arr. by John L. Bell, © 1990, Iona Community, GIA Publications, Inc., agent; verses and acc. by Marty Haugen, © 1993, GIA Publications, Inc.

ALLELUIA 397

Music: Alleluia II, Jacques Berthier, © 1984, Les Presses de Taizé, GIA Publications, Inc., agent

ALLELUIA 398

Music: A. Gregory Murray, OSB, © 1958, The Grail, GIA Publications, Inc., agent

ALLELUIA 399

Music: *Alleluia in C*, Howard Hughes, SM, © 1973, 1982, GIA Publications, Inc.

400 ALLELUIA

Cantor:
Al - le - lu - ia, al - le - lu - ia!

Assembly:
Al - le - lu - ia, al - le - lu - ia!

Cantor:
Al - le - lu - ia, al - le - lu - ia!

Assembly:
Al - le - lu - ia, al - le - lu - ia!

Cantor:
Al - le - lu - ia, al - le - lu - ia!

Assembly:
Al - le - lu - ia, al - le - lu - ia!

Cantor:
Al - le - lu - ia, al - le - lu - ia!

Assembly:
Al - le - lu - ia, al - le - lu - ia!

Music: *Joyful Alleluia;* Howard Hughes, SM, © 1973, 1979, GIA Publications, Inc.

401 ALLELUIA

Al - le - lu - ia, al - le - lu - ia, al - le - lu - ia.

Al - le - lu - ia, al - le - lu - ia, al - le - lu - ia!

Music: Alleluia 7; Jacques Berthier, © 1984, Les Presses de Taizé, GIA Publications, Inc., agent

402 ALLELUIA

Al - le - lu - ia, al - le - lu - ia, al - le - lu - ia.

Music: Mode II; acc. by Richard Proulx, © 1986, GIA Publications, Inc.

ALLELUIA 403

Al - le - lu - ia. Al - le -
lu - ia. Al - le - lu -
ia. Al - le - lu - ia.

Last time
Al - le - lu - ia. Al - le - lu - ia.

Text: Adapt. by Ralph C. Verdi, CPPS
Music: Ralph C. Verdi, CPPS
© 1977, GIA Publications, Inc.

ALLELUIA 404

Al - le - lu - ia, al - le -
lu - ia, al - le - lu - ia, al - le - lu - ia,
al - le - lu - ia.

Music: Richard Proulx, © 1980 ICEL

405 ALLELUIA

Al - le - lu - ia,
al - le - lu - ia, al - le - lu - ia, al - le -
lu - ia, al - le - lu - ia.

Music: Richard Proulx, © 1975, GIA Publications, Inc.

406 LENTEN ACCLAMATION

Refrain

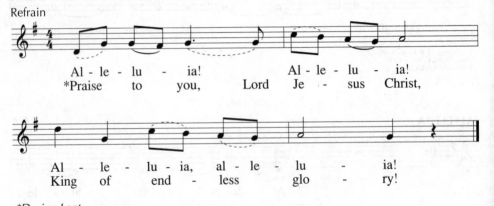

Al - le - lu - ia! Al - le - lu - ia!
*Praise to you, Lord Je - sus Christ,

Al - le - lu - ia, al - le - lu - ia!
King of end - less glo - ry!

*During Lent

Music: *Mass for John Carroll,* Michael Joncas, © 1990, GIA Publications, Inc.

407 LENTEN ACCLAMATION

Praise to you, Lord Je - sus, king of end - less glo - ry,
Sav - ior of the world, Sav - ior of the world.

Text: Marty Haugen
Music: Marty Haugen
© 1983, GIA Publications, Inc.

LENTEN ACCLAMATION 408

Glo - ry to you, O Word of God, Lord Je - sus Christ!

Text: ICEL, © 1969
Music: Richard Proulx, © 1975, GIA Publications, Inc.

GENERAL INTERCESSIONS 409

O Lord, hear our prayer.

Text: Ray East
Music: Ray East
© 1987, GIA Publications, Inc.

GENERAL INTERCESSIONS 410

O God, hear us; hear our prayer.

Text: Bob Hurd, © 1984
Music: Bob Hurd, © 1984; acc. by Dominic MacAller, © 1989, OCP Publications
Published by OCP Publications

GENERAL INTERCESSIONS 411

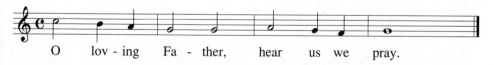

O lov - ing Fa - ther, hear us we pray.

Music: James Moore, © 1983, GIA Publications, Inc.

412 GENERAL INTERCESSIONS

Lord,   we   ask   you,   hear   our   prayer.

Music: From the *Litany of the Saints*

413 GENERAL INTERCESSIONS

Gra-cious Lord,   hear us we pray.

Music: Ronald F. Krisman, © 1977, GIA Publications, Inc.

414 GENERAL INTERCESSIONS

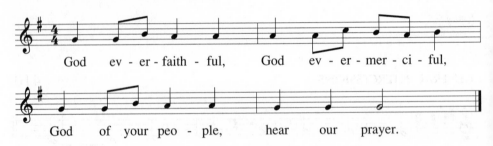

God   ev - er - faith - ful,   God   ev - er - mer - ci - ful,

God   of   your   peo - ple,   hear   our   prayer.

Text: Michael Joncas
Music: Michael Joncas
© 1990, GIA Publications, Inc.

415 GENERAL INTERCESSIONS

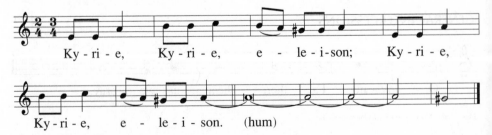

Ky - ri - e,   Ky - ri - e,   e - le - i - son;   Ky - ri - e,

Ky - ri - e,   e - le - i - son.   (hum)

Music: Jacques Berthier, © 1980, Les Presses de Taizé, GIA Publications, Inc., agent

GENERAL INTERCESSIONS 416

Ky - ri - e, Ky - ri - e, e - le - i - son. (hum)

Music: Jacques Berthier, © 1980, Les Presses de Taizé, GIA Publications, Inc., agent

PREFACE DIALOG 417

Priest: The Lord be with you. *Assembly:* And al - so with you.

Priest: Lift up your hearts. *Assembly:* We lift them up to the Lord.

Priest: Let us give thanks to the Lord our God.

Assembly: It is right to give him thanks and praise.

Music: *Sacramentary,* 1966

SANCTUS—PSALLITE MASS 418

Ho - ly, ho - ly, ho - ly.

Ho - ly, ho - ly, ho - ly. Ho-san-na,

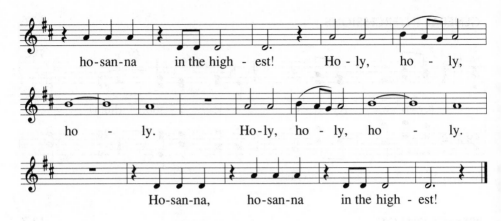

ho-san-na   in the high - est!   Ho - ly,   ho - ly,

ho   -   ly.   Ho-ly,   ho - ly,   ho   -   ly.

Ho-san-na,   ho-san-na   in the high - est!

Music: *The Psallite Mass,* Michael Joncas, © 1988, GIA Publications, Inc.

419 MEMORIAL ACCLAMATION

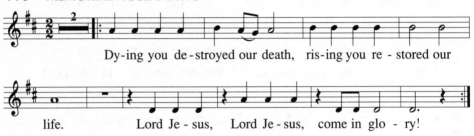

Dy-ing you de-stroyed our death,   ris-ing you re - stored our

life.   Lord Je - sus,   Lord Je - sus,   come in glo - ry!

Text: ICEL, © 1973
Music: *The Psallite Mass,* Michael Joncas, © 1988, GIA Publications, Inc.

420 AMEN

A - men,   a - men,   a   -   men.

Al-le-lu - ia,   al-le-lu - ia,   al-le-lu - ia!

Music: *The Psallite Mass,* Michael Joncas, © 1988, GIA Publications, Inc.

SANCTUS—AGAPÉ

Ho - ly, ho - ly, ho - ly, Lord,

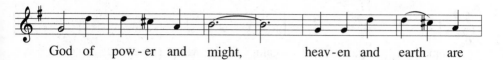

God of pow-er and might, heav-en and earth are

full of your glo-ry! Ho - san - na in the high - est!

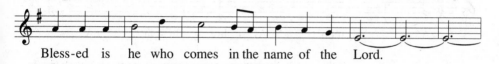

Bless-ed is he who comes in the name of the Lord.

Optional cut

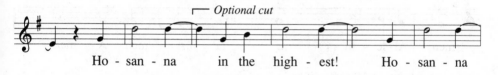

Ho - san - na in the high - est! Ho - san - na

End cut

in the high - est! Ho - san - na in the

high - est!

422 MEMORIAL ACCLAMATION

Christ has died, Christ is ris-en, Christ will come, Christ will

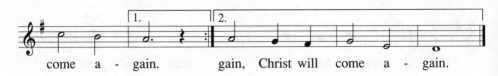

come a - gain.   gain, Christ will come a - gain.

Text: ICEL, © 1973
Music: *Agapé*, Marty Haugen, © 1993, GIA Publications, Inc.

423 DOXOLOGY AND GREAT AMEN

A - men! Al - le - lu - ia! A -

men! Al - le - lu - ia! ia! A - men! A - men!

Music: *Agapé*, Marty Haugen, © 1993, GIA Publications, Inc.

424 PREFACE DIALOG—EUCHARISTIC PRAYER FOR CHILDREN

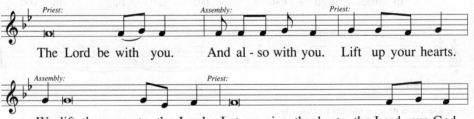

Priest: The Lord be with you. *Assembly:* And al - so with you. *Priest:* Lift up your hearts.

Assembly: We lift them up to the Lord. *Priest:* Let us give thanks to the Lord, our God.

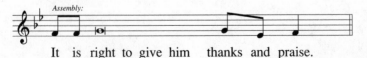

Assembly: It is right to give him thanks and praise.

Music: *Mass of Creation*, Marty Haugen, © 1984, GIA Publications, Inc.

CHILDREN'S ACCLAMATION 1   425

Ho - san-na in the high-est,   ho - san-na in the high-est!

Music: Eucharistic Prayer for Children, *Mass of Creation*, Marty Haugen, adapt. by Rob Glover, © 1989, GIA Publications, Inc.

SANCTUS   426

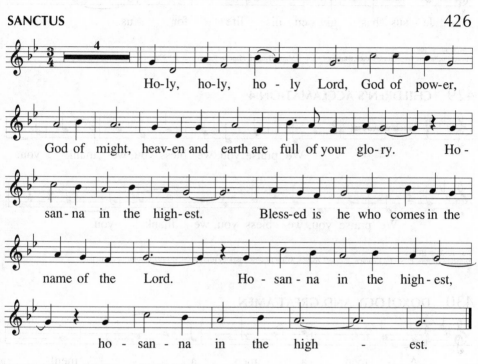

Ho - ly, ho - ly, ho - ly Lord, God of pow-er,

God of might, heav-en and earth are full of your glo - ry.   Ho -

san - na in the high-est.   Bless-ed is he who comes in the

name of the Lord.   Ho - san - na in the high - est,

ho - san - na in the high - est.

Music: *Mass of Creation*, Marty Haugen, © 1984, GIA Publications, Inc.

CHILDREN'S ACCLAMATION 2   427

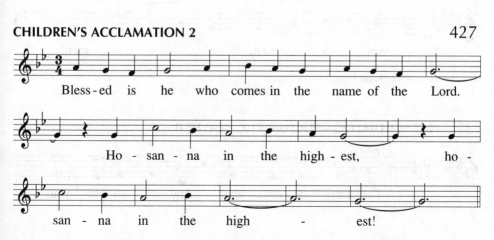

Bless - ed is he who comes in the name of the Lord.

Ho - san - na in the high - est,   ho -

san - na in the high - est!

Music: Eucharistic Prayer for Children, *Mass of Creation*, Marty Haugen, adapt. by Rob Glover, © 1989, GIA Publications, Inc.

428 CHILDREN'S ACCLAMATION 3

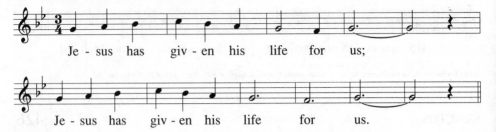

Je - sus has giv - en his life for us;

Je - sus has giv - en his life for us.

Text: ICEL, © 1975
Music: Eucharistic Prayer for Children, *Mass of Creation*, Marty Haugen, adapt. by Rob Glover, © 1989, GIA Publications, Inc.

429 CHILDREN'S ACCLAMATION 4

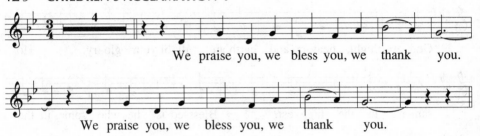

We praise you, we bless you, we thank you.

We praise you, we bless you, we thank you.

Text: ICEL, © 1975
Music: Eucharistic Prayer for Children, *Mass of Creation*, Marty Haugen, adapt. by Rob Glover, © 1989, GIA Publications, Inc.

430 DOXOLOGY AND GREAT AMEN

A - men, a - men, a - men!

A - men, a - men, a - men!

Music: *Mass of Creation*, Marty Haugen, © 1984, GIA Publications, Inc.

431 PREFACE DIALOG—EUCHARISTIC PRAYER II

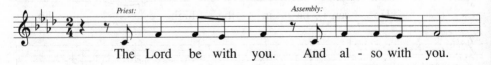

Priest: The Lord be with you. *Assembly:* And al - so with you.

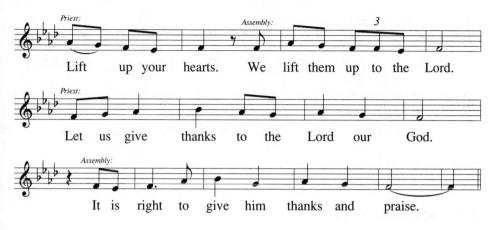

Lift up your hearts. We lift them up to the Lord.

Let us give thanks to the Lord our God.

It is right to give him thanks and praise.

Music: *Eucharistic Prayer II,* Marty Haugen, © 1990, GIA Publications, Inc.

ACCLAMATION 1   432

Let us give thanks to the Lord our God.

It is right to give him thanks and praise.

Music: *Eucharistic Prayer II,* Marty Haugen, © 1990, GIA Publications, Inc.

SANCTUS   433

Ho - ly, ho - ly, ho - ly Lord,

God of pow-er and might, heav-en and earth are

full of your glo - ry. Ho - san - na in the high - est.

Bless-ed is he, bless-ed is he who comes in the

name of the Lord. Ho - san - na in the

high - est. Ho - san - na in the high - est.

Music: *Eucharistic Prayer II*, Marty Haugen, © 1990, GIA Publications, Inc.

434 ACCLAMATION 2

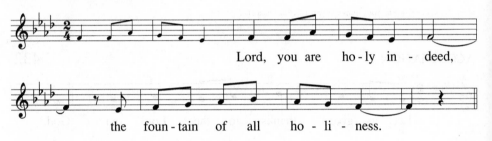

Lord, you are ho - ly in - deed,

the foun - tain of all ho - li - ness.

Music: *Eucharistic Prayer II*, Marty Haugen, © 1990, GIA Publications, Inc.

435 ACCLAMATION 3

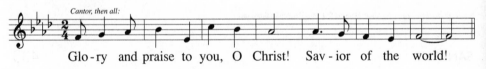

Glo - ry and praise to you, O Christ! Sav - ior of the world!

Music: *Eucharistic Prayer II*, Marty Haugen, © 1990, GIA Publications, Inc.

436 MEMORIAL ACCLAMATION

Let us pro - claim the mys - ter - y of faith:

Dy - ing you de -

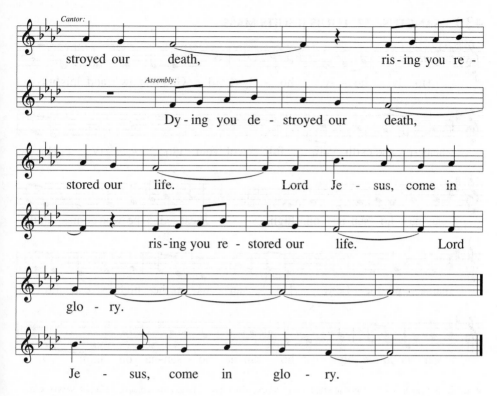

Cantor: stroyed our death, ris-ing you re-

Assembly: Dy-ing you de-stroyed our death,

stored our life. Lord Je-sus, come in

ris-ing you re-stored our life. Lord

glo-ry.

Je-sus, come in glo-ry.

Text: ICEL, © 1973
Music: *Eucharistic Prayer II,* Marty Haugen, ©1990, GIA Publications, Inc.

ACCLAMATION 4   437

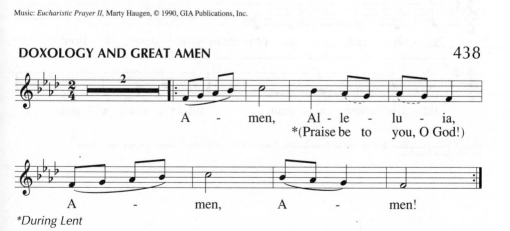

Cantor, then all: Good and gra-cious God, hear and re-mem-ber us.

Music: *Eucharistic Prayer II,* Marty Haugen, © 1990, GIA Publications, Inc.

DOXOLOGY AND GREAT AMEN   438

A - men, Al - le - lu - ia,
*(Praise be to you, O God!)

A - men, A - men!

*During Lent

Music: *Eucharistic Prayer II,* Marty Haugen, © 1990, GIA Publications, Inc.

439 SANCTUS—ST. LOUIS JESUITS MASS

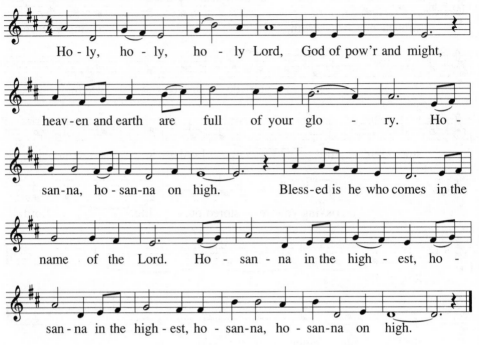

Ho - ly, ho - ly, ho - ly Lord, God of pow'r and might,

heav - en and earth are full of your glo - ry. Ho -

san - na, ho - san-na on high. Bless-ed is he who comes in the

name of the Lord. Ho - san - na in the high - est, ho -

san - na in the high - est, ho - san-na, ho - san-na on high.

Music: *St. Louis Jesuits Mass;* Robert J. Dufford, SJ and Daniel L. Schutte, © 1973, Robert J. Dufford, SJ and Daniel L. Schutte; acc. by Diana Kodner
Published by OCP Publications

440 WHEN WE EAT THIS BREAD

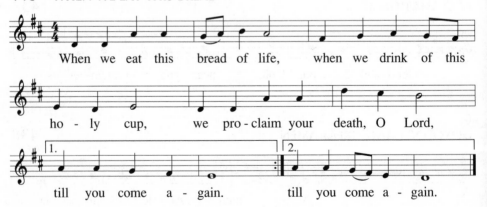

When we eat this bread of life, when we drink of this

ho - ly cup, we pro - claim your death, O Lord,

1. till you come a - gain.
2. till you come a - gain.

Text: ICEL, © 1973
Music: *St. Louis Jesuits Mass;* Robert J. Dufford, SJ and Daniel L. Schutte, © 1973, 1979, Robert J. Dufford, SJ and Daniel L. Schutte
Published by OCP Publications

AMEN 441

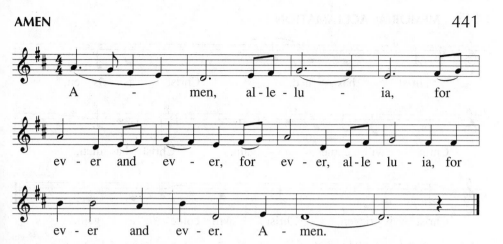

A - men, al-le-lu - ia, for ev - er and ev - er, for ev - er, al-le-lu - ia, for ev - er and ev - er. A - men.

Music: *St. Louis Jesuits Mass;* Robert J. Duffortd, SJ and Daniel L. Schutte, © 1973, Robert J. Duffortd, SJ and Daniel L. Schutte
Published by OCP Publications

SANCTUS—LAND OF REST 442

Ho - ly, ho - ly, ho - ly Lord, God of pow-er and might, heav - en and earth are full of your glo - ry. Ho - san - na in the high - est. Bless - ed is he who comes in the name of the Lord. Ho - san - na in the high - est, ho - san - na in the high - est.

Music: *Land of Rest,* adapt. by Marcia Pruner, © 1980, Church Pension Fund; acc. by Richard Proulx, © 1986, GIA Publications, Inc.

443 MEMORIAL ACCLAMATION

*Christ has died, Christ is ris-en,

Christ will come a-gain. Christ has died,

Christ is ris-en, Christ will come a-gain.

For a shorter version of this acclamation, sing the first two measures and the last two measures.

Text: ICEL, © 1973
Music: *Land of Rest,* adapt. by Richard Proulx, © 1986, GIA Publications, Inc.

444 AMEN

A - men, a - men, a - men.

Music: *Land of Rest,* adapt. by Richard Proulx, © 1986, GIA Publications, Inc.

445 SANCTUS—PLAINSONG

*Ho - ly, ho - ly, ho - ly Lord, God of pow'r and might,

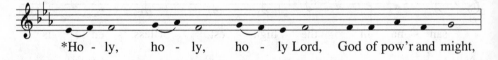

heav - en and earth are full of your glo - ry.

Ho-san-na in the high - est. Bless-ed is he who

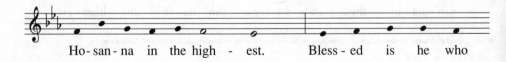

comes in the name of the Lord. Ho-san-na in the high - est.

May be sung unaccompanied.

Music: *Sacramentary*, 1974; adapt. by Robert J. Batastini, © 1975, GIA Publications, Inc.

MEMORIAL ACCLAMATION AND AMEN 446

Christ has died, Christ is ris - en, Christ will come a - gain.
A - men, a - men, a - men.

Text: ICEL, © 1973
Music: *Sacramentary*, 1974; adapt. by Robert J. Batastini, © 1980, GIA Publications, Inc.

SANCTUS—DEUTSCHE MESSE 447

Ho - ly, ho - ly, ho - ly Lord, God of pow'r and

might. Ho - ly, ho - ly, ho - ly Lord,

God of pow'r and might. Heav - en and earth are

full, full of your glo - ry. Ho -

san - na in the high - est, ho - san - na in the

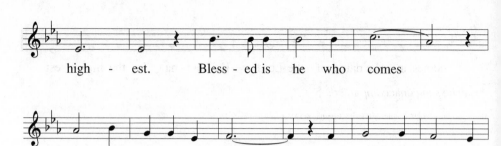

high - est. Bless - ed is he who comes

in the name of the Lord. Ho - san - na in the

high - est, ho - san - na in the high - est.

Music: *Deutsche Messe,* Franz Schubert, 1797-1828; adapt. by Richard Proulx, © 1985, 1989, GIA Publications, Inc.

448 MEMORIAL ACCLAMATION

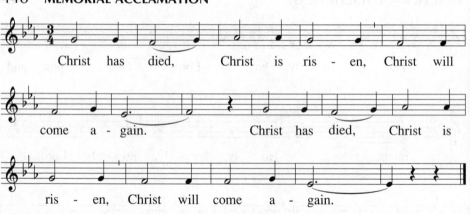

Christ has died, Christ is ris - en, Christ will

come a - gain. Christ has died, Christ is

ris - en, Christ will come a - gain.

Text: ICEL, © 1973
Music: *Deutsche Messe,* Franz Schubert, 1797-1828; adapt. by Richard Proulx, © 1985, 1995, GIA Publications, Inc.

449 AMEN

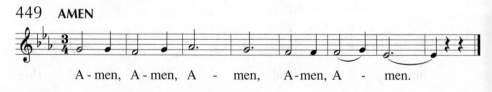

A - men, A - men, A - men, A - men, A - men.

Music: *Deutsche Messe,* Franz Schubert, 1797-1828, adapt. by Richard Proulx, © 1985, 1989, GIA Publications, Inc.

SANCTUS—A FESTIVAL EUCHARIST

Choir: Ho - ly, ho - ly, ho - ly Lord, God of pow'r and might,

All: ho - ly, ho - ly, ho - ly Lord, God of pow'r and might, *Choir:* heav - en and earth are full of your glo - ry. God of pow'r and might.

All: God of pow'r and might. *Choir:* Ho - san - na in the high - est, ho - san - na in the high - est, ho - san - na in the high - est.

All: Ho - san - na in the high - est, ho - san - na in the high - est, ho - san - na in the high - est. *Choir:* Bless-ed is he who comes in the name of the Lord.

All: Ho -

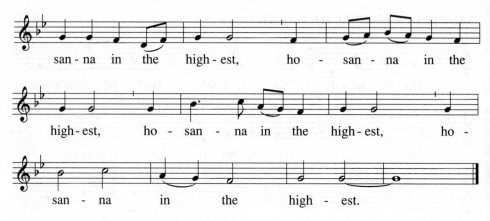

san - na in the high - est, ho - san - na in the

high - est, ho - san - na in the high - est, ho -

san - na in the high - est.

Music: *A Festival Eucharist,* Richard Proulx, © 1975, GIA Publications, Inc.

451 MEMORIAL ACCLAMATION

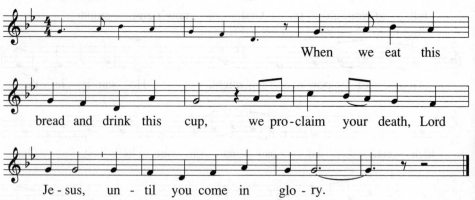

When we eat this

bread and drink this cup, we pro-claim your death, Lord

Je - sus, un - til you come in glo - ry.

Text: ICEL, © 1973
Music: *A Festival Eucharist,* Richard Proulx, © 1975, GIA Publications, Inc.

452 AMEN

A - men, a - men, a -

men, a - men.

Music: *A Festival Eucharist,* Richard Proulx, © 1975, GIA Publications, Inc.

SANCTUS—MASS IN HONOR OF ST. PAUL 453

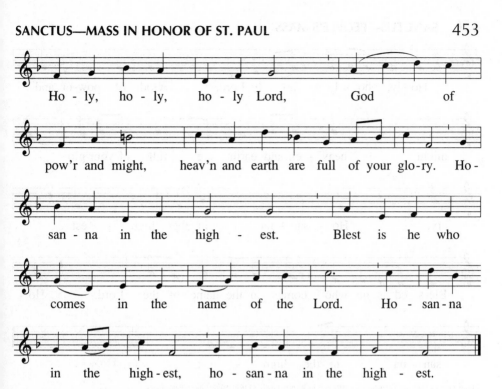

Ho - ly, ho - ly, ho - ly Lord, God of pow'r and might, heav'n and earth are full of your glo - ry. Ho - san - na in the high - est. Blest is he who comes in the name of the Lord. Ho - san - na in the high - est, ho - san - na in the high - est.

Music: *Mass in Honor of St. Paul,* Kevin Vogt, © 1995, GIA Publications, Inc.

MEMORIAL ACCLAMATION 454

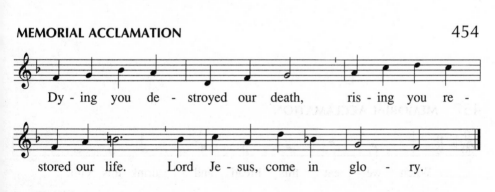

Dy - ing you de - stroyed our death, ris - ing you re - stored our life. Lord Je - sus, come in glo - ry.

Text: ICEL, © 1973
Music: *Mass in Honor of St. Paul,* Kevin Vogt, © 1995, GIA Publications, Inc.

AMEN 455

A - men, a - men, a - men.

Music: *Mass in Honor of St. Paul,* Kevin Vogt, © 1995, GIA Publications, Inc.

456 SANCTUS—PEOPLE'S MASS

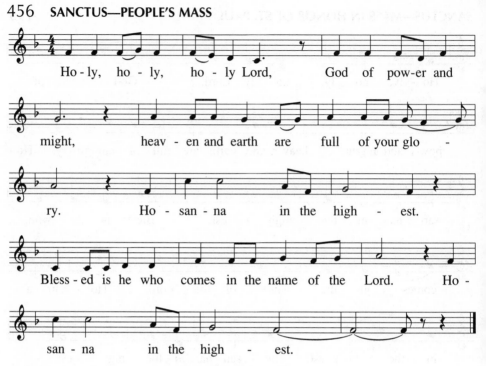

Ho-ly, ho-ly, ho-ly Lord, God of pow-er and

might, heav-en and earth are full of your glo -

ry. Ho - san - na in the high - est.

Bless-ed is he who comes in the name of the Lord. Ho-

san - na in the high - est.

Music: *People's Mass,* Jan Vermulst, 1925-1994, acc. by Richard Proulx, © 1970, World Library Publications

457 MEMORIAL ACCLAMATION

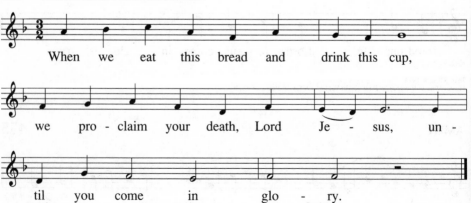

When we eat this bread and drink this cup,

we pro - claim your death, Lord Je - sus, un -

til you come in glo - ry.

Text: ICEL, © 1973
Music: *Danish Amen Mass,* Charles G. Frischmann and David Kraehenbuehl, © 1973, World Library Publications

AMEN 458

A - men,   a - men,   a -   men.

Music: Danish Amen

SANCTUS—MASS FOR THE CITY 459

Ho - ly, ho - ly, ho - ly Lord,   God   of pow-er and

might.   Heav - en and   earth   are

full   of   your glo - ry.   Ho - san - na, ho -

san - na, ho - san - na   in   the   high - est.

Bless - ed is   he   who comes in the name of the

Lord.   Ho - san - na, ho - san - na, ho -

san - na in the high - est. Ho - san - na, ho -

san - na, ho - san-na in the high - est.

Music: *Mass for the City*, Richard Proulx, © 1991, GIA Publications, Inc.

460   MEMORIAL ACCLAMATION 1

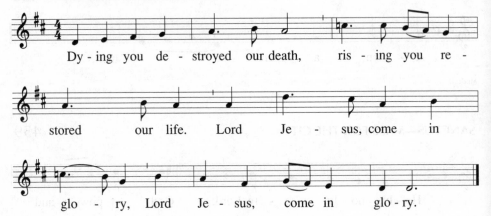

Dy - ing you de - stroyed our death,   ris - ing you re -
stored   our life.   Lord   Je - sus, come   in
glo - ry, Lord   Je - sus,   come in   glo - ry.

Text: ICEL, © 1973
Music: *Mass for the City,* Richard Proulx, © 1995, GIA Publications, Inc.

461   MEMORIAL ACCLAMATION 2

Lord,   by your   cross and res - ur - rec - tion   you have
set   us   free.   You are the   Sav-ior of   the   world.

Text: ICEL, © 1973
Music: *Mass for the City,* Richard Proulx, © 1995, GIA Publications, Inc.

462   AMEN

A - men,   a - men,   a -   men.

Music: *Mass for the City,* Richard Proulx, © 1995, GIA Publications, Inc.

463   MEMORIAL ACCLAMATION

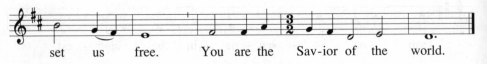

Christ   has   died,   al - le - lu - ia.   Christ is   ris - en,

al - le - lu - ia. Christ will come a - gain, al - le-

lu - ia, al - le - lu - ia.

Text: ICEL, © 1973
Music: Joe Wise; acc. by T.F. and R.P., © 1971, 1972, GIA Publications, Inc.

LORD'S PRAYER 464

Our Fa - ther, who art in heav - en,

hal-lowed be thy name; thy king - dom come; thy

will be done on earth as it is in heav - en.

Give us this day our dai - ly bread; and for - give us our

tres - pass - es as we for - give those who

tres - pass a - gainst us; and lead us not in - to temp-

ta - tion, but de - liv - er us from e - vil.

After the prayer "Deliver Us":

For the king - dom, the pow - er, and the

glo - ry are yours, now and for ev - er.

Music: *A Festival Eucharist,* Richard Proulx, © 1975, GIA Publications, Inc.

465 LORD'S PRAYER—LYRIC LITURGY

Priest:
Let us pray with con - fi - dence to the Fa - ther

in the words our Sav - ior gave us:

All:
Our Fa - ther, who art in heav - en, hal - lowed be thy

name; thy king - dom come; thy will be done on

earth as it is in heav - en. Give us this day our

dai - ly bread; and for - give us our tres - pass - es as we for -

give those who tres - pass a - gainst us; and

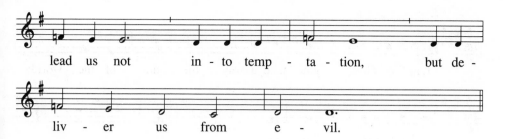

lead us not in - to temp - ta - tion, but de -

liv - er us from e - vil.

Music: *Lyric Liturgy,* Alexander Peloquin, © 1974, GIA Publications, Inc.

After the prayer "Deliver Us": **466**

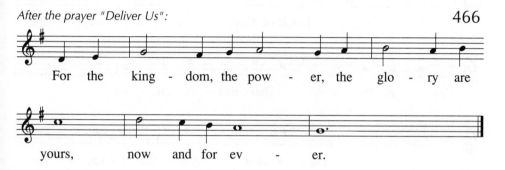

For the king - dom, the pow - er, the glo - ry are

yours, now and for ev - er.

Music: *Lyric Liturgy,* Alexander Peloquin, © 1974, GIA Publications, Inc.

RITE OF PEACE — 467

Priest: Lord, Jesus Christ... for ever and ever. *All:* **Amen.**

Priest: .... *Assembly:*

The peace of the Lord be with you al - ways. And al - so with you.

Music: *Lyric Liturgy,* Alexander Peloquin, © 1974, GIA Publications, Inc.

AGNUS DEI — 468

Cantor or choir, then all:

Lamb of God, you take a-way the sins of the world:

have mer - cy on us.

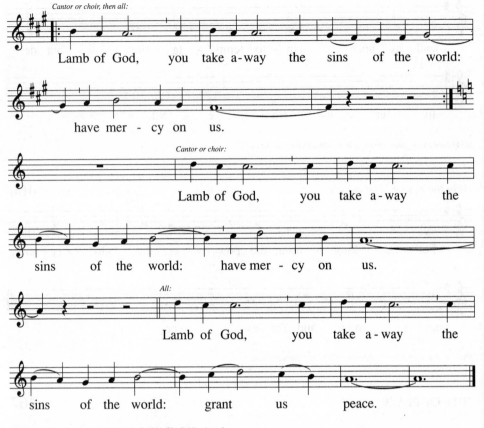

Cantor or choir, then all:

Lamb of God, you take a-way the sins of the world:

have mer - cy on us.

Cantor or choir:

Lamb of God, you take a-way the

sins of the world: have mer - cy on us.

All:

Lamb of God, you take a-way the

sins of the world: grant us peace.

Music: *Lyric Liturgy,* Alexander Peloquin, © 1974, GIA Publications, Inc.

469   LAMB OF GOD

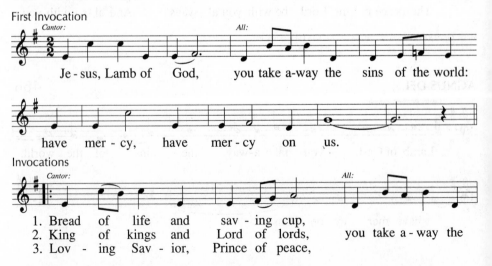

First Invocation

Cantor:

All:

Je - sus, Lamb of God, you take a-way the sins of the world:

have mer - cy, have mer - cy on us.

Invocations

Cantor:

All:

1. Bread of life and sav - ing cup,
2. King of kings and Lord of lords, you take a - way the
3. Lov - ing Sav - ior, Prince of peace,

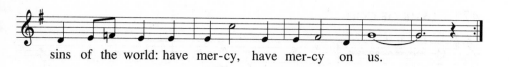

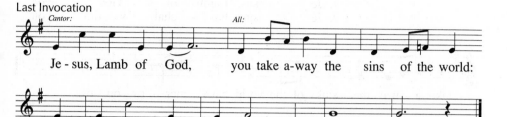

sins of the world: have mer-cy, have mer-cy on us.

Last Invocation

Cantor: *All:*

Je - sus, Lamb of God, you take a-way the sins of the world:

have mer - cy, and grant us your peace.

Music: *The Psallite Mass,* Michael Joncas, © 1988, GIA Publications, Inc.

LAMB OF GOD   470

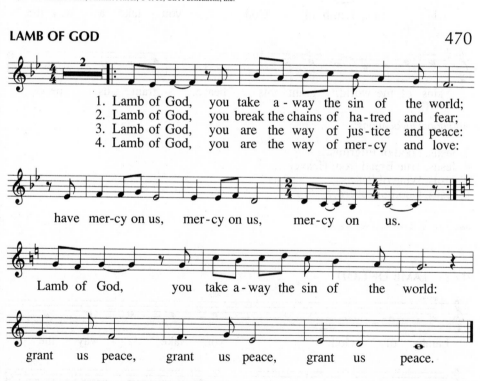

1. Lamb of God, you take a - way the sin of the world;
2. Lamb of God, you break the chains of ha - tred and fear;
3. Lamb of God, you are the way of jus - tice and peace:
4. Lamb of God, you are the way of mer - cy and love:

have mer-cy on us, mer-cy on us, mer-cy on us.

Lamb of God, you take a-way the sin of the world:

grant us peace, grant us peace, grant us peace.

Text: ICET; additional text by Marty Haugen, © 1990, GIA Publications, Inc.
Music: *Now the Feast and Celebration,* Marty Haugen, © 1990, GIA Publications, Inc.

471 LAMB OF GOD

1. Je - sus, Lamb of God you
2. Je - sus, Pas - chal vic - tim you

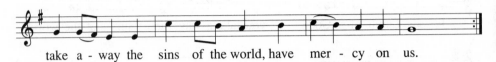

take a - way the sins of the world, have mer - cy on us.

Last time

Je - sus, Lamb of God you take a - way the

sins of the world, grant us peace, grant us peace.

Additional invocations:

3. Jesus, Food of Pilgrims…
4. Jesus, True Bread from Heaven…
5. Jesus, Wine of Peace…
6. Jesus, Good Shepherd…

Music: Tony Way, © 1995, GIA Publications, Inc.

472 LAMB OF GOD

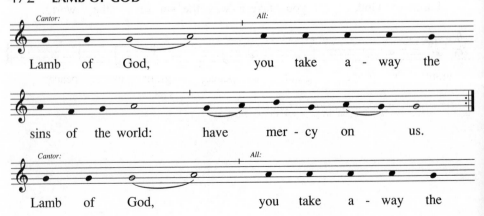

Lamb of God, you take a - way the

sins of the world: have mer - cy on us.

Lamb of God, you take a - way the

sins of the world: grant us peace.

Music: Agnus Dei XVIII, Vatican Edition; acc. by Robert J. Batastini, © 1993, GIA Publications, Inc.

LAMB OF GOD 473

Cantor:
Lamb of God, you take a-

way the sins of the world: have mer - cy on

Assembly:
us. Have mer - cy on us. *Lamb of God,

Cantor:
you take a - way the sins of the world: have

Assembly:
mer - cy on us. Have mer - cy on us.
repeat ad lib.

Cantor:
Lamb of God, you take a - way the sins of the

Assembly:
world: grant us peace. Grant us peace.

*Other titles, e.g., Bread of Life, Lord of Love, may be used.

Music: Howard Hughes, SM, © 1981, GIA Publications, Inc.

474 LAMB OF GOD

Lamb of God, you take a-way the sins of the world: have mer - cy on us. Lamb of God, you take a-way the sins of the world: grant us peace, grant us peace.

Music: Richard Proulx, © 1975, GIA Publications, Inc.

475 LAMB OF GOD

Choir or cantor:
*Lamb of God,

All:
you take a - way the sins of the world, *To repeat* have mer - cy on us.

Last time
world, grant *rall.* us peace.

Alternates: 1. Bread of life, 2. Prince of peace, 3. King of kings.

Music: *Festival Liturgy,* Richard Hillert, © 1983, GIA Publications, Inc.

LAMB OF GOD: MAY WE BE ONE

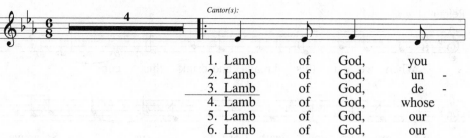

Cantor(s):

	Lamb	of	God,	
1.	Lamb	of	God,	you
2.	Lamb	of	God,	un -
3.	Lamb	of	God,	de -
4.	Lamb	of	God,	whose
5.	Lamb	of	God,	our
6.	Lamb	of	God,	our

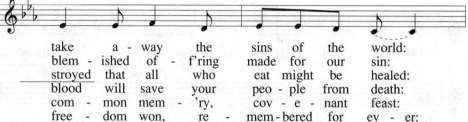

take	a - way	the	sins	of	the	world:
blem - ished	of - f'ring	made	for	our	sin:
stroyed	that all	who	eat	might	be	healed:
blood	will save	your	peo - ple	from	death:
com - mon	mem - 'ry,	cov - e - nant	feast:
free - dom	won,	re - mem - bered	for	ev - er:

All:

have mer - cy on us, have mer - cy on us.

Last time
Cantor(s):

Lamb of God, you take a-way the sins of the world,

All:

grant us peace, grant us peace.

Additional invocations:

Lamb of God, the shepherd of all who hunger and thirst…
Lamb of God, joy of the martyrs, song of the saints…
Lamb of God, all peoples will sing your victory song…
Lamb of God, unconquered light of the city of God…
Lamb of God, how blessed are those who are called to your feast…

Text: *Agnus Dei;* additional text by Rory Cooney
Music: Gary Daigle
© 1993, GIA Publications, Inc.

477 MAY WE BE ONE (COMMUNION HYMN)

Refrain

When we eat this bread and drink this cup, we pro-claim your death, Lord Je - sus. So as we share this feast may we be - come, heal-ing and light and peace. May we be one. one.

To verses / *Last time*

Verses

A - men, a - men.

A - men, a - men. A - men, a -

men. A - men, a - men.

D.C.

Text: Rory Cooney, b.1952
Tune: Gary Daigle, b.1957
© 1993, GIA Publications, Inc.

A Message Came to a Maiden Young   478

1. A mes - sage came to a maid - en young; The
2. No great - er news could a mes-sen - ger bring; For
3. He came, God's Word to the world here be - low; And
4. And some - times trum - pets from Si - on ring out, And

an - gel stood be - side her In shin - ing robes, and with
'twas from that young moth - er He came, who walked on the
round him there did gath - er A band who found that this
tramp - ing comes, and drum - ming; "Thy king - dom come," so we

gold - en tongue He told what should be - tide her:
earth as a king, And yet to all a broth - er:
teach - er to know Was e'en to know the Fa - ther:
cry; and they shout, "It comes!" and still 'tis com - ing.

The maid was lost in won - der; Her world was
His truth has spread like leav - en; 'Twill mar - ry
He healed the sick who sought him, For - gave the
Far, far a - head, to win us, Yet with us,

rent a - sun - der; Ah! how could she Christ's moth - er
earth to heav - en, Till all a - gree In char - i -
foes who fought him; Be - side the sea Of Gal - i -
nay with - in us; Till all shall see That King is

be By God's most high de - cree!
ty To dwell from sea to sea.
lee He set the na - tions free.
he, The Love from Gal - i - lee!

Text: St. 1, Dutch; para. E.B.G., 1928; sts. 2-4, Percy Dearmer, 1867-1936, © Oxford University Press
Tune: ANNUNCIATION, Irregular; traditional Dutch melody, 1896; harm. by David McK. Williams, b.1940, ©

479 O Come, Divine Messiah

1. O come, Di - vine Mes - si - ah, The
2. O come De - sired of na - tions, Whom
3. O come in peace and meek - ness, For

world in si - lence waits the day When
priest and proph - et long fore - told, Will
low - ly will your cra - dle be: Though

hope shall sing its tri - umph, And
break the cap - tive fet - ters, Re -
clothed in hu - man weak - ness We

sad - ness flee a - way.
deem the long - lost fold.
shall your God - head see.

Dear Sav - ior, haste! Come, come to earth. Dis - pel the

night and show your face, And bid us hail the dawn of

grace. O come, Di - vine Mes - si - ah, The

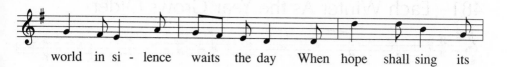

world in si - lence waits the day When hope shall sing its

tri - umph, And sad - ness flee a - way.

Text: *Venez, divin Messie;* Abbé Simon-Joseph Pellegrin, 1663-1745; tr. by S. Mary of St. Philip, 1877
Tune: VENEZ, DIVIN MESSIE, 7 8 7 6 with refrain; French Noël, 16th C.; harm. by Healey Willan, 1880-1968, © 1958,
Ralph Jusko Publications, Inc.

Savior of the Nations, Come 480

1. Sav - ior of the na - tions, come; Show the glo - ry
2. Not by hu - man flesh and blood, By the Spir - it
3. Won - drous birth! O won - drous child Of the Vir - gin
4. God Cre - a - tor is his source, Back to God he
5. Now your low - ly man - ger bright Hal - lows night with

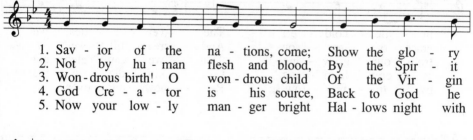

of the Son! Mar - vel now, O heav'n and earth,
of our God Was the word of God made flesh—
un - de - filed! Might - y God and man in one,
runs his course, Down to death and hell de - scends,
new - born light; Let no night this light sub - due,

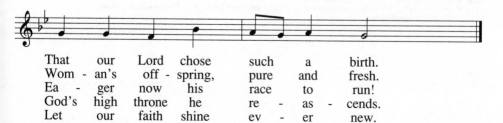

That our Lord chose such a birth.
Wom - an's off - spring, pure and fresh.
Ea - ger now his race to run!
God's high throne he re - as - cends.
Let our faith shine ev - er new.

Text: *Veni, Redemptor gentium;* ascr. to St. Ambrose, 340-397; tr. sts. 1-3a, William Reynolds, 1812-1876; sts. 3b-5, Martin L. Seltz, 1909-1967, alt.
Tune: NUN KOMM DER HEIDEN HEILAND, 77 77; *Geystliche gesangk Buchleyn,* Wittenberg, 1524

481 Each Winter As the Year Grows Older

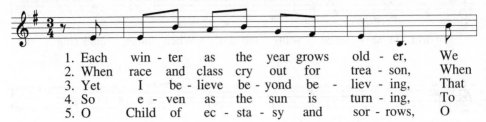

1. Each win - ter as the year grows old - er, We
2. When race and class cry out for trea - son, When
3. Yet I be - lieve be - yond be - liev - ing, That
4. So e - ven as the sun is turn - ing, To
5. O Child of ec - sta - sy and sor - rows, O

each grow old - er too. The chill sets in a
si - rens call for war, They o - ver - shout the
life can spring from death; That growth can flow - er
jour - ney to the north, The liv - ing flame, in
Prince of peace and pain, Bright - en to - day's world

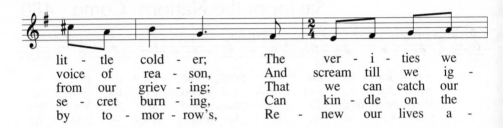

lit - tle cold - er; The ver - i - ties we
voice of rea - son, And scream till we ig -
from our griev - ing; That we can catch our
se - cret burn - ing, Can kin - dle on the
by to - mor - row's, Re - new our lives a -

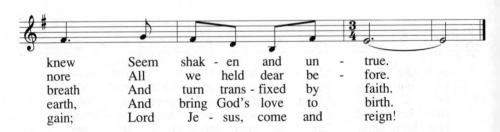

knew Seem shak - en and un - true.
nore All we held dear be - fore.
breath And turn trans - fixed by faith.
earth, And bring God's love to birth.
gain; Lord Je - sus, come and reign!

Text: William Gay, fl. 1969, © 1971, United Church Press
Tune: CAROL OF HOPE, 9 6 9 66; Annabeth Gay, b.1925, © 1971, United Church Press; acc. by Marty Haugen, b.1950, alt.,
© 1987, GIA Publications, Inc.

People, Look East   482

1. Peo - ple, look East. The time is near
2. Fur - rows, be glad. Though earth is bare.
3. Birds, though you long have ceased to build,
4. Stars, keep the watch. When night is dim
5. An - gels an - nounce with shouts of mirth

Of the crown - ing of the year.
One more seed is plant - ed there:
Guard the nest that must be filled.
One more light the bowl shall brim,
Him who brings new life to earth.

Make your house fair as you are a - ble,
Give up your strength the seed to nour - ish,
E - ven the hour when wings are fro - zen
Shin - ing be - yond the frost - y weath - er,
Set ev - 'ry peak and val - ley hum - ming

Trim the hearth and set the ta - ble.
That in course the flow'r may flour - ish.
He for fledg - ing time has cho - sen.
Bright as sun and moon to - geth - er.
With the word, the Lord is com - ing.

Peo - ple look East and sing to - day:

Love the Guest is on the way.
Love the Rose is on the way.
Love the Bird is on the way.
Love the Star is on the way.
Love the Lord is on the way.

Text: Eleanor Farjeon, 1881-1965, © David Higham Assoc. Ltd.
Tune: BESANÇON, 87 98 87; French traditional; harm. by Martin Shaw, 1875-1958, © Oxford University Press

483 Creator of the Stars of Night

1. Cre - a - tor of the stars of night,
2. In sor - row that the an - cient curse
3. When this old world drew on toward night,
4. At your great Name, O Je - sus, now
5. Come in your ho - ly might, we pray,
6. To God Cre - a - tor, God the Son,

1. Cre - á - tor ál - me sí - de - rum,
2. Qui daé - mo - nis ne fráu - di - bus
3. Com - mú - ne qui mún - di né - fas
4. Cú - jus po - té - stas gló - ri - ae.
5. Te de - pre - cá - mur, úl - ti - mae
6. Vír - tus, hó - nor, laus, gló - ri - a

Your peo - ple's ev - er - last - ing light,
Should doom to death a u - ni - verse,
You came; but not in splen - dor bright,
All knees must bend, all hearts must bow:
Re - deem us for e - ter - nal day;
And God the Spir - it, Three in One,

Ae - tér - na lux cre - dén - ti - um,
Per - í - ret ór - bis ím - pe - tu
Ut ex - pi - á - res, ad crú - cem
No - mén - que cum prí - mum só - nat,
Má - gnum di - é - i Jú - di - cem,
Dé - o Pá - tri cum Fí - li - o,

O Christ, Re - deem - er of us all,
You came, O Sav - ior, to set free
Not as a mon - arch, but the child
All things on earth with one ac - cord,
De - fend us while we dwell be - low
Praise, hon - or, might, and glo - ry be

Jé - su, Red - ém - ptor ó - mni - um,
A - mó - ris á - ctus lán - gui - di
E Vír - gi - nis sa - crá - ri - o
Et caé - li - tes et ín - fe - ri
Ár - mis su - pér - nae grá - ti - ae
Sán - cto sí - mul Pa - rá - cli - to

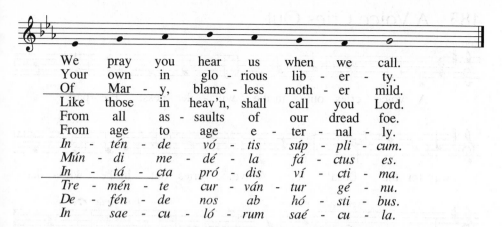

We   pray   you   hear   us   when   we   call.
Your   own   in   glo - rious   lib -   er -   ty.
Of   Mar - y,   blame - less   moth -   er   mild.
Like   those   in   heav'n, shall   call   you   Lord.
From   all   as - saults of   our   dread foe.
From   age   to   age   e -   ter -   nal - ly.
In -   tén - de   vó - tis   súp -   pli - cum.
Mún -   di   me -   dé - la   fá -   ctus   es.
In -   tá - cta   pró - dis   ví -   cti - ma.
Tre -   mén - te   cur - ván -   tur   gé -   nu.
De -   fén - de   nos   ab   hó -   sti - bus.
In   sae - cu -   ló - rum   saé -   cu -   la.

Text: *Conditor alme siderum,* Latin 9th C., alt. 1632; tr. *The Hymnal 1982,* © 1985, The Church Pension Fund
Tune: CONDITOR ALME SIDERUM, LM; Mode IV; acc. by Gerard Farrell, OSB, b.1919, © 1986, GIA Publications, Inc.

Wait for the Lord   484

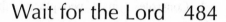

Wait   for   the Lord,   whose day   is   near.

Wait   for   the Lord: be   strong, take heart!

Text: Isaiah 40, Philippians 4, Matthew 6:33, 7:7; Taizé Community, 1984
Tune: Jacques Berthier, 1923-1994
© 1984, Les Presses de Taizé, GIA Publications, Inc., agent

485 A Voice Cries Out

Refrain

A voice cries out in the wil-der-ness: Pre-pare a way for the Lord! A voice cries out in the wil-der-ness: Make straight a high-way for God!

Last time

Verse 1
1. Con-sole my peo-ple, the ones dear to me: speak to the heart of Je-ru-sa-lem: the time of your mourn-ing is end-ed now, the Lord of life will come.

Verse 2
2. Ev-'ry val-ley is made a plain, ev-'ry moun-tain is lev-eled the glo-ry of God shall then be re-vealed, and the na-tions will sing in praise.

Verse 3

3. A voice shouts: "Cry!" O what shall I cry? All flesh is like grass and its flow-ers: the grass may with-er, the flow-er may fade, but the Word of the Lord is for - ev-er.

D.C.

Verse 4

4. Zi - on, shout from the moun - tain top, lift up your voice O Je - ru-sa-lem, and say to the peo-ple of God's own land, "Be-hold, be - hold your God!"

D.C.

Verse 5

5. The Lord will ap - pear as a shep-herd, hold-ing his lambs in his arms, keep-ing his flock so close to his heart lead-ing them all, old and young.

D.C.

Text: Isaiah 40:1-11; Michael Joncas, b.1951
Tune: Michael Joncas, b.1951

486 City of God, Jerusalem

1. Cit - y of God, Je - ru - sa - lem, Where he has set his
2. Sing and be glad, Je - ru - sa - lem, For God does not for -
3. Sor - row no more, Je - ru - sa - lem, Dis - card your rags of
4. Look all a - round, Je - ru - sa - lem, Sur - vey from west to

love;   Church of Christ that is one on earth With Je -
get;   He who said he would come to save Nev - er
shame!   Take your crown as a gift from God Who has
east;   Sons and daugh - ters of God the king Are in -

ru - sa - lem a - bove: Here as we walk this
failed his peo - ple yet.   Though we are tempt - ed
called you by his name.   Put off your sin, and
vit - ed to his feast.   Out of their ex - ile

chang - ing world Our joys are mixed with tears,   But the
by de - spair And daunt - ed by de - feat,   Our in -
wear the robe Of glo - ry in its place;   You will
far a - way His scat - tered fam - 'ly come,   And the

day will be soon when the Sav - ior re - turns
vin - ci - ble Lord will be seen in his strength,
shine in his light, you will share in his joy,
streets will re - sound with the song of the saints

And his voice will ban - ish our fears.
And his tri - umph will be com - plete.
You will praise his won - der - ful grace.
When the Sav - ior wel - comes us home.

Text: Baruch 4-5; Christopher Idle, b.1938, © 1982, Jubilate Hymns, Ltd. (Administered by Hope Publishing Co.)
Tune: PURPOSE, 8 6 8 7 8 6 12 8; Martin Shaw, 1875-1958, © Oxford University Press

When the King Shall Come Again   487

1. When the King shall come a - gain All his pow'r re -
2. In the des - ert trees take root Fresh from his cre -
3. Strength-en fee - ble hands and knees, Faint - ing hearts, be
4. There God's high - way shall be seen Where no roar - ing

veal - ing, Splen - dor shall an - nounce his reign,
a - tion; Plants and flow'rs and sweet - est fruit
cheer - ful! God who comes for such as these
li - on, Noth - ing e - vil or un - clean

Life and joy and heal - ing; Earth no
Join the cel - e - bra - tion; Riv - ers
Seeks and saves the fear - ful; Deaf ears,
Walks the road to Zi - on: Ran - somed

long - er in de - cay, Hope no more frus - trat - ed;
spring up from the earth, Bar - ren lands a - dorn - ing;
hear the si - lent tongues Sing a - way their weep - ing;
peo - ple home - ward bound All your prais - es voic - ing,

This is God's re - demp - tion day
Val - leys, this is your new birth,
Blind eyes, see the life - less ones
See your Lord with glo - ry crowned,

Long - ing - ly a - wait - ed.
Moun - tains, greet the morn - ing!
Walk - ing, run - ning, leap - ing.
Share in his re - joic - ing!

Text: Isaiah 35; Christopher Idle, b.1938, © 1982, Jubilate Hymns, Ltd. (Administered by Hope Publishing Co.)
Tune: GAUDEAMUS PARITER, 7 6 7 6 D; Johann Horn, c. 1495-1547

488 Comfort, Comfort, O My People

1. Com - fort, com - fort, O my peo - ple, Speak of peace, now
2. Hark, the voice of one who's cry - ing In the des - ert
3. O make straight what long was crook - ed, Make the rough - er

says our God; Com - fort those who sit in dark - ness,
far and near, Bid - ding all to full re - pent - ance
plac - es plain; Let your hearts be true and hum - ble,

Mourn - ing 'neath their sor - row's load. Speak un - to Je -
Since the king - dom now is here. O that warn - ing
As be - fits his ho - ly reign. For the glo - ry

ru - sa - lem Of the peace that waits for them;
cry o - bey! Now pre - pare for God a way;
of the Lord Now o'er earth is shed a - broad;

Tell of all the sins I cov - er, And that war - fare now is o - ver.
Let the val - leys rise to meet him And the hills bow down to greet him.
And all flesh shall see the to - ken That his word is nev - er bro - ken.

Text: Isaiah 40:1-8; *Tröstet, tröstet, meine Lieben*; Johann Olearius, 1611-1684; tr. by Catherine Winkworth, 1827-1878, alt.
Tune: GENEVA 42, 8 7 8 7 77 88; *Genevan Psalter*, 1551; harm. adapt. from Claude Goudimel, 1505-1572

489 Wake, O Wake, and Sleep No Longer

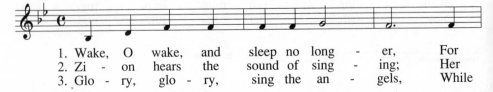

1. Wake, O wake, and sleep no long - er, For
2. Zi - on hears the sound of sing - ing; Her
3. Glo - ry, glo - ry, sing the an - gels, While

he who calls you is no stran - ger: A -
heart is thrilled with sud - den long - ing: She
mu - sic sounds from strings and cym - bals; All

wake, God's own Je - ru - sa - lem! Hear, the mid - night
stirs, and wakes, and stands pre-pared. Christ, her friend, and
hu - man - kind, with songs a - rise! Twelve the gates in -

bells are chim - ing The sig - nal for his roy - al com -
lord, and lov - er, Her star and sun and strong re - deem -
to the cit - y, Each one a pearl of shin - ing beau -

ing: Let voice to voice an - nounce his name! We
er— At last his might - y voice is heard. The
ty; The streets of gold ring out with praise. All

feel his foot-steps near, The Bride - groom at the door—
Son of God has come To make with us his home:
crea - tures round the throne A - dore the ho - ly One

Al - le - lu - ia! The lamps will shine With light di - vine
Sing Ho - san - na! The fight is won, The feast be - gun;
With re - joic - ing: A - men be sung By ev - 'ry tongue

As Christ the Sav - ior comes to reign.
We fix our eyes on Christ a - lone.
To crown their wel - come to the King.

Text: Matthew 25:1-13; *Wachet auf, ruft uns die Stimme*, Philipp Nicolai, 1556-1608; tr. and adapt. by Christopher Idle, b. 1938, © 1982, Hope
    Publishing Co.
Tune: WACHET AUF, 89 8 89 8 66 4 44 8; Philipp Nicolai, 1556-1608; harm. by J.S. Bach, 1685-1750

490 On Jordan's Bank

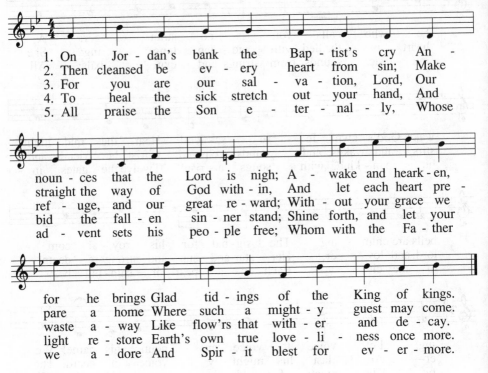

1. On Jor - dan's bank the Bap - tist's cry An -
2. Then cleansed be ev - ery heart from sin; Make
3. For you are our sal - va - tion, Lord, Our
4. To heal the sick stretch out your hand, And
5. All praise the Son e - ter - nal - ly, Whose

noun - ces that the Lord is nigh; A - wake and heark - en,
straight the way of God with - in, And let each heart pre -
ref - uge, and our great re - ward; With - out your grace we
bid the fall - en sin - ner stand; Shine forth, and let your
ad - vent sets his peo - ple free; Whom with the Fa - ther

for he brings Glad tid - ings of the King of kings.
pare a home Where such a might - y guest may come.
waste a - way Like flow'rs that with - er and de - cay.
light re - store Earth's own true love - li - ness once more.
we a - dore And Spir - it blest for ev - er - more.

Text: *Jordanis oras praevia;* Charles Coffin, 1676-1749; tr. by John Chandler, 1806-1876
Tune: WINCHESTER NEW, LM; adapt. from *Musikalisches Handbuch,* Hamburg, 1690

491 Prepare the Way of the Lord

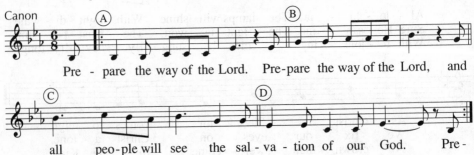

Canon

Pre - pare the way of the Lord. Pre-pare the way of the Lord, and

all peo-ple will see the sal - va - tion of our God. Pre-

Text: Luke 3:4,6; Taizé Community, 1984
Tune: Jacques Berthier, 1923-1994
© 1984, Les Presses de Taizé, GIA Publications, Inc., agent

Advent Gathering 492

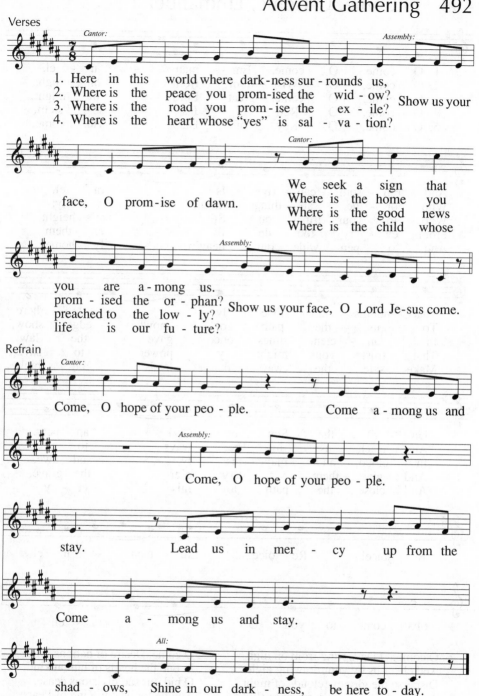

Verses

Cantor:

1. Here in this world where dark-ness sur - rounds us,
2. Where is the peace you prom-ised the wid - ow? Show us your
3. Where is the road you prom-ise the ex - ile?
4. Where is the heart whose "yes" is sal - va - tion?

face, O prom-ise of dawn.

Assembly:

Cantor:

We seek a sign that
Where is the home you
Where is the good news
Where is the child whose

Assembly:

you are a-mong us.
prom - ised the or - phan?
preached to the low - ly? Show us your face, O Lord Je-sus come.
life is our fu - ture?

Refrain

Cantor:

Come, O hope of your peo - ple. Come a - mong us and

Assembly:

Come, O hope of your peo - ple.

stay. Lead us in mer - cy up from the

Come a - mong us and stay.

All:

shad - ows, Shine in our dark - ness, be here to - day.

Text: Rory Cooney, b.1952
Tune: Gary Daigle, b.1957
© 1993, GIA Publications, Inc.

493   O Come, O Come, Emmanuel

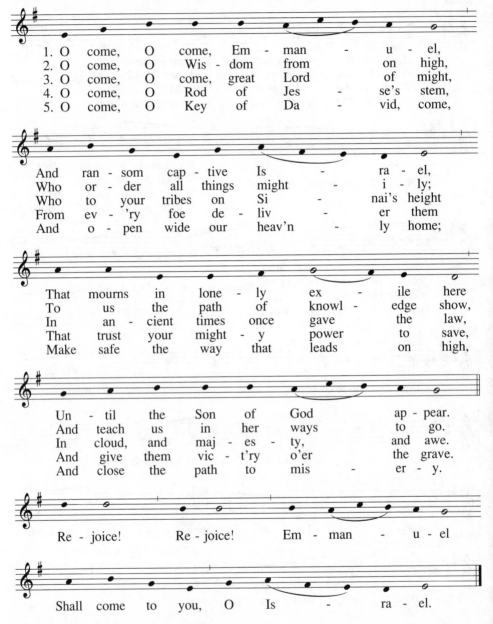

1. O come, O come, Em - man - u - el,
2. O come, O Wis - dom from on high,
3. O come, O come, great Lord of might,
4. O come, O Rod of Jes - se's stem,
5. O come, O Key of Da - vid, come,

And ran - som cap - tive Is - ra - el,
Who or - der all things might - i - ly;
Who to your tribes on Si - nai's height
From ev - 'ry foe de - liv - er them
And o - pen wide our heav'n - ly home;

That mourns in lone - ly ex - ile here
To us the path of knowl - edge show,
In an - cient times once gave the law,
That trust your might - y power to save,
Make safe the way that leads on high,

Un - til the Son of God ap - pear.
And teach us in her ways to go.
In cloud, and maj - es - ty,
And give them vic - t'ry o'er the grave.
And close the path to mis - er - y.

Re - joice!   Re - joice!   Em - man - u - el

Shall come to you, O Is - ra - el.

6. O come, O Dayspring from on high
   And cheer us by your drawing nigh;
   Disperse the gloomy clouds of night,
   And death's dark shadow put to flight.

7. O come, Desire of nations, bind
   In one the hearts of humankind;
   O bid our sad divisions cease,
   And be for us our King of Peace.

Text: *Veni, veni Emmanuel;* Latin 9th C.; tr. by John M. Neale, 1818-1866, alt.
Tune: VENI VENI EMMANUEL, LM with refrain; Mode I; adapt. by Thomas Helmore, 1811-1890; acc. by Richard Proulx, b.1937, © 1975,
   GIA Publications, Inc.

Awake! Awake, and Greet the New Morn   494

1. A - wake! a - wake, and greet the new morn, For
2. To us, to all in sor - row and fear, Em -
3. In dark - est night his com - ing shall be, When
4. Re - joice, re - joice, take heart in the night, Though

an - gels her - ald its dawn - ing, Sing out your joy, for
man - u - el comes a - sing - ing, His hum - ble song is
all the world is de - spair - ing, As morn - ing light so
dark the win - ter and cheer-less, The ris - ing sun shall

now he is born, Be - hold! the Child of our long - ing.
qui - et and near, Yet fills the earth with its ring - ing;
qui - et and free, So warm and gen - tle and car - ing.
crown you with light, Be strong and lov - ing and fear - less;

Come as a ba - by weak and poor, To bring all hearts to -
Mu - sic to heal the bro - ken soul And hymns of lov - ing
Then shall the mute break forth in song, The lame shall leap in
Love be our song and love our prayer, And love, our end - less

geth - er, He o - pens wide the heav'n - ly door And
kind - ness, The thun - der of his an - thems roll To
won - der, The weak be raised a - bove the strong, And
sto - ry, May God fill ev - 'ry day we share, And

lives now in - side us for ev - er.
shat - ter all ha - tred and blind - ness.
weap - ons be bro - ken a - sun - der.
bring us at last in - to glo - ry.

Text: Marty Haugen, b.1950
Tune: REJOICE, REJOICE, 9 8 9 8 8 7 8 9; Marty Haugen, b.1950
© 1983, GIA Publications, Inc.

495 My Soul in Stillness Waits

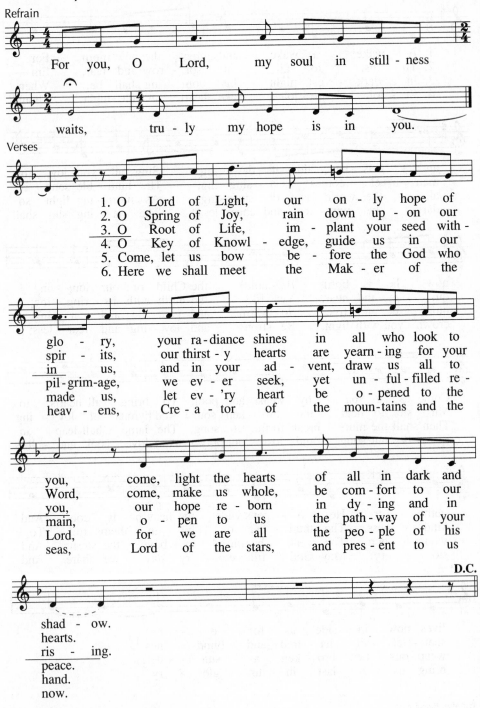

Refrain

For you, O Lord, my soul in still - ness waits, tru - ly my hope is in you.

Verses

1. O Lord of Light, our on - ly hope of
2. O Spring of Joy, rain down up - on our
3. O Root of Life, im - plant your seed with -
4. O Key of Knowl - edge, guide us in our
5. Come, let us bow be - fore the God who
6. Here we shall meet the Mak - er of the

glo - ry, your ra - diance shines in all who look to
spir - its, our thirst - y hearts are yearn - ing for your
in us, and in your ad - vent, draw us all to
pil - grim-age, we ev - er seek, yet un - ful - filled re -
made us, let ev - 'ry heart be o - pened to the
heav - ens, Cre - a - tor of the moun-tains and the

you, come, light the hearts of all in dark and
Word, come, make us whole, be com - fort to our
you, our hope re - born in dy - ing and in
main, o - pen to us the path - way of your
Lord, for we are all the peo - ple of his
seas, Lord of the stars, and pres - ent to us

D.C.

shad - ow.
hearts.
ris - ing.
peace.
hand.
now.

Text: Psalm 95 and "O" Antiphons; Marty Haugen, b.1950
Tune: Marty Haugen, b.1950
© 1982, GIA Publications, Inc.

Come, O Long Expected Jesus 496

1. Come, O long ex - pect - ed Je - sus, Born to set your
2. Born your peo - ple to de - liv - er; Born a child and

peo - ple free; From our fears and sins re - lease us;
yet a king! Born to reign in us for ev - er,

Free us from cap - tiv - i - ty. Is - rael's strength and
Now your gra - cious king - dom bring. By your own e -

con - so - la - tion, You, the hope of all the earth,
ter - nal Spir - it Rule in all our hearts a - lone;

Dear de - sire of ev - 'ry na - tion,
By your all suf - fi - cient mer - it

Come, and save us by your birth.
Raise us to your glo - rious throne.

Text: Haggai 2:7; Charles Wesley, 1707-1788, alt.
Tune: JEFFERSON, 8 7 8 7 D; William Walker's *Southern Harmony*, 1855; acc. by Theophane Hytrek, OSF, 1915-1992, © 1981, ICEL

497 The King Shall Come When Morning Dawns

1. The King shall come when morn - ing dawns And
2. Not, as of old, a lit - tle child, To
3. The King shall come when morn - ing dawns And
4. And let the end - less bliss be - gin, By
5. The King shall come when morn - ing dawns And

light tri - um - phant breaks. When beau - ty gilds the
suf - fer and to die, But crowned with glo - ry
earth's dark night is past; O haste the ris - ing
wea - ry saints fore - told, When right shall tri - umph
light and beau - ty brings. Hail, Christ, the Lord! Your

east - ern hills And life to joy a - wakes.
like the sun That lights the morn - ing sky.
of that morn Whose day shall ev - er last.
o - ver wrong, And truth shall be ex - tolled.
peo - ple pray: Come quick - ly, King of kings.

Text: John Brownlie, 1857-1925
Tune: MORNING SONG, CM; John Wyeth, 1770-1858; arr. by Robert J. Batastini, b.1942, © 1994, GIA Publications, Inc.

498 It Came upon the Midnight Clear

1. It came up - on the mid - night clear, That
2. Still through the clo - ven skies they come, With
3. Yet with the woes of sin and strife, The
4. For, lo, the days are has - tening on, By

glo - rious song of old, From
peace - ful wings un - furled, And
world has suf - fered long; Be -
proph - ets seen of old, When

an - gels bend - ing near the earth To
still their heav'n - ly mu - sic floats O'er
neath the heav'n - ly hymn have rolled Two
with the ev - er - cir - cling years Shall

touch their harps of gold: "Peace
all the wea - ry world: A -
thou - sand years of wrong; And
come the time fore - told, When

on the earth, good will to all From
bove its sad and low - ly plains They
war - ring hu - man - kind hears not The
peace shall o - ver all the earth Its

heaven's all gra - cious King"; The
bend on hov - 'ring wing, And
tid - ings which they bring; O
an - cient splen - dors fling, And

world in sol - emn still - ness lay, To
ev - er o'er its Ba - bel sounds The
hush the noise and cease your strife And
all the world give back the song Which

hear the an - gels sing.
bless - ed an - gels sing.
hear the an - gels sing.
now the an - gels sing.

Text: Edmund H. Sears, 1810-1876, alt.
Tune: CAROL, CMD; Richard S. Willis, 1819-1900

499 O Come, All Ye Faithful / Adeste Fideles

1. O come, all ye faith-ful, joy-ful and tri-um-phant, O
2. God of____ God,____ Light____ of____ Light,____
3. Sing, choirs of an-gels, sing in ex-ul-ta-tion,
4. Yea, Lord, we greet thee, born this hap-py morn-ing,
1. Ad-é-ste fi-dé-les, laé-ti, tri-um-phán-tes, Ve-
2. De-um de De-o, Lu-men de Lú-mi-ne,
3. Can-tet nunc i-o, cho-rus an-ge-lo-rum,
4. Er-go qui na-tus Di-e ho-di-ér-na,

come ye, O come ye to Beth - le-hem;
Lo! He comes forth from the Vir - gin's womb.
Sing, all ye cit-i-zens of heav'n a-bove!
Je - sus, to thee be all glo - ry giv'n;
ní - te, ve-ní-te in Béth - le-hem.
Ge - stant pu-él - lae ví - sce-ra.
Can - tet nunc au-la cae-lés - ti-um.
Je - su____ ti-bi sit gló - ri-a.

Come and be-hold him, born the King of an-gels;
Our ver-y God, be-got-ten not cre-a-ted,
Glo-ry to God, all glo-ry in the high-est;
Word of the Fa-ther, now in flesh ap-pear-ing;
Na-tum vi-dé-te, Re-gem an-ge-ló-rum.
De-um ve-rum, Gé-ni-tum, non fa-ctum.
Gló-ri-a, gló-ria, in ex-cél-sis De-o.
Pa-tris ae-ter-nae ver-bum ca-ro fa-ctum.

O come, let us a-dore him, O come, let us a-dore him,
Ve-ní-te a-do-ré-mus, ve-ní-te a-do-ré-mus,

O come, let us a-dore him, Christ, the Lord!
ve-ní-te a-do-ré-mus Dó - mi-num.

Text: *Adeste fideles;* John F. Wade, c.1711-1786; tr. by Frederick Oakeley, 1802-1880, alt.
Tune: ADESTE FIDELES, Irregular with refrain; John F. Wade, c.1711-1786

A Child Is Born in Bethlehem 500

1. A child is born in Beth - le - hem, al - le - lu - ia.
2. The babe who lies up - on the straw, al - le - lu - ia.
3. Up - on this joy - ful ho - ly night, al - le - lu - ia.
4. We praise you, Ho - ly Trin - i - ty, al - le - lu - ia.

1. *Pú - er ná - tus in Béth - le - hem, al - le - lú - ia.*
2. *Hic já - cet in prae - sé - pi - o, al - le - lú - ia.*
3. *In hoc na - tá - li gáu - di - o, al - le - lú - ia.*
4. *Lau - dé - tur sán - cta Trí - ni - tas, al - le - lú - ia.*

There - fore re - joice Je - ru - sa - lem, al - le - lu - ia,
Will rule the world for ev - er - more, al - le - lu - ia,
We bless your Name, O Lord of Light, al - le - lu - ia,
A - dor - ing you e - ter - nal - ly, al - le - lu - ia,

Un - de gáu - det Je - rú - sa - lem, al - le - lú - ia,
Qui ré - gnat sí - ne tér - mi - no, al - le - lú - ia,
Be - ne - di - cá - mus Dó - mi - no, al - le - lú - ia,
Dé - o di - cá - mus grá - ti - as, al - le - lú - ia,

al - le - lu - ia. Our joy - ful hearts we raise, Christ is born, O
al - le - lú - ia. In cór - dis jú - bi - lo Chrí - stum ná - tum

come a - dore him In new - found songs of praise.
a - do - ré - mus Cum nó - vo cán - ti - co.

Text: *Puer natus in Bethlehem;* Latin 14th C.; tr. by Ruth Fox Hume, b.1922, © 1964, GIA Publications, Inc.
Tune: PUER NATUS, 8 8 with alleluias and refrain; Mode I; acc. by Richard Proulx, b.1937, © 1986, GIA Publications, Inc.

501 The Virgin Mary Had a Baby Boy

1. The vir - gin Mar - y had a ba - by boy, the
2. The an - gels sang when the ba - by born, the
3. The wise men saw where the ba - by born, the

vir - gin Mar - y had a ba - by boy, the
an - gels sang when the ba - by born, the
wise men saw where the ba - by born, the

vir - gin Mar - y had a ba - by boy, and they
an - gels sang when the ba - by born, and they
wise men went where the ba - by born, and they

say that his name was Je - sus.
say that his name was Je - sus.
say that his name was Je - sus.

He come from the glo - ry, he come from the

glo - rious king - dom. Oh, yes! be - liev - er!

Oh, yes! be - liev - er! He come from the

glo - ry, he come from the glo - rious king - dom.

Text: West Indian carol, © 1945, Boosey and Co., Ltd.
Tune: West Indian carol, © 1945, Boosey and Co., Ltd.; acc. by Robert J. Batastini, b.1942, © 1993, GIA Publications, Inc.

Hark! The Herald Angels Sing 502

1. Hark! the her - ald an - gels sing, "Glo - ry to the
2. Christ, by high - est heaven a - dored, Christ the ev - er -
3. Hail the heav'n - born Prince of Peace! Hail the Sun of

new - born King; Peace on earth, and mer - cy mild
last - ing Lord: Late in time be - hold him come,
Right - eous - ness! Light and life to all he brings,

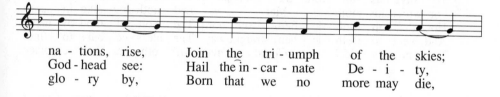

God and sin - ners rec - on - ciled!" Joy - ful, all you
Off - spring of the Vir - gin's womb. Veiled in flesh the
Ris'n with heal - ing in his wings. Mild he lays his

na - tions, rise, Join the tri - umph of the skies;
God - head see: Hail the in - car - nate De - i - ty,
glo - ry by, Born that we no more may die,

With the an - gel - ic host pro-claim, "Christ is born in Beth - le - hem!"
Pleased as man with us to dwell, Je - sus, our Em - man - u - el.
Born to raise us from the earth, Born to give us sec - ond birth.

Hark! the her-ald an - gels sing, "Glo-ry to the new-born King!"

Text: Charles Wesley, 1707-1788, alt.
Tune: MENDELSSOHN, 77 77 D with refrain; Felix Mendelssohn, 1809-1847

503 God Rest You Merry, Gentlemen

1. God rest you mer - ry, gen - tle-men, Let noth-ing you dis - may,
2. In Beth - le - hem in Ju - dah This bless-ed babe was born,
3. From God our great Cre - a - tor A bless-ed an - gel came,
4. The shep-herds at those tid - ings Re - joic-ed much in mind,
5. Now to the Lord sing prais - es, All you with - in this place,

For Je - sus Christ our Sav - ior Was born up - on this day,
And laid with - in a man - ger Up - on this bless - ed morn:
And un - to cer - tain shep - herds Brought tid - ings of the same,
And left their flocks a - feed - ing In tem-pest, storm, and wind,
And with true love and char-i - ty Each oth - er now em-brace;

To save us all from Sa - tan's power When we were gone a - stray.
For which his moth - er Mar - y Did noth-ing take in scorn.
How that in Beth - le - hem was born The Son of God by name.
And went to Beth - le - hem straight-way, The bless-ed babe to find.
This ho - ly tide of Christ - mas All oth - ers shall re - place.

O tid - ings of com - fort and joy, com-fort and

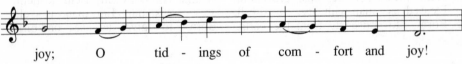

joy; O tid - ings of com - fort and joy!

Text: English carol, 18th C.
Tune: GOD REST YOU MERRY, 8 6 8 6 8 6 with refrain; English 18th C.; harm. by John Stainer, 1840-1901

Angels We Have Heard on High 504

1. An - gels we have heard on high Sweet - ly sing - ing
2. Shep-herds, why this ju - bi - lee? Why your joy - ous
3. Come to Beth - le - hem and see Him whose birth the
4. See him in a man - ger laid, Whom the choirs of

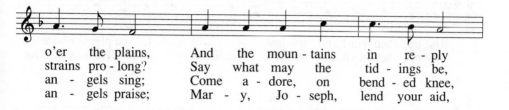

o'er the plains, And the moun - tains in re - ply
strains pro - long? Say what may the tid - ings be,
an - gels sing; Come a - dore, on bend - ed knee,
an - gels praise; Mar - y, Jo - seph, lend your aid,

Ech - o back their joy - ous strains.
Which in - spire your heav'n - ly song.
Christ, the Lord, the new - born King.
While our hearts in love we raise.

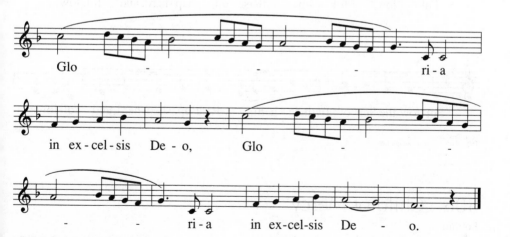

Glo - - - ri - a

in ex - cel - sis De - o, Glo - -

- - ri - a in ex-cel-sis De - o.

Text: *Les anges dans nos campagnes;* French, c. 18th C.; tr. from *Crown of Jesus Music*, London, 1862
Tune: GLORIA, 7 7 7 7 with refrain; French traditional

505 Rise Up, Shepherd, and Follow

Verses

Leader:

1. There's a star in the East on Christ-mas morn,
2. If you take good heed to the an - gel's words,

All: Leader:

Rise up, shep-herd, and fol-low, It will lead to the place where the
Rise up, shep-herd, and fol-low, You'll for-get your flocks, you'll for-

All:

Christ was born, Rise up, shep-herd, and fol-low.
get your herds, Rise up, shep-herd, and fol-low.

Refrain

Fol - low, fol - low, Rise up, shep-herd, and fol-low,

Fol-low the Star of Beth-le - hem, Rise up, shep-herd, and fol-low.

Text: Traditional
Tune: African-American spiritual

506 Child of Mercy

Refrain

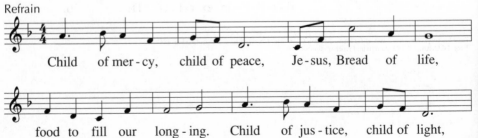

Child of mer-cy, child of peace, Je-sus, Bread of life,

food to fill our long-ing. Child of jus-tice, child of light,

Je-sus, sav - ing cup, Em - man - u - el, God with us.

Verses

1. All who walk in dark - ness have seen a great light, to
2. ⁊ A child is born to us, a son is giv - en us, up -
3. ⁊ We name him: "Won - der, coun - s'lor, he - ro, might-y God," The
4. We pro -claim good news to you, great ti - dings of joy: To

D.C.

those who dwell in fear, a light has shone!
on his shoul - der glo - ry rests!
Ho - ly One for ev - er: Prince of peace!
you is born a sav - ior: Christ the Lord!

Text: Isaiah 9:1, 5; David Haas, b.1957
Tune: David Haas, b.1957
© 1991, GIA Publications, Inc.

Gloria, Gloria   507

Canon—*4 voices*

Glo - ri - a, glo - ri - a, in ex - cel - sis De - o!

Glo - ri - a, glo - ri - a, al - le - lu - ia, al - le - lu - ia!

Tune: Jacques Berthier, 1923-1994, © 1979, 1988, Les Presses de Taizé, GIA Publications, Inc., agent

508 Angels, from the Realms of Glory

1. An - gels, from the realms of glo - ry,
2. Shep - herds, in the fields a - bid - ing,
3. Sag - es, leave your con - tem - pla - tions,
4. Though an in - fant now we view him,

Wing your flight o'er all the earth; You who sang cre -
Watch-ing o'er your flocks by night, God on earth is
Bright - er vi - sions beam a - far; Seek the great De -
He shall fill his heav'n-ly throne, Gath - er all the

a - tion's sto - ry, Now pro - claim Mes - si - ah's birth:
now re - sid-ing, Yon - der shines the in - fant light:
sire of na-tions, You have seen his morn - ing star:
na - tions to him; Ev - 'ry knee shall then bow down:

Come and wor - ship, come and wor - ship,

Wor - ship Christ, the new - born King.

Text: Sts. 1-3, James Montgomery, 1771-1854; st. 4, *Christmas Box*, 1825
Tune: REGENT SQUARE, 8 7 8 7 8 7; Henry Smart, 1813-1879

Infant Holy, Infant Lowly 509

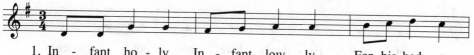

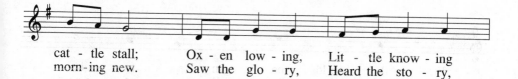

1. In - fant ho - ly, In - fant low - ly, For his bed a
2. Flocks were sleep - ing: Shep-herds keep - ing Vi - gil till the

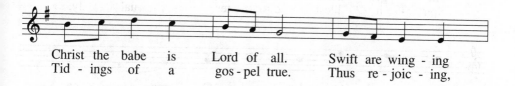

cat - tle stall; Ox - en low - ing, Lit - tle know - ing
morn-ing new. Saw the glo - ry, Heard the sto - ry,

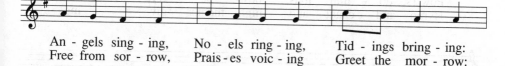

Christ the babe is Lord of all. Swift are wing - ing
Tid - ings of a gos - pel true. Thus re - joic - ing,

An - gels sing - ing, No - els ring - ing, Tid - ings bring - ing:
Free from sor - row, Prais-es voic - ing Greet the mor - row:

Christ the babe is Lord of all.
Christ the babe was born for you.

Text: Polish carol; para. by Edith M. G. Reed, 1885-1933
Tune: W ZLOBIE LEZY, 44 7 44 7 4444 7; Polish carol; harm. by A. E. Rusbridge, 1917-1969, © Bristol Churches Housing Assoc. Ltd.

510 Of the Father's Love Begotten

1. Of the Fa-ther's love be-got-ten,
2. O that birth for ev-er bless-ed,
3. Let the heights of heav'n a-dore him;
4. Christ, to you with God the Fa-ther,

Ere the worlds be-gan to be,
When the Vir-gin, full of grace,
An-gel hosts, his prais-es sing;
Spir-it blest e-ter-nal-ly,

He is Al-pha and O-me-ga,
By the Spir-it blest con-ceiv-ing,
Pow'rs, do-min-ions, bow be-fore him,
Hymn and chant and high thanks-giv-ing,

He the source, the end-ing he,
Bore the Sav-ior of our race;
And ex-tol our God and King;
And un-end-ing prais-es be:

Of the things that are, that have been,
And the Babe, the world's Re-deem-er,
Let no tongue on earth be si-lent,
Hon-or, glo-ry, and do-min-ion,

And that fu-ture years shall see,
First re-vealed his sa-cred face,
Ev-'ry voice in con-cert ring,
And e-ter-nal vic-to-ry,

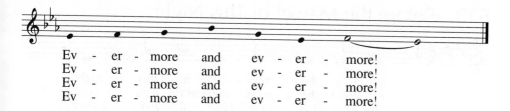

Ev - er - more and ev - er - more!
Ev - er - more and ev - er - more!
Ev - er - more and ev - er - more!
Ev - er - more and ev - er - more!

Text: *Corde natus ex Parentis;* Aurelius Prudentius, 348-413; tr. by John M. Neale, 1818-1866 and Henry W. Baker, 1821-1877
Tune: DIVINUM MYSTERIUM, 8 7 8 7 8 7 7; 12th C.; Mode V; acc. by Richard Proulx, b. 1937, © 1985, GIA Publications, Inc.

Gloria 511

¡Glo - ria, glo - ria, glo - ria   en las al - tur - as   a Dios!
Glo - ry, glo - ry, glo - ry,   glo - ry be to God on high!

Y_en la tie - rra paz pa-ra_a que - llos   que_a - ma el Se - ñor.
And on earth   peace to the peo - ple in whom God is well pleased.

Text: Luke 2:14
Tune: Pablo Sosa, © 1989, GIA Publications, Inc.

512 Before the Marvel of This Night

1. Be - fore the mar - vel of this night
2. A - wake the sleep - ing world with song,
3. The love that we have al - ways known,

A - dor - ing, fold your wings and bow,
This is the day the Lord has made.
Our con - stant joy and end - less light,

Then tear the sky a - part with light
As - sem - ble here, ce - les - tial throng,
Now to the love - less world be shown,

And with your news the world en - dow.
In roy - al splen - dor come ar - rayed.
Now break up - on its death - ly night.

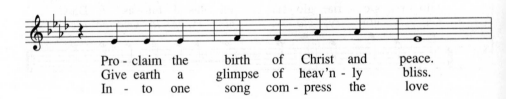

Pro - claim the birth of Christ and peace.
Give earth a glimpse of heav'n - ly bliss.
In - to one song com - press the love

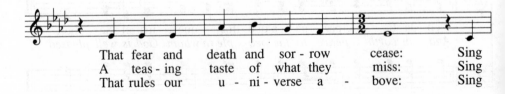

That fear and death and sor - row cease: Sing
A teas - ing taste of what they miss: Sing
That rules our u - ni - verse a - bove: Sing

peace,   sing peace,   sing   gift   of   peace,
bliss,   sing bliss,   sing   end - less   bliss,
love,   sing love,   sing   God   is   love,

Sing peace,   sing   gift   of   peace!
Sing bliss,   sing   end - less   bliss!
Sing love,   sing   God   is   love!

Text: Jaroslav J. Vajda, b.1919, © 1981
Tune: MARVEL, 8 8 8 8 8 8 8 6; Carl F. Schalk, b.1929, © 1981, GIA Publications, Inc.

Christ Was Born on Christmas Day   513

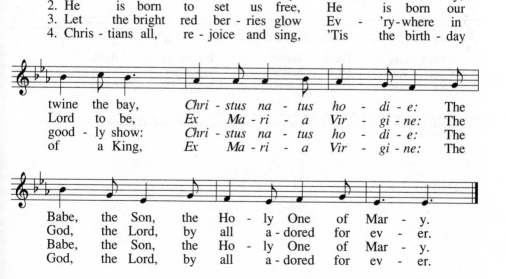

1. Christ   was born   on   Christ-mas day: Wreathe the   hol - ly,
2. He   is born   to   set   us   free,   He   is   born   our
3. Let   the bright   red   ber - ries glow   Ev - 'ry-where   in
4. Chris - tians all,   re - joice and sing,   'Tis   the birth - day

twine   the bay,   *Chri - stus na - tus ho - di - e:*   The
Lord   to   be,   *Ex   Ma - ri - a   Vir - gi - ne:*   The
good - ly show: *Chri - stus na - tus ho - di - e:*   The
of   a King,   *Ex   Ma - ri - a   Vir - gi - ne:*   The

Babe,   the Son,   the   Ho - ly One   of   Mar - y.
God,   the Lord,   by   all   a - dored for   ev - er.
Babe,   the Son,   the   Ho - ly One   of   Mar - y.
God,   the Lord,   by   all   a - dored for   ev - er.

Text: Traditional
Tune: RESONET IN LAUDIBUS, 777 11; German, 16th C.; harm. by Ralph Vaughan Williams, 1872-1958

514 Go Tell It on the Mountain

Refrain

Go tell it on the moun - tain, O - ver the hills and ev - 'ry - where; Go tell it on the moun - tain That Je - sus Christ is born!

Verses

1. While shep - herds kept their watch - ing O'er si - lent flocks by night, Be - hold through - out the heav - ens There shone a ho - ly light.
2. The shep - herds feared and trem - bled When lo! a - bove the earth Rang out the an - gel cho - rus That hailed our Sav - ior's birth.
3. Down in a low - ly man - ger The hum - ble Christ was born, And God sent us sal - va - tion That bless - ed Christ - mas morn.

D.C.

Text: African-American spiritual; adapt. by John W. Work, Jr., 1871-1925, © Mrs. John W. Work, III
Tune: GO TELL IT ON THE MOUNTAIN, 7 6 7 6 with refrain; African-American spiritual; harm. by Robert J. Batastini, b.1942, © 1995, GIA
   Publications, Inc.

Away in a Manger 515

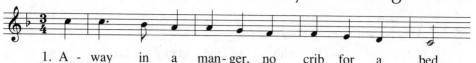

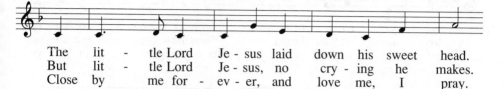

1. A - way in a man-ger, no crib for a bed,
2. The cat - tle are low-ing; the ba - by a - wakes,
3. Be near me, Lord Je - sus; I ask you to stay

The lit - tle Lord Je - sus laid down his sweet head.
But lit - tle Lord Je - sus, no cry - ing he makes.
Close by me for - ev - er, and love me, I pray.

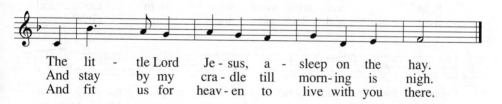

The stars in the bright sky looked down where he lay,
I love you, Lord Je - sus, look down from the sky,
Bless all the dear chil - dren in your ten - der care,

The lit - tle Lord Je - sus, a - sleep on the hay.
And stay by my cra - dle till morn-ing is nigh.
And fit us for heav - en to live with you there.

Text: St. 1-2, anonymous, st. 3, John T. McFarland, 1851-1913
Tune: MUELLER, 11 11 11 11; James R. Murray, 1841-1905; harm. by Robert J. Batastini, b. 1942, © 1994, GIA Publications, Inc.

516 Carol at the Manger

1. Ho-ly Child with-in the man-ger, Long a-go yet ev-er near; Come as friend to ev-'ry stran-ger, Come as hope for ev-'ry fear. As you lived to heal the bro-ken, Greet the out-cast, free the bound, Teach us now where you are found.

2. Once a-gain we tell the sto-ry— How your love for us was shown, When the Im-age of your glo-ry Wore an im-age like our own. Come, en-light-en with your wis-dom, Come, and fill us with your grace, May the fire of your com-pas-sion Kin-dle ev-'ry land and race.

3. Ho-ly Child with-in the man-ger, Lead us ev-er in your way, So we see in ev-'ry stran-ger How you come to us to-day. In our lives and in our liv-ing Give us strength to live as you, That our hearts might be for-giv-ing And our spir-its strong and true.

Text: Marty Haugen, b.1950
Tune: JOYOUS LIGHT, 8 7 8 7 D; Marty Haugen, b.1950
© 1987, GIA Publications, Inc.

Where Shepherds Lately Knelt   517

1. Where shep - herds late - ly knelt and
2. In that un - like - ly place I
3. How should I not have known I -
4. Can I, will I for - get how

kept the an - gel's word,   I come in
find him as they said: Sweet, new - born
sa - iah would be there,   His proph - e -
love was born and burned   Its way in -

half - be - lief, a pil - grim strange - ly
babe, how frail, and in a man - ger
cies ful - filled? With pound - ing heart, I
to my heart: un - asked, un - forced, un -

stirred;   But there is room
bed: A still, small voice
stare: A Child, a Son,
earned.   To die, to live,

and wel - come there for me,   But there is
to cry one day for me,   A still small
the Prince of Peace for me,   A Child, a
and not a - lone for me,   To die, to

room and wel - come there for me.
voice to cry one day for me.
Son, the Prince of Peace for me.
live, and not a - lone for me.

Text: Jaroslav J. Vajda, b.1919, © 1986
Tune: MANGER SONG, 12 12 10 10; Carl F. Schalk, b.1929, © 1986, GIA Publications, Inc.

518 Good Christian Friends, Rejoice

1. Good Chris - tian friends, re - joice
2. Good Chris - tian friends, re - joice
3. Good Chris - tian friends, re - joice
1. *Good Chris - tian friends, re - joice*
2. *Good Chris - tian friends, re - joice*
3. *Good Chris - tian friends, re - joice*

With heart and
With heart and
With heart and
With heart and
With heart and
With heart and

soul and voice;
soul and voice;
soul and voice;
soul and voice!
soul and voice!
soul and voice!

O give heed to what we say:
Now you hear of end - less bliss:
Now you need not fear the grave:
Raise your wea - ry hearts and see:
In the kind and just and true
Still be - fore us on the way,

Je - sus Christ is born to - day! Ox and ass be -
Je - sus Christ was born for this! He has o - pened
Je - sus Christ was born to save! Calls you one and
Je - sus Christ has come to free! When the cap - tives
Je - sus Christ is born a - new! In the low - ly,
Je - sus Christ is here to - day! In the break - ing

fore him bow, And he is in the man - ger now.
heav - en's door, And we are blest for ev - er - more.
calls you all To gain his ev - er - last - ing hall.
find re - lease, In feet that bring the word of peace,
weak and poor, The hum - ble stran - ger at our door,
of the bread, In life that cries out to the dead,

Christ is born to - day! Christ is born to - day!
Christ was born for this! Christ was born for this!
Christ was born to save! Christ was born to save!
Christ has come to free! Christ has come to free!
Christ is born a - new! Christ is born a - new!
Christ is born to - day! Christ is born to - day!

Text: *In dulci jubilo;* Latin and German, 14th C.; tr. by John M. Neale, 1818-1866; alt. verses, Marty Haugen, b.1950, © 1992, GIA Publications, Inc.
Tune: IN DULCI JUBILO, 66 77 78 55; Klug's *Geistliche Lieder,* Wittenberg, 1535; harm. by Robert L. Pearsall, 1795-1856

He Came Down 519

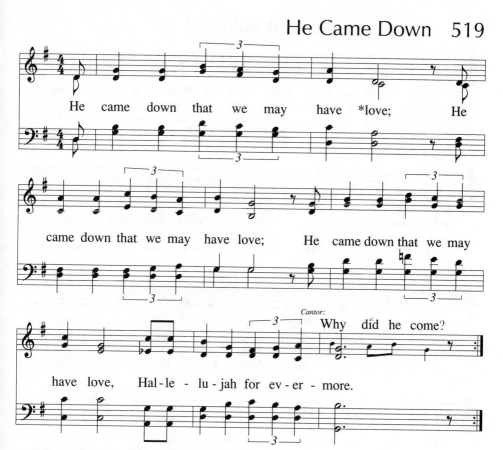

He came down that we may have *love; He
came down that we may have love; He came down that we may
have love, Hal-le-lu-jah for ev-er-more.

Cantor: Why did he come?

Substitute peace, joy, hope, life, *etc.*

Text: Cameroon traditional
Tune: Cameroon traditional; transcribed and arr. by John L. Bell, b.1949, © 1990, Iona Community, GIA Publications, Inc., agent

520 O Little Town of Bethlehem

1. O lit - tle town of Beth - le - hem, How
2. For Christ is born of Mar - y, And
3. How si - lent - ly, how si - lent - ly, The
4. O ho - ly Child of Beth - le - hem! De -

still we see thee lie! A - bove thy deep and
gath - ered all a - bove, While mor - tals sleep, the
won - drous gift is giv'n! So God im - parts to
scend to us we pray; Cast out our sin and

dream - less sleep The si - lent stars go by;
an - gels keep Their watch of won - d'ring love.
hu - man hearts The bless - ings of his heav'n.
en - ter in, Be born in us to - day.

Yet in the dark streets shin - eth The ev - er -
O morn - ing stars, to - geth - er Pro - claim the
No ear may hear his com - ing, But in this
We hear the Christ - mas an - gels The great glad

last - ing Light; The hopes and fears of
ho - ly birth! And prais - es sing to
world of sin, Where meek souls will re -
tid - ings tell; O come to us, a -

all the years Are met in thee to - night.
God the King, And peace to all on earth.
ceive him, still The dear Christ en - ters in.
bide with us, Our Lord Em - man - u - el!

Text: Phillips Brooks, 1835-1893
Tune: ST. LOUIS, 8 6 8 6 7 6 8 6; Lewis H. Redner, 1831-1908

Nativity Carol 521

Verses

1. Si - lent,   in the chill of mid - night,
2. "Fear not,"   said an - gel - ic voic - es;
3. Je - sus,   Lord of all cre - a - tion,

star - light   shines up - on a low - ly man - ger.
"tid - ings   of a won - drous love we bring you.
sleep now   close be - side your moth - er, Mar - y.

Won - der,   won - der of the a - ges;
Go   now,   find him in a man - ger;
Bring us   light a - mid the dark - ness,

heav - en breaks forth on the earth.
vis - it God's home on the earth."
prom - ise of life with - out end.

Refrain

For a child is born, the world re - joic - es! Shep - herds and

an - gels pro - claim his birth. This is Je - sus the Lord, our

Sav - ior and broth - er, bear - ing God's peace to the earth.

Text: Francis Patrick O'Brien, b.1958
Tune: Francis Patrick O'Brien, b.1958
© 1992, GIA Publications, Inc.

522 Silent Night, Holy Night

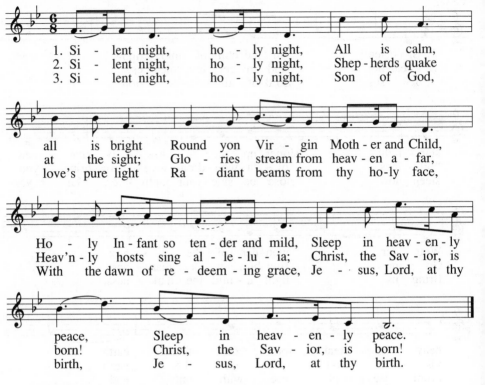

1. Si - lent night, ho - ly night, All is calm,
2. Si - lent night, ho - ly night, Shep - herds quake
3. Si - lent night, ho - ly night, Son of God,

all is bright Round yon Vir - gin Moth - er and Child,
at the sight; Glo - ries stream from heav - en a - far,
love's pure light Ra - diant beams from thy ho-ly face,

Ho - ly In - fant so ten - der and mild, Sleep in heav - en - ly
Heav'n - ly hosts sing al - le - lu - ia; Christ, the Sav - ior, is
With the dawn of re - deem - ing grace, Je - sus, Lord, at thy

peace, Sleep in heav - en - ly peace.
born! Christ, the Sav - ior, is born!
birth, Je - sus, Lord, at thy birth.

Text: *Stille Nacht, heilige Nacht;* Joseph Mohr, 1792-1849; tr. John F. Young, 1820-1885
Tune: STILLE NACHT, 66 89 66; Franz X. Gruber, 1787-1863

Night of Silence 523

1. Cold are the peo-ple, win-ter of life, We
2. Voice in the dis-tance, call in the night, On
3. Spir-it a-mong us, shine like the star, Your

trem-ble in shad-ows this cold end-less night,
wind you en-fold us, you speak of the light,
light that guides shep-herds and kings from a-far,

Fro-zen in the snow lie ros-es sleep-ing,
Gen-tle on the ear you whis-per soft-ly,
Shim-mer in the sky so emp-ty, lone-ly,

Flow-ers that will ech-o the sun-rise,
Ru-mors of a dawn so em-brac-ing,
Ris-ing in the warmth of your Son's love,

Fire of hope is our on-ly warmth,
Breath-less love a-waits dark-ened souls,
Star un-know-ing of night and day,

Wea-ry, its flame will be dy-ing soon.
Soon will we know of the morn-ing.
Spir-it we wait for your lov-ing Son.

Text: Daniel Kantor, b.1960
Tune: Daniel Kantor, b.1960
© 1984, GIA Publications, Inc.

524 Joy to the World

1. Joy to the world! the Lord is come:
2. Joy to the world! the Sav - ior reigns:
3. No more let sin and sor - rows grow,
4. He rules the world with truth and grace,

Let earth re - ceive her King;
Let us, our songs em - ploy;
Nor thorns in - fest the ground;
And makes the na - tions prove

Let ev - 'ry heart pre - pare him
While fields and floods, rocks, hills and
He comes to make his bless - ings
The glo - ries of his right - eous -

room, And heav'n and na - ture sing, And
plains Re - peat the sound - ing joy, Re -
flow Far as the curse is found, Far
ness, And won - ders of his love, And

heav'n and na - ture sing, And
peat the sound - ing joy, Re -
as the curse is found, Far
won - ders of his love, And

heav'n, and heav'n and na - ture sing.
peat, re - peat the sound - ing joy.
as, far as the curse is found.
won - ders, won - ders of his love.

Text: Psalm 98; Isaac Watts, 1674-1748
Tune: ANTIOCH, CM; arr. from George F. Handel, 1685-1759, in T. Hawkes' *Collection of Tunes*, 1833

The Aye Carol   525

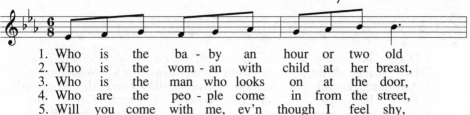

1. Who is the ba - by an hour or two old
2. Who is the wom - an with child at her breast,
3. Who is the man who looks on at the door,
4. Who are the peo - ple come in from the street,
5. Will you come with me, ev'n though I feel shy,

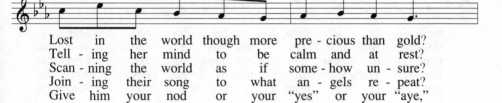

Looked for by shep - herds far strayed from their fold,
Giv - ing her milk to earth's heav - en - ly guest,
Wel - com - ing stran - gers, some rich but most poor,
Some to bring pres - ents and some just to meet,
Come to his cra - dle and come to his cry,

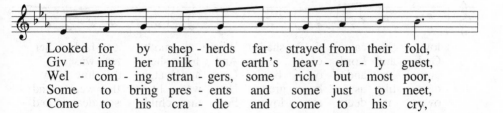

Lost in the world though more pre - cious than gold?
Tell - ing her mind to be calm and at rest?
Scan - ning the world as if some - how un - sure?
Join - ing their song to what an - gels re - peat?
Give him your nod or your "yes" or your "aye,"

This is God with us in Je - sus.
Mar - y, the moth - er of Je - sus.
Jo - seph, the fa - ther of Je - sus.
These are the new friends of Je - sus.
Give what you can give to Je - sus?

Text: John L. Bell, b.1949
Tune: AYE CAROL, 10 10 10 8; John L. Bell, b.1949
© 1987, Iona Community, GIA Publications, Inc., agent

526 Once in Royal David's City

1. Once in roy - al Da - vid's cit - y Stood a
2. He came down to earth from heav - en Who is
3. And through all his won - drous child - hood He would
4. For he is our child - hood's pat - tern, Day by
5. And our eyes at last shall see him, Through his

low - ly cat - tle shed, Where a moth - er laid her
God and Lord of all, And his shel - ter was a
hon - or and o - bey, Love and watch the low - ly
day like us he grew; He was lit - tle, weak, and
own re - deem - ing love; For that child so dear and

ba - by In a man - ger for his bed. Mar - y
sta - ble, And his cra - dle was a stall. With the
maid - en In whose gen - tle arms he lay. Chris - tian
help - less, Tears and smiles like us he knew: And he
gen - tle Is our Lord in heav'n a - bove: And he

was that moth - er mild, Je - sus
poor and mean and low - ly Lived on
chil - dren all should be Kind, o -
feels for all our sad - ness, And he
leads his chil - dren on To the

Christ her lit - tle Child.
earth our Sav - ior ho - ly.
be - dient, good as he.
shares in all our glad - ness.
place where he has gone.

Text: Cecil Frances Alexander, 1818-1895
Tune: IRBY, 8 7 8 7 77; Henry J. Gauntlett, 1805-1876; harm. by Arthur H. Mann, 1850-1929. © 1957, Novello and Co. Ltd.

Virgin-born, We Bow before You   527

1. Vir - gin - born, we bow be - fore you: Bless - ed was the
2. Bless - ed she by all cre - a - tion, Who brought forth the

womb that bore you; Mar - y, Moth - er meek and mild,
world's sal - va - tion. Bless - ed they who ev - er blest,

Bless - ed was she in her Child. Bless - ed
Love you most and serve you best. Vir - gin -

was the breast that fed you; Bless - ed
born, we bow be - fore you; Bless - ed

was the hand that led you; Bless - ed was the moth - er's
was the womb that bore you; Mar - y, Moth - er meek and

eye Watch - ing o'er your in - fan - cy.
mild, Bless - ed was she in her Child.

Text: Reginald Herber, 1783-1826, alt.
Tune: MON DIEU PRETE-MOI L'OREILLE, 88 77 D; attr. to Louis Bourgeois, c.1510-1561; harm. by Claude Goudimel, 1505-1572, alt.

528 Sing of Mary, Meek and Lowly

1. Sing of Mar - y meek and low - ly, Vir - gin - moth - er
2. Sing of Je - sus, son of Mar - y, In the home at
3. Glo - ry be to God the Fa - ther; Glo - ry be to

pure and mild, Sing of God's own Son most ho - ly,
Naz - a - reth. Toil and la - bor can - not wea - ry
God the Son; Glo - ry be to God the Spir - it;

Who be - came her lit - tle child. Fair - est child of
Love en - dur - ing un - to death. Con - stant was the
Glo - ry to the Three in One. From the heart of

fair - est moth - er, God the Lord who came to earth,
love he gave her, Though he went forth from her side,
bless - ed Mar - y, From all saints the song as - cends,

Word made flesh, our ver - y broth - er,
Forth to preach, and heal, and suf - fer,
And the church the strain re - ech - oes

Takes our na - ture by his birth.
Till on Cal - va - ry he died.
Un - to earth's re - mot - est ends.

Text: Roland F. Palmer, 1891-1985
Tune: PLEADING SAVIOR, 8 7 8 7 D; *Christian Lyre*, 1830; harm. by Richard Proulx, b.1937, © 1986, GIA Publications, Inc.

Songs of Thankfulness and Praise 529

1. Songs of thank - ful - ness and praise,   Je - sus, Lord, to
2. Man - i - fest   at   Jor - dan's stream,   Proph - et, Priest, and
3. Man - i - fest   in   mak - ing   whole   Pal - sied limbs and
4. Grant us grace to   see you, Lord,   Mir - rored in your

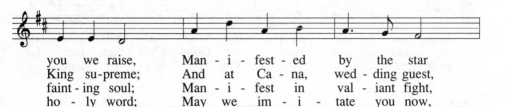

you we raise,   Man - i - fest - ed   by   the star
King su - preme;   And at Ca - na,   wed - ding guest,
faint - ing soul;   Man - i - fest in   val - iant fight,
ho - ly word;   May we im - i - tate you now,

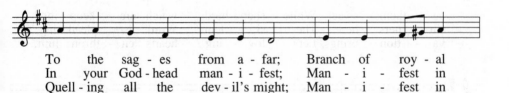

To   the sag - es   from a - far;   Branch of   roy - al
In   your God - head   man - i - fest;   Man - i - fest in
Quell - ing all the   dev - il's might;   Man - i - fest in
And on us your   grace en - dow;   That we like to

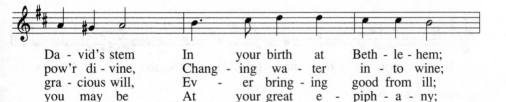

Da - vid's stem   In   your birth at   Beth - le - hem;
pow'r di - vine,   Chang - ing wa - ter   in - to wine;
gra - cious will,   Ev - er bring - ing   good from ill;
you may be   At   your great   e - piph - a - ny;

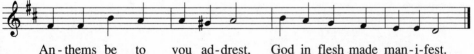

An - thems be to   you ad - drest,   God in flesh made man - i - fest.
An - thems be to   you ad - drest,   God in flesh made man - i - fest.
An - thems be to   you ad - drest,   God in flesh made man - i - fest.
And may praise you   ev - er blest,   God in flesh made man - i - fest.

Text: Christopher Wordsworth, 1807-1885
Tune: SALZBURG, 77 77 D; Jakob Hintze, 1622-1702, alt; harm. by J.S. Bach, 1685-1750

530 What Child Is This

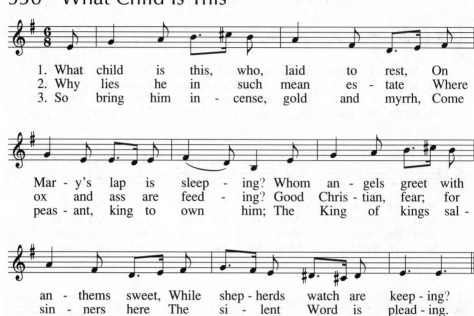

1. What child is this, who, laid to rest, On
2. Why lies he in such mean es - tate Where
3. So bring him in - cense, gold and myrrh, Come

Mar - y's lap is sleep - ing? Whom an - gels greet with
ox and ass are feed - ing? Good Chris - tian, fear; for
peas - ant, king to own him; The King of kings sal -

an - thems sweet, While shep - herds watch are keep - ing?
sin - ners here The si - lent Word is plead - ing.
va - tion brings, Let lov - ing hearts en - throne him.

This, this is Christ the King, Whom shep - herds guard and an - gels sing;

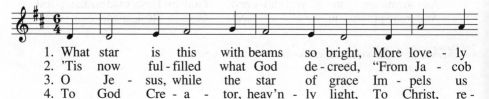

Haste, haste to bring him laud, The babe, the son of Mar - y.

Text: William C. Dix, 1827-1898
Tune: GREENSLEEVES, 8 7 8 7 with refrain; English melody, 16th C.; harm. by John Stainer, 1840-1901

531 What Star Is This

1. What star is this with beams so bright, More love - ly
2. 'Tis now ful - filled what God de - creed, "From Ja - cob
3. O Je - sus, while the star of grace Im - pels us
4. To God Cre - a - tor, heav'n - ly light, To Christ, re -

than	the	noon -	day	light?	'Tis	sent	to_an-nounce	a
shall	a	star	pro - ceed";	And	lo!	the	east -	ern
on	to	seek	your	face,	Let	not	our	sloth -	ful
vealed	in	earth -	ly	night,	To	God	the	Spir -	it

new -	born king,	Glad	tid - ings	of	our God	to	bring.
sag -	es stand,	To	read	in heav'n	the Lord's	com-mand.
hearts	re - fuse	The	guid - ance	of	your light	to	use.
blest	we raise	An	end - less song	of	thank - ful praise!

Text: *Quem stella sole pulchrior*, Charles Coffin, 1676-1749; tr. by John Chandler, 1806-1876, alt.
Tune: PUER NOBIS, LM; adapt. by Michael Praetorius, 1571-1621

Sion, Sing   532

Refrain

Cantor, then all:

Si - on, sing, break in - to song!

For with - in you is the Lord with sav - ing pow'r.

Verses

1. Rise and shine forth, for your light has come,
   and upon you breaks the glory of the Lord;
   For the darkness covers the earth,
   and the thick clouds, the people.

2. Wonder and thanksgiving shall fill your heart,
   As the wealth of nations enriches you;
   You shall be called the City of the Lord,
   Dear to the Holy One of Israel.

Text: Refrain, Zephaniah 3:14-17, Luke 1:28-35; verses, Isaiah 60:1-5, 14
Music: Lucien Deiss, CSSp, b.1921
© 1965, World Library Publications, Inc.

533 Brightest and Best

1. Bright-est and best of the stars of the morn-ing,
2. Cold on his cra-dle the dew-drops are shin-ing,
3. Shall we then yield him, in cost-ly de-vo-tion,
4. Vain-ly we of-fer each am-ple o-bla-tion,
5. Bright-est and best of the stars of the morn-ing,

Dawn on our dark-ness, and lend us thine aid;
Low lies his head with the beasts of the stall;
O-dors of E-dom, and of-f'rings di-vine,
Vain-ly with gifts would his fa-vor se-cure,
Dawn on our dark-ness, and lend us thine aid;

Star of the east, the ho-ri-zon a-dorn-ing,
An-gels a-dore him in slum-ber re-clin-ing,
Gems of the moun-tain, and pearls of the o-cean,
Rich-er by far is the heart's ad-o-ra-tion,
Star of the east, the ho-ri-zon a-dorn-ing,

Guide where our in-fant Re-deem-er is laid.
Mak-er and Mon-arch and Sav-ior of all.
Myrrh from the for-est, and gold from the mine?
Dear-er to God are the pray'rs of the poor.
Guide where our in-fant Re-deem-er is laid.

Bright-est and best of the stars of the morn-ing,

Dawn on our dark-ness, and lend us thine aid;

Star of the east, the ho-ri-zon a-dorn-ing,

Guide where our in-fant Re-deem-er is laid.

Text: Reginald Heber, 1783-1826, alt.
Tune: STAR IN THE EAST, 11 10 11 10 with refrain; *Southern Harmony*, 1835; harm. by Marty Haugen, b.1950, © 1987, GIA Publications, Inc.

As with Gladness Men of Old   534

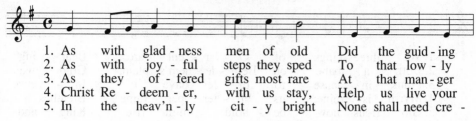

1. As   with   glad - ness   men   of   old   Did   the   guid - ing
2. As   with   joy - ful   steps they sped   To   that   low - ly
3. As   they   of - fered   gifts most rare   At   that   man - ger
4. Christ Re - deem - er,   with   us   stay,   Help   us   live your
5. In   the   heav'n - ly   cit - y   bright   None shall need cre -

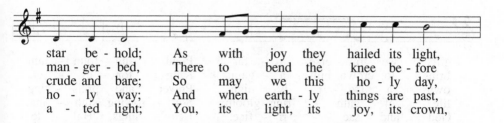

star   be - hold;   As   with   joy   they   hailed its   light,
man - ger - bed,   There   to   bend   the   knee   be - fore
crude and   bare;   So   may   we   this   ho - ly   day,
ho - ly   way;   And   when   earth - ly   things are   past,
a - ted   light;   You,   its   light,   its   joy,   its   crown,

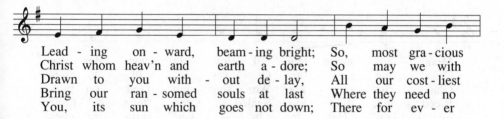

Lead - ing   on - ward,   beam - ing bright;   So,   most gra - cious
Christ whom heav'n and   earth   a - dore;   So   may   we with
Drawn   to   you   with - out   de - lay,   All   our   cost - liest
Bring   our   ran - somed   souls   at   last   Where they   need   no
You,   its   sun   which   goes   not down;   There   for   ev - er

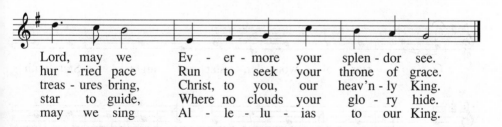

Lord,   may   we   Ev - er - more   your   splen - dor   see.
hur - ried pace   Run   to   seek   your   throne of   grace.
treas - ures bring,   Christ,   to   you,   our   heav'n - ly   King.
star   to   guide,   Where   no clouds   your   glo - ry   hide.
may   we   sing   Al - le - lu - ias   to   our   King.

Text: William C. Dix, 1837-1898
Tune: DIX, 77 77 77; arr. from Conrad Kocher, 1786-1872, by William H. Monk, 1823-1889

535   We Three Kings of Orient Are

1. We three kings of O - ri - ent are, Bear - ing
2. Born a babe on Beth - le - hem's plain, Gold we
3. Frank - in - cense to of - fer have I; In - cense
4. Myrrh is mine: its bit - ter per - fume Breathes a
5. Glo - rious now be - hold him rise, King and

gifts we trav - erse a - far Field and foun - tain,
bring to crown him a - gain; King for - ev - er,
owns a De - i - ty nigh, Prayer and prais - ing
life of gath - 'ring gloom; Sor - rowing, sigh - ing,
God and sac - ri - fice: Heav'n sings, "Hal - le -

Moor and moun - tain, Fol - low - ing yon - der star.
Ceas - ing nev - er, O - ver us all to reign.
Glad - ly rais - ing, Wor - ship - ing God on high.
Bleed - ing, dy - ing, Sealed in the stone cold tomb.
lu - jah!" "Hal - le - lu - jah!" earth re - plies.

O star of won - der, star of night, Star with

roy - al beau - ty bright, West - ward lead - ing, still pro -

ceed - ing, Guide us to the per - fect Light.

Text: Matthew 2:1-11; John H. Hopkins, Jr., 1820-1891
Tune: KINGS OF ORIENT, 88 44 6 with refrain; John H. Hopkins, Jr., 1820-1891

Lord, Today 536

Refrain

Lord, to-day we have seen your glo-ry, dawn fol-lows the night. We, your peo-ple who walked in dark-ness now have seen a great light.

Verses

1. A child is born, a Son giv-en
2. The Lord is king, the na-tions re-
3. O Beth-le-hem, you are from of
4. The days will come, the Lord prom-ised
5. New light has dawned up-on all the

us, on him do-min-ion shall rest.
joice, let all God's peo-ple be glad. The
old, too small a-mong Ju-dah's clans.
us, when God would raise up a shoot
just, glad-ness for up-right of heart. Re-

His name shall be Won-der-ful God,
heav-ens pro-claim jus-tice for all.
From you shall come a rul-er this day,
to rule the land, reign as a king,
joice in the Lord, you faith-ful ones.

D.C.

Coun-sel-or, Prince of Peace.
Glo-ry has filled the land.
shep-herd to guide the land.
whose name is Lord the Just.
Give thanks to God's great name.

Text: Mike Balhoff, b.1946
Tune: Darryl Ducote, b.1945, Gary Daigle, b.1957
© 1978, Damean Music. Distributed by GIA Publications, Inc.

537 The First Nowell

1. The first Now - ell, the an - gel did say, Was to
2. They look - ed up and saw a star Shin-ing
3. And by the light of that same star Three
4. This star drew nigh to the north - west, O'er
5. Then en - tered in those wise men three, Full
6. Then let us all with one ac - cord Sing

cer - tain poor shep-herds in fields as they lay; In
in the east, be - yond them far, And
wise men came from coun - try far; To
Beth - le - hem it took its rest; And
rev - 'rent - ly up - on their knee, And
prais - es to our heav - 'nly Lord; Who

fields where they lay keep-ing their sheep, On a
to the earth it gave great light, And
seek for a king was their in - tent, And to
there it did both stop and stay, Right
of - fered there, in his pres - ence, Their
with the Fa - ther we a - dore And

cold win - ter's night that was so deep.
so it con - tin - ued both day and night.
fol - low the star where - ev - er it went.
o - ver the place where Je - sus lay.
gold and myrrh and frank - in - cense.
Spir - it blest for ev - er - more.

Now - ell, Now - ell, Now - ell, Now - ell,

Born is the King of Is - ra - el.

Text: English Carol, 17th C.
Tune: THE FIRST NOWELL, Irregular; English Melody; harm. from *Christmas Carols New and Old*, 1871

When John Baptized by Jordan's River   538

1. When John bap - tized by Jor - dan's riv - er
2. There as the Lord, bap - tized and pray - ing,
3. O Son of Man, our na - ture shar - ing,

In faith and hope the peo - ple came, That John and
Rose from the stream, the sin - less one, A voice was
In whose o - be - dience all are blest, Sav - ior, our

Jor - dan might de - liv - er Their trou - bled
heard from heav - en say - ing, "This is my
sins and sor - rows bear - ing, Hear us and

souls from sin and shame. They came to seek a
own be - lov - ed Son." There as the Fa - ther's
grant us this re - quest: Dai - ly to grow, by

new be - gin - ning, The hu - man spir - it's age - less
word was spo - ken, Not in the pow'r of wind and
grace de - fend - ed, Filled with the Spir - it from a -

quest, Re - pent - ance, and an end of
flame, But of his love and peace the
bove; In Christ bap - tized, be - loved, be -

sin - ning, Re - nounc - ing ev - 'ry wrong con - fessed.
to - ken, Seen as a dove, the Spir - it came.
friend - ed, Chil - dren of God in peace and love.

Text: Timothy Dudley-Smith, b.1926, © 1984, Hope Publishing Co.
Tune: RENDEZ À DIEU, 9 8 9 8 D; Louis Bourgeois, c.1510-1561

539 Dust and Ashes

Verses

1. Dust and ash - es touch our face, mark our fail - ure and our
2. Dust and ash - es soil our hands— greed of mar - ket, pride of
3. Dust and ash - es choke our tongue in the waste - land of de -

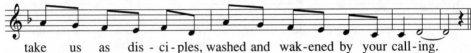

fall - ing. Ho - ly Spir - it, come, walk with us to - mor-row,
na - tion. Ho - ly Spir - it, come, walk with us to - mor-row,
pres-sion. Ho - ly Spir - it, come, walk with us to - mor-row,

take us as dis - ci - ples, washed and wak-ened by your call-ing.
as we pray and strug-gle through the mesh - es of op - pres-sion.
through all gloom and griev-ing to the paths of res - ur - rec - tion.

Refrain

Take us by the hand and lead us, lead us through the des - ert sands,

bring us liv - ing wa - ter, Ho-ly Spir - it, come.

Text: Brian Wren, b.1936, © 1989, Hope Publishing Co.
Tune: David Haas, b.1957, © 1991, GIA Publications, Inc.

Seek the Lord 540

Refrain

Seek the Lord while he may be found;

call to him while he is still near.

Verses 1, 2

1. To-day is the day and now the pro - per hour
2. As high as the sky is a - bove the earth,

to for - sake our sin - ful lives and turn to the Lord.
͞ so high a - bove our ways, the ways of the Lord.

Verse 3

3. Find - ing the Lord, let us cling to him. His

words, his ways lead us to life.

Verse 4

4. Some day we'll live in the house of God;

gaze on his face and praise his name.

Text: Isaiah 55:6-9; Roc O'Connor, SJ, b.1949
Tune: Roc O'Connor, SJ, b.1949; arr. by Peter Felice, alt.
© 1976, Robert F. O'Connor, SJ, and OCP Publications

541 Tree of Life

1. Tree of Life and awe-some mys - t'ry, In your
2. Seed that dies to rise in glo - ry, May we
3. We re - mem - ber truth once spo - ken, Love passed
4. Gen - tle Je - sus, might - y Spir - it, Come in -
5. Christ, you lead and we shall fol - low, Stum - bling

death we are re - born, Though you die in all of
see our - selves in you, If we learn to live your
on through act and word, Ev - 'ry per - son lost and
flame our hearts a - new, We may all your joy in -
though our steps may be, One with you in joy and

his - t'ry, Still you rise with ev - 'ry morn, Still you
sto - ry We may die to rise a - new, We may
bro - ken Wears the bod - y of our Lord, Wears the
her - it If we bear the cross with you, If we
sor - row, We the riv - er, you the sea, We the

rise with ev - 'ry morn.
die to rise a - new.
bod - y of our Lord.
bear the cross with you.
riv - er, you the sea.

Lenten Verses

General: Light of life beyond conceiving, Mighty Spirit of our Lord;
Give new strength to our believing, Give us faith to live your word.

1st Sunday: From the dawning of creation, You have loved us as your own;
Stay with us through all temptation, Make us turn to you alone.

2nd Sunday: In our call to be a blessing, May we be a blessing true;
May we live and die confessing Christ as Lord of all we do.

3rd Sunday: Living Water of salvation, Be the fountain of each soul;
Springing up in new creation, Flow in us and make us whole.

4th Sunday: Give us eyes to see you clearly, Make us children of your light;
Give us hearts to live more nearly As your gospel shining bright.

5th Sunday: God of all our fear and sorrow, God who lives beyond our death;
Hold us close through each tomorrow, Love as near as every breath.

Text: Marty Haugen, b.1950
Tune: THOMAS, 8 7 8 77; Marty Haugen, b.1950
© 1984, GIA Publications, Inc.

Adoramus Te Christe 542

Text: Antiphon from Good Friday Liturgy; *We adore you, O Christ, and we bless you, because by your holy cross you have redeemed the world.*
Tune: Marty Haugen, b.1950, © 1984, GIA Publications, Inc.

543 By the Babylonian Rivers

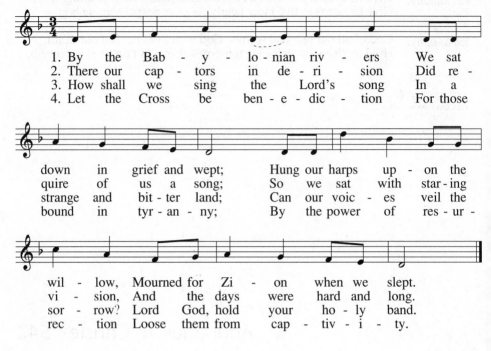

1. By the Bab - y - lo - nian riv - ers We sat
2. There our cap - tors in de - ri - sion Did re -
3. How shall we sing the Lord's song In a
4. Let the Cross be ben - e - dic - tion For those

down in grief and wept; Hung our harps up - on the
quire of us a song; So we sat with star - ing
strange and bit - ter land; Can our voic - es veil the
bound in tyr - an - ny; By the power of res - ur -

wil - low, Mourned for Zi - on when we slept.
vi - sion, And the days were hard and long.
sor - row? Lord God, hold your ho - ly band.
rec - tion Loose them from cap - tiv - i - ty.

Text: Psalm 137
Tune: KAS DZIEDAJA, 8 7 8 7; Latvian Folk Melody; acc. by Robert J. Batastini, b.1942, © 1995, GIA Publications, Inc.

544 O Sun of Justice

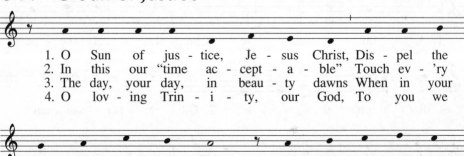

1. O Sun of jus - tice, Je - sus Christ, Dis - pel the
2. In this our "time ac - cept - a - ble" Touch ev - 'ry
3. The day, your day, in beau - ty dawns When in your
4. O lov - ing Trin - i - ty, our God, To you we

dark - ness of our hearts, Till your blest light makes
heart with sor - row, Lord, That, turned from sin, re -
light earth blooms a - new; Led back a - gain to
bow through end - less days, And in your grace new -

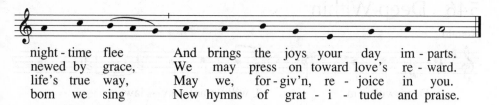

night - time	flee	And	brings	the	joys	your	day	im - parts.
newed by	grace,	We	may	press	on	toward	love's	re - ward.
life's true	way,	May	we,	for - giv'n,	re -	joice	in	you.
born we	sing	New	hymns	of	grat - i - tude			and praise.

Text: *Jam Christe sol justitiae;* Latin, 6th C.; tr. by Peter J. Scagnelli, b.1949, ©
Tune: JESU DULCIS MEMORIA, LM; Mode I; acc. by Richard Proulx, b.1937, © 1975, GIA Publications, Inc.

The Glory of These Forty Days   545

1. The glo - ry of these for - ty days We
2. A - lone and fast - ing, Mo - ses saw The
3. So Dan - iel trained his mys - tic sight, De -
4. Then grant that we like them be true, Con -

cel - e - brate with songs of praise; For Christ, by whom all
lov - ing God who gave the law; And to E - li - jah,
liv - ered from the li - on's might; And John, the Bride-groom's
sumed in fast and prayer with you; Our spir - its strength-en

things were made, Him - self has fast - ed and has prayed.
fast - ing, came The steeds and char - i - ots of flame.
friend, be - came The her - ald of Mes - si - ah's name.
with your grace, And give us joy to see your face.

Text: *Clarum decus jejunii;* ascr. to Gregory the Great, c.540-604; tr. by Maurice F. Bell, 1862-1947, © Oxford University Press
Tune: ERHALT UNS HERR, LM; Klug's *Geistliche Lieder,* 1543; harm. by J.S. Bach, 1685-1750

546 Deep Within

Refrain

Deep with-in I will plant my law,

not on stone, but in your heart.

Fol-low me, I will bring you back, you will

be my own, and I will be your God.

Verses

1. I will give you a new heart, a new spir-it with-
2. Seek my face, and see your
3. Re - turn to me, with all your

D.C.

in you, for I will be your strength.
God, for I will be your hope.
heart, and I will bring you back.

Text: Jeremiah 31:33, Ezekiel 36:26, Joel 2:12; David Haas, b.1957
Tune: David Haas, b.1957; acc. by Jeanne Cotter, b.1964
© 1987, GIA Publications, Inc.

Somebody's Knockin' at Your Door   547

Some-bod-y's knock-in' at your door; Some-bod-y's
knock-in' at your door; O sin-ner, why don't you
an-swer? Some-bod-y's knock-in' at your door.

Solo: *All:*

1. Knocks like Je - sus,
2. Can't you hear him?
3. Je - sus calls you,
4. Can't you trust him?

Some-bod-y's knock-in' at your door.

Solo: *All:*

Knocks like Je - sus,
Can't you hear him?
Je - sus calls you,
Can't you trust him?

Some-bod-y's knock-in' at your door.

O sin - ner, why don't you an - swer?

Some-bod - y's knock-in' at your door.

Text: African-American spiritual
Tune: SOMEBODY'S KNOCKIN', Irregular; African-American spiritual; harm. by Richard Proulx, b.1937, © 1986, GIA Publications, Inc.

548 Jesus, Tempted in the Desert

1. Je - sus, tempt - ed in the des - ert,
2. Je - sus, tempt - ed at the tem - ple,
3. Je - sus, tempt - ed on the moun - tain
4. When we face temp - ta - tion's pow - er,

Lone - ly, hun - gry, filled with dread: "Use your pow'r," the
High a - bove its an - cient wall: "Throw your - self from
By the lure of vast do - main: "Fall be - fore me!
Lone - ly, strug-gling, filled with dread, Christ, who knew the

tempt - er tells him; "Turn these bar - ren rocks to bread!"
loft - y tur - ret; An - gels wait to break your fall!"
Be my ser - vant! Glo - ry, fame, you're sure to gain!"
tempt - er's ho - ur, Come and be our liv - ing bread.

"Not a - lone by bread," he an - swers,
Je - sus shuns such emp - ty mar - vels,
Je - sus sees the daz - zling vi - sion,
By your grace, pro - tect, pre - serve us

"Can the hu - man heart be filled.
Feats that fick - le crowds re - quest:
Turns his eyes an - oth - er way:
Lest we fall, your trust be - tray.

On - ly by the Word that calls us
"God, whose grace pro - tects, pre - serves us,
"God a - lone de - serves our hom - age!
Yours, a - bove all oth - er voic - es,

Is our deep - est hun - ger stilled!"
We must nev - er vain - ly test."
God a - lone will I o - bey!"
Be the Word we hear, o - bey.

Text: Matthew 4:1-11, Luke 4:1-13; Herman G. Stuempfle, Jr., 1923–2007, © 1993, GIA Publications, Inc.
Tune: EBENEZER, 8 7 8 7 D; Thomas J. Williams, 1869-1944

Parce Domine 549

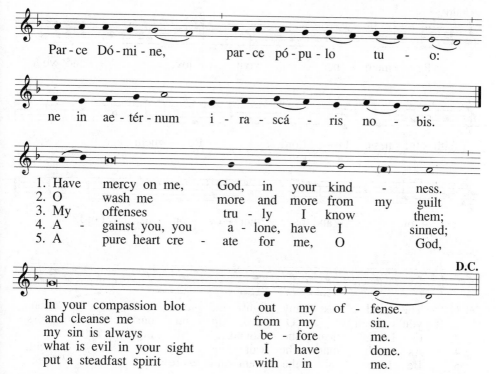

Par - ce Dó - mi - ne, par - ce pó - pu - lo tu - o:

ne in ae - tér - num i - ra - scá - ris no - bis.

1. Have mercy on me, God, in your kind - ness.
2. O wash me more and more from my guilt
3. My offenses tru - ly I know them;
4. A - gainst you, you a - lone, have I sinned;
5. A pure heart cre - ate for me, O God,

D.C.

In your compassion blot out my of - fense.
and cleanse me from my sin.
my sin is always be - fore me.
what is evil in your sight I have done.
put a steadfast spirit with - in me.

Text: *Spare your people, Lord, lest you be angry for ever,* Joel 2:17, Psalm 51:3-6, 12; tr. The Grail, © 1963, The Grail, GIA Publications, Inc., agent
Tune: PARCE DOMINE, Irregular; Mode I with Tonus Peregrinus; acc. by Robert LeBlanc, OSB, b.1948, © 1986, GIA Publications, Inc.

550 Remember Your Love

Refrain

Re - mem - ber your love and your faith - ful - ness, O Lord. Re - mem - ber your peo - ple and have mer - cy on us, Lord.

Verses

1. The Lord is my light and my sal - va - tion,
2. If you dwelt, O Lord, up - on our sin - ful - ness,
3. O Lord, hear the sound of my call
4. As watch - man who waits up - on the day - light,
5. Be - fore all the moun-tains were be - got - ten

whom should I fear? The Lord is my
then who could stand? But with you there is
and an - swer me. My heart cries
wait for the Lord. I trust in your
and earth took shape, e - ven then, O

D.C.

life and my ref - uge, when I call God hears.
mer - cy and for - give - ness and a guid - ing hand.
out for your pres - ence; it is you I seek.
kind - ness and re - demp - tion; and your faith - ful word.
Lord, you were our ref - uge through-out ev - 'ry age.

Text: Psalm 27; Mike Balhoff, b.1946
Tune: Darryl Ducote, b.1945, and Gary Daigle, b.1957
© 1978, Damean Music. Distributed by GIA Publications, Inc.

At the Cross Her Station Keeping 551

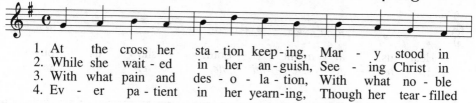

1. At the cross her sta - tion keep-ing, Mar - y stood in
2. While she wait - ed in her an-guish, See - ing Christ in
3. With what pain and des - o - la - tion, With what no - ble
4. Ev - er pa - tient in her yearn-ing, Though her tear - filled

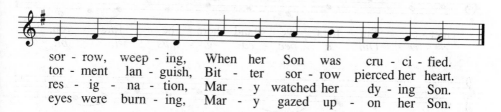

sor - row, weep - ing, When her Son was cru - ci - fied.
tor - ment lan - guish, Bit - ter sor - row pierced her heart.
res - ig - na - tion, Mar - y watched her dy - ing Son.
eyes were burn - ing, Mar - y gazed up - on her Son.

5. Who, that sorrow contemplating,
   On that passion meditating,
   Would not share the Virgin's grief?

6. Christ she saw, for our salvation,
   Scourged with cruel acclamation,
   Bruised and beaten by the rod.

7. Christ she saw with life-blood failing,
   All her anguish unavailing,
   Saw him breathe his very last.

8. Mary, fount of love's devotion,
   Let me share with true emotion
   All the sorrow you endured.

9. Virgin, ever interceding,
   Hear me in my fervent pleading:
   Fire me with your love of Christ.

10. Mother, may this prayer be granted:
    That Christ's love may be implanted
    In the depths of my poor soul.

11. At the cross, your sorrow sharing,
    All your grief and torment bearing,
    Let me stand and mourn with you.

12. Fairest maid of all creation,
    Queen of hope and consolation,
    Let me feel your grief sublime.

13. Virgin, in your love befriend me,
    At the Judgment Day defend me.
    Help me by your constant prayer.

14. Savior, when my life shall leave me,
    Through your mother's prayers receive me
    With the fruits of victory.

15. Let me to your love be taken,
    Let my soul in death awaken
    To the joys of Paradise.

Text: *Stabat mater dolorosa;* Jacopone da Todi, 1230-1306; trans. by Anthony G. Petti, 1932-1985, © 1971, Faber Music, Ltd.
Tune: STABAT MATER, 88 7; *Mainz Gesangbuch,* 1661; harm. by Richard Proulx, b.1937, © 1986, GIA Publications, Inc.

552 Hear Us, Almighty Lord / Attende Domine

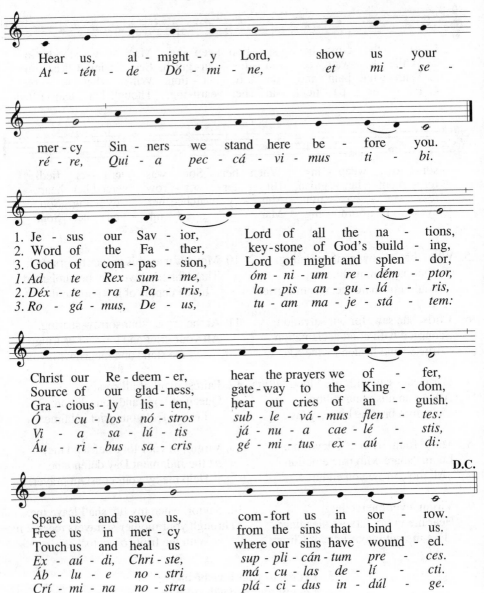

Hear us, al - might - y Lord, show us your
At - tén - de Dó - mi - ne, et mi - se -

mer - cy Sin - ners we stand here be - fore you.
ré - re, Qui - a pec - cá - vi - mus ti - bi.

1. Je - sus our Sav - ior, Lord of all the na - tions,
2. Word of the Fa - ther, key-stone of God's build - ing,
3. God of com - pas - sion, Lord of might and splen - dor,
1. Ad te Rex sum - me, óm - ni - um re - dém - ptor,
2. Déx - te - ra Pa - tris, la - pis an - gu - lá - ris,
3. Ro - gá - mus, De - us, tu - am ma - je - stá - tem:

Christ our Re - deem - er, hear the prayers we of - fer,
Source of our glad - ness, gate - way to the King - dom,
Gra - cious - ly lis - ten, hear our cries of an - guish.
Ó - cu - los nó - stros sub - le - vá - mus flen - tes:
Vi - a sa - lú - tis já - nu - a cae - lé - stis,
Áu - ri - bus sa - cris gé - mi - tus ex - aú - di:

D.C.

Spare us and save us, com - fort us in sor - row.
Free us in mer - cy from the sins that bind us.
Touch us and heal us where our sins have wound - ed.
Ex - aú - di, Chri - ste, sup - pli - cán - tum pre - ces.
Áb - lu - e no - stri má - cu - las de - lí - cti.
Crí - mi - na no - stra plá - ci - dus in - dúl - ge.

4. Humbly confessing that we have offended,
   Stripped of illusions, naked in our sorrow,
   Pardon, Lord Jesus, those your blood has ransomed.

5. Innocent captive, you were led to slaughter,
   Sentenced by sinners when they brought false witness.
   Keep from damnation those your death has rescued.

4. Tibi fatémur, crímina admíssa:
Contríto corde pándimus ocúlta:
Túa redémptor, píetas ignóscat.

5. Innocens captus, nec repúgnans ductus,
Téstibus falsis, pro ímpiis damnátus:
Quos redemísti, tu consérva, Christe.

Text: Latin, 10th C.; tr. by Ralph Wright, OSB, b.1938, © 1980, ICEL
Tune: ATTENDE DOMINE, 11 11 11 with refrain; Mode V; acc. by Richard Proulx, b.1937, © 1975, GIA Publications, Inc.

Lord, Who throughout These Forty Days 553

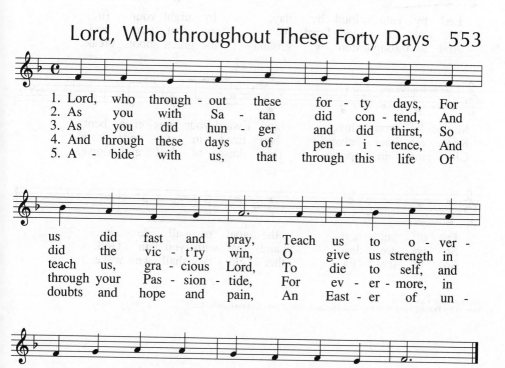

1. Lord, who through-out these for-ty days, For us did fast and pray, Teach us to o-ver-come our sins, And close by you to stay.
2. As you with Sa-tan did con-tend, And did the vic-t'ry win, O give us strength in you to fight, In you to con-quer sin.
3. As you did hun-ger and did thirst, So teach us, gra-cious Lord, To die to self, and so to live By your most ho-ly word.
4. And through these days of pen-i-tence, And through your Pas-sion-tide, For ev-er-more, in life and death, O Lord! with us a-bide.
5. A-bide with us, that through this life Of doubts and hope and pain, An East-er of un-end-ing joy We may at last at-tain!

Text: Claudia F. Hernaman, 1838-1898, alt.
Tune: ST. FLAVIAN, CM; *John's Day Psalter,* 1562; harm. based on the original *faux-bourdon* setting

554 Eternal Lord of Love

1. E - ter - nal Lord of love, be - hold your Church,
2. So dai - ly dy - ing to the way of self,
3. If dead in you, so in you we a - rise,

Walk - ing once more the pil - grim way of Lent,
So dai - ly liv - ing to your way of love,
You the first - born of all the faith - ful dead;

Led by your cloud by day, by night your fire,
We walk the road, Lord Je - sus, that you trod,
And as through ston - y ground the green shoots break,

Moved by your love and t'ward your pres - ence bent:
Know - ing our - selves bap - tized in - to your death:
Glo - rious in spring - time dress of leaf and flower,

Far off yet here the goal of all de - sire.
So we are dead and live with you in God.
So in the Fa - ther's glo - ry shall we wake.

Text: Thomas H. Cain, b.1931, © 1982
Tune: FENN HOUSE, 10 10 10 10 10 10; Michael Joncas, b.1951, © 1988, GIA Publications, Inc.

Return to God 555

Refrain

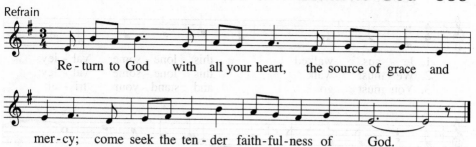

Re - turn to God with all your heart, the source of grace and

mer - cy; come seek the ten - der faith-ful-ness of God.

Verses

1. Now the time of grace has come,
   the day of salvation;
   come and learn now the way of our God.

2. I will take your heart of stone
   and place a heart within you,
   a heart of compassion and love.

3. If you break the chains of oppression,
   if you set the pris'ner free;
   if you share your bread with the hungry,
   give protection to the lost;
   give a shelter to the homeless,
   clothe the naked in your midst,
   then your light shall break forth like the dawn.

Text: Marty Haugen, b.1950
Tune: Marty Haugen, b.1950
© 1990, 1991, GIA Publications, Inc.

This Is the Time 556

Refrain

*Cantor or choir,
then all:*

This is the time of ful - fill - ment! The

reign of God is at hand!

Text: James J. Chepponis, b.1956
Tune: James J. Chepponis, b.1956
© 1994, GIA Publications, Inc.

557   Jesus Walked This Lonesome Valley

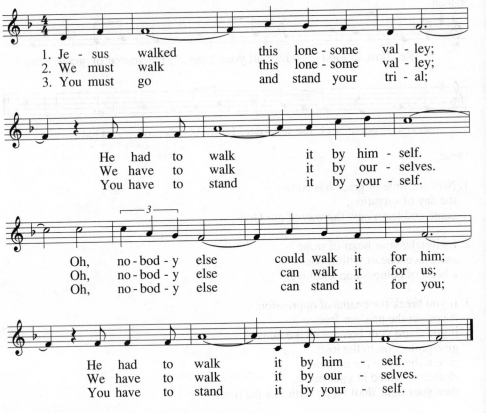

1. Je - sus walked this lone - some val - ley;
2. We must walk this lone - some val - ley;
3. You must go and stand your tri - al;

He had to walk it by him - self.
We have to walk it by our - selves.
You have to stand it by your - self.

Oh, no - bod - y else could walk it for him;
Oh, no - bod - y else can walk it for us;
Oh, no - bod - y else can stand it for you;

He had to walk it by him - self.
We have to walk it by our - selves.
You have to stand it by your - self.

Text: American Folk Hymn
Tune: LONESOME VALLEY, 8 8 10 8; American folk hymn; harm. by Richard Proulx, b.1937, © 1975, GIA Publications, Inc.

558   Grant to Us, O Lord

Refrain

Cantor, then all:

Grant to us, O Lord, a heart re - newed;

re - cre - ate in us your own Spir - it, Lord!

Text: Jeremiah 31:31-34
Tune: Lucien Deiss, CSSp, b.1921
© 1965, 1966, 1968, 1973, World Library Publications, Inc.

Again We Keep This Solemn Fast 559

1. A - gain we keep this sol - emn fast A
2. The law and proph - ets from of old In
3. More spar - ing, there - fore, let us make The
4. Let us a - void each harm - ful way That
5. We pray, O bless - ed Three in One, Our

gift of faith from a - ges past, This
fig - ured ways this Lent fore - told, Which
words we speak, the food we take, Our
lures the care - less mind a - stray; By
God while end - less a - ges run, That

Lent which binds us lov - ing - ly To
Christ, all a - ges' Lord and Guide, In
sleep, our laugh - ter, ev - 'ry sense; Learn
watch - ful prayer our spir - its free From
this, our Lent of for - ty days, May

faith and hope and char - i - ty.
these last days has sanc - ti - fied.
peace through ho - ly pen - i - tence.
schem - ing of the En - e - my.
bring us growth and give you praise.

Text: *Ex more docti mystico*; ascr. to Gregory the Great, c.540-604; tr. by Peter J. Scagnelli, b.1949, ©
Tune: ERHALT UNS HERR, LM; Klug's *Geistliche Lieder*, 1543; harm. by J.S. Bach, 1685-1750

560 Stations of the Cross

*	Kneel-ing in the gar - den grass,	Je - sus groans a -
1.	While the court and priests con - spire	How to slant the
2.	When the mas - sive cross of wood	Bends and bruis - es
3.	Je - sus falls be - neath the weight	Of the cross he's

gainst his death,	Let this cup of sor - row pass,
ev - i - dence	Je - sus calm - ly bears their ire
Je - sus' frame	Hear him seek e - ter - nal good
forced to bear	Yet its load of sin and hate

While he prays in that same breath:
As his prayer grows more in - tense:
As he prays in Yah - weh's name:
Do not crush his hope and prayer:

Not my will but yours be done.

This stanza begins the devotions. Stanzas 1-14 accompany each station.

Text: Thomas Troeger, © 1993, Oxford University Press
Tune: VIA CRUCIS, 77 77 with refrain; William P. Rowan, © 1995, GIA Publications, Inc.

1. **Jesus is condemned to death**

2. **Jesus carries his Cross**

3. **Jesus falls the first time**

4. **Jesus meets his afflicted mother**
Jesus reads in Mary's eyes
all the sorrow mothers bear,
and he prays his friend supplies
grace to strengthen her own prayer:
Not my will but yours be done.

5. **Simon of Cyrene helps Jesus to carry his Cross**
We with Simon of Cyrene
help the Savior bear the cross.
Step by step we slowly glean
what true faith and prayer will cost:
Not my will but yours be done.

6. **Veronica wipes the face of Jesus**
   Seek the courage and the grace
   that Veronica displays
   when she wipes the bleeding face
   of the one who bravely prays:
   　Not my will but yours be done.

7. **Jesus falls the second time**
   Jesus trips and falls again
   as he struggles through the street
   where the mob's unceasing din
   mocks the prayer his lips repeat:
   　Not my will but yours be done.

8. **Jesus meets the women of Jersusalem**
   Christ directs the women's tears
   toward the coming judgment day
   when God weighs our faithless years
   with our willingness to pray:
   　Not my will but yours be done.

9. **Jesus falls a third time**
   Jesus stumbles one last time
   nearly broken by the load
   yet by prayer finds strength to climb
   Calvary's final stretch of road:
   　Not my will but yours be done.

10. **Jesus is stripped of his clothes**
    Naked to the sun and clouds
    and the jeers and gawking stare
    of the soldiers and the crowds
    Christ continues with his prayer:
    　Not my will but yours be done.

11. **Jesus is nailed to the Cross**
    While the soldiers throw their dice
    they ignore their victim's groans,
    lost to them the sacrifice
    and the prayer that Jesus moans:
    　Not my will but yours be done.

12. **Jesus dies on the Cross**
    Jesus gives one loud last cry
    at the moment of his death
    while his prayer moves heaven's sky
    with his final, parting breath:
    　Not my will but yours be done.

13. **The body of Jesus is taken down from the Cross**
    As they take the body down
    and they wrap it in a sheet
    in their hearts they hear the sound
    that his lips no more repeat:
    　Not my will but yours be done.

14. **Jesus is laid in the tomb**
    Quiet is the hollowed cave.
    Peace and tears and grief descend.
    Mourners offer at the grave
    what they learned from Christ their friend:
    　Not my will but yours be done.

Text: Thomas Troeger, © 1993, Oxford University Press
Tune: VIA CRUCIS, 77 77 with refrain; William P. Rowan, © 1995, GIA Publications, Inc.

561　From Ashes to the Living Font

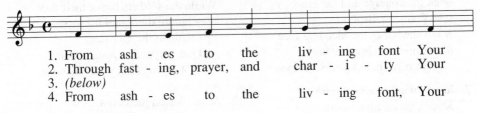

1. From ash - es to the liv - ing font Your
2. Through fast - ing, prayer, and char - i - ty Your
3. *(below)*
4. From ash - es to the liv - ing font, Your

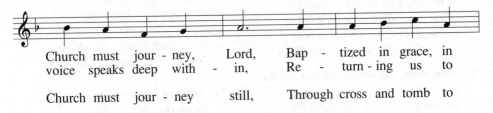

Church must jour - ney, Lord, Bap - tized in grace, in
voice speaks deep with - in, Re - turn - ing us to

Church must jour - ney still, Through cross and tomb to

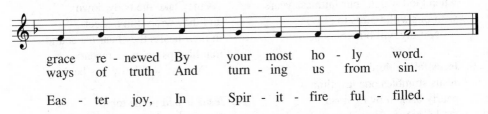

grace re - newed By your most ho - ly word.
ways of truth And turn - ing us from sin.

Eas - ter joy, In Spir - it - fire ful - filled.

Sundays I & II
3. From desert to the mountaintop
   In Christ our way we see,
   So, tempered by temptation's might
   We might transfigured be.

Sunday III
3. For thirsting hearts let waters flow
   Our fainting souls revive;
   And at the well your waters give
   Our everlasting life.

Sunday IV
3. We sit beside the road and plead,
   "Come, save us, David's son!"
   Now with your vision heal our eyes,
   The world's true Light alone.

Sunday V
3. Our graves split open, bring us back,
   Your promise to proclaim;
   To darkened tombs call out, "Arise!"
   And glorify your name.

Text: Alan J. Hommerding, b.1956, © 1994, World Library Publications, Inc.
Tune: ST. FLAVIAN, CM; *John's Day Psalter*, 1562; harm. based on the original *faux-bourdon* setting

Ride On, Jesus, Ride   562

Ride on, Je - sus, ride.   Ride on, Je - sus, ride.

Ride on, Je - sus, con - quering King,   Ride on, Je - sus ride.

1. King Je - sus rides on a milk white horse. Ride on, Je - sus,
2. My Je - sus lift - ed his throne a - bove. Ride on, Je - sus,
3. The chil - dren of Je - ru - sa - lem, Ride on, Je - sus,
4. ⁷ "Bless - ings on the Ho - ly One!" Ride on, Je - sus,
5. ⁷ Ride so hum - ble, ride so true, Ride on, Je - sus,
6. ⁷ Ride to set your peo - ple free, Ride on, Je - sus,
7. ⁷ Ride o - be - dient un - to death, Ride on, Je - sus,
8. ⁷ Ride a - gain in the hearts of us, Ride on, Je - sus,
9. ⁷ Now be - yond all time and space, Ride on, Je - sus,

ride. The riv - er Jor - dan he did cross.
ride. ⁷ See his mer - cy and his love.
ride, ⁷ strewed their branch - es on his way.
ride. ⁷ "Bless - ings on the Sav - ing One!"
ride. ⁷ Ride to bring the world to you, Ride on, Je - sus,
ride. ⁷ Ride the road to Cal - va - ry,
ride. ⁷ Ride to break the chains of death,
ride. ⁷ Ride a - gain in the hands of us,
ride. ⁷ Now in ev - 'ry land and race,

ride. Ride on, Je - sus, con - quering King. Ride on, Je - sus ride.

Text: African-American spiritual; verses 3-9, Marty Haugen, b.1950, © 1991, GIA Publications, Inc.
Tune: African-American spiritual; harm. by Barbara Jackson Martin, © 1987, GIA Publications, Inc.

563 All Glory, Laud, and Honor

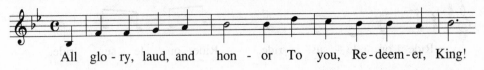

All glo-ry, laud, and hon-or To you, Re-deem-er, King!

To whom the lips of chil-dren Made sweet ho-san-nas ring.

1. You are the King of Is-ra-el, And Da-vid's roy-al Son,
2. The com-pa-ny of an-gels Are prais-ing you on high;
3. The peo-ple of the He-brews With palms be-fore you went:
4. To you be-fore your pas-sion They sang their hymns of praise:
5. Their prais-es you ac-cept-ed, Ac-cept the prayers we bring,

D.C.

Now in the Lord's Name com-ing, Our King and Bless-ed One.
And mor-tals, joined with all things Cre-a-ted, make re-ply.
Our praise and prayers and an-thems Be-fore you we pre-sent.
To you, now high ex-alt-ed, Our mel-o-dy we raise.
Great source of love and good-ness, Our Sav-ior and our King.

Text: *Gloria, laus et honor*; Theodulph of Orleans, c.760-821; tr. by John M. Neale, 1818-1866, alt.
Tune: ST. THEODULPH, 7 6 7 6 D; Melchior Teschner, 1584-1635

564 Jesu, Jesu

Refrain

Je-su, Je-su, fill us with your love, show

us how to serve the neigh-bors we have from you.

Verses

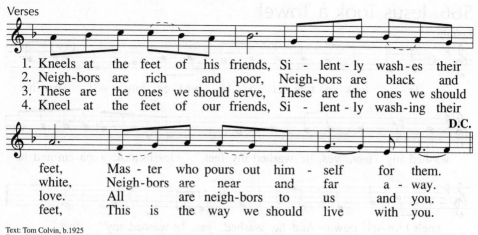

1. Kneels at the feet of his friends, Si - lent - ly wash - es their
2. Neigh-bors are rich and poor, Neigh-bors are black and
3. These are the ones we should serve, These are the ones we should
4. Kneel at the feet of our friends, Si - lent - ly wash-ing their

D.C.

feet, Mas - ter who pours out him - self for them.
white, Neigh-bors are near and far a - way.
love. All are neigh-bors to us and you.
feet, This is the way we should live with you.

Text: Tom Colvin, b.1925
Tune: CHEREPONI, Irregular; Ghana folk song; adapt. Tom Colvin, b.1925; acc. by Jane M. Marshall, b.1924
© 1969, and arr. © 1982, Hope Publishing Co.

Stay Here and Keep Watch 565

Ostinato Refrain

Stay here and keep watch with me. The hour has come.

Stay here and keep watch with me. Watch and pray.

Text: from Matthew 26; Taizé Community
Tune: Jacques Berthier, 1923-1994
© 1984, Les Presses de Taizé, GIA Publications, Inc., agent

566 Jesus Took a Towel

Refrain

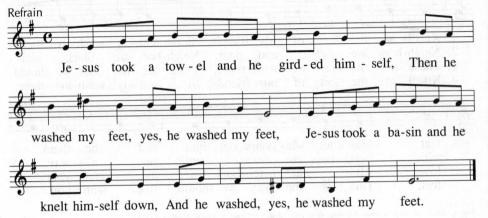

Je-sus took a tow-el and he gird-ed him-self, Then he washed my feet, yes, he washed my feet, Je-sus took a ba-sin and he knelt him-self down, And he washed, yes, he washed my feet.

Verses

1. The heavens are the Lord's, and the earth is his,
   The clouds are his chariot, glory his cloak;
   He made the mountains, set the limits of the sea;
   And he stooped and washed my feet.

2. The hour had come, the Pasch was near;
   Jesus loved his own, loved them to the end.
   O Lord, let me see, let me understand
   Why you stooped and washed my feet.

3. Jesus came to Peter; Peter said to him,
   "Do you wash my feet? Lord, do you wash my feet?"
   Jesus knelt down, but Peter cried out,
   "Lord, you'll never wash my feet!"

4. Jesus said to Peter, "Don't you understand?
   If you want to be mine, I must wash your feet."
   "Then not just feet, but my head and my hands!
   O Lord, I want to be yours."

5. He is King of kings and Lord of lords,
   Who dwells in light inaccessible;
   No one has seen him where he sits on high,
   Yet he stooped to wash my feet.

6. "Do you know, little children, what I've done for you?
   You call me Master, and you call me Lord.
   If I am your Master, and if I am your Lord,
   Then, what I've done, you must do."

7. Now friends, let's be glad, let our joy be full.
   For God is love, and he abides in us.
   He washed our feet, he washes them still
   When we do what he once did.

8. Who is like you, Lord, now enthroned on high,
   Where you look upon the heavens and the earth below?
   Before your face the earth trembles and quakes,
   Yet you stoop to wash my feet!

9. O the path is rugged, and the going is rough,
   The journey is long to our heav'nly home,
   Our feet are weary and covered with mud,
   So the Lord still washes our feet.

Text: John 13; Chrysogonus Waddell, OSCO, b.1930
Tune: JESUS TOOK A TOWEL, Irregular; Chrysogonus Waddell, OCSO, b.1930
© 1986, GIA Publications, Inc.

All You Who Pass This Way   567

Refrain

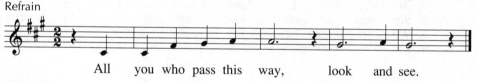

All you who pass this way, look and see.

Verses

1. Is any sorrow like the sorrow that afflicts me?

2. Women of Jerusalem!
   Do not weep for me, but for yourselves, and for your children.

3. Father, forgive them! They know not what they do.

4. My God, my God, why have you abandoned me?

5. Today you will be with me in paradise.

6. I am thirsty.

7. Father, into your hands I commend my spirit.

Text: From the Passion Gospels; Taizé Community, 1984
Tune: Jacques Berthier, 1923-1994
© 1984, Les Presses de Taizé, GIA Publications, Inc., agent

568 Calvary

Refrain

Cal - va - ry,   Cal - va - ry,   Cal - va -

ry,   Cal - va - ry,   Cal - va - ry,

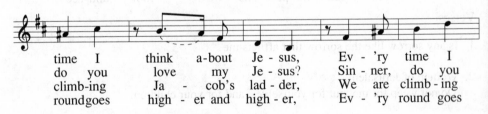

Cal - va - ry,   Sure - ly he died on   Cal - va - ry.

Verses

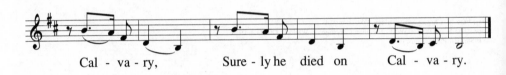

1. Ev - 'ry time I   think a-bout Je - sus,   Ev - 'ry
2. Sin - ner, do you   love my Je - sus?   Sin - ner,
3. We are climb-ing   Ja - cob's lad-der,   We are
4. Ev - 'ry round goes   high - er and high-er,   Ev - 'ry

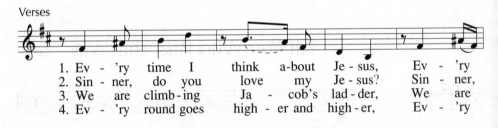

time I   think a-bout Je - sus,   Ev - 'ry time I
do you   love my Je - sus?   Sin - ner, do you
climb-ing   Ja - cob's lad-der,   We are climb-ing
round goes   high - er and high-er,   Ev - 'ry round goes

D.C.

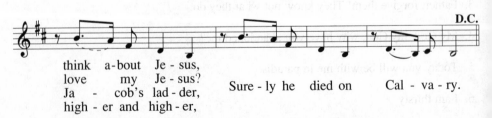

think a-bout Je - sus,
love my Je - sus?
Ja - cob's lad-der,   Sure - ly he died on   Cal - va - ry.
high - er and high-er,

Text: African-American spiritual
Tune: African-American spiritual

O Sacred Head Surrounded 569

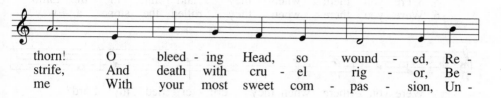

1. O Sa - cred Head sur-round - ed By crown of pierc - ing
2. I see your strength and vig - or All fad - ing in the
3. In this, your bit - ter pas - sion, Good Shep-herd, think of

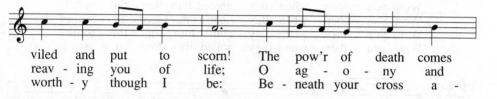

thorn! O bleed - ing Head, so wound - ed, Re -
strife, And death with cru - el rig - or, Be -
me With your most sweet com - pas - sion, Un -

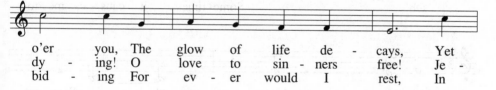

viled and put to scorn! The pow'r of death comes
reav - ing you of life; O ag - o - ny and
worth - y though I be: Be - neath your cross a -

o'er you, The glow of life de - cays, Yet
dy - ing! O love to sin - ners free! Je -
bid - ing For ev - er would I rest, In

an - gel hosts a - dore you, And trem - ble as they gaze.
sus, all grace sup - ply - ing, O turn your face on me.
your dear love con - fid - ing, And with your pres - ence blest.

Text: *Salve caput cruentatum;* ascr. to Bernard of Clairvaux, 1091-1153; tr. by Henry Baker, 1821-1877
Tune: PASSION CHORALE, 7 6 7 6 D; Hans Leo Hassler, 1564-1612; harm. by J. S. Bach, 1685-1750

570 Were You There

1. Were you there when they cru - ci - fied my Lord?
2. Were you there when they nailed him to the tree?
3. Were you there when they pierced him in the side?
4. Were you there when the sun re - fused to shine?
5. Were you there when they laid him in the tomb?
6. Were you there when they rolled the stone a - way?

Were you there when they cru - ci - fied my Lord?
Were you there when they nailed him to the tree?
Were you there when they pierced him in the side?
Were you there when the sun re - fused to shine?
Were you there when they laid him in the tomb?
Were you there when they rolled the stone a - way?

Oh! Some - times it caus - es me to

trem - ble, trem - ble, trem - ble, Were you

there when they cru - ci - fied my Lord?
there when they nailed him to the tree?
there when they pierced him in the side?
there when the sun re - fused to shine?
there when they laid him in the tomb?
there when they rolled the stone a - way?

Text: African-American spiritual
Tune: WERE YOU THERE, 10 10 with refrain; African-American spiritual; harm. by Robert J. Batastini, b.1942, © 1987, GIA Publications, Inc.

Crucem Tuam / O Lord, Your Cross   571

Ostinato Refrain

Cru - cem   tu - am   a - do - ra - mus Do - mi -
O   Lord,   your   cross,   we   a - dore   and   glo - ri -

ne,   res - ur - re - cti - o - nem   tu - am   lau - da - mus Do - mi -
fy,   for your ho - ly   res - ur - rec - tion,   we praise you   Lord   of

ne.   Lau - da - mus   et   glo - ri - fi - ca - mus.
life.   We praise   you   and   we glo - ri - fy   you.

Res - ur - re - cti - o - nem   tu - am   lau - da - mus   Do - mi - ne.
For your ho - ly   res - ur - rec - tion,   we praise you Lord of   life.

Text: Taizé Community, 1991
Tune: Jacques Berthier, 1923-1994
© 1991, Les Presses de Taizé, GIA Publications, Inc., agent

572 My Song Is Love Unknown

1. My song is love un - known, My
2. He came from his blest throne, My Sal -
3. Some - times they strew his way And
4. Why, what has my Lord done? What
5. They rise and needs will have My
6. In life, no house, no home My
7. Here might I stay and sing, No

Sav - ior's love for me, Love to the love - less
va - tion to be - stow, But all made strange, and
his sweet prais - es sing, Re - sound - ing all the
makes this rage and spite? He made the lame to
dear Lord made a - way; A mur - der - er they
Lord on earth might have; In death, no friend - ly
sto - ry so di - vine; Nev - er was love, dear

shown That they might love - ly be. O
none The longed - for Christ would know. But
day Ho - san - nas to their King. Then
run, He gave the blind their sight. Sweet
save: The prince of life they slay. Yet
tomb But what a stran - ger gave. What
King, Nev - er was grief like thine. This

who am I That for my sake My
O my friend, My friend in - deed, Who
"Cru - ci - fy!" Is all they breathe, And
in - jur - ies! Yet they at these Them -
cheer - ful he To suf - f'ring goes, That
may I say? Heav'n was his home; But
is my friend, In whose sweet praise I

Lord shall take Frail flesh, and die?
at my need His life did spend.
for his death They thirst and cry.
selves dis - please, And 'gainst him rise.
he his foes, From thence might free.
mine the tomb Where - in he lay.
all my days Could glad - ly spend.

Text: Samuel Crossman, c.1624-1683
Tune: LOVE UNKNOWN, 6 6 6 6 4 44 4; John Ireland, 1879-1962, © John Ireland Trust

Sing, My Tongue, the Song of Triumph 573

1. Sing, my tongue, the song of tri - umph,
2. He en - dured the nails, the spit - ting,
3. Faith - ful Cross, a - bove all oth - er,
4. Bend your boughs, O Tree of glo - ry!

Tell the sto - ry far and wide;
Vin - e - gar and spear and reed;
One and on - ly no - ble tree,
All you rig - id branch - es, bend!

Tell of dread and fi - nal bat - tle,
From that ho - ly bod - y bro - ken
None in fo - liage, none in blos - som,
For a while the an - cient tem - per

Sing of Sav - ior cru - ci - fied;
Blood and wa - ter forth pro - ceed:
None in fruit your peer may be;
That your birth be - stowed, sus - pend;

How up - on the cross a vic - tim
Earth and stars and sky and o - cean
Sweet the wood and sweet the i - ron
And the King of earth and heav - en

Van - quish - ing in death he died.
By that flood from stain are freed.
And your load, most sweet is he.
Gent - ly on your bos - om tend.

Text: *Pange, lingua, gloriosi lauream certaminis*; Venantius Fortunatus, c.530-609; tr. from *The Three Days*, 1981
Tune: PICARDY, 8 7 8 7 8 7; French Carol; harm. by Richard Proulx, b.1937, © 1986, GIA Publications, Inc.

574 Jesus, the Lord

Refrain

Je - sus. Je - sus. Let all cre-

a - tion bend the knee to the Lord.

3

Verse 1

1. In him we live, we move and have our

be - ing; in him the Christ, in him the

King. Je - sus, the Lord.

D.C.

Verses 2, 3

2. Though Son, he did not cling to
3. He lived o - be - dient - ly his

god - li - ness; but emp - tied him - self, be -
Fa - ther's will ac - cept - ing his death,

came a slave!
death on a tree!   Je - sus, the Lord.

D.C.

Text: *Jesus Prayer*, Philippians 2:5-11; Acts 17:28; Roc O'Connor, SJ, b.1949
Tune: Roc O'Connor, SJ, b.1949; arr. by Rick Modlin, b.1966
© 1981, 1994, Robert F. O'Connor, SJ, and OCP Publications

Come, Ye Faithful, Raise the Strain   575

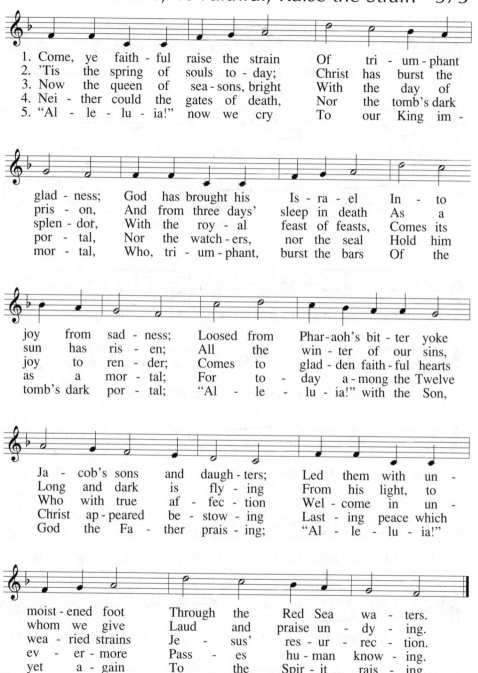

1. Come, ye faith - ful raise the strain Of tri - um - phant
2. 'Tis the spring of souls to - day; Christ has burst the
3. Now the queen of sea - sons, bright With the day of
4. Nei - ther could the gates of death, Nor the tomb's dark
5. "Al - le - lu - ia!" now we cry To our King im -

glad - ness; God has brought his Is - ra - el In - to
pris - on, And from three days' sleep in death As a
splen - dor, With the roy - al feast of feasts, Comes its
por - tal, Nor the watch - ers, nor the seal Hold him
mor - tal, Who, tri - um - phant, burst the bars Of the

joy from sad - ness; Loosed from Phar - aoh's bit - ter yoke
sun has ris - en; All the win - ter of our sins,
joy to ren - der; Comes to glad - den faith - ful hearts
as a mor - tal; For to - day a - mong the Twelve
tomb's dark por - tal; "Al - le - lu - ia!" with the Son,

Ja - cob's sons and daugh - ters; Led them with un -
Long and dark is fly - ing From his light, to
Who with true af - fec - tion Wel - come in un -
Christ ap - peared be - stow - ing Last - ing peace which
God the Fa - ther prais - ing; "Al - le - lu - ia!"

moist - ened foot Through the Red Sea wa - ters.
whom we give Laud and praise un - dy - ing.
wea - ried strains Je - sus' res - ur - rec - tion.
ev - er - more Pass - es hu - man know - ing.
yet a - gain To the Spir - it rais - ing.

Text: Exodus 15; Ασωμεν παντεξ λαοι; John of Damascus, c.675-c.749; tr. by John M. Neale, 1818-1886, alt.
Tune: GAUDEAMUS PARITER, 7 6 7 6 D; Johann Horn, c.1495-1547

576 This Is the Day

Refrain

This is the day the Lord has made; let us re-joice and be glad. This is the day the Lord has made; let us re-joice and be glad.

Verse 1

1. Give thanks to the Lord for he is good, his mer-cy en-dures for ev-er; let the house of Is-ra-el

D.C.

say: "His mer-cy en-dures for ev-er."

Verse 2

2. The Lord's right hand has struck with pow'r, the Lord's right hand is ex-alt-ed; I shall not die, but

D.C.

live and de-clare the works of the Lord.

Verse 3

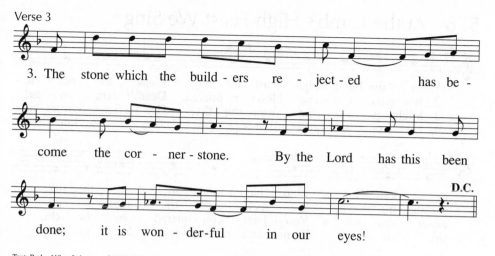

3. The stone which the build-ers re-ject-ed has be-

come the cor-ner-stone. By the Lord has this been

D.C.

done; it is won-der-ful in our eyes!

Text: Psalm 118, refrain trans. © 1969, ICEL; verses © Confraternity of Christian Doctrine, alt.
Tune: Michael Joncas, b.1951, © 1981, 1982; published by Cooperative Ministries, Inc., Exclusive agent: OCP Publications

Surrexit Christus 577

Ostinato Refrain

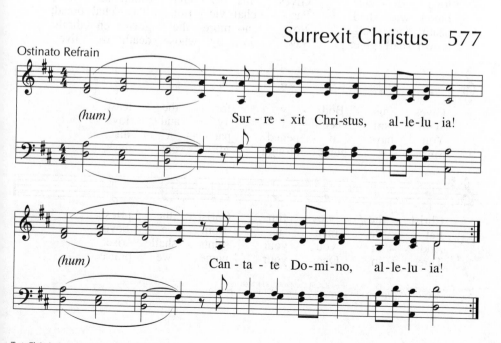

(hum)   Sur-re-xit Chri-stus, al-le-lu-ia!

(hum)   Can-ta-te Do-mi-no, al-le-lu-ia!

Text: *Christ is risen, sing to the Lord;* Daniel 3; Taizé Community, 1984
Tune: Jacques Berthier, 1923-1994
© 1984, Les Presses de Taizé, GIA Publications, Inc., agent

578 At the Lamb's High Feast We Sing

1. At the Lamb's high feast we sing Praise to our vic -
2. Where the Pas - chal blood is poured, Death's dark an - gel
3. Might - y vic - tim from the sky, Hell's fierce powers be -
4. East - er tri - umph, East - er joy, This a - lone can

to - rious King. Who has washed us in the tide
sheathes his sword; Is - rael's hosts tri - umph - ant go
neath you lie; You have con - quered in the fight,
sin de - stroy; From sin's power, Lord, set us free

Flow - ing from his pierc - ed side; Praise we him, whose
Through the wave that drowns the foe. Praise we Christ, whose
You have brought us life and light: Now no more can
New - born souls in you to be. Fa - ther, who the

love di - vine Gives his sa - cred Blood for wine,
blood was shed, Pas - chal vic - tim, Pas - chal bread;
death ap - pall, Now no more the grave en - thrall;
crown shall give, Sav - ior, by whose death we live,

Gives his Bod - y for the feast,
With sin - cer - i - ty and love
You have o - pened par - a - dise,
Spir - it, guide through all our days,

Christ the vic - tim, Christ the priest.
Eat we man - na from a - bove.
And in you your saints shall rise.
Three in One, your name we praise.

Text: *Ad regias agni dapes*; Latin, 4th C.; tr. by Robert Campbell, 1814-1868
Tune: SALZBURG, 77 77 D; Jakob Hintze, 1622-1702; harm. by J.S. Bach, 1685-1750

O Sons and Daughters 579

Al - le - lu - ia, al - le - lu - ia, al - le - lu - ia.

1. O sons and daugh - ters, let us sing!
2. That East - er morn, at break of day,
3. An an - gel clad in white they see,
4. That night the a - pos - tles met in fear;
5. When Thom - as, first the tid - ings heard,
6. "My wound - ed side, O Thom - as, see;

The King of heav'n the glo - rious King,
The faith - ful wom - en went their way
Who sat, and spoke un - to the three,
A - midst them came their Lord most dear,
How they had seen the ris - en Lord,
Be - hold my hands, my feet," said he,

D.C.

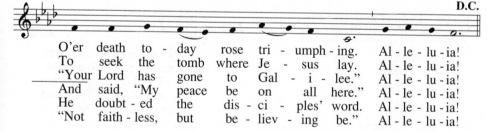

O'er death to - day rose tri - umph - ing. Al - le - lu - ia!
To seek the tomb where Je - sus lay. Al - le - lu - ia!
"Your Lord has gone to Gal - i - lee." Al - le - lu - ia!
And said, "My peace be on all here." Al - le - lu - ia!
He doubt - ed the dis - ci - ples' word. Al - le - lu - ia!
"Not faith - less, but be - liev - ing be." Al - le - lu - ia!

7. No longer Thomas then denied,
   He saw the feet, the hands, the side;
   "You are my Lord and God," he cried. Alleluia!

8. How blest are they who have not seen,
   And yet whose faith has constant been,
   For they eternal life shall win. Alleluia!

9. On this most holy day of days,
   To God your hearts and voices raise,
   In laud, and jubilee and praise. Alleluia!

Text: *O filii et filiae*; Jean Tisserand, d.1494; tr. by John M. Neale, 1818-1866, alt.
Tune: O FILII ET FILIAE, 888 with alleluias; Mode II; acc. by Richard Proulx, b.1937, © 1975, GIA Publications, Inc.

580 Resucitó

Refrain

Re - su - ci - tó, re - su - ci - tó, re - su - ci -
A - le - lu - ya, a - le - lu - ya, a - le - lu -

To verses | *Final ending*

tó, a - le - lu - ya. A - le - lu - ya.
ya, re - su - ci - tó.

Verses

1. La muer - te ¿dón - de es - tá la
2. Gra-cias se - an da - das al
3. A - le - grí - a, a - le - grí-a her -
4. Si con Él mo - ri - mos, ⁊ con Él vi -
1. And death now, van - ished is the
2. The king - dom, praise to God, the
3. Our glad - ness, bliss - ful in our
4. With him then, die and live with

muer - te? ¿Dón - de es - tá mi
Pa - dre que nos pa - só a su
ma - nos, que si hoy nos que -
vi - mos, ⁊ con Él can -
fear now, ban - ished are my
king - dom! Raised up to the
glad - ness, this will be our
him then, rise and sing our

D.C.

muer - te? ¿Dón - de su vic - to - ria?
rei - no dón - de se vi - ve de a - mor.
re - mos es que re - su - ci - tó.
ta - mos. ⁊ ¡A - le - lu - ya!
tears now, death has passed a - way.
king - dom, we shall live in love.
glad - ness, that he is a - live.
hymn then, sing al - le - lu - ia.

Text: Kiko Argüello, © 1972, Ediciones Musical PAX, U.S. agent: OCP Publications; trans. © 1988, OCP Publications
Tune: Kiko Argüello, © 1972, Ediciones Musical PAX, U.S. agent: OCP Publications; acc. by Diana Kodner

Alleluia, Alleluia, Give Thanks 581

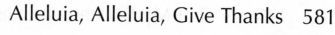

Refrain

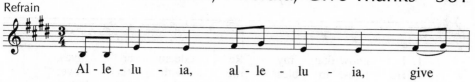

Al - le - lu - ia, al - le - lu - ia, give

thanks to the ris - en Lord. Al - le - lu - ia, al - le -

lu - ia, give praise to his Name.

Verses

1. Je - sus is Lord of all the earth.
2. Spread the good news o'er all the earth:
3. We have been cru - ci - fied with Christ.
4. God has pro - claimed his gra - cious gift:
5. Come, let us praise the liv - ing God,

D.C.

He is the King of cre - a - tion.
Je - sus has died and has ris - en.
Now we shall live for ev - er.
Life e - ter - nal for all who be - lieve.
Joy - ful - ly sing to our Sav - ior.

Text: Donald Fishel, b.1950, © 1973, Word of God Music
Tune: ALLELUIA NO. 1, 8 8 with refrain; Donald Fishel, b.1950, © 1973, Word of God Music; descant harm. by Betty Pulkingham, b.1929,
   Charles Mallory, b.1953, and George Mims, b.1938, © 1979, Celebration

582 I Know That My Redeemer Lives

1. I know that my Re - deem - er lives;
2. He lives, to bless me with his love;
3. He lives, and grants me dai - ly breath;
4. He lives, all glo - ry to his name;

What joy the blest as - sur - ance gives!
He lives, to plead for me a - bove;
He lives, and I shall con - quer death;
He lives, my Sav - ior still the same;

He lives, he lives, who once was dead;
He lives, my hun - gry soul to feed;
He lives, my man - sion to pre - pare;
What joy the blest as - sur - ance gives;

He lives, my ev - er - last - ing Head!
He lives, to help in time of need.
He lives, to bring me safe - ly there.
I know that my Re - deem - er lives!

Text: Samuel Medley, 1738-1799
Tune: DUKE STREET, LM; John Hatton, c.1710-1793

583 This Is the Feast of Victory

This is the feast of vic-to-ry for our God. Al-le-

To verses | Last time

lu - ia, al-le-lu - ia, al - le - lu - ia. lu - ia.

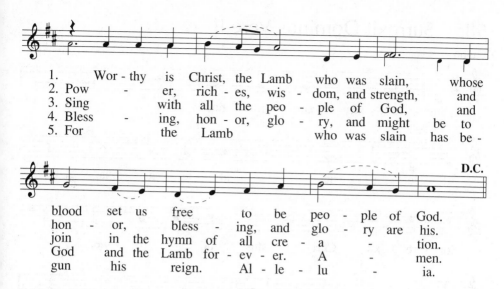

1. Wor - thy is Christ, the Lamb who was slain, whose
2. Pow - er, rich - es, wis - dom, and strength, and
3. Sing with all the peo - ple of God, and
4. Bless - ing, hon - or, glo - ry, and might be to
5. For the Lamb who was slain has be -

blood set us free to be peo - ple of God.
hon - or, bless - ing, and glo - ry are his.
join in the hymn of all cre - a - tion.
God and the Lamb for - ev - er. A - men.
gun his reign. Al - le - lu - ia.

Text: Based on Revelation 5, © 1978, *Lutheran Book of Worship*
Tune: FESTIVAL CANTICLE, Irregular; Richard Hillert, b.1923, © 1975, 1988, Richard Hillert

Regina Caeli / O Queen of Heaven   584

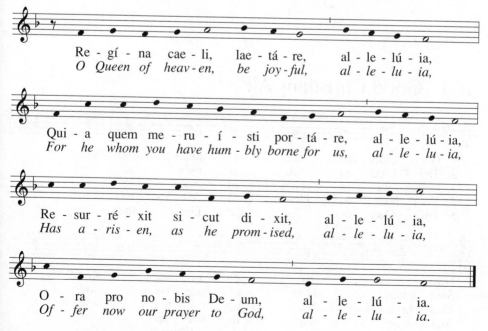

Re - gí - na cae - li, lae - tá - re, al - le - lú - ia,
O Queen of heav - en, be joy - ful, al - le - lu - ia,

Qui - a quem me - ru - í - sti por - tá - re, al - le - lú - ia,
For he whom you have hum - bly borne for us, al - le - lu - ia,

Re - sur - ré - xit si - cut di - xit, al - le - lú - ia,
Has a - ris - en, as he prom - ised, al - le - lu - ia,

O - ra pro no - bis De - um, al - le - lú - ia.
Of - fer now our prayer to God, al - le - lu - ia.

Text: Latin, 12th C.; tr. by C. Winfred Douglas, 1867-1944, alt.
Tune: REGINA CAELI, Irregular; Mode VI; acc. by Robert LeBlanc, OSB, b.1948, © 1986, GIA Publications, Inc.

585 Surrexit Dominus Vere II

Canon — *4 voices*

1. Sur - re - xit Do - mi - nus ve - re.
2. Al - le - lu - ia, al - le - lu - ia.
3. Sur - re - xit Chri - stus ho - di - e,
4. Al - le - lu - ia, al - le - lu - ia.

Text: *The Lord is truly risen! Christ is risen today!* Taizé Community, 1978
Tune: Jacques Berthier, 1923-1994
© 1978, Les Presses de Taizé, GIA Publications, Inc., agent

586 Good Christians All

1. Good Chris - tians all, re - joice and sing!
2. The Lord of life is ris'n to - day!
3. Praise we in songs of vic - to - ry
4. Your Name we bless, O ris - en Lord,
5. To God the Fa - ther, God the Son,

Now is the tri - umph of our King!
Sing songs of praise a - long his way;
That love, that life which can - not die,
And sing to - day with one ac - cord
To God the Spir - it, al - ways One,

To all the world glad news we bring:
Let all the earth re - joice and say:
And sing with hearts up - lift - ed high:
The life laid down, the life re - stored:
We sing for life in us be - gun:

Al - le - lu - ia, al - le - lu - ia, al - le - lu - ia!

Text: Cyril A. Alington, 1872-1955, alt., © 1956, *Hymns Ancient and Modern, Ltd.*; St. 5, Norman Mealy, b.1923, © 1971, Walton Music Corporation
Tune: GELOBT SEI GOTT, 888 with alleluias; Melchior Vulpius, c.1560-1616; acc. Robert J. Batastini, b.1942, © 1987, GIA Publications, Inc.

The Strife Is O'er 587

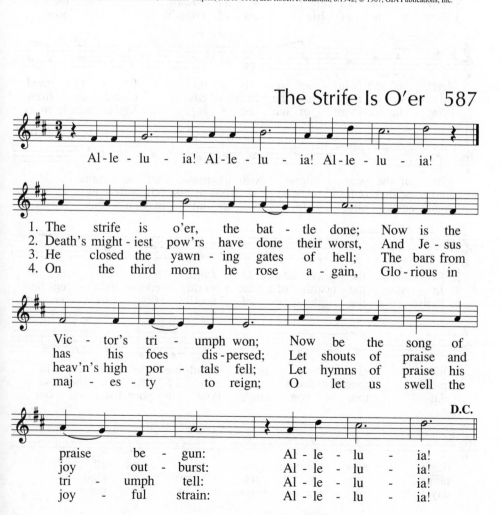

Al - le - lu - ia! Al - le - lu - ia! Al - le - lu - ia!

1. The strife is o'er, the bat - tle done; Now is the
2. Death's might - iest pow'rs have done their worst, And Je - sus
3. He closed the yawn - ing gates of hell; The bars from
4. On the third morn he rose a - gain, Glo - rious in

Vic - tor's tri - umph won; Now be the song of
has his foes dis - persed; Let shouts of praise and
heav'n's high por - tals fell; Let hymns of praise his
maj - es - ty to reign; O let us swell the

D.C.

praise be - gun: Al - le - lu - ia!
joy out - burst: Al - le - lu - ia!
tri - umph tell: Al - le - lu - ia!
joy - ful strain: Al - le - lu - ia!

Text: *Finita iam sunt praelia;* Latin, 12th C.; tr. by Francis Pott, 1832-1909, alt.
Tune: VICTORY, 888 with alleluias; Giovanni da Palestrina, 1525-1594; adapt. by William H. Monk, 1823-1889

588 Hail Thee, Festival Day

Hail thee, fes-ti-val day! Blest day that art hal-lowed for ev-er;

Day when our Lord was raised, break-ing the king-dom of death.

1. All the fair beau - ty of earth from the
3. God the Al-might - y, the Lord, the
5. Spir - it of life and of pow'r, now

death of the win - ter a - ris - ing! Ev - 'ry good
rul - er of earth and the heav - ens, Guard us from
flow in us, fount of our be - ing, Light that en -

D.C.

gift of the year now with its mas - ter re - turns.
harm with - out; cleanse us from e - vil with - in.
light - ens us all, life that in all may a - bide.

2. Rise from the grave now, O Lord, the au - thor of
4. Je - sus, the health of the world, en - light - en our
6. Praise to the giv - er of good! O Lov - er and

life and cre - a - tion. Tread-ing the path - way of
minds great Re-deem - er. Son of the Fa - ther su -
Au - thor of con - cord, Pour out your balm on our

D.C.

death, new life you give to us all.
preme, on - ly be - got - ten of God.
days; or - der our ways in your peace.

Text: *Salve festa dies*; Venantius Fortunatus, c.530-609; tr. composite
Tune: SALVE FESTA DIES, Irregular with refrain; Ralph Vaughan Williams, 1872-1958

Up from the Earth 589

1. Up from the earth, and surg-ing like a wave,
2. Up from the cross a bil-lion voic-es strain,
3. Up from the night Christ Morn-ing-star a - wakes.
4. Up from the tomb of all the past con - ceals!
5. Cry to the cross where ty - rants work their dread!

Rise up, O Christ! Your God de - fies the grave.
Cry for a hand to lift them from their pain.
O what a light up - on earth's dark - ness breaks!
See how our God a bright-er day re - veals.
Shout to the tombs where par - ents mourn their dead!

Up from the earth push blade and leaf and stem. They
Up from the cross but scarred in limbs and side, A
Up from the night Christ sows his life like wheat, And
Up from the tomb! Though death had bound us tight, Like
Sing to the earth, for God all new - ness gives! Al -

rise for Christ, and we shall rise with them!
wound-ed church brings heal - ing far and wide!
death it - self lies fal - low at his feet!
Laz - a - rus, we stum - ble in - to light!
le - lu - ia! Christ Lib - er - a - tor lives!

Text: Rory Cooney, b.1952
Tune: LIBERATOR, 10 10 10 10; Rory Cooney, b.1952
© 1987, North American Liturgy Resources. Published by OCP Publications.

590 Sing to the Mountains

Refrain

Sing to the moun-tains, sing to the sea. Raise your
voic - es, lift your hearts. This is the day the
Lord has made. Let all the earth re - joice.

Verse 1

1. I will give thanks to you, my Lord. You have
an - swered my plea. You have saved my
soul from death. You are my strength and my song. *D.C.*

Verse 2

2. Ho - ly, ho - ly, ho - ly Lord,
heav - en and earth are full of your glo - ry. *D.C.*

Verse 3

3. This is the day that the Lord has made. Let us be
glad and re - joice. He has turned all

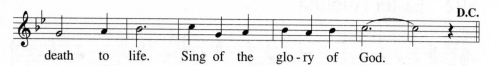

D.C.

death to life. Sing of the glo-ry of God.

Text: Psalm 118; Bob Dufford, SJ, b.1943
Tune: Bob Dufford, SJ, b.1943; acc. by Randall DeBruyn
© 1975, Robert J. Dufford, SJ, and OCP Publications

The Head That Once Was Crowned with Thorns   591

1. The head that once was crowned with thorns Is
2. The high-est place that heav'n af-fords Be-
3. The joy of all who dwell a-bove, The
4. To them the cross with all its shame, With
5. They suf-fer with their Lord be-low; They
6. The cross he bore is life and health, Though

crowned with glo-ry now; A roy-al di-a-
longs to him by right; The King of kings, and
joy of all be-low, To whom he man-i-
all its grace, is giv'n; Their name an ev-er-
reign with him a-bove; Their prof-it and their
shame and death to him, His peo-ple's hope, his

dem a-dorns The might-y vic-tor's brow.
Lord of lords, And heav'n's e-ter-nal light.
fests his love, And grants his name to know.
last-ing name; Their joy the joy of heav'n.
joy to know The mys-t'ry of his love.
peo-ple's wealth, Their ev-er-last-ing theme.

Text: Hebrews 2:9-10; Thomas Kelly, 1769-1855
Tune: ST. MAGNUS, CM; Jeremiah Clarke, 1670-1707

592 Easter Alleluia

Refrain

Al-le-lu-ia, al - le - lu-ia, al-le-lu - ia!

Verses

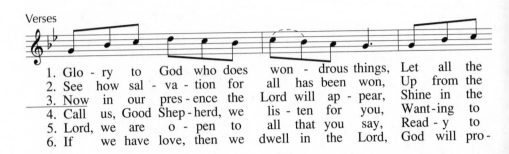

1. Glo - ry to God who does won - drous things, Let all the
2. See how sal - va - tion for all has been won, Up from the
3. Now in our pres - ence the Lord will ap - pear, Shine in the
4. Call us, Good Shep - herd, we lis - ten for you, Want-ing to
5. Lord, we are o - pen to all that you say, Read - y to
6. If we have love, then we dwell in the Lord, God will pro -

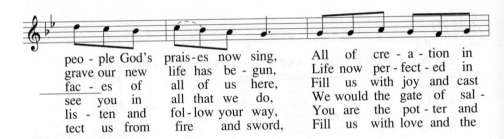

peo - ple God's prais-es now sing, All of cre - a - tion in
grave our new life has be - gun, Life now per - fect - ed in
fac - es of all of us here, Fill us with joy and cast
see you in all that we do, We would the gate of sal -
lis - ten and fol-low your way, You are the pot - ter and
tect us from fire and sword, Fill us with love and the

D.C.

splen - dor shall ring:
Je - sus, the Son:
out all our fear: Al - le - lu - ia!
va - tion pass through:
we are the clay:
peace of his word:

Text: Marty Haugen, b.1950
Tune: O FILII ET FILIAE; 10 10 10 with alleluias; adapt. by Marty Haugen, b.1950
© 1986, GIA Publications, Inc.

Jesus Christ Is Risen Today 593

1. Je - sus Christ is ris'n to - day, Al - le - lu - ia!
2. Hymns of praise then let us sing, Al - le - lu - ia!
3. But the pains which he en - dured, Al - le - lu - ia!
4. Sing we to our God a - bove, Al - le - lu - ia!

Our tri - um-phant ho - ly day, Al - le - lu - ia!
Un - to Christ, our heav'n-ly King, Al - le - lu - ia!
Our sal - va - tion have pro - cured; Al - le - lu - ia!
Praise e - ter - nal as his love; Al - le - lu - ia!

Who did once up - on the cross, Al - le - lu - ia!
Who en - dured the cross and grave, Al - le - lu - ia!
Now a - bove the sky he's King, Al - le - lu - ia!
Praise him, now his might con - fess, Al - le - lu - ia!

Suf - fer to re - deem our loss. Al - le - lu - ia!
Sin - ners to re - deem and save. Al - le - lu - ia!
Where the an - gels ev - er sing. Al - le - lu - ia!
Fa - ther, Son, and Spir - it blest. Al - le - lu - ia!

Text: St. 1, *Surrexit Christus hodie,* Latin, 14th C.; para. in *Lyra Davidica,* 1708, alt.; st. 2, 3, *The Compleat Psalmodist,* c.1750, alt.; st. 4, Charles Wesley, 1707-1788
Tune: EASTER HYMN, 77 77 with alleluias; *Lyra Davidica,* 1708

594 Christ the Lord Is Risen Today

1. Christ the Lord is ris'n to - day;
2. For the sheep the Lamb has bled,
3. Christ, the Vic - tim un - de - filed,
4. Chris - tians, on this hap - py day,
5. Hal - lowed, cho - sen dawn of praise,

Chris - tians, haste your vows to pay;
Sin - less in the sin - ner's stead;
God and sin - ners rec - on - ciled,
Raise your hearts with joy and say:
East - er, queen of all our days:

Make your joy and prais - es known;
Christ the Lord is ris'n on high;
When in fierce and blood - y strife
Christ the Lord is ris'n on high;
Zi - on's chil - dren now come forth;

At the Pas - chal Vic - tim's throne.
Now he lives no more to die.
Met to - geth - er death and life.
Now he lives no more to die.
East to west and south to north.

Al - le - lu - ia. Al - le - lu - ia. Al -

le - lu - ia. Al - le - lu - ia.

6. Let the people praise you, Lord,
   Be, by all that is, adored:
   Let the nations shout and sing;
   Glory to their Paschal King.

7. Hymns of glory, songs of praise,
   God on high, to you we raise:
   Risen Lord, we now adore,
   With the Spirit ever more.

Text: *Victimae paschali laudes*; ascr. to Wipo of Burgundy, d.1048; tr. by Jane E. Leeson, 1809-1881, alt.
Tune: SURGIT IN HAEC DIES, 77 77 with alleluias; 12th C.; acc. by Richard Proulx, b.1937, © 1980, GIA Publications, Inc.

Sing with All the Saints in Glory 595

1. Sing with all the saints in glo - ry, Sing the res - ur -
   rec - tion song! Death and sor - row, earth's dark sto - ry,
   To the for - mer days be - long. All a - round the
   clouds are break-ing, Soon the storms of time shall cease;
   In God's like-ness, we a - wak-en, Know-ing ev - er - last-ing peace.

2. O what glo - ry, far ex - ceed-ing All that eye has
   yet per - ceived! Ho - liest hearts for a - ges plead-ing,
   Nev - er that full joy con - ceived. God has prom - ised,
   Christ pre - pares it, There on high our wel - come waits;
   Ev - 'ry hum - ble spir - it shares it, Christ has passed the e - ter - nal gates.

3. Life e - ter - nal! heav'n re - joic - es: Je - sus lives who
   once was dead; Shout with joy, O death - less voic - es!
   Child of God, lift up your head! Pa - tri - archs from
   dis - tant a - ges, Saints all long - ing for their heav'n,
   Proph - ets, psalm-ists, seers, and sag - es, All a - wait the glo - ry giv'n.

4. Life e - ter - nal! O what won-ders Crowd on faith; what
   joy un - known, When, a - midst earth's clos - ing thun - ders,
   Saints shall stand be - fore the throne! O to en - ter
   that bright por - tal, See that glow - ing fir - ma - ment,
   Know, with you, O God im-mor-tal, Je - sus Christ whom you have sent!

Text: 1 Corinthians 15:20; William J. Irons, 1812-1883, alt.
Tune: HYMN TO JOY, 8 7 8 7 D; arr. from Ludwig van Beethoven, 1770-1827, by Edward Hodges, 1796-1867

596 Darkness Is Gone

1. Dark-ness is gone, day-light has come: God's
2. See now the cross, see now the grave: They,
3. Green-er the grass, bright-er the sun, The
4. The need-ed trust, the longed-for peace Are
5. "The King-dom comes!" the King pro-claims: Jus -
6. En-roll the drum, en-list the gong To

heir to heav'n and earth a - ris - es with the
va - cant, cel - e - brate how God's fool-ish-ness can
God-loved world pro-claims a new age has be -
passed as hands from sword and shack - le are re -
tice and joy a - bound where Christ-filled faith per -
cel - e - brate in sound that right has con - quered

dawn. Death los - es its sin - is - ter sting: God's
save. The crim - i - nal nailed as a fraud Is
gun. Cre - a - tion is decked for her guest Who,
leased. The vio - lence of hate reigns no more: The
tains. Re - lig - ion, re - mote and type - cast, Is
wrong. Join hands with the neigh-bor un - known, U -

prom - ise to do a new thing Is done, and Hal - le -
raised by the pow-er of God And lives. So, Hal - le -
freed from his grave clothes, is dressed In light and, Hal - le -
vic - t'ry of love is the core Of hope and, Hal - le -
gone and the fu - ture is vast. New tongues sing, "Hal - le -
nite through the love that is shown In Christ, for, Hal - le -

lu - jah! Earth joins heav'n to sing.
lu - jah! Scat - ter the news a - broad.
lu - jah! Tells that the earth is blessed.
lu - jah! Love means an o - pen door.
lu - jah! God is for us at last!"
lu - jah! Christ is our Lord a - lone.

Text: John L. Bell, b.1949
Tune: DAYLIGHT, Irregular; John L. Bell, b.1949
© 1988, Iona Community, GIA Publications, Inc., agent

Daylight Fades 597

1. Day - light fades in days when death - less Light has robbed earth's
2. Won - drous mys - t'ry of love's giv - ing! Our for - giv - ing
3. O Lord Je - sus, ris - en Sav - ior, Hear our joy - ful

night of fear; On the edge of all our twi - lights
Fa - ther's Son. Crushed in sor - row, raised to glo - ry
hymn of praise; Grant a sea - son of sal - va - tion,

East - er's an - gel shall ap - pear; When hearts bro - ken
Death had con - quered; life has won! Once in si - lence
Peace, and joy these East - er days. To our Fa - ther

by be - liev - ing Count their faith and hope as dead,
he sub - mit - ted, Now earth sings to him, our King;
and the Spir - it E - qual prais - es ev - er be;

Christ will greet them in each oth - er
Fear will ev - er flee de - feat - ed
Born a - gain, we sing God's good - ness

And in break - ing of the bread.
When a heart in love can sing!
Now and through e - ter - ni - ty.

Text: Luke 24:28-35; Peter J. Scagnelli, b.1949, ©
Tune: HYMN TO JOY, 8 7 8 7 D; arr. from Ludwig van Beethoven, 1770-1827, by Edward Hodges, 1796-1867

598 This Joyful Eastertide

1. This joy - ful East - er - tide A - way with sin and sor - row! My love, the Cru - ci - fied, Has sprung to life this mor - row:

2. My flesh in hope shall rest And for a sea - son slum - ber Till trump from east to west Shall wake the dead in num - ber:

3. Death's flood has lost its chill Since Je - sus crossed the riv - er; Lov - er of souls, from ill My pass - ing soul de - liv - er:

Had Christ, who once was slain, Not burst his three - day pris - on, Our faith had been in vain: But now has Christ a - ris - en, a - ris - en, a - ris - en; a - ris - en!

Text: George R. Woodward, 1848-1934
Tune: VRUECHTEN, 6 7 6 7 D; Melody in Oudaen's *David's Psalmen,* 1685; harm. by Paul G. Bunjes, b.1914, © 1969, Concordia Publishing House

That Easter Day with Joy Was Bright 599

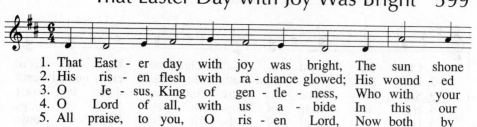

1. That East - er day with joy was bright, The sun shone
2. His ris - en flesh with ra - diance glowed; His wound - ed
3. O Je - sus, King of gen - tle - ness, Who with your
4. O Lord of all, with us a - bide In this our
5. All praise, to you, O ris - en Lord, Now both by

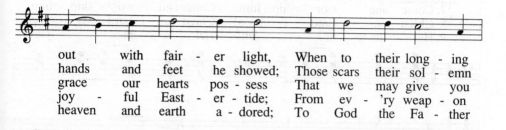

out with fair - er light, When to their long - ing
hands and feet he showed; Those scars their sol - emn
grace our hearts pos - sess That we may give you
joy - ful East - er - tide; From ev - 'ry weap - on
heaven and earth a - dored; To God the Fa - ther

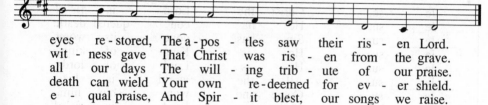

eyes re - stored, The a - pos - tles saw their ris - en Lord.
wit - ness gave That Christ was ris - en from the grave.
all our days The will - ing trib - ute of our praise.
death can wield Your own re - deemed for ev - er shield.
e - qual praise, And Spir - it blest, our songs we raise.

Text: *Claro paschali gaudio;* Latin 5th C.; tr. by John M. Neale, 1818-1866, alt.
Tune: PUER NOBIS, LM; adapt. by Michael Praetorius, 1571-1621

600 Christ the Lord Is Risen

1. Christ the Lord is ris'n! Christ the Lord is ris'n!
2. He has con - quered death. He has con - quered death.
3. Sin has done its worst. Sin has done its worst.
4. He is King of kings. He is King of kings.
5. He is Lord of lords. He is Lord of lords.
6. All the world is his. All the world is his.
7. Come and wor - ship him. Come and wor - ship him.
8. Christ our Lord is ris'n! Christ our Lord is ris'n!
9. Hal - le - lu - jah! Hal - le - lu - jah!

Je - su. Christ the Lord is ris'n!
Je - su. He has con - quered death.
Je - su. Sin has done its worst.
Je - su. He is King of kings.
Je - su. He is Lord of lords.
Je - su. All the world is his.
Je - su. Come and wor - ship him.
Je - su. Christ our Lord is ris'n!
Je - su. Hal - le - lu - jah!

Christ the Lord is ris'n! Je - su.
He has con - quered death. Je - su.
Sin has done its worst. Je - su.
He is King of kings. Je - su.
He is Lord of lords. Je - su.
All the world is his. Je - su.
Come and wor - ship him. Je - su.
Christ our Lord is ris'n! Je - su.
Hal - le - lu - jah! Je - su.

Text: Tom Colvin, b.1925.
Tune: GARU, 55 2 55 2; Ghanian folk song, adapt. by Tom Colvin, b.1925, arr. by Kevin R. Hackett
© 1969, Hope Publishing Company

Christ Is Alive   601

1. Christ is a - live! Let Chris - tians sing.
2. Christ is a - live! No long - er bound
3. In ev - 'ry in - sult, rift, and war,
4. Wom - en and men, in age and youth,
5. Christ is a - live, and comes to bring

The cross stands emp - ty to the sky.
To dis - tant years in Pal - es - tine,
Where col - or, scorn or wealth di - vide,
Can feel the Spir - it, hear the call,
Good news to this and ev - 'ry age,

Let streets and homes with prais - es ring.
But sav - ing, heal - ing here and now,
Christ suf - fers still, yet loves the more,
And find the way, the life, the truth,
Till earth and sky and o - cean ring

Love, drowned in death, shall nev - er die.
And touch - ing ev - 'ry place and time.
And lives, where ev - en hope has died.
Re - vealed in Je - sus, freed for all.
With joy, with jus - tice, love and praise.

Text: Romans 6:5-11; Brian Wren, b.1936, © 1975, Hope Publishing Co.
Tune: TRURO, LM; Williams' *Psalmodia Evangelica*, 1789

602 Christ the Lord Is Risen Today

1. Christ the Lord is ris'n to-day, Alle-
2. Lives a-gain our glo-rious King; Alle-
3. Love's re-deem-ing work is done, Alle-
4. Soar we now where Christ has led, Alle-

lu-ia! All on earth with an-gels say,
lu-ia! Where, O death, is now your sting?
lu-ia! Fought the fight, the bat-tle won.
lu-ia! Fol-l'wing our ex - alt-ed head;

Al - le-lu - ia! Raise your joys and
Al - le-lu - ia! Once he died our
Al - le-lu - ia! Death in vain for -
Al - le-lu - ia! Made like him, like

tri - umphs high, Al - le-lu - ia!
souls to save, Al - le-lu - ia!
bids him rise; Al - le-lu - ia!
him we rise, Al - le-lu - ia!

Sing, O heav'ns, and earth re - ply,
Where your vic - to - ry, O grave?
Christ has o - pened par - a - dise.
Ours the cross, the grave, the skies.

Al - le - lu - ia!

Text: Charles Wesley, 1707-1788
Tune: LLANFAIR, 77 77 with alleluias; Robert Williams, 1781-1821

I Will Be with You 603

Refrain

"I will be with you!" That is my prom-ise.

"I will be with you for ev - er - more."

Trust in my love. Bring me all your

cares, for I will be with you for ev - er - more.

Verses

1. You are my peo - ple, and I am your
2. You have re - ceived me, now go and spread my

God. I made you a prom-ise, to be with you al -
word. You are with - in me and I am in

ways, be - cause I real - ly love you. I real - ly
you,

D.S.

love you, and I will be with you for ev - er - more.

Text: James E. Moore, Jr., b.1951
Tune: James E. Moore, Jr., b.1951
© 1983, GIA Publications, Inc.

604 Go

1. Go ye there-fore and teach all na - tions,
2. If you love me, real - ly love me,

go, go, go. Go ye
feed my sheep. If you

there - fore and teach all na - tions, go,
love me, real - ly love me, feed

go, go. Bap - tiz - ing them in the
my sheep. And lo, I'll be with you for

name of the Fa - ther and Son and Ho - ly
ev - er and ev - er un - til the ends of the

Ghost. Go, go,
world, go, go,

go.
go.

Text: Leon Patillo
Tune: Leon Patillo
© 1981, 1982, Word Music, Inc.

Hail the Day That Sees Him Rise 605

1. Hail the day that sees him rise, Al - le - lu - ia!
2. There for him high tri - umph waits; Al - le - lu - ia!
3. High - est heav'n its Lord re - ceives, Al - le - lu - ia!
4. See, he lifts his hands a - bove. Al - le - lu - ia!
5. Still for us he in - ter - cedes, Al - le - lu - ia!
6. There we shall with him re - main, Al - le - lu - ia!

To his throne a - bove the skies; Al - le - lu - ia!
Lift your heads, e - ter - nal gates; Al - le - lu - ia!
Yet he loves the earth he leaves: Al - le - lu - ia!
See, he shows the prints of love. Al - le - lu - ia!
His pre - vail - ing death he pleads, Al - le - lu - ia!
Part - ners of his end - less reign; Al - le - lu - ia!

Christ, a - while to mor - tals given, Al - le - lu - ia!
He has con - quered death and sin; Al - le - lu - ia!
Though re - turn - ing to his throne, Al - le - lu - ia!
Hark, his gra - cious lips be - stow, Al - le - lu - ia!
Near him - self pre - pares our place, Al - le - lu - ia!
There his face un - cloud - ed see, Al - le - lu - ia!

Re - as - cends his na - tive heav'n. Al - le - lu - ia!
Take the King of glo - ry in. Al - le - lu - ia!
Still he calls the world his own. Al - le - lu - ia!
Bless - ings on his church be - low. Al - le - lu - ia!
He the first fruits of our race. Al - le - lu - ia!
Live with him e - ter - nal - ly. Al - le - lu - ia!

Text: Charles Wesley, 1707-1788, alt.
Tune: LLANFAIR, 77 77 with alleluias; Robert Williams, 1781-1821

606 A Hymn of Glory Let Us Sing

1. A hymn of glo - ry let us sing! New hymns through-out the world shall ring: Al - le - lu - ia! Al - le - lu - ia! Christ, by a road be - fore un - trod. As - cends un - to the throne of God.

2. The ho - ly ap - os - tol - ic band Up - on the Mount of Ol - ives stand. Al - le - lu - ia! Al - le - lu - ia! And with his faith - ful fol - l'wers see Their Lord as - cend in maj - es - ty.

3. To whom the shin - ing an - gels cry, "Why stand and gaze up - on the sky?" Al - le - lu - ia! Al - le - lu - ia! "This is the Sav - ior!" Thus they say, "This is his glo - rious tri - umph day!"

4. O ris - en Christ, as - cend - ed Lord, All praise to you let earth ac - cord: Al - le - lu - ia! Al - le - lu - ia! You are, while end - less a - ges run, With Fa - ther and with Spir - it one.

Al - le - lu - ia! Al - le - lu - ia! Al - le - lu - ia! Al - le - lu - ia!

Text: *Hymnum canamus gloria*; Venerable Bede, 673-735; tr. *Lutheran Book of Worship*, © 1978
Tune: LASST UNS ERFREUEN, LM with alleluias; *Geistliche Kirchengasange*, Cologne, 1623; harm. by Ralph Vaughan Williams

Lord, You Give the Great Commission 607

1. Lord, you give the great com-mis-sion: "Heal the
2. Lord, you call us to your serv-ice: "In my
3. Lord, you make the com-mon ho-ly: "This my
4. Lord, you show us love's true meas-ure: "Fa - ther,
5. Lord, you bless with words as - sur-ing: "I am

sick and preach the word." Lest the Church ne-
name bap - tize and teach." That the world may
bod - y, this my blood." Let us all, for
what they do, for - give." Yet we hoard as
with you to the end." Faith and hope and

glect its mis-sion, And the Gos - pel go un -heard,
trust your prom-ise, Life a - bun - dant meant for each,
earth's true glo - ry, Dai - ly lift life heav - en -ward,
pri - vate treas -ure All that you so free - ly give.
love re - stor-ing, May we serve as you in - tend,

Help us wit - ness to your pur-pose With re -
Give us all new fer - vor, draw us Clos - er
Ask - ing that the world a - round us Share your
May your care and mer - cy lead us To a
And, a - mid the cares that claim us, Hold in

newed in - teg - ri - ty;
in com - mun - i - ty;
chil - dren's lib - er - ty;   With the Spir - it's gifts em-
just so - ci - e - ty;
mind e - ter - ni - ty;

power us For the work of min - is - try.

Text: Jeffery Rowthorn, b.1934, © 1978, Hope Publishing Co.
Tune: ABBOT'S LEIGH, 8 7 8 7 D; Cyril V. Taylor, 1907-1991, © 1942, 1970, Hope Publishing Co.

608 Go to the World

1. Go to the world! Go in-to all the earth. Go preach the cross where Christ re-news life's worth, bap-tis-ing as the sign of our re-birth.
2. Go to the world! Go in-to ev-'ry place. Go live the Word of God's re-deem-ing grace. Go seek God's pres-ence in each time and space.
3. Go to the world! Go strug-gle, bless and pray; the nights of tears give way to joy-ous day, As ser-vant Church, you fol-low Christ's own way.
4. Go to the world! Go as the ones I send, for I am with you 'til the age shall end, When all the hosts of glo-ry cry "A-men!"

Al-le-lu-ia. Al-le-lu-ia.

Text: Sylvia G. Dunstan, 1955-1993, ©1991, GIA Publications, Inc.
Tune: SINE NOMINE, 10 10 10 with alleluias; Ralph Vaughan Williams, 1872-1958

Praise the Spirit in Creation 609

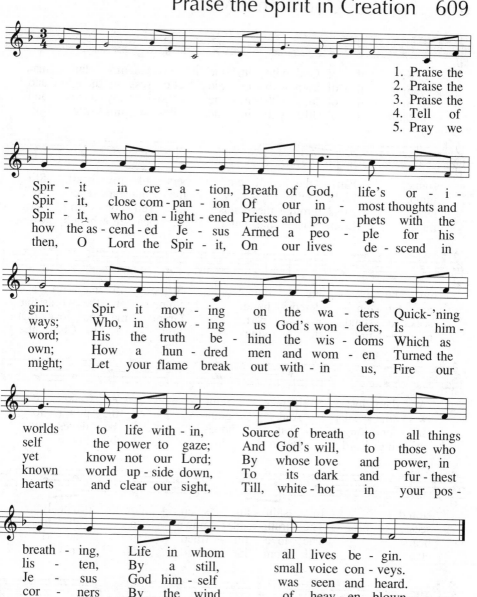

1. Praise the
2. Praise the
3. Praise the
4. Tell of
5. Pray we

1. Spir - it in cre - a - tion, Breath of God, life's or - i - gin: Spir - it mov - ing on the wa - ters Quick-'ning worlds to life with - in, Source of breath to all things breath - ing, Life in whom all lives be - gin.
2. Spir - it, close com - pan - ion Of our in - most thoughts and ways; Who, in show - ing us God's won - ders, Is him - self the power to gaze; And God's will, to those who lis - ten, By a still, small voice con - veys.
3. Spir - it, who en - light - ened Priests and pro - phets with the word; His the truth be - hind the wis - doms Which as yet know not our Lord; By whose love and power, in world up - side down, To its dark and fur - thest Je - sus God him - self was seen and heard.
4. Tell how the as - cend - ed Je - sus Armed a peo - ple for his own; How a hun - dred men and wom - en Turned the known world up - side down, To its dark and fur - thest cor - ners By the wind of heav - en blown.
5. Pray we then, O Lord the Spir - it, On our lives de - scend in might; Let your flame break out with - in us, Fire our hearts and clear our sight, Till, white - hot in your pos - ses - sion, We, too, set the world a - light.

Text: Michael Hewlett, b.1916, alt., © Oxford University Press
Tune: JULION, 8 7 8 7 8 7; David Hurd, b.1950, © 1983, GIA Publications, Inc.

610 Spirit of God within Me

1. Spir - it of God with-in me, Pos-sess my hu - man frame; Fan the dull em - bers of my heart, Stir up the liv - ing flame: Strive till that im - age A - dam lost, New mint - ed and re - stored, In shin - ing splen - dor bright-ly bears The like-ness of the Lord.

2. Spir - it of truth with-in me, Pos-sess my thought and mind; Light - en a - new the in - ward eye By Sa - tan ren - dered blind: Shine on the words that wis - dom speaks And grant me pow'r to see The truth made known to all in Christ, And in that truth be free.

3. Spir - it of love with-in me, Pos-sess my hands and heart; Break through the bonds of self - con - cern That seeks to stand a - part: Grant me the love that suf - fers long, That hopes, me the love that bears; The love ful - filled in sac - ri - fice, That cares as Je - sus cares.

4. Spir - it of life with-in me, Pos-sess this life of mine; Come as the wind of heav-en's breath, Come as the fire di - vine! Spir - it of Christ, the liv - ing Lord, Reign in this house of clay, Till from its dust with Christ I rise To ev - er - last - ing day.

Text: Timothy Dudley-Smith, b.1926, © 1968, Hope Publishing Co.
Tune: WILLOW RIVER, 7 6 8 6 8 6 8 6; Michael Joncas, b.1951, © 1985, 1988, GIA Publications, Inc.

Come, Holy Ghost 611

1. Come, Ho - ly Ghost, Cre - a - tor blest,
2. O Com - fort - er, to thee we cry,
3. O Ho - ly Ghost, through thee a - lone,
4. Praise we the Lord, Fa - ther and Son,

And in our hearts take up thy rest;
Thou heav'n - ly gift of God most high;
Know we the Fa - ther and the Son;
And Ho - ly Spir - it with them one;

Come with thy grace and heav'n - ly aid
Thou fount of life, and fire of love,
Be this our firm un - chang - ing creed,
And may the Son on us be - stow

To fill the hearts which thou hast made,
And sweet a - noint - ing from a - bove,
That thou dost from them both pro - ceed,
All gifts that from the Spir - it flow,

To fill the hearts which thou hast made.
And sweet a - noint - ing from a - bove.
That thou dost from them both pro - ceed.
All gifts that from the Spir - it flow.

Text: *Veni, Creator Spiritus;* attr. to Rabanus Maurus, 776-856; tr. by Edward Caswall, 1814-1878, alt.
Tune: LAMBILLOTTE, LM with repeat; Louis Lambillotte, SJ, 1796-1855, harm. by Richard Proulx, b.1937, © 1986, GIA Publications, Inc.

612 Send Us Your Spirit

Refrain

*1.
Come Lord Je-sus, send us your Spir-it, re-

2.
new the face of the earth. Come Lord

Je-sus, send us your Spir-it, re-new the face of the

earth.

Verses

1. Come to us, Spir-it of God, breathe in us
2. Fill us with the fire of your love, burn in us
3. Send us the wings of new birth, fill all the

now, we sing to-geth-er. Spir-it of
now, bring us to-geth-er. Come to us
earth with the love you have taught us. Let all cre-

hope and of light, fill our lives,
dwell in us, change our lives, O Lord,
a - tion now be shak-en with love,

D.C.

come to us, Spir-it of God.
come to us, Spir-it of God.
come to us, Spir-it of God.

*May be sung in canon.

Text: David Haas, b.1957
Tune: David Haas, b.1957; acc. by Jeanne Cotter, b.1964
© 1981, 1982, 1987, GIA Publications, Inc.

When God the Spirit Came 613

1. When God the Spir - it came Up - on his church out -
2. What cour - age, pow'r and grace That youth - ful church dis -
3. They saw God's Word pre - vail, His king - dom still in -
4. Their theme was Christ a - lone, The Lord who lived and
5. So to this pres - ent hour Our task is still the

poured In sound of wind and sign of flame They
played! To those of ev - 'ry tribe and race They
crease, No part of all his pur - pose fail, No
died, Who rose to his e - ter - nal throne At
same, In pen - te - cos - tal love and pow'r His

spread his truth a - broad, And filled with the
wit - nessed un - a - fraid, And filled with the
prom - ised bless - ing cease, And filled with the
God the Fa - ther's side; And filled with the
gos - pel to pro - claim, And filled with the

Spir - it Pro - claimed that Christ is Lord.
Spir - it They broke their bread and prayed.
Spir - it Knew love and joy and peace.
Spir - it The church was mul - ti - plied.
Spir - it Re - joice in Je - sus' Name.

Text: Acts 2; Timothy Dudley-Smith, b.1926, © 1984, Hope Publishing Co.
Tune: VINEYARD HAVEN, 6 6 8 6 6 6; Richard Dirksen, b.1921, © 1974, 1986, Harold Flammer, Inc.

614 Fire of God, Undying Flame

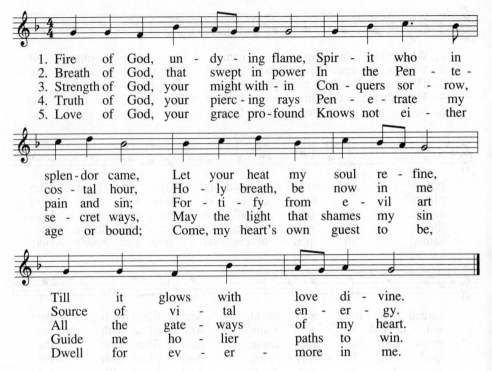

1. Fire of God, un - dy - ing flame, Spir - it who in
2. Breath of God, that swept in power In the Pen - te -
3. Strength of God, your might with - in Con - quers sor - row,
4. Truth of God, your pierc - ing rays Pen - e - trate my
5. Love of God, your grace pro - found Knows not ei - ther

splen - dor came, Let your heat my soul re - fine,
cos - tal hour, Ho - ly breath, be now in me
pain and sin; For - ti - fy from e - vil art
se - cret ways, May the light that shames my sin
age or bound; Come, my heart's own guest to be,

Till it glows with love di - vine.
Source of vi - tal en - er - gy.
All the gate - ways of my heart.
Guide me ho - lier paths to win.
Dwell for ev - er - more in me.

Text: Albert F. Bayly, 1901-1984, alt., © Oxford University Press
Tune: NUN KOMM DER HEIDEN HEILAND, 77 77; *Geystliche Gesangk Buchleyn*, Wittenberg, 1524

615 Veni Sancte Spiritus

Ostinato Refrain

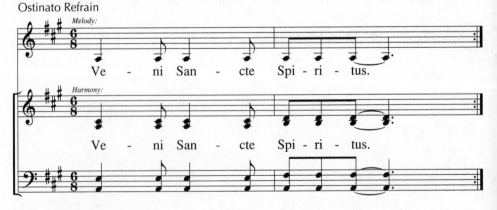

Melody:

Ve - ni San - cte Spi - ri - tus.

Harmony:

Ve - ni San - cte Spi - ri - tus.

Text: *Come Holy Spirit*; Verses drawn from the Pentecost Sequence; Taizé Community, 1978
Tune: Jacques Berthier, 1923-1994
© 1979, Les Presses de Taizé, GIA Publications, Inc., agent

O Holy Spirit, by Whose Breath 616

1. O Ho - ly Spir - it, by whose breath
2. You are the seek - er's sure re - source,
3. In you God's en - er - gy is shown,
4. Flood our dull sens - es with your light;
5. From in - ner strife grant us re - lease;
6. Praise to the Fa - ther, Christ the Word,

Life ris - es vi - brant out of death:
Of burn - ing love the liv - ing source,
To us your var - ied gifts made known.
In mu - tual love our hearts u - nite.
Turn na - tions to the ways of peace.
And to the Spir - it, God the Lord;

Come to cre - ate, re - new, in - spire;
Pro - tec - tor in the midst of strife,
Teach us to speak; teach us to hear;
Your pow'r the whole cre - a - tion fills;
To full - er life your peo - ple bring
To whom all hon - or, glo - ry be

Come, kin - dle in our hearts your fire.
The giv - er and the Lord of life.
Yours is the tongue and yours the ear.
Con - firm our weak, un - cer - tain wills.
That as one bod - y we may sing:
Both now and for e - ter - ni - ty.

Text: *Veni, Creator Spiritus;* attr. to Rabanus Maurus, 776-865; tr. by John W. Grant, b.1919, © 1971
Tune: VENI CREATOR SPIRITUS, LM; Mode VIII; setting by Richard J. Wojcik, b.1923, © 1975, GIA Publications, Inc.

617 Come Down, O Love Divine

1. Come down, O Love di - vine, Seek now this soul of
2. O let it free - ly burn, Till earth - ly pas - sions
3. And so the yearn - ing strong, With which the soul will

mine, And vis - it it with your own ar - dor glow-ing;
turn To dust and ash - es in its heat con - sum - ing;
long, Shall far out-pass the power of hu - man tell - ing;

O Com-fort - er, draw near, With - in my heart ap -
And let your glo - rious light Shine ev - er on my
For none can guess its grace, Till love cre - ates the

pear, And kin - dle it, your ho - ly flame be - stow-ing.
sight, And clothe me round, the while my path il - lum - ing.
place Where - in the Ho - ly Spir - it makes its dwell-ing.

Text: *Discendi, Amor Santo*; Bianco da Siena, d.c.1434; tr. by Richard F. Littledale, 1833-1890
Tune: DOWN AMPNEY, 66 11 D; Ralph Vaughan Williams, 1872-1958

How Wonderful the Three-in-One 618

1. How won - der - ful the Three - in - One, Whose
2. Be - fore the flow of dawn and dark, Cre -
3. The Lov - er's own Be - lov'd, in time, Be -
4. Their E - qual Friend all life sus - tains With
5. How won - der - ful the Liv - ing God: Di -

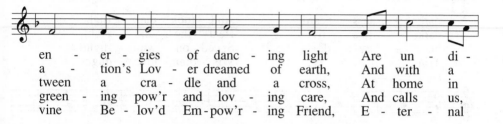

en - er - gies of danc - ing light Are un - di -
a - tion's Lov - er dreamed of earth, And with a
tween a cra - dle and a cross, At home in
green - ing pow'r and lov - ing care, And calls us,
vine Be - lov'd Em-pow'r - ing Friend, E - ter - nal

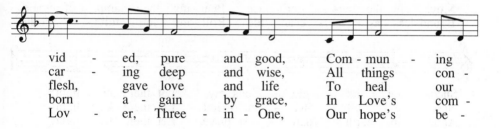

vid - ed, pure and good, Com - mun - ing
car - ing deep and wise, All things con -
flesh, gave love and life To heal our
born a - gain by grace, In Love's com -
Lov - er, Three - in - One, Our hope's be -

love in shared de - light.
ceived and brought to birth.
bro - ken - ness and loss.
mun - ing life to share.
gin - ning, way and end.

Text: Brian Wren, b.1936, © 1989, Hope Publishing Co.
Tune: PROSPECT, 8 8 8 8; *Southern Harmony*; arr. by Marty Haugen, b.1950, © 1991, GIA Publications, Inc.

619 God, Whose Almighty Word

1. God, whose al - might - y word
2. Sav - ior, you came to give
3. Spir - it of truth and love,
4. Gra - cious and ho - ly Three,

Cha - os and
Those who in
Life - giv - ing,
Glo - ri - ous

dark - ness heard,
dark - ness live
ho - ly dove,
Trin - i - ty,

And took their flight:
Heal - ing and sight,
Speed on your flight!
Wis - dom, love, might:

Hear us, we hum - bly pray,
Health to the sick in mind,
Move on the wa - ter's face
Bound-less as o - cean's tide

And where the gos - pel - day
Sight to the in - ward blind:
Bear - ing the lamp of grace
Roll - ing in full - est pride

Sheds not its glo - rious ray,
Now to all hu - man-kind
And, in earth's dark - est place,
Through the world far and wide,

Let there be light!
Let there be light!
Let there be light!
Let there be light!

Text: John Marriott, 1780-1825, alt.
Tune: ITALIAN HYMN, 66 4 666 4; Felice de Giardini, 1716-1796

Sing Praise to Our Creator   620

1. Sing praise to our Cre - a - tor, Re -
2. To Je - sus Christ give glo - ry, God's
3. Now praise the Ho - ly Spir - it Poured

deemed of A - dam's race; God's chil - dren by a -
co - e - ter - nal Son; As mem - bers of his
forth up - on the earth, Who sanc - ti - fies and

dop - tion, Bap - tized in liv - ing grace.
bod - y We are in Christ made one.
guides us, Con - firmed in our re - birth.

O most ho - ly Trin - i - ty, Un - di - vid - ed u - ni - ty;

Ho - ly God, might-y God, God im - mor - tal, be a-dored!

Text: Omer Westendorf, 1916-1998; © 1962, World Library Publications, Inc.
Tune: GOTT VATER SEI GEPRIESEN, 76 76 with refrain; *Limburg Gesangbuch,* 1838; harm. by Healey Willan, 1880-1968, © 1958,
   Ralph Jusko Publications, Inc.

621 This Holy Covenant Was Made

1. This ho-ly cov-e-nant was made: God our De-liv-'rance was o - beyed. Seas were part - ed; free-dom start - ed. By cloud and fi - re we were led. By quail and man - na we were fed. Al - le - lu - ia, Al - le - lu - ia. Al - le - lu - ia, Al - le - lu - ia, Al - le - lu - ia!

2. This ho-ly cov-e-nant was new At ta - ble with Christ's gath - ered few. Bless - ing spo - ken; bod - y bro - ken. By lift - ed cup our God for - gives. By Je - sus' grace a - lone we live.

3. This ho-ly cov-e-nant of flame Sears in our hearts the sav - ing name. Spir - it's fi - re, our de - si - re. By wind and tongue the Church is sealed. By might and pow - er here re - vealed.

Text: Sylvia Dunstan, 1955-1993, © 1991, GIA Publications, Inc.
Tune: LASST UNS ERFREUEN, LM with alleluias; Geistliche Kirchengesänge, 1623; harm. by Ralph Vaughan Williams, 1872-1958

Stand Up, Friends   622

Verses

1. Praise the God who chang - es plac - es,
2. Praise the Rab - bi, speak - ing, do - ing
3. Praise the Breath of Love, whose free - dom
4. Praise, un - til we join the sing - ing

Leaves the loft - y seat, Wel - comes us with
All that God in - tends, Dy - ing, ris - ing,
Spreads our wak - ing wings, Lift - ing ev - 'ry
Far be - yond our sight, With the End - ing

warm em - bra - ces, Stoops to wash our feet.
faith re - new - ing, Call - ing us his friends.
blight and bur - den Till the spir - it sings;
and Be - gin - ning Danc - ing in the light.

Refrain

Stand up, friends! Hold your heads high! Free-dom is our

song! Al - le - lu - ia! Free-dom is our song! Al-le - lu - ia!

1.

2.

ia!

D.C.   Final ending

Text: Brian Wren, b.1936, © 1986, Hope Publishing Co.
Tune: David Haas, b.1957, © 1993, GIA Publications, Inc.

623 God Is One, Unique and Holy

1., 4. God is One, u - nique and ho - ly,
2. God is One - ness - by - Com - mun - ion,
3. Through the pain that lov - ing Wis - dom

end - less dance of love and light,
nev - er dis - tant or a - lone,
could fore - see, but not fore - stall,

on - ly source of mind and bod - y,
at the heart of all be - long - ing:
God is One, though torn and an - guished

star - cloud, a - tom, day and night:
loy - al friend - ship, lov - ing home,
in the Christ's for - sak - en call;

ev - 'ry thing that is or could be
com - mon mind and shared a - gree - ment,
One through death and res - ur - rec - tion;

tells God's an - guish and de - light.
com - mon loaf and sung Sha - lom.
One in Spir - it, One for all.

Text: Brian Wren, b.1936, © 1983, Hope Publishing Co.
Tune: Gary Daigle, b.1957, © 1994, GIA Publications, Inc.

Holy, Holy, Holy! Lord God Almighty   624

1. Ho-ly, Ho-ly, Ho - ly!   Lord   God   Al - might - y!
2. Ho-ly, Ho-ly, Ho - ly!   all   the saints a - dore thee,
3. Ho-ly, Ho-ly, Ho - ly!   though the dark - ness hide thee,
4. Ho-ly, Ho-ly, Ho - ly!   Lord   God   Al - might - y!

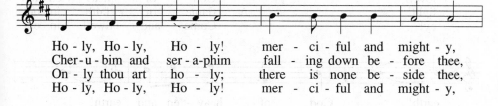

Ear - ly   in   the   morn - ing our song shall rise   to thee:
Cast - ing down their gold - en crowns a - round the glass - y sea;
Though the eye made blind by sin thy glo - ry may   not see,
All   thy works shall praise thy Name in earth, and sky, and sea;

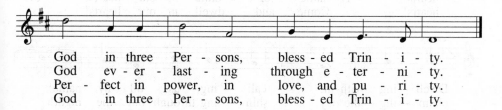

Ho - ly, Ho - ly,   Ho - ly!   mer - ci - ful and might - y,
Cher-u - bim and   ser - a-phim   fall - ing down be - fore thee,
On - ly thou art   ho - ly;   there is none be - side thee,
Ho - ly, Ho - ly,   Ho - ly!   mer - ci - ful and might - y,

God   in three Per - sons,   bless - ed Trin - i - ty.
God   ev - er - last - ing   through e - ter - ni - ty.
Per - fect in power,   in   love, and pu - ri - ty.
God   in three Per - sons,   bless - ed Trin - i - ty.

Text: Reginald Heber, 1783-1826, alt.
Tune: NICAEA, 11 12 12 10; John Bacchus Dykes, 1823-1876

625 Alleluia, Sing!

1. Bless - ed be our God! Bless - ed be our
2. Gift of love and peace! Gift of love and
3. Come, O Spir - it of truth! Come, O Spir - it of

God! Joy of our hearts, source of all life and
peace! Je - sus the Christ, Je - sus our hope and
truth! Prom - ise of hope, kind - ness and mer -

love! God of heav - en and
light! A flame of faith in our
cy! Come and dwell in our

earth! God of heav - en and earth!
hearts! A flame of faith in our hearts! Pro -
hearts! Come and dwell in our hearts!

Dwell - ing with-in, call - ing us all by name!
claim - ing the day, shin - ing through - out the night!
Jus - tice and peace, the king - dom of God in us!

Al - le - lu - ia, sing!

Al - le - lu - ia, sing!

Text: David Haas, b.1957
Tune: David Haas, b.1957
© 1988, GIA Publications, Inc.

Crown Him with Many Crowns   626

1. Crown him with man - y crowns, The Lamb up - on his
2. Crown him the Lord of life, Who tri - umphed o'er the
3. Crown him the Lord of love, Be - hold his hands and
4. Crown him the Lord of peace, Whose power a scep - ter
5. Crown him the Lord of years, The ris - en Lord sub -

throne; Hark! how the heav'n - ly an - them drowns All
grave, And rose vic - to - rious in the strife For
side, Rich wounds yet vis - i - ble a - bove In
sways From pole to pole, that wars may cease, Ab -
lime, Cre - a - tor of the roll - ing spheres, The

mu - sic but its own. A - wake, my soul, and sing Of
those he came to save. His glo - ries now we sing, Who
beau - ty glo - ri - fied. No an - gel in the sky Can
sorbed in prayer and praise. His reign shall know no end, And
Mas - ter of all time. All hail, Re - deem - er, hail! For

him who set us free, And hail him as your
died and rose on high, Who died, e - ter - nal
ful - ly bear that sight, But down - ward bends his
round his pierc - ed feet Fair flow'rs of Par - a -
you have died for me; Your praise and glo - ry

heav'n - ly King Through all e - ter - ni - ty.
life to bring, And lives that death may die.
burn - ing eye At mys - ter - ies so bright.
dise ex - tend Their fra - grance ev - er sweet.
shall not fail Through - out e - ter - ni - ty.

Text: Revelation 19:12; St. 1, 3-5, Matthew Bridges, 1800-1894; St. 2, Godfrey Thring, 1823-1903
Tune: DIADEMATA, SMD; George J. Elvey, 1816-1893

627 Rejoice, the Lord Is King

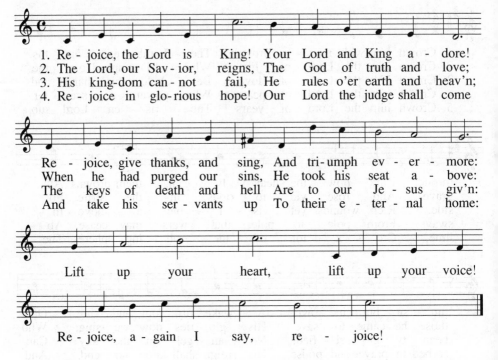

1. Re - joice, the Lord is King! Your Lord and King a - dore!
2. The Lord, our Sav - ior, reigns, The God of truth and love;
3. His king-dom can - not fail, He rules o'er earth and heav'n;
4. Re - joice in glo-rious hope! Our Lord the judge shall come

Re - joice, give thanks, and sing, And tri-umph ev - er - more:
When he had purged our sins, He took his seat a - bove:
The keys of death and hell Are to our Je - sus giv'n:
And take his ser - vants up To their e - ter - nal home:

Lift up your heart, lift up your voice!

Re - joice, a - gain I say, re - joice!

Text: Charles Wesley, 1707-1788
Tune: DARWALL'S 148TH, 6 6 6 6 88; John Darwall, 1731-1789; harm. from *The Hymnal 1940*

628 The King of Glory

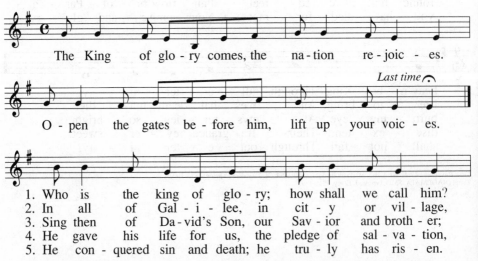

The King of glo - ry comes, the na - tion re - joic - es.

Last time

O - pen the gates be - fore him, lift up your voic - es.

1. Who is the king of glo - ry; how shall we call him?
2. In all of Gal - i - lee, in cit - y or vil - lage,
3. Sing then of Da - vid's Son, our Sav - ior and broth - er;
4. He gave his life for us, the pledge of sal - va - tion,
5. He con - quered sin and death; he tru - ly has ris - en.

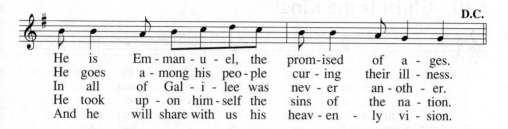

He is Em-man-u-el, the prom-ised of a-ges.
He goes a-mong his peo-ple cur-ing their ill-ness.
In all of Gal-i-lee was nev-er an-oth-er.
He took up-on him-self the sins of the na-tion.
And he will share with us his heav-en-ly vi-sion.

D.C.

Text: Willard F. Jabusch, b. 1930, © 1966, 1982, Willard F. Jabusch. Administered by OCP Publications.
Tune: KING OF GLORY, 12 12 with refrain; Israeli; harm. by Richard Proulx, b.1937, © 1986, GIA Publications, Inc.

To Jesus Christ, Our Sovereign King 629

1. To Je-sus Christ, our sov-'reign King, Who
2. Your reign ex-tend, O King be-nign, To
3. To you, and to your church, great King, We

is the world's sal-va-tion, All praise and hom-age
ev-'ry land and na-tion; For in your King-dom,
pledge our heart's ob-la-tion; Un-til be-fore your

do we bring And thanks and ad-o-ra-tion.
Lord di-vine, A-lone we find sal-va-tion.
throne we sing In end-less ju-bi-la-tion.

Christ Je-sus, Vic-tor! Christ Je-sus, Rul-er!

Christ Je-sus, Lord and Re-deem - er!

Text: Martin B. Hellrigel, 1891-1981, alt., © 1941, Irene C. Mueller
Tune: ICH GLAUB AN GOTT, 8 7 8 7 with refrain; *Mainz Gesangbuch*, 1870; harm. by Richard Proulx, b.1937, © 1986, GIA Publications, Inc.

630 Christ Is the King!

1. Christ is the King! O friends, re-joice:
2. O mag-ni-fy the Lord, and raise
3. They with a faith for ev-er new
4. O Chris-tian wom-en, Chris-tian men,
5. Christ through all a-ges is the same:

Broth-ers and sis-ters, with one voice
An-thems of joy and ho-ly praise
Fol-lowed the King, and round him drew
All the world o-ver, seek a-gain
Place the same hope in his great name,

Let the world know he is your choice.
For Christ's brave saints of an-cient days.
Thou-sands of men and wom-en true.
The Way dis-ci-ples fol-lowed then.
With the same faith his word pro-claim.

Al-le-lu-ia, al-le-lu-ia, al-le-lu-ia.

6. Let love's all reconciling might
Your scattered companies unite
In service to the Lord of light.
Alleluia, alleluia, alleluia.

7. So shall God's will on earth be done,
New lamps be lit, new tasks begun,
And the whole Church at last be one.
Alleluia, alleluia, alleluia.

Text: George K. A. Bell, 1883-1958, alt., © Oxford University Press
Tune: GELOBT SEI GOTT, 888 with alleluias; Melchior Vulpius, c.1560-1616

Jesus Shall Reign   631

1. Je - sus shall reign wher - e'er the sun
2. To him shall end - less prayer be made,
3. Peo - ple and realms of ev - 'ry tongue
4. Bless - ings a - bound wher - e'er he reigns;
5. Let ev - 'ry crea - ture rise and bring

Does his suc - ces - sive jour - neys run;
And prais - es throng to crown his head;
Dwell on his love with sweet - est song;
The pris - 'ner leaps to lose his chains;
Bless - ing and hon - or to our King;

His king - dom stretch from shore to shore,
His Name like sweet per - fume shall rise
And in - fant voic - es shall pro - claim
The wea - ry find e - ter - nal rest,
An - gels de - scend with songs a - gain,

Till moons shall wax and wane no more.
With ev - 'ry morn - ing sac - ri - fice.
Their ear - ly bless - ings on his Name.
And all who suf - fer want are blest.
And earth re - peat the loud A - men.

Text: Isaac Watts, 1674-1748, alt.
Tune: DUKE STREET, LM; John Hatton, c.1710-1793

632 All Hail the Power of Jesus' Name

Text: Edward Perronet, 1726-1792; alt. by John Rippon, 1751-1836, alt.
Tune: DIADEM, CM with repeats; from the *Primitive Baptist Hymn and Tune Book*, 1902; harm. by Robert J. Batastini, b.1942, © 1995, GIA Publications, Inc.

I Sing the Mighty Power of God   633

1. I sing the might-y pow'r of God That made the moun-tains rise, That spread the flow-ing seas a-broad, And built the loft-y skies. I sing the wis-dom that or-dained The sun to rule the day; The moon shines full at God's com-mand And all the stars o-bey.

2. I sing the good-ness of the Lord That filled the earth with food; That formed cre-a-tion with a word, And then pro-nounced it good. Lord, how your won-ders are dis-played Wher-e'er I turn my eye; If I sur-vey the ground I tread, Or gaze up-on the sky!

3. There's not a plant or flow'r be-low But makes your glo-ries known; And clouds a-rise, and tem-pests blow, By or-der from your throne; While all that bor-rows life from you Is ev-er in your care, And ev-'ry-where that I may be, O God, be pres-ent there.

Text: Isaac Watts, 1674-1748, alt.
Tune: ELLACOMBE, CMD; *Gesangbuch der Herzogl*, Wirtemberg, 1784

634 God, beyond All Names

Verses

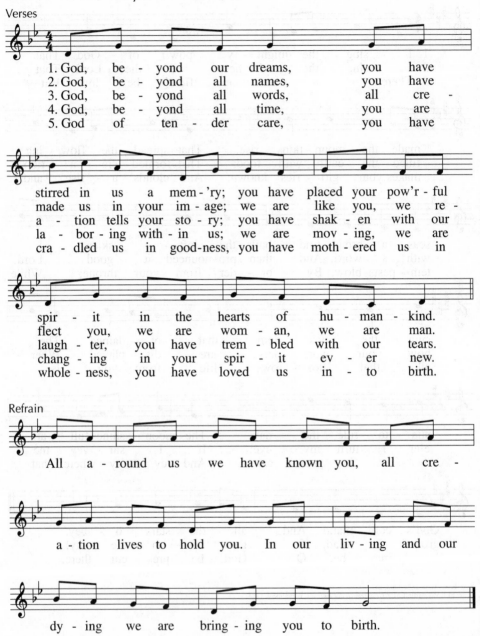

1. God, be - yond our dreams, you have
2. God, be - yond all names, you have
3. God, be - yond all words, all cre -
4. God, be - yond all time, you are
5. God of ten - der care, you have

stirred in us a mem - 'ry; you have placed your pow'r - ful
made us in your im - age; we are like you, we re -
a - tion tells your sto - ry; you have shak - en with our
la - bor - ing with - in us; we are mov - ing, we are
cra - dled us in good-ness, you have moth - ered us in

spir - it in the hearts of hu - man - kind.
flect you, we are wom - an, we are man.
laugh - ter, you have trem - bled with our tears.
chang - ing in your spir - it ev - er new.
whole - ness, you have loved us in - to birth.

Refrain

All a - round us we have known you, all cre -

a - tion lives to hold you. In our liv - ing and our

dy - ing we are bring - ing you to birth.

Text: Bernadette Farrell, b.1957
Tune: Bernadette Farrell, b.1957
© 1990, Bernadette Farrell, published by OCP Publications

All Things Bright and Beautiful 635

Refrain

All things bright and beau - ti - ful, All

crea - tures great and small, All things wise and

won - der - ful, The Lord God made them all.

Verses

1. Each lit - tle flow'r that o - pens, Each
2. The pur - ple - head - ed moun - tain, The
3. The cold wind in the win - ter, The
4. God gave us eyes to see them, And

lit - tle bird that sings, God made their glow - ing
riv - er run - ning by, The sun - set, and the
pleas-ant sum - mer sun, The ripe fruits in the
lips that we might tell How great is God Al -

D.C.

col - ors, God made their ti - ny wings.
morn - ing That bright - ens up the sky.
gar - den, God made them ev - 'ry one.
might - y, Who has made all things well.

Text: Cecil F. Alexander, 1818-1895, alt.
Tune: ROYAL OAK, 7 6 7 6 with refrain; English Melody; adapted by Martin Shaw, 1875-1958

636 Abundant Life

1. We can - not own the sun - lit sky, The
2. When bod - ies shiv - er in the night And
3. God calls hu - man - i - ty to join As

moon, the wild - flow'rs grow - ing, For we are
wea - ry, wait for morn - ing, When chil - dren
part - ners in cre - at - ing A fu - ture

part of all that is With - in life's
have no bread but tears, And war - horns
free from want or fear, Life's good - ness

riv - er flow - ing. With o - pen
sound their warn - ing, God calls hu -
cel - e - brat - ing, That new world

hands re - ceive and share The gifts of
man - i - ty to wake, To join in
beck - ons from a - far, In - vites our

God's cre - a - tion, That all may
com - mon la - bor, That all may
shared en - deav - or, That all may

have a - bun - dant life In
have a - bun - dant life In
have a - bun - dant life And

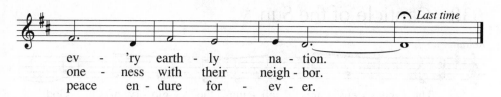

ev - 'ry earth - ly   na - tion.
one - ness with their   neigh - bor.
peace en - dure for - ev - er.

Text: Ruth Duck, b.1947, © 1992, GIA Publications, Inc.
Tune: LA GRANGE, 8 7 8 7 D; Marty Haugen, b.1950, © 1994, GIA Publications, Inc.

Many and Great   637

1. Man - y and great, O God, are your works, Mak - er of
2. Grant us com - mun - ion with you, our God, Though you tran -

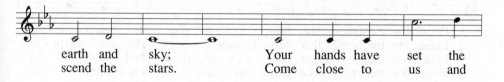

earth and sky;   Your hands have set the
scend the stars.   Come close to us and

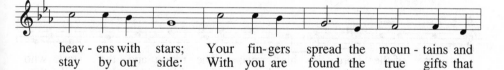

heav - ens with stars; Your fin - gers spread the moun - tains and
stay by our side: With you are found the true gifts that

plains. You mere - ly spoke and wa - ters were
last. Bless us with life which nev - er shall

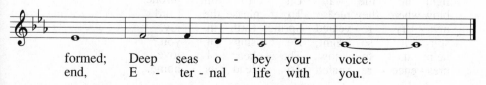

formed; Deep seas o - bey your voice.
end, E - ter - nal life with you.

Text: *Wakantanka tuku nitawa;* Dakota hymn; para. by Philip Frazier, 1892-1964, © 1916, Walton Music Corp.
Tune: LACQUIPARLE, 9 6 9 9 9 6; *Dakota Odowan,* 1879; acc. by John L. Bell, b.1949, © 1993, Iona Community, GIA Publications, Inc., agent

638 Canticle of the Sun

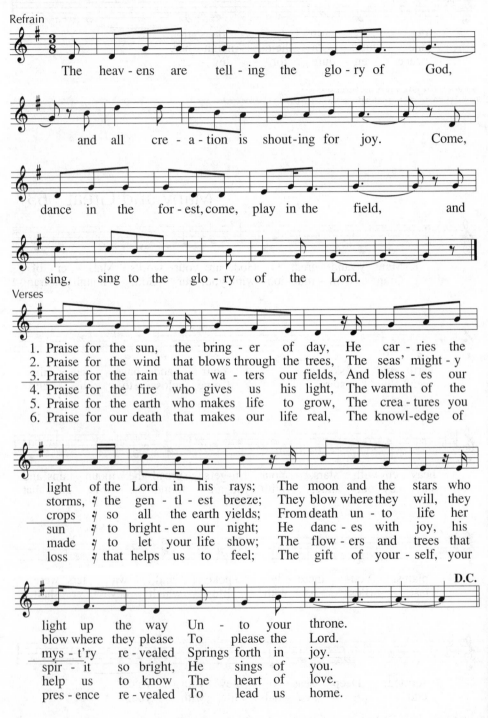

Refrain

The heav-ens are tell-ing the glo-ry of God, and all cre-a-tion is shout-ing for joy. Come, dance in the for-est, come, play in the field, and sing, sing to the glo-ry of the Lord.

Verses

1. Praise for the sun, the bring-er of day, He car-ries the light of the Lord in his rays; The moon and the stars who light up the way Un-to your throne.
2. Praise for the wind that blows through the trees, The seas' might-y storms, ꞔ the gen-tl-est breeze; They blow where they will, they blow where they please To please the Lord.
3. Praise for the rain that wa-ters our fields, And bless-es our crops ꞔ so all the earth yields; From death un-to life her mys-t'ry re-vealed Springs forth in joy.
4. Praise for the fire who gives us his light, The warmth of the sun ꞔ to bright-en our night; He danc-es with joy, his spir-it so bright, He sings of you.
5. Praise for the earth who makes life to grow, The crea-tures you made ꞔ to let your life show; The flow-ers and trees that help us to know The heart of love.
6. Praise for our death that makes our life real, The knowl-edge of loss ꞔ that helps us to feel; The gift of your-self, your pres-ence re-vealed To lead us home.

D.C.

Text: Marty Haugen, b.1950
Tune: Marty Haugen, b.1950
© 1980, GIA Publications, Inc.

The Stars Declare His Glory 639

1. The stars de - clare his glo - ry; The
2. The dawn re - turns in splen - dor, The
3. So shine the Lord's com - mand - ments To
4. So or - der too this life of mine, Di -

vault of heav - en springs Mute wit - ness of the
heav - ens burn and blaze, The ris - ing sun re -
make the sim - ple wise, More sweet than hon - ey
rect it all my days, The med - i - ta - tions

Mas - ter's hand In all cre - a - ted things, And
news the race That meas - ures all our days, And
to the taste, More rich than an - y prize, A
of my heart Be in - no - cence and praise, My

through the si - lenc - es of space Their
writes in fire a - cross the skies God's
law of love with - in our hearts, A
Rock, and my re - deem - ing Lord, In

sound - less mu - sic sings.
maj - es - ty and praise.
light be - fore our eyes.
all my words and ways.

Text: Psalm 19; Timothy Dudley-Smith, b.1926, © 1973, Hope Publishing Co.
Tune: ALDINE, 7 6 8 6 8 6; Richard Proulx, b.1937, © 1986, GIA Publications, Inc.

640 Sing Out, Earth and Skies

Verses

Cantor:

All:

1. Come, O God of all the earth: Come to us, O
2. Come, O God of wind and flame: Fill the earth with
3. Come, O God of flash-ing light: Twin-kling star and
4. Come, O God of snow and rain: Show-er down up-
5. Come, O Jus-tice, Come, O Peace: Come and shape our

Cantor:

Right-eous One; Come, and bring our love to birth:
right-eous-ness; Teach us all to sing your name:
burn-ing sun; God of day and God of night:
on the earth; Come, O God of joy and pain:
hearts a-new; Come and make op-pres-sion cease:

All:

In the glo-ry of your Son.
May our lives your love con-fess.
In your light we all are one.
God of sor-row, God of mirth.
Bring us all to life in you.

Refrain

Sing out, earth and skies! Sing of the God who

loves you! Raise your joy-ful cries!

Dance to the life a-round you!

Text: Marty Haugen, b.1950
Tune: SING OUT, 7 7 7 7 with refrain; Marty Haugen, b.1950
© 1985, GIA Publications, Inc.

I Have Loved You 641

Refrain

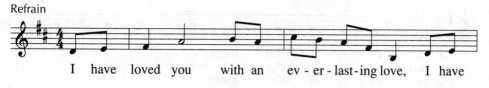

I have loved you with an ev-er-last-ing love, I have

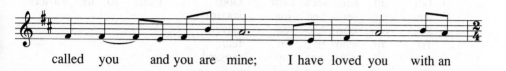

called you and you are mine; I have loved you with an

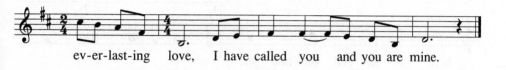

ev-er-last-ing love, I have called you and you are mine.

Verses

1. Seek the face of the Lord and long for
2. Seek the face of the Lord and long for
3. Seek the face of the Lord and long for

D.C.

him: He will bring you his light and his peace.
him: He will bring you his joy and his hope.
him: He will bring you his care and his love.

Text: Jeremiah 31:3, Psalm 24:3; Michael Joncas, b.1951
Tune: Michael Joncas, b.1951
© 1979, OCP Publications

642 Come to the Feast

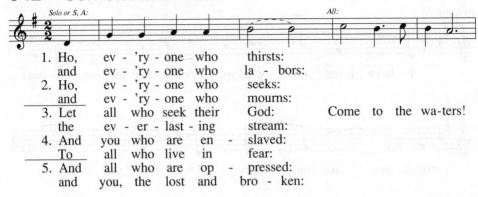

1. Ho,   ev - 'ry - one who   thirsts:
   and   ev - 'ry - one who   la - bors:
2. Ho,   ev - 'ry - one who   seeks:
   and   ev - 'ry - one who   mourns:
3. Let   all   who seek their   God: Come   to   the   wa-ters!
   the   ev - er - last - ing   stream:
4. And   you who   are   en - slaved:
   To   all   who   live   in   fear:
5. And   all   who   are   op - pressed:
   and   you,   the   lost   and   bro - ken:

here   is   an   end   to   hun - ger:
all   you who have   no   mon - ey:
hear   me and share the   rich - es:
now   is   an   end   to   sad - ness:
heed   now the   One who calls you: Come   to the feast!   Come   to the
drink   deep the   Cup that saves you:
this   is   the   feast   of   free - dom:
join   in   the   feast with cour - age:
this   is   the   feast   of   jus - tice:
this   is   the   feast   of   heal - ing:

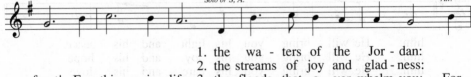

1. the   wa - ters   of   the   Jor - dan:
feast! For this   is   life: 2. the streams   of joy and   glad - ness:
3. the floods   that o - ver-whelm you: For
4. the   wa - ters that have freed   you:
5. to   die   and rise in   Je - sus:

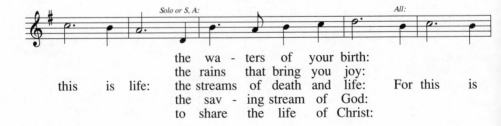

the   wa - ters   of   your birth:
the rains   that bring   you   joy:
this   is   life: the streams   of death and   life: For this   is
the sav - ing stream   of   God:
to   share   the   life   of Christ:

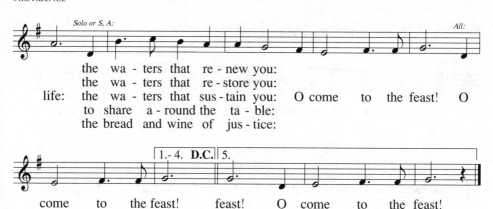

the wa - ters that re - new you:
the wa - ters that re - store you:
life: the wa - ters that sus - tain you: O come to the feast! O
to share a - round the ta - ble:
the bread and wine of jus - tice:

1.- 4. D.C. **5.**

come to the feast! feast! O come to the feast!

Text: Isaiah 55; Marty Haugen, b.1950
Tune: Marty Haugen, b.1950
© 1991, GIA Publications, Inc.

You Are All We Have 643

Refrain

You are all we have. You give us what we need. Our

lives are in your hands, O Lord, our lives are in your hands.

Verses

1. Protect me, Lord; I come to you for safety.
I say, "You are my God."
All good things, Lord, all good things
that I have come from you,
the God of my salvation.

2. How wonderful are your gifts to me,
how good they are!
I praise the Lord who guides me
and teaches me the way of truth and life.

3. You are near, the God I seek.
Nothing can take me from your side.
All my days I rest secure;
you will show me the path
that leads to life.

Text: Francis Patrick O'Brien, b.1958
Tune: Francis Patrick O'Brien, b.1958
© 1992, GIA Publications, Inc.

644 All You Who Are Thirsty

Refrain

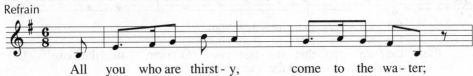

All   you   who are thirst - y,   come to the wa - ter;

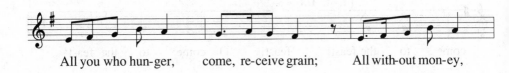

All you who hun-ger,   come, re-ceive grain;   All with-out mon-ey,

come with-out pay-ing;   All you who heed me,   come for rich fare.

Verses

Cantor or choir:

1. Come now and lis - ten that   you may have life;   my
2. Why spend your mon - ey for   what is not bread,   your
3. Drink of this wa - ter   a - bun-dant with life   and

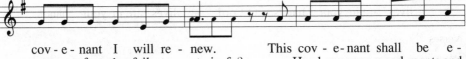

cov - e - nant I will re - new.   This cov - e-nant shall be e-
wag-es for what fails to sat-is-fy?   Heed my com-mand-ments and
eat of the bread I pro - vide.   I am the bread, and the

D.C.

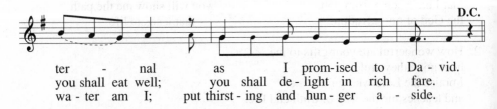

ter - nal   as   I prom-ised to Da - vid.
you shall eat well;   you shall de - light in rich   fare.
wa - ter am I;   put thirst - ing and hun - ger a - side.

Text: Isaiah 55; adapt. by Michael Connolly, b.1955
Tune: Michael Connolly, b.1955
© 1982, 1988, GIA Publications, Inc.

Who Can Measure Heaven and Earth 645

1. Who can meas - ure heav'n and earth? God was pre - sent
2. Who can tell what wis - dom brings, First of all cre -
3. Wis - dom in his plans he laid, Plant - ed her in
4. Wis - dom gives the sur - est wealth, Brings her chil - dren

at their birth; Who can num - ber seeds or sands?
at - ed things? One a - lone is tru - ly wise,
all he made; Grant - ed her to hu - man - kind,
life and health; Teach - es us to fear the Lord,

Ev - 'ry grain is in his hands: Through cre - a - tion's
Hid - den from our earth - bound eyes: Knowl - edge lies in
Sowed her truth in ev - 'ry mind: But with rich - est
Marks a u - ni - verse re - stored: Heav'n and earth she

count - less days Ev - 'ry dawn sings out his praise.
him a - lone— God, the Lord up - on his throne!
wis - dom blessed Those who love him first and best.
will out - last— Hap - py those who hold her fast!

Text: Ecclesiastes 1; Christopher Idle, b.1938, © 1982, Jubilate Hymns, Ltd. (Administered by Hope Publishing Co.)
Tune: DIX, 77 77 77; arr. from Conrad Kocher, 1786-1872, by William H. Monk, 1823-1889

646 God Is Working His Purpose Out

1. God is work - ing his pur - pose out As
2. From ut - most east to ut - most west, Wher -
3. March we forth in the strength of God, With the
4. All we can do is worth - less toil Un -

year suc - ceeds to year: God is work - ing his
ev - er foot has trod, By the mouth of man - y
ban-ner of Christ un - furled, That the light of the glo - rious
less God bless-es the deed: Vain - ly we hope for the

pur - pose out, And the time is draw - ing near;
mes - sen - gers Goes forth the voice of God;
gos - pel of truth May shine through-out the world;
har - vest - tide Till God gives life to the seed; Yet

Near - er and near - er draws the time, The time that shall sure - ly
Give ear to me, you con - ti - nents, You isles, give ear to
Fight we the fight with sor-row and sin To set their cap-tives
near - er and near - er draws the time, The time that shall sure - ly

be, When the earth shall be filled with the glo - ry of God As the
me, That the earth may be filled with the glo - ry of God As the
free, That the earth may be filled with the glo - ry of God As the
be, When the earth shall be filled with the glo - ry of God As the

1.- 3. | 4.

wa - ters cov-er the sea.
wa - ters cov-er the sea.
wa - ters cov-er the sea.
wa - ters cov-er the sea.

Text: Habakkuk 1:14; Arthur C. Ainger, 1841-1919, alt.
Tune: PURPOSE, Irregular; Martin Shaw, 1875-1958, © Oxford University Press

Light of Christ / Exsultet   647

Refrain

All:

The light of Christ sur - rounds us, the love of Christ en - folds us, the pow'r of Christ pro - tects us, the pres-ence of Christ watch-es o - ver us.

To verses

Last time

us, for ev-er, and ev-er, for ev-er, and ev-er. A - men.

Verses 1, 2, 3

Cantor or schola:

1. All the earth is a - blaze with the glo - ry of
2. Let us fill ev - 'ry space with the sound of our
3. As this can - dle shines out through the dark - ness of

D.C.

God, for the Light has come to burn a - way the dark - ness.
joy, prais-ing Christ, who is liv - ing now a - mong us.
night, may the love of Christ burn ev - er in our hearts.

Verse 4

4. In the east, the Morn-ing Star ris-es bright up - on you,

D.C.

in its peace - ful light shines the glo - ry of the Lord.

Text: Based on a prayer by James Dillet Freeman and the *Exsultet;* Marty Haugen, b.1950
Tune: Marty Haugen, b.1950

648 We Are Marching

We are march - ing* in the light of God, we are march - ing in the light of God. We are march - ing in the light of God, we are march - ing in the light of the light of God, we are march - ing in the light of God,

Alternate text: dancing, singing, praying

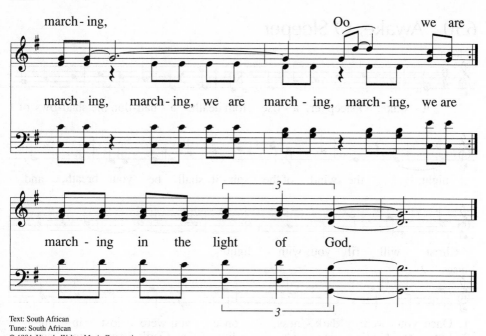

march - ing,   Oo   we are

march - ing,   march - ing,   we are   march - ing,   march - ing,   we are

march - ing   in   the   light   of   God.

The Lord Is My Light   649

Theme I

The   Lord   is my light,   my   light   and sal - va - tion: in

God   I   trust,   in   God   I   trust.

Last time

Theme II

The   Lord   is my light,   my   light   and sal - va - tion: in

God   I   trust,   in   God   I   trust.

Last time

The themes may be sung separately or together, in unison or in canon.

650 Awake, O Sleeper

Refrain

A - wake, O sleep-er, a - rise from death, a - ban-don the shad-ows of night; the wind of the spir - it shall be your breath, and Christ will fill you with light.

Verses 1, 2

1. Once you were dark - ness, once you were lost in the shad - ows. Once you were dark-ness, now you are chil - dren of light.
2. Live as God's peo - ple, live as God's jus - tice and mer - cy, filled with com - pas - sion, filled with the pow - er of love.

D.C.

Verse 3

3. Shine out with the splen-dor of love, shine with jus-tice and right-eous - ness. Sing the mu-sic your spir-it has heard, the songs of glo - ry and light.

D.C.

Text: Ephesians 5; Marty Haugen, b.1950
Tune: Marty Haugen, b.1950
© 1987, GIA Publications, Inc.

I Want to Walk as a Child of the Light 651

1. I want to walk as a child of the light.
2. I want to see the bright-ness of God.
3. I'm look - ing for the com - ing of Christ.

I want to fol - low Je - sus.
I want to look at Je - sus.
I want to be with Je - sus.

God set the stars to give light to the world. The
Clear sun of right-eous-ness shine on my path, And
When we have run with pa - tience the race, We

star of my life is Je - sus.
show me the way to the Fa - ther.
shall know the joy of Je - sus.

In him there is no dark - ness at all. The

night and the day are both a - like. The

Lamb is the light of the cit - y of God.

Shine in my heart, Lord Je - sus.

Text: Ephesians 5:8-10, Revelation 21:23, John 12:46, 1 John 1:5, Hebrews 12:1; Kathleen Thomerson, b.1934, © 1970, 1975, Celebration
Tune: HOUSTON, 10 7 10 8 9 9 10 7; Kathleen Thomerson, b.1934, © 1970, 1975, Celebration; acc. by Robert J. Batastini, b.1942, © 1987, GIA
Publications, Inc.

652 Praise to You, O Christ, Our Savior

Refrain

Praise to you, O Christ, our Sav-ior, Word of the Fa-ther,

call-ing us to life; Son of God who

leads us to free-dom: glo-ry to you, Lord Je-sus Christ!

Verses

1. You are the Word who calls us out of dark-ness;
2. You are the one whom proph-ets hoped and longed for;
3. You are the Word who calls us to be ser-vants;
4. You are the Word who binds us and u-nites us;

You are the Word who leads us in-to light; You are the Word who
You are the one who speaks to us to-day; You are the one who
You are the Word whose on-ly law is love; You are the Word made
You are the Word who calls us to be one; You are the Word who

D.C.

brings us through the des-ert: Glo-ry to you, Lord Je-sus Christ!
leads us to our fu-ture: Glo-ry to you, Lord Je-sus Christ!
flesh who lives a-mong us: Glo-ry to you, Lord Je-sus Christ!
teach-es us for-give-ness: Glo-ry to you, Lord Je-sus Christ!

Text: Bernadette Farrell, b.1957
Tune: Bernadette Farrell, b.1957
© 1986, Bernadette Farrell, published by OCP Publications

Word of God, Come Down on Earth 653

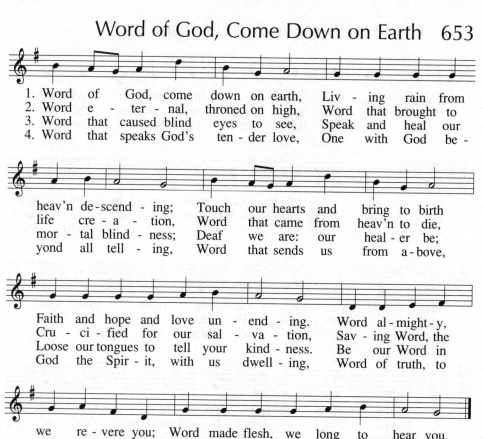

1. Word of God, come down on earth, Liv-ing rain from
2. Word e-ter-nal, throned on high, Word that brought to
3. Word that caused blind eyes to see, Speak and heal our
4. Word that speaks God's ten-der love, One with God be -

heav'n de-scend-ing; Touch our hearts and bring to birth
life cre-a-tion, Word that came from heav'n to die,
mor-tal blind-ness; Deaf we are: our heal-er be;
yond all tell-ing, Word that sends us from a-bove,

Faith and hope and love un-end-ing. Word al-might-y,
Cru-ci-fied for our sal-va-tion, Sav-ing Word, the
Loose our tongues to tell your kind-ness. Be our Word in
God the Spir-it, with us dwell-ing, Word of truth, to

we re-vere you; Word made flesh, we long to hear you.
world re-stor-ing, Speak to us, your love out-pour-ing.
pit-y spo-ken, Heal the world, by our sin bro-ken.
all truth lead us, Word of life, with one Bread feed us.

Text: James Quinn, SJ, b.1919, © 1969. Used by permission of Selah Publishing Co., Inc., Kingston, N.Y.
Tune: LIEBSTER JESU, 7 8 7 8 88; Johann R. Ahle, 1625-1673; harm. by George H. Palmer, 1846-1926

654　God Has Spoken by His Prophets

1. God has spo - ken by his proph - ets, Spo - ken
2. God has spo - ken by Christ Je - sus, Christ, the
3. God is speak - ing by his Spir - it, Speak-ing

his un - chang - ing Word; Each from age to age pro -
ev - er - last - ing Son, Bright-ness of the Fa - ther's
to the hearts of all, In the age - less Word ex -

claim - ing God, the one the right - eous, Lord.
glo - ry, With the Fa - ther ev - er one;
pound - ing God's own mes - sage for us all.

In the world's de - spair and tur - moil, One firm
Spo - ken by the Word In - car - nate, God of
Through the rise and fall of na - tions One sure

an - chor holds us fast; God is king, his throne e -
God, be - fore time was; Light of Light, to earth de -
faith yet stand - ing fast; God a - bides, his Word un -

ter - nal; God the first, and God the last.
scend - ing, He re - veals our God to us.
chang - ing; God the first, and God the last.

Text: George W. Briggs, 1875-1959, alt., © 1953, 1981, The Hymn Society (Administered by Hope Publishing Co.)
Tune: RUSTINGTON, 8 7 8 7 D; Charles H. H. Parry, 1848-1918

Your Word Went Forth   655

1. Your Word went forth and light a - woke. The dark-ness
2. Your Word went forth and shot a flame Of light from
3. Your Word goes forth and light e - rupts From kin - dled
4. Send forth your Word; your si - lence break. Shine in this

fled; Bright day was born And swift - ly sped A - cross pri -
light. Our flesh it wore And walked a - mong Us in this
speech And an - cient page, Your Spir - it's fire Ig - nit - ing
time In which our night Is ter - ror - torn By dreams of

me - val earth. It was cre - a - tion's morn.
dark - ened world Cre - a - tion to re - store.
hu - man words To light - en ev - 'ry age.
fier - y death. Come, be our life, our light.

Text: Psalm 119:130; Herman G. Stuempfle, Jr., 1923–2007
Tune: AWAKENING WORD, 8 4 4 4 6 6; Randall Sensmeier, b.1948
© 1993, GIA Publications, Inc.

656 Magnificat

1. My soul gives glo - ry to the Lord, In
God my Sav - ior I re - joice. My low - li -
ness he did re - gard, Ex - alt - ing me by
his own choice. From this day all shall call me
blest, For he has done great things for me, Of
all great names his is the best, For
it is ho - ly; strong is he.

2. His mer - cy goes to all who fear, From
age to age and to all parts. His arm of
strength to all is near; He scat - ters those who
have proud hearts. He casts the might - y from their
throne And rais - es those of low de - gree; He
feeds the hun - gry as his own, The
rich de - part in pov - er - ty.

3. He raised his ser - vant Is - ra - el, Re -
mem - b'ring his e - ter - nal grace, As from of
old he did fore - tell To A - bra - ham and
all his race. O Fa - ther, Son and Spir - it
blest, In three - fold Name are you a - dored, To
you be ev - 'ry prayer ad - dressed, From
age to age the on - ly Lord.

Text: Luke 1:46-55; J.T. Mueller, 1885-1967, alt., from *Praise God in Song*
Tune: MAGNIFICAT, LMD; Michael Joncas, b.1951
© 1979, 1988, GIA Publications, Inc.

Holy God, We Praise Thy Name   657

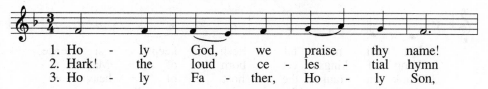

1. Ho - ly God, we praise thy name!
2. Hark! the loud ce - les - tial hymn
3. Ho - ly Fa - ther, Ho - ly Son,

Lord of all, we bow be - fore thee;
An - gel choirs a - bove are rais - ing;
Ho - ly Spir - it, Three we name thee,

All on earth thy scep - ter claim,
Cher - u - bim and Ser - a - phim
While in es - sence on - ly One,

All in heav'n a - bove a - dore thee;
In un - ceas - ing cho - rus prais - ing,
Un - di - vid - ed God we claim thee,

In - fi - nite thy vast do - main,
Fill the heav'ns with sweet ac - cord:
And a - dor - ing bend the knee,

Repeat ad lib.

Ev - er - last - ing is thy reign.
Ho - ly, ho - ly, ho - ly Lord!
While we own the mys - ter - y.

Text: *Grosser Gott, wir loben dich;* ascr. to Ignaz Franz, 1719-1790; tr. by Clarence Walworth, 1820-1900
Tune: GROSSER GOTT, 7 8 7 8 77; *Katholisches Gesangbuch*, Vienna, c.1774

658 Let All Mortal Flesh Keep Silence

1. Let all mor - tal flesh keep si - lence,
2. King of kings, yet born of Mar - y,
3. Rank on rank the host of heav - en
4. At his feet the six - winged ser - aph,

And with fear and trem - bling stand;
As of old on earth he stood,
Spreads its van - guard on the way,
Cher - u - bim with sleep - less eye,

Pon - der noth - ing earth - ly mind - ed,
Lord of lords in hu - man ves - ture,
As the Light of Light de - scend - ing
Veil their fac - es to the Pres - ence,

For with bless - ing in his hand
In the Bod - y and the Blood
From the realms of end - less day,
As with cease - less voice they cry,

Christ our God to earth de - scend -
He will give to all the faith -
That the pow'rs of hell may van -
"Al - le - lu - ia, al - le - lu -

ing, Our full hom - age to de - mand.
ful His own self for heav'n - ly food.
ish As the dark - ness clears a - way.
ia, Al - le - lu - ia, Lord, most high!"

Text: Liturgy of St. James, 5th C.; para. by Gerard Moultrie, 1829-1885
Tune: PICARDY, 8 7 8 7 8 7; French Carol; harm. by Richard Proulx, b.1937, © 1986, GIA Publications, Inc.

You Are the Voice 659

Refrain

You are the voice of the liv - ing God,

call - ing us now to live in your love, to be

chil - dren of God once a - gain!

Verses

Cantor:

1. Praise for the light that shines through the night, from
2. Praise for the wa - ter that springs from the sea, the
3. Praise for the sing - ing and praise for the dance, with

dark - ness to light, from death to new life, and
seed that gives life to all who be - lieve, God's
new heart and voice, all raise the song of

praise to the morn - ing that brings forth the sun, to
love o - ver - flow - ing, our hearts know the joy to be
praise to cre - a - tion; all heav - en and earth, come

All:

o - pen our eyes to the Lord! To
daugh - ters and sons of the Lord! To be
sing of the glo - ry of God! Come

D.C.

o - pen our eyes to the Lord! For
daugh - ters and sons of the Lord! For
sing of the glo - ry of God! For

Text: David Haas, b.1957
Tune: David Haas, b.1957; acc. by Jeanne Cotter, b.1964
© 1983, 1987, GIA Publications, Inc.

660 Laudate Dominum

Ostinato Refrain

Lau - da - te Do - mi - num, lau - da - te Do - mi - num om - nes

1.
gen - tes, al - le - lu - ia.

2.
al - le - lu - ia.

Text: Psalm 117, *Praise the Lord, all you peoples;* Taizé Community, 1980
Tune: Jacques Berthier, 1923-1994
© 1980, Les Presses de Taizé, GIA Publications, Inc., agent

661 Heavenly Hosts in Ceaseless Worship

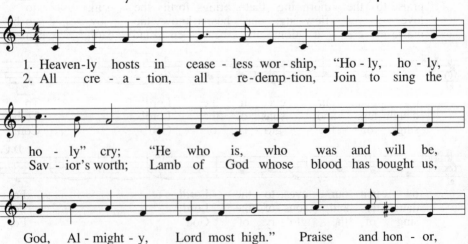

1. Heaven-ly hosts in cease - less wor - ship, "Ho - ly, ho - ly,
2. All cre - a - tion, all re - demp-tion, Join to sing the

ho - ly" cry; "He who is, who was and will be,
Sav - ior's worth; Lamb of God whose blood has bought us,

God, Al - might - y, Lord most high." Praise and hon - or,
Kings and priests, to reign on earth. Wealth and wis - dom,

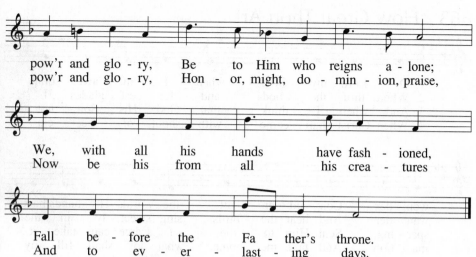

pow'r and glo - ry, Be to Him who reigns a - lone;
pow'r and glo - ry, Hon - or, might, do - min - ion, praise,

We, with all his hands have fash - ioned,
Now be his from all his crea - tures

Fall be - fore the Fa - ther's throne.
And to ev - er - last - ing days.

Text: Revelation 4-5; Timothy Dudley-Smith, b.1926, © 1975, Hope Publishing Co.
Tune: HEAVENLY HOSTS, 8 7 8 7 D; Noel H. Tredinnick, b.1949, © 1973, Hope Publishing Co.

Alabaré   662

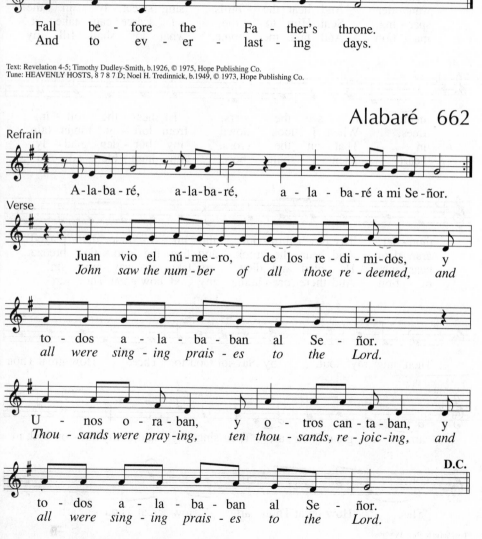

Refrain

A - la - ba - ré, a - la - ba - ré, a - la - ba - ré a mi Se - ñor.

Verse

Juan vio el nú - me - ro, de los re - di - mi - dos, y
John saw the num - ber of all those re - deemed, and

to - dos a - la - ba - ban al Se - ñor.
all were sing - ing prais - es to the Lord.

U - nos o - ra - ban, y o - tros can - ta - ban, y
Thou - sands were pray - ing, ten thou - sands, re - joic - ing, and

D.C.

to - dos a - la - ba - ban al Se - ñor.
all were sing - ing prais - es to the Lord.

Text: *I will praise the Lord;* Manuel José Alonso, José Pagán; trans. unknown
Tune: Manuel José Alonso, José Pagán, © 1979 and Ediciones Musical PAX; acc. by Diana Kodner
© 1979, Manuel José Alonso, José Pagán and Ediciones Musical PAX. Published by OCP Publications.

663 How Great Thou Art

1. O Lord my God, when I in awe-some
2. When thru the woods and for-est glades I
3. And when I think that God, His Son not
4. When Christ shall come with shout of ac-cla-

won-der Con-sid-er all the worlds Thy hands have
wan-der And hear the birds sing sweet-ly in the
spar-ing, Sent Him to die, I scarce can take it
ma-tion And take me home, what joy shall fill my

made, I see the stars, I hear the roll-ing
trees, When I look down from loft-y moun-tain
in That on the cross, my bur-den glad-ly
heart! Then I shall bow in hum-ble ad-o-

thun-der, Thy pow'r thru-out the un-i-verse dis-played!
gran-deur And hear the brook and feel the gen-tle breeze.
bear-ing, He bled and died to take a-way my sin!
ra-tion And there pro-claim, my God, how great Thou art!

Then sings my soul, my Sav-ior God, to Thee; How great Thou

art, how great Thou art! Then sings my soul, my Sav-ior God, to

Thee; How great Thou art, How great Thou art!

Text: Stuart K. Hine, 1899-1989
Tune: Stuart K. Hine, 1899-1989
© 1953, Stuart K. Hine. Assigned to Manna Music, Inc.

Cantemos al Señor / Let's Sing unto the Lord 664

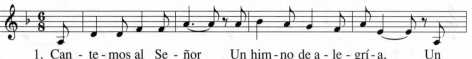

1. Can - te - mos al Se - ñor Un him - no de_a - le - grí - a, Un
2. Can - te - mos al Se - ñor Un him - no de_a - la - ban - za Que_ex-
1. *Let's sing un - to the Lord A hymn of glad re - joic - ing, Let's*
2. *Let's sing un - to the Lord A hymn of a - do - ra - tion, Ex -*

cán - ti - co de_a - mor Al na - cer el nue - vo dí - a. El
pre - se nues - tro_a - mor, Nues - tra fe_y nues - tra_es - pe - ran - za, En
sing a hymn of love, Join - ing hearts and hap - py voic - es. God
press un - to the Lord Our songs of faith and hope. Cre -

hi - zo_el cie - lo_el mar, El sol y las es - tre - llas Y
to - da la crea - ción Pre - go - na su gran - de - za, A -
made the sky a - bove, The stars, the sun, the o - ceans. Their
a - tion's broad dis - play Pro - claims the work of gran - deur, The

vio_en e - llos bon - dad, Pues sus o - bras e - ran be - llas.
sí nues - tro can - tar Va_a - nun - cian - do su be - lle - za.
good - ness does pro - claim The glo - ry of God's name.
bound - less love of One Who bless - es us with beau - ty.

¡A - le - lu - ya! ¡A - le - lu - ya! Can - te - mos al Se -
Al - le - lu - ia! Al - le - lu - ia! Let's sing un - to the

1.
ñor. ¡A - le - lu - ya!
Lord. Al - le - lu - ia!

2.
lu - ya!
lu - ia!

Text: Based on Psalm 19; Carlos Rosas, b.1939; trans. by Roberto Escamilla, Elise Eslinger, and George Lockwood, 1983,
© 1976, Resource Publications, Inc.
Tune: ROSAS, 6 7 6 8 D with refrain; Carlos Rosas, b.1939, © 1976, Resource Publications, Inc.; acc. by Diana Kodner, b.1957,
© 1993, GIA Publications, Inc.

665 When, in Our Music, God Is Glorified

1. When, in our mu - sic, God is glo - ri - fied,
2. How of - ten, mak - ing mu - sic, we have found
3. So has the Church, in lit - ur - gy and song,
4. And did not Je - sus sing a psalm that night
5. Let ev - 'ry in - stru-ment be tuned for praise!

And ad - o - ra - tion leaves no room for pride,
A new di - men - sion in the world of sound,
In faith and love, through cen - tu - ries of wrong,
When ut - most e - vil strove a - gainst the Light?
Let all re - joice who have a voice to raise!

It is as though the whole cre - a - tion cried:
As wor - ship moved us to a more pro - found
Borne wit - ness to the truth in ev - 'ry tongue:
Then let us sing, for whom he won the fight:
And may God give us faith to sing al - ways:

Al - le - lu - ia!

Text: Mark 14:26; Fred Pratt Green, b.1903, © 1972, Hope Publishing Co.
Tune: ENGELBERG, 10 10 10 with alleluia; Charles V. Stanford, 1852-1924

666 To God with Gladness Sing

1. To God with glad - ness sing, Your Rock and Sav - ior bless;
2. God cra - dles in his hand The heights and depths of earth;
3. Your heav'n - ly Fa - ther praise, Ac - claim his on - ly Son,

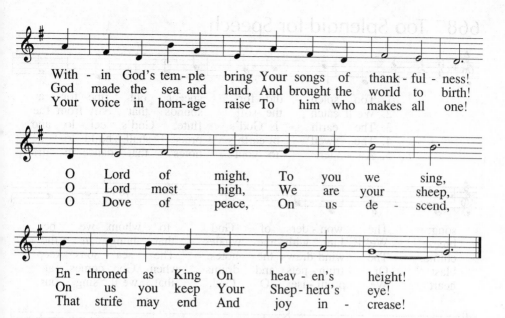

With - in God's tem - ple bring Your songs of thank - ful - ness!
God made the sea and land, And brought the world to birth!
Your voice in hom - age raise To him who makes all one!

O Lord of might, To you we sing,
O Lord most high, We are your sheep,
O Dove of peace, On us de - scend,

En - throned as King On heav - en's height!
On us you keep Your Shep - herd's eye!
That strife may end And joy in - crease!

Text: Psalm 95; James Quinn, SJ, b.1919, © 1969. Used by permission of Selah Publishing., Inc., Kingston, N.Y.
Tune: CYMBALA, 6 6 6 6 4 44 4; Michael Joncas, b.1951, © 1979, GIA Publications, Inc.

Jubilate Servite 667

Canon — 2 voices

Ju - bi - la - te De - o om - nis ter - ra.

Ser - vi - te Do - mi - no in lae - ti - ti - a.

Al - le - lu - ia, al - le - lu - ia, in lae - ti - ti - a.

Al - le - lu - ia, al - le - lu - ia, in lae - ti - ti - a!

Text: Psalm 100, *Rejoice in God, all the earth, Serve the Lord with gladness;* Taizé Community, 1978
Tune: Jacques Berthier, 1923-1994
© 1979, Les Presses de Taizé, GIA Publications, Inc., agent

668 Too Splendid for Speech

Text: Psalm 98; Thomas Troeger, b.1945, © 1985, Oxford University Press
Tune: COMMON PRAYER, 10 10 11 11; Todd Alan Constable, b.1964, © 1994, GIA Publications, Inc.

Joyful, Joyful, We Adore You 669

1. Joy - ful, joy - ful, we a - dore you, God of glo - ry,
2. All your works with joy sur - round you, Earth and heav'n re -
3. Al - ways giv - ing and for - giv - ing, Ev - er bless - ing,
4. Mor - tals join the might - y cho - rus, Which the morn - ing

Lord of love; Hearts un - fold like flowers be - fore you,
flect your rays, Stars and an - gels sing a - round you,
ev - er blest, Well - spring of the joy of liv - ing,
stars be - gan; God's own love is reign - ing o'er us,

Open - ing to the sun a - bove. Melt the clouds of
Cen - ter of un - bro - ken praise; Field and for - est,
O - cean depth of hap - py rest! Lov - ing Fa - ther,
Join - ing peo - ple hand in hand. Ev - er sing - ing,

sin and sad - ness; Drive the dark of doubt a - way;
vale and moun - tain, Flow - ery mead - ow, flash - ing sea,
Christ our broth - er, Let your light up - on us shine;
march we on - ward, Vic - tors in the midst of strife;

Giv - er of im - mor - tal glad - ness, Fill us with the light of day!
Chant - ing bird and flow - ing foun - tain, Prais - ing you e - ter - nal - ly!
Teach us how to love each oth - er, Lift us to the joy di - vine.
Joy - ful mu - sic leads us sun - ward In the tri - umph song of life.

Text: Henry van Dyke, 1852-1933, alt.
Tune: HYMN TO JOY, 8 7 8 7 D; arr. from Ludwig van Beethoven, 1770-1827, by Edward Hodges, 1796-1867

670 All Creatures of Our God and King

1. All crea - tures of our God and King, Lift
2. O rush - ing wind and breez - es soft, O
3. O flow - ing wa - ters, pure and clear, Make
4. Dear moth - er earth, who day by day Un -
5. O ev - 'ry one of ten - der heart, For -

up your voice and with us sing: Al - le - lu - ia! Al - le -
clouds that ride the winds a - loft: Al - le - lu - ia! Al - le -
mu - sic for your Lord to hear. Al - le - lu - ia! Al - le -
folds rich bless - ings on our way, Al - le - lu - ia! Al - le -
giv - ing oth - ers, take your part, Al - le - lu - ia! Al - le -

lu - ia! O burn - ing sun with gold - en beam And
lu - ia! O ris - ing morn, in praise re - joice, O
lu - ia! O fire so mas - ter - ful and bright, Pro -
lu - ia! The fruits and flow'rs that ver - dant grow, Let
lu - ia! All you who pain and sor - row bear, Praise

sil - ver moon with soft - er gleam:
lights of eve - ning, find a voice.
vid - ing us with warmth and light, Al - le -
them God's glo - ry al - so show.
God and cast on God your care.

lu - ia! Al - le - lu - ia! Al - le - lu - ia, al - le -

lu - ia, al - le - lu - ia!

6. And you, most kind and gentle death,
Waiting to hush our final breath,
 Alleluia! Alleluia!
You lead to heav'n the child of God,
Where Christ our Lord the way has trod.
 Alleluia! Alleluia!
 Alleluia, alleluia, alleluia!

7. Let all things their Creator bless,
And worship God in humbleness,
 Alleluia! Alleluia!
Oh praise the Father, praise the Son,
And praise the Spirit, Three in One!
 Alleluia! Alleluia!
 Alleluia, alleluia, alleluia!

Text: *Laudato si, mi Signor;* Francis of Assisi, 1182-1226; tr. by William H. Draper, 1855-1933, alt.
Tune: LASST UNS ERFREUEN, LM with alleluias; *Geistliche Kirchengesänge,* 1623; harm. by Ralph Vaughan Williams, 1872-1958

Cantai ao Senhor 671

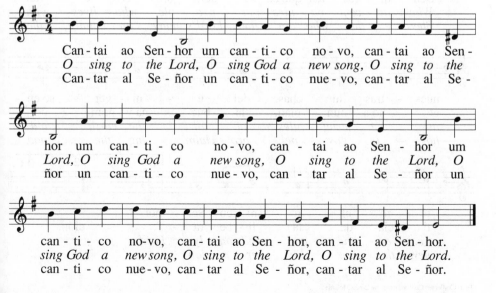

Can - tai ao Sen - hor um can - ti - co no - vo, can - tai ao Sen -
O sing to the Lord, O sing God a new song, O sing to the
Can - tar al Se - ñor un can - ti - co nue - vo, can - tar al Se -

hor um can - ti - co no - vo, can - tai ao Sen - hor um
Lord, O sing God a new song, O sing to the Lord, O
ñor un can - ti - co nue - vo, can - tar al Se - ñor un

can - ti - co no - vo, can - tai ao Sen - hor, can - tai ao Sen - hor.
sing God a new song, O sing to the Lord, O sing to the Lord.
can - ti - co nue - vo, can - tar al Se - ñor, can - tar al Se - ñor.

Text: Psalm 98; Anonymous
Tune: Traditional Brazilian, © Editora Sinodal, Sao Leopoldo; arr. by John L. Bell, b.1949, © 1991, Iona Community, GIA Publications, Inc., agent

672 Santo, Santo, Santo / Holy, Holy, Holy

1. San-to, san - to, san - to, san - to, san - to,
2. san - to, san - to, san - to, san - to,
1. *Ho - ly, ho - ly, ho - ly, ho - ly, ho - ly,*
2. *ho - ly, ho - ly, ho - ly, ho - ly,*

san - to_es nues - tro Dios, Se - ñor de to - da la
san - to_es nues - tro Dios, Se - ñor de to - da la_his -
ho - ly is our God, God, the Lord of earth and
ho - ly is our God, God, the Lord of all of

tie - rra. San-to, san - to_es nues - tro Dios. San-to,
to - ria. San-to, san - to_es nues - tro Dios.
heav - en. Ho - ly, ho - ly is our God. Ho - ly,
his - t'ry. Ho - ly, ho - ly is our God.

Que_a-com - pa - ña_a nues - tro pue - blo, que vi - ve_en
Ben - di - tos los que_en su nom - bre el e - van -
Who ac - com - pa - nies our peo - ple, who lives with -
Bless - ed those who in the Lord's name an - nounce the

nues - tras lu - chas, del u - ni - ver - so_en -
ge - lio_a - nun - cian, la bue - na_y gran no -
in our strug - gles, of all the earth and
ho - ly gos - pel, pro - claim - ing the good

te - ro el ú - ni - co Se - ñor.
ti - cia de la li - be - ra - ción.
heav - en the one and on - ly Lord.
news that our lib - er - a - tion comes.

Text: Guillermo Cuellar; trans. by Linda McCrae
Tune: Guillermo Cuellar; acc. by Diana Kodner, b.1957
© 1993, 1994, GIA Publications, Inc.

World without End 673

1. Praise to the Lord for the joys of the earth:
2. Praise to the Lord for the pro - gress of life:
3. Praise to the Lord for his care of our kind:
4. Praise to the Lord for the peo - ple we meet,
5. Praise to the Lord for the car - pen - ter's son,

Cy - cles of sea - son and rea - son and birth,
Cra - dle and grave, bond of hus - band and wife,
Faith for the faith - less and sight for the blind,
Safe in our homes or at risk in the street:
Dove - tail - ing wor - ship and work in - to one:

Con - trasts in out - look and land - scape and need,
Pain of youth grow - ing and wrin - kling of age,
Heal - ing, ac - cep - tance, dis - tur - bance, and change,
Kiss of a lov - er and friend - ship's em - brace,
Trades - man and teach - er and va - grant and friend,

Chal - lenge of fam - ine, pol - lu - tion, and greed.
Ques - tions in step with ex - pe - rience and stage.
All the e - mo - tions through which our lives range.
Smile of a stran - ger and words full of grace.
Source of all life in this world with - out end.

Text: John L. Bell, b.1949, © 1987, Iona Community, GIA Publications, Inc., agent
Tune: BONNIE GEORGE CAMPBELL, 10 10 10 10; Scottish Folk Song; acc. by John L. Bell, b.1949, © 1993, Iona Community,
    GIA Publications, Inc., agent

674 Christians, Lift Up Your Hearts

Refrain

Chris - tians, lift up your hearts, and make this a day of re - joic - ing; God is our strength and song; glo - ry and praise to his name!

Verses 1, 3, 5

1. This is the house of the Lord, where
3. Praise that his love o - ver - flowed in the
5. Come, Ho - ly Spir - it, to us, who

seek - ers and find - ers are wel - come; En - ter its
hearts of all who re - ceived him, Join - ing to -
live by your pres - ence with - in us, Come to di -

gates with your praise, fill all its courts with your song:
geth - er in peace those once di - vid - ed by sin:
rect our course, give us your life and your power:

D.C.

Verses 2, 4, 6

2. Strong and a - lert in his grace, God's peo - ple are
4. Those who are bur - dened with sin find here the
6. Al - might - y God, send us out to live to your

one in their wor - ship: Kept by his peace they de -
joy of for - give - ness, Lay - ing their sins be - fore
praise and your glo - ry; Yours is the pow'r and the

D.C.

part, read - y for serv - ing their Lord:
Christ, par - don and peace their re - ward:
might, ours be the cour - age and faith:

Text: John E. Bowers, b.1923, alt., © Canon John E. Bowers
Tune: SALVE FESTA DIES, Irregular with refrain; Ralph Vaughan Williams, 1872-1958

Magnificat 675

Canon

Ma - gni - fi - cat, ma - gni - fi - cat, Ma - gni - fi - cat a - ni - ma

me - a Do - mi - num. Ma - gni - fi - cat, ma - gni - fi - cat,

Ma - gni - fi - cat a - ni - ma me - a!

Text: Luke 1:46, *My soul magnifies the Lord*; Taizé Community, 1978
Tune: Jacques Berthier, 1923-1994
© 1979, Les Presses de Taizé, GIA Publications, Inc., agent

676 God, We Praise You

1. God, we praise you! God, we bless you! God, we
2. True a - pos - tles, faith - ful proph - ets, Saints who
3. Je - sus Christ, the king of glo - ry, Ev - er -
4. Christ, at God's right hand vic - to - rious, You will

name you sov-'reign Lord! Might - y King whom an - gels
set their world a - blaze, Mar - tyrs, once un - known, un -
last - ing Son of God, Hum - ble was your vir - gin
judge the world you made; Lord, in mer - cy help your

wor - ship, Fa - ther, by your church a - dored: All cre -
heed - ed, Join one grow - ing song of praise, While your
moth - er, Hard the lone - ly path you trod: By your
ser - vants For whose free - dom you have paid: Raise us

a - tion shows your glo - ry, Heav'n and
church on earth con - fess - es One ma -
cross is sin de - feat - ed, Hell con -
up from dust to glo - ry, Guard us

earth draw near your throne, Sing - ing "Ho - ly, ho - ly,
jes - tic Trin - i - ty: Fa - ther, Son, and Ho - ly
front - ed face to face, Heav - en o - pened to be -
from all sin to - day; King en - throned a - bove all

ho - ly, Lord of hosts, and God a - lone!"
Spir - it, God, our hope e - ter - nal - ly.
liev - ers, Sin - ners jus - ti - fied by grace.
prais - es, Save your peo - ple, God, we pray.

Text: Based on the *Te Deum*; Christopher Idle, b.1938, © 1982, Jubilate Hymns, Ltd. (Administered by Hope Publishing Co.)
Tune: NETTLETON, 8 7 8 7 D; Wyeth's *Repository of Sacred Music, Pt. II,* 1813

Sing a New Song to the Lord 677

1. Sing a new song to the Lord,
2. Now to the ends of the earth
3. Sing a new song and re - joice,
4. Join with the hills and the sea

He to whom won - ders be - long! Re -
See his sal - va - tion is shown; And
Pub - lish his prais - es a - broad! Let
Thun - ders of praise to pro - long! In

joice in his tri - umph and
still he re - mem - bers his
voic - es in cho - rus,
judge - ment and jus - tice he

tell of his power, O sing to the
mer - cy and truth, Un - chang - ing in
trum - pet and horn, Re - sound for the
comes to the earth, O sing to the

Lord a new song!
love to his own.
joy of the Lord!
Lord a new song!

Text: Psalm 98; Timothy Dudley-Smith, b.1926
Tune: CANTATE DOMINO (ONSLOW SQUARE), Irregular; David G. Wilson, b.1940
© 1973, Hope Publishing Co.

678 Canticle of the Turning

Verses

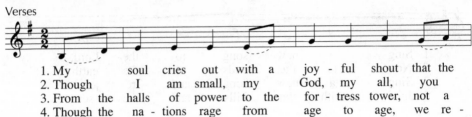

1. My soul cries out with a joy - ful shout that the
2. Though I am small, my God, my all, you
3. From the halls of power to the for - tress tower, not a
4. Though the na - tions rage from age to age, we re -

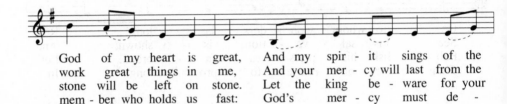

God of my heart is great, And my spir - it sings of the
work great things in me, And your mer - cy will last from the
stone will be left on stone. Let the king be - ware for your
mem - ber who holds us fast: God's mer - cy must de -

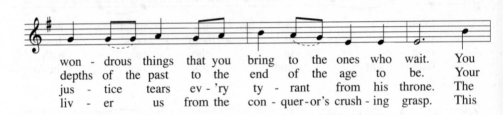

won - drous things that you bring to the ones who wait. You
depths of the past to the end of the age to be. Your
jus - tice tears ev - 'ry ty - rant from his throne. The
liv - er us from the con - quer-or's crush - ing grasp. This

fixed your sight on your ser - vant's plight, and my
ver - y name puts the proud to shame, and to
hun - gry poor shall weep no more, for the
sav - ing word that our fore - bears heard is the

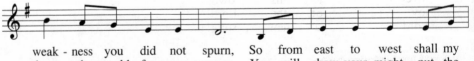

weak - ness you did not spurn, So from east to west shall my
those who would for you yearn, You will show your might, put the
food they can nev - er earn; There are ta - bles spread, ev - 'ry
prom - ise which holds us bound, 'Til the spear and rod can be

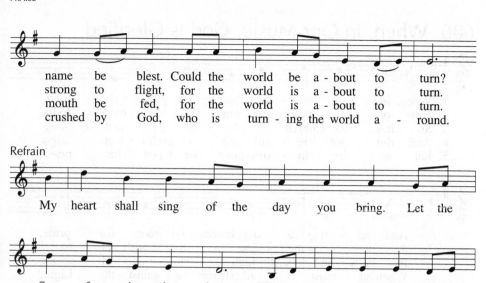

name	be	blest. Could the	world	be	a - bout	to	turn?
strong	to	flight, for the	world	is	a - bout	to	turn.
mouth	be	fed, for the	world	is	a - bout	to	turn.
crushed	by	God, who is	turn - ing the world	a	-	round.

Refrain

My heart shall sing of the day you bring. Let the

fires of your jus - tice burn. Wipe a - way all tears, for the

dawn draws near, and the world is a - bout to turn!

Text: Luke 1:46-58; Rory Cooney, b.1952
Tune: STAR OF THE COUNTY DOWN; Irish traditional; arr. by Rory Cooney, b.1952
© 1990, GIA Publications, Inc.

Jesus Christ, Yesterday, Today and for Ever 679

Ostinato Refrain

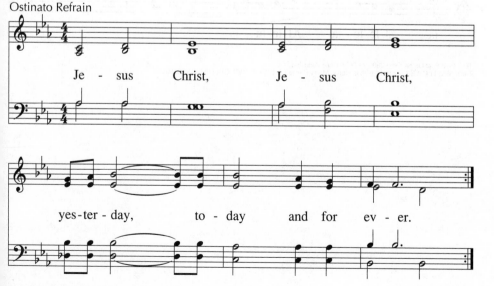

Je - sus Christ, Je - sus Christ,

yes-ter - day, to - day and for ev - er.

Text: Suzanne Toolan, SM, b.1927
Tune: Suzanne Toolan, SM, b.1927
© 1988, GIA Publications, Inc.

680 When, in Our Music, God Is Glorified

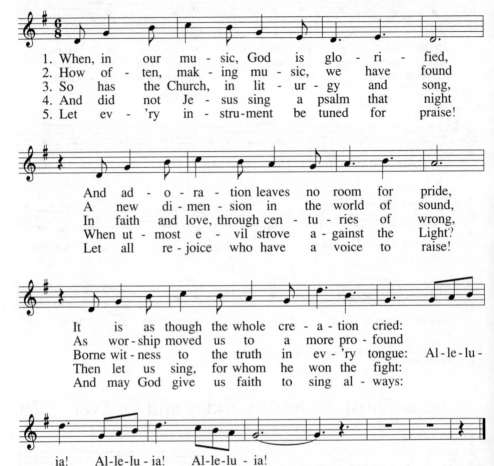

1. When, in our mu - sic, God is glo - ri - fied,
2. How of - ten, mak - ing mu - sic, we have found
3. So has the Church, in lit - ur - gy and song,
4. And did not Je - sus sing a psalm that night
5. Let ev - 'ry in - stru-ment be tuned for praise!

And ad - o - ra - tion leaves no room for pride,
A new di - men - sion in the world of sound,
In faith and love, through cen - tu - ries of wrong,
When ut - most e - vil strove a - gainst the Light?
Let all re - joice who have a voice to raise!

It is as though the whole cre - a - tion cried:
As wor - ship moved us to a more pro - found
Borne wit - ness to the truth in ev - 'ry tongue: Al - le - lu -
Then let us sing, for whom he won the fight:
And may God give us faith to sing al - ways:

ia! Al - le - lu - ia! Al - le - lu - ia!

Text: Fred Pratt Green, 1903-2000, © 1972, Hope Publishing Co.
Tune: MAYFLOWER, 10 10 10 with alleluias; Marty Haugen, b.1950, © 1989, GIA Publications, Inc.

Earth and All Stars 681

1. Earth and all stars, Loud rush-ing plan - ets
2. En - gines and steel, Loud pound-ing ham - mers
3. Class - rooms and labs, Loud boil-ing test tubes
4. Knowl-edge and truth, Loud sound-ing wis - dom

Sing to the Lord a new song!
Sing to the Lord a new song!
Sing to the Lord a new song!
Sing to the Lord a new song!

Hail, wind, and rain, Loud blow - ing snow - storm
Lime - stone and beams, Loud build - ing work - ers
Ath - lete and band, Loud cheer - ing peo - ple
Daugh - ter and son, Loud pray - ing mem - bers

Sing to the Lord a new song!
Sing to the Lord a new song!
Sing to the Lord a new song!
Sing to the Lord a new song!

God has done mar - vel - ous things.

I too sing prais - es with a new song!

Text: Herbert F. Brokering, b.1926
Tune: EARTH AND ALL STARS, 4 5 7 D with refrain; David N. Johnson
© 1968, Augsburg Publishing House

682 Joyfully Singing

Verses

1. Joy-ful-ly sing-ing to the Lord,
2. God, in your mer-cy, free our hearts to
3. Gath-er the na-tions to you, Lord,

prais-ing God on high, all of the earth in thank
praise your ho-ly name, help-ing the poor and low-
draw them to your care, com-ing from all the dis-

ful - ness joins in glad re - ply.
ly ones faith-ful - ly pro - claim.
tant lands glad - ly to de - clare.

Refrain

Bless-ed are your days, ho-ly are your nights,

won-drous is your love all of our lives.

Lord, bring us to-geth-er from east and from

the west. Show us your moun-tain, your

D.C.

dwell-ing place, your life of ho-li-ness.

Text: Mike Balhoff, b.1946, Gary Daigle, b.1957, Darryl Ducote, b.1945
Tune: Mike Balhoff, b.1946, Gary Daigle, b.1957, Darryl Ducote, b.1945
© 1985, Damean Music. Distributed by GIA Publications, Inc.

Sing Praise to God Who Reigns Above 683

1. Sing praise to God who reigns above, The God of all cre - a - tion, The God of pow'r, the God of love, The God of our sal - va - tion; With heal - ing balm my soul he fills, And ev - 'ry faith - less mur - mur stills: To God all praise and glo - ry.

2. What God's al - might - y pow'r has made, His gra - cious mer - cy keep - ing; By morn - ing glow or eve - ning shade His watch - ful eye ne'er sleep - ing; in the king - dom of his might, Lo! all is just and all is right: To God all praise and glo - ry.

3. Then all my glad - some way a - long, I sing a - loud your prais - es, That all may hear the grate - ful song My voice un - wea - ried rais - es; joy - ful in the Lord, my heart, Both soul and bod - y sing your part: To God all praise and glo - ry.

4. Let all who name Christ's ho - ly name, Give God all praise and glo - ry; All you who own his pow'r, pro - claim A - loud the won - drous sto - ry! Cast each false i - dol from its throne, The Lord is God, and he a - lone: To God all praise and glo - ry.

Text: *Sei Lob und Ehr' dem höchsten Gut;* Johann J. Schütz, 1640-1690; tr. by Frances E. Cox, 1812-1897
Tune: MIT FREUDEN ZART, 8 7 8 7 88 7; Bohemian Brethren's *Kirchengesänge,* 1566

684 Praise, My Soul, the King of Heaven

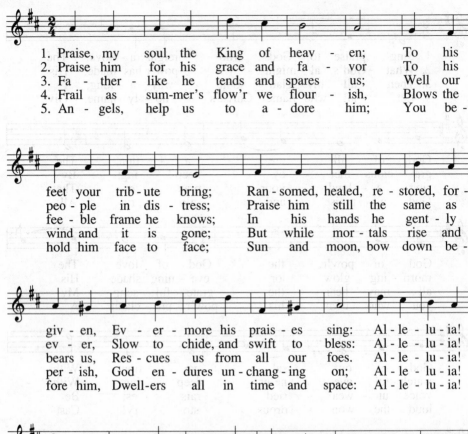

1. Praise, my soul, the King of heav - en; To his
2. Praise him for his grace and fa - vor To his
3. Fa - ther - like he tends and spares us; Well our
4. Frail as sum-mer's flow'r we flour - ish, Blows the
5. An - gels, help us to a - dore him; You be -

feet your trib - ute bring; Ran - somed, healed, re - stored, for -
peo - ple in dis - tress; Praise him still the same as
fee - ble frame he knows; In his hands he gent - ly
wind and it is gone; But while mor - tals rise and
hold him face to face; Sun and moon, bow down be -

giv - en, Ev - er - more his prais - es sing: Al - le - lu - ia!
ev - er, Slow to chide, and swift to bless: Al - le - lu - ia!
bears us, Res - cues us from all our foes. Al - le - lu - ia!
per - ish, God en - dures un - chang - ing on; Al - le - lu - ia!
fore him, Dwell-ers all in time and space: Al - le - lu - ia!

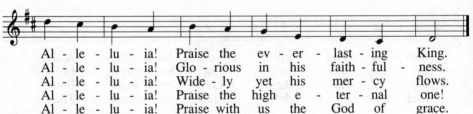

Al - le - lu - ia! Praise the ev - er - last - ing King.
Al - le - lu - ia! Glo - rious in his faith - ful - ness.
Al - le - lu - ia! Wide - ly yet his mer - cy flows.
Al - le - lu - ia! Praise the high e - ter - nal one!
Al - le - lu - ia! Praise with us the God of grace.

Text: Psalm 103; Henry F. Lyte, 1793-1847, alt.
Tune: LAUDA ANIMA, 8 7 8 7 8 7; John Goss, 1800-1880

The God of Abraham Praise 685

1. The God of A-braham praise, Who reigns en-throned a - bove;
2. The Lord, our God has sworn: I on that oath de - pend;
3. There dwells the Lord, our King, The Lord, our Right-eous-ness,
4. The God who reigns on high The great arch - an - gels sing,

The an - cient of e - ter - nal days, And God of love;
I shall, on ea - gle - wings up - borne, To heav'n as - cend:
Tri - umph-ant o'er the world and sin, The Prince of Peace;
And "Ho - ly, Ho - ly, Ho - ly," cry, "Al - might - y King!

The Lord, the great I AM, By earth and heav'n con - fessed
I shall be - hold God's face, I shall God's pow'r a - dore,
On Zi - on's sa - cred height The king - dom God main-tains,
Who was, and is, the same, For all e - ter - ni - ty,

We bow and bless the sa - cred name For ev - er blest.
And sing the won - ders of God's grace For ev - er - more.
And, glo - rious with the saints in light, For ev - er reigns.
Im - mor - tal God, the, great I AM, All glo - ry be."

Text: *Yigdal Elohim Hai*; ascr. to Daniel ben Judah Dayyan, fl.1400; para. by Thomas Olivers, 1725-1799, alt.
Tune: LEONI, 6 6 8 4 D; from the *Yigdal*; transcribed by Meyer Lyon, c.1751-1797

686 Sing a New Song

Refrain

Sing a new song un-to the Lord; let your song be
sung from moun-tains high. Sing a new song
un-to the Lord, sing-ing al - le - lu - ia.

Verses

1. Yah - weh's peo - ple dance for joy. O come be -
2. Rise, O chil - dren, from your sleep; your Sav - ior
3. Glad my soul for I have seen the glo - ry

fore the Lord. And play for him on
now has come. He has turned your
of the Lord. The trum - pet sounds; the

D.C.

glad tam - bou - rines, and let your trum - pet sound.
sor - row to joy, and filled your soul with song.
dead shall be raised. I know my Sav - ior lives.

Text: Psalm 98; Dan Schutte, b.1947
Tune: Dan Schutte, b.1947
© 1972, Daniel L. Schutte. Published by OCP Publications.

Sing Praise to the Lord 687

1. Sing praise to the Lord! praise God in the height;
2. Sing praise to the Lord! praise God up - on earth,
3. Sing praise to the Lord, all things that give sound;
4. Sing praise to the Lord! thanks - giv - ing and song

Re - joice in his word, you an - gels of light;
In tune - ful ac - cord, all you of new birth;
Each ju - bi - lant chord re - ech - o a - round;
To him be out - poured all a - ges a - long;

O heav - ens, a - dore him by whom you were made,
Praise him who has brought you his grace from a - bove,
Loud or - gans, his glo - ry tell forth in deep tone,
For love in cre - a - tion, for heav - en re - stored,

And wor - ship be - fore him in bright - ness ar - rayed.
Praise him who has taught you to sing of his love.
And trum - pets, the sto - ry of what God has done.
For grace of sal - va - tion, sing praise to the Lord!

Text: Psalm 150; Henry W. Baker, 1821-1877, alt.
Tune: LAUDATE DOMINUM, 10 10 11 11; Charles H. H. Parry, 1840-1918

688 Praise the Lord, My Soul

Refrain

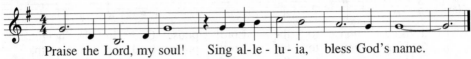

Praise the Lord, my soul! Sing al-le - lu - ia, bless God's name.

Verses

1. All praises to the Father of our Lord,
   a God so merciful and kind,
   who gives to us a new birth,
   who brings to us a new hope
   by raising his Son from death to life!

2. On this mountain God will prepare
   a banquet for all peoples:
   rich food and finest wine.
   On this mountain God will remove
   the mourning veil that covers all peoples
   and will destroy death for ever.

3. How great the sign of God's love for us
   in giving us his Son to be our bread:
   as promised us so long ago,
   revealed to us in these last days.
   How happy we who put our faith in him!

4. Ev'ry tear shall be wiped away
   and shame shall be no more
   for God's own chosen friends.
   Then they shall say:
   "This is the one we hoped for
   to bring us salvation.
   Now we rejoice that God has freed us."

5. And now we are God's work of art,
   a new creation formed in Christ the Lord.
   We know we are his children now.
   What we shall be in days to come,
   what tongue can tell?
   What ear has heard?

6. Taste and see the goodness of God!
   Happy those who take their shelter
   beneath his watchful care.
   Fear the Lord!
   Proud and rich may find themselves sent
       empty away;
   but those who seek the Lord lack nothing.

7. We come to you with hearts full of faith,
   your voice is calling us so deep within.
   We died with you as grain of wheat,
   we rise with you to fruitful lives,
   now make us children of the light!

Text: Tom Parker, b.1947
Tune: Tom Parker, b.1947
© 1981, GIA Publications, Inc.

There's a Spirit in the Air   689

1. There's a Spir - it in the air, Tell - ing Chris - tians
2. Lose your shy - ness, find your tongue; Tell the world what
3. When be - liev - ers break the bread, When a hun - gry
4. Still the Spir - it gives us light, See - ing wrong and
5. When a stran - ger's not a - lone, Where the home - less

ev - 'ry-where, "Praise the love that Christ re-vealed,
God has done: God in Christ has come to stay,
child is fed: Praise the love that Christ re-vealed,
set - ting right: God in Christ has come to stay,
find a home, Praise the love that Christ re-vealed,

Liv - ing, work - ing in our world."
Live to - mor - row's life to - day.
Liv - ing, work - ing in our world.
Live to - mor - row's life to - day.
Liv - ing, work - ing in our world.

6. May the Spirit fill our praise,
   Guide our thoughts and change our ways.
   God in Christ has come to stay,
   Live tomorrow's life today.

7. There's a Spirit in the air,
   Calling people ev'rywhere;
   Praise the love that Christ revealed;
   Living, working in our world.

Text: Brian Wren, b.1936, © 1969, 1995, Hope Publishing Co.
Tune: LAUDS, 77 77; John W. Wilson, 1905-1992, © 1979, Hope Publishing Co.

690 Sing Our God Together

Refrain

Sing*, O peo - ple, sing* our God to - geth - er,

raise your voic - es: sing al - le - lu - ia!

Verses

Solo: / *All:*

1. Sing with one an - oth - er: Sing the love that
2. Dance the steps of beau - ty: Dance the love that
3. Serve all those who suf - fer: Serve the love that
4. Shine as bright as day - break! Shine the love that
5. Teach the way of Je - sus: Teach the love that
6. Seek the chil - dren's wis - dom: Seek the love that
7. Live no more un - car - ing: Live the love that

Solo:

gave us breath! Sing, each sis - ter, broth - er:
gave us breath! Dance, de - light and du - ty:
gave us breath! Serve, that love might con - quer:
gave us breath! Shine as true as heart - ache!
gave us breath! Teach the way that frees us:
gave us breath! Seek God's way of free - dom:
gave us breath! Live your love un - spar - ing:

All: / **D.C.**

Sing the God be - yond all death!
Dance the God be - yond all death!
Serve the God be - yond all death!
Shine in God be - yond all death!
Teach the God be - yond all death!
Seek the God be - yond all death!
Live the God be - yond all death!

*After each verse, repeat key word in the refrain: (Dance/Dance our; Serve/Serve our;
Shine/Shine in; Teach/Teach our; Seek/Seek our; Live/Live our)*

Text: David Haas, b.1957, and Marty Haugen, b.1950
Tune: David Haas, b.1957, and Marty Haugen, b.1950
© 1993, GIA Publications, Inc.

Lift Up Your Hearts 691

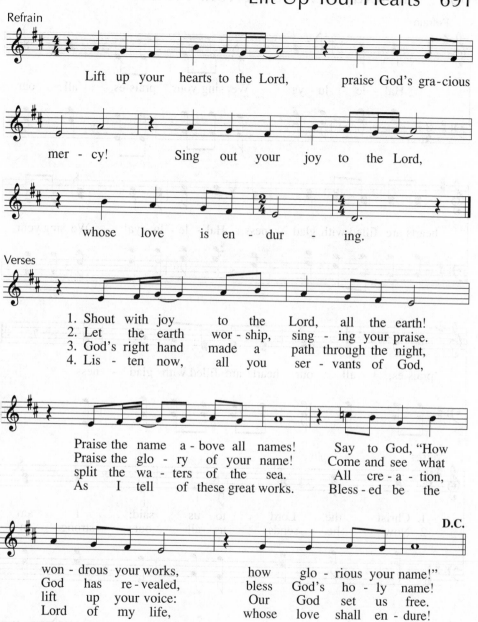

Refrain

Lift up your hearts to the Lord, praise God's gra-cious mer - cy! Sing out your joy to the Lord, whose love is en - dur - ing.

Verses

1. Shout with joy to the Lord, all the earth!
2. Let the earth wor - ship, sing - ing your praise.
3. God's right hand made a path through the night,
4. Lis - ten now, all you ser - vants of God,

Praise the name a - bove all names! Say to God, "How
Praise the glo - ry of your name! Come and see what
split the wa - ters of the sea. All cre - a - tion,
As I tell of these great works. Bless - ed be the

D.C.

won - drous your works, how glo - rious your name!"
God has re - vealed, bless God's ho - ly name!
lift up your voice: Our God set us free.
Lord of my life, whose love shall en - dure!

Text: Psalm 66; Roc O'Connor, SJ, b.1949
Tune: Roc O'Connor, SJ, b.1949; acc. by Robert J. Batastini, b.1942
© 1981, 1993, Robert F. O'Connor, SJ, and OCP Publications

692 Halleluya! We Sing Your Praises

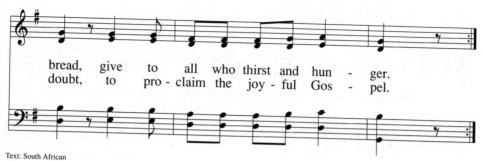

bread, give to all who thirst and hun - ger.
doubt, to pro - claim the joy - ful Gos - pel.

Text: South African
Tune: South African
© 1984, Utryck, Walton Music Corporation, agent

Jubilate Deo 693

Canon

Ju - bi - la - te De - o, ju - bi - la - te
In the Lord re - joic - ing! Christ is ris - en

De - o, al - le - lu - ia!
from the dead! Al - le - lu - ia!

Text: Psalm 100:1; tr. Taizé Community, 1990, © 1978, 1990, Les Presses de Taizé, GIA Publications, Inc., agent
Tune: Michael Praetorius, 1571-1621; acc. by Jacques Berthier, 1923-1994, © 1978, 1990, Les Presses de Taizé, GIA Publications, Inc., agent

694 We Praise You

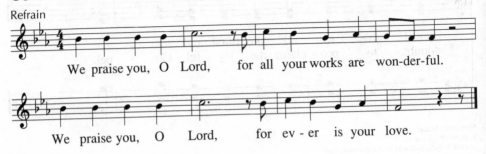

Refrain

We praise you, O Lord, for all your works are won-der-ful.

We praise you, O Lord, for ev - er is your love.

Verses

1. Your wisdom made the heavens and the earth, O Lord;
   You formed the land then set the lights;
   And like your love the sun will rule the day,
   And stars will grace the night.

2. You have chosen Jacob for yourself, O Lord;
   So tenderly you spoke his name;
   Then called a holy nation, Israel,
   To make them yours, you came.

3. You led us out of Egypt with a guiding hand.
   You raised your arm to set us free.
   And like a tender vine you planted us
   To grow unto the sea.

4. The nations fashion silver idols, golden gods;
   But none have hearing, speech or sight.
   Their makers shall be like their empty gods,
   The Lord alone brings life.

5. O House of Israel, now come to bless the Lord,
   O House of Aaron, bless God's name.
   O bless the Lord, all you who honor God,
   And praise his holy name.

*6. Happy is the home of you who fear the Lord;
   So fruitful shall your love become.
   Your children flourish like the olive plants,
   For ever are you one.

*7 . May the Lord God give you blessings all your days.
   May you see God fill your land
   Until your children bring their children home
   To show God's love again.

*Wedding verses

Text: Mike Balhoff, b.1946
Tune: Darryl Ducote, b.1945, Gary Daigle, b.1957
© 1978, Damean Music. Distributed by GIA Publications, Inc.

Praise to the Lord, the Almighty 695

1. Praise to the Lord, the Al - might - y, the king of cre - a - tion!
O my soul, praise him, for he is your health and sal - va - tion!
Come, all who hear: Broth - ers and sis - ters, draw near,
Praise him in glad ad - o - ra - tion!

2. Praise to the Lord, a - bove all things so might - i - ly reign - ing;
Keep - ing us safe at his side, and so gent - ly sus - tain - ing.
Have you not seen All you have need - ed has been
Met by his gra - cious or - dain - ing?

3. Praise to the Lord, who shall pros - per our work and de - fend us;
Sure - ly his good - ness and mer - cy shall dai - ly at - tend us.
Pon - der a - new What the Al - might - y can do,
Who with his love will be - friend us.

4. Praise to the Lord— O let all that is in us a - dore him!
All that has life and breath come now with prais - es be - fore him!
Let the "A - men!" Sound from his peo - ple a - gain—
Glad - ly with praise we a - dore him!

Text: *Lobe den Herren, den mächtigen König;* Joachim Neander, 1650-1680; tr. by Catherine Winkworth, 1827-1878, alt.
Tune: LOBE DEN HERREN, 14 14 47 8; *Stralsund Gesangbuch,* 1665; descant by C. S. Lang, 1891-1971, © 1953, Novello and Co. Ltd.

696 Glory and Praise to Our God

Refrain

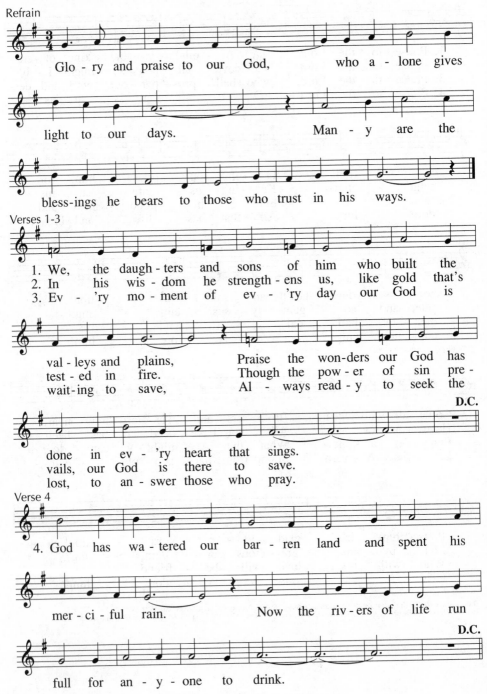

Glo - ry and praise to our God, who a - lone gives light to our days. Man - y are the bless-ings he bears to those who trust in his ways.

Verses 1-3

1. We, the daugh - ters and sons of him who built the
2. In his wis - dom he strength - ens us, like gold that's
3. Ev - 'ry mo - ment of ev - 'ry day our God is

val - leys and plains, Praise the won-ders our God has
test - ed in fire. Though the pow - er of sin pre -
wait-ing to save, Al - ways read - y to seek the

D.C.

done in ev - 'ry heart that sings.
vails, our God is there to save.
lost, to an - swer those who pray.

Verse 4

4. God has wa - tered our bar - ren land and spent his
mer - ci - ful rain. Now the riv - ers of life run

D.C.

full for an - y - one to drink.

Text: Psalm 65, 66; Dan Schutte, b.1947
Tune: Dan Schutte, b.1947; acc. by Sr. Theophane Hytrek, OSF, 1915-1992, alt.
© 1976, Daniel L. Schutte and OCP Publications

For the Beauty of the Earth   697

1. For the beau - ty of the earth, For the glo - ry
2. For the beau - ty of each hour Of the day and
3. For the joy of ear and eye, For the heart and
4. For the joy of hu - man love, Broth - er, sis - ter,
5. For your church, that ev - er - more Lifts its ho - ly
6. For your - self, best Gift Di - vine! To this world so

of the skies, For the love which from our birth
of the night, Hill and vale, and tree and flow'r,
mind's de - light, For the mys - tic har - mo - ny
par - ent, child, Friends on earth, and friends a - bove;
hands a - bove, Of - f'ring up on ev - 'ry shore
free - ly giv'n; Word In - car - nate, God's de - sign,

O - ver and a - round us lies:
Sun and moon, and stars of light:
Link - ing sense to sound and sight: Lord of all, to
For all gen - tle thoughts and mild:
Its pure sac - ri - fice of love:
Peace on earth and joy in heav'n:

you we raise This our hymn of grate - ful praise.

Text: Folliot S. Pierpont, 1835-1917
Tune: DIX, 7 7 7 7 77; arr. from Conrad Kocher, 1786-1872, by William H. Monk, 1823-1889

698 Amen Siakudumisa

Cantor:

Ma - si - thi.
O sing now.

Ma - si - thi.
O sing now.

A - men si - a - ku - du - mi - sa.
A - men sing prais - es to the Lord.

Si - a - ku - du - mi - sa
Sing prais - es to the Lord

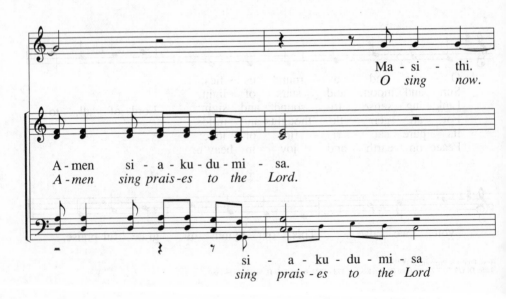

Ma - si - thi.
O sing now.

A - men si - a - ku - du - mi - sa.
A - men sing prais - es to the Lord.

si - a - ku - du - mi - sa
sing prais - es to the Lord

A-men ba - wo,   A-men ba - wo,
A-men sing praise,   *A-men sing praise,*

ba - wa, ba - wo,   ba - wo, ba -
O praise God's name,   *O praise God's*

(Omit last time)

Ma - si - thi.
O sing now.

A - men si - a - ku - du - mi - sa.
A - men sing prais - es to the Lord.

wo, si - a - ku - du - mi - sa.
name, sing prais - es to the Lord.

Text: *Amen. Praise the name of the Lord.* South African traditional; English text, *Hymnal Version*
Tune: Attr. to S. C. Molefe as taught by George Mxadana; arr. by John L. Bell, b.1949, © 1990, Iona Community, GIA Publications, Inc., agent

699 Christus Paradox

1. You, Lord, are both Lamb and Shep - herd.
2. Clothed in light up - on the moun - tain,
3. You, who walk each day be - side us,
4. Wor - thy is our earth - ly Je - sus!

You, Lord, are both prince and slave.
Stripped of might up - on the cross,
Sit in pow - er at God's side.
Wor - thy is our cos - mic Christ!

You, peace - mak - er and sword - bring - er
Shin - ing in e - ter - nal glo - ry,
You, who preach a way that's nar - row,
Wor - thy your de - feat and vic - t'ry.

Of the way you took and gave.
Beg - gar'd by a sol - dier's toss,
Have a love that reach - es wide.
Wor - thy still your peace and strife.

You, the ev - er - last - ing in - stant;
You, the ev - er - last - ing in - stant;
You, the ev - er - last - ing in - stant;
You, the ev - er - last - ing in - stant;

You, whom we both scorn and crave.
You, who are both gift and cost.
You, who are our pil - grim guide.
You, who are our death and life.

Text: Sylvia G. Dunstan, 1955-1993, © 1991, GIA Publications, Inc.
Tune: WESTMINSTER ABBEY, 8 7 8 7 8 7; adapt. from an anthem of Henry Purcell, 1659-1695

Now Thank We All Our God 700

1. Now thank we all our God With hearts and hands and
2. O may this gra-cious God Through all our life be
3. All praise and thanks to God The Fa - ther now be

voic - es, Who won - drous things has done, In
near us, With ev - er joy - ful hearts And
giv - en, The Son, and Spir - it blest, Who

whom his world re - joic - es; Who, from our moth-ers'
bless - ed peace to cheer us; Pre - serve us in his
reigns in high - est heav - en, E - ter - nal, Tri - une

arms, Hath blest us on our way With
grace, And guide us in dis - tress, And
God, Whom earth and heav'n a - dore; For

count-less gifts of love, And still is ours to - day.
free us from all sin, Till heav - en we pos - sess.
thus it was, is now, And shall be ev - er - more.

Text: *Nun danket alle Gott;* Martin Rinkart, 1586-1649; tr. by Catherine Winkworth, 1827-1878, alt.
Tune: NUN DANKET, 6 7 6 7 6 6 6 6; Johann Crüger, 1598-1662; harm. by A. Gregory Murray, OSB, 1905-1992

701 Table Prayer

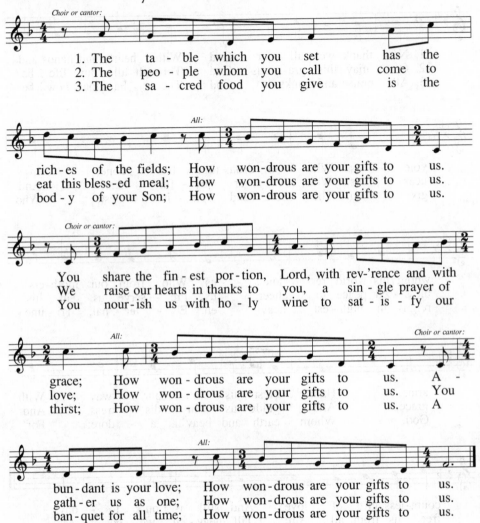

Choir or cantor:

1. The ta-ble which you set has the
2. The peo-ple whom you call come to
3. The sa-cred food you give is the

All:

rich-es of the fields; How won-drous are your gifts to us.
eat this bless-ed meal; How won-drous are your gifts to us.
bod-y of your Son; How won-drous are your gifts to us.

Choir or cantor:

You share the fin-est por-tion, Lord, with rev-'rence and with
We raise our hearts in thanks to you, a sin-gle prayer of
You nour-ish us with ho-ly wine to sat-is-fy our

All:

Choir or cantor:

grace; How won-drous are your gifts to us. A-
love; How won-drous are your gifts to us. You
thirst; How won-drous are your gifts to us. A

All:

bun-dant is your love; How won-drous are your gifts to us.
gath-er us as one; How won-drous are your gifts to us.
ban-quet for all time; How won-drous are your gifts to us.

Text: Mike Balhoff, b.1946, Gary Daigle, b.1957, Darryl Ducote, b.1945
Tune: Mike Balhoff, b.1946, Gary Daigle, b.1957, Darryl Ducote, b.1945
© 1985, Damean Music. Distributed by GIA Publications, Inc.

Blest Are You 702

Cantor or choir:

1., 5. Blest are you who made the u - ni - verse,
2. Through your good - ness we have bread to eat,
3. Through your good - ness we have wine to drink,
4. Here the stran - ger is a wel-come guest

You who see be - yond our death. Blest are you who dwells in
Seeds that died to bring life new. As the sep - 'rate grains be -
Fruit of vine-yard, work of hands. Let the fruits of all we
Here all hun - gers shall be fed. Come, and know the one who

each of us. Blest be you with ev - 'ry breath,
come one loaf, Gath - er us as one in you,
cel - e - brate Spread your love to ev - 'ry land,
brings you life In the break - ing of the bread,

All:

Blest be you with ev - 'ry breath.
Gath - er us as one in you.
Spread your love to ev - 'ry land.
In the break - ing of the bread.

Text: Berakhot and *Didache*; Marty Haugen, b.1950
Tune: Marty Haugen, b.1950
© 1993, GIA Publications, Inc.

703 In the Lord I'll Be Ever Thankful

Ostinato Refrain

In the Lord I'll be ev - er thank - ful, in the Lord I will re - joice! Look to God, do not be a - fraid; lift up your voic - es, the Lord is near; lift up your voic - es, the Lord is near.

Text: Taizé Community
Tune: Jacques Berthier, 1923-1994
© 1986, 1991, Les Presses de Taizé, GIA Publications, Inc., agent

For the Fruits of This Creation   704

1. For the fruits of this cre - a - tion, Thanks be to
2. In the just re - ward of la - bor, God's will is
3. For the har - vests of the Spir - it, Thanks be to

God;   For these gifts to ev - 'ry na - tion,
done;   In the help we give our neigh - bor,
God;   For the good we all in - her - it,

Thanks be to God;   For the plow - ing,
God's will is done;   In our world - wide
Thanks be to God;   For the won - ders

sow - ing, reap - ing, Si - lent growth while we are sleep - ing,
task of car - ing For the hun - gry and de - spair - ing,
that a - stound us, For the truths that still con-found us,

Fu - ture needs in earth's safe keep - ing, Thanks be to God.
In the har - vests we are shar - ing, God's will is done.
Most of all, that love has found us, Thanks be to God.

Text: Fred Pratt Green, 1903-2000, © 1970, Hope Publishing Co.
Tune: EAST ACKLAM, 8 4 8 4 888 4; Francis Jackson, b.1917, ©

705 Father, We Thank Thee, Who Hast Planted

1. Fa - ther, we thank thee, who hast plant - ed
2. Watch o'er thy Church, O Lord, in mer - cy,

Thy ho - ly Name with - in our hearts.
Save it from e - vil, guard it still,

Knowl - edge and faith and life im - mor - tal
Per - fect it in thy love, u - nite it,

Je - sus, thy Son, to us im - parts.
Cleansed and con - formed un - to thy will.

Thou, Lord, didst make all for thy pleas - ure,
As grain, once scat - ter'd on the hill - sides,

Didst give us food for all our days,
Was in this bro - ken bread made one,

Giv - ing in Christ the Bread e - ter - nal;
So from all lands thy Church be gath - er'd

Thine is the power, be thine the praise.
In - to thy king - dom by thy Son.

Text: From the *Didache*, c.110; tr. by F. Bland Tucker, 1895-1984, alt., © 1940, The Church Pension Fund
Tune: RENDEZ À DIEU, 9 8 9 8 D; *Genevan Psalter*, 1551; attr. to Louis Bourgeois, c.1510-1561

Come, Ye Thankful People, Come 706

1. Come, ye thank-ful peo-ple, come, Raise the song of
2. All the world is God's own field, Fruit un - to God's
3. For the Lord our God shall come, And shall take the
4. E - ven so, Lord, quick-ly come To your fi - nal

har - vest - home: All is safe-ly gath - ered in,
praise to yield; Wheat and tares to-geth - er sown,
har - vest home; From the field shall in that day
har - vest - home; Gath - er all your peo - ple in,

Ere the win - ter storms be - gin; God, our Mak - er,
Un - to joy or sor - row grown; First the blade, and
All of - fens - es purge a - way, Giv - ing an - gels
Free from sor - row, free from sin; There, for ev - er

does pro - vide For our wants to be sup - plied;
then the ear, Then the full corn shall ap - pear:
charge at last In the fire the tares to cast,
pu - ri - fied, In your pres-ence to a - bide:

Come to God's own tem - ple, come,
Lord of har - vest, grant that we
But the fruit - ful ears to store
Come, with all your an - gels, come,

Raise the song of har - vest - home.
Whole - some grain and pure may be.
In God's gar - ner ev - er - more.
Raise the glo - rious har - vest - home.

Text: Henry Alford, 1810-1871, alt.
Tune: ST. GEORGE'S WINDSOR, 77 77 D; George J. Elvey, 1816-1893

707 Let All Things Now Living

1. Let all things now liv-ing A song of thanks-giv-ing
2. His law he en - forc-es, The stars in their cours-es,

To God our Cre - a - tor tri - um-phant-ly raise;
The sun in its or - bit o - be-dient-ly shine,

Who fash-ioned and made us, Pro - tect-ed and stayed us,
The hills and the moun-tains, The riv - ers and foun-tains,

By guid - ing us on to the end of our days.
The depths of the o - cean pro - claim God di - vine.

God's ban - ners are o'er us, Pure light goes be - fore us,
We, too, should be voic - ing Our love and re - joic - ing

A pil - lar of fire shin-ing forth in the night:
With glad ad - o - ra - tion, a song let us raise:

Till shad-ows have van - ished And dark - ness is ban - ished,
Till all things now liv - ing U - nite in thanks-giv - ing,

As for - ward we trav - el from light in - to Light.
To God in the high-est, ho - san - na and praise.

Text: Katherine K. Davis, 1892-1980, © 1939, E.C. Schirmer Music Co.
Tune: ASH GROVE, 66 11 66 11 D; Welsh; harm. by Gerald H. Knight, 1908-1979, © The Royal School of Church Music

Thanks Be to You 708

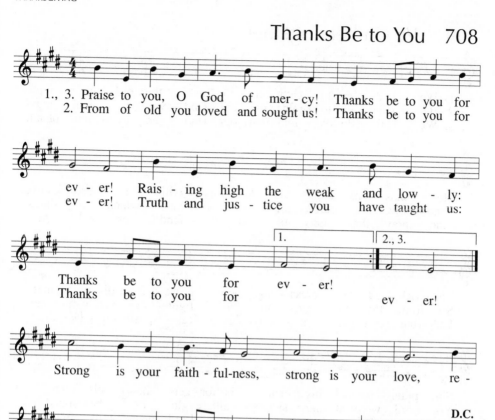

1., 3. Praise to you, O God of mer - cy! Thanks be to you for
2. From of old you loved and sought us! Thanks be to you for

ev - er! Rais - ing high the weak and low - ly:
ev - er! Truth and jus - tice you have taught us:

1.
Thanks be to you for ev - er!
2., 3.
Thanks be to you for ev - er!

Strong is your faith - ful-ness, strong is your love, re -

mem - b'ring your cov-e-nant of life with us.

Text: Marty Haugen, b.1950
Tune: Marty Haugen, b.1950

709 We Gather Together

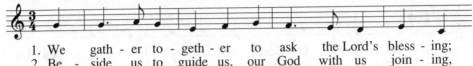

1. We gath - er to - geth - er to ask the Lord's bless - ing;
2. Be - side us to guide us, our God with us join - ing,
3. We all do ex - tol you our lead - er tri - um - phant,

He chas - tens and has - tens his will to make known;
Whose king - dom calls all to the love which en - dures.
And pray that you still our de - fend - er will be.

The wick - ed op - press - ing now cease from dis - tress - ing:
So from the be - gin - ning the fight we were win - ning:
Let your con - gre - ga - tion es - cape trib - u - la - tion:

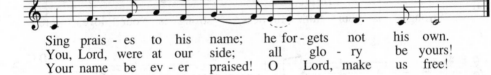

Sing prais - es to his name; he for - gets not his own.
You, Lord, were at our side; all glo - ry be yours!
Your name be ev - er praised! O Lord, make us free!

Text: *Wilt heden nu treden,* Netherlands folk hymn; tr. by Theodore Baker, 1851-1934, alt.
Tune: KREMSER, 12 11 12 11; *Neder-landtsch Gedenckclanck,* 1626; harm. by Edward Kremser, 1838-1914

710 Confitemini Domino / Come and Fill

Ostinato Refrain

Con - fi - te - mi - ni Do - mi - no
Come and fill our hearts with your peace.

quo - ni - am bo - nus. Con - fi - te - mi - ni
You a - lone, O Lord, are ho - ly. Come and fill our hearts

Do - mi - no, Al - le - lu - ia!
with your peace, *Al - le - lu* *-* *ia!*

Text: Psalm 137, *Give thanks to the Lord for he is good;* Taizé Community, 1982
Tune: Jacques Berthier, 1923-1994
© 1982, 1991, Les Presses de Taizé, GIA Publications, Inc., agent

Creating God 711

1. Cre - at - ing God, your fin - gers
2. Sus - tain - ing God, your hands up -
3. Re - deem - ing God, your arms em -
4. In - dwel - ling God, your gos - pel

trace The bold de - signs of far - thest space;
hold Earth's mys - t'ries known or yet un - told;
brace All now de - spised for creed or race;
claims One fam - 'ly with a bil - lion names;

Let sun and moon and stars and light And
Let wa - ters frag - ile blend with air, En -
Let peace, de - scend - ing like a dove, Make
Let ev - 'ry life be touched by grace Un -

what lies hid - den praise your might.
a - bling life, pro - claim your care.
known on earth your heal - ing love.
til we praise you face to face.

Text: Jeffery Rowthorn, b.1934, © 1979, Hymn Society of America, alt. (Admin. by Hope Publishing Co.)
Tune: PRESENCE, LM; David Haas, b.1957, © 1989, GIA Publications, Inc.

712 Lead Me, Guide Me

Refrain

Lead me, guide me, a - long the way, For if you
lead me, I can - not stray. Lord, let me walk each
day with thee. Lead me, oh Lord, lead me.

Verses

1. I am weak and I need thy strength and pow'r to
2. Help me tread in the paths of right - eous - ness, Be my
3. I am lost if you take your hand from me, I am

help me o - ver my weak - est hour. Help me through the
aid when Sa - tan and sin op - press. I am put - ting
blind with - out thy Light to see, Lord, just al - ways

D.C.

dark-ness thy face to see, Lead me, oh Lord, lead me.
all my trust in thee. Lead me, oh Lord, lead me.
let me thy ser - vant be. Lead me, oh Lord, lead me.

Text: Doris M. Akers, 1922-1995
Tune: Doris M. Akers, 1922-1995; harm. by Richard Smallwood
© 1953, Doris M. Akers, All rights administered by Unichappell Music, Inc.

Lord of all Hopefulness 713

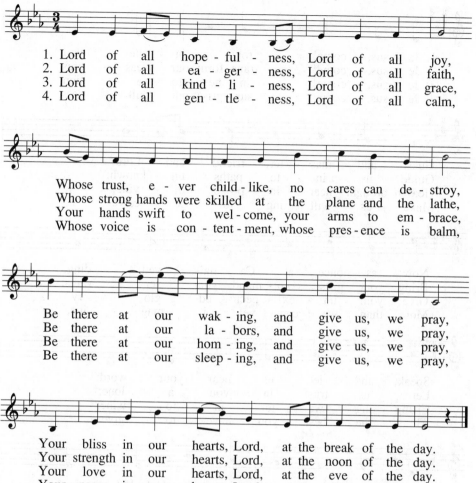

1. Lord of all hope-ful-ness, Lord of all joy,
2. Lord of all ea-ger-ness, Lord of all faith,
3. Lord of all kind-li-ness, Lord of all grace,
4. Lord of all gen-tle-ness, Lord of all calm,

Whose trust, e-ver child-like, no cares can de-stroy,
Whose strong hands were skilled at the plane and the lathe,
Your hands swift to wel-come, your arms to em-brace,
Whose voice is con-tent-ment, whose pres-ence is balm,

Be there at our wak-ing, and give us, we pray,
Be there at our la-bors, and give us, we pray,
Be there at our hom-ing, and give us, we pray,
Be there at our sleep-ing, and give us, we pray,

Your bliss in our hearts, Lord, at the break of the day.
Your strength in our hearts, Lord, at the noon of the day.
Your love in our hearts, Lord, at the eve of the day.
Your peace in our hearts, Lord, at the end of the day.

Text: Jan Struther, 1901-1953, © Oxford University Press
Tune: SLANE, 10 11 11 12; Gaelic; harm. by Erik Routley, 1917-1982, © 1975, Hope Publishing Co.

714 Jesus, Come! For We Invite You

1. Je - sus, come! for we in - vite you,
2. Je - sus, come! trans - form our pleas - ures,
3. Je - sus, come! in new cre - a - tion,
4. Je - sus, come! sur - prise our dull - ness,

Guest and mas - ter, friend and Lord;
Guide us in - to paths un - known;
Heav'n brought near in pow'r di - vine;
Make us will - ing to re - ceive

Now as once at Ca - na's wed - ding,
Bring your gifts, com - mand your ser - vants,
Give your un - ex - pect - ed glo - ry
More than we can yet i - mag - ine,

Speak, and let us hear your word:
Let us trust in you a - lone:
Chang - ing wa - ter in - to wine:
All the best you have to give:

Lead us through our need or doubt - ing,
Though your hand may work in se - cret,
Rouse the faith of your dis - ci - ples—
Let us find your hid - den rich - es,

Hope be born and joy re - stored.
All shall see what you have done.
Come, our first and great - est Sign!
Taste your love, be - lieve, and live!

Text: John 2; Christopher Idle, b.1938, © 1982, Jubilate Hymns, Ltd. (Administered by Hope Publishing Co.)
Tune: BEST GIFT, 8 7 8 7 8 7; Ronald F. Krisman, b.1946, © 1986, GIA Publications, Inc.

Healing River 715

1. O heal - ing riv - er, send down your
2. This land is parch-ing, this land is
3. Let the seed of free - dom, a - wake and

wa - ters, Send down your wa - ters up - on this
burn-ing, No seed is grow-ing in the bar - ren
flour-ish, Let the deep roots nour-ish, let the tall stalks

land. O heal - ing riv - er, send down your
ground. O heal - ing riv - er, send down your
rise. O heal - ing riv - er, send down your

wa - ters, And wash the blood from off the sand.
wa - ters, O heal-ing riv-er, send your wa - ters down.
wa - ters, O heal-ing riv-er, from out of the skies.

*The assembly echoes each phrase of the cantor at the interval of one half measure.

Text: Fran Minkoff
Tune: Fred Hellerman; arr. by Michael Joncas, b.1951
© 1964, Appleseed Music, Inc.

716 I Need You to Listen

Refrain

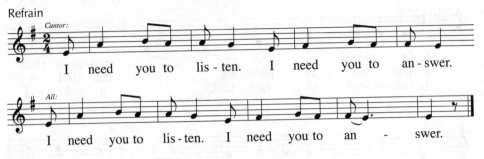

I need you to lis-ten. I need you to an-swer.

I need you to lis-ten. I need you to an - swer.

Verses

1. O God, I need you to. I want to see your face.
   It is this love I have. It makes me search for you.

2. Do not avoid my eyes or let me anger you.
   Do not toss me aside. O God, do not drop me.

3. You are the only hope I have; father, mother, they can leave me orphaned,
   but your love must never. Lead me to you, O God, along the smoothest road.

4. There are those who hate me. Do not leave me to them.
   They eat my life away by lying under oath or twisting evidence.

5. I trust your love. I will see your beauty after death in your land of life.
   My love will wait for you. It will be strong waiting. O God, my love will wait!

Text: Based on Psalm 27; Francis Patrick Sullivan, © 1983, The Pastoral Press
Tune: Marty Haugen, b.1950, © 1991, GIA Publications, Inc.

717 Come, My Way, My Truth, My Life

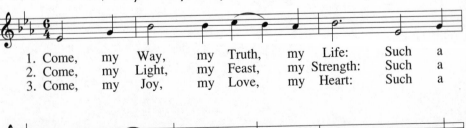

1. Come, my Way, my Truth, my Life: Such a
2. Come, my Light, my Feast, my Strength: Such a
3. Come, my Joy, my Love, my Heart: Such a

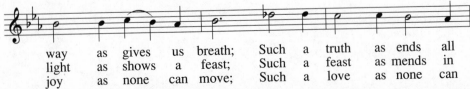

way as gives us breath; Such a truth as ends all
light as shows a feast; Such a feast as mends in
joy as none can move; Such a love as none can

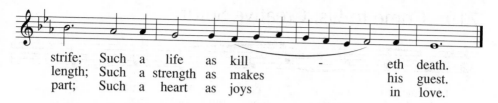

strife; Such a life as kill - eth death.
length; Such a strength as makes his guest.
part; Such a heart as joys in love.

Text: George Herbert, 1593-1632
Tune: THE CALL, 7 7 7 7; Ralph Vaughan Williams, 1872-1958

O Lord, Hear My Prayer 718

Ostinato Chorale

O Lord, hear my prayer, O Lord, hear my prayer:
*The Lord is my song, the Lord is my praise:

when I call an - swer me. O Lord, hear my prayer, O
all my hope comes from God. The Lord is my song, the

Lord, hear my prayer. Come and lis - ten to me. O
Lord is my praise: God, the well-spring of life. The

*Alternate text

Text: Psalm 102; Taizé Community, 1982
Tune: Jacques Berthier, 1923-1994

719 Come to Us, Creative Spirit

1. Come to us, cre - a - tive Spir - it,
2. Po - et, paint - er, mu - sic - mak - er,
3. Word from God e - ter - nal spring - ing,
4. In all plac - es and for ev - er

In our Fa - ther's house; Ev - 'ry hu -
All your treas - ures bring; Crafts - man, ac -
Fill our minds, we pray; And in all
Glo - ry be ex - pressed To the Son,

man tal - ent hal - low, Hid - den skills a -
tor, grace - ful danc - er, Make your of - fer -
ar - tis - tic vi - sion Give in - teg - ri -
with God the Fa - ther And the Spir - it

rouse, That with - in your earth - ly tem - ple,
ing; Join your hands in cel - e - bra - tion:
ty: May the flame with - in us burn - ing
blessed: In our wor - ship and our liv - ing

Wise and sim - ple, May re - joice.
Let cre - a - tion Shout and sing!
Kin - dle yearn - ing Day by day.
Keep us striv - ing For the best.

Text: David Mowbray, b.1938, © Stainer & Bell Publications (Administered by Hope Publishing Co.)
Tune: CASTLEWOOD, 8 5 8 5 84 3; Richard Proulx, b.1937, © 1986, GIA Publications, Inc.

Bwana Awabariki / May God Grant You a Blessing   720

Bwa - na a - wa - ba - ri - ki, Bwa - na
May   God   grant you a bless - ing,   may   God

a - wa - ba - ri - ki, Bwa - na a - wa - ba - ri - ki
grant you a bless - ing, may   God   grant you a bless - ing

mi - le - le.   U - ki - mcha Bwa - na.
ev - er - more.   Re - vere the Lord.

Bwa - na a - wa - ba - ri - ki.
May   God   grant you a bless - ing.

Text: Swahili folk hymn
Tune: Swahili melody

721 May the Lord, Mighty God

1., 3. May the Lord, might-y God, bless and
2. Lift your eyes and see God's face full of

keep you for - ev - er, grant you peace,
grace for - ev - er. May the Lord,

per - fect peace, cour-age in ev - 'ry en-deav - or.
might-y God, bless and keep you for-ev - er.

Text: Numbers 6:24-26; unknown
Tune: WEN-TI, Irregular; Chinese, Pao-chen Li; adapted by I-to Loh, © 1983, Abingdon Press; acc. by Diana Kodner, b.1957, © 1993,
    GIA Publications, Inc.

722 I Say "Yes," Lord / Digo "Sí," Señor

Verses

Cantor: *All:*

(Invocation) I say "Yes," my Lord. I say
            Di-go "Sí," Se - ñor. Di-go

Refrain

"Yes," my Lord. I say "Yes," my Lord, in
"Sí," Se - ñor. Di - go "Sí," Se - ñor, en

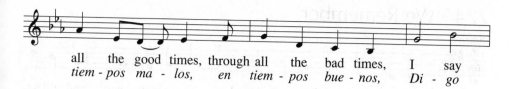

all the good times, through all the bad times, I say
tiem - pos ma - los, en tiem - pos bue - nos, Di - go

"Yes," my Lord, to ev - 'ry word you speak.
"Sí," Se - ñor, a to - do lo que ha - blas.

Text: Donna Peña, b.1955
Tune: Donna Peña, b.1955; arr. by Marty Haugen, b.1950
© 1989, GIA Publications, Inc.

We Walk By Faith 723

1., 5. We walk by faith, and not by sight: No
2. We may not touch his hands and side, Nor
3. Help then, O Lord, our un - be - lief, And
4. That when our life of faith is done In

gra - cious words we hear Of him who spoke as
fol - low where he trod; Yet in his prom - ise
may our faith a - bound; To call on you when
realms of clear - er light We may be - hold you

none e'er spoke, But we be - lieve him near.
we re - joice, And cry "My Lord and God!"
you are near, And seek where you are found:
as you are In full and end - less sight.

Text: Henry Alford, 1810-1871, alt.
Tune: SHANTI, CM; Marty Haugen, b.1950, © 1984, GIA Publications, Inc.

724 We Remember

Refrain

We re - mem-ber how you loved us to your death, and still we cel-e-brate, for you are with us here; and we be-lieve that we will see you when you come in your glo-ry, Lord. We re - mem-ber, we cel-e-brate, we be - lieve.

Verses

1. Here, a mil - lion wound - ed souls are
2. Now we re - cre - ate your love, we
3. Christ, the Fa - ther's great "A - men" to
4. See the face of Christ re - vealed in

1. yearn - ing just to touch you and be healed.
2. bring the bread and wine to share a meal.
3. all the hopes and dreams of ev - 'ry heart,
4. ev - 'ry per - son stand - ing by your side,

D.C.

1. Gath - er all your peo - ple, and hold them to your heart.
2. Sign of grace and mer - cy, the pres - ence of the Lord.
3. Peace be - yond all tell - ing, and free - dom from all fear.
4. Gift to one an - oth - er, and tem - ples of your love.

Text: Marty Haugen, b.1950
Tune: Marty Haugen, b.1950
© 1980, GIA Publications, Inc.

Mayenziwe / Your Will Be Done 725

Ma - ye - (Ma - ye) nzi - we 'nta - ndo ya - kho. Ma-
Your will (Your will) be done on earth, O Lord. Your

ye - (Ma - ye) nzi - we 'nta - ndo ya - kho. Ma - ye - nzi -
will (Your will) be done on earth, O Lord. Your will be

we 'nta - ndo ya - kho. Ma - ye - nzi - we 'nta -
done on earth, O Lord. Your will be done on

ndo ya - kho. Ma - ye - nzi - we 'nta - ndo ya - kho.
earth, O Lord. Your will be done on earth, O Lord.

Text: from the Lord's Prayer, South African
Tune: South African traditional, as taught by George Mxadana; transcribed by John L. Bell, b.1949; © 1990, Iona Community,
   GIA Publications, Inc., agent

726 A Living Faith

1. Faith of our fa - thers, liv - ing still
2. Faith of our moth - ers, dar - ing faith,
3. Faith of our broth - ers, sis - ters too,
4. Faith born of God, O call us yet;

In spite of dun - geon, fire and sword;
Your work for Christ is love re - vealed,
Who still must bear op - pres - sion's might,
Bind us with all who fol - low you,

O how our hearts beat high with joy,
Spread - ing God's word from pole to pole,
Rais - ing on high, in pris - ons dark,
Shar - ing the strug - gle of your cross

When - e'er we hear that glo - rious word:
Mak - ing love known and free - dom real:
The cross of Christ still burn - ing bright:
Un - til the world is made a - new,

Faith of our fa - thers, ho - ly faith,
Faith of our moth - ers, ho - ly faith,
Faith for to - day, O liv - ing faith,
Faith born of God, O liv - ing faith,

We will be true to you till death.

Text: St. 1, Frederick W. Faber, 1814-1863, alt.; sts. 2-4, Joseph R. Alfred, © 1981, alt.
Tune: ST. CATHERINE, LM with refrain; Henry F. Hemy, 1818-1888; adapt. by James G. Walton, 1821-1905

Pues Si Vivimos / If We Are Living 727

1. Pues si vi - vi - mos   pa - ra Él vi - vi - mos,
1. If   we are liv - ing   we are in   the Lord,
2. En es - ta vi - da,   fru - tos he - mos de dar;
2. Through-out our lives   we have fruit to bear.
3. En la tris - te - za   y en el   do - lor,
3. When there is sad - ness,   when there is pain
4. En es - te mun - do,   he - mos de en - con - trar
4. And   in this world   we will al - ways find

y si mo - ri - mos   pa - ra Él mo - ri - mos.
and if we die   we are in   the Lord,
las o - bras bue - nas   son pa - ra of - ren - dar.
All of our good works   are for us   to share.
en la be - lle - za   y en el   a - mor
in Christ the Lord,   we have love to gain.
gen - te que llo - ra   y sin con - so - lar.
those who are weep - ing,   sick in heart and mind.

Sea que vi - va - mos   o   que mu - ra - mos,
for   if we   live   or   if we   die
Ya sea que de - mos   o que re - ci - ba - mos,
Whe - ther we   give,   or   we re - ceive
Sea que su - fra - mos   o que go - ce - mos,
Whe - ther we   suf - fer   or   we re - joice,
Sea que a - yu - de - mos   o que al - i - men - te - mos,
They need our   help,   they need our   care.

so - mos del Señ - or,   so - mos del Señ - or.
we be - long to God,   we be - long to God.

Text: Verse 1, Romans 14:8; traditional Spanish; translation by Deborah L. Schmitz, b.1969, © 1994, GIA Publications, Inc.
Tune: Traditional Spanish; arr. by Diana Kodner, b.1957, © 1994, GIA Publications, Inc.

728 Seek Ye First the Kingdom of God

Canon

1. Seek ye first the king - dom of God
2. Ask, and it shall be giv - en un - to you,
3. You do not live by bread a - lone,
4. Where two or three are gath - ered in my name,

and his right - eous - ness,
seek, and ye shall find,
but by ev - 'ry word,
there am I in their midst;

and all these things shall be add - ed un - to you;
knock, and the door shall be o - pened un - to you;
that comes forth from the mouth of God;
and what - so - ev - er you ask I will do;

Al - le - lu, al - le - lu - ia. Al - le -

lu - ia, al - le - lu - ia, al - le -

lu - ia, al - le - lu, al - le - lu - ia.

May be sung as a two-voice canon.

Text: Matthew 6:33, 7:7; St. 1, adapt. by Karen Lafferty, b.1948; St. 2-4, anon.
Tune: SEEK YE FIRST, Irregular; Karen Lafferty, b.1948
© 1972, Maranatha! Music

Awake, O Sleeper, Rise from Death 729

1. A - wake, O sleep - er, rise from death,
2. To us on earth he came to bring
3. There is one Bod - y and one Hope,
4. Then walk in love as Christ has loved
5. For us Christ lived, for us he died

And Christ shall give you light.
From sin and fear re - lease,
One Spir - it and one Call,
Who died that he might save;
And con - quered in the strife.

So learn his love— its length and breadth,
To give the Spir - it's u - ni - ty,
One Lord, one Faith, and one Bap - tism,
With kind and gen - tle hearts for - give
A - wake, a - rise, go forth in faith,

Its full - ness, depth and height.
The ver - y bond of peace.
One Fa - ther of us all.
As God in Christ for - gave.
And Christ shall give you life.

Text: Ephesians 3-5; F. Bland Tucker, 1895-1984., © 1980, Augsburg Publishing House
Tune: AZMON, CM; Carl G. Gläser, 1784-1829; harm. by Lowell Mason, 1792-1872

730   Psalm of Hope

Refrain

A - maz - ing grace! how sweet the sound that saved and set me free. I once was lost, but now am found; was blind, but now I see.

Verses

1. My God, my God, why have you abandoned me?
   Far from my prayers, far from my cries, all day and night I call.
   Yet, our ancestors put their trust in you.
   You rescued them, you saved them from all foes.

2. But here am I, the scorn of all my people.
   They say, "if God is now your friend, let God rescue you."
   From my mother's womb you are my God.
   You held me up, you placed me in your arms.

3. The evildoers circle in around me.
   I am enslaved in chains of death, I can count all my bones.
   O my strength, hasten to my aid.
   Come save my life, come quickly to my help.

4. I shall proclaim your name to the full assembly.
   Those who fear God, exult and praise;
   Glorify the Lord. All generations, all children of the earth:
   Proclaim for ever the wondrous deeds of God.

*1. You did not turn your face from all your people.
   You rescued them from chains of death, you raised them from despair.
   Ev'ry nation on earth from end to end
   Shall turn to you and bow before your throne.

*2. And so my soul shall live for you, O Lord of hope.
   My children shall bring forth your deeds and magnify your name.
   All my descendants shall know your ways, O Lord.
   May they proclaim the justice you have shown.

*Alternate Easter verses used with vs. 4 above.

Text: Refrain, John Newton, 1725-1807; Verses, Psalm 22, adapted by Felix Goebel-Komala, b.1961
Tune: PSALM OF HOPE, Irregular with refrain; Felix Goebel-Komala, b.1961
© 1994, GIA Publications, Inc.

How Firm a Foundation 731

1. How firm a foun - da - tion, you saints of the Lord,
2. "Fear not, I am with you, O be not dis-mayed,
3. "When through the deep wa - ters I call you to go,
4. "The soul that on Je - sus still leans for re - pose,

Is laid for your faith in this ex - cel-lent Word!
For I am your God, and will still give you aid;
The riv - ers of woe shall not you o - ver - flow;
I will not, I will not de - sert to its foes;

What more can God say than to you has been said,
I'll strength - en you, help you, and cause you to stand,
For I will be with you, your trou - bles to bless,
That soul, though all hell should en - deav - or to shake,

To you who for ref - uge to Je - sus have fled?
Up - held by my right - eous, om - nip - o - tent hand.
And sanc - ti - fy to you, your deep - est dis - tress.
I'll nev - er, no nev - er, no nev - er for - sake!"

Text: 2 Peter 1:4; "K" in Rippon's *A Selection of Hymns*, 1787
Tune: FOUNDATION, 11 11 11 11; Funk's *Compilation of Genuine Church Music*, 1832; harm. by Richard Proulx, b.1937, © 1975, GIA Publications, Inc.

732 The Lord Is My Light

Verses 1, 3

1. The Lord is my light   and my sal - va - tion, the Lord is my
3. ⁏ Wait on the Lord   and be of good cour-age, O wait on the

light   and my sal - va - tion, the Lord is my light   and
Lord   and be of good cour - age, ⁏ wait on the Lord   and

my sal - va - tion;   whom   shall I   fear?
be of good cour - age.   He   shall strength-en   thine heart.

𝄪 Refrain

Whom shall I fear,   whom shall I   fear?   The Lord is the

strength   of   my   life;   whom   shall I   fear?

Verse 2

2. In the time of trou-ble   he shall hide me, O in the time of

trou-ble,   he shall hide me,   in the time of trou-ble,

D.S.

he shall hide me;   whom   shall I   fear?

Text: Lillian Bouknight
Tune: Lillian Bouknight; arr. by Paul Gainer
© 1980, Savgos Music, Inc.

How Can I Keep from Singing 733

1. My life flows on in end-less song A-
2. Through all the tu-mult and the strife, I
3. What, though my joys and com-fort die, The
4. The peace of Christ makes fresh my heart, A

bove earth's lam - en - ta - tion. I hear the real though
hear that mu - sic ring - ing; It sounds and ech - oes
Lord, my sav - ior liv - eth. What though the dark - ness
foun - tain ev - er spring-ing. All things are mine since

far - off hymn That hails a new cre - a - tion.
in my soul; How can I keep from sing-ing?
gath-er 'round? Songs in the night it giv - eth.
I am his; How can I keep from sing-ing?

No storm can shake my in-most calm, While to that rock I'm

cling - ing. Since Christ is Lord of heav-en and earth,

How can I keep from sing-ing?

Text: Robert Lowry, 1826-1899
Tune: HOW CAN I KEEP FROM SINGING, 8 7 8 7 with refrain; Robert Lowry, 1826-1899; harm. by Robert J. Batastini, b.1942, © 1988, GIA
Publications, Inc.

734   Be Not Afraid

pow'r of hell and death is at your side,

know that I am with you through it all.

Verse 3

3. Bless-ed are your poor, for the king-dom shall be

theirs. Blest are you that weep and mourn, for

one day you shall laugh. And if wick-ed tongues in -

sult and hate you all be-cause of me,

bless-ed, bless-ed are you!

Text: Isaiah 43:2-3, Luke 6:20ff; Bob Dufford, SJ, b.1943
Tune: Bob Dufford, SJ, b.1943; acc. by Sr. Theophane Hytrek, OSF, 1915-1992
© 1975, 1978, Robert J. Dufford, SJ, and OCP Publications

735 O God, Our Help in Ages Past

1. O God, our help in a - ges past, Our
2. Un - der the shad - ow of your throne Your
3. Be - fore the hills in or - der stood, Or
4. A thou - sand a - ges in your sight Are
5. Time, like an ev - er - roll - ing stream, Soon
6. O God, our help in a - ges past, Our

hope for years to come, Our shel - ter from the
saints have dwelt se - cure; Suf - fi - cient is your
earth re - ceived its frame, From ev - er - last - ing
like an eve - ning gone, Short as the watch that
bears us all a - way; We fly for - got - ten,
hope for years to come, Still be our guard while

storm - y blast, And our e - ter - nal home.
arm a - lone, And our de - fense is sure.
you are God, To end - less years the same.
ends the night Be - fore the ris - ing sun.
as a dream Dies at the op - 'ning day.
trou - bles last, And our e - ter - nal home.

Text: Psalm (89)90; Isaac Watts, 1674-1748
Tune: ST. ANNE, CM; attr. to William Croft, 1678-1727; harm. composite from 18th C. versions

736 Be Still and Know That I Am God

Canon

Be still and know that I am God.

Be still and know that I am God.

Text: Psalm 46:10; John L. Bell, b.1949
Tune: John L. Bell, b.1949
© 1989, Iona Community, GIA Publications, Inc., agent

Amazing Grace 737

1. A - maz - ing grace! how sweet the
2. 'Twas grace that taught my heart to
3. The Lord has prom - ised good to
4. Through man - y dan - gers, toils, and
5. When we've been there ten thou - sand

sound, That saved a wretch like me!
fear, And grace my fears re - lieved;
me, His word my hope se - cures;
snares, I have al - read - y come;
years, Bright shin - ing as the sun,

I once was lost, but now am
How pre - cious did that grace ap -
He will my shield and por - tion
'Tis grace has brought me safe thus
We've no less days to sing God's

found, Was blind, but now I see.
pear The hour I first be - lieved!
be As long as life en - dures.
far, And grace will lead me home.
praise Than when we'd first be - gun.

Text: St. 1-4, John Newton, 1725-1807; st. 5, attr. to John Rees, fl.1859
Tune: NEW BRITAIN, CM; *Virginia Harmony,* 1831; harm. by Edwin O. Excell, 1851-1921

738 With a Shepherd's Care

Refrain

With a shep-herd's care, God leads us. With a fa-ther's strength, God guides us. With a moth-er's love, God nur-tures us, and cra-dles us in gen - tle arms.

Verses

1. When we are lost, and can - not find the way, God
2. When we are weak, and cares press all a - round, God
3. When we are scared, and feel so all a - lone, God

cares for us and keeps us safe. For
strength - ens us to face each day. For
loves us and is by our side. For

God is our light and our faith - ful guide, and
God is our rock and our sav - ing help, and
God is our hope and our con - stant friend, and

D.C.

leads us with a shep - herd's care.
guides us with a fa - ther's strength.
nur - tures with a moth - er's love.

Text: James J. Chepponis, b.1956
Tune: James J. Chepponis, b.1956
© 1992, GIA Publications, Inc.

Surely It Is God Who Saves Me   739

1. Sure - ly it is God who
2. Make his deeds known to the

saves me; Trust-ing him, I shall not fear. For the
peo - ples; Tell out his ex - alt - ed Name. Praise the

Lord de - fends and shields me And his sav - ing help is
Lord, who has done great things; All his works his might pro -

near. So re - joice as you draw wa - ter From sal -
claim. Zi - on, lift your voice in sing - ing; For with

va - tion's liv - ing spring; In the day of your de -
you has come to dwell, In your ver - y midst, the

liv - 'rance Thank the Lord, his mer - cies sing.
great and Ho - ly One of Is - ra - el.

Text: Isaiah 12:1-6; Carl P. Daw, Jr., b.1944, © 1982, Hope Publishing Co.
Tune: RAQUEL, 8 7 8 7 D; Skinner Chávez-Melo, 1944-1992, © 1987, Estate of Skinner Chávez-Melo

740 On Eagle's Wings

Verse 3

3. You need not fear the ter - ror of the night, nor the ar - row that flies by day; though thou - sands fall a - bout you, near you it shall not come.

D.S.

Verse 4

4. For to his an - gels he's giv - en a com - mand to guard you in all of your ways; up - on their hands they will bear you up, lest you dash your foot a - gainst a stone.

D.S.

Coda

And hold you, hold you in the palm of his hand.

Text: Psalm 91; Michael Joncas, b.1951
Tune: Michael Joncas, b.1951
© 1979, OCP Publications

741 A Mighty Fortress Is Our God

1. A might-y for-tress is our God, A sword and
2. No strength of ours can match his might! We would be
3. Though hordes of dev-ils fill the land All threat-n'ing
4. God's Word for-ev-er shall a-bide, No thanks to

shield vic-to-rious, Who breaks the cruel op-pres-sor's
lost, re-ject-ed. But now a cham-pion comes to
to de-vour us, We trem-ble not, un-moved we
foes, who fear it; For God, our Lord, fights by our

rod And wins sal-va-tion glo-rious. The old sa-
fight, Whom God a-lone e-lect-ed. You ask who
stand; They can-not o-ver-pow'r us. Let this world's
side With weap-ons of the Spir-it. Were they to

tan-ic foe Has sworn to work us woe!
this may be? The Lord of hosts is he!
ty-rant rage; In bat-tle we'll en-gage!
take our house, Goods, hon-or, child, or spouse,

With craft and dread-ful might He arms him-
Christ Je-sus, might-y Lord, God's on-ly
His might is doomed to fail; God's judge-ment
Though life be wrenched a-way, They can-not

self to fight. On earth he has no e-qual.
Son, a-dored. He holds the field vic-to-rious.
must pre-vail! One lit-tle word sub-dues him.
win the day. The King-dom's ours for-ev-er!

Text: Psalm (45) 46; *Ein' feste Burg ins unser Gott;* Martin Luther, 1483-1546; tr. © 1978, *Lutheran Book of Worship*
Tune: EIN' FESTE BURG, 8 7 8 7 66 66 7; Martin Luther, 1483-1546; harm. by J.S. Bach, 1685-1750

There's a Wideness in God's Mercy 742

1. There's a wide-ness in God's mer-cy Like the wide-ness
2. For the love of God is broad-er Than the meas-ures
3. Trou-bled souls, why will you scat-ter Like a crowd of

of the sea; There's a kind-ness in God's jus-tice
of our mind, And the heart of the E-ter-nal
fright-ened sheep? Fool-ish hearts, why will you wan-der

Which is more than lib-er-ty. There is plen-ti-
Is most won-der-ful-ly kind. If our love were
From a love so true and deep? There is wel-come

ful re-demp-tion In the blood that has been shed;
but more sim-ple We should take him at his word,
for the sin-ner And more grac-es for the good;

There is joy for all the mem-bers
And our lives would be thanks-giv-ing
There is mer-cy with the Sav-ior,

In the sor-rows of the Head.
For the good-ness of our Lord.
There is heal-ing in his blood.

Text: Frederick W. Faber, 1814-1863, alt.
Tune: IN BABILONE, 8 7 8 7 D; *Oude en Nieuwe Hollanste Boerenlities*, c.1710

743 Love Divine, All Loves Excelling

1. Love di - vine, all loves ex - cel - ling,
2. Come, al - might - y to de - liv - er,
3. Fin - ish then your new cre - a - tion,

Joy of heav'n to earth come down!
Let us all your life re - ceive;
Pure and spot - less, gra - cious Lord,

Fix in us your hum - ble dwell - ing,
Sud - den - ly re - turn and nev - er,
Let us see your great sal - va - tion

All your faith - ful mer - cies crown.
Nev - er more your tem - ples leave.
Per - fect - ly in you re - stored.

Je - sus, source of all com - pas - sion,
Lord, we would be al - ways bless - ing,
Changed from glo - ry in - to glo - ry,

Love un - bound - ed, love all pure;
Serve you as your hosts a - bove,
Till in heav'n we take our place,

Vis - it us with your sal - va - tion,
Pray, and praise you with - out ceas - ing,
Till we sing be - fore the al - might - y

Let your love in us en - dure.
Glo - ry in your pre - cious love.
Lost in won - der, love and praise.

Text: Charles Wesley, 1707-1788, alt.
Tune: HYFRYDOL, 8 7 8 7 D; Rowland H. Prichard, 1811-1887

LOVE

God Is Love 744

Refrain

God is love, and all who live in love, live in God.

Verse 1

1. God is light, in God there is no dark-ness. Come
live in the love of the Lord.

Verse 2

2. Come to the Lord, re-ceive the light, and
live in the love of the Lord.

Verse 3

3. We are called to be God's own chil-dren, to
live in the love of the Lord.

Verse 4

4. All of you are one, u-nit-ed in Je-sus, to
live in the love of the Lord.

D.C.

Text: 1 John 1:5, 3:2, 4:15, Psalm 33:6, Galatians 3:28; David Haas, b.1957
Tune: David Haas, b.1957
© 1987, GIA Publications, Inc.

745 Love One Another

Refrain

Love one an - oth - er, for love is of God.

Love one an - oth - er, for God is love.

Verses

1. God loved the world so much he sent us his only son,
   that all who believe in him might have eternal life.

2. Since God has given his love to us, therefore let us love one another.
   If we love one another, God will love us, and live in us in perfect love.

3. Ev'ryone who loves is begotten of God and knows him as the Father.
   But they who do not love do not know God, for God is love.

4. Let not your hearts be troubled, for love has no room for fear.
   In love all fear is forgotten, for God is here with us.

5. God is love, and they who abide in love,
   abide in God, and God in them.

Text:1 John 4; James J. Chepponis, b.1956
Tune: James J. Chepponis, b.1956
© 1983, GIA Publications, Inc.

746 Ubi Caritas

Refrain

U - bi ca - ri - tas et a - mor,
Live in char - i - ty and stead - fast love,

u - bi ca - ri - tas De - us i - bi est.
live in char - i - ty; *God will dwell with you.*

Text: 1 Corinthians 13:2-8; *Where charity and love are found, God is there;* Taizé Community, 1978
Tune: Jacques Berthier, 1923-1994
© 1979, Les Presses de Taizé, GIA Publications, Inc., agent

Where Charity and Love Prevail 747

1. Where char - i - ty and love pre - vail,
2. With grate - ful joy and ho - ly fear
3. For - give we now each oth - er's faults
4. Let strife a - mong us be un - known,
5. Let us re - call that in our midst
6. No race nor creed can love ex - clude,

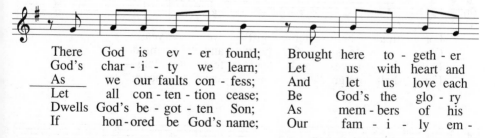

There God is ev - er found; Brought here to - geth - er
God's char - i - ty we learn; Let us with heart and
As we our faults con - fess; And let us love each
Let all con - ten - tion cease; Be God's the glo - ry
Dwells God's be - got - ten Son; As mem - bers of his
If hon - ored be God's name; Our fam - i - ly em -

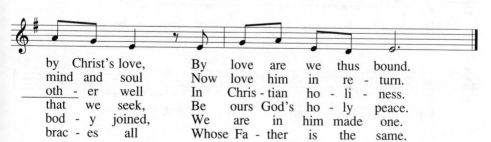

by Christ's love, By love are we thus bound.
mind and soul Now love him in re - turn.
oth - er well In Chris - tian ho - li - ness.
that we seek, Be ours God's ho - ly peace.
bod - y joined, We are in him made one.
brac - es all Whose Fa - ther is the same.

Text: *Ubi caritas;* trans. by Omer Westendorf, 1916-1998
Tune: CHRISTIAN LOVE, CM; Paul Benoit, OSB, 1893-1979
© 1960, 1961, World Library Publications, Inc.

748 May Love Be Ours

1. Not for tongues of heav - en's an - gels,
2. Love is hum - ble, love is gen - tle,
3. Nev - er jeal - ous, nev - er self - ish,
4. In the day this world is fad - ing,

Not for wis - dom to dis - cern,
Love is ten - der, true, and kind;
Love will not re - joice in wrong;
Faith and hope will play their part;

Not for faith that mas - ters moun - tains,
Love is gra - cious, ev - er pa - tient,
Nev - er boast - ful nor re - sent - ful,
But when Christ is seen in glo - ry,

For this bet - ter gift we yearn:
Gen - er - ous of heart and mind—
Love be - lieves and suf - fers long—
Love shall reign in ev - 'ry heart:

May love be ours, Lord; may love be ours.

May love be ours, O Lord.

Text: Timothy Dudley-Smith, b.1926, © 1985, Hope Publishing Co.
Tune: COMFORT, 8 7 8 7 with refrain; Michael Joncas, b.1951, © 1988, GIA Publications, Inc.

What Wondrous Love Is This   749

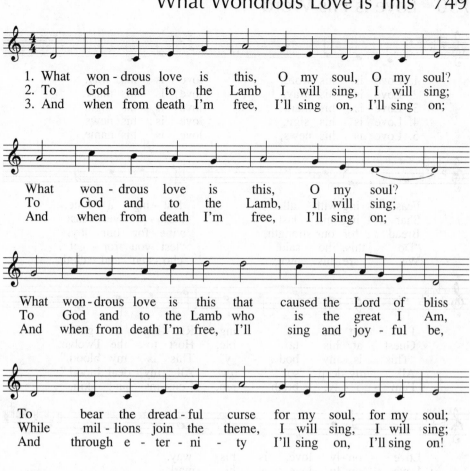

1. What won-drous love is this, O my soul, O my soul?
2. To God and to the Lamb I will sing, I will sing;
3. And when from death I'm free, I'll sing on, I'll sing on;

What won - drous love is this, O my soul?
To God and to the Lamb, I will sing;
And when from death I'm free, I'll sing on;

What won-drous love is this that caused the Lord of bliss
To God and to the Lamb who is the great I Am,
And when from death I'm free, I'll sing and joy - ful be,

To bear the dread - ful curse for my soul, for my soul;
While mil - lions join the theme, I will sing, I will sing;
And through e - ter - ni - ty I'll sing on, I'll sing on!

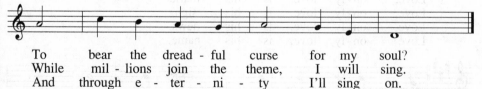

To bear the dread - ful curse for my soul?
While mil - lions join the theme, I will sing.
And through e - ter - ni - ty I'll sing on.

Text: Alexander Means, 1801-1853
Tune: WONDROUS LOVE, 12 9 12 12 9; *Southern Harmony*, 1835; harm. from *Cantate Domino, 1980*, © 1980, World Council of Churches

750 Love Is His Word

1. Love is his word, love is his way.
2. Love is his way, love is his mark.
3. Love is his mark, love is his sign.
4. Love is his sign, love is his news.
5. Love is his news, love is his name.

Feast - ing with all, fast - ing a - lone,
Shar - ing his last Pass - o - ver feast.
Bread for our strength, wine for our joy.
"Do this," he said, "lest you for - get
We are his own, cho - sen and called,

Liv - ing and dy - ing, Ris - ing a - gain.
Guest at his ta - ble, Host to the Twelve,
"This is my bod - y, This is my blood."
All my deep sor - row, All my dear blood."
Fam - i - ly, breth - ren, Cous - ins and kin.

Love, on - ly love, is his way.
Love, on - ly love, is his mark.
Love, on - ly love, is his sign.
Love, on - ly love, is his news.
Love, on - ly love, is his name.

Rich - er than gold is the love of my Lord,

bet - ter than splen - dor and wealth.

Rich - er than gold is the love of my Lord,

bet - ter   than   splen - dor   and   wealth.

6. Love is his name, love is his law.
   Hear his command, all who are his:
   "Love one another, I have loved you."
   Love, only love, is his law.

7. Love is his law, love is his word:
   Love of the Lord, Father and Word.
   Love of the Spirit, God ev'ry one.
   Love, only love, is his word.

Text: Luke Connaughton, 1917-1979, © 1970, Mayhew McCrimmon, Ltd.
Tune: JULINORMA, 4 4 8 5 4 7 with refrain; Robert M. Hutmacher, OFM, b.1948, © 1986, GIA Publications, Inc.

Lord of All Nations, Grant Me Grace   751

1. Lord of all na - tions, grant me grace To love all
2. Break down the wall that would di - vide Your chil - dren,
3. For - give me, Lord, where I have erred By love - less
4. Give me your cour - age, Lord, to speak When - ev - er
5. With your own love may I be filled And by your

peo - ple, ev - 'ry race To see each mor - tal as I
Lord, on ev - 'ry side. My neigh- bor's good let me pur -
act and thought-less word. Make me to see the wrong I
strong op - press the weak. Should I my - self as vic - tim
Ho - ly Spir - it willed, That all whose lives are touched by

ought, My kin - dred, whom your love has bought.
sue, Let Chris - tian love bind warm and true.
do Will cru - ci - fy my Lord a - new.
live, Re - mem - b'ring you, may I for - give.
mine, May know your heal - ing touch di - vine.

Text: Philippians 2:1-18; Olive W. Spannaus, b.1916, © 1969, Concordia Publishing House
Tune: BEATUS VIR, LM; Slovak; harm. by Richard Hillert, b.1923, © 1969, Concordia Publishing House

752 Where True Love and Charity Are Found / Ubi Caritas

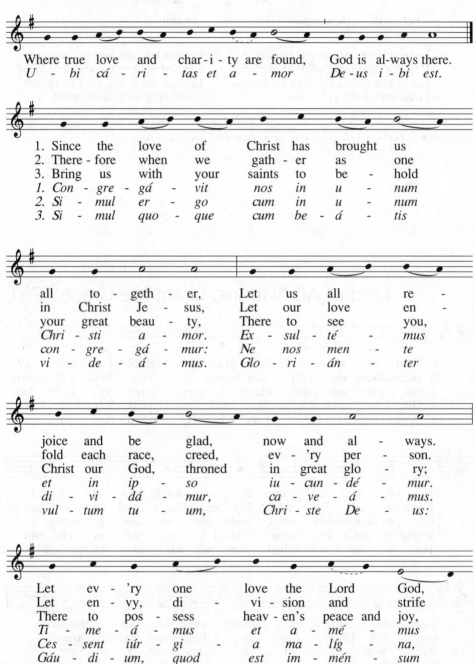

Where true love and char-i-ty are found, God is al-ways there.
U - bi cá - ri - tas et a - mor De-us i - bi est.

1. Since the love of Christ has brought us
2. There - fore when we gath - er as one
3. Bring us with your saints to be - hold
1. Con - gre - gá - vit nos in u - num
2. Si - mul er - go cum in u - num
3. Si - mul quo - que cum be - á - tis

all to - geth - er, Let us all re -
in Christ Je - sus, Let our love en -
your great beau - ty, There to see you,
Chri - sti a - mor. Ex - sul - té - mus
con - gre - gá - mur: Ne nos men - te
vi - de - á - mus. Glo - ri - án - ter

joice and be glad, now and al - ways.
fold each race, creed, ev - 'ry per - son.
Christ our God, throned in great glo - ry;
et in ip - so iu - cun - dé - mur.
di - vi - dá - mur, ca - ve - á - mus.
vul - tum tu - um, Chri - ste De - us:

Let ev - 'ry one love the Lord God,
Let en - vy, di - vi - sion and strife
There to pos - sess heav - en's peace and joy,
Ti - me - á - mus et a - mé - mus
Ces - sent iúr - gi - a ma - líg - na,
Gáu - di - um, quod est im - mén - sum

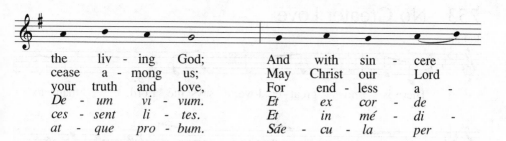

the   liv - ing   God;   And   with   sin - cere
cease   a - mong   us;   May   Christ   our   Lord
your   truth   and   love,   For   end - less   a -
De - *um*   *vi* - *vum.*   *Et*   *ex*   *cor* - *de*
ces - *sent*   *li* - *tes.*   *Et*   *in*   *mé* - *di* -
at - *que*   *pro* - *bum.*   *Sáe* - *cu* - *la*   *per*

D.C.

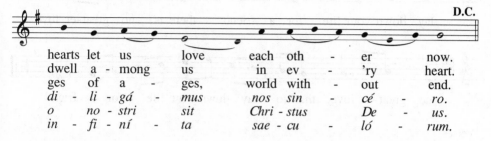

hearts let   us   love   each   oth - er   now.
dwell   a - mong   us   in   ev - 'ry   heart.
ges   of   a -   ges,   world   with - out   end.
di - *li* - *gá* -   *mus*   *nos*   *sin* - *cé* - *ro.*
o   *no* - *stri* *sit*   *Chri* - *stus* *De* - *us.*
in - *fi* - *ní* -   *ta*   *sae* - *cu* - *ló* - *rum.*

Text: Latin, 9th C.; tr. by Richard Proulx, b.1937, © 1975, 1986, GIA Publications, Inc.
Tune: UBI CARITAS, 12 12 12 12 with refrain; Mode VI; acc. by Richard Proulx, b.1937, © 1986, GIA Publications, Inc.

753 No Greater Love

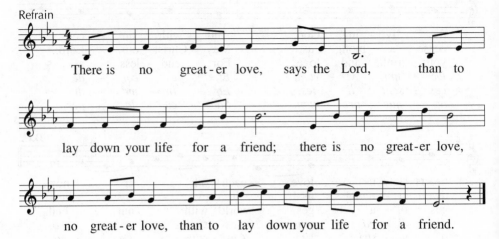

Refrain

There is no great-er love, says the Lord, than to

lay down your life for a friend; there is no great-er love,

no great-er love, than to lay down your life for a friend.

Verses

1. As the Father has loved me, so I have loved you.
   Live on in my love.
   You will live in my love if you keep my commands,
   even as I have kept my Father's.

2. All this I tell you that my joy may be yours
   and your joy may be complete.
   Love one another as I have loved you:
   This is my command.

3. You are my friends if you keep my commands;
   no longer slaves but friends to me.
   All I heard from my Father,
   I have made known to you: Now I call you friends.

4. It was not you who chose me, it was I who chose you,
   chose you to go forth and bear fruit.
   Your fruit must endure, so you will receive
   all you ask the Father in my name.

Text: John 15:9-17; Michael Joncas, b.1951
Tune: Michael Joncas, b.1951
© 1988, GIA Publications, Inc.

Precious Lord, Take My Hand 754

1. Pre - cious Lord, take my hand, Lead me on, let me
2. When my way grows drear, Pre - cious Lord, lin - ger
3. When the dark - ness ap-pears And the night draws

stand, I am tired, I am weak, I am
near, When my life is al - most
near, And the day is past and

worn. Through the storm, through the
gone, Hear my cry, hear my
gone, At the riv - er I

night, Lead me on to the light, Take my
call, Hold my hand lest I fall. Take my
stand, Guide my feet, hold my hand. Take my

hand, pre - cious Lord, lead me home.
hand, pre - cious Lord, lead me home.
hand, pre - cious Lord, lead me home.

Text: Thomas A. Dorsey, 1899-1993
Tune: PRECIOUS LORD 66 9 D; Thomas A. Dorsey, 1899-1993; arr. by Kelly Dobbs Mickus, b. 1966
© 1938, Unichappell Music, Inc.

755 Jesus, Lead the Way

1. Je - sus, lead the way Through our life's long day,
2. Je - sus be our light, In the midst of night,
3. When in deep - est grief, Strength - en our be - lief.
4. Je - sus, still lead on 'Til our rest be won:

When at times the way is cheer - less,
Let not faith - less fear o'er - take us,
When temp - ta - tions come al - lur - ing,
If you lead us through rough plac - es,

Help us fol - low, calm and fear - less;
Let not faith and hope for - sake us;
Make us pa - tient and en - dur - ing;
Grant us your re - deem - ing grac - es.

Guide us by your hand To the prom - ised land.
May we feel you near As we wor - ship here.
Lord we seek your grace In this ho - ly place.
When our course is o'er, O - pen heav - en's door.

Text: *Jesu, geh voran;* Nicholas L. von Zinzendorf, 1700-1760; tr. by Jane Borthwick, 1813-1897, alt.
Tune: ROCHELLE, 55 88 55; Adam Drese, 1620-1701; harm. alt.

756 Shepherd Me, O God

Refrain

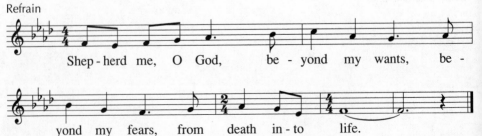

Shep - herd me, O God, be - yond my wants, be -

yond my fears, from death in - to life.

Verses

1. God is my shepherd, so nothing shall I want,
   I rest in the meadows of faithfulness and love,
   I walk by the quiet waters of peace.

2. Gently you raise me and heal my weary soul,
   you lead me by pathways of righteousness and truth,
   my spirit shall sing the music of your name.

3. Though I should wander the valley of death,
   I fear no evil, for you are at my side, your rod and your staff,
   my comfort and my hope.

4. You have set me a banquet of love in the face of hatred,
   crowning me with love beyond my pow'r to hold.

5. Surely your kindness and mercy follow me all the days of my life;
   I will dwell in the house of my God for evermore.

Text: Psalm 23; Marty Haugen
Music: Marty Haugen
© 1986, GIA Publications, Inc.

Nada Te Turbe / Nothing Can Trouble   757

Na - da te tur - be, na - da te_es-pan - te. Quien a Dios tie - ne
Noth-ing can trou-ble, noth-ing can fright-en. Those who seek God shall

na - da   le fal - ta.   So - lo Dios   bas - ta.
nev-er   go want - ing.   God a - lone   fills   us.

Text: St. Teresa of Jesus; Taizé Community, 1986, 1991
Tune: Jacques Berthier, 1923-1994
© 1986, 1991, Les Presses de Taizé, GIA Publications, Inc., agent

758 Eye Has Not Seen

Refrain

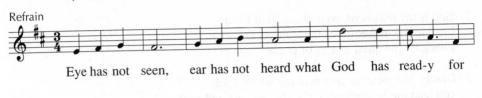

Eye has not seen, ear has not heard what God has read-y for

those who love him; Spir-it of love, come, give us the mind of

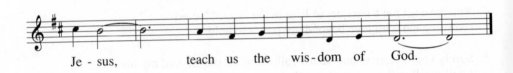

Je - sus, teach us the wis-dom of God.

Verses 1-3

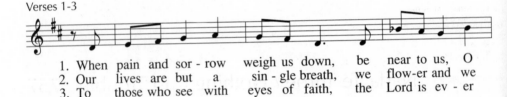

1. When pain and sor - row weigh us down, be near to us, O
2. Our lives are but a sin - gle breath, we flow-er and we
3. To those who see with eyes of faith, the Lord is ev - er

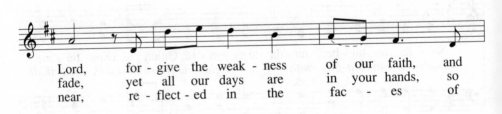

Lord, for - give the weak - ness of our faith, and
fade, yet all our days are in your hands, so
near, re - flect - ed in the fac - es of

D.C.

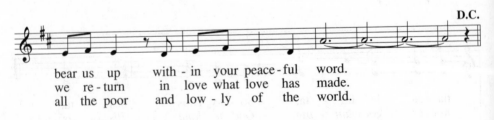

bear us up with - in your peace-ful word.
we re - turn in love what love has made.
all the poor and low - ly of the world.

Verse 4

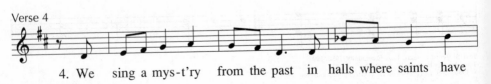

4. We sing a mys-t'ry from the past in halls where saints have

trod, yet ev - er new the mu - sic rings to

Je - sus, Liv - ing Song of God.

D.C.

Text: 1 Corinthians 2:9-10; Marty Haugen, b.1950
Tune: Marty Haugen, b.1950
© 1982, GIA Publications, Inc.

O Jesus, Joy of Loving Hearts 759

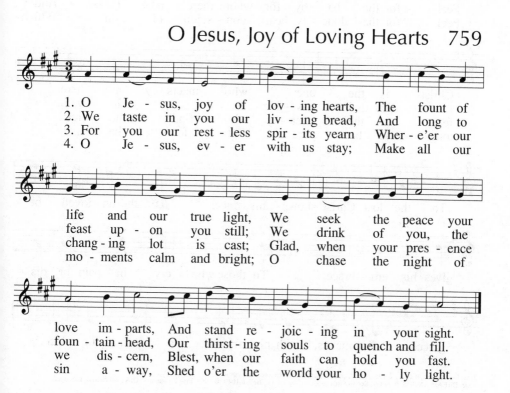

1. O Je - sus, joy of lov - ing hearts, The fount of
2. We taste in you our liv - ing bread, And long to
3. For you our rest - less spir - its yearn Wher - e'er our
4. O Je - sus, ev - er with us stay; Make all our

life and our true light, We seek the peace your
feast up - on you still; We drink of you, the
chang - ing lot is cast; Glad, when your pres - ence
mo - ments calm and bright; O chase the night of

love im - parts, And stand re - joic - ing in your sight.
foun - tain - head, Our thirst - ing souls to quench and fill.
we dis - cern, Blest, when our faith can hold you fast.
sin a - way, Shed o'er the world your ho - ly light.

Text: *Jesu, delcedo cordium*; attr. to Bernard of Clairvaux, 1091-1153; para. by Ray Palmer, 1808-1887, alt.
Tune: WAREHAM, LM; William Knapp, 1698-1768

760 A Touching Place

1. Christ's is the world in which we move,
2. Feel for the peo-ple we most a-void,
3. Feel for the par-ents who've lost their child,
4. Feel for the lives by life con-fused,

Christ's are the folk we're sum-moned to love,
Strange or be-reaved or nev-er em-ployed;
Feel for the wom-en whom men have de-filed,
Rid-dled with doubt, in lov-ing a-bused;

Christ's is the voice which calls us to care, And
Feel for the wom-en, and feel for the men Who
Feel for the ba-by for whom there's no breast, And
Feel for the lone-ly heart, con-scious of sin, Which

Christ is the one who meets us here.
fear that their liv-ing is all in vain.
feel for the wea-ry who find no rest.
longs to be pure but fears to be-gin.

To the lost Christ shows his face; To the un-loved he

gives his em-brace; To those who cry in pain or dis-

grace, Christ makes, with his friends, a touch-ing place.

Text: John L. Bell, b.1949, © 1989, Iona Community, GIA Publications, Inc., agent
Tune: DREAM ANGUS, Irregular; Scottish folk song; acc. by John L. Bell, b.1949, © 1993, Iona Community, GIA Publications, Inc., agent

My Shepherd Will Supply My Need 761

1. My Shep - herd will sup - ply my need; The
2. When I walk through the shades of death, Your
3. The sure pro - vi - sions of my God At -

God of love su - preme; In pas - tures green you
pres - ence is my stay; One word of your sup -
tend me all my days; O may your house be

make me feed, Be - side the liv - ing stream. You
port - ing breath Drives all my fears a - way. Your
my a - bode, And all my work be praise! There

bring my wan - d'ring spir - it back, When I for -
hand, in sight of all my foes, Does still my
would I find a set - tled rest, While oth - ers

sake your ways; In paths of truth and grace.
ta - ble spread; My cup with bless - ings
go and come, No more a stran - ger

mer - cy's sake, In paths of truth and grace.
o - ver - flows, Your oil a - noints my head.
nor a guest; But like a child at home.

Text: Psalm 23; Isaac Watts, 1674-1748, alt.
Tune: RESIGNATION, CMD; Funk's *Compilation of Genuine Church Music*, 1832; harm. by Richard Proulx, b.1937, © 1975, GIA Publications, Inc.

762 You Are Mine

Verses

1. I will come to you in the si - lence,
2. I am hope for all who are hope - less,
3. I am strength for all the de - spair - ing,
4. am the Word that leads all to free - dom, I

I will lift you from all your fear. In the
I am eyes for all who long to see.
heal - ing for the ones who dwell in shame.
am the peace the world can - not give.

You will hear my voice, I claim you as my choice, be
shad - ows of the night, I will be your light,
All the blind will see, the lame will all run free, and
I will call your name, em - brac - ing all your pain, stand

still and know I am here. *(To verse 2)*
come and rest in me. *(To refrain)*
all will know my name. *(To refrain)*
up, now walk, and live! *(To refrain)*

Refrain

Do not be a - fraid, I am with you. I have called you

each by name. Come and fol - low me, I will bring you

D.C.

home; I love you and you are mine.

4. I

Text: David Haas, b.1957
Tune: David Haas, b.1957
© 1991, GIA Publications, Inc.

Come to Me 763

Refrain

Come to me, come to me, come when you are wea - ry;
come to me, come to me, and I will give you rest.

Verses 1, 2

1. All who la - bor and are bur - dened,
2. Take my yoke up - on your shoul - ders,

all who la - bor and are bur - dened, let them come to me,
take my yoke up - on your shoul - ders, come and learn from me,

come to me, and I will give them rest.
learn from me, for I am gen - tle of heart.

Verse 3

3. For the heart I hold is hum - ble, yes, the

heart I hold is hum - ble, and my yoke is eas - y, my

bur - den light, and you will find rest for your souls.

D.C.

Text: Matthew 11:28-30; Michael Joncas, b.1951
Tune: Michael Joncas, b.1951
© 1989, GIA Publications, Inc.

764 There Is a Balm in Gilead

Refrain

There is a balm in Gil-e-ad To make the wound-ed whole,

There is a balm in Gil-e-ad To heal the sin-sick soul.

Verses

1. Some - times I feel dis - cour - aged   And
2. If you can - not preach like Pe - ter,   If you
3. Don't ev - er feel dis - cour - aged,   For

think my work's in vain,   But then the Ho - ly
can - not pray like Paul,   You can tell the love of
Je - sus is your friend;   And if you lack for

D.C.

Spir - it Re - vives my soul a - gain.
Je - sus, And say, "He died for all!"
knowl-edge He'll ne'er re - fuse to lend.

Text: Jeremiah 8:22, African-American spiritual
Tune: BALM IN GILEAD, Irregular; African-American spiritual; acc. by Robert J. Batastini, b.1942, © 1987, GIA Publications, Inc.

765 Shelter Me, O God

Refrain

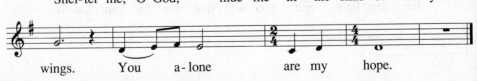

Shel-ter me, O God; hide me in the shad-ow of your

wings. You a-lone are my hope.

Verses

1. When my foes sur - round me, set me high a - bove their
2. As a moth - er gath - ers her young be - neath her
3. Though I walk in dark - ness, through the nee - dle's eye of

reach. Hear me when I call your name.
care, gath - er me in - to your arms.
death, you will nev - er leave my side.

Text: Psalm 16, 61, Luke 13:34; Bob Hurd, b.1950, © 1984
Tune: Bob Hurd, b.1950, © 1984; harm. by Dominic MacAller, © 1989, OCP Publications
Published by OCP Publications

The King of Love My Shepherd Is 766

1. The King of love my shep - herd is, Whose good-ness
2. Where streams of liv - ing wa - ter flow My ran-somed
3. Con - fused and fool - ish oft I strayed, But yet in
4. In death's dark vale I fear no ill With you, dear
5. You spread a ta - ble in my sight; Your sav - ing
6. And so through all the length of days Your good-ness

fails me nev - er; I noth - ing lack if
soul he's lead - ing, And where the ver - dant
love he sought me; And on his shoul - der
Lord, be - side me, Your rod and staff my
grace be - stow - ing; And O what trans - port
fails me nev - er; Good Shep - herd, may I

I am his, And he is mine for ev - er.
pas - tures grow With food ce - les - tial feed - ing.
gent - ly laid, And home, re - joic - ing, brought me.
com - fort still, Your cross be - fore to guide me.
of de - light From your pure chal - ice flow - ing!
sing your praise With - in your house for ev - er.

Text: Psalm 23; Henry W. Baker, 1821-1877, alt.
Tune: ST. COLUMBA, 8 7 8 7; Gaelic; harm. by A. Gregory Murray, OSB, 1905-1992, © Downside Abbey

767 Within Our Darkest Night

Within our darkest night, you kindle the fire that never dies away, never dies away. Within our darkest night, you kindle the fire that never dies away, never dies away.

Text: Taizé Community, 1991
Tune: Jacques Berthier, 1923-1994
© 1991, Les Presses de Taizé, GIA Publications, Inc., agent

I Heard the Voice of Jesus Say 768

1. I heard the voice of Je - sus say, "Come
2. I heard the voice of Je - sus say, "Be -
3. I heard the voice of Je - sus say, "I

un - to me and rest; Lay down, O wea - ry
hold, I free - ly give The liv - ing wa - ter;
am this dark world's light; Look un - to me, your

one, lay down Your head up - on my breast." I
thirst - y one, Stoop down, and drink, and live." I
morn shall rise, And all your day be bright." I

came to Je - sus as I was, So
came to Je - sus, and I drank Of
looked to Je - sus, and I found In

wea - ry, worn, and sad; I found in him a
that life - giv - ing stream; My thirst was quenched, my
him my star, my sun; And in that light of

rest - ing place, And he has made me glad.
soul re - vived, And now I live in him.
life I'll walk Till trav - 'ling days are done.

Text: Horatius Bonar, 1808-1889
Tune: KINGSFOLD, CMD; English; harm. by Ralph Vaughan Williams, 1872-1958

769 Come to Me, O Weary Traveler

1. Come to me, O wea - ry trav - 'ler; Come to me with
2. Do not fear, my yoke is eas - y; Do not fear, my
3. Take my yoke and leave your trou - bles; Take my yoke and
4. Rest in me, O wea - ry trav - 'ler; Rest in me and

your dis - tress; Come to me, you heav - y bur-dened;
bur - den's light; Do not fear the path be - fore you;
come with me. Take my yoke, I am be - side you;
do not fear. Rest in me, my heart is gen - tle;

Come to me and find your rest.
Do not run from me in fright.
Take and learn hu - mil - i - ty.
Rest and cast a - way your care.

Text: Matthew 11:28-30; Sylvia G. Dunstan, 1955-1993, © 1991, GIA Publications, Inc.
Tune: DUNSTAN, 8 7 8 7; Bob Moore, b.1962, © 1993, GIA Publications, Inc.

770 Jesus, Remember Me

Ostinato Refrain

Je - sus, re - mem - ber me when you come in - to your King - dom.

Je - sus, re - mem-ber me when you come in - to your King - dom.

Text: Luke 23:42; Taizé Community, 1981
Tune: Jacques Berthier, 1923-1994
© 1981, Les Presses de Taizé, GIA Publications, Inc., agent

I Will Not Die 771

Verses

1., 5. I will not die be-fore I've lived to see that land;
2. I will not rest un-til your dawn is in my eyes;
3. And I will breathe in that might - y wind of jus - tice;
4. You will stand up for the poor and the need - y;

firm as the earth, your own prom - ise.
that frag - ile light, new like morn - ing.
I'll know my name and rise up sing - ing.
you'll break the chains that bind your peo - ple.

I'll not let go un - til I've held it in my hand;
I will not sleep be-fore I've wak - ened to that sun - rise;
And I will call un - til my words bring on the thun - der;
For you are home for the lost and the des-p'rate;

that word of hope, and gen - tle laugh - ter.
and all the world knows your glo - ry.
washed in that rain, then I'll know you.
your strong right hand goes be - fore us.

Refrain

For your right hand has de - liv-ered us from death;

You have re - gard - ed our tears,

3

D.C.

you who are good - ness and grace.

Text: Tom Conry, b.1951, alt.
Tune: Tom Conry, b.1951; acc. by Patrick Loomis, 1951-1990
© 1984, 1990, TEAM Publications. Published by OCP Publications

772   Bring Forth the Kingdom

Verses

Cantor:

1. You are salt for the earth, O peo - ple:
2. You are a light on the hill, O peo - ple:
3. You are a seed of the Word, O peo - ple:
4. We are a blest and a pil - grim peo - ple:

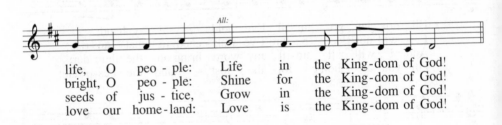

All: *Cantor:*

Salt for the King-dom of God! Share the fla - vor of
Light for the Cit - y of God! Shine so ho - ly and
Bring forth the King-dom of God! Seeds of mer - cy and
Bound for the King-dom of God! Love our jour-ney and

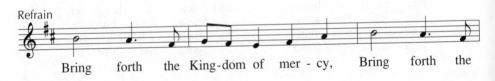

All:

life, O peo - ple: Life in the King-dom of God!
bright, O peo - ple: Shine for the King-dom of God!
seeds of jus - tice, Grow in the King-dom of God!
love our home - land: Love is the King-dom of God!

Refrain

Bring forth the King-dom of mer - cy, Bring forth the

King-dom of peace; Bring forth the King-dom of jus - tice,

Bring forth the Cit - y of God!

Text: Marty Haugen, b.1950
Tune: Marty Haugen, b.1950
© 1986, GIA Publications, Inc.

When Jesus Came Preaching 773

1. When Je - sus came preach-ing the   King-dom of God   With the
2. Since Je - sus came preach-ing the   King-dom of God,   What a
3. Still   Je - sus comes preach-ing the   King-dom of God   In   a

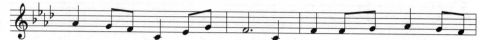

love   that has pow'r to per - suade, The   sick were made whole, both in
change in our lives he has made! How   man - y   have shared in the
world that is sick and a - fraid; His   gos - pel   has spread like the

bod - y and soul,   And   e - ven the de - mons o -
joy of their Lord,   In self - giv - ing have loved and o -
leav - en in bread   By the love that has a pow'r to per -

beyed.   But he need-ed a few he could trust to be true, To
beyed!   But let none of us doubt what re - li - gion's a-bout, Or by
suade.   So let none of us swerve from our mis - sion to serve, That has

share in his work from the start: When Je - sus came preach-ing the
what it is shamed and be - trayed: Do   just - ly, love mer - cy, walk
made us his Church from the start,   May Je - sus, the light of the

King - dom of God,   God's   gift to the hum-ble of   heart.
hum - bly with God,   Is   the   rule of life Je - sus o - beyed.
world, send us   out   In the strength of the hum-ble of   heart.

Text: Fred Pratt Green, b.1903, © 1974, Hope Publishing Co.
Tune: SAMANTHRA, 11 8 11 8 D; *Southern Harmony*, 1835; harm. by Austin C. Lovelace, b.1919, © 1986, GIA Publications, Inc.

774 Blest Are They

Verses 1-3

1. Blest are they, the poor in spir - it,
2. Blest are they, the low - ly ones,
3. Blest are they who show mer - cy,

theirs is the king - dom of God.
they shall in - her - it the earth.
mer - cy shall be theirs.

Blest are they, full of sor - row,
Blest are they who hun - ger and thirst,
Blest are they, the pure of heart,

they shall be con - soled.
they shall have their fill.
they shall see God!

𝄋 Refrain

Re - joice and be glad! Bless-ed are you,

ho - ly are you! Re - joice and be glad!

Yours is the king-dom of God!

Verses 4, 5

4. Blest are they who seek peace;
5. Blest are you who suf - fer hate,

they are the chil - dren of God.
all be - cause of me.

Re -

Blest are they who suf-fer in faith, the
joice and be glad, yours is the king-dom;

D.S.

glo-ry of God is theirs.
shine for all to see.

Text: Matthew 5:3-12; David Haas, b.1957
Tune: David Haas, b.1957; vocal arr. by David Haas and Michael Joncas, b.1951
© 1985, GIA Publications, Inc.

The Kingdom of God 775

1. The king-dom of God is jus-tice and joy;
2. The king-dom of God is mer-cy and grace;
3. The king-dom of God is chal-lenge and choice:
4. God's king-dom is come, the gift and the goal;

For Je-sus re-stores what sin would de-stroy.
The cap-tives are freed, the sin-ners find place,
Be-lieve the good news, re-pent and re-joice!
In Je-sus be-gun, in heav-en made whole.

God's pow-er and glo-ry in Je-sus we know;
The out-cast are wel-comed God's ban-quet to share;
God's love for us sin-ners brought Christ to his cross:
The heirs of the king-dom shall an-swer his call;

And here and here-af-ter the king-dom shall grow.
And hope is a-wak-ened in place of de-spair.
Our cri-sis of judge-ment for gain or for loss.
And all things cry "Glo-ry!" to God all in all.

Text: Bryn A. Rees, 1911-1983, © Mrs. Olwen Scott
Tune: LAUDATE DOMINUM, 10 10 11 11; Charles H. H. Parry, 1848-1918

776 Thy Kingdom Come

Verses

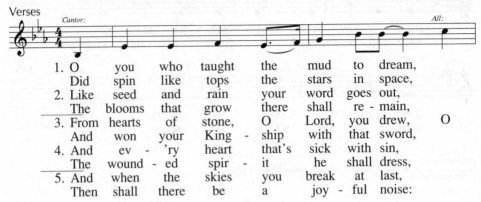

1. O you who taught the mud to dream,
   Did spin like tops the stars in space,
2. Like seed and rain your word goes out,
   The blooms that grow there shall re - main,
3. From hearts of stone, O Lord, you drew, O
   And won your King - ship with that sword,
4. And ev - 'ry heart that's sick with sin,
   The wound - ed spir - it he shall dress,
5. And when the skies you break at last,
   Then shall there be a joy - ful noise:

Lord, thy king-dom come.

And make the world with
Did guide their paths with
In gar - dens of the
Their scent the sign of your
The sword of sin that
That cut you down, O
The Heal - er King has
With balms of love and
Your king - dom come to
Your king - dom praise you

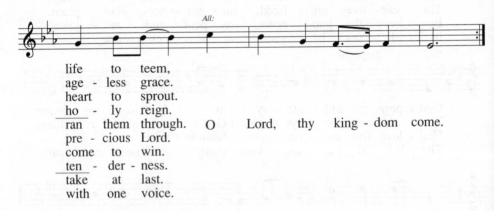

life to teem,
age - less grace.
heart to sprout.
ho - ly reign.
ran them through. O Lord, thy king - dom come.
pre - cious Lord.
come to win.
ten - der - ness.
take at last.
with one voice.

Refrain

We wait in joy, we wait in joy,

we wait in joy, like flow - ers wait the sun,

We wait in joy, we wait in joy, we wait in

joy and the spir-it, Lord, thy king-dom come!

Text: Rory Cooney, b.1952
Tune: Rory Cooney, b.1952
© 1983, North American Liturgy Resources. Published by OCP Publications.

777 Christ's Church Shall Glory

1. Christ's church shall glo - ry in his pow'r
2. Christ's peo - ple serve his way - ward world
3. Christ's liv - ing lamp shall bright - ly burn,
4. Christ's bod - y tri - umphs in his name;

And grow to his per - fec - tion; He is our
To whom he seems a stran - ger; He knows its
And to our earth - ly cit - y For - got - ten
One Fa - ther sov - 'reign giv - er, One Spir - it,

rock, our might - y tow'r Our life, our res - ur -
wel - come from of old, He shares our joy, our
beau - ty shall re - turn, And pu - ri - ty and
with his love a - flame, One Lord, the same for

rec - tion: So by his skill - ful hand
dan - ger: So strong, and yet so weak,
pit - y: To give the op - pressed their right
ev - er. To you, O God, our prize

The church of Christ shall stand; The mas - ter -
The church of Christ shall speak; His cross our
The church of Christ shall fight; And though the
The church of Christ shall rise Be - yond all

build - er's plan He works, as he be - gan,
great - est need, His word the vi - tal seed
years seem long He is our strength and song,
meas - ured height, To that e - ter - nal light

And soon will crown with splen - dor.
That brings a fruit - ful har - vest.
And he is our sal - va - tion.
Where Christ shall reign all - ho - ly.

Text: Christopher Idle, b.1938, © 1982, Jubilate Hymns, Ltd. (Administered by Hope Publishing Co.)
Tune: EIN' FESTE BURG, 8 7 8 7 66 66 7; Martin Luther, 1483-1546; harm. by J.S. Bach, 1685-1750

Christ Is Made the Sure Foundation 778

1. Christ is made the sure foun - da - tion,
2. To this tem - ple where we call you,
3. Here vouch - safe to all your ser - vants
4. Laud and hon - or to the Fa - ther,

Christ the head and cor - ner-stone; Cho - sen of the
Come, O Lord of hosts, to - day; With your wont - ed
What they ask of you to gain; What they gain from
Laud and hon - or to the Son, Laud and hon - or

Lord, and pre - cious, Bind - ing all the Church in one;
lov - ing kind - ness Hear your ser - vants as they pray,
you for ev - er With the bless - ed to re - tain,
to the Spir - it, Ev - er three and ev - er One,

Ho - ly Zi - on's help for ev - er,
And your full - est ben - e - dic - tion
And here - af - ter in your glo - ry
One in might and One in glo - ry,

And her con - fi - dence a - lone.
Shed in all its bright ar - ray.
Ev - er - more with you to reign.
While un - end - ing a - ges run.

Text: Latin hymn, c.7th C.; trans. by John M. Neale, 1818-1866, alt.
Tune: EDEN CHURCH, 8 7 8 7 8 7; Dale Wood, b.1934

779 As a Fire Is Meant for Burning

1. As a fire is meant for burn - ing With a
2. We are learn - ers; we are teach - ers; We are
3. As a green bud in the spring - time Is a

bright and warm-ing flame, So the church is meant for
pil - grims on the way. We are seek - ers; we are
sign of life re - newed, So may we be signs of

mis - sion, Giv - ing glo - ry to God's name.
giv - ers; We are ves - sels made of clay.
one - ness 'Mid earth's peo - ples, man - y hued.

Not to preach our creeds or cus - toms, But to
By our gen - tle, lov - ing ac - tions, We would
As a rain - bow lights the heav - ens When a

build a bridge of care, We join hands a - cross the
show that Christ is light. In a hum - ble, lis - t'ning
storm is past and gone, May our lives re - flect the

na - tions, Find-ing neigh - bors ev - 'ry - where.
Spir - it, We would live to God's de - light.
ra - diance Of God's new and glor - ious dawn.

Text: Ruth Duck, b.1947, © 1992, GIA Publications, Inc.
Tune: BEACH SPRING, 8 7 8 7 D; *The Sacred Harp*, 1844; harm. by Marty Haugen, b.1950, © 1985, GIA Publications, Inc.

Singing Songs of Expectation 780

1. Sing - ing songs of ex - pec - ta - tion,
2. One the light of God's own pres - ence,
3. One the strain the lips of thou - sands

On - ward goes the pil - grim band, Through the night of
O'er his ran - somed peo - ple shed, Chas - ing far the
Lift as from the heart of one; One the con - flict,

doubt and sor - row, March - ing to the prom - ised land.
gloom and ter - ror, Bright - 'ning all the path we tread:
one the per - il, One the march in God be - gun:

Clear be - fore us through the dark - ness Gleams and burns the
One the ob - ject of our jour - ney, One the faith which
One the glad - ness of re - joic - ing On the far e -

guid - ing light: Trust - ing God we march to - geth - er
nev - er tires, One the ear - nest look - ing for - ward,
ter - nal shore, Where the one al - might - y Fa - ther

Step - ping fear - less through the night.
One the hope our God in - spires.
Reigns in love for ev - er - more.

Text: Bernard Severin Ingeman, 1798-1862; tr. by Sabin Baring-Gould, 1834-1924, alt.
Tune: HOLY MANNA, 8 7 8 7 D; William Moore, fl. 1830; acc. by Marty Haugen, b.1950, © 1987, GIA Publications, Inc.

781 O Christ the Great Foundation

1. O Christ the great foun-da - tion On which your peo - ple stand To preach your true sal - va - tion In ev - 'ry age and land: Pour out your Ho - ly Spir - it To make us strong and pure, To keep the faith

2. Bap - tized in one con - fes - sion, One church in all the earth, We bear our Lord's im - pres - sion, The sign of sec - ond birth: One ho - ly peo - ple gath - ered In love be - yond our own, By grace we were

3. Where ty - rants' hold is tight - ened, Where strong de - vour the weak, Where in - no - cents are fright - ened, The right - eous fear to speak, There let your church a - wak - ing At - tack the pow'rs of sin And, all their ram -

4. This is the mo - ment glo - rious When he who once was dead Shall lead his church vic - to - rious, Their cham - pion and their head. The Lord of all cre - a - tion His heav'n - ly king - dom brings The fi - nal con -

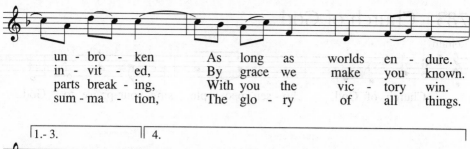

un - bro - ken	As	long	as	worlds	en - dure.
in - vit - ed,	By	grace	we	make	you	known.
parts break - ing,	With	you	the	vic - tory	win.
sum - ma - tion,	The	glo - ry	of	all	things.

1.- 3.   **4.**

A - men.

Text: Timothy T'ingfang Lew, 1891-1947, alt., © Christian Conference of Asia
Tune: ABREU; 76 76 D; Calvin Hampton, 1938-1984, © 1973, Concordia Publishing House

O Christ the Great Foundation   782

1. O   Christ the great foun - da - tion On   which your peo - ple stand
2. Bap - tized in   one con - fes - sion, One   church in   all   the earth,
3. Where ty - rants' hold is   tight - ened, Where strong de - vour the weak,
4. This   is   the mo - ment glo - rious When   he   who once was dead

To   preach your true sal - va - tion In   ev - 'ry age and   land:
We   bear   our Lord's im - pres - sion, The   sign   of   sec - ond   birth:
Where in - no - cents are fright - ened The   right-eous fear to   speak,
Shall lead   his church vic - to - rious, Their cham-pion and their   head.

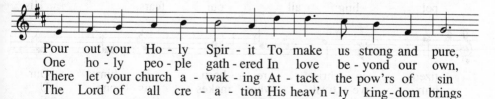

Pour   out your Ho - ly   Spir - it To   make   us strong and   pure,
One   ho - ly   peo - ple gath - ered In   love   be - yond our   own,
There   let your church a - wak - ing At - tack   the pow'rs of   sin
The   Lord of   all   cre - a - tion His heav'n - ly   king-dom brings

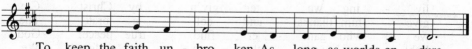

To   keep the faith un - bro - ken As   long as worlds en - dure.
By   grace we were in - vit - ed, By   grace we make you known.
And, all   their ram - parts break - ing, With   you the vic - tory   win.
The   fi - nal con - sum - ma - tion, The   glo - ry of   all   things.

Text: Timothy T'ingfang Lew, 1891-1947, alt., © Christian Conference of Asia
Tune: AURELIA, 7 6 7 6 D; Samuel Sebastian Wesley, 1810-1876

783 Church of God

Refrain

Church of God, cho - sen peo - ple, sing your praise to God.

He has called you out of dark-ness in - to his mar - vel-ous light.

Verses

1. Come, peo - ple of God, with joy - ful song, Praise
2. The church is built with liv - ing stones With
3. As heirs of Christ, re - deemed by love We
4. As wa - ter spring - ing from the rock Once
5. We gath - er here to wor - ship God, Our
6. May fra - grant smoke of in - cense rise To
7. The light of Christ has come to us Dis -

God the Fa - ther of all. Bap -
Christ as cor - ner - stone. In
wait for his re - turn; A
brought God's peo - ple life, The
eu - cha - rist to share. We
fill this house of prayer. May
pel - ling all our fears. His

tized in Christ, re - born in him, Our
him we trust who makes us one, U -
priest - ly peo - ple of - f'ring praise To
liv - ing wa - ter giv'n by Christ Cre -
give him thanks and cel - e - brate The
we who gath - er find true peace, God's
light re - veals the path of life. We

hearts	are	filled	with	joy.	He	cleans - es	our
nit - ing	us	in	love.	We	build	on the
God,	the	source	of	hope.	For	Je - sus is
ates	our	lives	a - new.	So	come	you who
mys - t'ry	of	his	love;	The	Word	is made
pres - ence	fill - ing	our	lives.	Our	hearts	lift with
fol - low	him	with	joy,	The	glo - ry of

sin,	Re - new - ing	our	lives.
rock	Of	faith	in	Christ.
Lord,	Our	Sav - ior	and	God.
thirst	To	springs	of	new	life.
flesh	And	giv - en	for	us.
praise,	Our	lips	sing	in	joy.
God,	The	light	of	the	world.

Text: Sr. Pamela Stotter
Tune: Margaret Daly
© 1980, International Commission on English in the Liturgy, Inc.

784 Not Alone Where Silent Woodlands

1. Not a - lone where si - lent wood - lands Shel - ter
2. Where the cit - y's cease-less clam - or Nev - er
3. Not a - lone where vast ca - the - drals Send their
4. Lord of life, a - mid the la - bor Fill - ing

crea - tures great and small; Not a - lone in peace - ful
ends by day, by night; Where the heav - ens' star - ry
arch - es soar - ing high; Not a - lone in hum - bler
all our crowd-ed days, There your love no less sus -

mead - ows Where the birds in con - cert call;
splen - dor Hides be - hind its gar - ish light;
chap - els Where the still - ness draws you nigh;
tains us; There our work may be your praise.

Not a - lone where rays of star - light Pierce the
Where the lurk - ing threat of vio - lence Dai - ly
Not a - lone in qui - et cham - bers Where we
Help us make each shop a tem - ple, Ev - 'ry

vel - vet skies of night, Can your peo - ple seek your
strikes the heart with fear; There, where life is bruised and
kneel in sol - i - tude Can our hearts pour out be -
desk a ho - ly place, Farms and fac - t'ries, homes and

pres - ence, God of mer - cy, God of might.
bro - ken, You, O God of grace, are near.
fore you Prayers of trust and grat - i - tude.
high - ways Shrines trans - fig - ured by your grace.

Text: Herman G. Stuempfle, Jr., 1923–2007, © 1993, GIA Publications, Inc.
Tune: NETTLETON, 8 7 8 7 D; Wyeth's *Repository of Sacred Music, Pt. II*, 1813

What Does the Lord Require 785

1. What does the Lord re - quire for praise and
2. Rul - ers of earth, give ear! should you not
3. Still down the a - ges ring the proph - et's
4. How shall our life ful - fill God's law so

of - fer - ing? What sac - ri - fice, de -
jus - tice know? Will God your plead - ing
stern com-mands: To mer - chant, work - er,
hard and high? Let Christ en - due our

sire or trib - ute bid you bring? Do
hear, while crime and cru - elty grow? Do
king, he brings God's high de - mands: Do
will with grace to for - ti - fy, Then

just - ly; Love mer - cy; Walk
just - ly; Love mer - cy; Walk
just - ly; Love mer - cy; Walk
just - ly, In mer - cy; We'll

hum - bly with your God.
hum - bly with your God.
hum - bly with your God.
hum - bly walk with God.

Text: Micah 6:6-8; Albert F. Bayly, 1901-1984, alt., © Oxford University Press
Tune: SHARPTHORNE, 6 6 6 6 33 6; Erik Routley, 1917-1982, © 1969, Hope Publishing Co.

786 Renew Your People

1. Lov - ing Fa - ther, gra-cious God,
2. Thank you for your gift of Love:
3. Fa - ther, make us car - ing neigh - bors;

praise and glo - ry to you. Bur-dened
Christ the Lord, Prince of Peace. Je - sus
teach us, Lord, how to give. Help us

by our sin and its dark - ness, we long for
is our friend and our Sav - ior; make us like
strive for true peace and jus - tice, liv - ing as

light, our souls re - new. Mer - ci - ful
him, your pow'r re - lease. Send us your
Christ taught us to live. May all our

Fa - ther, we ask of you, Sal - va - tion and heal-ing, our
Spir - it in all we do, With joy - ful de - vo-tion, our
ef - forts give praise to you, U - nite us in Spir - it, our

hearts re - new.
hearts re - new. Re - new your peo - ple, O
lives re - new.

Lord; re - new our lives with your Word.

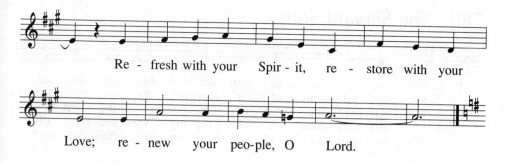

Re - fresh with your Spir - it, re - store with your
Love; re - new your peo-ple, O Lord.

Text: Lucia Welch
Tune: Randolph N. Currie, b.1943
© 1983, GIA Publications, Inc.

The Temple Rang with Golden Coins 787

1. The tem - ple rang with gold - en coins The
2. A wid - ow came with cop - per coins And
3. When Je - sus saw her cost - ly gift And
4. At last he brought his of - fer - ing And
5. Lord, help us all, with you, to yield What -

rich in bright ar - ray Con - trib - ut - ed from
of - fered them in praise. They were the last she
knew she had no more, He praised a love that
laid it on a tree; There gave him - self, his
ev - er love de - mands And free - ly give, as

gleam - ing hoards Their scales could scarce - ly weigh.
had to give Or save for dark - er days.
spared not self And called her rich, though poor.
life, his love For all hu - man - i - ty.
you have giv'n, With o - pen hearts and hands.

Text: Mark 12:41-44; Herman G. Stuempfle, Jr., 1923–2007; © 1993, GIA Publications, Inc.
Tune: LEWIS-TOWN, CM; William Billings, 1746-1800; harm. by Donald A. Busarow, b.1934, © 1978, *Lutheran Book of Worship*

788 The Servant Song

1., 6. Will you let me be your ser-vant, Let me be as
2. We are pil-grims on a jour-ney, We are trav-'lers
3. I will hold the Christ-light for you In the night-time
4. I will weep when you are weep-ing; When you laugh I'll
5. When we sing to God in heav-en We shall find such

Christ to you; Pray that I may have the grace to
on the road; We are here to help each oth-er
of your fear; I will hold my hand out to you,
laugh with you. I will share your joy and sor-row
har-mo-ny, Born of all we've known to-geth-er

Let you be my ser - vant, too.
Walk the mile and bear the load.
Speak the peace you long to hear.
'Til we've seen this jour - ney through.
Of Christ's love and ag - o - ny.

Text: Richard Gillard, b.1953
Tune: Richard Gillard, b.1953; harm. by Betty Pulkingham, b.1929
© 1977, Scripture in Song

789 We Are Your People

1. We are your peo - ple: Spir - it of grace,
2. Joined in com - mu-ni-ty, Treas-ured and fed,
3. Rich in di - ver-si-ty, Help us to live
4. Glad of tra - di - tion, Help us to see
5. Give, as we ven - ture Jus - tice and care
6. Spir - it, u - nite us, Make us, by grace,

You dare to make us To all our
May we dis - cov - er Gifts in each
Clos - er than neigh - bors, O - pen to
In all life's chang - ing Where you are
(Peace - ful, re - sist - ing, Wait - ing or
Will - ing and read - y, Christ's liv - ing

neigh - bors,	Christ's liv - ing	voice, hands	and face.
oth - er,	Will - ing to	lead and	be led.
stran - gers,	A - ble to	clash and	for - give.
lead - ing,	Where our best	ef - forts	should be.
risk - ing)	Wis - dom to	know when	and where.
bod - y,	Lov - ing the	whole hu -	man race.

Text: Brian Wren, b.1936, © 1975, Hope Publishing Co.
Tune: WHITFIELD, 5 4 5 5 7; John W. Wilson, 1905-1992, © 1980, Hope Publishing Co.

I Bind My Heart 790

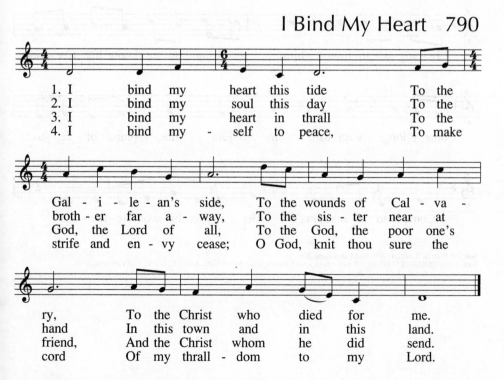

1. I	bind my	heart this tide	To the
2. I	bind my	soul this day	To the
3. I	bind my	heart in thrall	To the
4. I	bind my -	self to peace,	To make

Gal - i - le - an's	side,	To the wounds of	Cal - va -
broth - er far a -	way,	To the sis - ter	near at
God, the Lord of	all,	To the God, the	poor one's
strife and en - vy	cease;	O God, knit thou	sure the

ry,	To the Christ	who died for	me.
hand	In this town	and in this	land.
friend,	And the Christ	whom he did	send.
cord	Of my thrall - dom	to my	Lord.

Text: "Thraldom," The Tryst, 1907, Lauchlan McLean Watt, 1853-1931
Tune: Suzanne Toolan, SM, b.1927, © 1979, Resource Publications, Inc.

791 Glorious in Majesty

Verses

1. Glo-ri-ous in maj-es-ty, Ho-ly in his prais-es,
2. Vic-to-ry he won for us, Free-ing us from dark-ness,
3. One in love, as fam-i-ly, Liv-ing with each oth-er,

Je-sus, our Sav-ior and our King. Born a man, yet God of old,
Dy-ing and ris-ing from the dead. Liv-ing with the Fa-ther now,
Glad-ly we share each oth-er's pain. Yet he will not leave us so,

Let us all a-dore him: Filled with his Spir-it, let us sing.
Yet he is a-mong us: We are the bod-y, he the head.
Soon he is re-turn-ing, Tak-ing us back with him to reign.

Refrain

Liv-ing is to love him, serv-ing him to know his free-dom.

Come a-long with us to join the praise of Je-sus.

Come to Je-sus now, Go to live his word re-joic-ing.

Text: Jeff Cothran, fl.1972, © 1972, GIA Publications, Inc.
Tune: SHIBBOLET BASADEH, 7 6 8 D with refrain; Jewish melody; harm. by Jeff Cothran, fl.1972, © 1972, GIA Publications, Inc.

'Tis the Gift to Be Simple 792

'Tis the gift to be sim-ple, 'tis the gift to be free, 'tis the

gift to come down where we ought to be, and

when we find our-selves in the place just right, 'twill

be in the val - ley of love and de - light.

When true sim - plic - i - ty is gained to bow and to bend we

shan't be a-shamed, to turn, turn, will be our de-light till by

turn - ing, turn - ing, we come round right.

Text: Shaker Song, 18th. C.
Tune: SIMPLE GIFTS; acc. Margaret W. Mealy, b.1922, © 1984

793 Lord, Whose Love in Humble Service

1. Lord, whose love in hum-ble serv-ice Bore the weight of hu-man need, Who did on the Cross for-sak-en, Show us mer-cy's per-fect deed; We, your ser-vants, bring the wor-ship Not of voice a-lone, but heart: Con-se-crat-ing to your pur-pose Ev-'ry gift which you im-part.

2. Still your chil-dren wan-der home-less; Still the hun-gry cry for bread; Still the cap-tives long for free-dom; Still in grief we mourn our dead. As, O Lord, your deep com-pas-sion Healed the sick and freed the soul, Use the love your Spir-it kin-dles Still to save and make us whole.

3. As we wor-ship, grant us vi-sion, Till your love's re-veal-ing light, Till the height and depth and great-ness Dawns up-on our hu-man sight: Mak-ing known the needs and bur-dens Your com-pas-sion bids us bear, Stir-ring us to faith-ful serv-ice, Your a-bun-dant life to share.

4. Called from wor-ship in-to serv-ice Forth in your great name we go, To the child, the youth, the a-ged, Love in liv-ing deeds to show; Hope and health, good-will and com-fort, Coun-sel, aid, and peace we give That your chil-dren, Lord, in free-dom, May your mer-cy know and live.

Text: Albert F. Bayly, 1901-1984, © Oxford University Press, alt.
Tune: BEACH SPRING, 8 7 8 7 D; *The Sacred Harp*, 1844; harm. by Marty Haugen, b.1950, © 1985, GIA Publications, Inc.

God, Whose Giving Knows No Ending   794

1. God, whose giv-ing knows no end-ing, From your rich and end-less store: Na-ture's won-der, Je-sus' wis-dom, Cost-ly cross, grave's shat-tered door, Gift-ed by you, we turn to you, Of-f'ring up our-selves in praise; Thank-ful song shall rise for-ev-er, Gra-cious do-nor of our days.

2. Skills and time are ours for press-ing Toward the goals of Christ, your Son: All at peace in health and free-dom, Rac-es joined, the Church made one. Now di-rect our dai-ly la-bor, Lest we strive for self a-lone; Born with tal-ents, make us ser-vants Fit to an-swer at your throne.

3. Treas-ure, too, you have en-trust-ed, Gain through pow'rs your grace con-ferred; Ours to use for home and kin-dred, And to spread the Gos-pel Word. O-pen wide our hands in shar-ing, As we heed Christ's age-less call, Heal-ing, teach-ing, and re-claim-ing, Serv-ing you by lov-ing all.

Text: Robert L. Edwards, b.1915, © 1961, 1989, The Hymn Society of America (Administered by Hope Publishing Co.)
Tune: RUSTINGTON, 8 7 8 7 D; Charles H. H. Parry, 1848-1918

795 You Have Anointed Me

Verse 1

1. To bring glad tid - ings to the low - ly, to heal the bro - ken heart, You have a - noint - ed me. To pro - claim lib - er - ty to cap - tives, re - lease to pris - on - ers, You have a - noint - ed me.

Refrain

Your Spir - it, O God, is up - on me, You have a - noint - ed me.

Verse 2

2. To an - nounce a year of fa - vor, to com - fort those who mourn, You have a - noint - ed me. To give to them the oil of glad - ness, and

share a man-tle of joy, You have a - noint - ed me.

Text: Mike Balhoff, b.1946, Gary Daigle, b.1957, Darryl Ducote, b.1945
Tune: Mike Balhoff, b.1946, Gary Daigle, b.1957, Darryl Ducote, b.1945; acc. by Gary Daigle
© 1981, Damean Music. Distributed by GIA Publications, Inc.

Thuma Mina / Send Me, Jesus   796

1. Thu - ma mi - na, thu - ma mi - na,
2. Ndi - ya vu - ma, ndi - ya vu - ma,
1. *Send me, Je - sus; send me, Je - sus;*
2. *I am will - ing; I am will - ing;*

thu - ma mi - na, Nko - si yam.
ndi - ya vu - ma, Nko - si yam.
send me, Je - sus; send me, Lord.
I am will - ing, will - ing, Lord.

Cantor:

Thu-ma mi - na.

Text: Traditional South African
Tune: Traditional; transcribed from Lulu Dumazweni by John Bell, b.1949, © 1991, Iona Community, GIA Publications, Inc., agent

797 Good News

Verses

1. When Je - sus worked here on earth he
2. The eld - ers of the syn - a - gogue were
3. The way he lived was proof of it: he
4. So pass it on to - day, good friend: the

preached in his home - town, I - sa - iah's hopes
shocked by Mar - y's son, That he was des -
qui - et - ed our strife. The cross it - self he
mes - sage is the same. De - liv - 'rance Christ a -

now ful - filled, those claims of great re - nown.
tined to be the Christ for ev - 'ry - one.
would not flee e'en though it cost his life.
lone can give, for this to earth he came.

Refrain

To bring good news to the need - y, to make the

blind to see, the bro - ken hearts healed a - gain, to

1.
set the cap - tive free.

2.
cap - tive free.

Text: Howard S. Olson, b.1922
Tune: Almaz Belihu; Yemissrach Dimts Literature Program, Ethiopia
© 1993, Howard S. Olson

Go Make of All Disciples   798

1. "Go make of all dis - ci - ples:" We hear the call, O
2. "Go make of all dis - ci - ples:" Bap - tiz - ing in the
3. "Go make of all dis - ci - ples:" We at your feet would
4. "Go make of all dis - ci - ples:" We wel - come your com -

Lord, That comes from you, our Fa - ther, In
name Of Fa - ther, Son, and Spir - it— From
stay Un - til each life's vo - ca - tion Ac -
mand; "Lo, I am with you al - ways:" We

your e - ter - nal Word. In - spire our ways of
age to age the same. We call each new dis -
cents your ho - ly way. We cul - ti - vate the
take your guid - ing hand. The task looms large be -

learn - ing Through earn - est, fer - vent prayer, And
ci - ple To fol - low you, O Lord, Re -
na - ture God plants in ev - 'ry heart, Re -
fore us— We fol - low with - out fear. In

let our dai - ly liv - ing Re - veal you ev - 'ry-where.
deem - ing soul and bod - y By wa - ter and the Word.
veal - ing in our wit - ness The Mas - ter Teach-er's art.
heav'n and earth your pow - er Shall bring God's king - dom here.

Text: Matthew 28:19-20; Leon M. Adkins, 1896-1986, alt., © 1964, Abingdon Press
Tune: ELLACOMBE, 7 6 7 6 D; *Gesangbuch der Herzogl,* Wirtemberg, 1784

799 City of God

Verses 1, 2

1. A-wake from your slum-ber! A - rise from your
2. We are sons of the morn-ing; we are daugh-ters of

sleep! A new day is dawn - ing
day. The One who has loved us

for all those who weep. The peo - ple in
has bright-ened our way. The Lord of all

dark - ness have seen a great light. The Lord of our
kind - ness has called us to be a light for his

long - ing has con-quered the night.
peo - ple to set their hearts free.

Refrain

Let us build the cit-y of God. May our tears be

turned in - to danc - ing! For the Lord, our light and our

love, has turned the night in - to day!

Verse 3

3. God is light; in him there is no dark-ness. Let us walk in his light, his chil - dren, one and all.

O com-fort my peo-ple; make gen-tle your words. Pro - claim to my cit-y the day of her birth.

Verse 4

4. O cit-y of glad-ness, now lift up your voice. Pro - claim the good tid - ings that all may re - joice!

Text: Dan Schutte, b.1947
Tune: Dan Schutte, b.1947; acc. by Robert J. Batastini, b.1942
© 1981, Daniel L. Schutte and OCP Publications

800   You Are Called to Tell the Story

1. You are called to tell the sto - ry, pass - ing
2. You are called to teach the rhy - thm of the
3. You are called to set the ta - ble, bless - ing
4. May the One whose love is broad - er than the

words of life a - long, Then to
dance that nev - er ends, Then to
bread as Je - sus blessed, Then to
meas - ure of all space Give us

blend your voice with oth - ers as you
move with - in the cir - cle, hand in
come with thirst and hun - ger, need - ing
words to sing the sto - ry, move a -

sing the sa - cred song. Christ be
hand with stran - gers, friends. Christ be
care like all the rest, Christ be
mong us in this place. Christ be

known in all our sing - ing,
known in all our danc - ing,
known in all our shar - ing,
known in all our liv - ing,

fill - ing all with songs of love.
touch - ing all with hands of love.
feed - ing all with signs of love.
fill - ing all with gifts of love.

Text: Ruth Duck, b.1947, © 1992, GIA Publications, Inc.
Tune: GHENT, 8 7 8 7 8 7; M.D. Ridge, b.1938; acc. by Patrick Loomis, 1951-1990, © 1987, GIA Publications, Inc.

Moved by the Gospel, Let Us Move   801

1. Moved by the Gos - pel, let us move With
2. Let weav - ers form from bro - ken strands A
3. O Spir - it, breathe a - mong us here; In -

ev - 'ry gift and art. The im - age of cre -
tap - es - try of prayer. Let art - ists paint with
spire the work we do. May hands and voic - es,

a - tive love In - dwells each hu - man heart. The
skill - ful hands Their joy, la - ment, and care. Then
eye and ear At - test to life made new. In

Mak - er calls cre - a - tion good, So
mime the sto - ry: Christ has come. With
wor - ship and in dai - ly strife Cre -

let us now ex - press With sound and col - or,
rev - 'rence dance the word. With flute and or - gan,
ate a - mong us still. Great Art - ist, form our

stone and wood, The shape of ho - li - ness.
ching and drum God's praise be ev - er heard.
com - mon life Ac - cord - ing to your will.

Text: Ruth Duck, b.1947, © 1992, GIA Publications, Inc.
Tune: KINGSFOLD, CMD; English; harm. by Ralph Vaughan Williams, 1872-1958

802 Here I Am, Lord

Verses

1. I, the Lord of sea and sky, I have heard my
2. I, the Lord of snow and rain, I have borne my
3. I, the Lord of wind and flame, I will tend the

peo - ple cry. All who dwell in dark and sin
peo - ple's pain. I have wept for love of them.
poor and lame. I will set a feast for them.

My hand will save. I who made the
They turn a - way. I will break their
My hand will save. Fin - est bread I

stars of night, I will make their dark - ness bright.
hearts of stone, Give them hearts for love a - lone.
will pro - vide Till their hearts be sat - is - fied.

Who will bear my light to them? Whom shall I send?
I will speak my word to them. Whom shall I send?
I will give my life to them. Whom shall I send?

Refrain

Here I am, Lord. Is it I, Lord? I have heard you

call - ing in the night. I will go, Lord, if you

lead me. I will hold your peo - ple in my heart.

Text: Isaiah 6; Dan Schutte, b.1947
Tune: Dan Schutte, b.1947; arr. by Michael Pope, SJ, and John Weissrock
© 1981, OCP Publications

The Church of Christ in Every Age   803

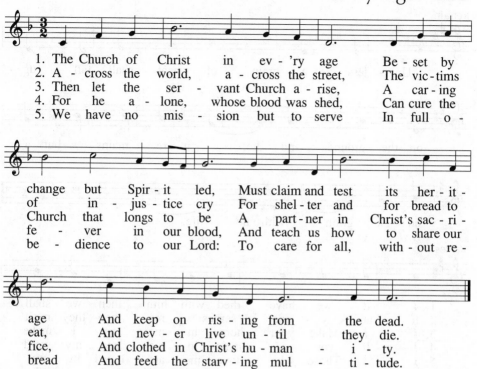

1. The Church of Christ in ev - 'ry age Be - set by
2. A - cross the world, a - cross the street, The vic - tims
3. Then let the ser - vant Church a - rise, A car - ing
4. For he a - lone, whose blood was shed, Can cure the
5. We have no mis - sion but to serve In full o -

change but Spir - it led, Must claim and test its her - it -
of in - jus - tice cry For shel - ter and for bread to
Church that longs to be A part - ner in Christ's sac - ri -
fe - ver in our blood, And teach us how to share our
be - dience to our Lord: To care for all, with - out re -

age And keep on ris - ing from the dead.
eat, And nev - er live un - til they die.
fice, And clothed in Christ's hu - man - i - ty.
bread And feed the starv - ing mul - ti - tude.
serve, And spread his lib - er - at - ing Word.

Text: Fred Pratt Green, 1903-2000, © 1971, Hope Publishing Co.
Tune: DUNEDIN, LM; Vernon Griffiths, 1894-1985, © 1971, Faber Music Ltd.

804 Unless a Grain of Wheat

Refrain

Un - less a grain of wheat shall fall upon the ground and die, it re - mains but a
sin - gle grain with no life.

Verses

1. If we have died with him then we shall
2. If an - y - one serves me then they must
3. Make your home in me as I make
4. If you re - main in me and my word
5. Those who love me are loved by my
6. Peace I leave with you, my peace I

live with him; if we hold firm, we shall
fol - low me; where - ev - er I am, my
mine in you; those who re - main in me
lives in you, then you will be my dis -
Fa - ther; we shall be with them and
give to you; peace which the world can - not

D.C.

reign with him.
ser - vants will be.
bear much fruit.
ci - ples.
dwell in them.
give is my gift.

Text: John 12:24; Bernadette Farrell, b.1957
Tune: Bernadette Farrell, b.1957
© 1983, Bernadette Farrell. Published by OCP Publications.

Those Who Love and Those Who Labor   805

1. Those who love and those who la-bor Fol-low in the
2. Where the man-y work to-geth-er, They with Christ him-
3. Let the seek-er nev-er fal-ter Till the truth is

way of Christ; Thus the first dis-ci-ples found him,
self a-bide, But the lone-ly work-ers al-so
found a-far With the wis-dom of the a-ges

Thus the gift of love suf-ficed. Je-sus says to
Find him ev-er at their side. Lo, the Prince of
Un-der-neath a gi-ant star, With the rich-est

those who seek him, I will nev-er pass you by;
com-mon wel-fare Dwells with-in the mar-ket strife;
and the poor-est, Of the sum of things pos-sessed,

Raise the stone and you shall find me;
Lo, the bread of heav'n is bro-ken
Like a child at first to won-der,

Cleave the wood, and there am I.
In the sac-ra-ment of life.
Like a king at last to rest.

Text: Geoffrey Dearmer, 1893-1996, © Oxford University Press
Tune: HYMN TO JOY, 8 7 8 7 D; arr. from Ludwig van Beethoven, 1770-1827, by Edward Hodges, 1796-1867

806 Jesu Tawa Pano / Jesus, We Are Here

Je - su   ta - wa pa - no;   Je - su   ta - wa pa - no;
Je - sus,   we   are   here;   Je - sus,   we   are   here;

Je - su   ta - wa pa - no;   ta - wa pa - no, mu   zi - ta re - nyu.
Je - sus,   we are here;   we are here   for   you.

Text: Zimbabwean; Patrick Matsikenyiri
Tune: Patrick Matsikenyiri
© 1990, 1996, General Board of Global Ministries, GBGMusik

807 You Walk Along Our Shoreline

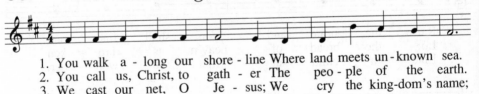

1. You walk a - long our   shore - line Where land meets un - known sea.
2. You call us, Christ, to   gath - er The   peo - ple of   the   earth.
3. We cast our net, O   Je - sus; We   cry the king-dom's name;

We   hear your voice of   pow - er, "Now come and fol - low   me.
We   can - not fish for   on - ly Those lives we think have   worth.
We   work for love and jus - tice; We   learn to hope through pain.

And   if   you still will   fol - low Through storm and wave and shoal,
We   spread your net of   gos - pel A -   cross the wa - ter's face,
You   call   us, Lord, to   gath - er God's   daugh - ters and God's sons,

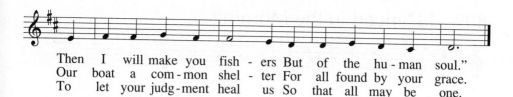

Then I will make you fish - ers But of the hu - man soul."
Our boat a com - mon shel - ter For all found by your grace.
To let your judg - ment heal us So that all may be one.

Text: Sylvia Dunston, 1955-1993, © 1991, GIA Publications, Inc.
Tune: AURELIA, 7 6 7 6 D; Samuel Sebastian Wesley, 1810-1876

Take Up Your Cross 808

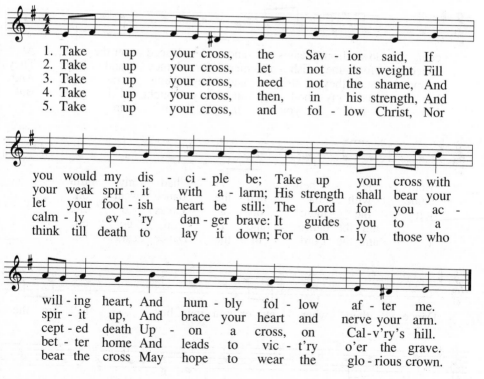

1. Take up your cross, the Sav - ior said, If
2. Take up your cross, let not its weight Fill
3. Take up your cross, heed not the shame, And
4. Take up your cross, then, in his strength, And
5. Take up your cross, and fol - low Christ, Nor

you would my dis - ci - ple be; Take up your cross with
your weak spir - it with a - larm; His strength shall bear your
let your fool - ish heart be still; The Lord for you ac -
calm - ly ev - 'ry dan - ger brave: It guides you to a
think till death to lay it down; For on - ly those who

will - ing heart, And hum - bly fol - low af - ter me.
spir - it up, And brace your heart and nerve your arm.
cept - ed death Up - on a cross, on Cal - v'ry's hill.
bet - ter home And leads to vic - t'ry o'er the grave.
bear the cross May hope to wear the glo - rious crown.

Text: Charles W. Everest, 1814-1877, alt.
Tune: ERHALT UNS HERR, LM; Klug's *Geistliche Lieder*, 1543; harm. by J.S. Bach, 1685-1750

809 I Danced in the Morning

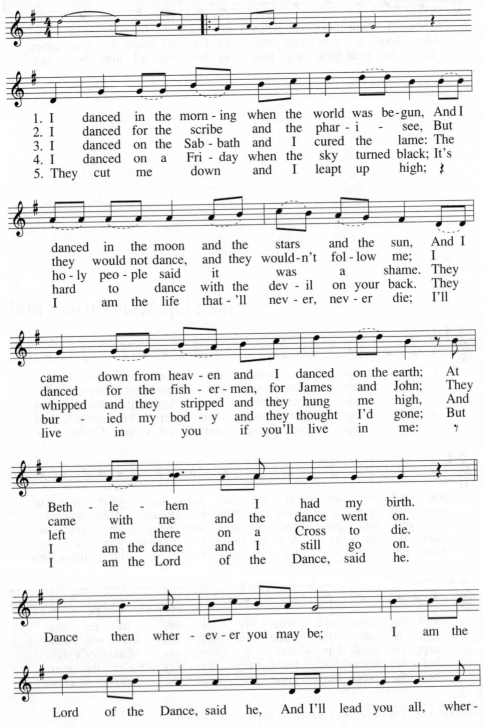

1. I danced in the morn-ing when the world was be-gun, And I
2. I danced for the scribe and the phar - i - see, But
3. I danced on the Sab - bath and I cured the lame: The
4. I danced on a Fri - day when the sky turned black; It's
5. They cut me down and I leapt up high;

danced in the moon and the stars and the sun, And I
they would not dance, and they would-n't fol - low me; I
ho - ly peo - ple said it was a shame. They
hard to dance with the dev - il on your back. They
I am the life that - 'll nev - er, nev - er die; I'll

came down from heav - en and I danced on the earth; At
danced for the fish - er - men, for James and John; They
whipped and they stripped and they hung me high, And
bur - ied my bod - y and they thought I'd gone; But
live in you if you'll live in me:

Beth - le - hem I had my birth.
came with me and the dance went on.
left me there on a Cross to die.
I am the dance and I still go on.
I am the Lord of the Dance, said he.

Dance then wher - ev - er you may be; I am the

Lord of the Dance, said he, And I'll lead you all, wher-

ev - er you may be, And I'll lead you all in the Dance, said he.

Text: Sydney Carter, b.1915, © 1963, Stainer & Bell, Ltd., London, England. (admin. by Hope Publishing Co.)
Tune: LORD OF THE DANCE, Irregular; adapted from a traditional Shaker melody by Sydney Carter, b.1915, © 1963, Stainer & Bell, Ltd., London, England. (admin. by Hope Publishing Co.)

Wherever He Leads 810

1. "Take up thy cross and fol - low Me," I
2. He drew me clos - er to His side, I
3. It may be through the shad - ows dim, Or
4. My heart, my life, my all I bring To

heard my Mas - ter say; "I gave My life to
sought His will to know, And in that will I
o'er the storm - y sea, I take my cross and
Christ who loves me so; He is my Mas - ter,

ran - som thee, Sur - ren - der your all to - day."
now a - bide, Wher - ev - er He leads I'll go.
fol - low Him, Wher - ev - er He lead - eth me.
Lord, and King, Wher - ev - er He leads I'll go.

Wher - ev - er He leads I'll go, Wher -

ev - er He leads I'll go, I'll fol - low my Christ who

loves me so, Wher - ev - er He leads I'll go.

Text: B. B. McKinney, 1886-1952
Music: FALLS CREEK; B. B. McKinney, 1886-1952
© 1936, 1964, Broadman Press

811 The Summons

1. Will you come and fol-low me If I but
2. Will you leave your-self be-hind If I but
3. Will you let the blind-ed see If I but
4. Will you love the 'you' you hide If I but
5. Lord, your sum-mons ech-oes true When you but

call your name? Will you go where
call your name? Will you care for
call your name? Will you set the
call your name? Will you quell the
call my name. Let me turn and

you don't know And nev-er be the same?
cruel and kind And nev-er be the same?
pris-'ners free And nev-er be the same?
fear in-side And nev-er be the same?
fol-low you And nev-er be the same.

Will you let my love be shown, Will you
Will you risk the hos-tile stare Should your
Will you kiss the lep-er clean, And do
Will you use the faith you've found To re-
In your com-pa-ny I'll go Where your

let my name be known, Will you let my
life at-tract or scare? Will you let me
such as this un-seen, And ad-mit to
shape the world a-round, Through my sight and
love and foot-steps show. Thus I'll move and

life be grown In you and you in me?
an-swer prayer In you and you in me?
what I mean In you and you in me?
touch and sound In you and you in me?
live and grow In you and you in me.

Text: John L. Bell, b.1949, © 1987, Iona Community, GIA Publications, Inc., agent
Tune: KELVINGROVE, 7 6 7 6 777 6; Scottish traditional; arr. by John L. Bell, b.1949, © 1987, Iona Community, GIA Publications, Inc., agent

Two Fishermen 812

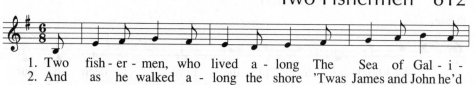

1. Two fish-er-men, who lived a-long The Sea of Gal-i-
2. And as he walked a-long the shore 'Twas James and John he'd
3. O Si-mon Pe-ter, An-drew, James And John be-lov-ed
4. And you, good Chris-tians, one and all Who'd fol-low Je-sus'

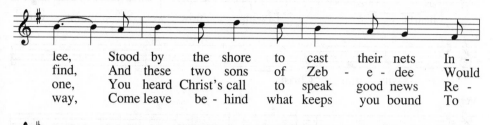

lee, Stood by the shore to cast their nets In-
find, And these two sons of Zeb-e-dee Would
one, You heard Christ's call to speak good news Re-
way, Come leave be-hind what keeps you bound To

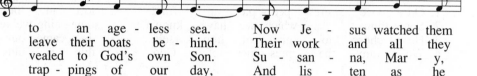

to an age-less sea. Now Je-sus watched them
leave their boats be-hind. Their work and all they
vealed to God's own Son. Su-san-na, Mar-y,
trap-pings of our day, And lis-ten as he

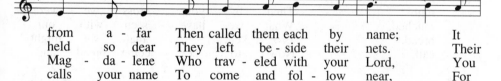

from a-far Then called them each by name; It
held so dear They left be-side their nets. Their
Mag-da-lene Who trav-eled with your Lord, You
calls your name To come and fol-low near, For

changed their lives, these sim-ple men; They'd nev-er be the same.
names they'd heard as Je-sus called; They came with-out re-gret.
min-is-tered to him with joy For he is God a-dored.
still he speaks in var-ied ways To those his call will hear.

Leave all things you have And come and fol-low

me, And come and fol-low me.

Text: Suzanne Toolan, SM, b.1927, © 1986, GIA Publications, Inc.
Tune: LEAVE ALL THINGS, CMD with refrain; Suzanne Toolan, SM, b.1927, © 1970, GIA Publications, Inc.

813 Now We Remain

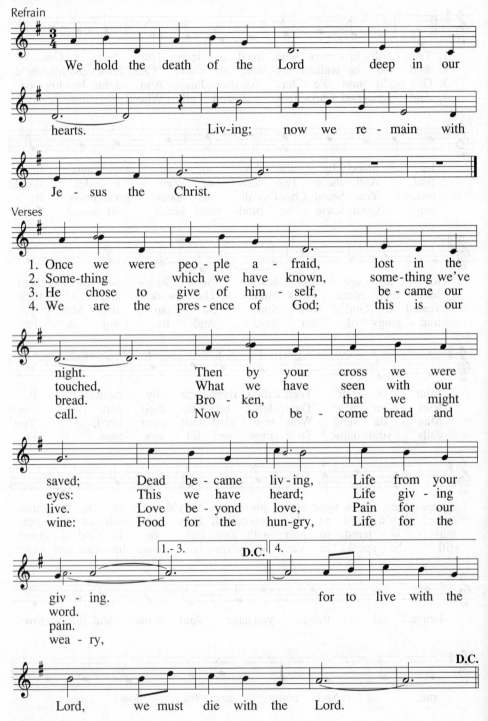

Refrain

We hold the death of the Lord deep in our hearts. Liv-ing; now we re-main with Je - sus the Christ.

Verses

1. Once we were peo - ple a - fraid, lost in the
2. Some-thing which we have known, some-thing we've
3. He chose to give of him - self, be - came our
4. We are the pres - ence of God; this is our

night. Then by your cross we were
touched, What we have seen with our
bread. Bro - ken, that we might
call. Now to be - come bread and

saved; Dead be - came liv-ing, Life from your
eyes: This we have heard; Life giv - ing
live. Love be - yond love, Pain for our
wine: Food for the hun-gry, Life for the

1.-3.
giv - ing.
word.
pain.
wea - ry,

D.C. 4.
for to live with the

D.C.
Lord, we must die with the Lord.

Text: Corinthians, 1 John, 2 Timothy; David Haas, b.1957
Tune: David Haas, b.1957
© 1983, GIA Publications, Inc.

The Love of the Lord 814

1. All that I count - ed as gain now I con - sid - er as loss, emp - ty and worth - less to me in the light of the love of the Lord.
2. Rich - es and hon - ors will fade, earth - ly de - light dis - ap - pear, fade like the grass of the field in the light of the love of the Lord.
3. Sil - ver and gold have I none, no land to count as my home, yet wealth be - yond meas - ure I own in the light of the love of the Lord.
4. Faith is the wealth I pos - sess Find - ing its source in my God: faith in the prom - ise of Christ is my life and my love of the Lord.

What more could bring us hope than to know the pow'r of his life? What more could bring us peace than to share in his suf - f'ring and death? What more could be our fi - nal wish than to live in the love of the Lord?

Text: Philippians 3:7-11; Michael Joncas, b.1951
Tune: Michael Joncas, b.1951

815 We Have Been Told

Refrain

We have been told, we've seen his face, and heard his voice a-live in our hearts; "Live in my love with all your heart, as the Fa-ther has loved me, so I have loved you."

Verse 1

1. "I am the vine, you are the branch-es, and all who live in me will bear great fruit."

Verses 2, 3

2. "You are my friends, if you keep my com-mands, no long-er slaves, I call you friends."
3. "No great-er love is there than this: to lay down one's life, for a friend."

Text: David Haas, b.1957
Tune: David Haas, b.1957; vocal arr. by David Haas and Marty Haugen, b.1950
© 1983, GIA Publications, Inc.

On the Journey to Emmaus   816

1. On the jour - ney to Em - ma - us with our
2. And our hearts burned with - in us as we
3. And that eve - ning at the ta - ble as he
4. On our jour - ney to Em - ma - us, in our

hearts cold as stone— The One who would
talked on the way, How all that was
blessed and broke bread, We saw it was
stor - ies and feast, With Je - sus we

save us had left us a - lone. Then a
prom - ised was ours on that day. So we
Je - sus a - ris'n from the dead; Though he
claim that the great - est is least: And his

stran - ger walks with us and, to our sur - prise, He
begged him, "Stay with us and grant us your word." We
van - ished be - fore us we knew he was near— The
words burn with - in us— let none be ig - nored— Who

o - pens our stor - ies and he o - pens our eyes.
wel - comed the stran - ger and we wel - comed the Lord.
life in our dy - ing and the hope in our fear.
wel - comes the stran - ger shall wel - come the Lord.

Text: Luke 24:13-35; Marty Haugen. b.1950
Tune: COLUMCILLE, Irregular; Gaelic, arr. by Marty Haugen, b.1950
© 1995, GIA Publications, Inc.

817 Lord, When You Came / Pescador de Hombres

Verses

1. Lord,   when you came to the sea - shore
2. Lord,   you knew what my boat car - ried:
3. Lord,   have you need of my la - bor,
4. Lord,   send me where you would have me,
1. *Tú*   *has ve - ni - do_a la_o - ri - lla,*
2. *Tú*   *sa - bes bien lo que ten - go,*
3. *Tú*   *ne - ce - si - tas mis ma - nos,*
4. *Tú*   *pes - ca - dor de_o - tros, ma - res,*

You weren't seek - ing   the wise or the wealth - y,
Nei - ther mon - ey   nor weap - ons for fight - ing,
Hands for serv - ice,   a heart made for lov - ing,
To a vil - lage,   or heart of the cit - y;
no_has bus - ca - do   *ni_a sa - bios, ni_a ri - cos,*
en mi bar - ca   *no_hay o - ro ni_es - pa - das,*
mi can - san - cio   *que_a o - tros des - can - se,*
an - sia_e - ter - na,   *al - mas que es - pe - ran.*

But on - ly ask - ing   that I might fol - low.
But nets for fish - ing,   my dai - ly la - bor.
My arms for lift - ing   the poor and bro - ken?
I will re - mem - ber   that you are with me.
tan só - lo quie - res   *que yo te si - ga.*
tan só - lo re - des   *y mi tra - ba - jo.*
a - mor que quie - ra   *se - guir a - man - do.*
A - mi - go bue - no,   *que_a - sí me lla - mas.*

Refrain

O Lord,   in my eyes you were gaz - ing,
Se - ñor   *me_has mi - ra - do_a los o - jos,*

Kind-ly smil - ing, my name you were
son - ri - en - do *has di - cho mi*

say - ing; All I treas - ured,
nom - bre, *en la a - re - na*

I have left on the sand there; Close to
he de - ja - do mi bar - ca, *jun - to a*

you, I will find oth - er seas.
ti *bus - ca - ré o - tro mar.*

Text: *Pescador de Hombres*, Cesáreo Gabaráin, © 1979, published by OCP Publications; trans. by Willard Francis Jabusch, b.1930, © 1982,
  administered by OCP Publications
Tune: Cesáreo Gabaráin, © 1979, published by OCP Publications; acc. by Diana Kodner, b.1957

818 God It Was

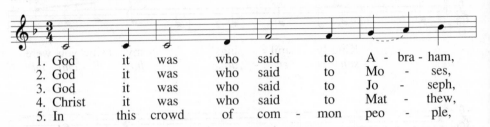

1. God it was who said to A - bra - ham,
2. God it was who said to Mo - ses,
3. God it was who said to Jo - seph,
4. Christ it was who said to Mat - thew,
5. In this crowd of com - mon peo - ple,

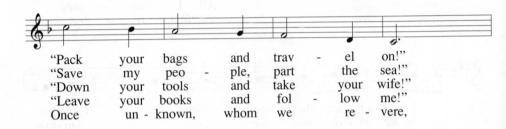

"Pack your bags and trav - el on!"
"Save my peo - ple, part the sea!"
"Down your tools and take your wife!"
"Leave your books and fol - low me!"
Once un - known, whom we re - vere,

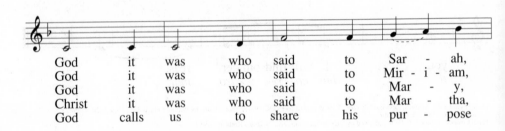

God it was who said to Sar - ah,
God it was who said to Mir - i - am,
God it was who said to Mar - y,
Christ it was who said to Mar - tha,
God calls us to share his pur - pose

"Smile and soon you'll bear a son!"
"Sing and dance to show you're free!"
"In your womb I'll start my life!"
"Lis - ten first, then make the tea!"
Start - ing now and start - ing here.

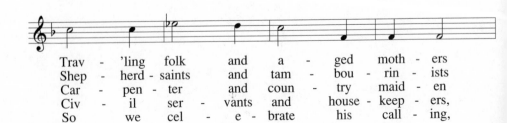

Trav - 'ling folk and a - ged moth - ers
Shep - herd - saints and tam - bou - rin - ists
Car - pen - ter and coun - try maid - en
Civ - il ser - vants and house - keep - ers,
So we cel - e - brate his call - ing,

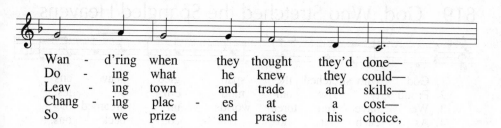

Wan - d'ring	when	they	thought	they'd	done—
Do - ing	what	he	knew	they	could—
Leav - ing	town	and	trade	and	skills—
Chang - ing	plac - es	at	a	cost—
So	we	prize	and	praise	his	choice,

This	is	how	God	calls	his	peo - ple,
This	is	how	God	calls	his	peo - ple,
This	is	how	God	calls	his	peo - ple,
This	is	how	Christ	calls	dis - ci - ples,
As	we	pray	that	through	this	com - pa - ny

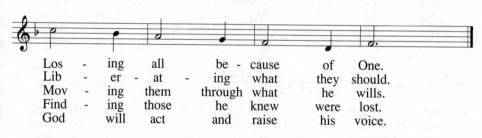

Los - ing	all	be - cause	of	One.
Lib - er - at - ing	what	they	should.
Mov - ing	them	through what	he	wills.
Find - ing	those	he	knew	were	lost.
God	will	act	and	raise	his	voice.

Text: John L. Bell, b.1949
Tune: JESUS CALLS US, Irregular; adapt. from a Gaelic Air by John L. Bell, b.1949
© 1989, Iona Community, GIA Publications, Inc., agent

819 God, Who Stretched the Spangled Heavens

1. God, who stretched the span - gled heav - ens
   In - fi - nite in time and place, Flung the suns in
   burn - ing ra - diance Through the si - lent
   fields of space; We, your chil - dren, in your like - ness,
   Share in - ven - tive pow'rs with you; Great Cre - a - tor,
   still cre - at - ing, Show us what we yet may do.

2. Proud - ly rise our mod - ern cit - ies,
   State - ly build - ings, row on row; Yet their win - dows,
   blank, un - feel - ing, Stare on can - yoned
   streets be - low, Where the lone - ly drift un - no - ticed
   In the cit - y's ebb and flow, Lost to pur - pose
   and to mean - ing, Scarce - ly car - ing where they go.

3. We have ven - tured worlds un - dreamed of
   Since the child - hood of our race; Known the ec - sta -
   sy of wing - ing Through un - trav - eled
   realms of space; Probed the se - crets of the at - om,
   Yield - ing un - i - mag - ined pow'r, Fac - ing us with
   life's de - struc - tion Or our most tri - um - phant hour.

4. As each far ho - ri - zon beck - ons,
   May it chal - lenge us a - new, Chil - dren of cre -
   a - tive pur - pose, Serv - ing oth - ers,
   hon - oring you. May our dreams prove rich with prom - ise,
   Each en - deav - or, well be - gun: Great Cre - a - tor,
   give us guid - ance Till our goals and yours are one.

Text: Catherine Cameron, b.1927, © 1967, Hope Publishing Co.
Tune: HOLY MANNA, 8 7 8 7 D; William Moore, fl.1830; harm. by Charles Anders, b.1929, © 1969, *Contemporary Worship I: Hymns*

We Are Called 820

1. Come! Live in the light! Shine with the
2. Come! O - pen your heart! Show your
3. Sing! Sing a new song! Sing of that

joy and the love of the Lord! We are called
mer - cy to all those in fear! We are called
great day when all will be one! God will reign,

to be light for the king - dom, to
to be hope for the hope - less so all
and we'll walk with each oth - er as

live in the free - dom of the cit - y of God!
ha - tred and blind - ness will be no more!
sis - ters and broth - ers u - nit - ed in love!

We are called to act with jus - tice, we are called to

love ten - der - ly, we are called to serve one an - oth - er;

to walk hum - bly with God!

Text: Micah 6:8; David Haas, b.1957
Tune: David Haas, b.1957
© 1988, GIA Publications, Inc.

821 Freedom Is Coming

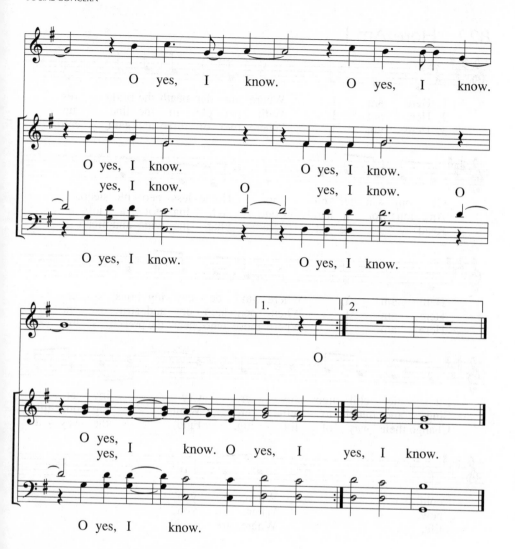

Text: South African
Tune: South African
© 1984, Utryck, Walton Music Corporation, agent

822 Here Am I

1. Here am I, Where un-der-neath the bridg - es
2. Here am I, With peo-ple in the line - up,
3. Here am I, Where two or three are gath - ered,

Of our win-ter cit - ies Home-less peo-ple sleep.
Anx-ious for a hand - out, Ach - ing for a job.
Read-y to be al - tered, Shar - ing wine and bread.

Here am I, Where in de-cay-ing hous - es
Here am I, When pen-sion-ers and strik - ers
Here am I, Where those who hear the preach - ing

Lit - tle chil-dren shiv - er, Cry - ing at the
Sing and march to-geth - er, Want - ing some-thing
Change their way of liv - ing, Find the way to

cold. Where are you?
new. Where are you?
life. Where are you?

Text: Brian Wren, b.1936
Tune: STANISLAUS, 3 7 6 5 D 3; Daniel Charles Damon, b.1955
© Words 1983, music 1995, Hope Publishing Co.

For the Healing of the Nations 823

1. For the heal-ing   of the na-tions, Lord, we pray with
2. Lead us now, Lord,   in-to free-dom, From de-spair your
3. All that kills a -   bun-dant liv-ing, Let it from the
4. You, cre-a-tor God, have writ-ten Your great name on

one ac-cord;   For a just and   e-qual shar-ing
world re-lease;   That re-deemed from war and ha-tred,
earth be banned; Pride of stat-us,   race or school-ing,
hu-man-kind;   For our grow-ing   in your like-ness

Of the things that earth af-fords.   To a life of
All may come and go in peace.   Show us how through
Dog-mas that ob - scure your plan.   In our com-mon
Bring the life of Christ to mind: That by our re -

love and ac-tion   Help us rise and pledge our word.
care and good-ness Fear will die and hope in-crease.
quest for jus-tice May we hal-low   life's brief span.
sponse and serv-ice Earth its des-ti - ny may find.

Text: Fred Kaan, b.1929, alt., © 1968, Hope Publishing Co.
Tune: ST. THOMAS, 8 7 8 7 8 7; John Wade, 1711-1786

824 God Made from One Blood

1. God made from one blood all the fam - 'lies of
2. We turn to you, God, with our thanks and our
3. We learn through our fam - 'lies how close - ness and
4. Give, Lord, to each fam - 'ly in con - flict and
5. Then wid - en that wis - dom and grace to in -

earth, The cir - cles of nur - ture that
tears For all of the fam - 'lies we've
trust In - crease when our ac - tions are
storm A sense of your wis - dom and
clude The rac - es and view - points our

raised us from birth, Com - pan - ions who
known through the years, The in - ti - mate
lov - ing and just. Yet fam - 'lies have
grace that trans - form Sharp an - ger to
fam - 'lies ex - clude Till peace in each

join us to walk through each stage Of
net - works on whom we de - pend Of
al - so dis - tort - ed their roles, Mis -
in - sight which strength - ens the heart And
home bears and nur - tures the bud Of

child - hood and youth and a - dult - hood and age.
par - ent and part - ner and room - mate and friend.
treat - ing their mem - bers and bruis - ing their souls.
makes clear the place where re - build - ing can start.
peace shared by all you have made from one blood.

Text: Thomas H. Troeger, b.1945, © 1991, Oxford University Press
Tune: FOUNDATION, 11 11 11 11; Funk's *Compilation of Genuine Church Music*, 1832; harm. by Richard Proulx, b.1937,
© 1975, GIA Publications, Inc.

If You Believe and I Believe 825

If you be-lieve and I be-lieve And we to-geth-er pray, The Ho-ly Spir-it must come down And set God's peo-ple free, And set God's peo-ple free, And set God's peo-ple free; The Ho-ly Spir-it must come down And set God's peo-ple free.

Text: Zimbabwean traditional
Tune: Zimbabwean traditional; adapt. of English traditional; as taught by Tarasai; arr. by John L. Bell, b.1949, © 1991, Iona Community, GIA Publications, Inc., agent

826 God of Day and God of Darkness

1. God of day and God of dark - ness,
Now we stand be - fore the night;
As the shad - ows stretch and deep - en,
Come and make our dark - ness bright.
All cre - a - tion still is groan - ing
For the dawn - ing of your might,
When the Sun of peace and jus - tice
Fills the earth with ra - diant light.

2. Still the na - tions curse the dark - ness,
Still the rich op - press the poor;
Still the earth is bruised and bro - ken
By the ones who still want more.
Come and wake us from our sleep - ing,
So our hearts can - not ig - nore
All your peo - ple lost and bro - ken,
All your chil - dren at our door.

3. Show us Christ in one an - oth - er,
Make us ser - vants strong and true;
Give us all your love of jus - tice
So we do what you would do.
Let us call all peo - ple ho - ly,
Let us pledge our lives a - new,
Make us one with all the low - ly,
Let us all be one in you.

4. You shall be the path that guides us,
You the light that in us burns;
Shin - ing deep with - in all peo - ple,
Yours the love that we must learn,
For our hearts shall wan - der rest - less
'Til they safe to you re - turn;
Find - ing you in one an - oth - er,
We shall all your face dis - cern.

5. Praise to you in day and dark - ness,
You our source and you our end;
Praise to you who love and nur - ture us
As a fa - ther, moth - er, friend.
Grant us all a peace - ful rest - ing,
Let each mind and bod - y mend,
So we rise re - freshed to - mor - row,
Hearts re - newed to King - dom tend.

Text: Marty Haugen, b.1950, © 1985, 1994, GIA Publications, Inc.
Tune: BEACH SPRING, 8 7 8 7 D; The Sacred Harp, 1844; harm. by Marty Haugen, b.1950, © 1985, GIA Publications, Inc.

Now Join We to Praise the Creator   827

1. Now join we to praise the cre - a - tor,
2. We thank you, O God, for your good - ness,
3. But al - so of need and star - va - tion
4. We cry for the plight of the hun - gry
5. The song grows in depth and in wide - ness:
6. Then teach us, O Lord of the har - vest,

Our voic - es in wor - ship and song;
For the joy and a - bun - dance of crops,
We sing with con - cern and de - spair,
While har - vests are left on the field,
The earth and its peo - ple are one.
To be hum - ble in all that we claim;

We stand to re - call with thanks - giv - ing
For food that is stored in our lard - ers,
Of skills that are used for de - struc - tion,
For or - chards ne - glect - ed and wast - ing,
There can be no thanks with - out giv - ing,
To share what we have with the na - tions,

That to God all sea - sons be - long.
For all we can buy in the shops.
Of land that is burnt and laid bare.
For pro - duce from mar - kets with - held.
No words with - out deeds that are done.
To care for the world in your name.

Text: Fred Kaan, b.1929, © 1968, Hope Publishing Co.
Tune: HARVEST, 9 8 9 8; Geoffrey Laycock, b.1927, © 1971, Faber Music Ltd.

828 God, Whose Purpose Is to Kindle

1. God, whose pur - pose is to kin - dle:
2. God, who in your ho - ly gos - pel
3. God, who still a sword de - liv - ers

Now ig - nite us with your fire; While the earth a -
Wills that all should tru - ly live, Make us sense our
Rath - er than a plac - id peace, With your sharp - ened

waits your burn - ing, With your pas - sion us in - spire.
share of fail - ure, Our tran - quil - li - ty for - give.
word dis - turb us, From com - pla - cen - cy re - lease!

O - ver - come our sin - ful calm - ness,
Teach us cour - age as we strug - gle
Save us now from sat - is - fac - tion,

Stir us with your sav - ing name; Bap - tize with your
In all lib - er - at - ing strife; Lift the small - ness
When we pri - vate - ly are free, Yet are un - dis -

fier - y Spir - it, Crown our lives with tongues of flame.
of our vi - sion By your own a - bun - dant life.
turbed in spir - it By our neigh - bor's mis - er - y.

Text: Luke 12:49; David E. Trueblood, b.1900; © 1967, David Elton Trueblood
Tune: HOLY MANNA, 8 7 8 7 D; William Moore, fl.1830; harm. by Charles Anders, b.1929, © 1969 *Contemporary Worship I:Hymns*

How Long, O Lord, How Long 829

1. "How   long,   O   Lord,   how   long,"   The
2. How   long,   O   Lord,   how   long   Must
3. How   long,   O   Lord,   how   long   Will
4. How   long,   O   Lord,   how   long   Will
5. How   long,   O   Lord,   how   long   Must
6. "How   long,   O   Lord,   how   long?"   We
7. How   long,   O   Lord,   how   long?   Grant
8. How   long,   O   Lord,   how   long   Will

starv - ing   mil - lions   cry,   "Shall   fam - ine's   blight   our
home - less   peo - ple   lie   With - out   a   bed   in
jus - tice   bow   to   greed,   And   wealth   and   pow - er
walls   we   build   di - vide,   And   pride   of   gen - der,
war   its   car - nage   spread   And   leave   be - hind   in
cry   in   our   de - spair;   Yet,   nailed   up - on   the
strength of   heart   and   nerve   To   share   your   work   of
e -   vil's   pow'r   pre - vail?   We   hope   in   Christ   who

lives   de - stroy,   Our   chil - dren   waste   and   die?"
street and   camp   While   oth - ers   pass   them   by?
forge   the   chains   That   hold   the   poor   in   need?
race   or   class   An -   oth - er's   worth   de - ride?
ru -   ined   rows   The   har - vest   of   the   dead?
cross   we   see   The   em - blem   of   your   care.
truth   and   love,   To   suf - fer   and   to   serve.
con - quered death,   Whose   pur - pose   can - not   fail.

Text: Herman G. Stuempfle, Jr., 1923–2007, © 1993, GIA Publications, Inc.
Tune: SOUTHWELL; Damon's *Psalmes*, 1579

830 Make Me a Channel of Your Peace

Verses 1, 2, 4

1. Make me a chan-nel of your peace. Where
2. Make me a chan-nel of your peace. Where
4. Make me a chan-nel of your peace. It

there is ha-tred, let me bring your love. Where
there's de-spair in life, let me bring hope. Where
is in par-don-ing that we are par-doned, in

there is in-ju-ry, your par-don, Lord, And
there is dark-ness, on-ly light, And
giv-ing of our-selves that we re-ceive, and in

1.
where there's doubt, true faith in you.
where there's sad-ness, ev-er joy.
dy-ing that we're born to e-ter-nal life.
2., 4.

Verse 3

3. Oh, Mas-ter, grant that I may nev-er seek So much to be con-

soled as to con-sole. To be un-der-stood as to under-

D.C.

stand. To be loved as to love with all my soul.

Text: *Prayer of St. Francis;* adapt. by Sebastian Temple, 1928-1997
Tune: Sebastian Temple, 1928-1997; acc. by Robert J. Batastini, b.1942
© 1967, OCP Publications
Dedicated to Mrs. Frances Tracy

Let There Be Peace on Earth 831

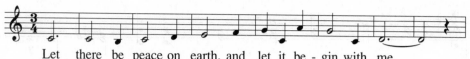

Let there be peace on earth, and let it be - gin with me.

Let there be peace on earth, the peace that was meant to be. With

God as our Fa - ther, broth - ers all are we.
fam - 'ly

Let me walk with my broth-er in per-fect har-mo - ny.
us each oth - er

Let peace be - gin with me; let this be the mo - ment now.

With ev - 'ry step I take, let this be my sol - emn vow; To

take each mo - ment, and live each mo - ment in peace e - ter - nal - ly!

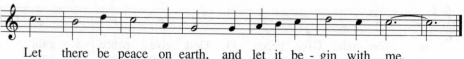

Let there be peace on earth, and let it be - gin with me.

Text: Sy Miller, 1908-1941, Jill Jackson, © 1955, 1983, Jan-Lee Music
Tune: Sy Miller, 1908-1941, Jill Jackson © 1955, 1983, Jan-Lee Music; acc. by Diana Kodner, b.1957, © 1993 GIA Publications, Inc.
Used with permission

832 Dona Nobis Pacem in Terra

Do - na no - bis pa - cem in ter - ra,

do - na no - bis pa - cem, Do - mi - ne.

Music: The Iona Community, © 1987, The Iona Community, GIA Publications, Inc., agent

833 O God of Love, O King of Peace

1. O God of love, O King of peace, Make
2. Whom shall we trust but you, O Lord? Where
3. Where saints and an - gels dwell a - bove, All

wars through-out the world to cease; Our vio - lent ways help
rest but on your faith - ful word? None ev - er called on
hearts are joined in ho - ly love; O bind us in that

us con - tain; Give peace, O God, give peace a - gain!
you in vain; Give peace, O God, give peace a - gain!
heav'n - ly chain; Give peace, O God, give peace a - gain!

*May be sung as a two- or four-voice canon.

Text: Henry W. Baker, 1821-1877
Tune: TALLIS' CANON, LM; Thomas Tallis, c.1505-1585

O God of Every Nation 834

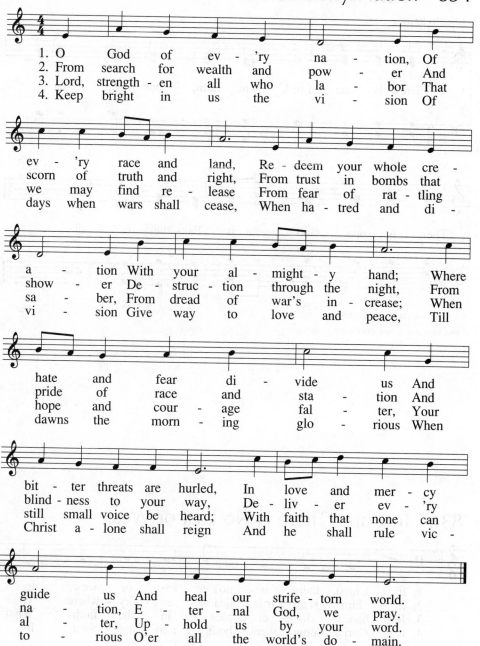

1. O God of ev-'ry na - tion, Of
2. From search for wealth and pow - er And
3. Lord, strength-en all who la - bor That
4. Keep bright in us the vi - sion Of

ev-'ry race and land, Re-deem your whole cre -
scorn of truth and right, From trust in bombs that
we may find re - lease From fear of rat - tling
days when wars shall cease, When ha - tred and di -

a - tion With your al - might - y hand; Where
show - er De - struc - tion through the night, From
sa - ber, From dread of war's in - crease; When
vi - sion Give way to love and peace, Till

hate and fear di - vide us And
pride of race and sta - tion And
hope and cour - age fal - ter, Your
dawns the morn - ing glo - rious When

bit - ter threats are hurled, In love and mer - cy
blind - ness to your way, De - liv - er ev - 'ry
still small voice be heard; With faith that none can
Christ a - lone shall reign And he shall rule vic -

guide us And heal our strife - torn world.
na - tion, E - ter - nal God, we pray.
al - ter, Up - hold us by your word.
to - rious O'er all the world's do - main.

Text: William W. Reid, b.1923, alt., © 1958, 1986, The Hymn Society (Administered by Hope Publishing Co.)
Tune: PASSION CHORALE, 7 6 7 6 D; Hans Leo Hassler, 1564-1612; harm. by J. S. Bach, 1685-1750

835 There Is One Lord

Ostinato Refrain

There is one Lord, one faith, one bap-tis-m,

There is one God who is Fa-ther of all.

Text: Ephesians 4; Taizé Community, 1984
Tune: Jacques Berthier, 1923-1994
© 1984, Les Presses de Taizé, GIA Publications, Inc., agent

836 In Christ There Is No East or West

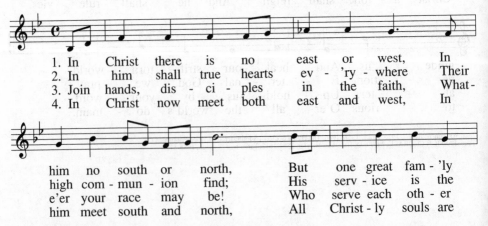

1. In Christ there is no east or west, In
2. In him shall true hearts ev-'ry-where Their
3. Join hands, dis-ci-ples in the faith, What-
4. In Christ now meet both east and west, In

him no south or north, But one great fam-'ly
high com-mun-ion find; His serv-ice is the
e'er your race may be! Who serve each oth-er
him meet south and north, All Christ-ly souls are

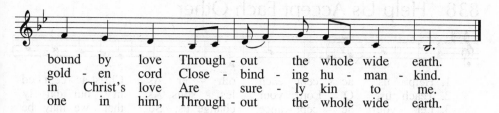

bound   by   love   Through - out   the   whole   wide   earth.
gold - en   cord   Close - bind - ing   hu - man - kind.
in   Christ's   love   Are   sure - ly   kin   to   me.
one   in   him,   Through - out   the   whole   wide   earth.

Text: Galatians 3:23; John Oxenham, 1852-1941
Tune: MC KEE, CM; African-American; adapt. by Harry T. Burleigh, 1866-1949

Diverse in Culture, Nation, Race   837

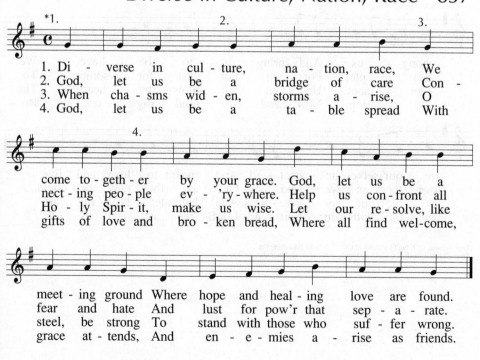

1. Di - verse in cul - ture, na - tion, race, We
2. God, let us be a bridge of care Con -
3. When cha - sms wid - en, storms a - rise, O
4. God, let us be a ta - ble spread With

come to - geth - er by your grace. God, let us be a
nect - ing peo - ple ev - 'ry - where. Help us con - front all
Ho - ly Spir - it, make us wise. Let our re - solve, like
gifts of love and bro - ken bread, Where all find wel - come,

meet - ing ground Where hope and heal - ing love are found.
fear and hate And lust for pow'r that sep - a - rate.
steel, be strong To stand with those who suf - fer wrong.
grace at - tends, And en - e - mies a - rise as friends.

May be sung as a two- or four-voice canon.

Text: Ruth Duck, b.1947, © 1992, GIA Publications, Inc.
Tune: TALLIS' CANON, LM; Thomas Tallis, c.1510-1583

838 Help Us Accept Each Other

1. Help us ac-cept each oth-er As Christ ac-cept-ed
2. Teach us, O Lord, your les-sons, As in our dai-ly
3. Let your ac-cept-ance change us, So that we may be
4. Lord, for to-day's en-coun-ters With all who are in

us; Teach us as sis-ter, broth-er, Each
life We strug-gle to be hu-man And
moved In liv-ing sit-u-a-tions To
need, Who hun-ger for ac-cept-ance, For

per-son to em-brace. Be pres-ent, Lord, a-
search for hope and faith. Teach us to care for
do the truth in love; To prac-tice your ac-
right-eous-ness and bread, We need new eyes for

mong us, And bring us to be-lieve We
peo-ple, For all, not just for some; To
cept-ance, Un-til we know by heart The
see-ing, New hands for hold-ing on; Re-

are our-selves ac-cept-ed And meant to love and live.
love them as we find them, Or, as they may be-come.
ta-ble of for-give-ness And laugh-ter's heal-ing art.
new us with your Spir-it; Lord, free us, make us one!

Text: Romans 15:7; Fred Kaan, b.1929, © 1975, Hope Publishing Co.
Tune: ELLACOMBE, 7 6 7 6 D; *Gesangbuch der Herzogl*, Wirtemberg, 1784

Father, Lord of All Creation   839

1. Fa - ther, Lord of all cre - a - tion,
2. Je - sus Christ, the man for oth - ers,
3. Ho - ly Spir - it, rush - ing, burn - ing

Ground of be - ing, life and love; Height and depth be -
We, your peo - ple, make our prayer: Give us grace to
Wind and flame of Pen - te - cost, Fire our hearts a -

yond de - scrip-tion On - ly life in you can prove:
love all oth - ers, Those whose bur - dens we can share.
fresh with yearn-ing To re - gain what we have lost.

You are mor - tal life's de - pend - ence:
Where your name binds us to - geth - er
May your love u - nite our ac - tion,

Thought, speech, sight are ours by grace; Yours is ev - 'ry
You, Lord Christ, will sure - ly be; Where no self - ish -
Nev - er - more to speak a - lone: God, in us a -

hour's ex - ist - ence, Sov - 'reign Lord of time and space.
ness can sev - er, There your love we all may see.
bol - ish fac - tion. God, through us your love make known.

Text: Stewart Cross, 1928-1989, ©
Tune: GENEVA, 8 7 8 7 D; George H. Day, 1883-1966, © 1942, The Church Pension Fund

840 We Are Many Parts

Refrain

We are man-y parts, we are all one bod-y, and the gifts we have we are giv-en to share. May the Spir-it of love make us one in-deed; one, the love that we share, one, our hope in de-spair, one, the cross that we bear.

Verses

1. God of all, we look to you, we would be your
2. So my pain is pain for you, in your joy is
3. All you seek-ers, great and small, seek the great-est

D.C.

ser-vants true, let us be your love to all the world.
my joy, too; all is brought to-geth-er in the Lord.
gift of all; if you love, then you will know the Lord.

Text: 1 Corinthians 12, 13; Marty Haugen, b.1950
Tune: Marty Haugen, b.1950
© 1980, 1986, GIA Publications, Inc.

Many Are the Lightbeams 841

1. Man - y are the light - beams from the one light.
2. Man - y are the branch - es of the one tree.
3. Man - y are the gifts giv'n, love is all one.
4. Man - y ways to serve God, the Spir - it is one;
5. Man - y are the mem - bers, the bod - y is one;

Our one light is Je - sus.
Our one tree is Je - sus.
Love's the gift of Je - sus.
ser - vant spir - it of Je - sus.
mem - bers all of Je - sus.

Man - y are the light - beams from the one
Man - y are the branch - es of the one
Man - y are the gifts giv'n, love is all
Man - y ways to serve God, the Spir - it is
Man - y are the mem - bers, the bod - y is

light; we are one in Christ.
tree; we are one in Christ.
one; we are one in Christ.
one; we are one in Christ.
one; we are one in Christ.

Text: *De unitate ecclesiae,* Cyprian of Carthage, 252 A.D.; by Anders Frostenson © A-F Foundation Hymns and Songs
Tune: Olle Widestrand ©; acc. by Marty Haugen, b.1950, © 1987, GIA Publications, Inc.

842 This Is the Day When Light Was First Created

1. This is the day when light was first cre - a - ted,
2. This is the day of our com - plete sur - pris - ing,
3. We join to praise, with ev - 'ry race and na - tion,
4. This is the day of wor - ship and of vi - sion,
5. We pray that this, the day of re - cre - a - tion,

Sym - bol and gift of or - der and de - sign.
Re - peat of Eas - ter: Christ has come to life!
The God who with the world his Spir - it shares;
Great birth - day of the church in ev - 'ry land.
May hal - low all the week that is to come.

In light is God's in - ten - tion clear - ly stat - ed,
Now is the feast of love's re - volt and ris - ing
Strong wind of change and earth's il - lu - mi - na - tion,
Let Chris - tians all con - fess their sad di - vi - sion,
Help us, O Lord, to lay a good foun - da - tion

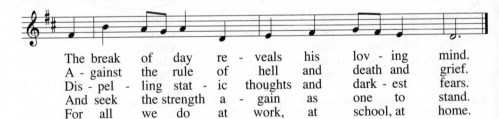

The break of day re - veals his lov - ing mind.
A - gainst the rule of hell and death and grief.
Dis - pel - ling stat - ic thoughts and dark - est fears.
And seek the strength a - gain as one to stand.
For all we do at work, at school, at home.

Text: Fred Kaan, b.1929, © 1968, Hope Publishing Co.
Tune: NORTHBROOK, 11 10 11 10; Reginald S. Thatcher, 1888-1957, © Oxford University Press

On This Day, the First of Days 843

1. On this day, the first of days,
2. On this day the e - ter - nal Son
3. Word - made - flesh, all prais - es be!
4. Ho - ly Spir - it, you im - part
5. God, the bless - ed Three in One,

God our Mak - er's name we praise;
O - ver death his tri - umph won;
You from sin have set us free;
Gifts of love to ev - 'ry heart;
May your ho - ly will be done;

Who, cre - a - tion's Lord and Spring,
On this day the Spir - it came
And with you we die and rise
Give us light and grace, we pray,
In your word our souls are free,

Did the world from dark - ness bring.
With its gifts of liv - ing flame.
Un - to God in sac - ri - fice.
Fill our hearts this ho - ly day.
As we praise the Trin - i - ty.

Text: *Die parente temporum; Le Mans Breviary*, 1748; tr. by Henry W. Baker, 1821-1877
Tune: LÜBECK, 77 77; *Freylinghausen's Gesangbuch*, 1704

844 God Is Here! As We His People

1. God is here! As we his peo-ple Meet to
2. Here are sym-bols to re-mind us Of our
3. Here our chil-dren find a wel-come In the
4. Lord of all, of church and king-dom, In an

of - fer praise and prayer, May we find in ful - ler
life - long need of grace; Here are ta - ble, font and
Shep - herd's flock and fold; Here, as bread and wine are
age of change and doubt, Keep us faith - ful to the

meas-ure What it is in Christ we share:
pul - pit, Here the cross has cen - tral place:
tak - en, Christ sus - tains us as of old:
gos - pel, Help us work your pur - pose out:

Here, as in the world a - round us, All our
Here in hon - es - ty of preach-ing, Here in
Here the ser - vants of the Ser - vant Seek in
Here, in this day's ded - i - ca - tion, All we

var - ied skills and arts Wait the com - ing
si - lence as in speech, Here in new - ness
wor - ship to ex - plore What it means in
have to give, re - ceive; We who can - not

of his Spir - it In - to o - pen minds and hearts.
and re - new-al God the Spir - it comes to each.
dai - ly liv-ing To be - lieve and to a - dore.
live with-out you, We a - dore you! We be - lieve!

Text: Fred Pratt Green, 1903-2000, © 1979, Hope Publishing Co.
Tune: ABBOT'S LEIGH, 8 7 8 7 D; Cyril V. Taylor, 1907-1991, © 1942, 1970, Hope Publishing Co.

All Who Hunger, Gather Gladly 845

1. All who hun - ger, gath - er glad - ly;
2. All who hun - ger, nev - er stran - gers,
3. All who hun - ger, sing to - geth - er;

Ho - ly man - na is our bread. Come from wil - der -
Seek - er, be a wel-come guest. Come from rest - less -
Je - sus Christ is liv - ing bread. Come from lone - li -

ness and wan - d'ring. Here, in truth, we will be fed.
ness and roam - ing. Here, in joy, we keep the feast.
ness and long - ing. Here, in peace, we have been led.

You that yearn for days of full - ness,
We that once were lost and scat - tered
Blest are those who from this ta - ble

All a - round us is our food. Taste and see the
In com - mun - ion's love have stood. Taste and see the
Live their days in grat - i - tude. Taste and see the

grace e - ter - nal. Taste and see that God is good.
grace e - ter - nal. Taste and see that God is good.
grace e - ter - nal. Taste and see that God is good.

Text: Sylvia G. Dunstan, 1955-1993, © 1991, GIA Publications, Inc.
Tune: HOLY MANNA, 8 7 8 7 D; William Moore, fl.1830; harm. by Charles Anders, b.1929, © 1969, Comtemporary Worship I: Hymns

846   All Are Welcome

1. Let us build a house where love can dwell And
2. Let us build a house where proph - ets speak, And
3. Let us build a house where love is found In
4. Let us build a house where hands will reach Be -
5. Let us build a house where all are named, Their

all can safe - ly live, A place where saints and
words are strong and true, Where all God's chil - dren
wa - ter, wine and wheat: A ban - quet hall on
yond the wood and stone To heal and strength-en,
songs and vi - sions heard And loved and treas - ured,

chil - dren tell How hearts learn to for -
dare to seek To dream God's reign a -
ho - ly ground, Where peace and jus - tice
serve and teach, And live the Word they've
taught and claimed As words with - in the

give. Built of hopes and dreams and vi - sions,
new. Here the cross shall stand as wit - ness
meet. Here the love of God, through Je - sus,
known. Here the out - cast and the stran - ger
Word. Built of tears and cries and laugh-ter,

Rock of faith and vault of grace; Here the
And as sym - bol of God's grace; Here as
Is re - vealed in time and space; As we
Bear the im - age of God's face; Let us
Prayers of faith and songs of grace, Let this

love of Christ shall end di - vi - sions:
one we claim the faith of Je - sus:
share in Christ the feast that frees us:
bring an end to fear and dan - ger:
house pro - claim from floor to raft - er:

All are wel-come, all are wel-come, all are wel-come

in this place.

Text: Marty Haugen, b. 1950
Tune: TWO OAKS, 9 6 8 6 8 7 10 with refrain; Marty Haugen, b. 1950
© 1994, GIA Publications, Inc.

Come, Rejoice before Your Maker   847

1. Come,   re - joice be - fore   your Mak - er
2. Know   for cer - tain,   our   Cre - a - tor
3. Come   with grate - ful   hearts   and voic - es
4. For   the Lord   our   God   is gra - cious

All   you peo - ples   of   the   earth;   Serve   the Lord your
Is   the true and   on - ly   God;   We   the crea - tures
En - ter now God's courts   with   praise;   Show your thank - ful -
Ev - er - last - ing   is   God's love,   And   to ev - 'ry

God   with glad - ness, Come   re - joic - ing   with   a   song!
of   our Mak - er   Sheep   with - in   the   Shep - herd's fold.
ness   with glad - ness, Give   due hon - or   to   God's name.
gen - er - a - tion   That   great faith - ful - ness   en - dures.

Text: Psalm 100; Michael Baughen, b.1930, alt.
Tune: JUBILATE DEO, 8 7 8 7; Noel H. Tredinnick, b.1949
© 1973, Jubilate Hymns, Ltd. (Administered by Hope Publishing Co.)

848 As We Gather at Your Table

1. As we gath - er at your Ta - ble, As we
2. Turn our wor - ship in - to wit - ness In the
3. Gra - cious Spir - it, help us sum - mon Oth - er

lis - ten to your Word, Help us know, O God, your
sac - ra - ment of life; Send us forth to love and
guests to share that feast Where tri - um - phant Love will

pres - ence: Let our hearts and minds be stirred. Nour - ish
serve you, Bring - ing peace where there is strife. Give us,
wel - come Those who had been last and least. There no

us with sa - cred sto - ry Till we
Christ, your great com - pas - sion To for -
more will en - vy blind us Nor will

claim it as our own; Teach us through this ho - ly
give as you for - gave; May we still be - hold your
pride our peace de - stroy, As we join with saints and

ban - quet How to make Love's vic - tory known.
im - age In the world you died to save.
an - gels To re - peat the sound - ing joy.

Text: Carl P. Daw, Jr. b.1944; © 1989, Hope Publishing Co.
Tune: NETTLETON, 8 7 8 7 D; Wyeth's *Repository of Sacred Music, Pt. II*, 1813

All People That on Earth Do Dwell   849

1. All peo - ple that on earth do dwell,
2. Know that the Lord is God in - deed;
3. O en - ter then his gates with praise;
4. For why? the Lord our God is good:
5. To Fa - ther, Son, and Ho - ly Ghost,
* Praise God, from whom all bless - ings flow;

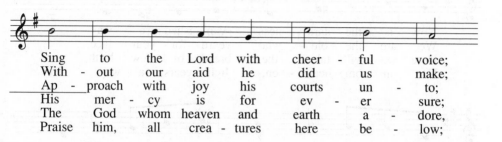

Sing to the Lord with cheer - ful voice;
With - out our aid he did us make;
Ap - proach with joy his courts un - to;
His mer - cy is for ev - er sure;
The God whom heaven and earth a - dore,
Praise him, all crea - tures here be - low;

Him serve with mirth, his praise forth tell,
We are his folk, he does us feed,
Praise, laud, and bless his Name al - ways,
His truth at all times firm - ly stood,
From us and from the an - gel host
Praise him a - bove, you heav'n - ly host:

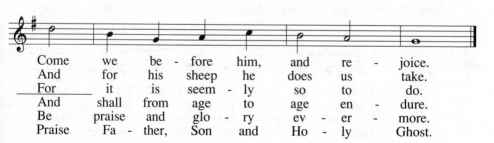

Come we be - fore him, and re - joice.
And for his sheep he does us take.
For it is seem - ly so to do.
And shall from age to age en - dure.
Be praise and glo - ry ev - er - more.
Praise Fa - ther, Son and Ho - ly Ghost.

*May be sung alone or as an alternate to stanza 5.

Text: Psalm (99)100; William Kethe, d. c.1593; Doxology, Thomas Ken, 1637-1711
Tune: OLD HUNDREDTH, LM; Louis Bourgeois, c.1510-1561

850 Gather Us In

1. Here in this place new light is stream - ing,
2. We are the young— our lives are a mys - t'ry,
3. Here we will take the wine and the wa - ter,
4. Not in the dark of build - ings con - fin - ing,

Now is the dark - ness van - ished a - way,
We are the old— who yearn for your face,
Here we will take the bread of new birth,
Not in some heav - en, light - years a - way, But

See in this space our fears and our dream - ings,
We have been sung through - out all of his - t'ry,
Here you shall call your sons and your daugh - ters,
here in this place the new light is shin - ing,

Brought here to you in the light of this day.
Called to be light to the whole hu - man race.
Call us a - new to be salt for the earth.
Now is the King - dom, now is the day.

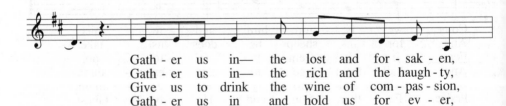

Gath - er us in— the lost and for - sak - en,
Gath - er us in— the rich and the haugh - ty,
Give us to drink the wine of com - pas - sion,
Gath - er us in and hold us for ev - er,

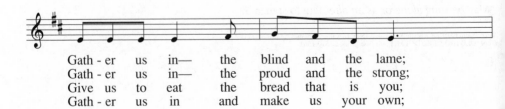

Gath - er us in— the blind and the lame;
Gath - er us in— the proud and the strong;
Give us to eat the bread that is you;
Gath - er us in and make us your own;

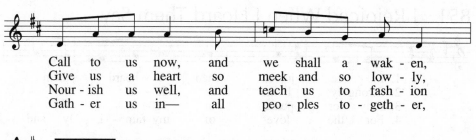

Call to us now, and we shall a - wak - en,
Give us a heart so meek and so low - ly,
Nour - ish us well, and teach us to fash - ion
Gath - er us in— all peo - ples to - geth - er,

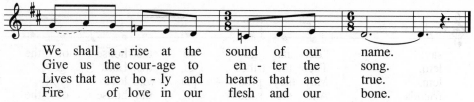

We shall a - rise at the sound of our name.
Give us the cour-age to en - ter the song.
Lives that are ho - ly and hearts that are true.
Fire of love in our flesh and our bone.

851 I Rejoiced When I Heard Them Say

1. I re - joiced when I heard them
2. Strong-ly built is Je - ru - sa -
3. Pray for peace in Je - ru - sa -
4. For the love of my fam - i - ly and

say: "Let us go to the house of the
lem, There the tribes of the Lord go
lem, May they pros - per who love you
friends And the sake of the house of the

Lord." Our feet are stand - ing with - in your
up, Seek-ing their jus - tice and bring - ing
well; E - ter - nal peace be with - in your
Lord, I ev - er pray for your health and

gates, O Je - ru - sa - lem.
thanks, O Je - ru - sa - lem.
walls, O Je - ru - sa - lem.
peace, O Je - ru - sa - lem.

I re - joiced when I heard them say:

"Let us go to the house of the Lord!"

I re - joiced when I heard them say:

"Let us go to the house of the Lord!"

Text: Psalm 121; Richard Proulx, b.1937
Tune: MA YEDIDUT; Chassidic Melody, arr. by Richard Proulx, b.1937
© 1993, GIA Publications, Inc.

Only-begotten, Word of God Eternal 852

1. On - ly - be - got - ten, Word of God e -
2. Ho - ly this tem - ple where our Lord is
3. Lord, we be - seech you, as we throng your
4. God in Three Per - sons, Fa - ther ev - er -

ter - nal, Lord of cre - a - tion, mer - ci - ful and
dwell - ing, This is none oth - er than the gate of
tem - ple, By your past bless - ings, by your pres - ent
liv - ing, Son co - e - ter - nal, ev - er - bless - ed

might - y, Hear now your ser - vants, when their tune - ful
heav - en; Stran - gers and pil - grims, seek - ing homes e -
boun - ty, Smile on your chil - dren, and with ten - der
Spir - it, Yours be the glo - ry, praise and ad - or -

voic - es Rise to your pres - ence.
ter - nal, Pass through its por - tals.
mer - cy Hear our pe - ti - tions.
a - tion, Now and for ev - er.

Text: *Christe cunctorum dominator alme*; Latin, 9th C.; tr. by Maxwell J. Blacker, 1822-1888
Tune: ISTE CONFESSOR, 11 11 11 5; Rouen Church Melody; harm. by Carl Schalk, b.1929, © 1969, Concordia Publishing House

853 Now the Feast and Celebration

Refrain

Now the feast and cel - e - bra-tion, all of cre - a - tion

sings for joy, to the God of life and love and free-dom;

praise and glo - ry for - ev - er - more!

Verse 1

1. Now is the feast of the Lamb once slain,

whose blood has freed and u - nit - ed us

D.C.

to be one great peo - ple of God.

Verse 2

2. Pow-er and rich-es, wis - dom and might, all hon - or and

D.C.

glo - ry to Christ for - ev - er.

Verse 3

3. For God has come to dwell with us, to make us

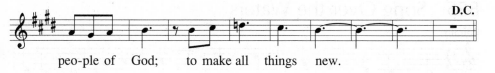

peo-ple of God; to make all things new.

Text: Marty Haugen, b.1950
Tune: Marty Haugen, b.1950
© 1990, GIA Publications, Inc.

I Come with Joy 854

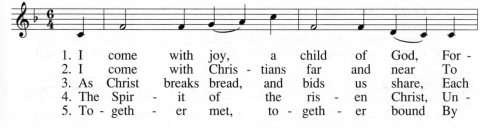

1. I come with joy, a child of God, For-
2. I come with Chris - tians far and near To
3. As Christ breaks bread, and bids us share, Each
4. The Spir - it of the ris - en Christ, Un-
5. To - geth - er met, to - geth - er bound By

giv - en, loved, and free, The life of Je - sus
find, as all are fed, The new com - mu - ni -
proud di - vi - sion ends. The love that made us,
seen, but al - ways near, Is in such friend - ship
all that God has done, We'll go with joy, to

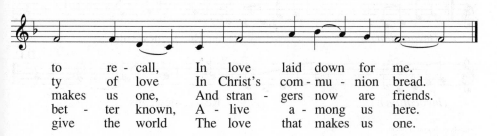

to re - call, In love laid down for me.
ty of love In Christ's com - mu - nion bread.
makes us one, And stran - gers now are friends.
bet - ter known, A - live a - mong us here.
give the world The love that makes us one.

Text: Brian Wren, b.1936, © 1971, Hope Publishing Co.
Tune: LAND OF REST, CM; American; harm. by Annabel M. Buchanan, 1888-1983, © 1938, 1966, J. Fisher and Bro.

855 Song Over the Waters

Refrain

God, you have moved up-on the wa-ters, you have sung in the
rush of wind and flame; and in your love, you have called us sons and
daugh-ters, make us peo-ple of the wa-ter and your name.

Verses

1. Come fill our wait - ing hearts with the
2. Give us a thirst for love, give us a
3. You are the breath of life, you are the
4. Come, o - pen ev - 'ry heart, come now and

spir - it of Je - sus, let us shine with your
hun - ger for jus - tice, make us one with the
hope of the hope - less, come and fill us with
wake us to won - der, make us ves - sels of

D.C.

light and peace.
mind of Christ.
light and peace.
light and peace.

Sprinkling Rite

Cantor: All:

(Invocation)   Re - new us!

Cantor: All: D.C.

(Invocation)   Re - new us!

Text: Marty Haugen, b.1950
Tune: Marty Haugen, b.1950
© 1987, GIA Publications, Inc.

This Day God Gives Me   856

1. This day God gives me Strength of high
2. This day God sends me Strength as my
3. God's way is my way, God's shield is
4. Ris - ing I thank you, Might - y and

heav - en, Sun and moon shin - ing,
guar - dian, Might to up - hold me,
'round me, God's host de - fends me,
strong One, King of cre - a - tion,

Flame in my hearth, Flash - ing of light - ning,
Wis - dom as guide. Your eyes are watch - ful,
Sav - ing from ill. An - gels of heav - en,
Giv - er of rest, Firm - ly con - fess - ing

Wind in its swift - ness, Depths of the
Your ears are lis - t'ning, Your lips are
Drive from me al - ways All that would
God in three Per - sons, One - ness of

o - cean, Firm - ness of earth.
speak - ing, Friend at my side.
harm me, Stand by me still.
God - head, Trin - i - ty blest.

Text: Ascribed to St. Patrick; James Quinn, SJ, b.1919, © 1969. Used by permission of Selah Publishing Co., Inc., Kingston, N.Y.
Tune: ANDREA, 5 5 5 4 D; David Haas, b.1957, © 1993, GIA Publications, Inc.

857 Today I Awake

1. To - day I a - wake and God is be - fore me. At
2. To - day I a - rise and Christ is be - side me. He
3. To - day I af - firm the Spir - it with - in me At
4. To - day I en - joy the Trin - i - ty round me, A -

night, as I dreamt, he sum-moned the day; For
walked through the dark to scat - ter new light. Yes,
wor - ship and work, in strug - gle and rest. The
bove and be - neath, be-fore and be - hind; The

God nev - er sleeps but pat - terns the morn - ing With
Christ is a - live, and beck - ons his peo - ple To
Spir - it in - spires all life which is chang - ing From
Mak - er, the Son, the Spir - it to - geth - er— They

slith - ers of gold or glo - ry in gray.
hope and to heal, re - sist and in - vite.
fear - ing to faith, from bro - ken to blest.
called me to life and call me their friend.

Text: John L. Bell, b.1949
Tune: SLITHERS OF GOLD, 11 10 11 10; John L. Bell, b.1949
© 1989, Iona Community, GIA Publications, Inc., agent

When Morning Gilds the Skies 858

1. When morn - ing gilds the skies, My heart, a -
2. To God, the Word, on high The hosts of
3. Let earth's wide cir - cle round In joy - ful
4. Be this while life is mine My can - ti -

wak - ing, cries, "May Je - sus Christ be praised!" A -
an - gels cry: "May Je - sus Christ be praised!" Let
notes re - sound: "May Je - sus Christ be praised!" Let
cle di - vine: "May Je - sus Christ be praised!" Be

like at work and prayer To Je - sus I re -
mor - tals, too, up - raise Their voice in hymns of
air, and sea, and sky, From depth to height, re -
this the e - ter - nal song, Through all the a - ges

pair: "May Je - sus Christ be praised!"
praise: "May Je - sus Christ be praised!"
ply: "May Je - sus Christ be praised!"
long: "May Je - sus Christ be praised!"

Text: *Wach ich früh Morgens auf; Katholiches Gesangbuch*, 1828; tr. by Edward Caswall, 1814-1878
Tune: LAUDES DOMINI, 66 6 D; Joseph Barnby, 1838-1896

859 Morning Has Broken

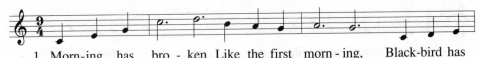

1. Morn-ing has bro-ken Like the first morn-ing, Black-bird has
2. Sweet the rain's new fall Sun-lit from heav-en, Like the first
3. Mine is the sun-light! Mine is the morn-ing Born of the

spo-ken Like the first bird. Praise for the sing-ing! Praise for the
dew-fall On the first grass. Praise for the sweet-ness Of the wet
one light E-den saw play! Praise with e-la-tion, Praise ev-'ry

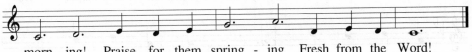

morn-ing! Praise for them, spring-ing Fresh from the Word!
gar-den, Sprung in com-plete-ness Where his feet pass.
morn-ing, God's re-cre-a-tion Of the new day!

Text: Eleanor Farjeon, 1881-1965, *The Children's Bells*, © David Higham Assoc., Ltd.
Tune: BUNESSAN, 5 5 5 4 D; Gaelic; acc. by Marty Haugen, b.1950, © 1987, GIA Publications, Inc.

860 Father, We Praise You

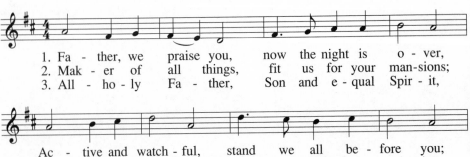

1. Fa-ther, we praise you, now the night is o-ver,
2. Mak-er of all things, fit us for your man-sions;
3. All-ho-ly Fa-ther, Son and e-qual Spir-it,

Ac-tive and watch-ful, stand we all be-fore you;
Ban-ish our weak-ness, health and whole-ness send-ing;
Trin-i-ty bless-ed, send us your sal-va-tion;

Sing - ing we of - fer pray'r and med - i -
Bring us to heav - en, where your saints u -
Yours is the glo - ry, gleam - ing and re -

ta - tion: Thus we a - dore you.
nit - ed Joy with - out end - ing.
sound - ing Through all cre - a - tion.

Text: *Nocte Surgentes;* Attr. to St. Gregory the Great, 540-604; tr. by Percy Dearmer, 1867-1936, alt., © Oxford University Press
Tune: CHRISTE SANCTORUM, 11 11 11 5; *La Feillees Methode du plain-chant*, 1782

Kindle a Flame to Lighten the Dark 861

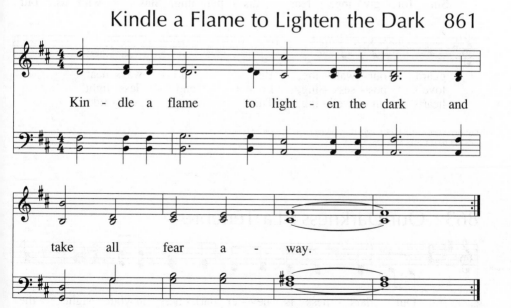

Kin - dle a flame to light - en the dark and

take all fear a - way.

Text: John L. Bell, b.1949
Tune: John L. Bell, b.1949

862 Day Is Done

1. Day is done, but love un-fail-ing Dwells ev - er
2. Dark de-scends, but light un-end-ing Shines through our
3. Eyes will close, but you un-sleep-ing Watch by our

here; Shad - ows fall, but hope, pre - vail - ing,
night; You are with us, ev - er lend - ing
side; Death may come, in love's safe keep - ing

Calms ev - 'ry fear. God, our Mak - er, none for-sak - ing,
New strength to sight: One in love, your truth con-fess - ing,
Still we a - bide. God of love, all e - vil quell-ing,

Take our hearts, of Love's own mak - ing, Watch our sleep-ing,
One in hope of heav - en's bless-ing, May we see, in
Sin for - giv - ing, fear dis - pel - ling, Stay with us, our

guard our wak - ing, Be al - ways near.
love's pos - sess - ing, Love's end - less light!
hearts in - dwell - ing, This e - ven - tide.

Text: James Quinn, SJ, b.1919, © 1969, Used with permission of Selah Publishing Co., Inc.
Tune: AR HYD Y NOS, 8 4 8 4 888 4; Welsh

863 Our Darkness / La Ténèbre

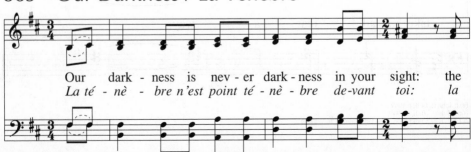

Our dark - ness is nev - er dark - ness in your sight: the
La té - nè - bre n'est point té - nè - bre de-vant toi: la

deep - est night is clear as the day - light.
nuit com - me le jour est lu - miè - re.

Text: Taizé Community
Tune: Jacques Berthier, 1923-1994
© 1991, Les Presses de Taizé, GIA Publications, Inc., agent

At Evening 864

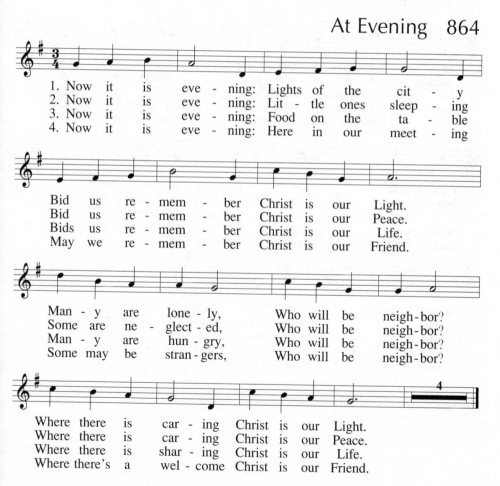

1. Now it is eve - ning: Lights of the cit - y
2. Now it is eve - ning: Lit - tle ones sleep - ing
3. Now it is eve - ning: Food on the ta - ble
4. Now it is eve - ning: Here in our meet - ing

Bid us re - mem - ber Christ is our Light.
Bid us re - mem - ber Christ is our Peace.
Bids us re - mem - ber Christ is our Life.
May we re - mem - ber Christ is our Friend.

Man - y are lone - ly, Who will be neigh-bor?
Some are ne - glect - ed, Who will be neigh-bor?
Man - y are hun - gry, Who will be neigh-bor?
Some may be stran - gers, Who will be neigh-bor?

Where there is car - ing Christ is our Light.
Where there is car - ing Christ is our Peace.
Where there is shar - ing Christ is our Life.
Where there's a wel - come Christ is our Friend.

Text: Fred Pratt Green, 1903-2000, © 1974, Hope Publishing Co.
Tune: EVENING HYMN, 5 5 5 4 D; David Haas, b.1957, © 1985, GIA Publications, Inc.

865 Christ, Mighty Savior

1. Christ, might-y Sav-ior, Light of all cre-
2. Now comes the day's end as the sun is
3. There-fore we come now eve - ning rites to
4. Give heed, we pray you, to our sup-pli-
5. Though bod-ies slum-ber, hearts shall keep their

a - tion, You make the day - time
set - ting: Mir - ror of day - break,
of - fer, Joy - ful - ly chant - ing
ca - tion: That you may grant us
vig - il, For ev - er rest - ing

ra - diant with the sun - light And to the
pledge of res-ur-rec-tion; While in the
ho - ly hymns to praise you, With all cre -
par - don for of-fens-es, Strength for our
in the peace of Je - sus, In light or

night give glit - ter-ing a-dorn-ment,
heav - ens choirs of stars ap-pear-ing
a - tion join - ing hearts and voic - es
weak hearts, rest for ach-ing bod - ies,
dark - ness wor - ship-ing our Sav - ior

Stars in the heav - ens.
Hal - low the night - fall.
Sing - ing your glo - ry.
Sooth - ing the wea - ry.
Now and for-ev - er.

Text: *Christe, lux mundi*; Mozarabic Rite, 10th C.; tr. by Alan G. McDougall, 1895-1964, rev. by Anne K. LeCroy, b.1930, and others, ©
Tune: MIGHTY SAVIOR, 11 11 11 5; David Hurd, b.1950, © 1985, GIA Publications, Inc.

The Day You Gave Us, Lord, Is Ended 866

1. The day you gave us, Lord, is end-ed, The
2. We thank you that your Church, un-sleep-ing While
3. A-cross each con-ti-nent and is-land As
4. The sun that bids us rest is wak-ing Your
5. So be it, Lord; your throne shall nev-er, Like

dark - ness falls at your be - hest; To
earth rolls on - ward in - to light, Through
dawn leads on an - oth - er day, The
friends be - neath the west - ern sky, And
earth's proud em - pires, pass a - way: Your

you our morn - ing hymns as - cend-ed, Your
all the world its watch is keep-ing, And
voice of prayer is nev - er si - lent, Nor
hour by hour fresh lips are mak-ing Your
king - dom stands, and grows for ev - er, Till

praise shall sanc - ti - fy our rest.
rests not now by day or night.
dies the strain of praise a - way.
won - drous do - ings heard on high.
all your crea - tures own your sway.

Text: John Ellerton, 1826-1893, alt.
Tune: ST. CLEMENT, 9 8 9 8; Clement C. Scholefield, 1839-1904

867 Praise and Thanksgiving

1. Praise and thanks - giv - ing, Fa - ther, we of - fer,
2. Lord, bless the la - bor We bring to serve you,
3. Fa - ther, pro - vid - ing Food for your chil - dren,
4. Then will your bless - ing Reach ev - 'ry peo - ple,

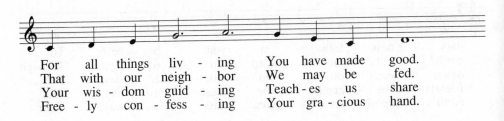

For all things liv - ing You have made good.
That with our neigh - bor We may be fed.
Your wis - dom guid - ing Teach - es us share
Free - ly con - fess - ing Your gra - cious hand.

Har - vest of sown fields, Fruits of the or - chard,
Sow - ing or till - ing, We would work with you,
One with an - oth - er, So that re - joic - ing
Where you are reign - ing No one will hun - ger,

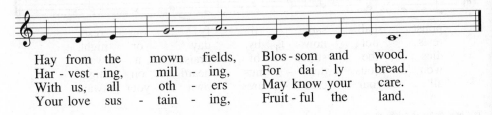

Hay from the mown fields, Blos - som and wood.
Har - vest - ing, mill - ing, For dai - ly bread.
With us, all oth - ers May know your care.
Your love sus - tain - ing, Fruit - ful the land.

Text: Albert F. Bayly, 1901-1984, © 1988, Oxford University Press
Tune: BUNESSAN, 5 5 5 4 D; Gaelic; harm. by A. Gregory Murray, OSB, 1905-1992, © Downside Abbey

When the Lord in Glory Comes 868

1. When the Lord in glo - ry comes not the trum - pets, not the
   shout the heav-ens raise, not the cho - rus, not the
2. When the Lord is seen a - gain not the glo - ries of his
   pomp and pow'r a - lone, not the splen-dors of his
3. When the Lord to hu - man eyes shall be-stride our nar - row
   man by all de - nied, not the vic - tim cru - ci -

drums, not the an - them, not the psalm, not the
praise, not the si - lenc - es sub - lime, not the
reign, not the light - nings through the storm, not the
throne, not his robe and di - a - dems, not the
skies, not the child of hum - ble birth, not the
fied, but the God who died to save, but the

1., 3., 5.

2., 4., 6.

thun - der, not the calm, not the
sounds of space and
ra - diance of his form, not his
gold and not the
car - pen - ter of earth, not the
vic - tor of the

time,

gems,

grave,

but his voice when he ap - pears shall be
but his face up - on my sight shall be
he it is to whom I fall, Je - sus

All:

mu - sic to my ears— but his voice when he ap -
dark - ness in - to light— but his face up - on my
Christ, my All in all— he it is to whom I

pears shall be mu - sic to my ears.
sight shall be dark - ness in - to light.
fall, Je - sus Christ, my All in all.

Text: Timothy Dudley-Smith, b.1926, © 1967, Hope Publishing Co.
Tune: ST. JOHN'S, 77 77 77 D; Bob Moore, b.1962, © 1993, GIA Publications, Inc.

869 Mine Eyes Have Seen the Glory

1. Mine eyes have seen the glo - ry of the
2. I have seen him in the watch - fires of a
3. He has sound - ed forth the trum - pet that shall
4. In the beau - ty of the lil - ies Christ was

com - ing of the Lord; He is tram - pling out the
hun - dred cir - cling camps; They have build - ed him an
nev - er call re - treat; He is sift - ing out all
born a - cross the sea, With a glo - ry in his

vin - tage where the grapes of wrath are stored; He hath
al - tar in the eve - ning dews and damps; I can
hu - man hearts be - fore his judg - ment seat; O be
bos - om that trans - fig - ures you and me; As he

loosed the fate - ful light - ning of his ter - ri - ble swift
read the right - eous sen - tence by the dim and flar - ing
swift, my soul, to an - swer him; be ju - bi - lant, my
died to make us ho - ly, let us die that all be

sword; His truth is march - ing on.
lamps; His day is march - ing on.
feet! Our God is march - ing on.
free! While God is march - ing on.

Glo - ry! Glo - ry! Hal - le - lu - jah! Glo - ry!

Glo - ry! Hal - le - lu - jah! Glo - ry! Glo - ry!

Hal - le - lu - jah! His truth is march-ing on.

Text: Julia W. Howe, 1819-1910
Tune: BATTLE HYMN OF THE REPUBLIC, 15 15 15 6 with refrain; attr. to William Steffe, d.1911

Soon and Very Soon 870

1. Soon and ver - y soon we are goin' to see the King,
2. No more cry - in' there we are goin' to see the King,
3. No more dy - in' there we are goin' to see the King,
4. Soon and ver - y soon we are goin' to see the King,

Soon and ver - y soon we are goin' to see the King,
No more cry - in' there we are goin' to see the King,
No more dy - in' there we are goin' to see the King,
Soon and ver - y soon we are goin' to see the King,

Soon and ver - y soon we are goin' to see the King,
No more cry - in' there we are goin' to see the King,
No more dy - in' there we are goin' to see the King, Hal-le-
Soon and ver - y soon we are goin' to see the King,

1., 2.
lu - jah, Hal-le-lu - jah, we're goin' to see the King!

3.,4.
Hal - le - lu - jah, Hal - le - lu -

jah, Hal - le - lu - jah, Hal - le - lu - jah.

Text: Andraé Crouch
Tune: Andraé Crouch
© 1976, Bud John Songs, Inc./Crouch Music/ASCAP

871 Jerusalem, My Happy Home

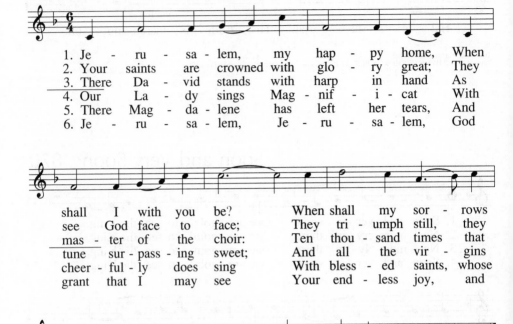

1. Je - ru - sa - lem, my hap - py home, When
2. Your saints are crowned with glo - ry great; They
3. There Da - vid stands with harp in hand As
4. Our La - dy sings Mag - nif - i - cat With
5. There Mag - da - lene has left her tears, And
6. Je - ru - sa - lem, Je - ru - sa - lem, God

shall I with you be? When shall my sor - rows
see God face to face; They tri - umph still, they
mas - ter of the choir: Ten thou - sand times that
tune sur - pass - ing sweet; And all the vir - gins
cheer - ful - ly does sing With bless - ed saints, whose
grant that I may see Your end - less joy, and

have an end? Your joys when shall I see?
still re - joice: In that most ho - ly place.
we were blest That might this mu - sic hear.
join the song While sit - ting at her feet.
har - mo - ny In ev - 'ry street does ring.
of the same Par - tak - er ev - er be!

Text: Joseph Bromehead, 1747-1826, alt.
Tune: LAND OF REST, CM; American; harm. by Richard Proulx, b.1937, © 1975, GIA Publications, Inc.

872 We Shall Rise Again

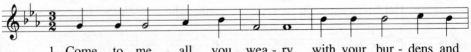

1. Come to me, all you wea - ry, with your bur - dens and
2. Though we walk through the dark - ness, e - vil we do not
3. We de - pend on God's mer - cy, mer - cy which nev - er
4. Do not fear death's do - min - ion, look be - yond earth and
5. At the door there to greet us, mar - tyrs, an - gels, and

pain.   Take my yoke on your shoul - ders and
fear.   You are walk - ing be - side us with your
fades.   We re - mem - ber our cov - e - nant and the
grave.   See the bright - ness of Je - sus shin - ing
saints,   And our fam - 'ly and loved ones, ev - 'ry -

learn from me: I am gen - tle and hum - ble,
rod and your staff. On - ly good - ness and kind - ness
prom - ise Je - sus made: If we die with Christ Je - sus,
out to light our way. Lov - ing Fa - ther and Spir - it,
one freed from their chains. We shall feel their ac - cep - tance,

and your soul will find rest, For my yoke is
fol - low us all our lives. We shall dwell in the
we shall live with him, And if we are
lov - ing Je - sus the Son, All God's peo - ple to -
and the joy of new life. We shall join in the

eas - y and my bur - den is light.
Lord's house for so man - y years to come!
faith - ful, we shall reign with him!
geth - er, we shall live on as one!
gath - er - ing, re - u - nit - ed in God's love!

We shall rise a-gain on the last day with the faith - ful, rich and

poor. Com-ing to the house of Lord Je - sus, we will find an o - pen

door there, we will find an o - pen door.

Text: Matthew 11:29-30, Psalm 23, John 11, 2 Timothy 2; Jeremy Young, b.1948
Tune: RESURRECTION; Irregular with refrain; Jeremy Young, b.1948
©1987, GIA Publications, Inc.

873 Steal Away to Jesus

Refrain

Steal a-way, steal a-way, steal a-way to Je-sus!

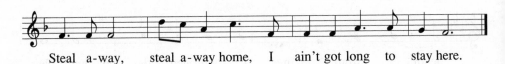

Steal a-way, steal a-way home, I ain't got long to stay here.

Verses

1. My Lord, he calls me, He calls me by the thun-der; The
2. Green trees are bend-ing, Poor sin-ners stand a trem-bling; The
3. My Lord, he calls me, He calls me by the light-ning; The

D.C.

trum-pet sounds with-in my soul; I ain't got long to stay here.

Text: African-American spiritual
Tune: African-American spiritual

Lord, Bid Your Servant Go in Peace 874

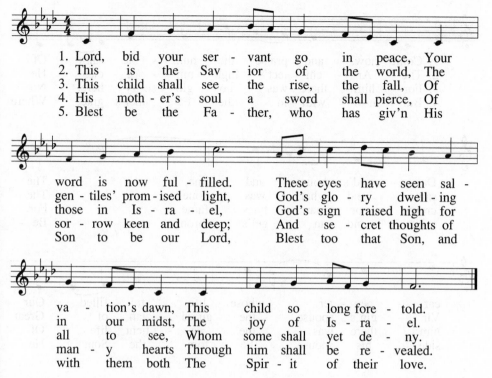

1. Lord, bid your ser - vant go in peace, Your word is now ful - filled. These eyes have seen sal - va - tion's dawn, This child so long fore - told.

2. This is the Sav - ior of the world, The gen - tiles' prom - ised light, God's glo - ry dwell - ing in our midst, The joy of Is - ra - el.

3. This child shall see the rise, the fall, Of those in Is - ra - el, God's sign raised high for all to see, Whom some shall yet de - ny.

4. His moth - er's soul a sword shall pierce, Of sor - row keen and deep; And se - cret thoughts of man - y hearts Through him shall be re - vealed.

5. Blest be the Fa - ther, who has giv'n His Son to be our Lord, Blest too that Son, and with them both The Spir - it of their love.

Text: Luke 2:29-32, 34-35; *Nunc dimittis*; James Quinn, SJ, b.1919, alt., © 1969. Used by permission of Selah Publishing Co., Inc.
Tune: MORNING SONG, CM; Wyeth's *Repository of Sacred Music*, 1813; harm. by Richard Proulx, b.1937, © 1975, GIA Publications, Inc.

875 Come Now, and Praise the Humble Saint

1. Come now, and praise the hum - ble saint Of
2. The Ar - chi - tect's high mir - a - cles He
3. For him there was no glo - ry here, No
4. But now with - in the Fa - ther's grace Where

Da - vid's house and line, The
saw, and what was done, The
crown or mar - tyr's fame, For
saints and an - gel's throng, Be -

car - pen - ter whose life ful - filled Our
Vir - gin's spouse, the guard - ian of Great
him there was the pa - tient life Of
side his spouse, be - fore the Son, He

gra - cious God's de - sign.
Da - vid's great - er Son.
faith and hum - ble name.
joins the heav'n - ly song.

Text: G. W. Williams, b.1922, © 1979, Hymn Society of America (Admin. by Hope Publishing Co.)
Tune: LAND OF REST, CM; American; harm. by Richard Proulx, b.1937, © 1975, GIA Publications, Inc.

No Wind at the Window 876

1. No wind at the win - dow, No knock on the
2. "O Mar - y, O Mar - y, Don't hide from my
3. "This child must be born that The king - dom might
4. No pay - ment was prom - ised, No prom - is - es

door; No light from the lamp - stand, No
face. Be glad that you're fa - vored And
come: Sal - va - tion for man - y, De -
made; No wed - ding was dat - ed, No

foot on the floor; No dream born of
filled with God's grace. The time for re -
struc - tion for some; Both end and be -
blue - print dis - played. Yet Mar - y, con -

tired - ness, No ghost raised by fear: Just an
deem - ing The world has be - gun; And
gin - ning, Both mes - sage and sign; Both
sent - ing To what none could guess, Re -

an - gel and a wom - an And a voice in her ear.
you are re - quest - ed To moth - er God's son.
vic - tor and vic - tim, Both yours and di - vine."
plied with con - vic - tion, "Tell God I say yes."

Text: John L. Bell, b.1949
Tune: COLUMCILLE, Irregular; Gaelic; arr. by John L. Bell, b.1949
© 1992, Iona Community, GIA Publications, Inc., agent

877 Praise We the Lord This Day

1. Praise we the Lord this day, This day so long fore - told, Whose prom - ise shone with cheer - ing ray On wait - ing saints of old.
2. The Proph - et gave the sign For faith - ful folk to read: A vir - gin, born of Da - vid's line, Shall bear the prom - ised Seed.
3. Ask not how this should be, But wor - ship and a - dore Like her whom God's own maj - es - ty Came down to shad - ow o'er.
4. She meek - ly bowed her head To hear the gra - cious word, Mar - y, the pure and low - ly maid, The fa - vored of the Lord.
5. Bless - ed shall be her name In all the Church on earth, Through whom that won - drous mer - cy came, The in - car - nate Sav - ior's birth.
6. O Christ, the Vir - gin's Son, We praise you and a - dore, You are with God the Fa - ther One And Spir - it ev - er - more.

Text: Matthew 1:23; *Hymns for the Festivals and Saints' Days*, 1846
Tune: SWABIA, SM; Johann M. Speiss, 1715-1772; adapt. by William H. Havergal, 1793-1870

When Jesus Came to Jordan   878

1. When Je - sus came to Jor - dan To
2. He came to share re - pen - tance With
3. He came to share temp - ta - tion, Our
4. So when the Dove de - scend - ed On

be bap - tized by John, He did not come for
all who mourn their sins, To speak the vi - tal
ut - most woe and loss; For us and our sal -
him, the Son of Man, The hid - den years had

par - don, But as his Fa - ther's Son.
sen - tence With which good news be - gins.
va - tion To die up - on the cross.
end - ed, The age of grace be - gan.

Text: Fred Pratt Green, b.1903, © 1980, Hope Publishing Co.
Tune: DE EERSTEN ZIJN DE LAATSTEN, 7 6 7 6; Frits Mehrtens, 1922-1975, © Interkerkelijke Stichting voorhet Kerklied

879 The Great Forerunner of the Morn

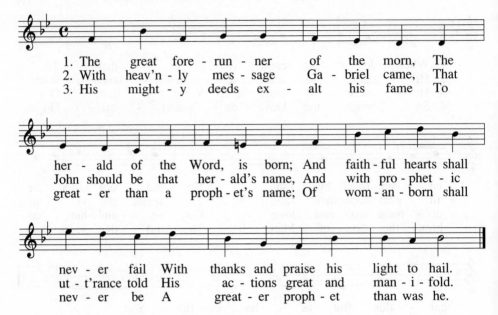

1. The great fore - run - ner of the morn, The
2. With heav'n - ly mes - sage Ga - briel came, That
3. His might - y deeds ex - alt his fame To

her - ald of the Word, is born; And faith - ful hearts shall
John should be that her - ald's name, And with pro - phet - ic
great - er than a proph - et's name; Of wom - an - born shall

nev - er fail With thanks and praise his light to hail.
ut - t'rance told His ac - tions great and man - i - fold.
nev - er be A great - er proph - et than was he.

Text: *Praecursor altus luminis;* Venerable Bede, 673-735; tr. by John M. Neale, 1818-1866, alt.
Tune: WINCHESTER NEW, LM; adapt. from *Musikalisches Handbuch,* Hamburg, 1690

Two Noble Saints 880

1. Two no-ble saints both root-ed In faith and ho-ly
2. The words of Paul as-sure us Of Christ's re-deem-ing

love, By hope of God u - nit - ed They
word; The works of Pe - ter show us How

reach to heaven a - bove. One on a cross is
we may serve the Lord. So praise we the Cre -

mar - tyred, One by the sword is slain; Both
a - tor, And praise we Christ the Son, Who

tri - umph in their dy - ing, Both glo - rious saint-hood gain.
with the Ho - ly Spir - it, Now reign, blest Three in One.

Text: Based on *Decora lux aeternitatis auream*, by Anne K. LeCroy, b.1930, ©
Tune: ELLACOMBE, 7 6 7 6 D; *Gesangbuch der Herzogl*, Wirtemberg, 1784

881 Transform Us

1. Trans-form us as you, trans - fig - ured,
2. Trans-form us as you, trans - fig - ured,
3. Trans-form us as you, trans - fig - ured,

Stood a - part on Ta - bor's height.
Once spoke with those ho - ly ones.
Would not stay with - in a shrine.

Lead us up our sa - cred moun - tains,
We, sur - round - ed by the wit - ness
Keep us from our great temp - ta - tion—

Search us with re - veal - ing light.
Of those saints whose work is done,
Time and truth we quick - ly bind,

Lift us from where we have fall - en,
Live in this world as your Bod - y,
Lead us down those dai - ly path - ways

Full of ques - tions, filled with fright.
Cho - sen daugh - ters, cho - sen sons.
Where our love is not con - fined.

Text: Sylvia Dunstan, 1955-1993, © 1993, GIA Publications, Inc.
Tune: PICARDY, 8 7 8 7 8 7; French Carol; harm. by Richard Proulx, b.1937, © 1986, GIA Publications, Inc.

'Tis Good, Lord, to Be Here 882

1. 'Tis good, Lord, to be here! Your
2. 'Tis good, Lord, to be here, Your
3. Ful - fill - er of the past! Prom -
4. Be - fore we taste of death, We
5. 'Tis good, Lord, to be here! Yet

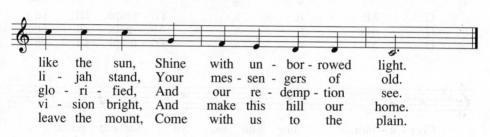

glo - ry fills the night; Your face and gar - ments,
beau - ty to be - hold, Where Mo - ses and E -
ise of things to be! We hail your bod - y
see your king - dom come; We long to hold the
we may not re - main; But since you bid us

like the sun, Shine with un - bor - rowed light.
li - jah stand, Your mes - sen - gers of old.
glo - ri - fied, And our re - demp - tion see.
vi - sion bright, And make this hill our home.
leave the mount, Come with us to the plain.

Text: Luke 9:32-33; Joseph A. Robinson, 1858-1933, alt., © Esme. D. E. Bird
Tune: SWABIA, SM; Johann M. Speiss, 1715-1772; adapt. by William H. Havergal, 1793-1870

883 Hail, Holy Queen Enthroned Above

1. Hail, ho-ly Queen en-throned a-bove, O Ma-ri-a.
2. The cause of joy to all be-low, O Ma-ri-a.
3. O gen-tle, lov-ing, ho-ly one, O Ma-ri-a.

1. Hail, Queen of mer-cy and of love, O Ma-ri-a.
2. The spring through which all grac-es flow, O Ma-ri-a.
3. The God of light be-came your Son, O Ma-ri-a.

1. Tri-umph, all ye Cher-u-bim,
2. An-gels, all your prais-es bring,
3. Tri-umph, all ye Cher-u-bim,

1. Sing with us, ye Ser-a-phim, Heav'n and earth re-sound the hymn:
2. Earth and heav-en, with us sing, All cre-a-tion ech-o-ing:
3. Sing with us, ye Ser-a-phim, Heav'n and earth re-sound the hymn:

1. Sal-ve, Sal-ve, Sal-ve, Re-gi-na.
2. Sal-ve, Sal-ve, Sal-ve, Re-gi-na.
3. Sal-ve, Sal-ve, Sal-ve, Re-gi-na.

Text: *Salve, Regina, mater misericordia;* c.1080; tr. *Roman Hymnal,* 1884; st. 2-3 adapt. by M. Owen Lee, CSB, b.1930
Tune: SALVE REGINA COELITUM, 8 4 8 4 777 4 5; *Choralmelodien zum Heiligen Gesänge,* 1808; harm. by Healey Willan, 1880-1968, © Willis Music Co.

Lift High the Cross 884

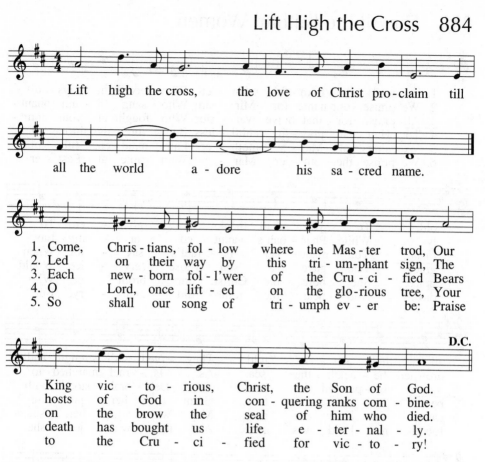

Lift high the cross, the love of Christ pro-claim till
all the world a-dore his sa-cred name.

1. Come, Chris-tians, fol-low where the Mas-ter trod, Our
2. Led on their way by this tri-um-phant sign, The
3. Each new-born fol-l'wer of the Cru-ci-fied Bears
4. O Lord, once lift-ed on the glo-rious tree, Your
5. So shall our song of tri-umph ev-er be: Praise

D.C.

King vic-to-rious, Christ, the Son of God.
hosts of God in con-quering ranks com-bine.
on the brow the seal of him who died.
death has bought us life e-ter-nal-ly.
to the Cru-ci-fied for vic-to-ry!

Text: 1 Corinthians 1:18; George W. Kitchin, 1827-1912, and Michael R. Newbolt, 1874-1956, alt.
Tune: CRUCIFER, 10 10 with refrain; Sydney H. Nicholson, 1875-1947

885 For All the Faithful Women

1. For all the faith-ful wom-en Who served in days of old, To you shall thanks be giv-en; To all, their sto-ry told. They served with strength and glad-ness In tasks your wis-dom gave. To you their lives bore wit-ness, Pro-claimed your pow'r to save.

2. We praise your name for Mir-iam Who sang tri-um-phant-ly While Phar-oah's vaunt-ed ar-my Lay drowned be-neath the sea. As Is-rael marched to free-dom, Her chains of bond-age gone, So may we reach the king-dom Your might-y arm has won.

3. All praise for that brave war-rior Who fought at your com-mand; You made her Is-rael's sav-ior When foes op-pressed the land. As Deb-orah stood with val-or Up-on the bat-tle-field, May we, in e-vil's ho-ur, Truth's sword with bold-ness wield.

4. To Han-nah, pray-ing child-less Be-fore the throne of grace, You gave a son whose serv-ice Would be be-fore your face. Grant us her per-se-ver-ance; Lord, teach us how to pray, To trust in your de-liv-'rance When dark-ness hides our way.

5. We sing of Mar-y, moth-er, Fair maid-en, full of grace. She bore the Christ, our broth-er, Who came to save our race. May we, with her, sur-ren-der Our-selves to your com-mand And lay up-on your al-tar Our gifts of heart and hand.

6. We praise the oth-er Mar-y Who came at East-er dawn And near the tomb did tar-ry, But found her Lord was gone. And then with joy she saw him In res-ur-rec-tion light. May we, by faith be-hold him, The day who ends all night.

Text: Herman G. Stuempfle, Jr., 1923–2007, © 1993, GIA Publications, Inc.
Tune: AURELIA, 7 6 7 6 D; Samuel Sebastian Wesley, 1810–1876

Ye Watchers and Ye Holy Ones   886

1. Ye watch - ers and ye ho - ly ones,
2. O high - er than the cher - u - bim,
3. Re - spond, ye souls in end - less rest,
4. O friends, in glad - ness let us sing,

Bright ser - aphs, cher - u - bim, and thrones,
More glo - rious than the ser - a - phim,
Ye pa - tri - archs and proph - ets blest,
Su - per - nal an - thems ech - o - ing,

Raise the glad strain,
Lead their prais - es,
Al - le - lu - ia, Al - le - lu - ia!
Al - le - lu - ia,

Cry out, do - min - ions, prince - doms, powers,
O bear - er of the e - ter - nal Word,
Ye ho - ly Twelve, ye mar - tyrs strong,
To God the Fa - ther, God the Son,

Vir - tues, arch - an - gels, an - gels' choirs,
Most gra - cious, mag - ni - fy the Lord,
All saints tri - um - phant, raise in song,
And God the Spir - it, Three in One,

Al - le - lu - ia, Al - le - lu - ia, Al - le - lu - ia,

Al - le - lu - ia, Al - le - lu - ia!

Text: Athelstan A. Riley, 1858-1945
Tune: LASST UNS ERFREUEN, LM with alleluias; *Geistliche Kirchengasänge,* Cologne, 1623; harm. by Ralph Vaughan Williams, 1872-1958

887 By All Your Saints Still Striving

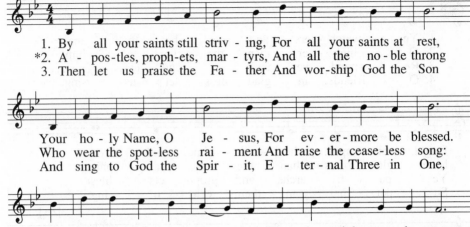

1. By all your saints still striv - ing, For all your saints at rest,
*2. A - pos-tles, proph-ets, mar - tyrs, And all the no - ble throng
3. Then let us praise the Fa - ther And wor-ship God the Son

Your ho - ly Name, O Je - sus, For ev - er-more be blessed.
Who wear the spot-less rai - ment And raise the cease-less song:
And sing to God the Spir - it, E - ter-nal Three in One,

You rose, our King vic - to - rious, That they might wear the crown
For them and those whose wit - ness Is on - ly known to you
Till all the ran-somed num - ber Who stand be - fore the throne,

And ev - er shine in splen - dor Re - flect-ed from your throne.
By walk-ing in their foot - steps We give you praise a - new.
A - scribe all pow'r and glo - ry And praise to God a - lone.

This stanza may be replaced by an appropriate stanza taken from the following pages.

Text: Based on Horatio Nelson, 1823-1913, by Jerry D. Godwin, b.1944, © 1985, The Church Pension Fund
Tune: ST. THEODULPH, 7 6 7 6 D; Melchior Teschner, 1584-1635

January 25: Conversion of Paul

Praise for the light from heaven
  And for the voice of awe:
Praise for the glorious vision
  The persecutor saw.
O Lord, for Paul's conversion,
  We bless your Name today.
Come shine within our darkness
  And guide us in the Way.

February 22: Chair of Peter

We praise you, Lord, for Peter,
  So eager and so bold:
Thrice falling, yet repentant,
  Thrice charged to feed your fold.
Lord, make your pastors faithful
  To guard your flock from harm
And hold them when they waver
  With your almighty arm.

March 19: Joseph, Husband of Mary

All praise, O God, for Joseph,
  The guardian of your Son,
Who saved him from King Herod,
  When safety there was none.
He taught the trade of builder,
  When they to Naz'reth came,
And Joseph's love made "Father"
  To be, for Christ, God's name.

March 25: Annunciation of Our Lord

We sing with joy of Mary
  Whose heart with awe was stirred
When, youthful and unready,
  She heard the angel's word;
Yet she her voice upraises
  God's glory to proclaim,
As once for our salvation
  Your mother she became.

April 25: Mark

For Mark, O Lord, we praise you,
  The weak by grace made strong:
His witness in his Gospel
  Becomes victorious song.
May we, in all our weakness,
  Receive your power divine,
And all, as faithful branches,
  Grow strong in you, the Vine.

May 3: Philip and James

We praise you, Lord, for Philip,
  Blest guide to Greek and Jew,
And for young James the faithful,
  Who heard and followed you,
O grant us grace to know you,
  The victor in the strife,
That we with all your servants
  May wear the crown of life.

May 14: Matthias

For one in place of Judas,
  The apostles sought God's choice:
The lot fell to Matthias
  For whom we now rejoice.
May we like true apostles
  Your holy Church defend,
And not betray our calling
  But serve you to the end.

June 11: Barnabas

For Barnabas we praise you,
  Who kept your law of love
And, leaving earthly treasures,
  Sought riches from above.
O Christ, our Lord and Savior,
  Let gifts of grace descend,
That your true consolation
  May through the world extend.

June 24: Birth of John the Baptist

All praise for John the Baptist,
  Forerunner of the Word,
Our true Elijah, making
  A highway for the Lord.
The last and greatest prophet,
  He saw the dawning ray
Of light that grows in splendor
  Until the perfect day.

June 29: Peter and Paul

We praise you for Saint Peter;
  We praise you for Saint Paul.
They taught both Jew and Gentile
  that Christ is all in all.
To cross and sword they yielded
  And saw the kingdom come:
O God, your two apostles
  Won life through martyrdom.

July 3: Thomas

All praise, O Lord, for Thomas
  Whose short-lived doubtings prove
Your perfect twofold nature,
  The depth of your true love.
To all who live with questions
  A steadfast faith afford;
And grant us grace to know you,
  Made flesh, yet God and Lord.

July 22: Mary Magdalene

All praise for Mary Magd'lene,
  Whose wholeness was restored
By you, her faithful Master,
  Her Savior and her Lord.
On Easter morning early,
  A word from you sufficed:
Her faith was first to see you,
  Her Lord, the risen Christ.

July 25: James

O Lord, for James, we praise you,
  Who fell to Herod's sword.
He drank the cup of suff'ring
  And thus fulfilled your word.
Lord, curb our vain impatience
  For glory and for fame,
Equip us for such suff'rings
  As glorify your Name.

August 24: Bartholomew

Praised for your blest apostle
  Surnamed Bartholomew;
We know not his achievements
  But know that he was true,
For he at the Ascension
  Was an apostle still.
May we discern your presence
  And seek, like him, your will.

September 21: Matthew

We praise you, Lord, for Matthew,
  Whose gospel words declare
That, worldly gain forsaking,
  Your path of life we share.
From all unrighteous mammon,
  O raise our eyes anew,
That we, whate'er our station
  May rise and follow you.

October 18: Luke

For Luke, beloved physician,
  All praise; whose Gospel shows
The healer of the nations,
  The one who shares our woes.
Your wine and oil, O Savior,
  Upon our spirits pour,
And with true balm of Gilead
  Anoint us evermore.

October 28: Simon and Jude

Praise, Lord, for your apostles,
  Saint Simon and Saint Jude.
One love, one hope impelled them
  To tread the way, renewed.
May we with zeal as earnest
  The faith of Christ maintain,
Be bound in love together,
  And life eternal gain.

November 30: Andrew

All praise, O Lord, for Andrew,
  The first to follow you;
He witnessed to his brother,
  "This is Messiah true."
You called him from his fishing
  Upon Lake Galilee;
He rose to meet your challenge,
  "Leave all and follow me."

December 26: Stephen

All praise, O Lord, for Stephen
  Who, martyred, saw you stand
To help in time of torment,
  To plead at God's right hand.
Like you, our suff'ring Savior,
  His enemies he blessed,
With "Lord, receive my spirit,"
  His faith, in death, confessed.

December 27: John

For John, your loved disciple,
  Exiled to Patmos' shore,
And for his faithful record,
  We praise you evermore;
Praise for the mystic vision
  His words to us unfold.
Instill in us his longing,
  Your glory to behold.

December 28: Holy Innocents

Praise for your infant martyrs,
  Whom your mysterious love
Called early from life's conflicts
  To share your peace above.
O Rachel, cease your weeping;
  They're free from pain and cares.
Lord, grant us crowns as brilliant
  And lives as pure as theirs.

Give Thanks to God on High 888

1. Give thanks to God on high For saints of
2. Their vi - sion long ful - filled, Our prayer is
3. New tasks to - day are ours Who serve a
4. Give thanks to God on high For all the

oth - er days, Whose hope it was to
still the same; Up - on their work of
world in pain, New calls to chal - lenge
fu - ture sends, In praise of Christ to

live and die In love's con - sum - ing blaze,
faith to build, Their word of truth pro - claim,
all our pow'rs Of heart and hand and brain,
live and die Who calls his ser - vants friends,

For Christ and his king - dom, His glo - ry and his praise.
For Christ and his king - dom, And for his ho - ly name.
For Christ and his king - dom, While life and breath re - main.
For Christ and his king - dom, Whose glo - ry nev - er ends.

Text: Timothy Dudley-Smith, b.1926, © 1985, Hope Publishing Co.
Tune: BALDWIN, 6 6 8 6 6 6; James J. Chepponis, b.1956, © 1987, GIA Publications, Inc.

889　For All the Saints

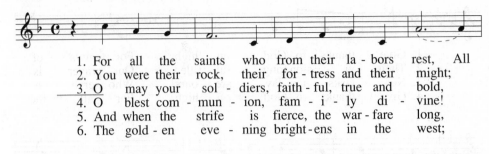

1. For all the saints who from their la - bors rest, All
2. You were their rock, their for - tress and their might;
3. O may your sol - diers, faith - ful, true and bold,
4. O blest com - mun - ion, fam - i - ly di - vine!
5. And when the strife is fierce, the war - fare long,
6. The gold - en eve - ning bright - ens in the west;

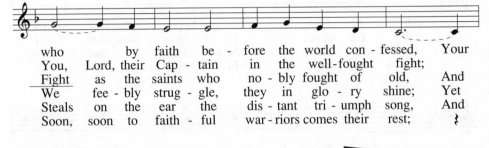

who by faith be - fore the world con - fessed, Your
You, Lord, their Cap - tain in the well-fought fight;
Fight as the saints who no - bly fought of old, And
We fee - bly strug - gle, they in glo - ry shine; Yet
Steals on the ear the dis - tant tri - umph song, And
Soon, soon to faith - ful war - riors comes their rest;

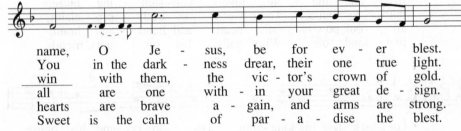

name, O Je - sus, be for ev - er blest.
You in the dark - ness drear, their one true light.
win with them, the vic - tor's crown of gold.
all are one with - in your great de - sign.
hearts are brave a - gain, and arms are strong.
Sweet is the calm of par - a - dise the blest.

Al - le - lu - ia! Al - le - lu - ia!

7. But then there breaks a yet more glorious day:
   The saints triumphant rise in bright array;
   The King of glory passes on his way.
   Alleluia! Alleluia!

8. From earth's wide bounds, from ocean's farthest coast,
   Through gates of pearl streams in the countless host,
   Singing to Father, Son, and Holy Ghost:
   Alleluia! Alleluia!

Text: William W. How, 1823-1897
Tune: SINE NOMINE, 10 10 10 with alleluias; Ralph Vaughan Williams, 1872-1958

Immaculate Mary 890

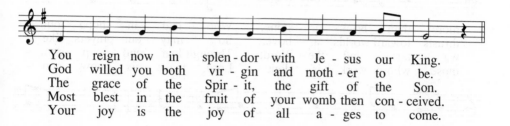

1. Im - mac - u - late Mar - y, your prais - es we sing;
2. Pre - des - tined for Christ by e - ter - nal de - cree,
3. To you by an an - gel, the Lord God made known
4. Most blest of all wom - en, you heard and be - lieved,
5. The an - gels re - joiced when you brought forth God's Son;

You reign now in splen - dor with Je - sus our King.
God willed you both vir - gin and moth - er to be.
The grace of the Spir - it, the gift of the Son.
Most blest in the fruit of your womb then con - ceived.
Your joy is the joy of all a - ges to come.

A - ve, A - ve, A - ve, Ma - ri - a.

A - ve, A - ve, Ma - ri - a.

6. Your child is the Savior, all hope lies in him:
   He gives us new life and redeems us from sin.

7. In glory for ever now close to your Son,
   All ages will praise you for all God has done.

Text: St. 1, Jeremiah Cummings, 1814-1866, alt.; St. 2-7, Brian Foley, b.1919, © 1971, Faber Music Ltd.
Tune: LOURDES HYMN, 11 11 with refrain; *Grenoble*, 1882

891 For Builders Bold

1. For build - ers bold whose vi - sion pure Saw
2. As here they raised a soar - ing spire Which
3. Here saints new - born you gen - er - ate Through
4. We come, O Lord, in - her - i - tors From

more than brick or stone, Who laid in hope foun -
thrusts toward worlds a - bove, So may our prayers, like
wa - ter and the Word; Through loaf and cup com -
those whose work is done. Lord, make us now con -

da - tions sure With Christ the cor - ner - stone; For
tongues of fire, Leap kin - dled by your love. And
mu - ni - cate The gift of Christ the Lord. We
trib - u - tors To years be - yond our own. Let

those who hon - ored your com - mands And trust - ed
let your liv - ing Word de - scend As seed on
gath - er, Christ's own fam - i - ly; Christ's meal of
faith's en - kin - dled flame not fail; Let love's best

your strong Word, Who of - fered faith - ful
wait - ing hearts And, fruit - ful there, its
love we share. Come, help us live in
gifts in - crease. Let hope in Christ's sure

hearts and hands, We give you thanks, O Lord.
grace ex - tend To earth's most dis - tant parts.
u - ni - ty, Each oth - er's bur - dens bear.
Word pre - vail Till earth and time shall cease.

Text: Herman G. Stuempfle, Jr., 1923–2007, © 1993, GIA Publications, Inc.
Tune: FOREST GREEN, CMD; English, harm. by Ralph Vaughan Williams, 1872–1958, alt.

What Is This Place 892

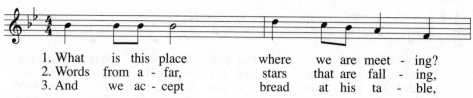

1. What is this place where we are meet - ing?
2. Words from a - far, stars that are fall - ing,
3. And we ac - cept bread at his ta - ble,

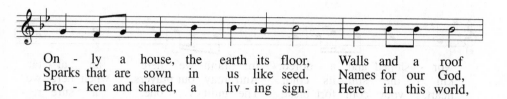

On - ly a house, the earth its floor, Walls and a roof
Sparks that are sown in us like seed. Names for our God,
Bro - ken and shared, a liv - ing sign. Here in this world,

shel - ter - ing peo - ple, Win - dows for light, an o - pen door.
dreams, signs and won - ders Sent from the past are all we need.
dy - ing and liv - ing, We are each oth - er's bread and wine.

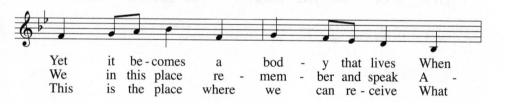

Yet it be - comes a bod - y that lives When
We in this place re - mem - ber and speak A -
This is the place where we can re - ceive What

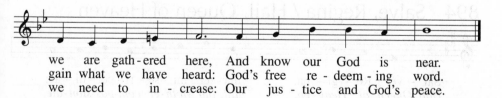

we are gath - ered here, And know our God is near.
gain what we have heard: God's free re - deem - ing word.
we need to in - crease: Our jus - tice and God's peace.

Text: *Zomaar een dak boven wat hoofen;* Huub Oosterhuis, b.1933; trans. by David Smith, b.1933, © 1967, Gooi en Sticht, bv., Baarn,
The Netherlands. Exclusive English language agent: OCP Publications
Tune: KOMT NU MET ZANG, 9 8 9 8 9 66; Valerius' *Neder-landtsche gedenck-klanck;* acc. by Robert J. Batastini, b.1942, © 1987,
GIA Publications, Inc.

893 How Blessed Is This Place

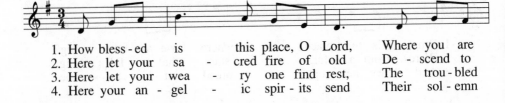

1. How bless-ed is this place, O Lord, Where you are
2. Here let your sa - cred fire of old De - scend to
3. Here let your wea - ry one find rest, The trou - bled
4. Here your an - gel - ic spir - its send Their sol - emn

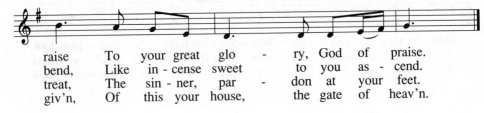

wor - shiped and a - dored; In faith we here an al - tar
kin - dle spir-its cold; And may our prayers, when here we
heart, your com - fort blest, The guilt-y one, a sure re -
praise with ours to blend, And grant the vi - sion, in - ly

raise To your great glo - ry, God of praise.
bend, Like in - cense sweet to you as - cend.
treat, The sin - ner, par - don at your feet.
giv'n, Of this your house, the gate of heav'n.

Text: Ernest E. Ryden, 1886-1981, alt., © sts. 1-3, Lutheran Church in America, © st. 4, 1958, Service Book and Hymnal
Tune: O WALY WALY, LM; English; harm. by Martin West, b.1929, © 1983, Hope Publishing Co.

894 Salve, Regina / Hail, Queen of Heaven

Sal - ve, Re - gí - na, ma - ter mi - se - ri - cór - di - ae:
Hail, Queen of Heav - en, hail, our Moth-er com-pas-sion-ate,

Vi - ta, dul - cé - do et spes no - stra sal - ve.
True life and com - fort and our hope, we greet you!

Ad te cla - má - mus, éx - su - les fí - li - i He - vae.
To you we ex - iles, chil-dren of Eve, raise our voic - es.

BLESSED VIRGIN MARY

Ad te sus-pi-rá-mus, ge-mén-tes et flen-tes
We send up sighs to you, as mourn-ing and weep-ing,

in hac la-cri-má-rum val-le. E-ia er-go,
we pass through this vale of sor-row. Then turn to us,

ad-vo-cá-ta no-stra, il-los tu-os mi-se-ri-
O most gra-cious Wom-an, those eyes of yours, so full of

cór-des ó-cu-los ad nos con-vér-te.
love and ten-der-ness, so full of pit-y.

Et Je-sum, be-ne-dí-ctum fru-ctum ven-tris tu-i,
And grant us af-ter these, our days of lone-ly ex-ile,

no-bis post hoc ex-sí-li-um o-stén-de.
the sight of your blest Son and Lord, Christ Je-sus.

O cle-mens, O pi-a,
O gen-tle, O lov-ing,

O dul-cis Vir-go Ma-rí-a.
O ho-ly, sweet Vir-gin Mar-y.

Text: Latin, c.1080, tr. by John C. Selner, SS, b.1904, © 1954, GIA Publications, Inc.
Tune: SALVE REGINA, Irregular; Mode V; acc. by Gerard Farrell, OSB, b.1919, © 1986, GIA Publications, Inc.

895 Sing We of the Blessed Mother

1. Sing we of the bless-ed Moth-er Who re-ceived the
an - gel's word, And o - be - dient to the sum - mons
Bore in love the in - fant Lord; Sing we of the
joys of Mar - y At whose breast that child was fed
Who is Son of God e - ter - nal
And the ev - er - last - ing Bread.

2. Sing we, too, of Mar-y's sor-rows, Of the sword that
pierced her through, When be - neath the cross of Je - sus
She his weight of suf - f'ring knew, Looked up - on her
Son and Sav - ior Reign-ing from the aw - ful tree,
Saw the price of our re - demp - tion
Paid to set the sin - ner free.

3. Sing a - gain the joys of Mar - y When she saw the
ris - en Lord, And in prayer with Christ's a - pos - tles,
Wait - ed on his prom - ised word: From on high the
blaz - ing glo - ry Of the Spir - it's pres - ence came,
Heav'n - ly breath of God's own be - ing,
To - kened in the wind and flame.

4. Sing the great - est joy of Mar - y When on earth her
work was done, And the Lord of all cre - a - tion
Brought her to his heav'n - ly home: Vir - gin Moth - er,
Mar - y bless-ed, Raised on high and crowned with grace,
May your Son, the world's re - deem - er,
Grant us all to see his face.

Text: George B. Timms, 1910-1997, © 1975, Oxford University Press
Tune: OMNE DIE, 8 7 8 7 D; *Trier Gesängbuch,* 1695

Ave Maria   896

Verses

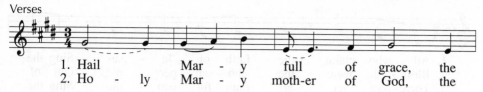

1. Hail Mar - y full of grace, the
2. Ho - ly Mar - y moth-er of God, the

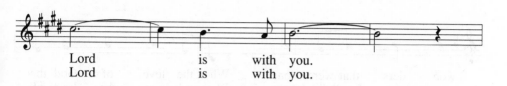

Lord is with you.
Lord is with you.

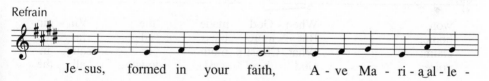

Bless - ed are you a - mong all wom-en,
Pray for us sin - ners, pray for us sin - ners,

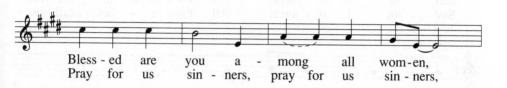

Blest is the fruit of your womb.
Now and at the hour of our death.

Refrain

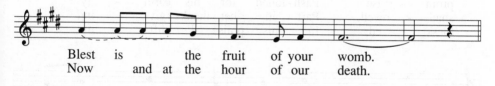

Je-sus, formed in your faith, A - ve Ma - ri-a al-le -

lu - ia. Je-sus, born in your love,

A - ve Ma - ri-a al-le - lu - ia.

Text: Hail Mary; additional text by Dan Kantor, b.1960
Tune: Dan Kantor, b.1960; arr. by Rob Glover
© 1993, GIA Publications, Inc.

897 All Who Claim the Faith of Jesus

1. All who claim the faith of Je - sus Sing the
2. Bless - ed were the cho - sen peo - ple Out of
3. There - fore let all faith - ful peo - ple Sing the
4. "Mag - ni - fy, my soul, God's great - ness; In my

won - ders that were done When the love of God the
whom the Lord did come; Bless - ed was the land of
hon - or of her name; Let the Church, in her fore -
Sav - ior I re - joice; All the a - ges call me

Fa - ther O'er our sins the vic - t'ry
prom - ise Fash - ioned for his earth - ly
shad - owed, Part in her thanks - giv - ing
bless - ed, In his praise I lift my

won, When God made the Vir - gin
home; But more bless - ed far the
claim; What Christ's moth - er sang in
voice; God has cast down all the

Mar - y Moth - er of the on - ly Son.
moth - er, She who bore him in her womb.
glad - ness Let Christ's peo - ple sing the same:
might - y, And the low - ly are his choice."

Text: Vincent Stuckey Stratton Coles, 1845-1929, alt.; St. 4, F. Bland Tucker, 1895-1984
Tune: TILLFLYKT, 87 87 87; *Sionstoner,* 1889; harm. by Marty Haugen, b.1950, © 1987, GIA Publications, Inc.

Ave Maria 898

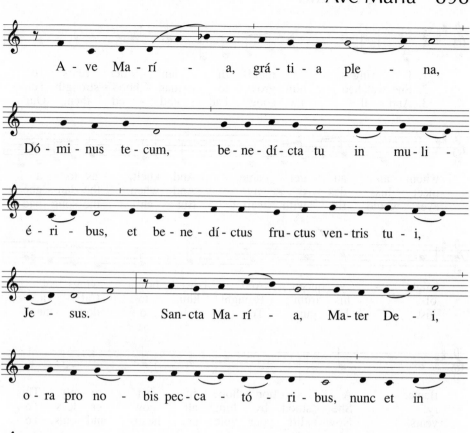

A - ve Ma - rí - a, grá - ti - a ple - na,

Dó - mi - nus te - cum, be - ne - dí - cta tu in mu - li -

é - ri - bus, et be - ne - dí - ctus fru - ctus ven - tris tu - i,

Je - sus. San - cta Ma - rí - a, Ma - ter De - i,

o - ra pro no - bis pec - ca - tó - ri - bus, nunc et in

ho - ra mor - tis no - strae. A - men.

Text: Luke 1:29; Latin, 13th C.
Tune: AVE MARIA, Irregular; Mode I; acc. by Robert LeBlanc, b.1948, © 1986, GIA Publications, Inc.

899   I Sing a Maid

1. I sing a maid of ten - der years To
2. She watched him grow to man - hood's strength To
3. And if the song had end - ed then, Our

whom an an - gel came, And knelt, as to a
meet his des - ti - ny. And when the dan - ger
eyes would fill with tears, But ah! the song had

might - y queen, And bowed bright wings of
of his truth Brought him to Cal - va -
just be - gun To ech - o down the

flame: A na - tion's hope in her re - ply, This
ry, She stood by him all pow - er - less To
years! Now lift your voic - es, hearts and souls, To

maid of match - less grace; For God's own son be -
ease his dy - ing pain, 'Til in the dark - est
sing with one ac - cord To hon - or Mar - y,

came her child, And she his rest - ing place.
hour of all, She held her son a - gain.
Moth - er of The Christ, the Ris - en Lord!

Text: M. D. Ridge, b.1938, © 1987, GIA Publications, Inc.
Tune: THE FLIGHT OF THE EARLS, CMD; traditional Celtic melody; harm. by Michael Joncas, b.1951, © 1987, GIA Publications, Inc.

O Sanctissima / O Most Virtuous 900

1. O san - ctís - si - ma, O pi - ís - si - ma,
2. Tu so - lá - ti - um Et re - fú - gi - um,
3. Ec - ce dé - bi - les, Per - quam flé - bi - les,
4. Vir - go ré - spi-ce, Ma - ter, ád - spi-ce,

1. *O most vir - tu-ous And most pi - ous,*
2. *Our pro - tec - tion and Con - so - la - tion,*
3. *See us pow - er-less In our hope - less-ness:*
4. *Maid - en, look on us, Moth - er, care for us.*

Dul - cis vir - go Ma - rí - a!
Vir - go ma - ter Ma - rí - a!
Sal - va nos, Ma - rí - a!
Au - di nos, Ma - rí - a!

Dear - est maid - en, sweet Mar - y,
Vir - gin moth - er, good Mar - y,
Aid us, save us, Mar - y!
Hear our pleas, O Mar - y!

Ma - ter a - má - ta, In - te - me - rá - ta,
Quid - quid op - tá - mus, Per te spe - rá - mus,
Tol - le lan - guó - res, Sa - na do - ló - res,
Tu me - di - cí - nam, Por - tas di - ví - nam;

Moth - er af - fec - tion-ate, Vir - gin in - vi - o - late,
What - e'er our souls de - sire, May you help us to ac - quire.
Wipe a - way the tears we shed, Heal us of our grief and dread.
Balm and our sur - e - ty, Gate-way to di - vin - i - ty,

O - ra, o - ra pro no - bis.
O - ra, o - ra pro no - bis.
O - ra, o - ra pro no - bis.
O - ra, o - ra pro no - bis.

In - ter - cede and pray for us, O Mar - y!
In - ter - cede and pray for us, O Mar - y!
In - ter - cede and pray for us, O Mar - y!
In - ter - cede and pray for us, O Mar - y!

Text: St. 1, *Stimmen der Völker in Liedern*, 1807; st. 2, *Arundel Hymnal*, 1902; tr. Neil Borgstrom, b.1953, © 1994, GIA Publications, Inc.
Tune: O DU FRÖLICHE, 55 7 55 7; Tattersall's *Improved Psalmody*, 1794

901   We Are God's Work of Art /
Somos la Creación de Dios

Refrain

We are God's work of art, fash-ioned in
So - mos la crea - ción de Dios, co - mo en

Christ, fash - ioned to shine with good - ness and light.
Cris - to, el nos hi - zo bri - llar con su luz.

As it was from the start— formed by this
A - sí fue al co - men - zar, con gran a -

great, great love, we are God's
mor, el nos for - mó, so - mos gran - des

great, won - drous work of art.
o - bras del ar - te del Se - ñor.

Verses

1. When we were dead in sin, you brought us to life in Christ,
   and raised us up, up to the heavens.

1. *Cuando en pecado morimos,*
   nos trajo la vida en Cristo y nos llevó a las alturas.

2. How rich is the grace of God, how strong is the love of God,
   to send us Christ for our salvation.

2. *Qué rica es la gracia de Dios qué fuerte es su amor,*
   envió a Cristo para nuestra salvacion.

3. We are strangers no longer, outcasts no longer,
   we are saints in the house of God.

3. *No somos extranjeros, no mas desterrados,*
   somos santos en la casa del Señor.

4. We are the temple that our God has fashioned,
   in Christ we are the dwelling place of love.

4. *Somos el templo que_el Señor hizo,*
   en Cristo somos morada de su_amor.

5. From the foundation of the world you have chosen us,
   destined in love to be your sons and daughters.
   You have revealed to us the myst'ry of grace, to unite all things in Christ.

5. *Desde_el principio del mundo nos escogiste el destino de ser tus hijos y tus hijas.*
   Nos reveló el misterio de gracia, para unir todas las cosas en Cristo.

Text: Ephesians 2:1, 4-7, 10, 19, 21-22; Marty Haugen, b.1950; Spanish trans. by Donna Peña, b.1955
Tune: Marty Haugen, b.1950
© 1991, GIA Publications, Inc.

Come and Let Us Drink of That New River   902

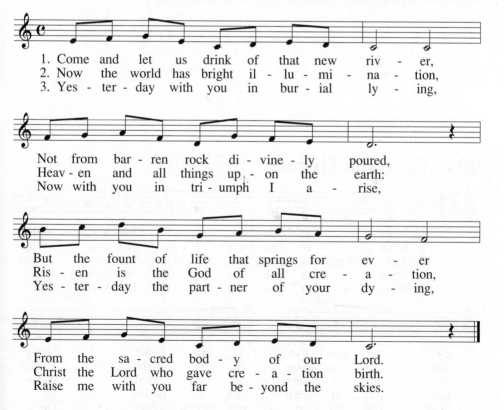

1. Come and let us drink of that new riv - er,
   Not from bar - ren rock di - vine - ly poured,
   But the fount of life that springs for ev - er
   From the sa - cred bod - y of our Lord.

2. Now the world has bright il - lu - mi - na - tion,
   Heav - en and all things up - on the earth:
   Ris - en is the God of all cre - a - tion,
   Christ the Lord who gave cre - a - tion birth.

3. Yes - ter - day with you in bur - ial ly - ing,
   Now with you in tri - umph I a - rise,
   Yes - ter - day the part - ner of your dy - ing,
   Raise me with you far be - yond the skies.

Text: John of Damascus, c.675-746; tr. by John M. Neale, 1818-1866, adapt. by Anthony G. Petti, 1932-1985, © 1971, Faber Music Ltd.
Tune: NEW RIVER, 10 9 10 9; Kenneth D. Smith, b.1928

903 Baptized in Water

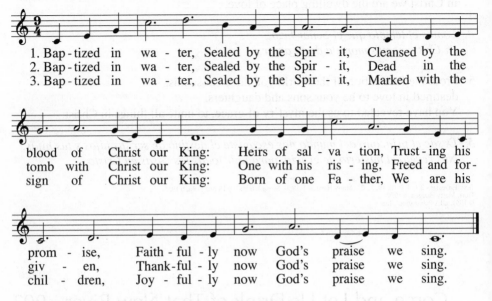

1. Bap-tized in wa-ter, Sealed by the Spir-it, Cleansed by the
2. Bap-tized in wa-ter, Sealed by the Spir-it, Dead in the
3. Bap-tized in wa-ter, Sealed by the Spir-it, Marked with the

blood of Christ our King: Heirs of sal-va-tion, Trust-ing his
tomb with Christ our King: One with his ris-ing, Freed and for-
sign of Christ our King: Born of one Fa-ther, We are his

prom-ise, Faith-ful-ly now God's praise we sing.
giv-en, Thank-ful-ly now God's praise we sing.
chil-dren, Joy-ful-ly now God's praise we sing.

Text: Michael Saward, b.1932, © 1982, Jubilate Hymns, Ltd. (admin. by Hope Publishing Co.)
Tune: BUNESSAN, 5 5 8 D; Gaelic melody; acc. by Marty Haugen, b.1950, © 1987, GIA Publications, Inc.

904 Covenant Hymn

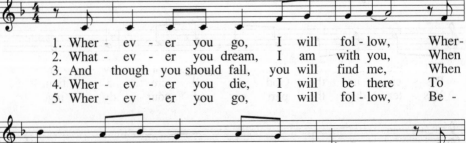

1. Wher-ev-er you go, I will fol-low, Wher-
2. What-ev-er you dream, I am with you, When
3. And though you should fall, you will find me, When
4. Wher-ev-er you die, I will be there To
5. Wher-ev-er you go, I will fol-low, Be-

ev-er you live is my home. Though
stars call your name in the night. Though
no oth-er friend can you claim, When
sing you to sleep with a psalm, To
hold! The ho-ri-zon shines clear. The

days   be   of   bless - ing   or   sor - row,   Though
shad - ows   and   mist   cloud   the   fu - ture,   To -
foes   beat   you   down   or   be - tray   you   And
soothe   you   with   tales   of   our   jour - ney,   Your
pos - si - ble gleams   like   a   cit - y: To -

house   be   of   can - vas   or   stone,   Though
geth - er   we   bear   there   a   light.   Like
oth - ers   de - sert   you   in   shame.   When
fears   and   your   doubts   I   will   calm.   We'll
geth - er   we've   noth - ing   to   fear.   So

E - den   be   lost   to   the   past,   Though
A - bram   and   Sar - ah   we   stand,   With
home   and   dreams   aren't   e - nough,   And
live   when   jour - neys   are   done   For -
speak   with   words   bold   and   true   The

moun - tains   be - fore   us   be   vast,   Wher -
on - ly   a   prom - ise   in   hand.   But
you   run   a - way   from   my   love,   I'll
ev - er   in   mem - 'ry   as   one.   And
mes - sage   my   heart   speaks   to   you.   You

ev - er   you   go,   I   am   with you,   I
lead   where   you   dream: I   will   fol - low.   To
raise   you   from   where   you   have   fall - en.   ʒ
we   will   be   bur - ied   to - geth - er,   And
won't   be   a - lone,   I   have   prom - ised.   Wher -

nev - er   will   leave   you   a - lone.
dream   with   you   is   my   de - light.
Faith - ful   to   you   is   my   name.
wak - en   to   greet   a   new   dawn.
ev - er   you   go,   I   am   here.

Text: Ruth 1:16; Rory Cooney, b.1952
Tune: Gary Daigle, b.1957
© 1993, GIA Publications, Inc.

905 Blessed Be God, Who Chose You in Christ

Refrain

Bless-ed be God, who chose you in Christ to be filled with the Spir-it of love. Bless-ed be God, who chose you in Christ to pro-claim to all na-tions His deeds.

Verses

1. We come to you, Lord Jesus.
   You have filled us with new life,
   as children of the Father, and one in you.

The cantor concludes each verse:
Send forth your Holy Spirit, renew the face of the earth.

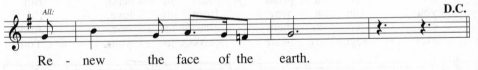

Re - new the face of the earth.

2. From all who have been baptized in water and the Holy Spirit,
   you have formed one people,
   united in your Son, Jesus Christ.
   Send forth...

3. You have set us free, and filled our hearts
   with the Spirit of your love,
   that we may live in your peace.
   Send forth...

4. You call those who have been baptized
   to announce the Good News of
   Jesus Christ to people ev'rywhere.
   Send forth...

Text: Adapted from the Rite of Baptism, James J. Chepponis, b.1956
Tune: James J. Chepponis, b.1956
© 1982, GIA Publications, Inc.

We Know That Christ Is Raised 906

1. We know that Christ is raised and dies no
2. We share by wa - ter in his sav - ing
3. The Fa - ther's splen - dor clothes the Son with
4. A new cre - a - tion comes to life and

more. Em - braced by death, he broke its
death. Re - born, we share with him an
life. The Spir - it's fis - sion shakes the
grows As Christ's new bod - y takes on

fear - ful hold, And our de - spair he turned to
East - er life As liv - ing mem - bers of our
Church of God. Bap-tized, we live with God the
flesh and blood. The u - ni - verse re - stored and

blaz - ing joy. Al - le - lu - ia!
Sav - ior Christ. Al - le - lu - ia!
Three in One. Al - le - lu - ia!
whole will sing: Al - le - lu - ia!

Text: Romans 6:4, 9; John B. Geyer, b.1932, ©
Tune: ENGELBERG, 10 10 10 with alleluia; Charles V. Stanford, 1852-1924

907 O Breathe on Me, O Breath of God

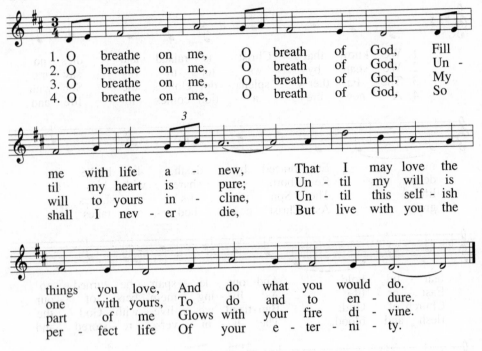

1. O breathe on me, O breath of God, Fill me with life a - new, That I may love the things you love, And do what you would do.
2. O breathe on me, O breath of God, Un - til my heart is pure; Un - til my will is one with yours, To do and to en - dure.
3. O breathe on me, O breath of God, My will to yours in - cline, Un - til this self - ish part of me Glows with your fire di - vine.
4. O breathe on me, O breath of God, So shall I nev - er die, But live with you the per - fect life Of your e - ter - ni - ty.

Text: Edwin Hatch, 1835-1889
Tune: ST. COLUMBA, CM; Gaelic; harm. by A. Gregory Murray, OSB, 1905-1992, © Downside Abbey

908 In Memory of You / Ave Verum

Refrain

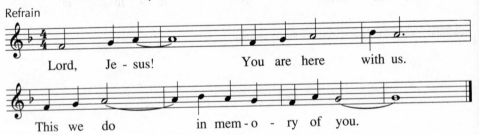

Lord, Je - sus! You are here with us.

This we do in mem - o - ry of you.

Verses

Ave verum Corpus natum de Maria Virgine:
Vere passum immolatum in cruce pro homine:
Cujus latus perforatum fluxit aqua et sanguine:
Esto nobis praegustatum mortis in examine.
O Jesus dulcis! O Jesu pie! O Jesu fili Mariae.

Hail, true body, born of the Virgin Mary,
Truly suffering, sacrificed on the cross for us.
Whose side, when pierced, flowed with water and blood:
Be for us a foretaste in death's agony.
O Jesu sweet, O Jesu pure, O Jesu, Son of Mary.

Text: Refrain, Alexander Peloquin, 1918-1997; verses ascr. to Innocent VI, d.1362
Tune: Refrain, Alexander Peloquin, 1918-1997; verses, Chant mode VI
© 1976, GIA Publications, Inc.

Pan de Vida 909

Refrain

*Pan de Vi - da, cuer-po del Se - ñor,

cup of bless - ing, blood of Christ the Lord.

At this ta - ble the last shall be first, **po -

der es ser - vir, por-que Dios es a - mor.

Verses

1. We are the dwell-ing of God,
***2. Us - te - des me lla - man "Se - ñor," me in-
3. There is no Jew or Greek,

fra - gile and wound-ed and weak. We are the
cli - no_a la - var - les los pies: Ha - gan lo
there is no slave or free; there is no

bod - y of Christ, called to be the com -
mis - mo, hu - mil - des, sir - vién - do - se
wom-an or man; on - ly heirs of the

D.C.

pas - sion of God.
u - nos a o - tros.
prom - ise of God.

*Bread of Life, body of the Lord, **power is for service, because God is Love.
***You call me "Lord," and I bow to wash your feet:
you must do the same, humbly serving each other.

Text: John 13:1-15, Galatians 3:28-29; Bob Hurd, b.1950, and Pia Moriarty, b.1948
Tune: Bob Hurd, b.1950; acc. by Craig S. Kingsbury, b.1952
© 1988, Bob Hurd and Pia Moriarty. Published by OCP Publications.

910 Take and Eat

Refrain

Take and eat; take and eat: this is my bod - y giv-en up for you. Take and drink; take and drink: this is my blood giv - en up for you.

Verses

1. I am the Word that spoke and light was made;
2. I am the way that leads the ex - ile home;
3. I am the Lamb that takes a - way your sin;
4. I am the cor - ner - stone that God has laid;
5. I am the light that came in - to the world;
6. I am the first and last, the Liv - ing One;

I am the seed that died to be re - born;
I am the truth that sets the cap - tive free;
I am the gate that guards you night and day;
A cho - sen stone and pre - cious in his eyes;
I am the light that dark - ness can - not hide;
I am the Lord who died that you might live;

I am the bread that comes from heav'n a - bove;
I am the life that rais - es up the dead;
You are my flock: you know the shep-herd's voice;
You are God's dwell - ing place, on me you rest;
I am the morn - ing star that nev - er sets;
I am the bride-groom, this my wed - ding song;

D.C.

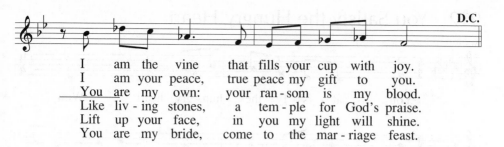

I   am the vine   that fills your cup with joy.
I   am your peace,   true peace my gift to you.
You are my own: your ran-som is my blood.
Like liv-ing stones,   a tem-ple for God's praise.
Lift up your face,   in you my light will shine.
You are my bride,   come to the mar-riage feast.

Text: Verse text, James Quinn, SJ, b.1919, © 1989. Used by permission of Selah Publishing Co., Inc.; refrain text, Michael Joncas, b.1951, © 1989,
    GIA Publications, Inc.
Tune: Michael Joncas, b.1951, © 1989, GIA Publications, Inc.

Let Us Break Bread Together   911

1. Let us break bread to-geth-er on our knees;
2. Let us drink wine to-geth-er on our knees;
3. Let us praise God to-geth-er on our knees;

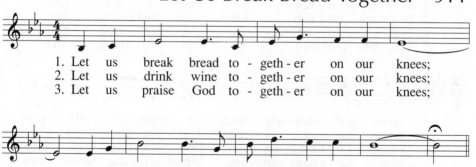

Let us break bread to-geth-er on our knees;
Let us drink wine to-geth-er on our knees;
Let us praise God to-geth-er on our knees;

When I fall on my knees, With my face to the ris-ing

sun, O Lord, have mer-cy on me.

Text: American folk hymn
Tune: LET US BREAK BREAD, 10 10 6 8 7; American folk hymn; harm. by David Hurd, b.1950, © 1968, GIA Publications, Inc.

912 You Satisfy the Hungry Heart

Refrain

You sat-is-fy the hun-gry heart With gift of fin-est wheat; Come give to us, O sav-ing Lord, The bread of life to eat.

Verses

1. As when the shep - herd calls his sheep, They
2. With joy - ful lips we sing to you Our
3. Is not the cup we bless and share The
4. The mys - t'ry of your pres - ence, Lord, No
5. You give your - self to us, O Lord; Then

know and heed his voice; So when you call your
praise and grat - i - tude, That you should count us
blood of Christ out - poured? Do not one cup, one
mor - tal tongue can tell: Whom all the world can -
self - less let us be, To serve each oth - er

D.C.

fam - 'ly, Lord, We fol - low and re - joice.
wor - thy, Lord, To share this heav'n - ly food.
loaf, de - clare Our one - ness in the Lord?
not con - tain Comes in our hearts to dwell.
in your name In truth and char - i - ty.

Text: Omer Westendorf, 1916-1998
Tune: BICENTENNIAL, CM with refrain; Robert E. Kreutz, 1922-1996
© 1977, Archdiocese of Philadelphia

I Received the Living God   913

Refrain

I re-ceived the liv-ing God, and my heart is full of joy. I re-ceived the liv-ing God, and my heart is full of joy.

Verses

1. Je-sus said: "I am the Bread Knead-ed long to give you life; You who will par-take of me Need not ev-er fear to die."
2. Je-sus said: "I am the Way, And my Fa-ther longs for you; So I come to bring you home To be one with him a-new."
3. Je-sus said: "I am the Truth; If you fol-low close to me, You will know me in your heart, And my word shall make you free."
4. Je-sus said: "I am the Life Far from whom no thing can grow, But re-ceive this liv-ing bread, And my Spir-it you shall know."

D.C.

Text: Bernard Geoffroy, tr. anonymous
Tune: LIVING GOD, 7777 with refrain; Dom Clément Jacob, adapt.; harm. by Richard Proulx, b. 1937, © 1986, GIA Publications, Inc.

914 Alleluia! Sing to Jesus

1. Al - le - lu - ia! sing to Je - sus! His the scep - ter, his the throne; Al - le - lu - ia! his the tri - umph, His the vic - to - ry a - lone; Hark! the songs of peace - ful Zi - on Thun - der like a might - y flood; Je - sus out of ev - 'ry na - tion Has re - deemed us by his blood.

2. Al - le - lu - ia! not as or - phans Are we left in sor - row now; Al - le - lu - ia! he is near us, Faith be - lieves, nor ques - tions how: Though the cloud from sight re - ceived him, When the for - ty days were o'er, Shall our hearts for - get his prom - ise, "I am with you ev - er - more"?

3. Al - le - lu - ia! Bread of An - gels, Here on earth our food, our stay! Al - le - lu - ia! here the sin - ful Flee to you from day to day: In - ter - ces - sor, friend of sin - ners, Earth's re - deem - er, plead for me, Where the songs of all the sin - less Sweep a - cross the crys - tal sea.

4. Al - le - lu - ia! King e - ter - nal, You the Lord of lords we own; Al - le - lu - ia! born of Mar - y, Earth your foot - stool, heav'n your throne: You, with - in the veil, have en - tered, Robed in flesh, our great high priest; Here on earth both priest and vic - tim In the eu - cha - ris - tic feast.

Text: Revelation 5:9; William C. Dix, 1837-1898
Tune: HYFRYDOL, 8 7 8 7 D; Rowland H. Prichard, 1811-1887

One Bread, One Body 915

Refrain

One bread, one bod-y, one Lord of all,
one cup of bless - ing which we bless. And
we, though man-y, through-out the earth,
we are one bod - y in this one Lord.

Verses

1. Gen - tile   or   Jew,   ser - vant   or   free,
2. Man - y   the   gifts,   man - y   the   works,
3. Grain for   the   fields,   scat-tered   and   grown,

D.C.

wom - an   or   man   no   more.
one   in   the   Lord   of   all.
gath - ered   to   one   for   all.

Text: 1 Corinthians 10:16; 17, 12:4, Galatians 3:28; the *Didache* 9; John Foley, SJ, b.1939
Tune: John Foley, SJ, b.1939

916 In Christ There Is a Table Set for All

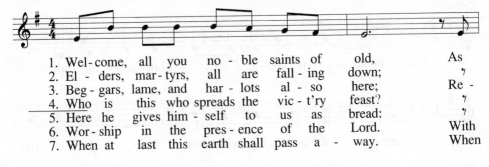

1. Wel-come, all you no - ble saints of old, As
2. El - ders, mar - tyrs, all are fall - ing down; ,
3. Beg - gars, lame, and har - lots al - so here; Re -
4. Who is this who spreads the vic - t'ry feast? ,
5. Here he gives him - self to us as bread: ,
6. Wor - ship in the pres - ence of the Lord. With
7. When at last this earth shall pass a - way. When

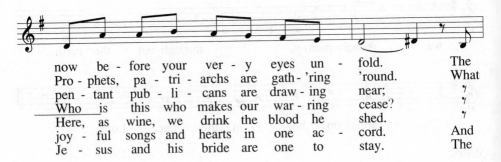

now be - fore your ver - y eyes un - fold. The
Pro - phets, pa - tri - archs are gath - 'ring 'round. What
pen - tant pub - li - cans are draw - ing near; ,
Who is this who makes our war - ring cease? ,
Here, as wine, we drink the blood he shed. ,
joy - ful songs and hearts in one ac - cord. And
Je - sus and his bride are one to stay. The

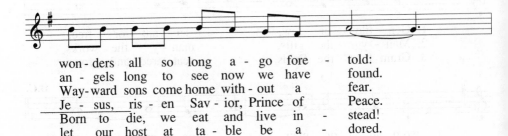

won - ders all so long a - go fore - told:
an - gels long to see now we have found.
Way-ward sons come home with - out a fear.
Je - sus, ris - en Sav - ior, Prince of Peace.
Born to die, we eat and live in - stead!
let our host at ta - ble be a - dored.
feast of love is just be - gun that day.

In Christ there is a ta - ble set for all.

Text: Robert J. Stamps
Tune: CENÉDIUS, Irregular, Robert J. Stamps
© 1972, Dawn Treader Music

Draw Us in the Spirit's Tether 917

1. Draw us in the Spir-it's teth - er, For when
2. As dis - ci - ples used to gath - er In the
3. All our meals and all our liv - ing Make as

hum - bly in your name, Two or
name of Christ to sup, Then with
sac - ra - ments of you, That by

three are met to - geth - er, You are in the
thanks to God the Fa - ther Break the bread and
car - ing, help-ing, giv - ing, We may be dis -

midst of them; Al - le - lu - ia! Al - le - lu - ia!
bless the cup, Al - le - lu - ia! Al - le - lu - ia!
ci - ples true. Al - le - lu - ia! Al - le - lu - ia!

Touch we now your gar - ment's hem.
So now bind our friend - ship up.
We will serve with faith a - new.

Text: Percy Dearmer, 1867-1936, alt., © Oxford University Press
Tune: UNION SEMINARY, 8 7 8 7 44 7; Harold Friedell, 1905-1958, © 1957, H. W. Gray Co., Inc.; harm. by Jet Turner, 1928-1984, © Chalice Press

918 Seed, Scattered and Sown

Refrain

Seed, scat-tered and sown, wheat, gath-ered and grown, bread, bro-ken and shared as one, the Liv-ing Bread of God. Vine, fruit of the land, wine, work of our hands, one cup that is shared by all; the Liv-ing Cup, the Liv-ing Bread of God.

Verses

D.C.

1. Is not the bread we break a shar-ing in our Lord?
Is not the cup we bless the blood of Christ out-poured?

2. The seed which falls on rock will with-er and will die.
The seed with-in good ground will flow-er and have life.

3. As wheat up-on the hills was gath-ered and was grown,
So may the church of God be gath-ered in-to one.

Text: *Didache* 9, 1 Corinthians 10:16-17, Mark 4:3-6; Dan Feiten
Tune: Dan Feiten; keyboard arr. by Eric Gunnison, R.J. Miller
© 1987, Ekklesia Music, Inc.

Taste and See 919

Refrain

Taste and see, taste and see the good-ness of the Lord.

Taste and see, taste and see the good-ness of the Lord.

Verses

1. I will nev - er stop thank - ing my God
2. Join the sing - ing in praise of our God;
3. Look to God and be ra - diant with joy;
4. God of jus - tice, rain down on the poor,

with my words of praise.   My
tell the world of the Name.   I
you will nev - er know shame.   The
giv - ing hope to their days.   Come

soul will boast,   will boast in the Lord.   The
cried to the Lord: "Have mer-cy on me."   God
weight of your bur - den   is light to the Lord.   With
vis - it your peo - ple,   each child of the earth;   come

D.C.

low - ly will hear me and be lift - ed in praise.
calmed all my fears and then set me free.
ten - der com - pas - sion God will call you by name.
vis - it us now and bring us to a new birth.

Text: Psalm 34:1-3; Francis Patrick O'Brien, b.1958
Tune: Francis Patrick O'Brien, b.1958
© 1992, GIA Publications, Inc.

920 Life-giving Bread, Saving Cup

Refrain

Life-giv-ing bread, sav-ing cup, we of-fer in thanks-giv-ing, O God.

Life-giv-ing bread, sav-ing cup, we of-fer as a sign of our love.

Verses

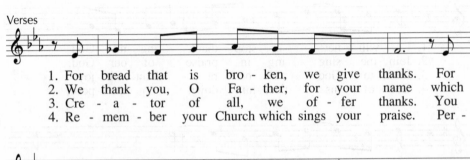

1. For bread that is bro-ken, we give thanks. For
2. We thank you, O Fa-ther, for your name which
3. Cre-a-tor of all, we of-fer thanks. You
4. Re-mem-ber your Church which sings your praise. Per-

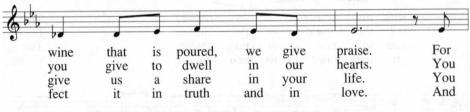

wine that is poured, we give praise. For
you give to dwell in our hearts. You
give us a share in your life. You
fect it in truth and in love. And

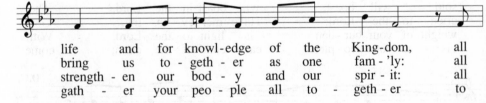

life and for knowl-edge of the King-dom, all
bring us to-geth-er as one fam-'ly: all
strength-en our bod-y and our spir-it: all
gath-er your peo-ple all to-geth-er to

D.C.

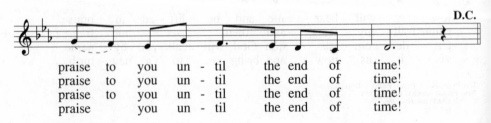

praise to you un-til the end of time!
praise to you un-til the end of time!
praise to you un-til the end of time!
praise you un-til the end of time!

Text: Adapted from the *Didache*, 2nd C.; James J. Chepponis, b.1956
Tune: James J. Chepponis, b.1956
© 1987, GIA Publications, Inc.

As the Grains of Wheat   921

Refrain

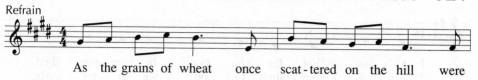

As the grains of wheat once scat-tered on the hill were

gath-ered in - to one to be - come our bread;

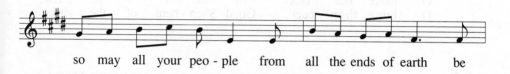

so may all your peo - ple from all the ends of earth be

gath - ered in - to one in you.

Verses

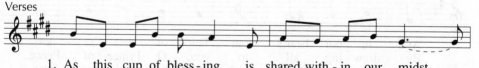

1. As this cup of bless-ing is shared with-in our midst,
2. Let this be a fore-taste of all that is to come when

D.C.

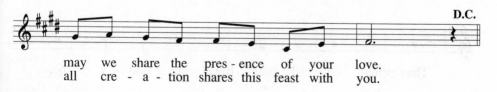

may we share the pres - ence of your love.
all cre - a - tion shares this feast with you.

Text: Marty Haugen, b.1950
Tune: Marty Haugen, b.1950
© 1990, GIA Publications, Inc.

922 At That First Eucharist

1. At that first Eu - cha - rist be - fore you died,
2. For all your church, O Lord, we in - ter - cede;
3. We pray for those who wan - der from the fold;

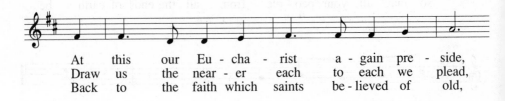

O Lord, you prayed that all be one in you;
O make our lack of char - i - ty to cease;
O bring them back, Good Shep - herd of the sheep,

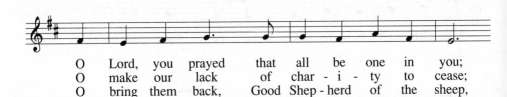

At this our Eu - cha - rist a - gain pre - side,
Draw us the near - er each to each we plead,
Back to the faith which saints be - lieved of old,

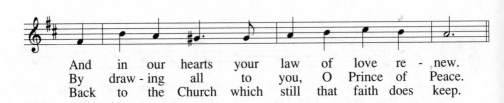

And in our hearts your law of love re - new.
By draw - ing all to you, O Prince of Peace.
Back to the Church which still that faith does keep.

Thus may we all one Bread, one Bod - y be;

Through this blest Sac - ra - ment of U - ni - ty.

Text: William H. Turton, 1859-1938, alt.
Tune: UNDE ET MEMORES, 10 10 10 10 with refrain; William H. Monk, 1823-1889, alt.

O Taste and See 923

Refrain

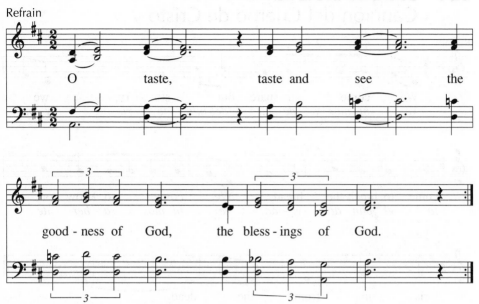

O   taste,   taste and   see   the

good - ness of   God,   the bless - ings   of   God.

Verses

1. I will sing God's praises all the days that I shall live.
   My soul will glory in my God, the lowly will hear and be glad.
   O glorify God's name with me, together let us rejoice.

2. For God has heard my anguished cries, and delivered me from all my foes.
   O look to God that you might shine, your faces be radiant with joy.

3. When the poor cry out, God hears and saves them,
   rescues them from their distress.
   God's angel watches near to those who look to their God to save them.

4. O taste and see that God is good, how happy the ones who find refuge.
   The mighty shall grow weak and hungry, those who seek God lack nothing.

5. Come, my children, hear me, I will teach you the fear of God.
   Come, all of you who thirst for life and seek joy in all of your days.

6. For God is close to the brokenhearted, near to those crushed in spirit.
   The hand of God redeems your life, a refuge for all those who seek.

Text: Psalm 34:2-4, 5-6, 7-8, 9, 11, 12-13, 19; Marty Haugen, b.1950
Tune: Marty Haugen, b.1950
© 1993, GIA Publications, Inc.

924 Song of the Body of Christ / Canción del Cuerpo de Cristo

Refrain

We come to share our sto - ry, we
Ve - ni-mos a de - cir del mis - te - rio, y par -

come to break the bread, We come to know our
tir el pan de vi - da. Ve - ni-mos a sa - ber de

ris - ing from the dead.
nues - tra e - ter - ni - dad.

Verses

1. We come as your peo - ple, we
2. We are called to heal the bro - ken, to be
3. Bread of life and cup of prom - ise, in this
4. You will lead and we shall fol - low, you will
5. We will live and sing: "A - lo - ha," "Al - le -
   (live and sing your prais - es,)

come as your own, u - nit - ed with each
hope for the poor, we are called to feed the
meal we all are one. In our dy - ing and our
be the breath of life; liv - ing wa - ter, we are
lu - ia" is our song. May we live in love and

D.C.

oth - er, love finds a home.
hun - gry at our door.
ris - ing, may your king - dom come.
thirst - ing for your light.
peace our whole life long.

Verses

1. Ve - ni - mos, co - mo su pueb - lo en es -
2. Nos lla - ma pa - ra cu - rar y
3. Pan de vi - da y co - pa de pro - me - sa, so - mos
4. Nos guia - rás y te se - gui - re - mos, por - que
5. Vi - vi - re - mos can - tan - do "A - lo - ha." "A - le -

pí - ri - tu de ver - dad. U - ni - dos en su a -
ser su es - per - an - za. So - mos su - yos pa - ra_a - li - men
u - no en es - ta co - mi - da. Ven - drá su rei - no_en
e - res la luz que bus - ca - mos. En el di - a o en la
lu - ya" es nues - tra can - ción. Por siem - pre vi - vi -

D.C.

mor, so - mos un co - ra - zón.
tar a los po - bres.
nues - tra trans - for - ma - ción.
no - che, bri - lla - rás.
re - mos en su paz.

Text: David Haas, b.1957, Spanish translation by Donna Peña, b.1955
Tune: NO KE ANO' AHI AHI, Irregular, Hawaiian traditional, arr. by David Haas, b.1957
© 1989, GIA Publications, Inc.

925 Take the Bread, Children

1. Take the bread, chil - dren, take the bread,
2. Bless the bread, chil - dren, bless the bread,
3. Break the bread, chil - dren, break the bread,
4. Give the bread, chil - dren, give the bread,
5. Eat the bread, chil - dren, eat the bread,

Take the bread, chil - dren, take the bread, For the
Bless the bread, chil - dren, bless the bread, For the
Break the bread, chil - dren, break the bread, For the
Give the bread, chil - dren, give the bread, For the
Eat the bread, chil - dren, eat the bread, For the

Fa - ther of us all Is the One who gives the
bless - ing of the Lord Comes in bread and in the
break - ing is the sign All is mine and all is
gift of moth - er earth Is the sign of dai - ly
ta - ble of the Lord Is the way you take the

1.- 4.

call, Take the bread, chil - dren, take the
Word, Bless the bread, chil - dren, bless the
thine, Break the bread, chil - dren, break the
birth, Give the bread, chil - dren, give the
Word, Eat the bread,

5.

bread.
bread.
bread.
bread.
chil - dren, eat the bread.

Text: Herbert Brokering, b.1926, © 1981
Tune: BREAD, 88 77 8; Carl F. Schalk, b.1929, © 1981, GIA Publications, Inc.

All Who Hunger 926

Verses

Cantor(s):

1. All who hun-ger, gath - er glad - ly; ho - ly man - na
2. All who hun-ger, nev - er stran-gers, seek-er, be a
3. All who hun-ger, sing to - geth - er; Je - sus Christ is

is our bread. Come from wil - der - ness and wan-d'ring.
wel - come guest. Come from rest - less - ness and roam - ing.
liv - ing bread. Come from lone - li - ness and long - ing.

Here, in truth, we will be fed. You that yearn for
Here, in joy, we keep the feast. We that once were
Here, in peace, we have been led. Blest are those who

days of full-ness, all a - round us is our food.
lost and scat-tered in com-mun-ion's love have stood.
from this ta - ble live their lives in grat - i - tude.

Refrain

All:

Taste and see the grace e - ter-nal. Taste and see that God is good.

927 Bread to Share

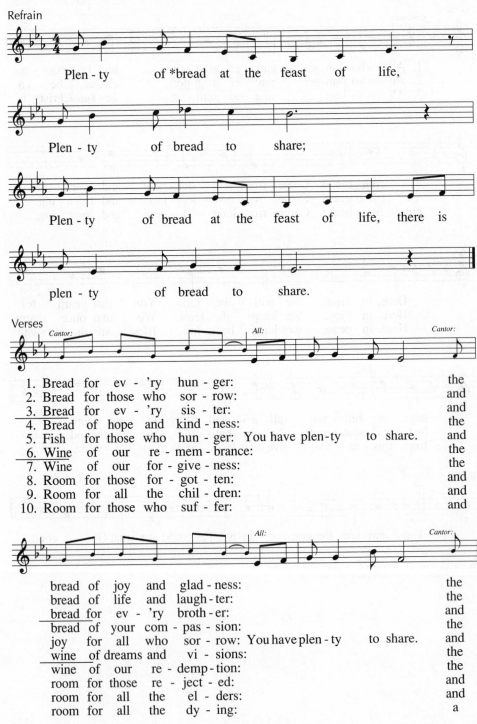

Refrain

Plen-ty of *bread at the feast of life,
Plen-ty of bread to share;
Plen-ty of bread at the feast of life, there is
plen-ty of bread to share.

Verses

Cantor: ... *All:* ... *Cantor:*

1. Bread for ev-'ry hun-ger: the
2. Bread for those who sor-row: and
3. Bread for ev-'ry sis-ter: and
4. Bread of hope and kind-ness: the
5. Fish for those who hun-ger: You have plen-ty to share. and
6. Wine of our re-mem-brance: the
7. Wine of our for-give-ness: the
8. Room for those for-got-ten: and
9. Room for all the chil-dren: and
10. Room for those who suf-fer: and

All: ... *Cantor:*

bread of joy and glad-ness: the
bread of life and laugh-ter: the
bread for ev-'ry broth-er: and
bread of your com-pas-sion: the
joy for all who sor-row: You have plen-ty to share. and
wine of dreams and vi-sions: the
wine of our re-demp-tion: the
room for those re-ject-ed: and
room for all the el-ders: and
room for all the dy-ing: a

Use bread, fish, wine, or room according to the preceeding verse.

bread of grace and mer - cy:
bread of strength and jus - tice:
bread for free - dom's jour - ney:
bread of love and wel - come:
faith for un - be - liev - ers: You have plen-ty to share, you have
wine of cel - e - bra - tion:
wine of our to - mor - rows:
room for all the out - casts:
room for all the lone - ly:
room that sings of new life:

D.C.

plen - ty of bread to share.

Text: John 6:1-15; Marty Haugen, b.1950
Tune: Marty Haugen, b.1950
© 1995, GIA Publications, Inc.

Eat This Bread 928

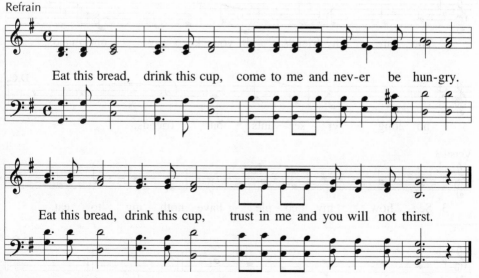

Refrain

Eat this bread, drink this cup, come to me and nev-er be hun-gry.

Eat this bread, drink this cup, trust in me and you will not thirst.

Text: John 6; adapt. by Robert J. Batastini, b.1942, and the Taizé Community
Tune: Jacques Berthier, 1923-1994
© 1984, Les Presses de Taizé, GIA Publications, Inc., agent

929 Let Us Be Bread

Refrain

Let us be bread, blessed by the Lord, bro-ken and shared,

life for the world. Let us be wine, love free-ly poured.

Let us be one in the Lord.

Verse 1

1. I am the bread of life, bro-ken for all.

Eat now and hun-ger no more. *D.C.*

Verse 2

2. You are my friends if you keep my com-mands,

no long - er ser-vants but friends. *D.C.*

Verse 3

3. See how my peo-ple have noth-ing to eat.

Give them the bread that is you. *D.C.*

Verse 4

4. As God has loved me so I have loved you.

D.C.

Go and live on in my love.

Text: Thomas J. Porter, b.1958
Tune: Thomas J. Porter, b.1958
© 1990, GIA Publications, Inc.

Jesus Is Here Right Now   930

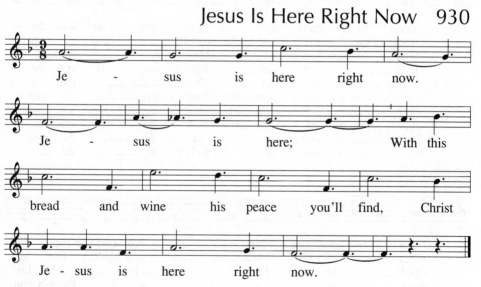

Je - sus is here right now.

Je - sus is here; With this

bread and wine his peace you'll find, Christ

Je - sus is here right now.

Verses

1. Do not let your old hearts be troubled.
   Have faith in God and have faith in me.
   In my Father's house there are many mansions;
   otherwise, how could I have told you so?

2. I am indeed going to prepare a place for you,
   and then I shall come back to take you with me;
   that where I am you also may be.
   For you know the way that leads to where I go.

Text: Leon C. Roberts; verses, John 14:1-4
Tune: Leon C. Roberts
© 1986, GIA Publications, Inc.

931 I Am the Bread of Life / Yo Soy el Pan de Vida

1.___ I am the Bread of life. You who
2. The bread that___ I will give is my
3. Un - less___ you___ eat of the
4.___ I am the Res - ur - rec - tion,___
5. Yes, Lord,___ I be - lieve that___

1.___ Yo soy el pan de vi – da. El que
2. El pan que___ yo da - ré___ es mi
3.___ Mien - tras no co - mas el___
4.___ Yo soy la re - su - rrec - ción.___
5.___ Sí, Se - ñor, yo cre - o que___

come to me shall not hun - ger;___ and who be -
flesh for the life of the world,___ and if you
flesh of the Son of Man___ and___
I___ am the life.___ If you be -
you___ are the Christ,___ the___

vie - ne_a mí no ten – drá ham - bre.___ El que
cuer - po___ vi - da del mun - do,___ y el que
cuer - po del hi - jo del hom - bre,___ y___
Yo___ soy la vi - da.___ El que
tú e - res el Cris - to,___ El___

lieve in me shall not thirst.___ No one can come to
eat___ of this bread,___ you shall___ live for
drink___ of his blood,_ and drink___ of his
lieve___ in___ me,___ e - ven___ though you
Son___ of___ God,___ Who___ has___

cree_en mí no ten - drá sed.___ Na - die___ vie - ne_a
co - ma___ de mi car – ne___ ten - drá vi - da_e -
be - bas___ de su san - gre y be - bas___ de su
cree___ en___ mí,___ aun - que___ mu - rie -
Hi - jo de Dios,___ que vi - no al

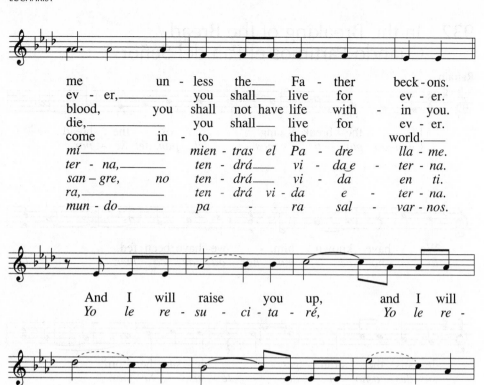

me   un - less   the___   Fa - ther   beck - ons.
ev - er,___   you   shall___   live   for   ev - er.
blood,   you   shall   not have life   with - in you.
die,___   you   shall___   live   for   ev - er.
come   in - to___   the___   world.___
mí___   mien - tras el Pa - dre   lla - me.
ter - na,___   ten - drá___   vi - da e - ter - na.
san – gre,   no   ten - drá___   vi - da   en ti.
ra,___   ten - drá vi - da   e - ter - na.
mun - do___   pa - ra   sal - var - nos.

And   I   will   raise   you   up,   and I will
Yo   le   re - su - ci - ta - ré,   Yo le re -

raise   you   up,   and I will raise   you
su - ci - ta - ré,   Yo le re - su - ci - ta -

up   on   the   last   day.
ré   el   di - a   de El.

Text: John 6; Suzanne Toolan, SM, b.1927
Tune: BREAD OF LIFE, Irregular with refrain; Suzanne Toolan, SM, b.1927

932 In the Breaking of the Bread /
Cuando Partimos el Pan del Señor

Refrain

In the break - ing of the bread
Cuan-do par - ti - mos el pan del Se - ñor,

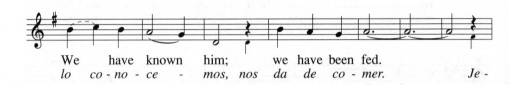

We have known him; we have been fed. *Je-*
lo co - no - ce - mos, nos da de co - mer.

Je - sus the stran - ger, Je - sus the Lord,
sús des - co-no - ci - do, Je - sús, Se - ñor,

Be our com - pan - ion, be our hope.
nues-tro com-pa - ñe - ro, y fuen-te de fe.

Verses

1. Bread for the jour - ney, strength for our years,
1. *Pan pa - ra el via - je, Pan de la vi - da,*
2. Bread of the prom - ise, peo - ple of hope,
2. *Pan del pro - me - sa, Pan de es - pe - ran - za,*

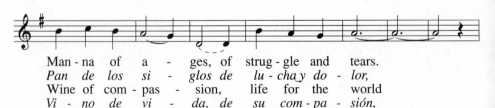

Man - na of a - ges, of strug - gle and tears.
Pan de los si - glos de lu - cha y do - lor,
Wine of com - pas - sion, life for the world
Vi - no de vi - da, de su com - pa - sión,

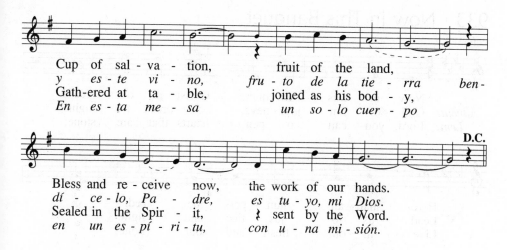

Cup of sal - va - tion,   fruit of the land,
y es - te vi - no,   *fru - to de la tie - rra ben -*
Gath-ered at ta - ble,   joined as his bod - y,
En es - ta me - sa   *un so - lo cuer - po*

D.C.

Bless and re - ceive now,   the work of our hands.
dí - ce - lo, Pa - dre,   *es tu - yo, mi Dios.*
Sealed in the Spir - it,   sent by the Word.
en un es - pí - ri - tu,   *con u - na mi - sión.*

Original Verses:

1. Once I was helpless, sad and confused; darkness surrounded me, courage removed.
And then I saw him by my side. Carry my burden, open my eyes.

2. There is no sorrow, pain or woe; there is no suffering he did not know.
He did not waver; he did not bend. He is the victor. He is my friend.

Text: Bob Hurd, b.1950, and Michael Downey, © 1984, 1987; Spanish text by Stephen Dean and Kathleen Orozco, © 1989, OCP Publications
Tune: Bob Hurd, b.1950, © 1984; acc. by Dominic MacAller, b.1959, © 1984, OCP Publications
Published by OCP Publications

933 Now in This Banquet

Refrain

Now in this ban-quet, Christ is our bread;
Advent: God of our jour-neys, day-break to night;
Lent: Lord, you can o-pen hearts that are stone;

Here shall all hun-gers be fed.
Lead us to jus-tice and light.
Live in our flesh and our bone;

Bread that is bro-ken, wine that is poured,
Grant us com-pas-sion, strength for the day,
Lead us to won-der, mys-t'ry and grace,

Love is the sign of our Lord.
Wis-dom to walk in your way.
One in your lov-ing em-brace.

Verses 1, 2

1. You who have touched us and graced us with love,
2. Let our hearts burn with the fire of your love;

D.C.

make us your peo-ple of good-ness and light.
o-pen our eyes to the glo-ry of God.

Verse 3

3. God who makes the blind to see, God who makes the

*May be sung in canon.

lame to walk, bring us danc - ing in - to day,

D.C.

lead your peo - ple in your way.

Verse 4

4. Hope for the hope - less, light for the blind,

D.C.

"Strong" is your name, Lord, "Gen - tle" and "Kind."

Verse 5

5. Call us to be your light, call us to be your love,

D.C.

make us your peo - ple a - gain.

Verse 6

6. Come, O Spir - it! re - new our hearts!

D.C.

We shall a - rise to be chil - dren of light.

Text: Marty Haugen, b.1950
Tune: Marty Haugen, b.1950
© 1986, GIA Publications, Inc.

934 In Paradisum / May Choirs of Angels

In pa - ra - dí - sum de - dú - cant te án - ge - li:
May choirs of an - gels es - cort you in - to par - a - dise:

in tu - o ad - vén - tu su - scí - pi - ant te
and at your ar - ri - val may the mar - tyrs re - ceive

már - ty - res, et per - dú - cant te in
and wel - come you; may they bring you home in -

ci - vi - tá - tem san - ctam Je - rú - sa - lem.
to the ho - ly cit - y, Je - ru - sa - lem.

Cho - rus an - ge - ló - rum te su -
May the ho - ly an - gels wel -

scí - pi - at, et cum Lá - za - ro quon - dam
come you, and with Laz - a - rus, who lived in

páu - pe - re ae - tér - nam
pov - er - ty, may you have

há - be - as ré - qui - em.
ev - er - last - ing rest.

Text: *In Paradisum*, tr. © 1986, GIA Publications, Inc.
Tune: Mode VII; acc. by Richard Proulx, b.1937, © 1986, GIA Publications, Inc.

Song of Farewell 935

Refrain

Dy-ing you de-stroyed our death! Ris-ing you re-stored our life!

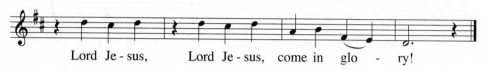

Lord Je-sus, Lord Je-sus, come in glo - ry!

Verses

1. May Christ who died for you lead you into his kingdom;
   may Christ who died for you lead you this day into paradise.

2. May Christ, the Good Shepherd, lead you home today
   and give you a place within his flock.

Alternate children s verse:
2. May Christ, the Good Shepherd, take you on his shoulders
   and bring you home, bring you home today.

3. May the angels lead you into paradise;
   may the martyrs come to welcome you
   and take you to the Holy City, the new and eternal Jerusalem.

4. May the choirs of angels come to meet you,
   may the choirs of angels come to meet you;
   where Lazarus is poor no longer, may you have eternal life in Christ.

Alternate children s verse:
4. May the choirs of angels come to meet you,
   may the choirs of angels come to meet you;
   and with all God's children may you have eternal life in Christ.

Text: Memorial Acclamation, © 1973, ICEL; *In paradisum;* Michael Marchal, b.1951, © 1988, GIA Publications, Inc.
Tune: Michael Joncas, b.1951, © 1988, GIA Publications, Inc.

936 I Know That My Redeemer Lives

Cantor:
I know that my Re-deem-er lives, and on the last day

I shall rise a-gain; in my bod-y I shall look on God, my

All:
Sav - ior, in my bod-y I shall look on God, my

Cantor:
Sav - ior. I my-self shall see him; my own eyes will

gaze on him, my own eyes will gaze on him; in my

All:
bod-y I shall look on God, my Sav - ior, in my bod-y I shall

Cantor:
look on God, my Sav - ior. This is the hope I

cher-ish, this is the hope I cher-ish in my heart;

in my bod-y I shall look on God, my Sav - ior,

All:
in my bod-y I shall look on God, my Sav - ior.

Text: *Rite of Funerals,* © 1970, ICEL
Tune: *Music for Rite of Funerals and Rite of Baptism for Children,* Howard Hughes, SM, b.1930, © 1977, ICEL

Rest in Peace 937

1. Rest in peace, earth's jour - ney end - ed,
2. Hap - py soul, to Christ u - nit - ed,
3. May we meet, dear Lord, in heav - en,

You whom Christ re - deemed, de - fend - ed:
Calm - er now and clear - er sight - ed:
Each for - giv - ing, each for - giv - en,

To the place where saints are one,
Your new jour - ney now be - gins,
Each more gift - ed to pur - sue

Safe - ly brought by him a - lone— May he grant us
Freed from earth's be - set - ting sins: Press - ing on to -
All you have for us to do. By your Spir - it's

like pro - tec - tion— Rest in peace, Rest in peace,
wards per - fec - tion, Hap - py soul, Hap - py soul,
sure di - rec - tion May we meet, May we meet,

Rest in peace, earth's jour - ney end - ed.
Hap - py soul, to Christ u - nit - ed.
May we meet, dear Lord, in heav - en.

Text: Fred Pratt Green, b.1903, © 1982, Hope Publishing Co.
Music: MOEHR, Russell Schulz-Widmar, b.1944, © 1987, GIA Publications, Inc.

938   May the Angels Lead You into Paradise

Cantor, then all:

May the an-gels lead you in-to par-a-dise;

may the mar-tyrs come to wel-come you and

take you to the ho-ly cit-y, the

new and e-ter-nal Je-ru-sa-lem.

Text: *In paradisum; Rite of Funerals,* © 1970, ICEL
Tune: *Music for Rite of Funerals and Rite of Baptism for Children,* Howard Hughes, SM, b.1930, © 1977, ICEL

939   May Saints and Angels Lead You On

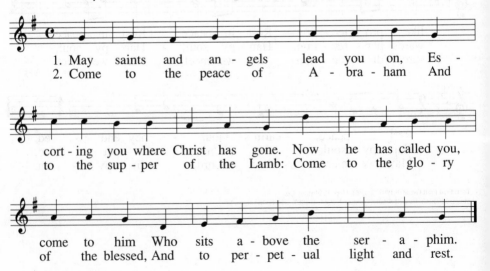

1. May saints and an-gels lead you on, Es-
2. Come to the peace of A-bra-ham And

cort-ing you where Christ has gone. Now he has called you,
to the sup-per of the Lamb: Come to the glo-ry

come to him Who sits a-bove the ser-a-phim.
of the blessed, And to per-pet-ual light and rest.

Text: *In Paradisum,* © 1985, ICEL
Tune: TALLIS' CANON, LM; Thomas Tallis, c.1505-1585

Keep in Mind   940

Refrain

Keep in mind that Je-sus Christ has died for
us and is ris-en from the dead. He
is our sav-ing Lord, he is joy for all a-ges.

Verse 1

D.C.

1. If we die with the Lord, we shall live with the Lord.
   If we en-dure with the Lord, we shall reign with the Lord.

Verses 2, 3

D.C.

2. In Christ all our sor-row, in Christ all our joy.
   In him hope of glo-ry, in him all our love.
3. In Christ our re-demp-tion, in Christ all our grace.
   In him our sal-va-tion, in him all our peace.

Text: 2 Timothy 2:8-12, Lucien Deiss, CSSp, b.1921
Tune: Lucien Deiss, CSSp, b.1921
© 1965, World Library Publications, Inc.

941 A Nuptial Blessing

Refrain

May God bless you, hold and keep you; may God's mer-cy shine on you, guide your work and guard your rest-ing, keep your love for ev - er new.

Verses

1. May God satisfy your longing, be refreshment at your table,
   and provide your daily bread,
   guard your going and your coming, be the solace in your silence:
   life within the lives you wed.

2. May God join your hopeful spirits, fill your hearts with truth and courage,
   trust to share both joy and tears,
   teach love to your children's children; may your household learn to witness
   living faith through all your years.

3. May God make your home a refuge where you warmly welcome strangers
   and the lowly find a place;
   make you caring, kind companions, help you meet the needs of neighbors,
   finding Christ in every face.

Text: Vicki Klima, b.1952; adapt. by Michael Joncas, b.1951, and George Szews, b.1951
Tune: Michael Joncas, b.1951
© 1989, GIA Publications, Inc.

When Love Is Found   942

1. When love is found and hope comes home,
2. When love has flow'red in trust and care,
3. When love is tried as loved-ones change,
4. When love is torn and trust be - trayed,
5. Praise God for love, praise God for life,

Sing and be glad that two are one.
Build both each day that love may dare
Hold still to hope though all seems strange,
Pray strength to love till tor - ments fade,
In age or youth, in calm or strife.

When love ex - plodes and fills the sky,
To reach be - yond home's warmth and light,
Till ease re - turns and love grows wise
Till lov - ers keep no score of wrong
Lift up your hearts let love be fed

Praise God and share our Mak - er's joy.
To serve and strive for truth and right.
Through lis - t'ning ears and o - pened eyes.
But hear through pain love's Eas - ter song.
Through death and life in bro - ken bread.

Text: Brian Wren, b.1936
Tune: O WALY WALY, LM; English; harm. by Martin West, b.1929
© 1983, Hope Publishing Co.

943 Wherever You Go

1. Wher-ev-er you go I shall go.

Wher-ev-er you live so shall I live.

Your peo-ple will be my peo - ple, and

your God will be my God too.

2. Wher-ev-er you die I shall die

and there shall I be bur-ied be-side you.

We will be to-geth-er for ev - er, and

our love will be the gift of our life.

Text: Ruth 1:16, 17; Weston Priory, Gregory Norbet, OSB, b.1940
Tune: Gregory Norbet, OSB, b.1940; arr. by Mary David Callahan, b.1923
© 1972, 1981, The Benedictine Foundation of the State of Vermont, Inc.

Bridegroom and Bride 944

1. God, in the plan-ning and pur-pose of life,
2. Je - sus was found, at a sim - i - lar feast,
3. There - fore we pray that his spir - it pre - side
4. Praise then the Mak - er, the Spir - it, the Son,

Hal - lowed the un - ion of hus - band and wife:
Tak - ing the roles of both wait - er and priest,
O - ver the wed - ding of bride-groom and bride,
Source of the love through which two are made one.

This we em - bod - y where love is dis - played,
Turn - ing the world - ly to - wards the di - vine,
Ful - fill - ing all that they've hoped will come true,
God's is the glo - ry, the good - ness, and grace

Rings are pre - sent - ed and prom - is - es made.
Tears in - to laugh - ter and wa - ter to wine.
Light - ing with love all they dream of and do.
Seen in this mar - riage and known in this place.

Text: John L. Bell, b.1949, © 1989, Iona Community, GIA Publications, Inc., agent
Tune: SLANE, 10 10 10 10; Irish traditional; harm. by Erik Routley, 1917-1982, © 1975, Hope Publishing Co.

945 Blessing the Marriage

1. That hu - man life might rich - er be, That
2. As two we love are wed this day And
3. Par - ents and fam - i - lies they leave, Their
4. This is as God meant it to be, That
5. Then, bless the bride - groom, bless the bride, The

chil - dren may be named and known, That love finds its own
we stand wit - ness to their vow, We call on God, the
own new fam - i - ly to make; And, shar - ing what their
man and wom - an should be one And live in love and
dreams they dream, the hopes they share; And thank the Lord whose

sanc - tua - ry, That those in love stay not a - lone.
Trin - i - ty, To sanc - ti - fy their pledg - es now.
pasts have taught, They shape it for the fu - ture's sake.
love through life, As Christ on earth has taught and done.
love in - spires The joy their lips and ours de - clare.

Praise, praise the Mak - er, Spir - it, Son,

bless - ing this mar - riage now be - gun.

Text: John L. Bell, b.1949, © 1989, Iona Community, GIA Publications, Inc., agent
Tune: SUSSEX CAROL, 8 8 8 8 8 88; harm. by Ralph Vaughan Williams, 1872-1958

Love Is the Sunlight 946

1. Love is the sun - light Shaped of your splen - dor,
2. Love is the spa - cious Qui - et of shad - ows,
3. May we in glad - ness Grow in your sun - shine,

Love is the star bright Born of your hand,
Love is the gra - cious Shade of re - lease,
May we in sad - ness Rest in your shade,

Bless-ing of heav - en Gra - cious - ly giv - en,
Mist of the morn - ing, Mid - day a - dorn - ing,
Giv - ing and gain - ing, Ev - er re - main - ing,

Ra - diant with glo - ry From your com - mand.
Cool with the twi - light Breath of your peace.
One in the mar - riage Your love has made.

Text: Borghild Jacobson, © 1981, Concordia Publishing House
Tune: BUNESSAN, 5 5 5 4 D; Gaelic; harm. by A. Gregory Murray, OSB, 1905-1992, © Downside Abbey

947 Out of the Depths

1. Out   of the depths, O   God, we call to you.
2. Out   of the depths of   fear, O God, we speak.
3. God   of the lov - ing   heart, we praise your name.

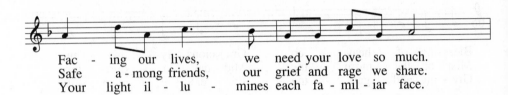

Wounds   of the past re-main, af - fect-ing all we do.
Break - ing the si - len-ces, the sear-ing truth we seek.
Dance   through our lives and loves; a - noint with Spir - it flame.

Fac - ing our lives,   we need your love so much.
Safe   a - mong friends, our grief and rage we share.
Your   light il - lu -   mines each fa - mil - iar face.

Here in this com-mun - i-ty,   heal us by your touch.
Here in this com-mun - i-ty,   hold us in your care.
Here in this com-mun - i-ty,   meet us with your grace.

Text: Psalm 130:1; Ruth Duck, b.1947, © 1992, GIA Publications, Inc.
Tune: FENNVILLE, 10 12 10 12; Robert J. Batastini, b.1942, © 1994, GIA Publications, Inc.

948 Lord Jesus Christ, Lover of All

Lord   Je - sus Christ,   lov - er of all,   trail

wide   the hem   of your gar - ment. Bring heal-ing,   bring peace.

Text: John L. Bell, b.1949
Tune: John L. Bell, b.1949
© 1987, Iona Community, GIA Publications, Inc., agent

Your Hands, O Lord, in Days of Old   949

1. Your hands, O Lord, in days of old Were strong to heal and save; They tri - umphed o - ver pain and death, Fought dark - ness and the grave. To you they went, the blind, the mute, The pal - sied, and the lame, The lep - er set a - part and shunned The sick and those in shame.

2. And then your touch brought life and health, Gave speech, and strength, and sight; And youth re - newed and health re - stored, Claimed you, the Lord of light: And so, O Lord, be near to bless, Al - might - y now as then, In ev - 'ry street, in ev - 'ry home, In ev - 'ry trou - bled friend.

3. O be our might - y heal - er still, O Lord of life and death; Re - store and strength - en, soothe and bless, With your al - might - y breath: On hands that work and eyes that see, Your heal - ing wis - dom pour, That whole and sick, and weak and strong, May praise you ev - er - more.

Text: Matthew 14:35-36; Edward H. Plumtre, 1821-1891, alt., © 1986, GIA Publications, Inc.
Tune: MOZART, CMD; adapt. from Wolfgang A. Mozart, 1756-1791

950 O Christ, the Healer

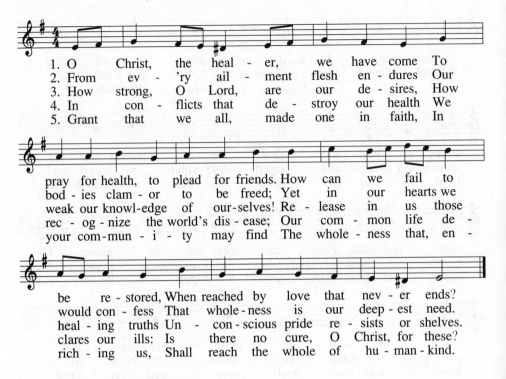

1. O Christ, the heal - er, we have come To
2. From ev - 'ry ail - ment flesh en - dures Our
3. How strong, O Lord, are our de - sires, How
4. In con - flicts that de - stroy our health We
5. Grant that we all, made one in faith, In

pray for health, to plead for friends. How can we fail to
bod - ies clam - or to be freed; Yet in our hearts we
weak our knowl-edge of our-selves! Re - lease in us those
rec - og - nize the world's dis - ease; Our com - mon life de -
your com - mun - i - ty may find The whole - ness that, en -

be re - stored, When reached by love that nev - er ends?
would con - fess That whole - ness is our deep - est need.
heal - ing truths Un - con - scious pride re - sists or shelves.
clares our ills: Is there no cure, O Christ, for these?
rich - ing us, Shall reach the whole of hu - man - kind.

Text: Fred Pratt Green, 1903-2000, © 1969, Hope Publishing Co.
Tune: ERHALT UNS HERR, LM; Klug's *Geistliche Lieder*, 1543; harm. by J.S. Bach, 1685-1750

951 He Healed the Darkness of My Mind

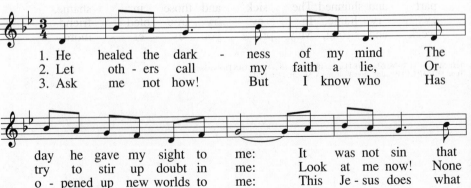

1. He healed the dark - ness of my mind The
2. Let oth - ers call my faith a lie, Or
3. Ask me not how! But I know who Has

day he gave my sight to me: It was not sin that
try to stir up doubt in me: Look at me now! None
o - pened up new worlds to me: This Je - sus does what

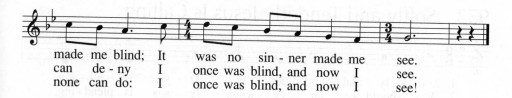

made me blind; It was no sin - ner made me see.
can de - ny I once was blind, and now I see.
none can do: I once was blind, and now I see!

Text: John 9; Fred Pratt Green, 1903-2000, © 1982, Hope Publishing Co.
Tune: ARLINGTON, LM; David Haas, b.1957, © 1988, GIA Publications, Inc.

Forgive Our Sins 952

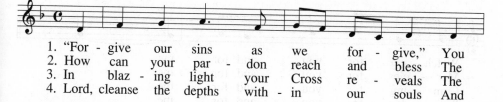

1. "For - give our sins as we for - give," You
2. How can your par - don reach and bless The
3. In blaz - ing light your Cross re - veals The
4. Lord, cleanse the depths with - in our souls And

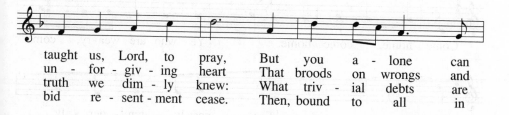

taught us, Lord, to pray, But you a - lone can
un - for - giv - ing heart That broods on wrongs and
truth we dim - ly knew: What triv - ial debts are
bid re - sent - ment cease. Then, bound to all in

grant us grace To live the words we say.
will not let Old bit - ter - ness de - part?
owed to us, How great our debt to you!
bonds of love, Our lives will spread your peace.

Text: Rosamund E. Herklots, 1905-1987, © Oxford University Press
Tune: DETROIT, CM; Supplement to Kentucky Harmony, 1820; harm. by Gerald H. Knight, 1908-1979, © The Royal School of Church Music

953 Softly and Tenderly Jesus Is Calling

1. Soft - ly and ten - der - ly Je - sus is call - ing,
2. Why should we tar - ry when Je - sus is plead - ing,
3. Time is now fleet - ing, the mo - ments are pass - ing,
4. O for the won - der - ful love He has prom - ised,

Call - ing for you and for me; See, on the
Plead - ing for you and for me? Why should we
Pass - ing from you and from me; Shad - ows are
Prom - ised for you and for me; Though we have

por - tals He's wait - ing and watch - ing,
lin - ger and heed not His mer - cies,
gath - er - ing, death - beds are com - ing,
sinned He has mer - cy and par - don,

Watch - ing for you and for me.
Mer - cies for you and for me?
Com - ing for you and for me.
Par - don for you and for me.

Come home, come home, Ye who are wea - ry, come

home; Ear - nest - ly, ten - der - ly,

Je - sus is call - ing— Call - ing, "O sin - ner, come home!"

Text: Will L. Thompson, 1847-1909
Tune: Will L. Thompson, 1847-1909

Come, You Sinners, Poor and Needy 954

1. Come, you sin - ners, poor and need - y,
2. Come, you thirst - y, come, and wel - come,
3. Come, you wea - ry, heav - y lad - en,

Weak and wound - ed, sick and sore, Je - sus, Son of
God's free boun - ty glo - ri - fy; True be - lief and
Lost and ru - ined by the fall; If you tar - ry

God, will save you, Full of pit - y, love, and pow'r.
true re - pent - ance, Ev - 'ry grace that brings you nigh.
till you're bet - ter, You will nev - er come at all.

I will a - rise and go to Je - sus, He will em - brace me

in his arms; In the arms of my dear

Sav - ior; O there are ten thous - sand charms.

Text: Joseph Hart, 1712-1768, alt.
Tune: RESTORATION, 8 7 8 7 with refrain; American; harm. by George Mims, b.1938, © 1979, Church of the Redeemer, Houston

955 Our Father, We Have Wandered

1. Our Fa - ther, we have wan - dered And
2. And now at length dis - cern - ing The
3. O Lord of all the liv - ing, Both

hid - den from your face; In fool - ish - ness have
e - vil that we do, Be - hold us, Lord, re -
ban - ished and re - stored, Com - pas - sion - ate, for -

squan - dered Your leg - a - cy of grace. But
turn - ing With hope and trust to you. In
giv - ing And ev - er car - ing Lord, Grant

now, in ex - ile dwell - ing, We
haste you come to meet us And
now that our trans - gress - ing, Our

rise with fear and shame, As dis - tant but com -
home re - joic - ing bring, In glad - ness there to
faith - less - ness may cease. Stretch out your hand in

pell - ing, We hear you call our name.
greet us With calf and robe and ring.
bless - ing, In par - don and in peace.

Text: Kevin Nichols, b.1929, © 1980, ICEL
Tune: PASSION CHORALE, 7 6 7 6 D; Hans Leo Hassler, 1564-1612; harm. by J.S. Bach, 1685-1750

The Master Came to Bring Good News 956

1. The Mas - ter came to bring good news, The
2. The Law's ful - filled through Je - sus Christ, The
3. To seek the sin - ners Je - sus came, To
4. For - give us, Lord, as we for - give And

news of love and free - dom, To heal the sick and
man who lived for oth - ers, The law of Christ is:
live a - mong the friend - less, To show them love that
seek to help each oth - er. For - give us, Lord, and

seek the poor, To build the peace - ful king - dom.
Serve in love Our sis - ters and our broth - ers.
they might share The king - dom that is end - less.
we shall live To pray and work to - geth - er.

Fa - ther, for - give us! Through Je - sus hear us!

As we for - give one an - oth - er!

Text: Ralph Finn, b.1941, © 1965, GIA Publications, Inc.
Tune: ICH GLAUB AN GOTT, 8 7 8 7 with refrain; *Mainz Gesangbuch*, 1870; harm. by Richard Proulx, b.1937, © 1986, GIA Publications, Inc.

957 Ashes

1. We rise a-gain from ash - es, from the good we've failed to do. We rise a-gain from ash - es, to cre-ate our-selves a - new. If all our world is ash - es, then must our lives be true, An of - fer-ing of ash - es, an of - fer-ing to you.

2. We of - fer you our fail - ures, we of - fer you at-tempts, The gifts not ful - ly giv - en, the dreams not ful - ly dreamt. Give our stum - bl - ings di - rec - tion, give our vi - sions wid - er view, An of - fer-ing of ash - es, an of - fer-ing to you.

3. Then rise a-gain from ash - es, let heal - ing come to pain, Though spring has turned to win - ter, and sun - shine turned to rain. The rain we'll use for grow - ing, and cre - ate the world a - new From an of - fer-ing of ash - es, an of - fer-ing to you.

4. ⎨ Thanks be to the Fa - ther, who made us like him - self. Thanks be to the Son, who saved us by his death. Thanks be to the Spir - it, who cre - ates the world a - new From an of - fer-ing of ash - es, an of - fer-ing to you.

Text: Tom Conry, b.1951
Tune: Tom Conry, b.1951; acc. by Michael Joncas, b.1951
© 1978, OCP Publications

Healer of Our Every Ill 958

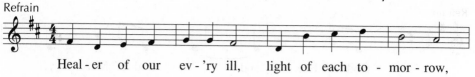

Refrain

Heal - er of our ev - 'ry ill, light of each to - mor - row,

give us peace be - yond our fear, and hope be - yond our sor - row.

Verses

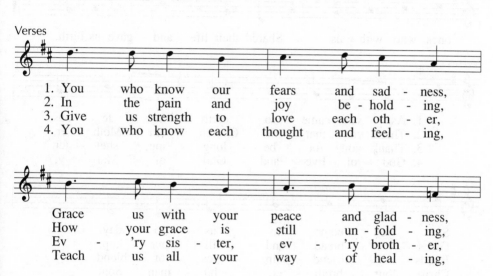

1. You   who know   our   fears   and sad - ness,
2. In   the pain   and   joy   be - hold - ing,
3. Give   us strength   to   love   each oth - er,
4. You   who know   each   thought   and feel - ing,

Grace   us with   your   peace   and glad - ness,
How   your grace   is   still   un - fold - ing,
Ev - 'ry   sis - ter,   ev - 'ry   broth - er,
Teach   us all   your   way   of heal - ing,

D.C.

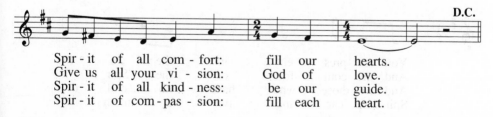

Spir - it   of all com - fort: fill   our   hearts.
Give us   all your vi - sion: God   of   love.
Spir - it   of all kind - ness: be   our   guide.
Spir - it   of com - pas - sion: fill   each   heart.

Text: Marty Haugen, b.1950
Tune: Marty Haugen, b.1950
© 1987, GIA Publications, Inc.

959 God of Eve and God of Mary

Refrain

God of Eve and God of Mar - y,
God of love and moth - er earth, Thank you for the
ones who with us Shared their life and gave us birth.

Verses

1. As you came to earth in Je - sus,
2. Thank you, that the Church, our Moth - er,
3. Thank you for be - long - ing, shel - ter,
4. God of Eve and God of Mar - y,

So you come to us to - day;
Gives us bread and fills our cup,
Bonds of friend - ship, ties of blood,
Christ our broth - er, hu - man Son.

You are pres - ent in the car - ing
And the com - fort of the Spir - it
And for those who have no chil - dren,
Spir - it, car - ing like a moth - er,

D.C.

That pre - pares us for life's way.
Warms our hearts and lifts us up.
Yet are par - ents un - der God.
Take our love and make us one.

Text: Fred Kaan, b.1929, © 1989, Hope Publishing Co.
Tune: FARRELL, 8 7 8 7 with refrain; Thomas J. Porter, b.1958, © 1994, GIA Publications, Inc.

God of Adam, God of Joseph 960

Refrain

God of A - dam, God of Jo - seph,
God of sow - ing, soil and seed, Thank you for your
world of prom - ise: Milk and hon - ey, wine and bread.

Verses

1. God, you make us your com - pan - ions,
2. May your pas - sion for cre - a - tion
3. Thank you for all men en - trust - ed
4. Ab - ba (Fa - ther), God of Jo - seph,

Shar - ers of your lov - ing cup;
Be re - flect - ed in our own;
With the charge of fa - ther - hood,
Hu - man Christ whose name we bear,

Thank you for the gen - er - a - tions,
For our role in birth and nur - ture
And for those who have no chil - dren,
Spir - it, womb of life and wis - dom:

D.C.

Weave of names and threads of hope.
Make through us your pres - ence known.
Yet are par - ents un - der God.
Thank you, God, for who we are!

Text: Fred Kaan, b.1929, © 1989, Hope Publishing Co.
Tune: FARRELL, 8 7 8 7 with refrain; Thomas J. Porter, b.1958, © 1994, GIA Publications, Inc.

961 Our Father, by Whose Name

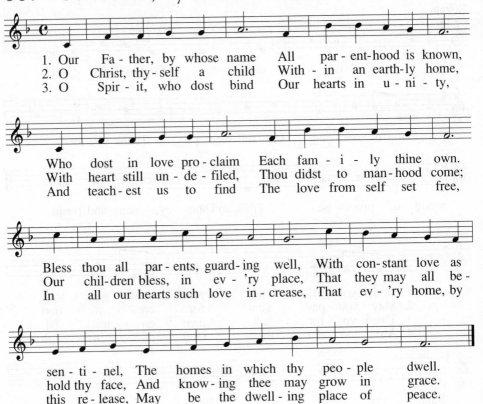

1. Our Fa - ther, by whose name All par - ent-hood is known,
2. O Christ, thy - self a child With - in an earth - ly home,
3. O Spir - it, who dost bind Our hearts in u - ni - ty,

Who dost in love pro - claim Each fam - i - ly thine own.
With heart still un - de - filed, Thou didst to man - hood come;
And teach - est us to find The love from self set free,

Bless thou all par - ents, guard - ing well, With con - stant love as
Our chil - dren bless, in ev - 'ry place, That they may all be -
In all our hearts such love in - crease, That ev - 'ry home, by

sen - ti - nel, The homes in which thy peo - ple dwell.
hold thy face, And know - ing thee may grow in grace.
this re - lease, May be the dwell - ing place of peace.

Text: F. Bland Tucker, 1895-1984, alt., © 1941, The Church Pension Fund
Tune: RHOSYMEDRE, 6 6 6 6 888; John Edwards, 1806-1885

O Saving Victim / O Salutaris 962

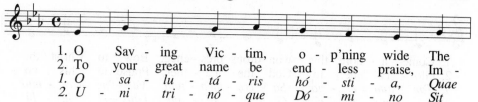

1. O Sav - ing Vic - tim, o - p'ning wide The
2. To your great name be end - less praise, Im -
1. O sa - lu - tá - ris hó - sti - a, Quae
2. U - ni tri - nó - que Dó - mi - no Sit

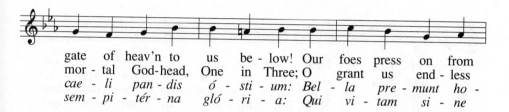

gate of heav'n to us be - low! Our foes press on from
mor - tal God-head, One in Three; O grant us end - less
cae - li pan - dis ó - sti - um: Bel - la pre - munt ho -
sem - pi - tér - na gló - ri - a: Qui vi - tam si - ne

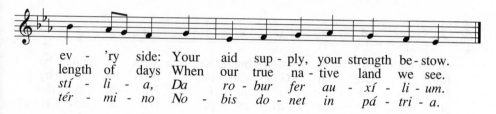

ev - 'ry side: Your aid sup - ply, your strength be - stow.
length of days When our true na - tive land we see.
stí - li - a, Da ro - bur fer au - xí - li - um.
tér - mi - no No - bis do - net in pá - tri - a.

Text: Thomas Aquinas, 1227-1275; tr. by Edward Caswall, 1814-1878, alt.
Tune: DUGUET, LM; Dieu donne Duguet, d.1767

963 Come Adore / Tantum Ergo

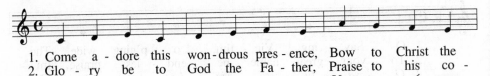

1. Come a-dore this won-drous pres-ence, Bow to Christ the
2. Glo - ry be to God the Fa - ther, Praise to his co -
1. *Tan - tum er - go Sa - cra - mén - tum Ve - ne - ré - mur*
2. *Ge - ni - tó - ri, Ge - ni - tó - que Laus et ju - bi -*

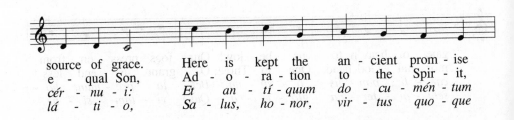

source of grace. Here is kept the an - cient prom - ise
e - qual Son, Ad - o - ra - tion to the Spir - it,
cér - nu - i: Et an - tí - quum do - cu - mén - tum
lá - ti - o, Sa - lus, ho - nor, vir - tus quo - que

Of God's earth - ly dwell-ing-place. Sight is blind be -
Bond of love, in God-head one. Blest be God by
No - vo ce - dat rí - tu - i: Prae - stet fi - des
Sit et be - ne - dí - cti - o: Pro - ce - dén - ti

fore God's glo - ry, Faith a - lone may see his face.
all cre - a - tion Joy - ous - ly while a - ges run.
sup - ple - mén - tum Sén - su - um de - fé - ctu - i.
ab u - tró - que Com - par sit lau - dá - ti - o.

Text: Thomas Aquinas, 1227-1274; tr. by James Quinn, SJ, b.1919, © 1969. Used by permission of Selah Publishing Co., Inc.
Tune: ST. THOMAS, 8 7 8 7 8 7; John F. Wade, 1711-1786

This Is My Song 964

1. This is my song, O God of all the na - tions,
2. My coun - try's skies are blu - er than the o - cean,
3. This is my prayer, O God of all earth's king - doms,

A song of peace for lands a - far and mine.
And sun - light beams on clo - ver - leaf and pine.
Your king - dom come; on earth your will be done.

This is my home, the coun - try where my heart is;
But oth - er lands have sun - light too, and clo - ver,
Let Christ be lift - ed up till all shall serve him,

Here are my hopes, my dreams, my ho - ly shrine;
And skies are ev - 'ry - where as blue as mine.
And hearts u - nit - ed learn to live as one.

But oth - er hearts in oth - er lands are beat - ing
So hear my song, O God of all the na - tions,
So hear my prayer, O God of all the na - tions.

With hopes and dreams as true and high as mine.
A song of peace for their land and for mine.
My - self I give you; let your will be done.

Text: St. 1-2, Lloyd Stone, 1912-1993, st. 3, Georgia Harkness, 1891-1974, © 1964, Lorenz Publishing Co.
Tune: FINLANDIA, 11 10 11 10 11 10; Jean Sibelius, 1865-1957

965 America the Beautiful

1. O beau - ti - ful for spa - cious skies, For
2. O beau - ti - ful for pil - grim feet, Whose
3. O beau - ti - ful for he - roes proved In
4. O beau - ti - ful for pa - triot dream That

am - ber waves of grain, For pur - ple moun - tain
stern, im - pas-sioned stress A thor - ough - fare for
lib - er - at - ing strife, Who more than self their
sees be - yond the years Thine al - a - bas - ter

maj - es - ties A - bove the fruit - ed plain! A -
free - dom beat A - cross the wil - der - ness! A -
coun - try loved, And mer - cy more than life! A -
cit - ies gleam, Un - dimmed by hu - man tears! A -

mer - i - ca! A - mer - i - ca! God
mer - i - ca! A - mer - i - ca! God
mer - i - ca! A - mer - i - ca! May
mer - i - ca! A - mer - i - ca! God

shed his grace on thee, And crown thy good with
mend thine ev - 'ry flaw, Con - firm thy soul in
God thy gold re - fine, Till all suc - cess be
shed his grace on thee, And crown thy good with

broth - er - hood From sea to shin - ing sea.
self - con - trol, Thy lib - er - ty in law.
no - ble - ness, And ev - 'ry gain di - vine.
broth - er - hood From sea to shin - ing sea.

Text: Katherine L. Bates, 1859-1929
Tune: MATERNA, CMD; Samuel A. Ward, 1848-1903

God of Our Fathers 966

1. God of our fa - thers, whose al - might - y hand
2. Your love di - vine has led us in the past,
3. From war's a - larms, from dead - ly pes - ti - lence,
4. Re - fresh your peo - ple on their toil - some way,

Leads forth in beau - ty all the star - ry band
In this free land by you our lot is cast;
Your might - y arm our ev - er sure de - fense;
Lead us from night to nev - er - end - ing day;

Of shin - ing worlds in splen - dor through the skies,
Be our strong rul - er, guar - dian, guide, and stay,
Your true re - lig - ion in our hearts in - crease,
Fill all our lives with heav'n - born love and grace,

Our grate - ful songs be - fore your throne a - rise.
Your word our law, your paths our cho - sen way.
Your boun - teous good - ness nour - ish us in peace.
Un - til at last, we meet be - fore your face.

Text: Daniel C. Roberts, 1841-1907
Tune: NATIONAL HYMN, 10 10 10 10; George W. Warren, 1828-1902

967 The God of All Eternity

1. The God of all e - ter - ni - ty,
2. What shall we of - fer God to - day—
3. God does not share our doubts and fears,
4. Let faith or for - tune rise or fall,
5. God grant that we, in this new year,

Un - bound by
Our dreams of
Nor shrinks from
Let dreams and
May show the

space yet al - ways near,
what we can - not see,
the un - known or strange:
dread both have their day;
world the King - dom's face,

Is pres - ent
Or, with eyes
The one who
Those whom God
And let our

where his peo - ple meet
fas - tened to the past,
fash - ioned heav'n and earth
loves walk un - a - fraid
work and wor - ship thrive

To cel - e -
Our dread of
Makes all things
With Christ their
As signs of

brate the com - ing year.
what is yet to be?
new and ush - ers change.
guide and Christ their way.
hope and means of grace.

Text: John L. Bell, b.1949, © 1989, Iona Community, GIA Publications, Inc., agent
Tune: O WALY WALY, 8 8 8 8; English traditional; arr. by John L. Bell, b.1949, © 1989, Iona Community, GIA Publications, Inc., agent

Greet Now the Swiftly Changing Year 968

1. Greet now the swift - ly chang - ing year With
2. This Je - sus came to wage sin's war; The
3. His love a - bun - dant far ex - ceeds The
4. With such a Lord to lead our way In
5. "All glo - ry be to God on high And

joy and pen - i - tence sin - cere; Re - joice, re-joice, with
Name of names for us he bore; Re - joice, re-joice, with
vol - ume of a whole year's needs; Re - joice, re-joice, with
want and in pros - per - i - ty, What need we fear in
peace on earth," the an - gels cry; Re - joice, re-joice, with

thanks em - brace An - oth - er year of grace.
thanks em - brace An - oth - er year of grace.
thanks em - brace An - oth - er year of grace.
earth or space In this new year of grace?
thanks em - brace An - oth - er year of grace.

Text: Slovak, 17th C.; tr. Jaroslav J. Vajda, b.1919, alt. © 1969, Concordia Publishing House
Tune: SIXTH NIGHT, 88 86; Alfred V. Fedak, © 1989, Selah Publishing Co.

Appendix

969   PASSION SUNDAY (PALM SUNDAY)

Passion or Palm Sunday is the last Sunday in Lent. Its closeness to the end of Lent has given this liturgy two distinct features: the procession with palms and the gospel reading of the Lord's passion. The blessing and carrying of palms celebrates Jesus' entrance into Jerusalem to accomplish his paschal mystery. The reading of the passion comes as a conclusion to all the gospel readings of the Lenten Sundays: these scriptures yearly prepare catechumens and the faithful to approach the celebration of Christ's death and resurrection. That celebration takes place most especially in the sacraments of initiation at the Easter Vigil.

COMMEMORATION OF THE LORD'S ENTRANCE INTO JERUSALEM

This rite may be very simple or may involve the entire assembly in a procession with the blessing of palms and the gospel reading of Jesus' entrance into Jerusalem.

OPENING ANTIPHON
The following or another appropriate acclamation may be sung.

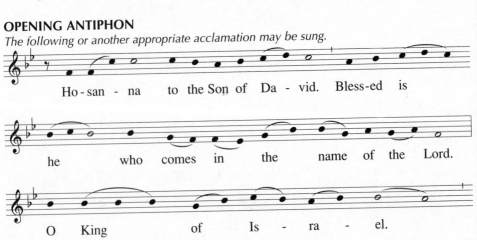

Ho-san-na to the Son of Da-vid. Bless-ed is he who comes in the name of the Lord. O King of Is-ra-el.

Ho - san - na   in   the   high - est.

Music: Chant Mode VII; adapt. and acc. by Richard Proulx, © 1985, GIA Publications, Inc.

BLESSING OF BRANCHES
All hold branches as these are blessed. The branches may be of palm or from a tree that is native to the area. The green or flowering branches signify the victory of life.

PROCESSION
All join in the procession or at least in the song. Such a movement of people expresses the experience of Lent: the church has been called to move on, to go ever further toward the paschal mystery of death and resurrection. The hymn, "All Glory, Laud, and Honor" (no. 563) or another appropriate song is sung during the procession.

The commemoration of the Lord's entrance into Jerusalem, whether this is done in a simple or solemn manner, concludes with the opening prayer of the Mass.

EASTER TRIDUUM   970

"The Easter Triduum of the passion and resurrection of Christ is...the culmination of the entire liturgical year. What Sunday is to the week, the solemnity of Easter is to the liturgical year." (General Norms for the Liturgical Year, #18)
        Lent ends quietly on Thursday afternoon. The church enters the Triduum ("three days"). On Thursday night the church begins a time of prayer and fasting, a time of keeping watch, that lasts into the great Vigil between Saturday and Sunday. The church emphasizes that the fasting of Good Friday and, if possible, of Holy Saturday are integral to the keeping of these days and the preparation for the sacraments of initiation celebrated at the Vigil. On Thursday night and on Friday afternoon or evening the church gathers to pray and to remember the many facets of the single mystery.

HOLY THURSDAY: EVENING MASS OF THE LORD'S SUPPER   971

On Thursday night Lent has ended and the church, at this Mass of the Lord's Supper, enters into the Easter Triduum. From the very first moment the all-embracing experience of these three days is proclaimed: "We should glory in the cross of our Lord Jesus Christ. For he is our salvation, our life, and our resurrection. Through him we are saved and made free." This is the whole of the great Triduum. On Thursday night, the liturgy draws us toward this through the scriptures, through the mandatum or washing of the feet which is the direct expression of our service to one another and the world, through the eucharistic banquet itself.

WASHING OF FEET

The homily is followed by the washing of feet, the mandatum (from the Latin word for "command": "A new commandment I give to you..."). This is a simple gesture of humble service: the priest washes the feet of various members of the assembly. Such a gesture, with the song which accompanies it, speaks directly of the way of life Christians seek.

Appropriate songs are: Ubi Caritas, no. 746 or 752, and Jesus Took a Towel, no. 566.

The Mass continues with the general intercessions.

972 TRANSFER OF THE HOLY EUCHARIST

When the communion rite is concluded, the eucharistic bread that remains is solemnly carried from the altar. The following hymn accompanies the procession.

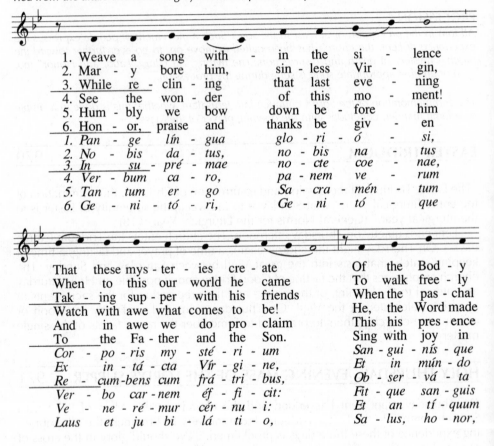

1. Weave a song with - in the si - lence
2. Mar - y bore him, sin - less Vir - gin,
3. While re - clin - ing that last eve - ning
4. See the won - der of this mo - ment!
5. Hum - bly we bow down be - fore him
6. Hon - or, praise and thanks be giv - en

1. Pan - ge lín - gua glo - ri - ó - si,
2. No - bis da - tus, no - bis na - tus
3. In su - pré - mae no - cte coe - nae,
4. Ver - bum ca - ro, pa - nem ve - rum
5. Tan - tum er - go Sa - cra - mén - tum
6. Ge - ni - tó - ri, Ge - ni - tó - que

That these mys - ter - ies cre - ate   Of the Bod - y
When to this our world he came   To walk free - ly
Tak - ing sup - per with his friends   When the pas - chal
Watch with awe what comes to be!   He, the Word made
And in awe we do pro - claim   This his pres - ence
To the Fa - ther and the Son.   Sing with joy in

Cor - po - ris my - sté - ri - um   San - gui - nís - que
Ex in - tá - cta Vír - gi - ne,   Et in mún - do
Re - cum - bens cum frá - tri - bus,   Ob - ser - vá - ta
Ver - bo car - nem éf - fi - cit: Fit - que san - guis
Ve - ne - ré - mur cér - nu - i: Et an - tí - quum
Laus et ju - bi - lá - ti - o,   Sa - lus, ho - nor,

Text: *Pange lingua*, Thomas Aquinas, 1227-1274; tr. by Ralph Wright, OSB, b.1938. © 1989, GIA Publications, Inc.
Tune: PANGE LINGUA, 8 7 8 7 8 7; Mode III; acc. by Eugene Lapierre, © 1964, GIA Publications, Inc.

The liturgy has no concluding rite, no dismissal. Rather, the church continues to watch and pray throughout the Triduum.

973 GOOD FRIDAY

In Good Friday's liturgy of the word and veneration of the cross there is great solemnity: a pondering of the "mystery of our faith," the passion, death and resurrection of our Lord Jesus Christ. Fasting and praying during these days, the catechumens and the baptized assemble on Good Friday in the afternoon or evening for a time of prayer together. This begins a time of silence.

LITURGY OF THE WORD

GENERAL INTERCESSIONS
As at Sunday liturgy, the word service concludes with prayers of intercession. Today these prayers take a more solemn form as the church lifts up to God its own needs and those of the world.

974 VENERATION OF THE CROSS
An ancient liturgical text reads: "See here the true and most revered Tree. Hasten to kiss it and to cry out with faith: You are our help, most revered Cross." For many centuries the church has solemnly venerated the relic or image of the cross on Good Friday. It is not present as a picture of suffering only but as a symbol of Christ's passover, where "dying he destroyed our death and rising restored our life." It is the glorious, the life-giving cross that the faithful venerate with song, prayer, kneeling and a kiss.

As the cross is shown to the assembly, the following is sung.

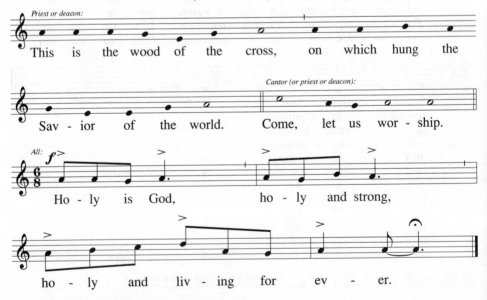

Music: Howard Hughes, SM, © 1979, 1985, GIA Publications, Inc.

As the assembly comes forward to venerate the cross, appropriate hymns and songs may be sung.

HOLY COMMUNION

This liturgy concludes with a simple communion rite. All recite the Lord's Prayer and receive holy communion. There is no concluding rite or dismissal for the church continues to be at prayer throughout the Triduum.

HOLY SATURDAY   975

The church continues to fast and pray and to make ready for this night's great Vigil. Saturday is a day of great quiet and reflection. Catechumens, sponsors and some of the faithful may assemble during the day for prayer, the recitation of the Creed, and for the rite of Ephpheta (opening of ears and mouth).

EASTER VIGIL   976

The long preparation of the catechumens, the lenten disciplines and fast of the faithful, the vigiling and fasting and prayer that have gone on since Thursday night—all culminate in the great liturgy of this night. On this night the church assembles to spend much time listening to scriptures, praying psalms, acclaiming the death and resurrection of the Lord. Only then are the catechumens called forward and prayed over, challenged to renounce evil and affirm their faith in God, led to the font and baptized in the blessed water. The newly baptized are then anointed with chrism and the entire assembly joins in intercession and finally in the eucharist.

INTRODUCTORY RITE

BLESSING OF THE FIRE AND LIGHTING OF THE PASCHAL CANDLE
The night vigil begins with the kindling of new fire and the lighting of the assembly's paschal candle.

PROCESSION
The ministers and assembly go in procession to the place where the scriptures will be read. The following is sung during the procession.

Priest or deacon: Christ our light.   All: Thanks be to God.

EASTER PROCLAMATION: THE EXSULTET
In this ancient text the church gives thanks and praise to God for all that is recalled this night: Adam's fall, the deliverance from Egypt, the passover of Christ, the wedding of earth and heaven, our reconciliation.

LITURGY OF THE WORD
At the Vigil, the liturgy of the word is an extended time of readings, silence and the chanting of psalms. On this night when the faithful know the death and resurrection of the Lord in baptism and eucharist, the church needs first to hear these scriptures which are the foundation of our life together: the creation story, Abraham and Isaac, the dividing of the sea, the poetry of Isaiah and Baruch and Ezekiel, the proclamation of Paul to the Romans and the gospel account of Jesus' resurrection.

977 LITURGY OF BAPTISM

After the homily the catechumens are called forward. The assembly chants the litany of the saints, invoking the holy women and men of all centuries. Patron saints of the church and of the catechumens and the faithful may be included in the litany.

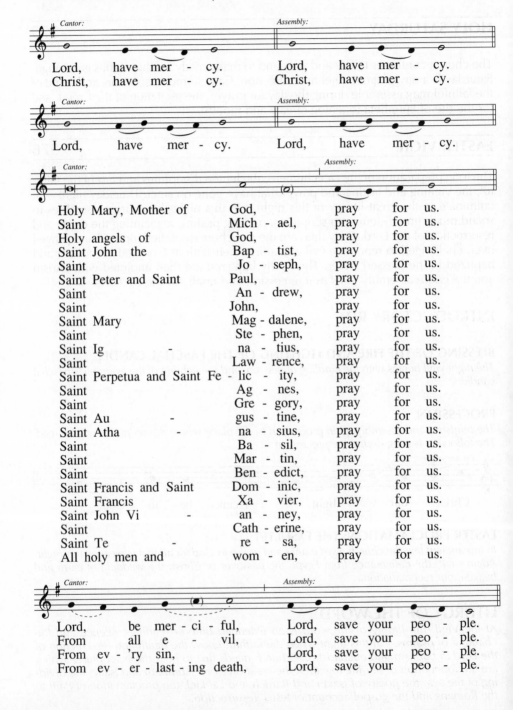

Cantor:	Assembly:
Lord, have mer - cy.	Lord, have mer - cy.
Christ, have mer - cy.	Christ, have mer - cy.

Cantor:	Assembly:
Lord, have mer - cy.	Lord, have mer - cy.

Cantor:	Assembly:
Holy Mary, Mother of God,	pray for us.
Saint Mich - ael,	pray for us.
Holy angels of God,	pray for us.
Saint John the Bap - tist,	pray for us.
Saint Jo - seph,	pray for us.
Saint Peter and Saint Paul,	pray for us.
Saint An - drew,	pray for us.
Saint John,	pray for us.
Saint Mary Mag - dalene,	pray for us.
Saint Ste - phen,	pray for us.
Saint Ig - na - tius,	pray for us.
Saint Law - rence,	pray for us.
Saint Perpetua and Saint Fe - lic - ity,	pray for us.
Saint Ag - nes,	pray for us.
Saint Gre - gory,	pray for us.
Saint Au - gus - tine,	pray for us.
Saint Atha - na - sius,	pray for us.
Saint Ba - sil,	pray for us.
Saint Mar - tin,	pray for us.
Saint Ben - edict,	pray for us.
Saint Francis and Saint Dom - inic,	pray for us.
Saint Francis Xa - vier,	pray for us.
Saint John Vi - an - ney,	pray for us.
Saint Cath - erine,	pray for us.
Saint Te - re - sa,	pray for us.
All holy men and wom - en,	pray for us.

Cantor:	Assembly:
Lord, be mer - ci - ful,	Lord, save your peo - ple.
From all e - vil,	Lord, save your peo - ple.
From ev - 'ry sin,	Lord, save your peo - ple.
From ev - er - last - ing death,	Lord, save your peo - ple.

By your com - ing as man, Lord, save your peo - ple.
By your death and ris - ing to new life, Lord, save your peo - ple.
By your gift of the Ho - ly Spir - it, Lord, save your peo - ple.

Be merciful to us sin - ers. Lord, hear our prayer.
Give new life to these
chosen ones by the grace of bap - tism. Lord, hear our prayer.
Jesus, Son of the liv - ing God. Lord, hear our prayer.

Christ, hear us. Christ, hear us.

Lord Je - sus, hear our prayer. Lord Je - sus, hear our prayer.

Text: *Litany of the Saints, Roman Missal*
Music: *Litany of the Saints, Roman Missal*

BLESSING OF WATER
978

The priest gives thanks and praise to God over the waters of baptism. This acclamation is sung by all.

Springs of wa - ter, bless the Lord. Springs of wa - ter, bless the Lord.

Give him glo - ry and praise for ev - er.

Give him glo - ry and praise for ev - er.

Springs of wa - ter, bless the Lord.

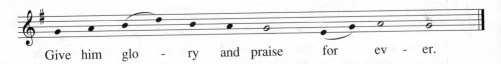

Give him glo - ry and praise for ev - er.

Text: Refrain trans. © 1973, ICEL
Tune: Richard Proulx, b.1937, © 1985, GIA Publications, Inc.

RENUNCIATION OF SIN AND PROFESSION OF FAITH

Each candidate for baptism is asked to reject sin and the ways of evil and to testify to faith in Father, Son and Holy Spirit. All join to affirm this faith.

979   THE BAPTISMS

One by one the candidates are led into the waters, or they bend over the font, and water is poured over them as the priest says: "N., I baptize you in the name of the Father, and of the Son, and of the Holy Spirit." After each baptism, the assembly sings an acclamation.

Cantor, then All:

1.   2.

You have put on Christ, in him you have been bap - tized.

Al - le - lu - ia, al - le - lu - ia.

*May be sung in canon.

Text: ICEL, © 1969
Music: Howard Hughes, SM, © 1977, ICEL

Each of the newly baptized is then clothed in a baptismal garment.

RECEPTION INTO FULL COMMUNION

Those who have been previously baptized are now called forward to profess their faith and to be received into the full communion of the Roman Catholic Church.

CONFIRMATION

Infants who have been baptized are anointed with chrism. Children and adults are usually confirmed: the priest prays and lays hands on them, then anoints each of the newly baptized with chrism saying: "N., be sealed with the Gift of the Holy Spirit."

RENEWAL OF BAPTISMAL PROMISES

All of the faithful repeat and affirm the rejection of sin made at baptism and profess faith in the Father, Son and Holy Spirit. The assembly is sprinkled with the baptismal water. The newly baptized then take their places in the assembly and, for the first time, join in the prayer of the faithful, the prayers of intercession.

LITURGY OF THE EUCHARIST

The gifts and table are prepared and the eucharist is celebrated in the usual way.

Sequence for Easter

980

1. Chris-tians, praise the pas-chal vic-tim! Of - fer thank-ful sac - ri -fice!
1. *Ví - cti - mae Pa-schá - li lau - des im - mó-lent Chri-sti - á - ni.*

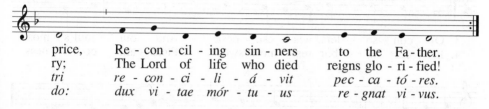

2. Christ the Lamb has saved the sheep, Christ the just one paid the
3. Death and life fought bit - ter - ly For this won-drous vic - to -
2. *A - gnus ré - de - mit ó - ves: Chri - stus ín - no - cens Pá -*
3. *Mors et vi - ta du - él - lo con - fli - xé - re mi - rán -*

price, Re - con - cil - ing sin - ners to the Fa - ther.
ry; The Lord of life who died reigns glo - ri - fied!
tri re - con - ci - li - á - vit pec - ca - tó - res.
do: dux vi - tae mór - tu - us re - gnat vi - vus.

4. O Mar - y, come and say what you saw at break of day.
6. Bright an - gels tes - ti - fied, Shroud and grave clothes side by side!
4. *Dic no - bis Ma - rí - a, quid vi - dí - sti in vi - a?*
6. *An - gé - li - cos te - stes, su - dá - ri - um, et ve - stes.*

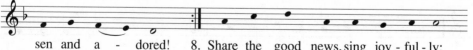

5. "The emp - ty tomb of my liv - ing Lord! I saw Christ Je - sus ri -
7. "Yes, Christ my hope rose glo - ri - ous - ly. He goes be - fore you in -
5. *Se - púl - crum Chri - sti vi - vén - tis, et gló - ri - am vi - di*
7. *Sur - ré - xit Chri-stus spes me - a: prae-cé - det su - os in*

sen and a - dored! 8. Share the good news, sing joy - ful - ly:
to Ga - li - lee." 8. *Scí - mus Chrí - stum sur - re - xís - se*
re - sur - gén - tis.
Ga - li - láe - am.

His death is vic - to - ry! Lord Je - sus, Vic - tor King, Show us mer - cy.
a mór - tu - is ve - re: tu no - bis vi - ctor Rex, mi - se - ré - re.

Text: Sequence for Easter, ascr. to Wipo of Burgundy, d.1048; tr. by Peter J. Scagnelli, b.1949, © 1983
Tune: Mode I; acc. by Richard Proulx, b.1937, © 1975, GIA Publications, Inc.

981 Sequence for Pentecost

1. Ho - ly Spir - it, Lord Di - vine, Come, from heights of
2. Come, O Fa - ther of the poor, Come, whose treas - ured

heav'n and shine, Come with bless - ed ra - diance bright!
gifts en - dure, Come, our heart's un - fail - ing light!

3. Of con - so - lers, wis - est, best, And our soul's most
4. In our la - bor rest most sweet, Pleas - ant cool - ness

wel - come guest, Sweet re - fresh - ment sweet re - pose.
in the heat, Con - so - la - tion in our woes.

5. Light most bless - ed, shine with grace In our heart's most
6. Left with - out your pres - ence here, Life it - self would

se - cret place, Fill your faith - ful through and through.
dis - ap - pear, Noth - ing thrives a - part from you!

7. Cleanse our soil - ed hearts of sin, Ar - id souls re -
8. Bend the stub - born heart and will, Melt the fro - zen,

fresh with - in, Wound - ed lives to health re - store.
warm the chill, Guide the way - ward home once more!

9. On the faith - ful who are true And pro -
10. Give us vir - tue's sure re - ward, Give us

fess their faith in you, In your sev'n - fold gift de - scend!
your sal - va - tion, Lord, Give us joys that nev-er end!

Text: Sequence for Pentecost, 13th. C.; tr. by Peter J. Scagnelli; b.1949, © 1983
Tune: Mode I; acc. by Adriaan Engels, 1906-2003, © Interkerkelijke Stichting voor het Kerklied Den Haag

SERVICE MUSIC

2 Text: Antiphons © 1974, ICEL; Verses © 1963, 1993, The Grail, GIA Publications Inc., agent. Music: © 1974, ICEL

4 Text: © 1969, James Quinn, SJ. Used by permission of Selah Publishing Co., Inc., (North American agent, Kingston NY 12401. All rights reserved. Used by permission.) Music: © 1987, GIA Publications, Inc.

6 Text: © 1974, ICEL. Music © 1986, GIA Publications, Inc.

7 Text: © 1992, GIA Publications, Inc.

8 © 1979, GIA Publications, Inc.

10 © 1979, GIA Publications, Inc.

13 Text trans.: © WGS (William G. Storey). Music acc.: © 1975, GIA Publications, Inc.

15 Text: © 1963, 1993, The Grail, GIA Publications, Inc., agent. Music: © 1985, GIA Publications, Inc.

16 Text: © 1974, ICEL. Music: © 1986, GIA Publications, Inc.

17 Text: © 1992, GIA Publications, Inc.

19 through 20: © 1979, GIA Publications, Inc.

22 Text: © 1967, Benedictine Nuns of St. Mary's Abbey, West Malling, Kent. Music: © 1982, GIA Publications, Inc.

25 through 26: Text: © 1974, ICEL. Music: © 1986, GIA Publications, Inc.

27 © 1979, GIA Publications, Inc.

28 Antiphon text: © 1969, 1981, ICEL. Antiphon Music: © 1975, GIA Publications. Psalm tone: © 1979, Robert Knox Kennedy. Gelineau tone and psalm text: © 1963,1993, The Grail, GIA Publications, Inc., agent

29 Antiphon I text: © 1974, ICEL. Antiphon II text: © 1969, ICEL. Antiphon Music: © 1986, GIA Publications, Inc. Psalm tone: © L.J. Carey and Co. Ltd. Gelineau tone and psalm text: © 1963, 1993, The Grail, GIA Publications, Inc., agent

30 © 1980, GIA Publications, Inc.

31 Antiphon I: © 1963, The Grail, GIA Publications, Inc., agent. Antiphon II text: © 1969, 1981, ICEL. Antiphon II music: © 1986, GIA Publications, Inc. Psalm tone: © 1975, GIA Publications, Inc. Text and Gelineau tone: © 1963, 1993, The Grail, GIA Publications, Inc., agent

32 © 1990, GIA Publications, Inc.

33 Antiphon text: © 1981, ICEL. Antiphon Music: © 1995, GIA Publications, Inc. Psalm tone: © Gethsemani Abbey. Gelineau tone and psalm text: © 1963, 1993, The Grail, GIA Publications, Inc., agent

34 Antiphon I text: © 1974, ICEL. Antiphons II-IV text: © 1969, 1981, ICEL. Antiphon music: © 1986, GIA Publications, Inc. Psalm tone: © 1969, Ampleforth Abbey Trust. Gelineau tone and psalm text: © 1963, 1993, The Grail, GIA Publications, Inc., agent.

35 Text: © 1993, GIA Publications, Inc. Refrain trans.: © 1969, ICEL. Music: © 1993, GIA Publications, Inc.

36 Refrain III trans.: © 1969, ICEL. Text and music: © 1988, GIA Publications, Inc.

37 Refrain trans.: © 1969, ICEL. Text and music: © 1993, GIA Publications, Inc.

38 Refrain trans.: © 1969, ICEL. Text: © 1963, 1993, The Grail, GIA Publications, Inc., agent. Music: © 1994, GIA Publications, Inc.

39 Antiphon I-IV texts: © 1969, ICEL. Antiphon I music © 1975, GIA Publications, Inc. Antiphon II-IV music: © 1986, GIA Publications, Inc. Psalm tone: © L.J. Carey and Co. Ltd. Gelineau tone and psalm text: © 1963, 1993, The Grail, GIA Publications, Inc., agent.

40 Refrain trans.: © 1969, ICEL. Text and music: © 1983, GIA Publications, Inc.

41 Refrain trans.: © 1969, ICEL. Text: © 1963, 1993, The Grail, GIA Publications, Inc., agent. Music: © 1994, GIA Publications, Inc.

42 Refrain music: © 1975, GIA Publications, Inc. Refrain text and psalm text: © 1963, 1993 The Grail, GIA Publications, Inc., agent

43 Refrain trans.: © 1969, ICEL. Text and music: © 1983, GIA Publications, Inc.

44 © 1994, GIA Publications, Inc.

45 Antiphon III-IV texts: © 1969, ICEL. Antiphon III-IV music and psalm tone: © 1975, GIA Publications, Inc. Antiphons I-II: © 1963, The Grail, GIA Publications, Inc., agent. Gelineau tone and psalm text: © 1963, 1993, The Grail, GIA Publications, Inc., agent.

46 © 1988, 1993, GIA Publications, Inc.

47 Refrain I trans.: © 1969, ICEL. Text and music: © 1993, GIA Publications, Inc.

48 Refrain text: © 1969, ICEL. Text: © 1963, 1993, The Grail, GIA Publications, Inc., agent. Music: © 1975, GIA Publications, Inc.

49 Refrain trans.: © 1969, ICEL. Text: © The Grail, GIA Publications, Inc., agent. Music: © 1995, GIA Publications, Inc.

50 Refrain text: © 1963, The Grail, GIA Publications, Inc., agent. Text: © 1963, 1993, The Grail, GIA Publications, Inc., agent. Music: © 1975, GIA Publications, Inc.

51 Refrain trans.: © 1969, ICEL. Text: © 1963, 1993, The Grail, GIA Publications, Inc., agent. Music: © 1995, GIA Publications, Inc.

52 © 1988, 1993, GIA Publications, Inc.

53 Refrain trans.: © 1969, ICEL. Text and music: © 1982, GIA Publications, Inc.

54 Refrain trans.: © 1969, ICEL. Text and music: © 1985, GIA Publications, Inc.

55 Antiphon I-II texts: © 1969, ICEL. Antiphon music © 1975, GIA Publications, Inc. Text: © 1963, 1993, The Grail, GIA Publications, Inc., agent

56 Text: From *The Jerusalem Bible,* by Alexander Jones, ed. Copyright © 1966, Darton, Longman and Todd, Ltd. and Doubleday, a division of Bantam Doubleday Dell Publishing Group, Inc. Used by permission of Doubleday, a division of Bantam Doubleday Dell Publishing Group, Inc. Music: © 1993, GIA Publications, Inc.

57 © 1983, GIA Publications, Inc.

58 Antiphon text: © 1981, ICEL. Antiphon music: © 1995, GIA Publications, Inc. Text: © 1963, 1993, The Grail, GIA Publications, Inc., agent

59 Refrain trans.: © 1969, ICEL. Text: © 1963, 1993, The Grail, GIA Publications, Inc., agent. Music: © 1995, GIA Publications, Inc.

60 Psalm text: © 1963, 1993, The Grail, GIA Publications, Inc., agent. Refrain text and music: © 1985, Paul Inwood. Published by OCP Publications, P.O. Box 13248, Portland, OR 97213-0248. All rights reserved. Used with permission.

61 © 1993, GIA Publications, Inc.

62 Text: From *New American Bible* © 1970, Confraternity of Christian Doctrine, Washington DC 20017-1194. Refrain trans: © 1969, ICEL. Music: © 1980, GIA Publications, Inc.

63 Antiphon I-II texts: © 1969, 1981, ICEL. Antiphon III text: © 1974, ICEL. Antiphon I music: © 1975, GIA Publications, Inc. Antiphon II-III music: © 1986, GIA Publications, Inc. Psalm tone: © L.J. Carey and Co. Ltd. Gelineau tone and psalm text: © 1963, 1993, The Grail, GIA Publications, Inc., agent

64 Refrain trans.: © 1969, ICEL. Text and music: © 1993, GIA Publications, Inc.

65 Refrain trans.: © 1969, ICEL. Text: © 1963, 1993, The Grail, GIA Publications, Inc., agent. Music: © 1995, GIA Publications, Inc.

66 Refrain I trans.: © 1969, ICEL. Refrains II, III, verses and music: © 1987, 1994, GIA Publications, Inc.

67 Antiphon texts: © 1969, 1981, ICEL. Antiphon music: © 1975, GIA Publications. Text: © 1963, 1993, The Grail, GIA Publications, Inc., agent.

68 Refrain trans.: © 1969, ICEL. Text: © 1963, 1993, The Grail, GIA Publications, Inc., agent. Music: © 1995, GIA Publications, Inc.

69 © 1978, 1990, John B. Foley SJ and OCP Publications, P.O. Box 13248, Portland, OR 97213-0248. All rights reserved. Used with permission.

70 Refrain trans.: © 1969, ICEL. Text and music: © 1980, GIA Publications, Inc.

71 Refrain trans.: © 1969, ICEL. Text: © 1963, 1993, The Grail GIA Publications, Inc., agent. Music: © 1995, GIA Publications, Inc.

72 © 1981, Stephen Dean. Published by OCP Publications, P.O. Box 13248, Portland, OR 97213-0248. All rights reserved. Used with permission.

73 Antiphon texts: © 1969, 1981, ICEL. Antiphon music © 1975 GIA Publications, Inc. Psalm tone: © 1986, GIA Publications, Inc Gelineau tone and psalm text: © 1963, 1993, The Grail, GIA Publications, Inc., agent

74 © 1971, 1991, North American Liturgy Resources. Published by OCP Publications, PO Box 13248, Portland OR 97213-0248. All rights reserved. Used with permission.

75 Antiphon texts: © 1969, 1981, ICEL. Antiphon I music: © 1986 GIA Publications, Inc. Antiphon II music: © 1975, GIA Publications Inc. Text: © 1963, 1993, The Grail, GIA Publications, Inc., agent.

76 and 77: Antiphon text: © 1969, 1981, ICEL. Antiphon music: © 1975, GIA Publications, Inc. Text: © 1963, 1993, The Grail, GIA Publications, Inc., agent.

78 Refrain trans.: © 1969, ICEL. Text: © 1963, 1993, The Grail GIA Publications, Inc. Music: © 1995, GIA Publications, Inc.

79 Antiphon text: © 1969, 1981, ICEL. Antiphon music: © 1975 GIA Publications, Inc. Text: © 1963, 1993, The Grail, GIA Publications Inc., agent

80 Refrain trans.: © 1969, ICEL. Text and music: © 1983, GIA Publications, Inc.

81 Refrain trans.: © 1969, ICEL. Text: © 1963, 1993, The Grail GIA Publications, Inc., agent. Music: © 1994, GIA Publications, Inc.

Acknowledgments/*continued*

82 Antiphons II, IV text: © 1969, 1981, ICEL. Antiphon III text: © 1969, ICEL. Antiphon II, III music: © 1975, GIA Publications, Inc. Antiphon IV music: © 1986, GIA Publications, Inc. Antiphon V: © 1979, 1995, GIA Publications, Inc. Psalm Tone: © Gethsemani Abbey. Antiphon I, psalm text and Gelineau tone: © 1963, 1993, The Grail, GIA Publications, Inc., agent

83 Refrain trans.: © 1969, ICEL. Text and music: © 1983, GIA Publications, Inc.

84 Refrain trans.: © 1969, ICEL. Text: © 1963, 1993, The Grail, GIA Publications, Inc., agent. Music: © 1995, GIA Publications, Inc., agent.

85 © 1987, GIA Publications, Inc.

86 Refrain trans.: © 1969, ICEL. Text: © 1963, 1986, The Grail, GIA Publications, Inc., agent. Music: © 1994, GIA Publications, Inc.

87 Antiphon text: © 1969, 1981, ICEL. Antiphon music: © 1975, GIA Publications, Inc. Text: © 1963, 1993, The Grail, GIA Publications, Inc., agent

88 © 1989, GIA Publications, Inc.

89 Antiphon I text: © 1969, 1981, ICEL. Antiphon I music: © 1975, GIA Publications, Inc. Antiphon II: © 1979, GIA Publications, Inc. Psalm tone: © 1986, GIA Publications, Inc. Gelineau tone and psalm text: © 1963, The Grail, GIA Publications, Inc., agent

90 Verses trans.: © 1970, Confraternity of Christian Doctrine, Washington, DC 20017-1194; refrain text and music: © 1987, GIA Publications, Inc.

91 Refrain trans.: © 1969, ICEL. Text and music: © 1993, GIA Publications, Inc.

92 Refrain trans.: © 1969, ICEL. Text: © 1963, 1993, The Grail, GIA Publications, Inc., agent. Music: © 1994, GIA Publications, Inc.

93 © 1982, GIA Publications, Inc.

94 Refrain trans.: © 1969, ICEL. Text: © 1963, 1993, The Grail, GIA Publications, Inc., agent. Music: © 1994, GIA Publications, Inc.

95 Antiphon texts: © 1969, 1981, ICEL. Antiphon music: © 1975, GIA Publications, Inc. Psalm tone: © 1969, Ampleforth Abbey Trust. Gelineau tone and psalm text: © 1963, 1993 The Grail, GIA Publications, Inc., agent

96 Refrain trans.: © 1969, 1981, ICEL. Text: © 1963, 1993, The Grail, GIA Publications, Inc., agent. Refrain music: © 1991, GIA Publications, Inc.

97 Refrain trans.: © 1969, ICEL. Text: © 1963, 1993, The Grail, GIA Publications, Inc., agent. Refrain music: © 1994, GIA Publications, Inc.

98 Refrain trans.: © 1969, 1981, ICEL. Text: © 1963, 1993, The Grail, GIA Publications, Inc., agent. Refrain music: © 1975, GIA Publications, Inc.

99 Refrain trans.: © 1969, ICEL. Text: © 1963, 1993, The Grail, GIA Publications, Inc., agent. Refrain music: © 1995, World Library Publications, a division of J.S. Paluch Company, Inc. Schiller Park, IL 60176. All rights reserved. Used by permission

100 through 101: Refrain trans.: © 1969, ICEL. Text: © 1963, 1993, The Grail, GIA Publications, Inc., agent. Refrain music: © 1995, GIA Publications, Inc.

102 © 1987, 1994, GIA Publications, Inc.

103 Refrain trans.: © 1969, ICEL. Text: © 1963, 1993, The Grail, GIA Publications, Inc., agent. Refrain music: © 1995, GIA Publications, Inc.

104 Refrain trans.: © 1969, 1981, ICEL. Text: © 1963, 1993, The Grail, GIA Publications, Inc., agent. Refrain music: © 1975, GIA Publications, Inc.

105 Refrain trans.: © 1969, 1981, ICEL. Text: © 1963, 1993, The Grail, GIA Publications, Inc., agent. Refrain music: © 1975, GIA Publications, Inc.

106 Refrain trans.: © 1969, ICEL. Text: © 1963, 1993, The Grail, GIA Publications, Inc., agent. Refrain music: © 1994, GIA Publications, Inc.

107 © 1982, GIA Publications, Inc.

108 Refrain trans.: © 1969, ICEL. Text: © 1963, 1993, The Grail, GIA Publications, Inc., agent. Refrain music: © 1995, GIA Publications, Inc.

109 Refrain trans.: © 1969, 1981, ICEL. Text: © 1963, 1993, The Grail, GIA Publications, Inc., agent. Refrain music: © 1986, GIA Publications, Inc.

110 Psalm tone: © Gethsemani Abbey. Antiphon, psalm text and Gelineau tone: © 1963, 1993, The Grail, GIA Publications, Inc., agent

111 © 1987, GIA Publications, Inc.

112 Refrain trans.: © 1969, ICEL. Text and music: © 1983, GIA Publications, Inc.

113 Antiphon texts: © 1969, 1981, ICEL. Text: © 1963, 1993, The Grail, GIA Publications, Inc., agent. Antiphon I music: © 1975, GIA Publications, Inc. Antiphon II music: © 1986, GIA Publications, Inc.

114 Refrain texts: © 1969, ICEL. Verse text and music: © 1978, 1993, Damean Music. Distributed by GIA Publications, Inc.

115 Antiphon I text: © 1974, ICEL. Antiphon II text: © 1969, 1981, ICEL. Antiphon music: © 1986, GIA Publications, Inc. Psalm tone: © 1969, Ampleforth Abbey Trust. Gelineau tone and psalm text: © 1963, 1993, The Grail, GIA Publications, Inc., agent.

116 Antiphon text: © 1974, ICEL. Antiphon music: © 1986, GIA Publications, Inc. Psalm tone: © Gethsemani Abbey. Gelineau tone and psalm text: © 1963, 1993, The Grail, GIA Publications, Inc., agent.

117 Refrain trans.: © 1969, ICEL. Text: © 1963, 1993, The Grail, GIA Publications, Inc., agent. Music: © 1995, GIA Publications, Inc.

118 Refrain trans.: © 1969, ICEL. Text: © 1963, 1993, The Grail, GIA Publications, Inc., agent. Alt. text and music: © 1988, 1994, GIA Publications, Inc.

119 Antiphon texts: © 1969, 1981, ICEL. Antiphon I music: © 1975, GIA Publications, Inc. Antiphon II music: © 1986, GIA Publications, Inc. Verse text: © 1963, 1993, The Grail, GIA Publications, Inc., agent

120 Antiphon texts: © 1969, 1981, ICEL. Antiphon I and III music: © 1986, GIA Publications, Inc. Antiphon II music: © 1975, 1995, GIA Publications, Inc. Psalm tone: © L.J. Carey and Co. Ltd. Gelineau tone and psalm text: © 1963, 1993, The Grail, GIA Publications, Inc., agent

121 Refrain trans.: © 1969, ICEL. Text and music: © 1993, GIA Publications, Inc.

122 Antiphon III text: © 1974, ICEL. Psalm tone and Antiphon III music: © 1986, GIA Publications, Inc. Antiphons I-II, Gelineau tone and psalm text: © 1963, 1993, The Grail, GIA Publications, Inc., agent

123 © 1980, GIA Publications, Inc.

124 Refrain trans.: © 1969, ICEL. Text: © 1963, 1993, The Grail, GIA Publications, Inc., agent. Music: © 1994, GIA Publications, Inc.

125 Refrain trans.: © 1969, 1981, ICEL. Refrain music: © 1975, GIA Publications, Inc. Text: © 1963, 1993, The Grail, GIA Publications, Inc., agent

126 Psalm tone: © 1975, GIA Publications, Inc. Antiphons, Gelineau tone and psalm text: © 1963, 1993, The Grail, GIA Publications, Inc., agent

127 Refrain trans.: © 1969, ICEL. Text: © 1963, 1993, The Grail, GIA Publications, Inc., agent. Music: © 1995, GIA Publications, Inc.

128 Refrain trans.: © 1969, ICEL. Text and music: © 1993, GIA Publications, Inc.

129 © 1983, 1994, GIA Publications, Inc.

130 Refrain trans.: © 1969, ICEL. Verse trans.: © 1970, Confraternity of Christian Doctrine, Washington DC 20017-1194. Music: © 1976, GIA Publications, Inc.

131 Antiphon III-IV texts: © 1969, 1981, ICEL. Antiphon III music: © 1975, GIA Publications, Inc. Antiphon IV music: © 1986, GIA Publications, Inc. Antiphons I-II and psalm text: © 1963, 1993, The Grail, GIA Publications, Inc., agent

132 Refrain trans.: © 1969, ICEL. Text: © 1989, GIA Publications, Inc. Music: © 1989, 1994, GIA Publications, Inc.

133 through 134: Antiphon text: © 1969, 1981, ICEL. Antiphon music: © 1975, GIA Publications, Inc. Text: © 1963, 1993, The Grail, GIA Publications, Inc., agent.

135 © 1983, 1994, GIA Publications, Inc.

136 Refrain trans.: © 1969, ICEL. Text: © 1963, 1993, The Grail, GIA Publications, Inc., agent. Music: © 1995, GIA Publications, Inc.

137 Antiphon texts: © 1969, 1981, ICEL. Antiphon I-II music: © 1975, GIA Publications, Inc. Antiphon III music: © 1986, GIA Publications, Inc. Text: © 1963, 1993, The Grail, GIA Publications, Inc., agent

138 © 1983, GIA Publications, Inc.

139 Psalm tone: © 1975, GIA Publications, Inc. Antiphons, Gelineau tone and psalm texts: © 1963, 1993, The Grail, GIA Publications, Inc., agent

140 © 1993, GIA Publications, Inc.

141 Antiphon texts: © 1969, 1981, ICEL. Antiphon I-II music: © 1986, GIA Publications, Inc. Antiphon III music and psalm tone: © 1975, GIA Publications, Inc. Gelineau tone and psalm text: © 1963, 1993, The Grail, GIA Publications, Inc., agent

142 Refrain trans.: © 1969, ICEL. Text: © 1963, 1993, The Grail, GIA Publications, Inc., agent. Music: © 1995, GIA Publications, Inc.

143 Refrain trans.: © 1969, ICEL. Text and music: © 1983, GIA Publications, Inc.

144 Refrain trans.: © 1969, 1981, ICEL. Text: © 1963, 1993, The Grail, GIA Publications, Inc., agent. Music: © 1971, GIA Publications, Inc.

145 Refrain trans.: © 1969, 1981, ICEL. Text: © 1963, 1993, The Grail, GIA Publications, Inc., agent. Music: © 1975, GIA Publications, Inc.

146 Refrain trans.: © 1969, ICEL. Text and music: © 1985, GIA Publications, Inc.

147 through 148: Refrain trans.: © 1969, 1981, ICEL. Text: © 1963, 1993, The Grail, GIA Publications, Inc., agent. Music: © 1975, GIA Publications, Inc.

Acknowledgments/*continued*

Acknowledgments/*continued*

248 © Refrain trans: © 1969, 1981, ICEL. Refrain music: © 1975, GIA Publications, Inc. Text and Music: © 1963, 1993, The Grail, GIA Publications, Inc.

249 © 1985, GIA Publications, Inc. Lent acc.: © 1970, GIA Publications, Inc.

254 Refrain trans.: © 1974, ICEL. Refrain music: © 1986, GIA Publications, Inc. Text and music: © 1963, The Grail, GIA Publications, Inc., agent.

255 © 1985, GIA Publications, Inc. Lent acc.: © 1970, GIA Publications, Inc.

259 Refrain trans.: © 1969, ICEL. Text: © 1963, 1993, The Grail, GIA Publications, Inc., agent. Music: © 1994, GIA Publications, Inc.

264 Refrain trans.: © 1969, ICEL. Text: © 1963, 1993, The Grail, GIA Publications, Inc., agent. Music: © 1994, GIA Publications, Inc.

265 © 1985, GIA Publications, Inc. Lent acc.: © 1970, GIA Publications, Inc.

272 (A)Refrain trans.: © 1969, ICEL. Refrain music: © 1975, GIA Publications, Inc. Text and Music: © 1963, 1993, The Grail, GIA Publications, inc., agent. (B) © 1983, GIA Publications, Inc.

273 © 1985, GIA Publications, Inc. Lent acc.: © 1970, GIA Publications, Inc.

277 © 1984, GIA Publications, Inc.

278 (A) © 1984, GIA Publications, Inc. (B) © 1990, GIA Publications, Inc. (C) & (D) © 1993, GIA Publications, Inc.

279 © 1984, GIA Publications, Inc.

280 © 1975, 1993, GIA Publications, Inc.

281 © 1993, GIA Publications, Inc.

284 (A) Text: © 1985, ICEL. Music: © 1990, GIA Publications, Inc. (B) © 1990, GIA Publications, Inc. (C) © 1975, GIA Publications, Inc.

286 Text: © 1985, ICEL. Music: © 1990, GIA Publications, Inc.

377 Refrain trans.: © 1973, ICEL. Text and Music: © 1994, GIA Publications, Inc.

379 Text and music: © 1975, GIA Publications, Inc.

385 through 386: © 1990, Iona Community, GIA Publications, Inc., agent.

388 © 1981, 1982, Peter Jones. Published by OCP Publications, P.O. Box 13248, Portland, OR 97213-0248. All rights reserved. Used with permission.

395 © 1985, Fintan O'Carroll and Christopher Walker. Published by OCP Publications, P.O. Box 13248, Portland, OR 97213-0248. All rights reserved. Used with permission.

396 Text and music: © 1990, Iona Community, GIA Publications, Inc., agent. Verses and acc.: © 1993, GIA Publications, Inc.

397 © 1984, Les Presses de Taizé, GIA Publications, Inc., agent

398 © 1958, The Grail, GIA Publications, Inc., agent

401 © 1984, Les Presses de Taizé, GIA Publications, Inc., agent

404 © 1980, ICEL.

410 Text and music: © 1984, Bob Hurd. Acc.: © 1989, OCP Publications. Published by OCP Publications, P.O. Box 13248, Portland, OR 97213-0248. All rights reserved. Used with permission.

415 through 416: © 1980, Les Presses de Taizé, GIA Publications, Inc., agent

439 through 441: Text and Music: © 1973, Robert J. Dufford and Daniel L. Schutte. Published by OCP Publications, P.O. Box 13248, Portland, OR 97213-0248. All rights reserved. Used with permission.

442 © 1980, The Church Pension Fund. Acc.: © 1986, GIA Publications, Inc.

456 © 1970, World Library Publications, a division of J.S. Paluch Company, Inc. Schiller Park, IL 60176. All rights reserved. Used by permission

457 © 1973, World Library Publications, a division of J.S. Paluch Company, Inc. Schiller Park, IL 60176. All rights reserved. Used by permission

478 Text: sts. 2-4 © 1928, Oxford University Press. Harm.: © David McK. Williams

479 Harm.: © 1958, Basilian Fathers, assigned 1958 to Ralph Jusko Publications

481 Text and music: © 1971, United Church Press. Acc. © 1987, GIA Publications, Inc.

482 Text: © David Higham Assoc. Ltd. Harm.: © Oxford University Press

483 Text: © 1985, The Church Pension Fund. Acc.: © 1986, GIA Publications, Inc.

484 © 1984, Les Presses de Taizé, GIA Publications, Inc., agent

485 © 1981, 1982, Michael Joncas and Cooperative Ministries, Inc., OCP Publications, agent, , P.O. Box 13248, Portland, OR 97213-0248. All rights reserved. Used with permission.

486 Text: © 1982, Jubilate Hymns, Ltd. Admin. by Hope Publishing Co., Carol Stream, IL 60188. All rights reserved. Used by permission. Music: from *Enlarged Songs of Praise* © Oxford University Press

487 Text: © 1982, Jubilate Hymns, Ltd. Admin. byHope Publishing Co., Carol Stream, IL 60188. All rights reserved. Used by permission.

489 Text: © 1982, Hope Publishing Co., Carol Stream, IL 60188. All rights reserved. Used by permission

491 © 1984, Les Presses de Taizé, GIA Publications, Inc., agent

492 © 1993, GIA Publications, Inc.

493 Acc. © 1975, GIA Publications, Inc.

494 © 1983, GIA Publications, Inc.

495 © 1982, GIA Publications, Inc.

496 © 1981, ICEL.

497 © 1994, GIA Publications, Inc.

500 Text: © 1964, GIA Publications, Inc. Acc.: © 1986, GIA Publications, Inc.

501 Text and music: © 1945, Boosey and Co. Ltd. Copyright renewed. Reprinted by permission of Boosey & Hawkes, Inc. Acc. © 1993, GIA Publications, Inc.

506 © 1991, GIA Publications, Inc.

507 © 1979, 1988, Les Presses de Taizé, GIA Publications, Inc., agent

509 Harm.: © Bristol Churches Housing Assoc. Ltd.

510 © 1985, GIA Publications, Inc.

511 Tune: © 1989, GIA Publications, Inc.

512 Text: © 1981, Jaroslav Vajda. Music: © 1981, GIA Publications, Inc.

514 Text: © Mrs. John W. Work III. Music: © 1995, GIA Publications, Inc.

515 Music: © 1994, GIA Publications, Inc.

516 © 1987, GIA Publications, Inc.

517 Text: © 1986, Jaroslav J. Vajda. Music: © 1986, GIA Publications, Inc.

518 Alternate text: © 1992, GIA Publications, Inc.

519 Text: © 1990, Iona Community, GIA Publications, Inc., agent

521 © 1992, GIA Publications, Inc.

523 © 1984, GIA Publications, Inc.

525 © 1987, Iona Community, GIA Publications, Inc., agent

526 Harm.: © 1957, Novello and Co. Ltd. 8/9 Frith Street, London

528 Harm.: © 1986, GIA Publications, Inc.

532 © 1965, World Library Publications, a division of J.S. Paluch Company, Inc. Schiller Park, IL 60176. All rights reserved. Used by permission

533 Harm.: © 1987, GIA Publications, Inc.

536 © 1978, Damean Music. Distributed by GIA Publications, Inc.

538 Text: © 1984, Hope Publishing Co., Carol Stream, IL 60188. All rights reserved. Used by permission

539 Text: © 1989, Hope Publishing Co., Carol Stream, IL 60188. All rights reserved. Used by permission. Music: © 1991, GIA Publications, Inc.

540 © 1976, Robert F. O'Connor, SJ, and OCP Publications, P.O. Box 13248, Portland, OR 07213-0248. All rights reserved. Used with permission.

541 © 1984, GIA Publications, Inc.

542 Music: © 1984, GIA Publications, Inc.

543 Music: © 1995, GIA Publications, Inc.

544 Text: © Peter J. Scagnelli. Acc.: © 1975, GIA Publications, Inc.

545 Text: from *The English Hymnal* © Oxford University Press

546 © 1987, GIA Publications, Inc.

547 Harm.: © 1986, GIA Publications, Inc.

548 Text: © 1993, GIA Publications, Inc.

549 Text: © 1963, The Grail, GIA Publications, Inc., agent. Acc.: © 1986, GIA Publications, Inc.

550 © 1978, Damean Music. Distributed by GIA Publications, Inc.

551 Text: © 1971, Faber Music Ltd. London. Reprinted from *New Catholic Hymnal* by permission of the publishers. Harm.: © 1986, GIA Publications, Inc.

552 Text: © 1980, ICEL. Acc.: © 1975, GIA Publications, Inc.

554 Text: © 1982, Thomas H. Cain. Music: © 1988, GIA Publications, Inc.

555 © 1990, 1991, GIA Publications, Inc.

556 © 1994, GIA Publications, Inc.

557 © 1975, GIA Publications, Inc.

558 © 1965, 1966, 1968, 1973, World Library Publications, a division of J.S. Paluch Company, Inc. Schiller Park, IL 60176. All rights reserved. Used by permission

559 Text: © Peter J. Scagnelli

560 Text: © Oxford University Press. Music: © 1995, GIA Publications, Inc.

561 Text: © 1994, World Library Publications, a division of J.S. Paluch Company, Inc. Schiller Park, IL 60176. All rights reserved. Used by permission

Acknowledgments/*continued*

Acknowledgments/*continued*

Acknowledgments/*continued*

Scripture Passages Related to Hymns/*continued*

PHILIPPIANS
2:1-18	Lord of All Nations, Grant Me Grace 751
2:5-7	Stand Up, Friends 622
2:5-8	Psalm 8: How Great Is Your Name 31
2:8-8	Hark! The Herald Angels Sing 502
2:9-10	All Hail the Power of Jesus' Name 632
2:10-11	Creator of the Stars of Night 483
3:7-11	The Love of the Lord 814
4:4-5	Rejoice, the Lord Is King 627

COLOSSIANS
1:16-16	Ye Watchers and Ye Holy Ones 886
1:17-17	Psalm 8: How Great Is Your Name 31
1:18-18	Christ the Lord Is Risen Today 594
1:18-18	Christ the Lord Is Risen Today 602
2:13-13	Good Christians All 586
3:12-21	Our Father, by Whose Name 961
3:13-14	Forgive Our Sins 952
3:16-16	Come, Rejoice before Your Maker 847

1 THESSALONIANS
13:18-18	When the Lord in Glory Comes 868

2 THESSALONIANS
2:15-15	God Is Here! As We His People 844

1 TIMOTHY
6:12-12	Faith of Our Fathers 726

2 TIMOTHY
2:	Now We Remain 813
2:	We Shall Rise Again 872
2:8-12	Keep in Mind 940
2:12-12	The Head That Once Was Crowned with Thorns 591
4:3-7	Faith of Our Fathers 726
4:6-8	Two Noble Saints 880

TITUS
2:14-14	God Is Here! As We His People 844

HEBREWS
1:3-3	Rejoice, the Lord Is King 627
2:9-10	The Head That Once Was Crowned with Thorns 591
9:	The King of Glory 628
9:11-14	Alleluia, Sing to Jesus 914
10:	The King of Glory 628
10:7-7	Psalm 40: Here I Am 74
11:	Faith of Our Fathers 726
12:1-1	For All the Saints 889
12:1-1	I Want to Walk as a Child of the Light 651
12:1-3	Holy God, We Praise Thy Name 657
12:18-19	How Blessed Is This Place 893
13:6-6	My Shepherd Will Supply My Need 761
13:8-8	I Know That My Redeemer Lives 582

JAMES
1:17-17	America the Beautiful 965
1:17-17	For the Beauty of the Earth 697
1:17-17	I Sing the Mighty Power of God 633
5:13-16	Your Hands, O Lord, in Days of Old 949

1 PETER
1:3-5	Praise the Lord, My Soul 688
2:4-6	Christ's Church Shall Glory in His Power 777
2:4-6	O Christ the Great Foundation 781
2:4-7	For Builders Bold 891
2:4-7	Christ Is Made the Sure Foundation 778
2:4-8	O Christ the Great Foundation 781 782
2:5-5	Take and Eat 910
2:9-9	Light of Christ / Exsultet 647
2:9-10	God Is Here! As We His People 844

2 PETER
1:16-18	Transform Us 881
1:19-19	Take and Eat 910
1:19-19	Up from the Earth 589

1 JOHN
1:	Now We Remain 813
1:	City of God 799
1:5-5	God Is Love 744
1:5-5	I Want to Walk as a Child of the Light 651
1:5-5	Our Darkness / La Ténèbre 863
2:27-27	Come, Holy Ghost 611
3:2-2	God Is Love 744
3:18-18	Faith of Our Fathers 726
4:	God Is Love 744
4:	Where Charity and Love Prevail 747
4:7-7	Love One Another 745
4:7-17	Love Divine, All Loves Excelling 743
4:9-10	What Wondrous Love Is This 749
4:10-16	Where True Love and Charity Are Found / Ubi Caritas 752
4:12-12	Love One Another 745
4:12-12	Ubi Caritas 746
4:16-16	Many Are the Lightbeams 841
4:16-16	Ubi Caritas 746
4:20-21	Now Join We to Praise the Creator 827
5:4-4	How Long, O Lord, How Long 829
5:6-8	Come and Let Us Drink of That New River 902
5:13-13	Good Christians All 586
9:12-16	Easter Alleluia 592

REVELATION
1:8-8	Of the Father's Love Begotten 510
1:18-18	Rejoice, the Lord Is King 627
1:18-18	The Strife Is O'er 587
2:10-10	For All the Saints 889
3:20-20	Somebody's Knockin' at Your Door 547
4:	God, We Praise You 676
4:	Heavenly Hosts in Ceaseless Worship 661
4:	Holy God, We Praise Thy Name 657
4:	Holy, Holy, Holy! Lord God Almighty 624
4:8-8	Of the Father's Love Begotten 510
5:	Heavenly Hosts in Ceaseless Worship 661
5:	Holy God, We Praise Thy Name 657
5:	This Is the Feast of Victory 583
5:9-9	Alleluia, Sing to Jesus 914
5:9-9	At the Lamb's High Feast We Sing 578
5:9-9	Crown Him with Many Crowns 626
5:9-9	To Jesus Christ, Our Sovereign King 629
5:11-12	Alabaré 662
5:11-13	Now the Feast and Celebration 853
5:11-14	All Hail the Power of Jesus' Name 632
5:13-13	All Glory, Laud, and Honor 563
6:2-2	Ride On, Jesus, Ride 562
7:2-4	For All the Saints 889
7:9-14	For All the Saints 889
8:3-4	How Blessed Is This Place 893
14:17-20	Mine Eyes Have Seen the Glory 869
15:4-4	Holy, Holy, Holy! Lord God Almighty 624
19:1-7	Revelation 19:1-7 213
19:6-9	Wake, O Wake, and Sleep No Longer 489
19:11-16	Let All Mortal Flesh Keep Silence 658
19:11-16	The King Shall Come When Morning Dawns 497
19:12-12	Crown Him with Many Crowns 626
19:16-16	Christ the Lord Is Risen 600
21:1-4	Jerusalem, My Happy Home 871
21:1-5	What Is This Place 892
21:9-13	Wake, O Wake, and Sleep No Longer 489
21:23-23	I Want to Walk as a Child of the Light 651
22:	Jerusalem, My Happy Home 871
22:1-1	Come and Let Us Drink of That New River 902
22:5-5	Light of Christ / Exsultet 647
22:5-5	Our Darkness / La Ténèbre 863
22:17-17	In Christ There Is a Table Set for All 916
22:17-17	We Know That Christ Is Raised 906
22:20-20	Each Winter As the Year Grows Older 481
22:20-20	Soon and Very Soon 870

The following hymns and psalms are suggested for the Sundays of the three-year lectionary cycle. Those with an asterisk (*) are directly related to the scriptures of the day, while the others are suggested because of their relationship to the predominant focus of the day's readings.

ADVENT I
A - Wake, O Wake and Sleep No Longer 489
Psalm 122: I Rejoiced When I Heard 165
B - Wake, O Wake and Sleep No Longer 489
Psalm 80: Lord, Make Us Turn to You 108
C - When the Lord in Glory Comes 868
Psalm 25: To You, O Lord 50 51 53
Psalm 25: Levanto Mi Alma 52

ADVENT II
A - On Jordan's Bank* 490
A Voice Cries Out* 485
Psalm 72: Justice Shall Flourish 101
Psalm 72: In His Days Justice Will Flourish 102
B - Comfort, Comfort, O My People* 488
On Jordan's Bank* 490
A Voice Cries Out* 485
Psalm 85: Lord, Let Us See Your Kindness 112 113
114
C - City of God, Jerusalem* 486
On Jordan's Bank* 490
A Voice Cries Out* 485
Psalm 126: The Lord Has Done Great Things 169
170 171

ADVENT III
A - When the King Shall Come Again* 487
Psalm 146: O Lord, Come and Save Us 195
B - On Jordan's Bank* 490
A Voice Cries Out* 485
Luke 1:46-55/Magnificat 209 211
Luke 1:46-55/Magnificat/Holy Is Your Name 210
C - On Jordan's Bank* 490
A Voice Cries Out* 485
Isaiah 12: Cry Out with Joy and Gladness 205

ADVENT IV
A - Savior of the Nations, Come 480
Psalm 24: Let the Lord Enter 48
B - No Wind at the Window* 876
A Message Came to a Maiden Young* 478
Psalm 89: For Ever I Will Sing 117 118 119
C - Savior of the Nations, Come 480
Psalm 80: Lord, Make Us Turn to You 108

CHRISTMAS
see nos. 498-524
Vigil - Psalm 89: For Ever I Will Sing 117 118 119
Midnight - Psalm 96: Today Is Born Our Savior 130
131
Dawn - Psalm 97: A Light Will Shine 134
Day - Psalm 98: All the Ends of the Earth 135 136 137

HOLY FAMILY
see nos. 525-526
Psalm 128: O Happy Are Those 172

MARY, MOTHER OF GOD
see nos. 527-528
Psalm 67: May God Bless Us in His Mercy 94 95

EPIPHANY
see nos. 529-537
Psalm 72: Every Nation on Earth 102
Psalm 72: Lord, Every Nation on Earth 103

BAPTISM OF THE LORD
When John Baptized by Jordan's River* 538
Psalm 29: The Lord Will Bless His People 58

ASH WEDNESDAY
Dust and Ashes 539
Psalm 51: Be Merciful, O Lord 82 83

LENT I
A - Jesus, Tempted in the Desert* 548
Psalm 51: Be Merciful, O Lord 82 83
B - Lord, Who throughout These Forty Days* 553
This Is the Time* 556
Psalm 25: Your Ways, O Lord 53
C - Jesus, Tempted in the Desert* 548
Psalm 91: Be with Me 123

LENT II
A - 'Tis Good, Lord, to Be Here* 882
Transform Us* 881
Psalm 33: Let Your Mercy Be on Us 66
Psalm 33: Lord, Let Your Mercy 68
B - 'Tis Good, Lord, to Be Here* 882
Transform Us* 881
Psalm 116: I Will Walk in the Presence 153 154
C - 'Tis Good, Lord, to Be Here* 882
Transform Us* 881
Psalm 27: The Lord Is My Light 55 57 238

LENT III
A - I Heard the Voice of Jesus Say* 768
Psalm 95: If Today You Hear His Voice 127 128
Psalm 95: If Today You Hear God's Voice 129
B - Christ Is Made the Sure Foundation 778
Psalm 19: Lord, You Have the Words 39 40
C - Eternal Lord of Love 554
Psalm 103: The Lord Is Kind and Merciful 140 141
143

LENT IV
A - He Healed the Darkness of My Mind* 951
Psalm 23: The Lord Is My Shepherd 44 45
Psalm 23: My Shepherd Is the Lord 45
Psalm 23: Nada Me Falta 46
Psalm 23: Shepherd Me, O God 756
B - What Wondrous Love Is This 749
Psalm 137: Let My Tongue Be Silent 182 183
C - Our Father, We Have Wandered* 955
Psalm 34: Taste and See 70 71 72 73

LENT V
A - I Am the Bread of Life/Yo Soy el Pan de Vida*
931
Psalm 130: With the Lord There Is Mercy 174 175
176
B - Unless a Grain of Wheat* 804
Psalm 51: Create a Clean Heart 82
Psalm 51: Create in Me a Clean Heart 84, 85
C - Forgive Our Sins* 952
Psalm 126: The Lord Has Done Great Things 169
170 171

PASSION SUNDAY
see nos. 562-563
Psalm 22: My God, My God 42 43

Hymns and Psalms for the Church Year/*continued*

HOLY THURSDAY
see nos. 564-566
  Psalm 116: Our Blessing Cup   152 153 155

GOOD FRIDAY
see nos. 567-574
  Psalm 31: I Put My Life in Your Hands/Pongo Mi Vida
    61
  Psalm 31: Father, I Put My Life in Your Hands   62 63

EASTER VIGIL
see nos. 575-602
  I.   Psalm 104: Lord, Send Out Your Spirit   144 145
        146
        or Psalm 33: The Earth Is Full of the Goodness   66
        67
  II.   Psalm 16: Keep Me Safe, O God   34 35 36
  III. Exodus 15: Let Us Sing to the Lord   201
        Exodus 15: Song at the Sea   202
  IV.   Psalm 30: I Will Praise You, Lord   59 60
  V.   Isaiah 12: You Will Draw Water   204
  VI.   Psalm 19: Lord, You Have the Words   39 40
  VII. Psalm 42/43: Like a Deer That Longs   77
        or Psalm 51: Create a Clean Heart   82
        Psalm 51: Create in Me a Clean Heart   84 85

EASTER
see nos. 575-602
  Psalm 118: This Is the Day   158 160

EASTER II
  A - O Sons and Daughters*   579
      We Walk by Faith*   723
      Psalm 118: Give Thanks to the Lord   159
  B - O Sons and Daughters*   579
      We Walk by Faith*   723
      Psalm 118: Give Thanks to the Lord   159
  C - O Sons and Daughters*   579
      We Walk by Faith*   723
      Psalm 118: Give Thanks to the Lord   159

EASTER III
  A - On the Journey to Emmaus*   816
      Psalm 16: Lord, You Will Show   34
      Psalm 16: You Will Show Me the Path of Life   36
  B - On the Journey to Emmaus*   816
      Psalm 4: Lord, Let Your Face Shine on Us   29
      Psalm 4: Lord, Let Your Face Shine upon Us   30
  C - You Walk along Our Shoreline   807
      Psalm 30: I Will Praise You, Lord   59 60

EASTER IV
  A - Christus Paradox   699
      Psalm 23: The Lord Is My Shepherd   44 45
      Psalm 23: My Shepherd Is the Lord   45
      Psalm 23: Nada Me Falta   46
      Psalm 23: Shepherd Me, O God   756
  B - Christus Paradox   699
      Psalm 118: The Stone Rejected   161
  C - Christus Paradox   699
      Psalm 100: We Are God's People   138

EASTER V
  A - Come, My Way, My Truth, My Life*   717
      I Know That My Redeemer Lives*   582
      Psalm 33: Let Your Mercy Be on Us   66
      Psalm 33: Lord, Let Your Mercy   68
  B - We Have Been Told*   815
      Psalm 22: I Will Praise You, Lord   41
  C - Lord of All Nations, Grant Me Grace   751

Love Is His Word*   750
Psalm 145: I Will Praise Your Name   192 193 194

EASTER VI
  A - Come Down, O Love Divine*   617
      If You Believe and I Believe   825
      Psalm 66: Let All the Earth   93
  B - No Greater Love*   753
      Psalm 98: The Lord Has Revealed   137
  C - Come Down, O Love Divine   617
      Unless a Grain of Wheat   804
      Psalm 67: O God, Let All the Nations Praise You
        94 95

ASCENSION
see nos. 603-608
  Psalm 47: God Mounts His Throne   79 80

EASTER VII
  A - Alleluia! Sing to Jesus   914
      Psalm 27: I Believe That I Shall See   55
      Psalm 27: In the Land of the Living   56
  B - Alleluia! Sing to Jesus   914
      Psalm 103: The Lord Has Set His Throne   141 142
  C - Alleluia! Sing to Jesus   914
      Psalm 97: The Lord Is King   133

PENTECOST
see nos. 609-617
  Vigil - Psalm 104: Lord, Send Out Your Spirit   144 145
        146
  Day - Psalm 104: Lord, Send Out Your Spirit   144 145
        146

TRINITY SUNDAY
see nos. 618-625
  A - What Wondrous Love Is This   749
      Daniel 3:52-57/Song of the Three Children   206
  B - Go*   604
      Go to the World*   608
      Psalm 33: Happy Are the People   66
      Psalm 33: Happy the People   67
  C - Alleluia, Sing!   625
      Psalm 8: O Lord, Our God   31
      Psalm 8: How Glorious Is Your Name   32

BODY AND BLOOD
  A - I Am the Bread of Life/Yo Soy el Pan de Vida*   931
      Psalm 147: Praise the Lord   198 199
  B - Take and Eat*   910
      Psalm 116: The Name of God   152
      Psalm 116: I Will Take the Cup of Salvation   153
  C - Plenty of Bread   927
      Psalm 110: You Are a Priest for Ever   148

ORDINARY TIME

SECOND SUNDAY
  A - When Jesus Came to Jordan*   878
      Psalm 40: Here I Am   74
      Psalm 40: Here Am I   75
  B - Those Who Love and Those Who Labor*   805
      Psalm 40: Here I Am   74
      Psalm 40: Here Am I   75
  C - Jesus, Come! For We Invite You*   714
      Psalm 96: Proclaim to All the Nations   132

THIRD SUNDAY
  A - Two Fishermen*   812
      The Summons   811
      You Walk along Our Shoreline   807

Hymns and Psalms for the Church Year/*continued*

Psalm 27: The Lord Is My Light 55 57
B - Two Fishermen* 812
The Summons 811
You Walk along Our Shoreline 807
Psalm 25: Teach Me Your Ways 54
C - You Have Anointed Me* 795
Good News* 797
Psalm 19: Your Words, Lord, Are Spirit and Life 40

FOURTH SUNDAY
A - Blest Are They* 774
Psalm 146: Happy the Poor 196
B - When Jesus Came Preaching 773
Psalm 95: If Today You Hear His Voice 127 128
Psalm 95: If Today You Hear God's Voice 129
C - God Has Spoken by His Prophets 654
May Love Be Ours* 748
Psalm 71: I Will Sing 99

FIFTH SUNDAY
A - Bring Forth the Kingdom* 772
Psalm 112: A Light Rises in the Darkness 149
B - Your Hands, O Lord, in Days of Old* 949
Psalm 147: Praise the Lord 198
C - You Walk along Our Shoreline* 807
Lord, When You Came/Pescador de Hombres* 817
Psalm 138: In the Sight of the Angels 184 185

SIXTH SUNDAY
A - What Does the Lord Require 785
Deep Within 546
Eye Has Not Seen* 758
Psalm 119: Happy Are They 162
B - Your Hands, O Lord, in Days of Old* 949
Psalm 32: I Turn to You 64
C - Blest Are They* 774
Psalm 1: Happy Are They 28

SEVENTH SUNDAY
A - Lord of All Nations, Grant Me Grace* 751
Psalm 103: The Lord Is Kind and Merciful 140 141 143
B - Your Hands, O Lord, in Days of Old 949
Psalm 41: Lord, Heal My Soul 76
C - Lord of All Nations, Grant Me Grace* 751
Psalm 103: The Lord Is Kind and Merciful 140 141 143

EIGHTH SUNDAY
A - Seek Ye First the Kingdom of God* 728
Psalm 62: Rest in God 87
Psalm 62: In God Alone 88
B - Christ Is the King 630
Psalm 103: The Lord Is Kind and Merciful 140 141 143
C - Help Us Accept Each Other 838
Psalm 92: Lord, It Is Good 124 125

NINTH SUNDAY
A - Christ Is Made the Sure Foundation 778
Psalm 31: Lord, Be My Rock of Safety 63
B - I Danced in the Morning 809
Psalm 81: Sing with Joy to God 109
C - Surely It Is God Who Saves Me 739
Psalm 117: Go Out to All the World 157

TENTH SUNDAY
A - Come, You Sinners, Poor and Needy* 954
God It Was 818
Psalm 50: To the Upright 81

B - The Master Came to Bring Good News 956
Psalm 130: With the Lord There Is Mercy 174 175 176
C - Your Hands, O Lord, in Days of Old* 949
Psalm 30: I Will Praise You, Lord 59, 60

ELEVENTH SUNDAY
A - When Jesus Came Preaching 773
Psalm 100: We Are God's People 138
B - The Kingdom of God* 775
Psalm 92: Lord, It Is Good 124 125
C - There's a Wideness in God's Mercy 742
Psalm 32: Lord, Forgive the Wrong 65

TWELFTH SUNDAY
A - Be Not Afraid 734
Psalm 69: Lord, in Your Great Love 98
B - How Firm a Foundation* 731
Psalm 107: Give Thanks to the Lord 147
C - Take Up Your Cross* 808
Wherever He Leads* 810
Psalm 63: My Soul Is Thirsting 89 90 91

THIRTEENTH SUNDAY
A - Take Up Your Cross* 808
Wherever He Leads* 810
Psalm 89: For Ever I Will Sing 117 118 119
B - Draw Us in the Spirit's Tether* 917
Psalm 30: I Will Praise You, Lord 59, 60
C - Jesus, Lead the Way 755
Psalm 16: You Are My Inheritance 34 36

FOURTEENTH SUNDAY
A - Come to Me, O Weary Traveler* 769
Come to Me* 763
I Heard the Voice of Jesus Say* 768
Psalm 145: I Will Praise Your Name for Ever 192
Psalm 145: I Will Praise Your Name 193 194
B - God Has Spoken by His Prophets 654
Psalm 123: Our Eyes Are Fixed on the Lord 168 264
C - Lord, You Give the Great Commission 607
Psalm 66: Let All the Earth 93

FIFTEENTH SUNDAY
A - Word of God, Come Down on Earth* 653
Psalm 65: The Seed That Falls on Good Ground 92
B - Go to the World 608
Psalm 85: Lord, Let Us See Your Kindness 112 113 114
C - Lord of All Nations, Grant Me Grace* 751
We Are Your People 789
Psalm 69: Turn to the Lord in Your Need 97

SIXTEENTH SUNDAY
A - Come, Ye Thankful People, Come* 706
Psalm 86: Lord, You Are Good and Forgiving 115
B - There's a Wideness in God's Mercy* 742
Psalm 23: My Shepherd Is the Lord 45
Psalm 23: The Lord Is My Shepherd 44 45
Psalm 23: Shepherd Me, O God 756
C - God It Was 818
Psalm 15: The Just Will Live 33

SEVENTEENTH SUNDAY
A - The Kingdom of God 775
Psalm 119: Lord, I Love Your Commands 163
B - Bread to Share 927
Psalm 145: The Hand of the Lord Feeds Us 191
C - Seek Ye First the Kingdom of God* 728
Psalm 138: Lord, on the Day I Called for Help 184

Hymns and Psalms for the Church Year/*continued*

EIGHTEENTH SUNDAY
A - Bread to Share* 927
    Psalm 145: The Hand of the Lord Feeds Us 191
B - All Who Hunger 926 845
    Psalm 78: The Lord Gave Them Bread 105
C - The Love of the Lord 814
    Psalm 95: If Today You Hear His Voice 127 128
    Psalm 95: It Today You Hear God's Voice 129

NINTEENTH SUNDAY
A - How Firm a Foundation* 731
    Psalm 85: Lord, Let Us See Your Kindness 112 113
    114
B - I Am the Bread of Life/Yo Soy el Pan de Vida* 931
    Psalm 34: Taste and See 70 71 72 73 248
C - What Does the Lord Require 785
    God Whose Giving Knows No Ending 794
    Psalm 33: Happy Are the People 66
    Psalm 33: Happy the People 67

TWENTIETH SUNDAY
A - Your Hands, O Lord, in Days of Old 949
    Psalm 67: O God, Let All the Nations Praise You
    94 95
B - I Am the Bread of Life/Yo Soy el Pan de Vida* 931
    Psalm 34: Taste and See 70 71 72 73 248
C - God, Whose Purpose Is to Kindle* 828
    Psalm 40: Lord, Come to My Aid 75

TWENTY-FIRST SUNDAY
A - O Christ the Great Foundation 781 782
    Psalm 138: Lord, Your Love Is Eternal 184
B - I Am the Bread of Life/Yo Soy el Pan de Vida* 931
    Psalm 34: Taste and See 70 71 72 73 248
C - In Christ There Is a Table Set for All 916
    Psalm 117: Go Out to All the World 157

TWENTY-SECOND SUNDAY
A - Take Up Your Cross* 808
    Wherever He Leads* 810
    Psalm 63: My Soul Is Thirsting 89 90 91
B - Deep Within 546
    Psalm 15: The Just Will Live 33
C - Gather Us In 850
    Psalm 68: You Have Made a Home for the Poor 96

TWENTY-THIRD SUNDAY
A - Draw Us in the Spirit's Tether* 917
    Seek Ye First* 728
    Forgive Our Sins 952
    Psalm 95: If Today You Hear His Voice 127 128
    Psalm 95: If Today You Hear God's Voice 129
B - When the King Shall Come Again* 487
    Psalm 146: Praise the Lord, My Soul 195
C - Take Up Your Cross* 808
    Wherever He Leads* 810
    Psalm 90: In Every Age 120

TWENTY-FOURTH SUNDAY
A - Forgive Our Sins* 952
    Psalm 103: The Lord Is Kind and Merciful 140 141
    143
B - Take Up Your Cross* 808
    Wherever He Leads* 810
    Psalm 115: I Will Walk in the Presence 153 154
C - Our Father, We Have Wandered* 955
    Psalm 51: I Will Rise and Go to My Father 82
    Psalm 51: I Will Arise and Go to My God 85

TWENTY-FIFTH SUNDAY
A - For the Fruits of This Creation 704
    Psalm 145: The Lord Is Near 191
B - The Church of Christ in Every Age* 803
    Psalm 54: The Lord Upholds My Life 86
C - God, Whose Giving Knows No Ending 794
    The Love of the Lord 814
    Psalm 113: Praise the Lord 151

TWENTY-SIXTH SUNDAY
A - In Christ There Is a Table Set for All 916
    Psalm 25: Remember Your Mercies 54
B - The Love of the Lord 814
    Psalm 19: The Precepts of the Lord 39
C - God, Whose Purpose Is to Kindle 828
    Come, You Sinners, Poor and Needy 954
    Psalm 146: Praise the Lord, My Soul 195

TWENTY-SEVENTH SUNDAY
A - O Christ the Great Foundation* 781 782
    Psalm 80: The Vineyard of the Lord 106
B - Our Father, by Whose Name 961
    When Love Is Found 942
    Psalm 128: May the Lord Bless and Protect 172
    Psalm 128: May the Lord Bless Us 173
C - The Church of Christ in Every Age 803
    Psalm 95: If Today You Hear His Voice 127 128
    Psalm 95: If Today You Hear God's Voice 129

TWENTY-EIGHTH SUNDAY
A - City of God, Jerusalem* 486
    Gather Us In* 850
    Psalm 23: I Shall Live in the House of the Lord 45
B - The Summons 811
    The Love of the Lord 814
    Psalm 90: Fill Us with Your Love, O Lord 120 121
C - Your Hands, O Lord, in Days of Old 949
    Psalm 98: The Lord Has Revealed to the Nations
    137

TWENTY-NINTH SUNDAY
A - Sing Praise to God Who Reigns Above 683
    Psalm 96: Give the Lord Glory and Honor 131 132
B - Lord, Whose Love in Humble Service 793
    'Tis the Gift to Be Simple 792
    Psalm 33: Let Your Mercy Be on Us 66
    Psalm 33: Lord, Let Your Mercy Be on Us 68
C - Sing Praise to God Who Reigns Above 683
    Psalm 121: Our Help Comes from the Lord 164

THIRTIETH SUNDAY
A - Lord of All Nations, Grant Me Grace* 751
    Psalm 18: I Love You, Lord, My Strength 38
B - Your Hands, O Lord, in Days of Old 949
    Amazing Grace 737
    Psalm 126: The Lord Has Done Great Things 169
    170 171
C - What Does the Lord Require 785
    'Tis the Gift to Be Simple 792
    Psalm 34: The Lord Hears the Cry of the Poor 71

THIRTY-FIRST SUNDAY
A - What Does the Lord Require 785
    'Tis the Gift to Be Simple 792
    Psalm 131: My Soul Is Still 178
    Psalm 131: In You, Lord 179
B - Lord of All Nations, Grant Me Grace 751
    Psalm 18: I Love You, Lord, My Strength 38
C - Come, You Sinners, Poor and Needy 954
    Psalm 145: I Will Praise Your Name 192 193 194

Hymns and Psalms for the Church Year/*continued*

THIRTY-SECOND SUNDAY
A - Wake, O Wake, and Sleep No Longer* 489
    Who Can Measure Heaven and Earth 645
    Psalm 63: My Soul Is Thirsting 89 90 91
B - The Temple Rang with Golden Coins* 787
    Psalm 146: Praise the Lord, My Soul 195
C - Jesus, Lead the Way 755
    Soon and Very Soon 870
    Psalm 17: Lord, When Your Glory Appears 37

THIRTY-THIRD SUNDAY
A - God, Whose Giving Knows No Ending* 794
    Psalm 128: O Happy Are Those Who Fear the Lord
      172
B - The King Shall Come When Morning Dawns 497
    When the Lord in Glory Comes 868
    Psalm 16: Keep Me Safe, O God 34 35 36
C - Be Not Afraid 734
    How Can I Keep from Singing 733
    Psalm 98: The Lord Comes to Rule the Earth 135

CHRIST THE KING
see nos. 626-632
A- Lord, Whose Love in Humble Service 793
    A Touching Place 760
    Psalm 23: The Lord Is My Shepherd 44 45
    Psalm 23: My Shepherd Is the Lord 45
    Psalm 23: Nada Me Falta 46
    Psalm 23: Shepherd Me, O God 756
B- To Jesus Christ, Our Sovereign King 629
    Psalm 93: The Lord Is King for Evermore 126
C- Jesus, Remember Me* 770
    Psalm 122: I Rejoiced When I Heard 165
    Psalm 122: I Was Glad 166
    Psalm 122: Let Us Go Rejoicing 167

FEB. 2: PRESENTATION OF THE LORD
Lord, Bid Your Servant Go in Peace* 874
Psalm 24: Who Is This King 49

MARCH 19: JOSEPH, HUSBAND OF MARY
Come Now, and Praise the Humble Saint 875
Psalm 89: The Son of David 119

MARCH 25: ANNUNCIATION OF OUR LORD
see nos. 875-876
Psalm 40: Here I Am 74
Psalm 40: Here Am I 75

JUNE 24: BIRTH OF JOHN THE BAPTIST
see nos. 878-879
    Vigil - Psalm 71: Since My Mother's Womb 100
    Day - Psalm 139: I Praise You 187

JUNE 29: PETER AND PAUL
Two Noble Saints 880
Vigil - Psalm 19: Their Message Goes Out 39
Day - Psalm 34: The Angel of the Lord 73

JULY 4: INDEPENDENCE DAY
see nos. 964-966
Psalm 85: The Lord Speaks of Peace 113

AUGUST 6: TRANSFIGURATION
see nos. 881-882
Psalm 97: The Lord Is King 133

AUGUST 15: ASSUMPTION
Hail, Holy Queen Enthroned Above 883
Vigil - Psalm 132: Lord, Go Up 180
Day - Psalm 45: The Queen Stands 78

LABOR DAY
Those Who Love and Those Who Labor 805
Psalm 90: Lord, Give Success 120

SEPTEMBER 14: TRIUMPH OF THE CROSS
Lift High the Cross 884
Psalm 78: Do Not Forget 104

NOVEMBER 1: ALL SAINTS
see nos. 885-889
Psalm 24: O God, This Is the People 47

NOVEMBER 9: DEDICATION
OF ST. JOHN LATERAN
see nos. 891-893
1Chr 29: We Praise Your Glorious Name 203

THANKSGIVING DAY
see nos. 700-709
Psalm 67: The Earth Has Yielded 95
1Chr 29: We Praise Your Glorious Name 203
Psalm 145: I Will Praise Your Name 192 193 194

DECEMBER 8: IMMACULATE CONCEPTION
Immaculate Mary 890
Psalm 98: Sing to the Lord a New Song 135 136 137

985 Liturgical Index

Liturgical Index/*continued*

790 I Bind My Heart
809 I Danced in the Morning
641 I Have Loved You
768 I Heard the Voice of Jesus Say
716 I Need You to Listen
557 Jesus Walked This Lonesome Valley
770 Jesus, Remember Me
548 Jesus, Tempted in the Desert
574 Jesus, the Lord
712 Lead Me, Guide Me
884 Lift High the Cross
553 Lord, Who throughout These Forty Days
572 My Song Is Love Unknown
753 No Greater Love
933 Now in This Banquet
544 O Sun of Justice
955 Our Father, We Have Wandered
947 Out of the Depths
549 Parce Domine
39 Psalm 19: Lord, You Have the Words
40 Psalm 19: Lord, You Have the Words
41 Psalm 22: I Will Praise You, Lord
52 Psalm 25: Levanto Mi Alma
51 Psalm 25: To You, O Lord
55 Psalm 27: I Believe That I Shall See
56 Psalm 27: In the Land of the Living
57 Psalm 27: The Lord Is My Light
59 Psalm 30: I Will Praise You, Lord
60 Psalm 30: I Will Praise You, Lord
64 Psalm 32: I Turn to You, Lord
73 Psalm 34: Taste and See
76 Psalm 41: Lord, Heal My Soul
83 Psalm 51: Be Merciful, O Lord
84 Psalm 51: Create in Me
85 Psalm 51: Create in Me
254 Psalm 51: Give Back to Me
88 Psalm 62: In God Alone
106 Psalm 80: The Vineyard of the Lord
123 Psalm 91: Be with Me
129 Psalm 95: If Today You Hear God's Voice
127 Psalm 95: If Today You Hear His Voice
128 Psalm 95: If Today You Hear His Voice
140 Psalm 103: The Lord Is Kind and Merciful
143 Psalm 103: The Lord Is Kind and Merciful
153 Psalm 116: I Will Take the Cup of Salvation
168 Psalm 123: Our Eyes Are Fixed on the Lord
169 Psalm 126: The Lord Has Done Great Things
170 Psalm 126: The Lord Has Done Great Things
171 Psalm 126: The Lord Has Done Great Things
175 Psalm 130: I Place All My Trust
175 Psalm 130: I Place All My Trust
177 Psalm 130: If You, O God, Laid Bare Our Guilt
174 Psalm 130: With the Lord There Is Mercy
176 Psalm 130: With the Lord There Is Mercy
182 Psalm 137: Let My Tongue Be Silent
183 Psalm 137: Let My Tongue Be Silent
189 Psalm 141: Evening Offering
188 Psalm 141: Let My Prayer Rise Like Incense

730 Psalm of Hope
550 Remember Your Love
786 Renew Your People
555 Return to God
540 Seek the Lord
547 Somebody's Knockin' at Your Door
565 Stay Here and Keep Watch
685 The God of Abraham Praise
238 The Lord Is My Light
649 The Lord Is My Light
732 The Lord Is My Light
742 There's a Wideness in God's Mercy
556 This Is the Time
882 'Tis Good, Lord, to Be Here
541 Tree of Life
749 What Wondrous Love Is This
(also Cross, Mercy, Sin, Social Concern)

PALM SUNDAY

542 Adoramus Te Christe
563 All Glory, Laud, and Honor
626 Crown Him with Many Crowns
564 Jesu, Jesu
574 Jesus, the Lord
884 Lift High the Cross
569 O Sacred Head Surrounded
43 Psalm 22: My God, My God
562 Ride On, Jesus, Ride
541 Tree of Life
570 Were You There
(also Lent, Christ the King, Easter Triduum)

EASTER TRIDUUM

HOLY THURSDAY

542 Adoramus Te Christe
922 At That First Eucharist
917 Draw Us in the Spirit's Tether
564 Jesu, Jesu
566 Jesus Took a Towel
884 Lift High the Cross
607 Lord, You Give the Great Commission
750 Love Is His Word
753 No Greater Love
813 Now We Remain
153 Psalm 116: I Will Take the Cup of Salvation
155 Psalm 116: Our Blessing-Cup
152 Psalm 116: The Name of God
918 Seed, Scattered and Sown
573 Sing, My Tongue, the Song of Triumph
565 Stay Here and Keep Watch
746 Ubi Caritas
815 We Have Been Told
747 Where Charity and Love Prevail
752 Where True Love and Charity Are Found / Ubi Caritas
(also Ministry, Service, Good Friday, Eucharist)

GOOD FRIDAY

542 Adoramus Te Christe
567 All You Who Pass This Way
957 Ashes
551 At the Cross Her Station Keeping
568 Calvary
571 Crucem Tuam / O Lord, Your Cross
790 I Bind My Heart
557 Jesus Walked This Lonesome Valley
884 Lift High the Cross
572 My Song Is Love Unknown
753 No Greater Love
569 O Sacred Head Surrounded
549 Parce Domine

42 Psalm 22: My God, My God
43 Psalm 22: My God, My God
62 Psalm 31: Father, I Put My Life in Your Hands
63 Psalm 31: Father, I Put My Life in Your Hands
61 Psalm 31: I Put My Life in Your Hands
573 Sing, My Tongue, the Song of Triumph
560 Stations of the Cross
565 Stay Here and Keep Watch
541 Tree of Life
570 Were You There
749 What Wondrous Love Is This
943 Wherever You Go

EASTER VIGIL

644 All You Who Are Thirsty
642 Come to the Feast
571 Crucem Tuam / O Lord, Your Cross
592 Easter Alleluia
201 Exodus 15: Let Us Sing to the Lord
202 Exodus 15: Song at the Sea
205 Isaiah 12: Cry Out with Joy and Gladness
204 Isaiah 12: You Will Draw Water
647 Light of Christ / Exsultet
34 Psalm 16: In You, My God
35 Psalm 16: Keep Me Safe, O God
36 Psalm 16: You Will Show Me the Path of Life
67 Psalm 33: Happy the People
77 Psalm 42-43: Like a Deer That Longs
84 Psalm 51: Create in Me
254 Psalm 51: Give Back to Me
144 Psalm 104: Lord, Send Out Your Spirit
145 Psalm 104: Lord, Send Out Your Spirit
146 Psalm 104: Lord, Send Out Your Spirit
377 Rite of Sprinkling-Haugen
585 Surrexit Dominus Vere II
(also Easter Season)

EASTER SEASON

606 A Hymn of Glory Let Us Sing
581 Alleluia, Alleluia, Give Thanks
379 Asperges Me
578 At the Lamb's High Feast We Sing
395 Celtic Alleluia
601 Christ Is Alive!
600 Christ the Lord Is Risen
594 Christ the Lord Is Risen Today
602 Christ the Lord Is Risen Today
865 Christ, Mighty Savior
288 Cleanse Us, Lord
902 Come and Let Us Drink of That New River
575 Come, Ye Faithful, Raise the Strain
626 Crown Him with Many Crowns
571 Crucem Tuam / O Lord, Your Cross
596 Darkness Is Gone
597 Daylight Fades
592 Easter Alleluia
586 Good Christians All
605 Hail the Day That Sees Him Rise
588 Hail Thee, Festival Day
931 I Am the Bread of Life
809 I Danced in the Morning
582 I Know That My Redeemer Lives
916 In Christ There Is a Table Set for All
932 In the Breaking of the Bread
593 Jesus Christ Is Risen Today

Liturgical Index/*continued*

Liturgical Index/*continued*

Liturgical Index/*continued*

Liturgical Index/*continued*

Topical Index/*continued*

Topical Index/*continued*

Topical Index/*continued*

Topical Index/*continued*

Topical Index/*continued*

Topical Index/*continued*

Topical Index/*continued*

Topical Index/*continued*

Topical Index/*continued*

Topical Index/*continued*

Topical Index/*continued*

Topical Index/*continued*

Topical Index/*continued*

Topical Index/*continued*

Topical Index/*continued*

Topical Index/*continued*

SEEKING
760   A Touching Place
926   All Who Hunger
845   All Who Hunger, Gather Gladly
779   As a Fire Is Meant for Burning
642   Come to the Feast
641   I Have Loved You
716   I Need You to Listen
817   Lord, When You Came / Pescador de Hombres
757   Nada Te Turbe / Nothing Can Trouble
718   O Lord, Hear My Prayer
47   Psalm 24: We Long to See Your Face
56   Psalm 27: In the Land of the Living
77   Psalm 42-43: Like a Deer That Longs
91   Psalm 63: My Soul Is Thirsting
98   Psalm 69: Lord, in Your Great Love
110   Psalm 84: How Lovely Is Your Dwelling Place
112   Psalm 85: Lord, Let Us See Your Kindness
175   Psalm 130: I Place All My Trust
195   Psalm 146: O Lord, Come and Save Us
728   Seek Ye First the Kingdom of God
840   We Are Many Parts
643   You Are All We Have

SERVICE
849   All People That on Earth Do Dwell
887   By All Your Saints Still Striving
777   Christ's Church Shall Glory in His Power
674   Christians, Lift Up Your Hearts
719   Come to Us, Creative Spirit
847   Come, Rejoice before Your Maker
208   Daniel 3: Benedicite
917   Draw Us in the Spirit's Tether
823   For the Healing of the Nations
791   Glorious in Majesty
798   Go Make of All Disciples
819   God, Who Stretched the Spangled Heavens
794   God, Whose Giving Knows No Ending
829   How Long, O Lord, How Long
836   In Christ There Is No East or West
564   Jesu, Jesu
566   Jesus Took a Towel
707   Let All Things Now Living
817   Lord, When You Came / Pescador de Hombres
793   Lord, Whose Love in Humble Service
607   Lord, You Give the Great Commission
750   Love Is His Word
841   Many Are the Lightbeams
781   O Christ the Great Foundation
909   Pan de Vida
609   Praise the Spirit in Creation
41   Psalm 22: I Will Praise You, Lord
139   Psalm 100: Arise, Come to Your God
181   Psalm 134: In the Silent Hours of Night
727   Pues Sí Vivimos / If We Are Living
690   Sing Our God Together
788   The Church of Christ in Every Age
788   The Servant Song
689   There's a Spirit in the Air
842   This Is the Day When Light Was First Created
792   'Tis the Gift to Be Simple
881   Transform Us
820   We Are Called
840   We Are Many Parts

789   We Are Your People
815   We Have Been Told
892   What Is This Place
613   When God the Spirit Came
912   You Satisfy the Hungry Heart

SHARING
921   As the Grains of Wheat
848   As We Gather at Your Table
864   At Evening
945   Blessing the Marriage
702   Blest Are You
927   Bread to Share
823   For the Healing of the Nations
929   Let Us Be Bread
827   Now Join We to Praise the Creator
867   Praise and Thanksgiving
727   Pues Sí Vivimos / If We Are Living
925   Take the Bread, Children
840   We Are Many Parts
785   What Does the Lord Require
800   You Are Called to Tell the Story

SHEPHERD
849   All People That on Earth Do Dwell
922   At That First Eucharist
592   Easter Alleluia
471   Lamb of God-Way
569   O Sacred Head Surrounded
45   Psalm 23: My Shepherd Is the Lord
46   Psalm 23: Nada Me Falta
44   Psalm 23: The Lord Is My Shepherd
272 A   Psalm 23: The Lord Is My Shepherd
139   Psalm 100: Arise, Come to Your God
138   Psalm 100: We Are God's People
505   Rise Up, Shepherd, and Follow
756   Shepherd Me, O God
766   The King of Love My Shepherd Is
666   To God with Gladness Sing
517   Where Shepherds Lately Knelt
738   With a Shepherd's Care
912   You Satisfy the Hungry Heart

SICKNESS
(see Comfort, Healing, Suffering; Liturgical Index: Pastoral Care of the Sick)

SIN
729   Awake, O Sleeper, Rise from Death
600   Christ the Lord Is Risen
952   Forgive Our Sins
824   God Made from One Blood
828   God, Whose Purpose Is to Kindle
951   He Healed the Darkness of My Mind
782   O Christ the Great Foundation
915   One Bread, One Body
549   Parce Domine
64   Psalm 32: I Turn to You, Lord
65   Psalm 32: Lord, Forgive the Wrong
83   Psalm 51: Be Merciful, O Lord
85   Psalm 51: Create in Me
254   Psalm 51: Give Back to Me
82   Psalm 51: Have Mercy, Lord
116   Psalm 88: Day and Night
173   Psalm 128: Blest Are Those Who Love You
175   Psalm 130: I Place All My Trust
177   Psalm 130: If You, O God, Laid Bare Our Guilt
188   Psalm 141: Let My Prayer Rise Like Incense
956   The Master Came to Bring Good News
742   There's a Wideness in God's Mercy
776   Thy Kingdom Come
666   To God with Gladness Sing
541   Tree of Life
538   When John Baptized by Jordan's River

SOCIAL CONCERN
941   A Nuptial Blessing
760   A Touching Place
926   All Who Hunger
644   All You Who Are Thirsty
779   As a Fire Is Meant for Burning
864   At Evening
927   Bread to Share
543   By the Babylonian Rivers
678   Canticle of the Turning
516   Carol at the Manger
777   Christ's Church Shall Glory in His Power
799   City of God
642   Come to the Feast
711   Creating God
917   Draw Us in the Spirit's Tether
539   Dust and Ashes
481   Each Winter As the Year Grows Older
928   Eat This Bread
839   Father, Lord of All Creation
704   For the Fruits of This Creation
823   For the Healing of the Nations
821   Freedom Is Coming
791   Glorious in Majesty
604   Go
824   God Made from One Blood
826   God of Day and God of Darkness
966   God of Our Fathers
819   God, Who Stretched the Spangled Heavens
794   God, Whose Giving Knows No Ending
828   God, Whose Purpose Is to Kindle
797   Good News
715   Healing River
838   Help Us Accept Each Other
822   Here Am I
802   Here I Am, Lord
733   How Can I Keep from Singing
829   How Long, O Lord, How Long
790   I Bind My Heart
722   I Say "Yes," Lord / Digo "Sí," Senor
771   I Will Not Die
825   If You Believe and I Believe
836   In Christ There Is No East or West
682   Joyfully Singing
861   Kindle a Flame to Lighten the Dark
831   Let There Be Peace On Earth
751   Lord of All Nations, Grant Me Grace
817   Lord, When You Came / Pescador de Hombres
607   Lord, You Give the Great Commission
209   Luke 1:46-55/Magnificat
211   Luke 1:46-55/Magnificat
210   Luke 1:46-55/Magnificat/Holy Is Your Name
656   Magnificat
725   Mayenziwe/ Your Will Be Done
869   Mine Eyes Have Seen the Glory
827   Now Join We to Praise the Creator
781   O Christ the Great Foundation
782   O Christ the Great Foundation
950   O Christ, the Healer
816   On the Journey to Emmaus
867   Praise and Thanksgiving
103   Psalm 72: Lord, Every Nation on Earth
112   Psalm 85: Lord, Let Us See Your Kindness
113   Psalm 85: Lord, Let Us See Your Kindness
141   Psalm 103: The Lord Has Set His Throne
149   Psalm 112: A Light Rises in the Darkness

Topical Index/*continued*

Topical Index/*continued*

Topical Index/*continued*

Topical Index/*continued*

Index of Composers, Authors and Sources/*continued*

Index of Composers, Authors and Sources/*continued*

SM (SHORT METER)

829	SOUTHWELL
877 882	SWABIA

CM (COMMON METER - 86 86)

524	ANTIOCH
729	AZMON
912	BICENTENNIAL
747	CHRISTIAN LOVE
952	DETROIT
854 871 875	LAND OF REST
787	LEWIS-TOWN
836	MC KEE
497 874	MORNING SONG
737	NEW BRITAIN
723	SHANTI
735	ST. ANNE
907	ST. COLUMBA
553 561	ST. FLAVIAN
591	ST. MAGNUS

CMD (COMMON METER DOUBLE)

498	CAROL
633	ELLACOMBE
7 891	FOREST GREEN
17 768 801	KINGSFOLD
812	LEAVE ALL THINGS
965	MATERNA
949	MOZART
761	RESIGNATION

LM (LONG METER - 88 88)

951	ARLINGTON
751	BEATUS VIR
483	CONDITOR ALME SIDERUM
962	DUGUET
582 631	DUKE STREET
803	DUNEDIN
545 559 808 950	ERHALT UNS HERR
13 544	JESU DULCIS MEMORIA
893 942	O WALY WALY
849	OLD HUNDREDTH
711	PRESENCE
531 599	PUER NOBIS
837 939	TALLIS' CANON
22	TE LUCIS ANTE TERMINUM
601	TRURO
616	VENI CREATOR SPIRITUS
759	WAREHAM
490 879	WINCHESTER NEW

LM WITH REFRAIN

726	ST. CATHERINE
493	VENI VENI EMMANUEL

5 5 5 4 D

856	ANDREA
4 859 867	BUNESSAN
864	EVENING HYMN
946	LOVE IS THE SUNLIGHT

6 6 6 6 4 44 4

666	CYMBALA
572	LOVE UNKNOWN

6 6 8 6 6 6

888	BALDWIN
613	VINEYARD HAVEN

7 6 7 6 D

782 807 885	AURELIA
798 838 880	ELLACOMBE
487 575	GAUDEAMUS PARITER
569 834 955	PASSION CHORALE
563 887	ST. THEODULPH

7 6 7 6 WITH REFRAIN

514	GO TELL IT ON THE MOUNTAIN
635	ROYAL OAK

7 7 7 7 WITH REFRAIN

504	GLORIA
913	LIVING GOD
640	SING OUT

7 7 77

689	LAUDS
843	LUBECK
480 614	NUN KOMM DER HEIDEN HEILAND

7 7 77 D

529 578	SALZBURG
706	ST. GEORGE'S WINDSOR

7 7 77 WITH ALLELUIAS

593	EASTER HYMN
602 605	LLANFAIR
594	SURGIT IN HAEC DIES

8 4 8 4 888 4

704	EAST ACKLAM
862	AR HYD Y NOS

8 7 8 7 WITH REFRAIN

748	COMFORT
959 960	FARRELL
530	GREENSLEEVES
733	HOW CAN I KEEP FROM SINGING
629 956	ICH GLAUB AN GOTT
954	RESTORATION

8 7 8 7

769	DUNSTAN
847	JUBILATE DEO
543	KAS DZIEDAJA
766	ST. COLUMBA

8 7 8 7 D

607 844	ABBOT'S LEIGH
779 793 826	BEACH SPRING
548	EBENEZER
839	GENEVA
661	HEAVENLY HOSTS
780 819 828 845	HOLY MANNA
743 914	HYFRYDOL
595 597 669 805	HYMN TO JOY
742	IN BABILONE
496	JEFFERSON
516	JOYOUS LIGHT
636	LA GRANGE
676 784 848	NETTLETON
895	OMNE DIE
528	PLEADING SAVIOR
739	RAQUEL
654 794	RUSTINGTON

8 7 8 7 8 7

714	BEST GIFT
778	EDEN CHURCH
800	GHENT
609	JULION
684	LAUDA ANIMA
972	PANGE LINGUA
573 658 881	PICARDY
508	REGENT SQUARE
823 963	ST. THOMAS
897	TILLFLYKT
699	WESTMINSTER ABBEY

8 8 8 8

967	O WALY WALY
618	PROSPECT

888 WITH ALLELUIAS

586 630	GELOBT SEI GOTT
579	O FILII ET FILIAE
587	VICTORY

9 8 9 8

827	HARVEST
866	ST. CLEMENT

Metrical Index of Tunes/*continued*

10 10 10 WITH ALLELUIAS
665 906 ENGELBERG
680 MAYFLOWER
592 O FILII ET FILIAE
608 889 SINE NOMINE

10 10 10 10
673 BONNIE GEORGE CAMPBELL
589 LIBERATOR
966 NATIONAL HYMN
944 SLANE

10 10 WITH REFRAIN
884 CRUCIFER
570 WERE YOU THERE

10 10 11 11
668 COMMON PRAYER
687 775 LAUDATE DOMINUM

11 10 11 10
842 NORTHBROOK
857 SLITHERS OF GOLD

11 10 11 10 WITH REFRAIN
663 O STORE GUD
533 STAR IN THE EAST

11 11 11 11
731 824 FOUNDATION
515 MUELLER

11 11 11 5
860 CHRISTE SANCTORUM
852 ISTE CONFESSOR
865 MIGHTY SAVIOR

IRREGULAR WITH REFRAIN
499 ADESTE FIDELES
931 BREAD OF LIFE
730 PSALM OF HOPE
872 RESURRECTION
588 674 SALVE FESTA DIES
678 STAR OF THE COUNTY DOWN

IRREGULAR
478 ANNUNCIATION
898 AVE MARIA
764 BALM IN GILEAD
677 CANTATE DOMINO
916 CENEDIUS
564 CHEREPONI
816 876 COLUMCILLE
596 DAYLIGHT
760 DREAM ANGUS
810 FALLS CREEK
583 FESTIVAL CANTICLE
850 GATHER US IN
818 JESUS CALLS US
566 JESUS TOOK A TOWEL
809 LORD OF THE DANCE
851 MA YEDIDUT
924 NO KE ANO' AHI AHI
549 PARCE DOMINE
646 PURPOSE
584 REGINA CAELI
894 SALVE REGINA
728 SEEK YE FIRST
792 SIMPLE GIFTS
547 SOMEBODY'S KNOCKIN'
537 THE FIRST NOWELL

ONE OF A KIND

SMD (SHORT METER DOUBLE)
626 DIADEMATA

CM WITH REPEATS
632 DIADEM

LM WITH ALLELUIAS
606 621 670 886 LASST UNS ERFREUEN

LM WITH REPEAT
611 LAMBILLOTTE

LMD (LONG METER DOUBLE)
656 MAGNIFICAT

3 7 6 5 D 3
822 HERE AM I

4 4 8 5 4 7
750 JULINORMA

44 7 44 7 4444 7
509 W ZLOBIE LEZY

4 5 7 D WITH REFRAIN
681 EARTH AND ALL STARS

5 4 5 5 7
789 WHITFIELD

5 5 8 D
903 BUNESSAN

55 7 55 7
900 O DU FROLICHE

55 88 55
755 ROCHELLE

6 6 6 6 33 6
785 SHARPTHORNE

6 6 6 6 88
627 DARWALL'S 148TH

6 6 6 6 888
961 RHOSYMEDRE

6 6 8 4 D
685 LEONI

6 7 6 7 D
598 VRUECHTEN

6 7 6 7 6 6 6 6
700 NUN DANKET

6 7 6 8 D WITH REFRAIN
664 ROSAS

66 4 666 4
619 ITALIAN HYMN

66 6 D
858 LAUDES DOMINI

66 77 78 55
518 IN DULCI JUBILO

66 89 66
522 STILLE NACHT

66 9 D
754 PRECIOUS LORD

66 11 D
617 DOWN AMPNEY

66 11 66 11 D
707 ASH GROVE

7 6 7 6
878 DE EERSTEN ZIJN DE LAATSTEN

Metrical Index of Tunes/*continued*

Metrical Index of Tunes/*continued*

Psalm Refrains Set to Music/*continued*

Lord, it is good to give thanks to you. 124 125
Lord, let us see your kindness. 112
Lord, let us see your kindness. Lord, grant us your salvation.
  113 114
Lord, let your face shine on us. 29 30
Lord, make us turn to you, show us your face, and we shall
  be saved. 107 108
Lord, on the day I called for help, you answered me. 184
Lord, send out your Spirit and renew the face of the earth.
  144 145 146
Lord, when your glory appears, my joy will be full. 37
Lord, you are good and forgiving. 115
Lord, you have the words of everlasting life. 39 40
Lord, you will show us the path of life. 34
Lord, your love is eternal; do not forsake the work of your
  hands. 184

May God bless us in his mercy. 94 95 259
May the Lord bless and protect us all the days of our life.
  172 173
My God, my God, why have you abandoned me? 42 43
My refuge, my stronghold, my God in whom I trust! 122
My shepherd is the Lord, nothing indeed shall I want. 45
My soul is thirsting for you, O Lord. 89 90 91
My soul rejoices in my God. 209 656

Night holds no terrors for me sleeping under God's wings.
  122

O Dios mío, levanto mi alma, levanto a ti Señor, mi sal-
  vación. 52
O God, O God, let all the nations praise you. 94 95
O God, this is the people that longs to see your face. 47
O happy are those who fear the Lord and walk in his ways.
  172
O Lord, come and save us. 195
O Lord, our God, how glorious is your name in all the earth!
  32
O Lord, our God, how wonderful your name in all the earth!
  31
O Lord, our God, unwearied is your love for us. 115
Open wide your gates; let the King of Glory in! 47
Our blessing cup is a communion with the blood of Christ.
  152 153 155
Our eyes are fixed on the Lord, pleading for his mercy. 168
  264
Our help comes from the Lord, the maker of heaven and
  earth. 164
Out of the depths I cry to you, O Lord. 175

Parce Dómine, parce pópulo tuo: ne in aetérnum irascáris
  nobis. 549
Pongo mi vida en tus manos. 61
Praise and exalt him for ever. 208
Praise the Lord who lifts up the poor. 151
Praise the Lord, Jerusalem. 199
Praise the Lord, my soul! Praise the Lord! 195
Praise the Lord, who heals the brokenhearted. 198
Proclaim the greatness of God; rejoice in God, my Savior!
  211
Proclaim to all the nations the marvelous deeds of the Lord!
  132

Remember your love and your faithfulness, O Lord.
  Remember your people and have mercy on us, Lord. 550
Remember your mercies, O Lord. 54
Rest in God alone, my soul. 87

Shepherd me, O God, beyond my wants, beyond my fears,
  from death into life. 756
Since my mother's womb, you have been my strength. 100
Sing a new song unto the Lord. 686
Sing to the Lord a new song, for God has done wonderful
  deeds. 135 136 137
Sing with joy to God! Sing to God, our help! 109

Taste and see the goodness of the Lord. 70 71 72 73 248 919
  923
Teach me your ways, O Lord. 54
The angel of the Lord will rescue those who fear him. 73
The earth has yielded its fruits; God has blessed us. 95
The earth is full of the goodness of God. 66 67
The hand of the Lord feeds us: he answers all our needs. 191
The just will live in the presence of the Lord. 33
The Lord comes to the earth to rule the earth with justice.
  135
The Lord gave them bread from heaven. 105
The Lord has done great things for us; we are filled with joy.
  169 170 171
The Lord has revealed to the nations, revealed his saving
  power. 137
The Lord has set his throne in heaven. 141 142
The Lord hears the cry of the poor. 69 71
The Lord is kind and merciful. 141 143
The Lord is kind and merciful; slow to anger, rich in kind-
  ness. 140
The Lord is King for evermore. 126
The Lord is king, the most high over all the earth. 133
The Lord is my light and my salvation, of whom should I be
  afraid? 57 272
The Lord is my light and my salvation. 55 238
The Lord is my shepherd, I shall not want. 44
The Lord is my shepherd, nothing shall I want; he leads me
  by safe paths, nothing shall I fear. 45
The Lord is my shepherd; there is nothing I shall want. 45
  272
The Lord is near to all who call on him. 191
The Lord is risen, alleluia. 2
The Lord speaks of peace to his people. 113
The Lord upholds my life. 86
The Lord will bless his people with peace. 58
The Lord's kindness is everlasting to those who fear him.
  141
The precepts of the Lord give joy to the heart. 39
The queen stands at your right hand, arrayed in gold. 78
The seed that falls on good ground will yield a fruitful har-
  vest. 92
The Son of David will live for ever. 119
The stone rejected by the builders has become the corner-
  stone. 161
The vineyard of the Lord is the house of Israel. 106
Their message goes out through all the earth. 39
This is the day the Lord has made, let us rejoice and be glad.
  158 160 576 590
To the upright I will show the saving power of God. 81
To you glory and praise for evermore. 206 207
To you, O Lord, I lift my soul. 50 51 53
Today if you hear the voice of the Lord, harden not your
  hearts. 2
Today is born our Savior, Christ the Lord. 130 131
Turn to the Lord in your need and you will live. 97

We are God's people, the flock of the Lord. 138
We praise your glorious name, O mighty God! 203
Who is this King of Glory? It is the Lord. 49
With the Lord there is mercy and the fullness of redemption.
  174 175 176

You are a priest for ever, in the line of Melchizedek. 148
You are my inheritance, you, O Lord. 34 36
You will draw water joyfully from the springs of salvation.
  204
You will show me the path of life, you, my hope and my shel-
  ter; in your presence is endless joy, at your side is my
  home forever. 36
Your ways, O Lord, are love and truth, to those who keep
  your covenant. 53
Your word went forth and light awoke. 655
Your words, Lord, are spirit and life. 39

Index of First Lines and Common Titles/*continued*

Index of First Lines and Common Titles/*continued*

Index of First Lines and Common Titles/*continued*

Index of First Lines and Common Titles/*continued*

Index of First Lines and Common Titles/*continued*